CONSTITUTIONALISM AND THE RULE OF LAW

Rule of law and constitutionalist ideals are understood by many, if not most, as necessary to create a just political order. Defying the traditional division between normative and positive theoretical approaches, this book explores how political reality on the one hand, and constitutional ideals on the other, mutually inform and influence each other. Seventeen chapters from leading international scholars cover a diverse range of topics and case studies to assess the assumption that the best normative theories, including those regarding the role of constitutions, constitutionalism and the rule of law, conceive of the ideal and the real as mutually regulating.

MAURICE ADAMS is Professor of General Jurisprudence and Professor of Democratic Governance and Rule of Law at the Law School of Tilburg University. His research has a particular focus on comparative law, and on the relation between constitutional law and political theory.

ANNE MEUWESE is Professor of European and Comparative Public Law at the Law School of Tilburg University. She is co-chair of the ECPR Standing Group on Regulatory Governance. Her work has been published in a number of renowned law journals.

ERNST HIRSCH BALLIN is Professor of Dutch and European Constitutional Law at Tilburg University and Professor of Human Rights Law at the University of Amsterdam. Prior to returning to academia in 2011 he was Dutch Minister of Justice (1989–1994, 2006–2010) and Minister of the Interior and Kingdom Affairs (2010).

CONSTITUTIONALISM AND THE RULE OF LAW

Bridging Idealism and Realism

Edited by

MAURICE ADAMS
Tilburg University

ANNE MEUWESE
Tilburg University

ERNST HIRSCH BALLIN
Tilburg University, University of Amsterdam

CAMBRIDGE
UNIVERSITY PRESS

CAMBRIDGE
UNIVERSITY PRESS

University Printing House, Cambridge CB2 8BS, United Kingdom

One Liberty Plaza, 20th Floor, New York, NY 10006, USA

477 Williamstown Road, Port Melbourne, VIC 3207, Australia

4843/24, 2nd Floor, Ansari Road, Daryaganj, Delhi – 110002, India

79 Anson Road, #06–04/06, Singapore 079906

Cambridge University Press is part of the University of Cambridge.

It furthers the University's mission by disseminating knowledge in the pursuit of education, learning, and research at the highest international levels of excellence.

www.cambridge.org
Information on this title: www.cambridge.org/9781107151857
10.1017/9781316585221

First published 2017

A catalogue record for this publication is available from the British Library.

Library of Congress Cataloging-in-Publication Data
Names: Adams, Maurice, 1964– editor. | Meuwese, Anne Claartje Margreet, 1980– editor. | Hirsch Ballin, Ernst Maurits Henricus, 1950– editor.
Title: Constitutionalism and the Rule of Law : Bridging Idealism and Realism / edited by Maurice Adams, Anne Meuwese, Ernst Hirsch Ballin.
Description: Cambridge [UK] ; New York : Cambridge University Press, 2016.
Identifiers: LCCN 2016032454 | ISBN 9781107151857 (hardback)
Subjects: LCSH: Constitutional law. | Constitutional law – Philosophy. | Rule of law. | State, The. | Idealism. | Realism.
Classification: LCC K3165 .C6235 2016 | DDC 342.001–dc23
LC record available at https://lccn.loc.gov/2016032454

ISBN 978-1-107-15185-7 Hardback

CONTENTS

CONTRIBUTORS

MAURICE ADAMS is Professor of General Jurisprudence and Professor of Democratic Governance and Rule of Law ('vfonds' chair) at the Law School of Tilburg University (the Netherlands).

ERNST HIRSCH BALLIN is Professor of Dutch and European Constitutional Law at Tilburg University and Professor of Human Rights Law at the University of Amsterdam (both in the Netherlands).

ADRIAAN BEDNER is Associate Professor of Indonesian Law and Society at the Van Vollenhoven Institute for Law, Governance and Development at the Law School of Leiden University (the Netherlands).

SUMIT BISARYA is Senior Project Manager for the Constitution Building Programme at the International Institute for Democracy and Electoral Assistance (IDEA) in The Hague (the Netherlands).

ELLIOT BULMER is a Programme Officer in the Constitution Building Programme at the International Institute for Democracy and Electoral Assistance (IDEA) in The Hague (the Netherlands).

TOM GINSBURG is the Leo Spitz Professor of International Law and Professor of Political Science at the University of Chicago and a member of the American Academy of Arts and Sciences.

NICK HULS is Honorary Professor in Socio-Legal Studies at the Erasmus School of Law and Leiden University Law School (both in the Netherlands) since his retirement in 2014. He is also an Honorary Professor at the University of Pretoria School of Law (South Africa).

DIMITRY KOCHENOV is Visiting Professor and Martin and Kathleen Crane Fellow in Law and Public Affairs at the Woodrow Wilson School,

Princeton University (USA). He holds a Chair of EU Constitutional Law in Groningen (the Netherlands).

MARTIN KRYGIER is Gordon Samuels Professor of Law and Social Theory at the University of New South Wales (Australia).

RANDALL LESAFFER is Professor of Legal History at Tilburg University (the Netherlands) and part-time Professor of International and European Legal History at the University of Leuven (Belgium).

FENG LIN is Professor of Law at the City University of Hong Kong and Director of the Centre for Chinese and Comparative Law.

PETER L. LINDSETH is Olimpiad S. Ioffe Professor of International and Comparative Law and Director of International Programs at the University of Connecticut School of Law (USA). In 2014 he was Royal Netherlands Academy of Arts and Sciences (KNAW) Visiting Professor at Tilburg University (the Netherlands).

JÖRG LUTHER is Professor of European and Comparative Public Law at the Law School of Tilburg University (the Netherlands).

ANNE MEUWESE is Professor of European and Comparative Public Law at the Law School of Tilburg University (the Netherlands).

SHAVANA MUSA is a Lecturer in Law at the University of Manchester (United Kingdom).

KIM LANE SCHEPPELE is the Laurance S. Rockefeller Professor of Sociology and International Affairs in the Woodrow Wilson School and the University Center for Human Values at Princeton University (USA).

GERHARD VAN DER SCHYFF is Associate Professor in the Department of Public Law, Jurisprudence and Legal History at the Law School of Tilburg University (the Netherlands).

ADAM SHINAR is Assistant Professor at the Radzyner School of Law, Interdisciplinary Center Herzliya (Israel).

GÁBOR ATTILA TÓTH is chair at the Department of Constitutional Law, University of Debrecen and lecturer at the Eötvös Loránd University in Budapest and the Rajk László College for Advanced Studies (all in Hungary).

MILA VERSTEEG is Professor of Law at the University of Virginia School of Law (USA).

PIERRE DE VOS holds the Claude Leon Foundation Chair in Constitutional Governance at the Faculty of Law of the University of Cape Town (South Africa).

ACKNOWLEDGEMENTS

The editors of this volume gratefully acknowledge the support of the vfonds, the Dutch National Foundation for Peace, Freedom and Veteran Care. This support made it possible to hold a workshop at Tilburg University in October 2014, where drafts of most chapters in this volume were discussed. Edwin Alblas, a research assistant at Tilburg Law School, provided invaluable assistance during the editing process. The editors of Cambridge University Press, Elizabeth Spicer and Bethany Johnson in particular, were of great patience and help during the entire period that work on this volume took place. Without the support of the persons and organizations mentioned, this volume would not have been possible. The editors' thanks go to all of them.

PART I

Realism and Idealism in Constitutionalism and the Rule of Law

Theory and History

1

The Ideal and the Real in the Realm of Constitutionalism and the Rule of Law: An Introduction

MAURICE ADAMS, ERNST HIRSCH BALLIN AND ANNE MEUWESE*

Introduction

Recent years have witnessed a multiplication of initiatives promoting constitutionalism and the rule of law. Both are understood, by many if not most, as necessary to create and sustain a just political order. If constitutionalism refers to a range of ideas and patterns of behaviour about how a government should be regulated in its powers in order to effectuate the fundamental principles of a political regime,[1] it is usually a national constitution that shapes constitutionalism in concrete legal terms. A more abstract definition, which applies not only to nation states but also to a post-national order, identifies constitutionalism as 'an overarching legal framework that determines the relationships of the different levels of law and the distribution of powers among their institutions'.[2]

* Many thanks to Sven Braspenning (formerly of Antwerp and Tilburg Universities), Hans Lindahl and Maarten Stremler (both Tilburg University) for suggestions and commenting on a previous version of this chapter.

1 Cf. K. E. Whittington, 'Constitutionalism' in K. E. Whittington, R. D. Kelemen and G. A. Caldeira (eds.), *The Oxford Handbook of Law and Politics* (Oxford University Press, 2008), p. 281.

2 N. Krisch, *Beyond Constitutionalism: The Pluralist Structure of Postnational Law* (Oxford University Press, 2010), p. 23. We use in this volume a rather material definition of a constitution, not necessarily confined to the single fundamental document – the Constitution with a capital C – that sets out the rules that regulate the government of a specific nation-state. Although national Constitutions get prime attention in most of the chapters in this volume, there is also reference to rules not encapsulated in a Constitution, but which nevertheless refer to a system of government: for example in the form of constitutional conventions, case law, (secondary) legislation, and soft law instruments of some sort, be they from national, supra- or international origin.

On the inter- and supra-national level, a rule of law discourse appears to prominently have taken on the task of expressing the norms and values that are deemed necessary for a just political order to exist.[3] And although the precise meaning of the phrase 'rule of law' is much debated,[4] nowadays there seems to be some agreement that it encompasses fundamental rights protection, judicial review, the division of powers, as well as a variety of governance requirements[5] – values that are in some form also legally protected by constitutional norms. In this sense these norms are, as Ginsburg and Versteeg put it in their contribution to this volume, 'the law that must rule, if the [rule of law] is to be achieved.' This can be taken to imply that constitutional norms tend to be of a more concrete and legal nature than the more process-oriented rule of law principles and instruments; constitutions function as a legal source for furthering the rule of law. Still, rule of law arrangements sometimes do have a concrete legal character and constitutional norms can be less than specific. In any event, the terms constitutionalism and rule of law are often used interchangeably.[6] But in whichever

[3] Often to be found in preambles, as in the *Statute of the Council of Europe*, the *European Convention on Human Rights*, the *Treaty on European Union*, the *Charter of Fundamental Rights of the European Union*, or the *Universal Declaration of Human Rights*. Also in national constitutions many times reference is being made to the rule of law or similar concepts, albeit in different meanings. See the examples in *European Commission for Democracy through Law* (Venice Commission), *Report on the Rule of Law*, Strasbourg, CDL-AD(2011)003rev, 8–9 April 2011 and the analysis in the report of the Netherlands Advisory Council for International Affairs, 'The Rule of Law: Safeguard for European Citizens and Foundation for European Cooperation' (No. 87, January 2014).

[4] R. H. Fallon, '"The Rule of Law" as a Concept in Constitutional Discourse', *Columbia Law Review*, 97 (1997), 1–56; M. Rosenfeld, 'The Rule of Law and the Legitimacy of Constitutional Democracy', *Southern California Law Review*, 74 (2001), 1307–52, and B. Z. Tamanaha, *On the Rule of Law. History, Politics, Theory* (Cambridge University Press, 2004), pp. 91–113. See also F. Venter, 'The Rule of Law as a Global Norm for Constitutionalism' in J. R. Silkenat, J. E. Hickey Jr. and P. D. Bairenboim (eds.), *The Legal Doctrines of the Rule of Law and the Legal State (Rechtsstaat)* (Springer: Heidelberg, 2014), pp. 92–5.

[5] Cf. M. D. McCubbins, D. B. Rodriguez and B. R. Weingast, 'The Rule of Law Unplugged', *Emory Law Journal*, 59 (2010), 1455.

[6] L. Catá Becker, 'Theocratic Constitutionalism: An Introduction to a New Global Legal ordening', *Indiana Journal of Global Legal Studies*, 16 (2009), 99–101. Also quoted by Venter, 'The Rule of Law', p. 96. Both terms also play a role in efforts to translate the German (and Dutch) concept of the *Rechtsstaat*. Whereas in academic publications the translation 'constitutional state' is quite popular, the Treaty on European Union lists 'the rule of law' among the values of the Union as the equivalent and translation of 'Rechtsstaat'. On how the rule of law relates to conceptions of *Rechtsstaat* or *état de droit*, see: R. Grote, 'Rule of Law, Rechtsstaat and

way one balances or differentiates these notions, the key observation must be that they are inseparably conjoined, albeit more so in their ends than in their means: the core function of either concept is to channel, discipline, constrain, inform and, as Krygier puts it, 'temper' the exercise of power, not to serve it.[7]

Clearly no constitution is a machine 'that would go of itself',[8] but little is known about the mechanisms that facilitate (or hinder) constitutions and rule of law arrangements. What makes a 'living constitution',[9] or, under what conditions can a rule of law instrument be considered effective? Is a constitution that purposely takes a 'light touch' approach to actually imposing rule of law values more or less effective in putting the ideal behind those values into practice? Adams and Van der Schyff, in the context of the Dutch example, suggest that the answer may well depend on the degree of constitutional literacy in a society. And to what extent is a semi-legal or evolutionary approach, for example by building on transnational rule of law peer review procedures, conducive to development in this domain? Meuwese, in her chapter, argues that the community of states willing to engage in dialogue should indeed be considered as a potential source of authority in this context.

État de droit' in C. Starck (ed.), *Constitutionalism, Universalism and Democracy. A comparative analysis* (Baden-Baden: Nomos Verlag 1999), pp. 269–306; N. W. Barber, 'The *Rechtsstaat* and the Rule of Law', *University of Toronto Law Journal*, 53 (2003), 443–54, and M. Loughlin, *Foundations of Public Law* (Oxford University Press, 2010), pp. 312–41.

7 See the chapter by Krygier in this volume. See also M. Krygier, 'Rule of Law (and Rechtsstaat)' in J. R. Silkenat, J. E. Hickey Jr. and P. D. Bairenboim (eds.), *The Legal Doctrines*, p. 46, and M. Krygier, 'Rule of Law' in M. Rosenfeld and A. Sajó (eds.), *The Oxford Handbook on Comparative Constitutional Law* (Oxford University Press, 2012), p. 245. Krygier points out that the rule of law can also be understood to deal with sources of social powers other than the state (family, companies), which is many times the realm of private law. Our focus is nevertheless on the public law realm, realising that public law and private law are getting more and more mixed (e.g., through *Drittwirkung* of fundamental rights). Cf. also Bingham: '[A]ll persons and authorities within the state, whether public or private, should be bound by and entitled to the benefit of laws publicly made, taking effect (generally) in the future and publicly administered in the courts'. T. Bingham, *The Rule of Law* (London: Penguin Books, 2010), p. 8.

8 M. G. Kammen, *A Machine That Would Go of Itself: The Constitution in American Culture* (New Brunswick: Transaction Publishers 2006).

9 The phrase living constitution was of course prominently used by B. Ackerman, 'The Living Constitution', *Harvard Law Review*, 120 (2007), 1737–812. See also D. A. Strauss, *The Living Constitution* (Oxford University Press, 2010).

Realising that full constitutional or rule of law compliance is like chasing a will-o'-the-wisp, in this volume we will close in on the aforementioned facilitating or hindering mechanisms by charting an underexplored tension. We are interested in the way constitutional norms and rule of law ideals or aspirations interact with the network of understandings and practices that inform and structure the concomitant political and social reality. The volume explores this tension through a combination of theoretical considerations and, mostly, case studies.[10] This approach provides an opportunity to uncover microfoundations of the mutually regulating relationship between the real and the ideal in this context.

The theme of this volume builds on work in the domains of political theory and philosophy and, if to a lesser extent, legal philosophy. In this introductory chapter, we will first, briefly and in general terms, present and discuss the distinction between idealism and realism, and the tension it inevitably engenders, as it is presented in political theory and legal philosophy. In doing so, we will break down the strict separation between positive and normative theory and show how the positive and the normative, a distinction that relates to the real and the ideal, are structurally related. In the following two sections we will then consider how this tension-fraught relationship presents itself in the constitutional and rule of law realm and can be used for our aims. Finally, we will put flesh on the bones of this volume by presenting and connecting its different contributions, and by introducing the structure of this volume. Given the setup of this introductory chapter, the way the terms that are central to this volume – realism and idealism – are deployed, will take shape as our discussion unfolds.

Positive and normative political theory

Traditionally, practical domains of inquiry are subdivided into two categories, according to their purpose and method: *positive* theory and

[10] Note that the aim is not to chart constitutional or rule of law *compliance* or implementation, although some of the chapters may shed a light on the conditions or mechanisms that either support or hinder constitutional compliance. See on this F. Schauer, 'Comparative Constitutional Compliance: Notes towards a Research Agenda' in M. Adams and J. A. Bomhoff (eds.), *Practice and Theory in Comparative Law* (Cambridge University Press, 2012), pp. 212–29.

normative theory.[11] In the domain of political theory, where the distinction between these two types of inquiry is generally acknowledged, positive political theory (often called political science) concerns the study of governments, public policies and political processes, systems and behaviour. Broadly speaking, positive political theory aims first and foremost to describe its objects, explain why they are the way they are, and how they (and their consequences) are expected to persist or change in the future. It includes such methods as literature review, document analysis, behavioural experiments and observations, survey research and interviewing, statistical analysis, and modelling and simulations. Normative political theory (frequently called political philosophy)[12] approaches the same objects from a normative point of view. Not only does it aim to describe its objects, it also wants to evaluate, criticise or justify the way they are or have come about, provide a picture of what they ought to be and possibly provide suggestions or prescriptions on how to accomplish this prospect. The methods used are mostly hermeneutic and interpretative, with an emphasis on literature review. Normative political theory, then, does not primarily try to describe or explain how our actual political world works; it rather aims to provide compelling reasons in favour of a desirable or ideal world.[13]

The distinction between positive and normative theory is also known in the field of law. One of the best-known proponents of a descriptive approach to law is, of course, Hans Kelsen. His 'pure theory of law' (*Reine Rechtslehre*) is the methodological foundation of a type of legal scholarship that aspires to be free of what Kelsen calls ideology; the aim is to describe the law *as it is*, not *as it ought to be*.[14] Normative theories of law steer a different course, and explicitly involve evaluative and prescriptive

[11] On this S. Braspenning, *Normative Democratic Theory and the Realities of Public Moral Disagreement* (Brussels: UPA 2012), pp. 11–13.

[12] See R. Goodin, P. Pettit and T. Pogge, *A Companion to Contemporary Political Philosophy* (Oxford: Blackwell, 2007), p. xvi. We here use normative political theory and political philosophy as synonyms.

[13] Z. Stemplowska, 'What's Ideal About Ideal Theory?', *Political Studies Review*, 10 (2008), 327–8.

[14] H. Kelsen, *Reine Rechtlehre (Mit einem Anhang: Das Problem der Gerechtigkeit* (Wien: Verlag Franz Deuticke, 1976 (unchanged from the 1961 (second) edition): 'Der Haupteinwand, der gegen die Naturrechtslehre im allgemeinen zu erheben ist: dass aus dem Sein kein Sollen, aus Tatsachen keine normen gefolgert werden können.' (p. 409). Kelsen's critique is first and foremost directed at theories of natural law, but is in our opinion not restricted to such theories.

questions:[15] What ought to be the sources of sovereignty and legitimacy? Which procedures should be followed? How should the rulers and the ruled act publicly and privately? And how should these two spheres of acting be distinguished?

Positive and normative theory, and the distinction between 'is' and 'ought', are traditionally understood as separate ontological domains that cannot be reduced to one another, and this of course also holds for *statements* concerning what 'is' and what 'ought' to be.[16] This dichotomy, however, is untenable, because even descriptive accounts of the objects of political science or legal scholarship are unavoidably interpretative and evaluative. '[T]he evaluations of the theorist himself are an indispensable and decisive component in the selection or formation of any concepts for use in description of such aspects of human affairs as law and legal order.'[17] Indeed, as John Finnis reminds his readers, law 'does not come neatly demarcated from other features of social life and practice'.[18] The descriptive theorist is therefore always in the business of making judgements of importance and significance in his description of law. If someone sees the ideal of law as pertaining to, for example creating a stable social order – as H. L. A. Hart does[19] – then such a view about the purpose of law will inevitably enter one's descriptive concept of law, even to the point of controlling it.[20]

[15] See the work by R. Dworkin and J. Finnis for example. R. Dworkin, *Taking Rights Seriously* (Cambridge, MA: Harvard University Press, 1978); R. Dworkin *Law's Empire* (London: Fontana Press, 1986) and J. Finnis, *Natural Law and Natural Rights* (Oxford University Press, 1980). More general normative theories, like John Rawls's theory of justice, are usually seen as contributions to political philosophy, not to legal scholarship. The line between these different disciplinary approaches is however not always easy to draw.

[16] As is well known, already Hume famously argued that the latter cannot *logically* be derived from the former. See *A Treatise of Human Nature*, see especially book III, part I, section I.

[17] Finnis, *Natural Law*, p. 16. [18] *Ibid.*, p. 4.

[19] H. L. A. Hart, *The Concept of Law* (Oxford University Press, 1961), p. 78 ff. (this feature of law pertaining to social stability seems also part and parcel of Hart's 'minimum content of natural law'). Finnis, *Natural Law*, pp. 6–7.

[20] Admittedly, the 'theory-ladenness of observation' does not make the distinction between is and ought (or fact and value) in all circumstances useless. For even though some distinctions may be inaccurate or problematic at a deeper theoretical level (the level we are focusing at here), this does not necessarily prevent one from making them useful for some contexts or uses. See, e.g., H. Putnam, *The Collapse of the Fact/Value Dichotomy and Other Essays* (Cambridge, MA: Harvard University Press, 2002) and P. A. Railton, *Facts, Values, and Norms: Essays toward a Morality of Consequence*

will fail; and indeed, we may be able to find no satisfactory answer at all. But we must try to postpone the day of reckoning as long as possible, and try to arrange society so that it never comes.'[35] Rawls, so it turns out, was aware of the substantial but nevertheless limited use of his normative theory in non-ideal circumstances, but this did not drive him to cynicism. Instead he clings on to his hope for a just and fair society, building on man as being to some extent reasonable,[36] and gives some priority to morality in political reasoning.[37]

This *prima facie* comparison of Schmitt and Rawls confirms that although views on meta-theoretical political issues revolve around typical concepts such as political possibility, the meaning of these concepts is informed by substantive views of the political itself, which in turn are influenced by an image of man as being either evil or reasonable. And while theories like Rawls's prioritise morality over politics, they too derive a part of their purpose from what is considered to be politically or realistically possible (and from a picture or representation of what has not or not fully been realised).[38] Moreover, both Rawls and Schmitt think that only by exploring the limits of what seems realistically possible in political terms can there be any hope of making sense of what the concept of the political truly entails as a practical concept, which is highly dependent on particular circumstances. This shared insight can and

[35] *Ibid.*

[36] See also the Introduction to the 2005 edition of Rawls, *Political Liberalism*, first published in 1993, almost a quarter century after *A Theory of Justice*: 'The wars of this century with their extreme violence and increasing destructiveness, culminating in the manic evil of the Holocaust, raise in an acute way the question whether political relations must be governed by power and coercion alone. If a reasonably just society that subordinates power to its aims is not possible and people are largely amoral, if not incurably cynical and self-centered, one might ask with Kant whether it is worthwhile for human beings to live on the earth. We must start with the assumption that a reasonably just political society is possible, and for it to be possible, human beings must have a moral nature, not of course a perfect such nature, yet one that can understand, act on, and be sufficiently moved by a reasonable political conception of right and justice to support a society guided by its ideals and principles. *Theory* [*of Justice*] and PL [*Political Liberalism*] try to sketch what the more reasonable conceptions of justice for a democratic regime are and to present a candidate for the most reasonable. They also consider how citizens need to be conceived to construct [. . .] those more reasonable conceptions, and what their moral psychology has to be to support a reasonably just political society over time. The focus on these questions no doubt explains in part what seems to many readers the abstract and unworldly character of these texts. I do not apologize for that.' Rawls, *Political Liberalism*, p. lx.

[37] Williams, 'Realism and Moralism', p. 2.

[38] Similar: D. Runciman, 'Political Theory and Real Politics in the Age of the Internet', *the Journal of Political Philosophy*, 24 (2016).

ought to be translated to our thinking about constitutionalism and the rule of law.

Constitutions and the Rule of Law as Institutionalised Ideals

Constitutional norms and rule of law arrangements are mostly thoroughly normative, and grounded in liberal convictions. As such they tune in with Rawlsian normative or ideal theory as described in the previous paragraph. In this vein, idealism, in its most transcendental and general but also most fundamental sense, here refers to a situation where the protection of the values of personal freedom and autonomy is prime, and in which equality – everyone deserves equal respect as autonomous and thus free persons – is the most genuine form of morality which should be protected by the constitution and its concomitant rules and legislation. This morality derives from historical, social and political events, documents (e.g., the *Declaration of Independence*, the *Declaration des Droits de l'Homme et du Citoyen*, the *International Covenant on Civil and Political Rights*, the *European Convention for the Protection of Human Rights and Fundamental Freedoms* and the *Charter of Fundamental Rights of the European Union*), judicial decisions, and institutions, but also from society as a 'fair system of cooperation'.[39]

This transcendental ideal functions as a kind of master ideal or *Grundnorm*, and is not so much concerned with practical politics or laws really, but free floating from this. '[Ideals] function as judgments upon us, and inform the concrete goals we set before us, but they ought not to be confused with those goals. (. . .) [Ideals] are not situational, and in themselves do not help to make the discriminations which are necessary in action.'[40] This approach is not unlike the role of 'regulative ideals' in the Kantian sense, where the ideal aspect gives an orientation and the regulative aspect guides the approach.[41] This also tunes in with one of the other roles Rawls identifies – next to the already mentioned 'exploratory role' – for political philosophy, which he calls 'orientation'.[42] Indeed, an

[39] To use Rawls' terminology. See Rawls, *Political Liberalism*, p. 15.

[40] P. Selznick, 'The Iron Law of Bureaucracy', *Modern Review*, 3 (1950), 161. Also quoted in M. Krygier, *Philip Selznick; Ideals in the World* (Stanford University Press, 2012), p. 40.

[41] D. M. Emmet, *The Role of the Unrealisable. A Study in Regulative Ideals* (New York: St. Martin's Press, 1994), p. 9.

[42] Political philosophy 'may contribute to how people think of their political and social institutions as a whole' and 'understand themselves as members having a certain political status – in a democracy, that of equal citizenship – and how this status affects their

important necessary condition of rendering something meaningful is the mapping of its structure and how it relates to us through this structure; in short, how it provides an orientation for thought.

If the just-quoted evaluation by Selznick is correct, constitutional norms and rule of law arrangements are the institutionalised translations of the master ideal. They will take on a variety of more-concrete shapes in different contexts and settings, often in full awareness of the fact that in practice neither the master ideal nor the aims of these more concrete arrangements will be fully achieved.[43] Furthermore, the images of what should be part and parcel of these arrangements, and how they are to be understood, will differ significantly in time and place.

Institutionalisation is in any case key, not just to provide concrete shape and legal authority to the ideals that are deemed important, but also to avoid the complete 'ethicalisation' of the rule of law and constitutional practice. If constitutionalism and the rule of law are being considered the rule of the 'good' law, then to explain its nature is to propound a complete social philosophy.[44] This has to be avoided, not just because as a result the terms lack any useful function, but also because such a position runs the danger that those accidentally in power will determine what this social philosophy consists of; the rule of law is then exchanged for the rule of man, and abuse and arbitrariness lurks around the corner.[45] It would indeed be a mistake to think of concrete institutions and practices *solely* as instruments in the realisation of certain ideals or moral values – in whatever form they are expressed – whose justification is given independently of these institutions and practices.[46] At the same time, constitutions and the rule of law are of course informed by particular conceptions of what constitutes a good society. As Bisarya and Bulmer put it in their chapter: as soon as we ask 'What is the rule of law actually *for*?', it emerges that the rule of law is rarely pursued as an end in itself, but is valued for its contribution to other desired outcomes in terms

relation to their social world.' To this end it may offer a 'unified framework' for reflection. Rawls, *Justice as Fairness*, pp. 2–3.

43 Cf. Taekema, who describes ideals as desirable states of affairs which are difficult to realize completely, and which provide direction in problematic situations. S. Taekema, 'What Ideals Are' in W. van der Burg and S. Taekema (eds.), *The Importance of Ideals* (Brussels: Peter Lang, 2004), p. 39.

44 As Raz once put it. J. Raz, 'The Rule of Law and Its Virtue' in *The Authority of Law* (Oxford University Press, 1979), p. 211.

45 See Krygier in his chapter about the relation between the rule of law and arbitrariness.

46 Bell, 'Under an Empty', p. 15.

of good governance and the capacity of states to 'deliver the goods' in terms of public services and development outcomes.

Constitutions and the Rule of Law as Practical Ideals

Constitutional norms and rule of law arrangements can, we contend, be understood as *practical* ideals, i.e., directed at reality. They thus not merely inform and set the goals of what society should be striving for, but are at the same time determined by political disagreements and the tensions that beset political life,[47] and this not only at the outset, when they were conceived, but also during their life span through interpretation and implementation. This places them between the purely ideal on the one hand and the real on the other. They do not merely refer to social and political reality in a formal way, as if this reality were nothing more than its addressee. On the contrary, if they aim to stabilise or transform a concrete social and political reality, they must be sensitive to this reality. And this sensitivity is key to what realism, as opposed to idealism, stands for here: an approach to constitutional norms and rule of law arrangements that does not float free from the forces of politics,[48] but one that is thoroughly shaped by it.

This dual nature of constitutional norms and rule of law arrangements, and especially the practical questions it gives rise to, can be illustrated by the work of Russell Hardin. As Hardin states, '[o]ne of the oldest and most honoured traditions in political philosophy is the odd claim that a constitution or the very act of forming a government is metaphorically a big contract [between constituents or elite groups].'[49] As contracts, which are supposed to be explicitly agreed upon by its signees, constitutions are thought to be thoroughly normative and therefore binding and followed. Hardin himself however compares constitutions not so much to contracts, but rather with social conventions whose norms are not regulated or fixed or contracted, but emerge spontaneously. Since these conventional norms are as a result in touch with recent changes in society, relying as they are on a far wider input of understanding and experience than available to, say, a particular group of constitution drafters at a particular moment.[50]

[47] See also Shinar in this volume.

[48] Cf. E. Rossi and M. Sleat, 'Realism in Normative Political Theory', *Philosophy Compass*, 9/10 (2014), 689–700.

[49] See R. Hardin, 'Why a Constitution?' in B. Grofman and D. Wittman (eds.), *The Federalist Papers and the New Institutionalism* (New York: Agathon Press, 1989), p. 100.

[50] *Ibid.*, p. 115.

As such, when compared to contractual norms, they can according to Hardin better provide the seed for understanding why an arrangement not formally agreed to is nevertheless being experienced as legitimate, that is, when it works to mutual advantage.[51] In other words, since constitutions only work when they are backed by the groups they serve, they must reflect what is perceived to be the public good and promote what seems mutually advantageous. Under these conditions they might well enjoy public support or at least public acquiescence. 'Constitutions must (. . .) be self-enforcing, meaning that it is in the interest of all powerful factions to abide by the provisions of the constitution.'[52] From all this it also follows that 'the appeal of conventions is greater, because they need not be constrained by 'mistaken ideal conceptions',[53] conceptions which do not have the capacity to bind people. In a similar fashion, Hardin observes that '[a] constitution can include anything people might want. But if it is filled with *perversities*, it is likely to fail to coordinate us.'[54] Hardin's thesis seems primarily intended as a sociological or causal explanation for the effectiveness of constitutions.

Jeff King points out that there are two possible readings of Hardin's constitutional theory. The first is the weaker reading, which is unproblematic: if a constitution must work for it to be successful or useful or accepted, it should not attempt the impossible.[55] Societal stability, which Hardin believes to be the main purpose of a constitution, can then be a realistic end to reach for, and a 'precursor for whatever else a state may wish to do.'[56] The second, stronger, reading is more sceptical and tunes in with Hardin's view that too much presence of (mistaken) aspirational

[51] R. Hardin, 'Why a Constitution?' in D. J. Galligan and M. Versteeg (eds.), *Social and Political Foundations of Constitutions* (Cambridge University Press, 2013), p. 61. See on Hardin's coordination thesis also D. Galligan and M. Versteeg, 'Theoretical Perspectives on the Social and Political Foundations of Constitutions' in D. J. Galligan and M. Versteeg (eds.), pp. 24–39.

[52] T. Ginsburg, 'Constitutional endurance' in T. Ginsburg and R. Dixon (eds.), *Comparative Constitutional Law* (Cheltenham: Edward Elgar, 2011), p. 116. See also Z. Elkins, T. Ginsburg and J. Melton, *The Endurance of National Constitutions* (Cambridge University Press, 2009).

[53] R. Hardin, *Liberalism, Constitutionalism, and Democracy* (Oxford University Press, 1999), p. 118.

[54] Hardin 2013, p. 62 (emphasis added).

[55] J. King, 'Constitutions as Mission Statements' in: D. J. Galligan and M. Versteeg (eds.), *Social and Political Foundations of Constitutions*, pp. 73–103. We add that acceptance here is not the same as complete agreement with the constitution by its addressees, but rather, at the minimum, tacit agreement with a power structure to the extent that it seems practical and/or prudent. See Galligan and Versteeg, 'Theoretical Perspectives', p. 25.

[56] King, 'Constitutions as Mission Statements', p. 79.

ideals in a constitution create cynicism or at least a lack of (popular) constitutional commitment. However, such a view could, King believes, encourage constitutional conservatism rather than a proactive view on constitutions. It might well strip constitutions of any ideal aspirations. To be sure, if Hardin believes that unrealistic constitutional idealism, based on significantly false assumptions, would peel the meaning of constitutions to such an extent that it even creates cynicism in this regard, his point is understandable. A good example of this might well be the following provision, which is Article 33 of the current Syrian Constitution (2012):

1. Freedom shall be a sacred right and the state shall guarantee the personal freedom of citizens and preserve their dignity and security;
2. Citizenship shall be a fundamental principle which involves rights and duties enjoyed by every citizen and exercised according to law;
3. Citizens shall be equal in rights and duties without discrimination among them on grounds of sex, origin, language, religion or creed;
4. The state shall guarantee the principle of equal opportunities among citizens.[57]

The Syrian Constitution appears to be what Loewenstein would call a 'semantic constitution': an unrealistic and meaningless piece of paper.[58] It seems clear that Hardin would condemn this provision, because it is in all respects out of tune with even the most minimal understanding of the Syrian reality. But would Hardin also condemn it if it were not Syrian but part and parcel of the South African Constitution, which was charged with performing a 'fanciful' transformative task[59] and contains quite some idealistic norms which in practice will almost certainly only to

[57] *Constitution of the Syrian Arab Republic*, 26 February 2012. Translation on the UNHCR-website: www.refworld.org/cgi-bin/texis/vtx/rwmain?docid=5100f02a2. On this E. M. H. Hirsch Ballin, *De Grondwet in politiek en samenleving* (The Hague: Boom, 2013), p. 21 (Dutch).

[58] K. Loewenstein, *Political Power and the Governmental Process* (The University of Chicago Press, 1957), p. 149.

[59] See on this also C. Sunstein, 'Social and economic rights? Lessons from South Africa', *Constitutional Forum*, 11 (2000–01), 123–32. The phrase 'transformative constitutionalism' comes from K. Klare, 'Legal Culture and Transformative Constitutionalism', *South African Journal on Human Rights*, 14 (1998), 146–88: 'By transformative constitutionalism I mean a long-term project of constitutional enactment, interpretation, and enforcement committed (. . .) to transforming a country's political and social institutions and power relationships in a democratic, participatory, and egalitarian direction.' p. 150. South Africa might represent what Loewenstein would call a nominal constitution, referring to a situation where the factual state of affairs does not, or not yet, permit

a certain extent be realised? This example reveals an element that is not too clear in Hardin's theory, regardless of the weak or strong reading: What constitutes too much unrealistic idealism – 'perversities' – in a constitution or rule of law instrument? To what extent can constitutional norms and rule of law arrangements not also try to prescribe norms or values that run against what seems realistically possible? And under what conditions can legitimacy also be generated, not just by acquiescence, but by the aspirations of a constitution itself? Even if quite a few of the South African constitutional provisions fall short, because they represent 'mistaken ideal conceptions', the history of South Africa might well suggest that the current constitutionalism was, and still is, immensely meaningful as a source of legitimacy.

Charting the Tension between the Real and Ideal in the Constitutional and Rule of Law Realm

There is a growing voice of dissent against idealism and ideal theory, or at least the kind of theory that does not have the pretence of constructing feasible or realistic recommendations.[60] In the constitutional context, the provision from the Syrian Constitution that was quoted above may well be understood as feeding such a point of view. The adherents of this position, often called realists, argue, just as Hardin seems to be doing in the constitutional realm, that 'taking an unattainable standard as the polestar is likely to produce, at best the frustration of political aims, at worst, destructive distortions of politics.'[61] From this point of view, if an ideal leads to political or constitutional proposals that cannot be materialised, it might lose legitimacy and value as a regulative standard.

It seems obvious that the more the constitutional and rule of law debates are informed by (political) reality, the more practical they are.

a fulfilling integration of the constitutional norms into the dynamics of political life. Loewenstein, *Political Power,* p. 149.

60 See, e.g., W. A. Galston, 'Realism in Political Theory', *European Journal of Political Theory*, 9 (2010), 385–411; C. Mouffe, *On the political* (London: Routledge, 2005) and R. Geuss, *Philosophy and Real Politics* (Princeton University Press, 2008). The debate between realism and idealism is also prominently present in international relations theory and practice. See R. M. A. Crawford, *Idealism and Realism in International Relations: Beyond the Discipline* (London: Routledge, 2000); D. Bell (ed.), *Political Thought and International Relations. Variations on a Realist Theme* (Oxford University Press, 2008) and J. S. Barkin, *Realist Constructivism: Rethinking International Relations Theory* (Cambridge University Press, 2010).

61 Galston, 'Realism in Political', 395.

Case sensitivity seems crucial here; what is a good for one society is not necessarily fitting or desirable for another. Indeed, comparing the (particular) realities of everyday to what lies at the limits of the practical and to the possibilities of the normative also constitutes, we contend, the core of almost any constitutional and rule of law scholarship and practice. So we do acknowledge the contingencies and specific circumstances of each case as such, and no claim in this realm can be plausible if it does not take account of these different levels of understanding and their internal relationship. This approach is similar to the exploratory role Rawls believed to be so valuable in the context of political philosophy.

Even so, assuming the 'fanciful' or ideal as an integral part of constitutional and rule of law analysis can at the same time make clear just how crucial or determinative certain constraints are to shaping what we consider desirable or just when they are present.[62] So even if they do not amount to sufficient conditions for making sense of value judgements, we deem ideals indispensable as regulative ideas, whether they can be realised or not: to move through the field of values and norms without the orientation provided by the ideal is, ultimately, to move blindly.

Political Moderation as a Means to Bridge Realism and Idealism

The various chapters in this volume trace and discuss the aforementioned interplay across four main, and many times overlapping, categories: mechanisms of institutional change, constitutional design, (judicial) levers for enforcing political moderation and positive constitutionalism and citizenship.

Mechanisms of Institutional Change

Bisarya and Bulmer, in their chapter, stress that it is never a constitution *by itself* that can establish the necessary bridging between idealism and realism. Krygier, in a similar vein, writes that legal texts and institutions can never be the answer on their own for the bridging to be done; they depend for their success on the deeper socio-cultural elements that make for institutional foundation or evolution in this regard. Building on the work of the French administrative law scholar Maurice Hauriou

[62] Cf. Stemplowska, 'What's Ideal About', 327. Similar: A. Swift, 'The Value of Philosophy in Nonideal Circumstances', *Social Theory and Practice*, 34 (2008), 363–87 and I. Robeyns, 'Are Transcendental Theories of Injustice Redundant?', *Journal of Economic Methodology*, 19 (2012), 159–63.

(1856–1929), Lindseth claims one can view the process of institutional and constitutional contestation and change as operating along three inter-related dimensions: (a) the *functional* (in which existing institutional structures are brought under pressure and transformed as a consequence of social demands), as well as by constraints imposed by the availability (or lack) of resources and technology; (b) the *political*, in which actors struggle over the allocation of scarce institutional advantages and resources in responding to the just mentioned functional pressures; and (c) the *cultural*, encompassing the ways in which competing notions of legitimacy are then mobilised by social and political actors either to justify or to resist changes in institutional and legal categories or structures. Almost all of the chapters can be read in view of these dimensions of institutional change Lindseth sets out. It is moreover important to note, and also central to this volume, that the changing structures of (constitutional) governance – the real – will never be perfectly congruent with prevailing understandings of legitimate or ideal governance – the ideal. The perceived disconnect between these two inevitably will lead to a dialectic in which both structures of governance and understandings of a legitimate legal and political order establish themselves in the face of the reciprocal influences of the other.

An interesting contrast in this regard can be seen between the South African and Dutch approach to constitutionalism. De Vos points out that unlike traditional liberal constitutions, the South African Constitution is by many understood to contain a strong commitment to creating a more just society, i.e., more equal, caring, social, redistributive, multicultural etc., than before the demise of Apartheid. The Dutch Constitution, on the contrary, as Adams and Van der Schyff make clear, is not intended as the main or sole source of rule of law values in the Netherlands. The Dutch Constitution does not function as a strong normative document;[63] it comes close to being a codification of political practice and creates an incomplete constitutional framework to be further developed by sheer political – legislative or non-legislative – means. The underlying and questionable assumption appears to be that Dutch democratic culture is so strong that the Constitution can be safely ignored. However, the demise of the old political structures that formed the basis of Dutch

[63] The expression of its normativity differs essentially from that of neighbouring Belgium for instance, especially in the realm of the relations between the different constituent parts of the Belgian federation. See M. Adams, 'Disabling Constitutionalism', *International Journal of Constitutional Law*, 12 (2014), 279–302.

governance, and the key to its political stability, now points to the need to develop a stronger constitutional culture to help fill the vacuum left by the dissolution of these old power structures. Adams and Van der Schyff remind the reader that under the current political conditions, the Dutch Constitution runs the risk of falling prey to deliberate political manipulation.

De Vos makes clear that the South African Constitutional Court, which up until the present day had to work within a context of one-party-dominance in parliament, is taking tentative and pragmatic steps to protect democracy while at the same time avoiding a head-on confrontation with the dominant party. By involving politicians in the appointment of judges and by ensuring this happens in a way that, over time, will make the judiciary more representative of the general population in terms of race and gender (but also in terms of sexual orientation, class, rural representation, language and the like), De Vos argues that the Constitution provides political cover for judges to do their job. It potentially also helps to prevent the appointment of judges whose views about the world and the role of law in regulating the world are completely out of kilter with the norms embodied in the Constitution and with the broad values of the majority of citizens. Once appointed, judges will often try to navigate the waters between upholding the high principles of the Constitution and at the same time trying not to alienate the overwhelming majority of voters and the political elites. And although the South African Constitutional Court seems to have been skilful in navigating these waters, the political system and culture have not been entirely successful in producing the more egalitarian society in which the human dignity of all South Africans are equally respected and protected.

Feng Lin provides insights into the tensions and interactions between idealism and realism in the Chinese constitutional realm from a variety of perspectives: a historical one, a practical one and a theoretical one. The issue of 'constitutional enforcement' is central to the institutional developments in China. Out of all the well-established constitutional supervision models in the world which may serve as inspiration, the most recent proposal and a very concrete attempt to bridge the 'ideal' and the 'real', presented to the Central Government by a group of leading constitutional scholars is to establish a special committee under the National People's Congress (NPC) for this purpose. The tensions explored in this chapter are mainly between judicial activism and the Communist Party's attachment to the status quo and between transplantation of foreign models and Chinese domestic reality. Lin identifies the

Judicial and Other Levers for Enforcing Political Moderation

Recent decades have seen the emergence of judicial constitutional review in political systems worldwide. While by the middle of the nineteenth century this competence had only been available for courts in the United States (since 1803), Greece (1847) and Norway (since 1866), today more than 80 countries have some form of it. Add to this the increasing tendency among international and supranational courts to act as constitutional courts,[65] and the picture is complete: constitutional review by the judiciary has gathered momentum and is *en vogue*. Lesaffer and Musa, in their chapter, point out that it was the emergence of international human rights, from 1960s onwards, that provided for a new allocation of power by adding a layer, next to the introduction in the late eighteenth century of a constitutional separation of powers, of legal protection above the state. It was this development which subsequently led to the rise of judicial constitutional review in many countries.

Judicial independence and impartiality are seen as central elements of almost any rule of law conception. As the 'Venice Commission' of the Council of Europe made clear a few years ago, this means that the judiciary must be 'free from external pressure, and is not controlled by the other branches of government, especially the executive branch. This requirement is an integral part of the fundamental democratic principle of the separation of powers. Courts should not be subject to political influence or manipulation. "Impartial" means that the judiciary is not – even in appearance – prejudiced as to the outcome of the case.'[66]

Hungary turns out to be a worrisome case in this regard. The parliamentary majority is, since the constitutional transformation in 2011 (and its subsequent changes), able to nominate candidates for the Constitutional Court without working together with the opposition. The membership of the Court has moreover been enlarged from 11 to 15, and the president of the Court will no longer be elected by his fellow justices but by parliament too. Partly as a result of this court-packing activity, the parliamentary majority has been able to elect 11 new justices. The Hungarian Fundamental Law also affects the competences of the Constitutional Court. As a result, *a priori* judicial constitutional control, instead of being a protective tool for the minority, is now in the

[65] E.g., the European Court of Justice, the European Court of Human Rights, the Dispute Settlement Body of the World Trade Organisation, and the International Criminal Court.

[66] *European Commission for Democracy through Law* (Venice Commission), *Report on the Rule of Law*, Strasbourg, CDL-AD(2011)003rev, April 2011, 12.

hands of the parliamentary majority. Moreover, the *ex post* review of the unconstitutionality of legislation is restricted: the Fundamental Law abolishes the *actio popularis*. Only the Government, the Commissioner for Fundamental Rights, and one quarter of the members of parliament can turn to the Constitutional Court, which means that according to the existing division of seats in parliament all the opposition parties would have to agree on a petition for *ex post* constitutional review.

Judicial constitutional review is of course not the only mechanism for enforcing a constitution or for elevating the rule of law to a higher level. Mechanisms of a more political nature, such as peer review or international pressure by the international community, might also play a role. Hungary is not just an interesting case, then, for its domestic reforms of the judiciary (see above), but also for the calls it triggers on the European Commission to take action when a EU Member State starts to deviate from the common values expressed in Article 2 of the Treaty of the European Union (TEU).[67] To what extent can a legal or extra-legal (political) external leverage make a difference here? Meuwese in her contribution to this volume discusses the role that peer review may play in either developing constitutionalism or challenging more concrete governmental actions across the globe. Examples are the OECD peer reviews, never directly aimed at rule of law promotion, but with spillover capacities to that effect, the African Peer Review Mechanism and the EU Rule of Law monitor.

The last of these plays a prominent role in Kochenov's analysis of the various institutional responses to the European Union's systemic deficiencies regarding the rule of law, which as the author shows, stretch far beyond enforcement issues and beyond the Hungarian case. The chapter critically evaluates the European Commission's recent 'pre-Article 7' proposal, putting it in the context of its deficiencies. Kochenov argues that solving the EU's vulnerability on the Rule of Law front will require a reinvention of the place that values actually occupy in the edifice of EU integration. As such the EU's efforts constitute a relevant test case for the capacity of transnational mechanisms to contribute to the reconciliation of the constitutional 'real' and 'ideal'. Scheppele argues that the European Union, despite being known as 'constitutionally pluralist' can and should

[67] 'The Union is founded on the values of respect for human dignity, freedom, democracy, equality, the rule of law and respect for human rights, including the rights of persons belonging to minorities. These values are common to the Member States in a society in which pluralism, non-discrimination, tolerance, justice, solidarity and equality between women and men prevail.'

enforce rule of law standards on the direct basis of treaty-based 'acquis' of European values. One concrete mechanism for doing so is the 'systemic infringement procedure' – bundling together a group of complaints into a single infringement action so as to demonstrate a pattern of violation of fundamental principles and rights – which has been teased in the EU context as a new constitutional mechanism for upholding the rule of law. This concerns a practical application of the idea that the 'ideal' is furthered not always by enforcing individual constitutional norms but by institutional means that can absorb a set of 'real' circumstances.

Turning to how extra-judicial, transnational mechanisms play out at the state level outside of Europe, Rwanda comes to mind too. As Huls in his chapter points out, Rwanda wants to play a more prominent role in the United Nations – it already occupied a UN Security Council seat in 1994–1995 and in 2013–2014 – and the President has signed many human rights treaties. The country reports regularly to the Monitoring Groups of the UN in Geneva and also promises to perform better in the future. At the same time, its track record is diffuse in this regard: it does not have a prominent place on the scorecards of institutes that measure civil liberties and political rights (Freedom House) and voice and accountability (World Bank Institute). In the 2014 Report on Rwanda by the US State Department, an overview of the concerns of the international community can be found: the State security forces (SSF) operate in a way that is insufficiently checked by the judiciary; cruel, inhuman or degrading treatment of punishment of prisoners is forbidden in the Constitution, but government action against abuses is rare; press freedom is limited and sometimes journalists are harassed. Rwanda does therefore not qualify for financial support by the US Millennium Challenge Corporation. At the same time, Huls writes, the Rwandan government is very smart in exploiting the guilt feelings of the superpowers, who did nothing during the 1994 genocide and therefore do not experience the legitimacy to criticise the present government. In any case, illiberal peace building sacrifices individual freedoms, but apparently secures negative peace in the form of stability and abatement of armed violence.

The role of extra-judicial, international levers is also addressed by Luther, when he deals with the case of the Italian constitution and its reform. His chapter reminds readers that idealism and realism are concepts that have been both opposed and composed mainly in Europe. In Italy idealism and realism have been bridged throughout history mainly through legal doctrines and practices of the 'living law' (*diritto vivente*).

The focus of the chapter is on the controversial recent reforms, which seem to reduce both regionalism and bicameralism and propose a stronger government, prioritising 'real efficiency' to 'ideal justice'. Or, in the words of the author, these recent developments show a lack of idealism *and* realism. This appears to be why the author, in the final part of his chapter, turns to the pressures the international context can exert. The setting of pluralist constitutionalism in Europe offers opportunities for comparative dialogues and interaction, and even for mechanisms of interference (see also the chapters by Meuwese, Kochenov and Scheppele).

Luther also appeals to extra-legal mechanisms and instruments such as indicators, rankings and peer reviews, which are increasingly being used to shape the practice of constitutionalism and rule of law across countries.[68] The standards and norms used in these exercises represent an ideal that is often left implicit and assumed to be shared among participants. For instance, a rule of law indicator might measure the number of judges in a country as a percentage of the total population as an indication of the degree of judicial protection. The ideal percentage is not stated (and obviously does not exist) but it is implied that below a certain ratio the situation is non-ideal (as compared to the measurable realities of other countries). Rankings also may employ measurements of the faith that professionals have in, say, legal certainty in a country, thus using beliefs about the ideal to capture the real. And mechanisms such as the World Justice Project produce a Rule of Law ranking every year, with the intention of using the possibility of visible improvement as an incentive for countries to make progress. As such, these transnational mechanisms are rather explicitly aimed at bringing the 'real' and the 'ideal' closer together.

Ginsburg and Versteeg in their chapter take a critical look at this blossoming global practice by offering a first, preliminary empirical exploration of the relationship between constitutions and the rule of law. Since the indexes by the World Governance Indicator project of the World Bank (WGI), the Heritage Foundation and the World Justice Project (WJP) are closely correlated, they use the former, while zooming in on three constitutional features: the direct protection of the rule of law in the constitution, the inclusion of rights and the establishment of constitutional review. They find that a number of features that are

[68] E. M. H. Hirsch Ballin, 'Mutual Trust: The Virtue of Reciprocity – Strengthening the Acceptance of the Rule of Law through Peer Review' in C. Closa and D. Kochenov (eds.), *Reinforcement of the Rule of Law Oversight in the European Union* (Cambridge University Press 2016).

commonly associated with the rule of law in an ideal sense do not appear to be linked to respect for the rule of law in practice. For instance, the presence of constitutional rights and judicial review do not appear to lead to higher rule of law scores. This leads them to conclude that while it is plausible that written constitutions are necessary for building respect for the rule of law, it is clear that they are not a sufficient condition.

Positive Constitutionalism and Citizenship

The theme of political moderation and constitutional design as key for realising constitutional norms and rule of law values also prominently emerges in Krygier's chapter [Krygier prefers the term 'tempering power' in this context.] Applied to constitutionalism and the rule of law, tempering can, according to him, better suggest some judicious combination of mix, balance, moderation and self-knowledge. Contrary to the popular view of constitutions and rule of law arrangements as imposing negative constraints on those in power, the ambition to 'temper' power is consistent with acknowledging that among what is hoped for from constitutionalism and the rule of law are salutary forms of *strengthening* the power to which it is applied.

Building on Stephen Holmes' work, Krygier focuses on what Holmes calls 'positive constitutionalism', i.e., the much-overlooked potential of constitutional provisions to achieve cooperation and support, and deploy it towards socially desirable ends, and to prevent 'social chaos and private oppression, immobilism, unaccountability, instability, and the ignorance and stupidity of politicians'.[69] To quote Holmes again: 'If we think of constitutional rules as scripts, rather than ropes (. . .) it is easier to understand why powerful actors, looking for protocols to facilitate rapid coordination, might be willing to incorporate them into their motivations as obligatory principles of conduct. They are not incapacitating, but capacitating. They are not shackles making unwanted action impossible, but guidelines making wanted action feasible. Seen in this way, their binding power becomes more commonsensical than mysterious.'[70]

[69] S. Holmes, *Passions and Constraint. On the Theory of Liberal Democracy* (University of Chicago Press, 1995), p. 51.

[70] S. Holmes, 'Constitutions and Constitutionalism' in M. Rosenfeld and A. Sajó (eds.), *Th Oxford Handbook of Comparative Constitutional Law* (Oxford University Press, 2012), p. 202. Also quoted by Krygier in this volume.

This insight is speaking in situations of extreme societal stress. Krygier refers to the post-9/11 situations about which also Stephen Holmes has written extensively, where 'defenders of unchecked (or only weakly checked) executive discretion in the war on terror typically ignore the liberal paradox and its corollary, that legal and constitutional restraints can increase the government's capacity to manage risk and crisis'.[71] His argument is that emergency situations are precisely those situations when measures to discipline the exercise of power are most needed. Holmes points out that, when faced with a disorienting crisis, embracing a strict adherence to rules and protocols provides decision-makers with a kind of artificial 'cool head'[72]; 'only those who fail to appreciate the gravity of a looming threat would advocate a wholesale dispensing with rules that professionals have developed over time to reduce the error rate of rapid-fire choices made as crises unfold'.[73] Though most of the chapters in this volume do not deal with emergency situations, some of them can be read with an eye to how governments use constitutional and rule of law guarantees towards what they understand as socially desirable ends.

In this respect, positive or enabling constitutionalism might be especially relevant for those countries that suffer under ethnic divisions, or a divided citizenship. Choudhry says it like this: 'To some extent, the constitution can foster the development of a common political identity by creating institutional spaces for shared decision making among members of different ethnocultural groups. Concrete experiences of shared decision-making within the framework of the rule of law, and without resource to force or fraud, can serve as the germ of a nascent sense of political community.' It can 'constitute a demos by encoding and projecting a certain vision of political community with the view of altering the very self-understanding of citizens'.[74] Thus understood, citizenship can function as the gateway to safeguarding human rights within the context of the constitutional systems of states and other political unions.[75]

[71] S. Holmes, 'In Case of Emergency: Misunderstanding Tradeoffs in the War on Terror', *California Law Review*, 97 (2009) 304–5.

[72] *Ibid.*, 302. [73] *Ibid.*, 303.

[74] S. Choudhry, 'Bridging Comparative Politics and Comparative Constitutional Law: Constitutional Design in Divided Societies' in S. Choudhry (ed.), *Constitutional Design for Divided Societies. Integration or Accommodation?* (Oxford University Press, 2008), p. 6.

[75] E. M. H. Hirsch Ballin, *Citizens' Rights and the Right to Be a Citizen* (Leiden/Boston: Brill Nijhoff, 2013), p. 141. See also historical examples of American practice in this regard, in B. Ackerman, *We the People, Volume 3: The Civil Rights Revolution* (Cambridge, MA: Belknap Press, 2014).

The opposite can however also be true, and in many of the chapters examples can be found of how citizenship is deliberatively used as a constitutional category to engineer or realise nationalistic or exclusionary aims.[76] Take Hungary again: the 2011 Fundamental Law states that there is 'one single Hungarian nation that belongs together' and it consists of all ethnic Hungarians regardless of their habitual residence. It thus includes Hungarians living abroad, even without an effective link to the State. At the same time, members of ethnic minorities living within the territory of the Hungarian state are not a constituent part of the Hungarian nation. A constitution, Tóth writes, that identifies the nation as an 'intellectual and spiritual' community for some groups, can by definition not be understood as a representative of integrative constitutions, but must rather be seen as descendant of the Eastern European nationalist ideas and movements from the previous two centuries. Tóth is critical of the role of the Hungarian Constitutional Court in this regard, when he writes that the Court had a Janus-faced constitutional adjudicatory role, since it was not able to escape from intolerant social attitudes or inappropriate political expectations. As a result, the Court for example never clashed with the legislature in order to support women's rights, and despite several petitions, the problems relating to the exclusion and discrimination of Roma remained absolutely hidden.

In this regard, Rwanda is also an important and very complicated example. Due to the disastrous genocide in 1994, the post-genocide government aimed to overcome the problems that racial hatred had caused in the past. The Constitution, Huls writes, is a pamphlet under the battle cry 'Never again genocide'. And since divisionism and genocide ideology are seen as the main contributing forces behind the 1994 genocide, they therefore are vigorously oppressed. But the laws based on these principles are heavily criticised because they are so broadly formulated that they also function as vehicles to stifle free speech and political opposition. Combined with a not very clear-cut separation of powers and a strict media law, Huls writes in his chapter, there is the risk of creating resentment in the Hutu part of the population if they have no avenues to voice their grievances. At the same time, Huls acknowledges that we

[76] This is what Nils Butenschøn has called the Janus-faced nature of citizenship, whose function 'to exclude people is just as important as the function to include [them].' N. Butenschøn, 'Citizenship and Human Rights. Some Thoughts on a Complex Relationship' in M. Bergsmo (ed.), *Human Rights and Criminal Justice for the Downtrodden. Essays in Honour of Asbjorn Eide* (Leiden: Martinus Nijhoff Publishers, 2003), p. 556.

cannot ignore the reality of the history of Rwandan politics. How could the new government in 1994 promote a majoritarian form of democracy in the aftermath of a genocide in which the majority almost completely eradicated the minority?

The Arab examples are also telling here, because while the Egyptian Constitution clearly emphasises its rule of law objectives, and also contains strong guarantees for critical features of the rule of law (an independent judiciary, *nullem crimen sine lege* and other due process rights), it is, Bisarya and Bulmer write, the Tunisian Constitution that is more likely to lead to political moderation. And the reason for this is that the Tunisian Constitution provides greater opportunities for sociological divides to negotiate their differences through politics. And this is mainly due to a more *inclusionary* approach towards the representation or recognition of significant groups in society – including minorities and the political opposition – resulting, for example, from political party and electoral system regulation (i.e., through not banning religious parties and a strongly proportional electoral system).

Structure of this Volume

Given the fact that the variables across constitutional and rule of law cultures and approaches are great and thus difficult to control for through quantitative approaches,[77] we have opted for a mainly, though not exclusively, qualitative and interpretative approach. Also, through the case studies and transnational chapters in this volume, we opt for a 'bottom-up' approach, starting from political practice and reality instead of starting from abstract principles. Case sensitivity is key here. This means that, next to more theoretical considerations, we need some conception of the function of constitutional and rule of law norms and ideals within a particular context, in order to make sense of them.[78] This also calls for an historical approach to their emergence or transformation (i.e., the social and political values they fulfil or the constellations of political power they were meant to justify), an approach which is

[77] Schauer, 'Comparative Constitutional Compliance', pp. 227–9. Compare also Lindseth (quoting Thompson) in his chapter to this volume: 'Where a historical problem is big enough to matter, causation is invariably multiple, the factors intertwined and interdependent'.

[78] A. Sangiovanni, 'Normative Political Theory: A Flight from Reality?' in D. Bell (ed.), *Political Thought and International Relations. Variations on a Realist Theme* (Oxford University Press, 2008), p. 234.

available in most of the chapters. The 'transnational chapters' analyse – some more explicitly so than others – instances of rule of law promotion, a phenomenon which embodies the practical attempt to bring the real closer to the ideal on a global scale.

Taken as a whole, the volume thus uses theory and historical background (Part I), rich or thick descriptions in country case studies (Part II) and dynamics triggered by new transnational mechanisms (Part III) to further understanding with regard to the tension of idealist and realist perspectives and practices in the context of constitutionalism and the rule of law. More specifically, the theoretical part, after introducing the theme of the volume, focuses on conceptualising rule of law and constitutional discourses (Krygier), institutional analysis and constitutional change (Lindseth) and the historical setting as critically recounted in opposing narratives (Lesaffer/Musa). The country studies form the core of the volume, and represent transitional settings (Egypt/Tunisia, China, Indonesia, Rwanda), high-stakes settings where constitutional frameworks need to do some heavy lifting (Israel) as well as case studies from European countries, displaying a wide variety of historical and cultural factors (Italy, Hungary, Netherlands). Finally, the dynamics involving the ideal and the real in the European Union's recent crisis in which rule of law values are at stake are addressed by both Scheppele and Kochenov. The two final chapters zoom in on mechanisms which possibly make use of the mutually regulative relationship between the ideal and the real when shaping transnational debates: peer review mechanisms (Meuwese) and indicator-based rule of law rankings (Ginsburg/Versteeg).

2

Tempering Power

MARTIN KRYGIER*

If ideals are to be taken seriously, there must be genuine concern for their embodiment in action, and especially in the routines of institutional life.

(Philip Selznick, TVA and the Grass Roots, x)

John Dewey was famously hostile to attempts to carve up the world, and approaches to the world, with 'pernicious dualisms'. His objection was that such dualisms set up and reify as dichotomies in thought things that are not in fact dichotomous in life. Thus they block recognition of continuities and interdependencies.

Forced confrontations between realism and idealism are apt examples. For realism and idealism do better together than apart, and not merely as separate and independent viewpoints that might be gathered together but as interdependent ingredients of a whole that is generally more satisfactory than the sum of its parts taken separately. Realistic-idealism is not an oxymoron, but a salutary combination. Ideals are part of the human world. 'Realism' that does not take their existence and significance into account is empirically impoverished and programmatically unhelpful. Conversely, idealism is at worst empty or at best Utopian, if undisciplined by the real. Utopias might have their attractions and uses as regulative principles,[1] but not as practical ideals, intended to be made good (even if only partially) in the real world. And constitutionalism and the rule of law are intensely practical ideals.

* The first version of this article was delivered at the Tilburg Rule of Law Workshop *Bridging Idealism and Realism in Constitutionalism and Rule of Law*, 2–3 October 2014. It was also discussed at a seminar at Scuola Superiore Sant'Anna, Pisa, 4 June 2015. I am grateful to the participants in the workshop, and particularly my discussant, Hans Lindahl, to colleagues in the Sant'Anna seminar, particularly Gianluigi Palombella and Giuseppe Martinico, and to my colleagues Arthur Glass and Theunis Roux, for their comments.

[1] See L. Kołakowski, 'The Death of Utopia Reconsidered' in *Modernity on Endless Trial* (University of Chicago Press, 1990).

Though closely related, they are not identical. So the first section of this chapter sketches some areas of overlap and distinction between constitutionalism and the rule of law. The second suggests one central aim they have in common: hostility to arbitrariness in the exercise of power. I then discuss different interpretations of this value, to illustrate the mutual and indispensable intertwinings of realism and idealism involved in its pursuit. One of these interpretations, usually captured with terms such as 'limiting', 'curbing', 'restraining' power, prides itself on its tough-minded realism, and in truth it does focus on significant aspects of reality that should never be ignored. At the same time, however it misses fundamental elements of what it seeks to describe and diminishes an ideal central to it. More readily to encompass that ideal I introduce the idea of *tempering* power, rather than 'limiting . . . ', etc., and propose some reasons to prefer this term. Central among them is its ready availability for larger purposes, more positive ideals, for constitutionalism and the rule of law, than the crimped, negative, implications of the concepts in common use. This more positive spin turns out more protective as well, so long as it neither forgets nor undermines the realistic foundations on which it depends.

Constitutionalism and the Rule of Law

Constitutionalism and the rule of law have different historical, institutional and discursive/rhetorical trajectories and incarnations, but they are also closely related, and they overlap. There is a certain, perhaps necessary, vagueness to both ideals and many of their concerns are shared. A great deal that can be said of one can be said, in the same terms, of the other; both terms being protean and their concerns interwoven, few differences are categorical or uncontroversial.

Moreover, whatever else differentiates or connects them, they both have to do with the exercise of power. For centuries the power in question was taken to be that of the state, but in recent decades (and arguably in the pre-Westphalian past), it has been acknowledged that states are/were not the only entities to which constitutionalism can be ascribed. There are supra- and infra-state levels of governance that can plausibly be regarded as subjects of constitutionalism. That might be a bitter pill for many to swallow, but it seems unavoidable.[2] This is equally, I would

[2] See N. Walker, 'The Idea of Constitutional Pluralism', *Modern Law Review*, 65 (2002), 317–59; N. Walker 'Taking Constitutionalism Beyond the State', *Political Studies*, 56

argue even more starkly, true of the rule of law too, though recognition of this is still uncommon.[3] The rule of law can only with considerable artificiality be cabined within the boundaries, and activities, of nation states. And within those boundaries, the 'public law presumption', that ties the rule of law to the state and is so common in rule of law discussions, is misplaced.[4]

For what it is worth, my own preference is to understand the rule of law as the more encompassing notion, which extends to relations among citizens as much as it does to acts of governments or governance, indeed to the activities of all persons and institutions capable of exercising significant power in a society. To say that the rule of law is strongly or weakly in evidence is to appraise a social *state of affairs*, with complex, multi-layered elements of various provenances, rather than simply to characterise any particular set of legal institutions. The rule of law is 'a contingent reality, real *insofar as* certain things go on', to borrow a phrase from another author and context.[5] You have it insofar as, to the extent that, power is routinely exercised in ways consistent with the ideal, and certain other ways of exercising power – wildly, capriciously, wilfully, arbitrarily, say – are rare. Since many of the major threats to the ideal of the rule of law come from outside governments, and many means of achieving that ideal are also to be found in the wider society, the rule of law must be sought there too. Not merely in 'law in the books', but not merely in 'law in action' either. For the rule of law can be subverted by things other than law.

To the extent that non-governmental organisations are in a position to exercise significant power in ways that offend the values of the rule of law, they diminish its sway, whatever the state of legal rules or institutions. Once, but far from always in human history, one might have been confident that governments were uniquely more powerful than all other forces, and that is why they were rightly the centre of attention for anyone concerned with the values of the rule of law. But it is an

(2008), 519–543 and A. Peters, 'Compensatory Constitutionalism: The Function and Potential of Fundamental International Norms and Structures', *Leiden Journal of International Law*, 19 (2006), 579–610.

[3] See M. Krygier, 'Four Puzzles about the Rule of Law: Why, What, Where? and Who Cares?' in J. E. Fleming, ed., *Getting to the Rule of Law, Nomos no.50* (New York University Press, 2011), pp. 64–104 at 85–91.

[4] See L. M. Austin and D. Klimchuk (eds.), *Private Law and the Rule of Law* (Oxford University Press, 2014).

[5] Gianfranco Poggi coins the phrase to describe Durkheim's conception of society. See G. Poggi, *Durkheim* (Oxford University Press, 2000), p. 85.

empirical and variable matter whether threats to those values are going to come from governments or somewhere else or both. And today things are more complicated. If non-governmental power is arbitrarily exercised by oligarchs, Mafiosi, warlords, tribal elders, Al Qaeda, NGOs, business executives, currency speculators, international ratings agencies, financial institutions or indeed university administrators, it too has the potential to bring with it the vices of arbitrariness mentioned above. Banks can do a lot of damage too, and in recent relatively unregulated years and countries, they have. We have an interest in tempering power that has significant public consequence, whoever or whatever wields it.

And if one thinks of what might be necessary to approach the ideal the rule of law is supposed to serve, it is plain that legal texts and institutions can never be the answer on their own. Governments and laws should be viewed, not as the always-necessary centrepieces of power-tempering craftsmanship to which other measures are inferior or supplementary addenda, but as implements among several, in some respects and particular circumstances of potentially unique importance, but dependent for their success on many other things, and often arguably not more important for the achievement of its own goal than those others.

Though I am not the only person to argue it, it is certainly controversial whether the concept of the rule of law should extend so far. Even more so, in this case I think rightly, of constitutionalism. Given the long political associations of constitutionalism and its modern association with written constitutions addressed to governments, my own bias would be to treat the rule of law as the larger notion, and see central aspects of constitutionalism as part of that large enterprise. Margaret Jane Radin has recently argued powerfully that mass-market 'contractual' boilerplate can offend the rule of law.[6] This does not seem strained because, while we may not always talk this way, it squares with the understanding of rule of law as not merely a 'mode of governance', but also and more deeply a 'mode of association', to use Postema's distinction.[7] It seems to me less plausible to see such contractual boilerplate as an offence against constitutionalism, however, because the connection with governance is tighter there. But stipulations are vain in these contested and changing fields, so I just state my preference.

[6] See M. J. Radin, 'Boilerplate: A Threat to the Rule of Law?' in L. M. Austin and D. Klimchuk (eds.), *Private Law and the Rule of Law*, pp. 288–305.

[7] G. J. Postema, 'Fidelity in Law's Commonwealth' in Austin and Klimchuk (eds.), *Private Law and the Rule of Law*, p. 24.

Constitutionalism, as the name suggests, focuses on the ways the exercise of public power is *constituted*, made up. It is an ideal having to do with the legal architecture and frame of a polity, its institutional design, foundations, structure, as well as the character of its major institutions and their occupants, their interrelations among themselves and with the subjects of power.

It is also an old ideal, incarnations of which have altered dramatically in recent centuries. 'Old-fashioned, historic' constitutions are often unwritten or spread among an array of documents.[8] They do not claim to found, but rather to express, to codify, the nature of an existing political order. A few such constitutions remain – in the United Kingdom, the Netherlands, New Zealand, the Nordic countries – but they have been outflanked, if not completely surpassed by constitutions of a different sort. For since the American Constitution, constitutionalism has typically incorporated what Martin Loughlin describes as

> [T]he establishment of the altogether novel idea of a constitution. Political constitutions were no longer to be conceived as some ideal expression of a nation's culture, manners and traditional forms of rule. A constitution in the modern sense was to be a document drafted in the name of the people to establish and regulate the powers of the main institutions of government, to specify the relationship between government and citizen, and to take effect as fundamental law.[9]

Thus, though it was not always so, from the end of the eighteenth century and now around the globe, constitutionalism has had a recognisable and single centrepiece: a written document, the constitution. That in turn has a central subject: institutions of governance. Constitutional law is fundamentally a branch, and a fundamental branch, of public law.

If a constitution of this sort is to contribute to constitutional***ism***, it must be real and not sham;[10] the architecture must not be that of a Potemkin village, or its later legal parallel, a Soviet constitution. It must be implemented and effective in the institutions and practices of the political order; it must *count* both within the offices of state, in their interactions with the lives of citizens and in the interactions among citizens themselves. So too, of course, the rule of law.

8 L. F. M. Besselink, 'The Notion and Nature of the European Constitution after the Reform Treaty' (2008), 3. available at SSRN: http://papers.ssrn.com/sol3/papers.cfm?abstract_id=1086189.

9 M. Loughlin, 'The Constitutional Imagination', *Modern Law Review*, 78(1) (2015), 2.

10 See D. S. Law and M. Versteeg, 'Sham Constitutions', *California Law Review*, 101 (2013), 863–952.

The ideal of the rule of law differs in several ways from constitutionalism, however, particularly of the modern variety. Apart from the issue of modes of association that I have already mentioned, constitutionalism involves locating, allocating, distributing and channelling jurisdiction and powers among specified, 'constituted' legal institutions. Today it typically also specifies certain fundamental rights of citizens that agencies of government are legally obliged to respect.

Constitutionalism has to do with the frame and architecture of governance, always formal and often substantive. The rule of law is less architectonically focussed, more process-oriented, than constitutionalism. Whatever the constitutional frame, the rule of law is primarily concerned with *ways* in which power is exercised, specifically non-arbitrary ways. Not every aspect of the rule of law is a constitutional matter, and not everything likely to be found, in a modern constitution at any rate, is part of the rule of law. Though they should not be inconsistent with the ideal of tempering power common to both, constitutions have other purposes such as clear and functional allocation of jurisdiction and competences, about which the ideal of the rule of law might be agnostic. Again, constitutions typically specify permissible *content* of laws, whereas many accounts of the rule of law limit it more austerely to matters of form and procedure.[11] And finally, on many mainstream views the rule of law has a great deal to do with the *character* of laws, with formal or procedural aspects of the system of legal rules, that allow subjects to be able confidently to predict the operations of public power when they plan to act. That confidence depends in part upon legal rules and institutions (and I would add other social institutions and practices as well) being of some kinds – knowable, relatively clear, predictable, coherent – and not others. These characteristics are rarely mentioned in constitutions, unless through medium of a rule of law clause.

Again, the rule of law does not necessarily have a specific or even any documentary anchor or focal point, such as a written constitution, though many contemporary constitutions specify the rule of law as a constitutional principle, and many people believe written constitutions are good for the rule of law. And while a written constitution is not necessary for the rule of law, without the latter you might well have a constitution but no *-ism*, as is the case in many constitution-rich constitutionalism-poor despotisms

[11] See L. L. Fuller, *The Morality of Law*, 2nd edn (New Haven, CT: Yale University Press, 1969); J. Raz, 'The Rule of Law and Its Virtue' in J. Raz (ed.), *The Authority of Law* (Oxford, Clarendon Press, 1979), pp. 210–29 and J. Waldron, 'The Rule of Law and the Importance of Procedure' in J. Fleming, *Getting to the Rule of Law, Nomos no. 50* (New York University Press, 2011), pp. 3–31.

around the world. Further if, as Neil Walker argues, 'a *sine qua non* of constitutional status in *all* circumstances . . . is the existence of a self-conscious discourse of constitutionalism,'[12] it is not obvious that the existence of the rule of law requires there to be a discourse of rule of law, though it may well help.

Other differences could be identified, though given the overlaps none is clear-cut. In any event, they are not my special concern. For if constitutionalism and the rule of law are not identical, they are pretty clearly in the same line of business. A central part of that business is to channel, discipline, constrain and inform – rather than merely serve – the exercise of power, in ways that prevent it from being arbitrary.

Arbitrary Power

Over centuries, as countless thinkers have observed, a pervasive problem with power is that left to their own devices, power-holders cannot be relied on to avoid exercising it capriciously, and at worst wildly. And as too many people over too many centuries have not only observed but experienced, capricious power is terribly unsettling and wild power is simply terrible. More generally, the potential is alive even when power is not wild but merely, to use the more commonly identified term for this order of vice, arbitrary. Arbitrary power is not necessarily wild but it is usually and already objectionable, and that for many reasons.[13]

Arbitrariness is notoriously under-theorised,[14] and I will not deliver conceptual purity here. I just mention three ways in which power can be exercised, any one of which can and has been described as arbitrary and each of which has figured as the antihero in one or other invocation of the rule of law. I think they are all bad and so an exercise of power which is arbitrary in any of these senses is to be treated, at the very least, with great suspicion; better still, the possibility of such exercise of power should be reliably limited.

The first has to do with whether power-wielders are subject to any routine, regular control or limit or accountability to something other than their own 'will' or 'pleasure,' to use traditional terms of suspicion, or caprice, or desire. In the words of the Indian Supreme Court, interpreting

[12] Walker, 'The Idea of Constitutional Pluralism', 343.

[13] I discuss four of these reasons at some length in 'Four Puzzles about the Rule of Law', pp. 78–81.

[14] See T. Endicott, 'Arbitrariness,' *University of Oxford Legal Research Paper Series Paper No 2/2014*, http://ssrn.com/abstract=2378858.

contribution of constitutionalism and the rule of law is to try to reduce the suffering of the weak by restricting what the strong can do. On this interpretation, the point is to *block* and *limit* the possibility of unruly power, to curb and restrain power exercise. This is not a new view, and it is still popular among liberals, even more among neo-liberals. Thus Hayek once more: 'The effective limitation of power is the most important problem of social order'.[24] It is the job of constitutionalism and the rule of law to impose the limits: 'Constitutionalism means limited government. . . . indeed, what function is served by a constitution which makes omnipotent government possible? Is its function to be merely that governments work smoothly and efficient, whatever their aims?'[25] When questions are posed in such starkly dichotomous terms, what surprise that they are merely rhetorical?

And it is not just 'neos' who think this way. Thus Judith Shklar, a profound analyst and exponent of liberalism, reads Montesquieu to argue that the rule of law

> [R]eally has only one aim, to protect the ruled against the aggression of those who rule. While it embraces all people, it fulfills only one fundamental aim, freedom from fear, which, to be sure, was for Montesquieu supremely important. ... [t]his whole scheme is ultimately based on a very basic dichotomy. The ultimate spiritual and political struggle is always between war and law . . . The institutions of judicial citizen protection may create rights, but they exist in order to avoid what Montesquieu took to be the greatest of human evils, constant fear created by the threats of violence and the actual cruelties of the holders of military power in society.[26]

Shklar's own choice between these two accounts is clear: 'If one then begins with the fear of violence, the insecurity of arbitrary government, and the discriminations of injustice, one may work one's way up to finding a significant place for the Rule of Law, and for the boundaries it has historically set upon these the most enduring of our political troubles.'[27] As befits a devotee of 'the liberalism of fear' who 'begins with what is to be avoided,' Shklar insists that the prevention of evil, rather than a quest for the good, is the signal virtue of the rule of law.

[24] F. Hayek, *Law, Legislation, and Liberty*, vol. 3 (University of Chicago Press, 1979), p. 128

[25] F. Hayek, *Law, Legislation, and Liberty*, vol. 2 (University of Chicago Press, 1973), p. 1.

[26] J. N. Shklar, 'Political Theory and the Rule of Law' in J. N. Shklar and S. Hoffmann (ed.), *Political Thought and Political Thinkers* (University of Chicago Press, 1998), pp. 24–5.

[27] *Ibid.*, p. 36.

A similar, if less passionate, thought underlies the somewhat tepid praise (two cheers) for the rule of law offered by the legal philosopher, Joseph Raz. He describes it as 'a purely negative value . . . merely designed to minimize the harms to freedom and dignity which the law might cause in its pursuit of its goals however laudable these might be.'[28] Shklar does not share Raz's lukewarm tone, but the precious service she lauds is also negative. The bottom line is 'damage control'.[29]

This negative, constraining, controlling aspect of the rule of law is both realistic and of fundamental importance. It responds to 'the circumstances of politics' as they often have been found to be.[30] It finds in constitutionalism and the rule of law expressions of 'a politics of scepticism as opposed to a "politics of faith" and of absolute ends.'[31] More deeply, it is a realistically pessimistic reflection on dangers, not contingently visited upon us from elsewhere, but endemic to the human predicament, of the sort famously expressed by Alexander Hamilton in *The Federalist No. 51*:

> If men were angels, no government would be necessary. If angels were to govern men, neither external nor internal controls on government would be necessary. In framing a government which is to be administered by men over men, the great difficulty lies in this: you must first enable the government to control the governed; and in the next place oblige it to control itself. A dependence on the people is, no doubt, the primary

[28] J. Raz, 'The Rule of Law', p. 228.

[29] J. N. Shklar, 'The Liberalism of Fear' in Shklar and Hoffmann (eds.), *Political Thought*, p. 9.

[30] See J. Waldron, *Law and Disagreement* (Oxford University Press, 1999).

[31] See A. Craiutu, *A Virtue for Courageous Minds. Moderation in French Political Thought, 1748–1830* (Princeton University Press, 2012), p. 5. Craiutu goes beyond this sceptical perspective, however. He speaks frequently and more interchangeably than I of both moderation and tempering (both as character traits and institutional arrangements), with the former making the conceptual running and the latter supporting or exemplifying moderation but carrying no conceptual emphasis. He may or may not be interested in the sort of distinctions I want to make in this section, but there is little of substance that separates us. Indeed, though I only came across his book while revising the manuscript of this chapter, I would fully endorse the dual argument that he, unlike Shklar, finds and applauds in Montesquieu (at 64): 'Montesquieu's pluralist perspective followed, to some extent, in the footsteps of Hobbes, who also believed that in the political sphere there is always a *summum malum* on which people agree. In Montesquieu's political writings, this absolute evil was despotism, characterized by cruelty and arbitrary power, and the political good was defined by the absence of cruelty. Nonetheless, one might argue that Montesquieu made an equally important argument for the existence of a *positive* political good – moderate government – which represents much more than the opposite of a despotism based upon fear and arbitrary power.'

> control on the government; but experience has taught mankind the necessity of auxiliary precautions.[32]

The exercise of public power carries terrible risks. It is wise to be aware of them and to think seriously and realistically about what may be done to minimise them, both because they are directly threatening in themselves and because where such threats are realised, nothing much else good will occur. Partisans of both constitutionalism and the rule of law are clearly deeply informed by such thought. It is aptly identified as realistic, in the sense identified by Philip Selznick, according to which it is

> not enough to think of specific evils as problems to be solved or as obstacles to be overcome. Rather, the perspective of moral realism treats some transgressions as dynamic and inescapable. They can be depended on to arise, in one form or another, despite our best efforts to put them down.[33]

And not just 'moral realism' but specifically *political* realism is necessary in the case of constitutionalism and the rule of law, for thinking about such things is not, as both Bernard Williams and Jeremy Waldron have emphasised against much conventional academic unwisdom, 'just applied moral philosophy'.[34] Politics and the wielding of power more generally are, after all, not simply – perhaps not primarily – a matter of the ideal ends we should seek, but of conflict, violence, oppression, domination, their consequences, and what might be needed and feasible to avoid them.[35] The liberalism of fear articulated by Shklar and others is a sober, sombre response to such realities.

So realism has a kind of foundational priority over other concerns, not necessarily chronological but normative, or to use Rawls' term, lexical: you can be realistic (in a normatively limited sense) without further ideals, but practical ideals are always precarious in the absence of realism. However, a purely negative, defensive, interpretation of the liberalism of fear can also reduce and distort one's understanding of politics, and of law. This negative perspective does not exhaust realism, and it most certainly should not exclude idealism. Violence and oppression are not

[32] A. Hamilton, *The Federalist Papers, No. 51* (New York, New American Library, 1961), p. 322.

[33] P. Selznick, *The Moral Commonwealth* (Berkeley, University of California Press, 1992), p. 175.

[34] J. Waldron, 'Political Theory: An Inaugural Lecture', *Journal of Political Philosophy*, 21(1) (2013), 1–23.

[35] See B. Williams, 'The Liberalism of Fear' in *In the Beginning Was the Deed: Realism and Moralism in Political Argument* (Princeton University Press, 2005), pp. 52–61.

the sum of what politics and power well exercised can and often do deliver, and limitation of power is not the sum of what constitutionalism and the rule of law can contribute to a well-ordered polity.

Tempering

That is one reason the umbrella term that I have come to prefer for such contributions is *tempering* power, rather than limiting it, or any of the other words – taming, restraining, controlling, etc. – commonly invoked. Not that they are wrong, but they are insufficient to grasp some core features of both constitutionalism and the rule of law. For the rule of law and constitutionalism are not merely about constraint, they also depend upon, and in turn are intended to produce, salutary positive results impossible without them.

To speak of tempering power is not likely to raise alarm, particularly since Aquinas and Bracton in the thirteenth century, and Montesquieu in the eighteenth, not to mention many Greeks and Romans before them, did so. Still, though only a word, and a metaphor at that, this is not the most common way of putting things, and typically, even where the word is used in connection with the rule of law, it is not chosen for a distinctive purpose; it seems simply to be thrown in to amplify common concerns, e.g. 'constrain, moderate, temper, etc'.

Thus Montesquieu lauds both the tempering and moderating of power, but for him moderation is the concept that does the work, 'tempering' is conceptual embroidery. I might have followed him, since I certainly favour moderated power too.[36] But for reasons I will seek to explain, this terminological difference has a few implications. Even moderation misses something, though not nearly as much as is missed in locutions such as limit, restrain, constrain, restrict and curb. As we have seen, these are the terms typically used by people who think themselves realists about power, the rule of law and constitutionalism. Though there is something to their boast, indeed something important as we have seen, I think they are wrong to think so well of themselves. The rule of law and constitutionalism can and should serve larger, more positive, ideals as well.

Since the Greeks, temperance has after all been considered one of the primary, cardinal virtues. Used in reference to persons, it certainly included restraint, particularly self-restraint, and was the opposite of

[36] See Craiutu, *A Virtue for Courageous Minds*.

hubris, but it also suggested moderation and self-knowledge as positive self-generated virtues, aspects of the character of people and institutions, not necessarily imposed. The example of self-knowledge is important. As Helen North comments on the Greek tragedians,

> If the Aeschylean conception of sōphrōsynē [glossed by Cicero and writers thereafter as *temperantia*] can be glossed by the Apolline 'Nothing in excess' and 'Think mortal thoughts', the Sophoclean virtue is closer to 'Know thyself.' The failure in sōphrōsynē that marks such heroes as Ajax, Antigone, Oedipus, Electra, and Deianaira is a failure in self-knowledge, amounting sometimes to delusion, sometimes almost to madness. The hero is blind to something essential in himself or his situation, and tragedy arises from the interplay between his circumstances and his admirable but imperfect nature.[37]

Many aspects of both constitutionalism and the rule of law are intended to encourage such virtues of moderation and thoughtful self-knowledge, not merely to curb wild power. They are *encouraged* by constitutional and rule of law practices and institutions, not contained or constrained by them.

The examples so far only relate to personal behaviour. There are also institutional senses of tempering, and they seem to me helpful for two reasons. First, tempering suggests both a moderating balance of elements (e.g. justice with mercy; strength with moderation), a *blending*. In early medieval representations, *Temperantia* held a mixing bowl, 'in keeping with the translation of "temperamentum" as measure/proper mixture/moderation.'[38] This is missed in much of the conventional language of constitutionalism and the rule of law. Indeed, though negative constraining conceptions of constitutionalism often speak of separation of powers, as everyone knows that is not enough: mixing is key. As Craiutu observes: 'Montesquieu in fact favoured a blending rather than a strict separation of powers and referred in his book to *pouvoirs distribués* and not *pouvoirs séparés.*'[39]

In Lorenzetti's marvellous *Allegory of Good Government*, in Siena's town hall, *Temperantia* holds an hourglass rather than a mixing bowl, to make an allied point. Among the fresco's seven 'virtues of good government', she is immediately flanked by Justitia on one side holding

[37] P. P. Wiener, *Dictionary of the History of Ideas*, vol. IV (New York, Charles Scribner's Sons, 1973), p. 367.

[38] G. Dohrn-van Rossum, *History of the Hour: Clocks and Modern Temporal Orders* (University of Chicago Press, 1996), p. 5.

[39] Craiutu, *A Virtue for Courageous Minds*, p. 49.

the severed head of some felon and Magnanimita disbursing coins from a large dish, on the other. The juxtaposition is unlikely to be accidental. Justice is good, magnanimity is good, but temperance with measured patience mediates between them. There is nothing of this in the conventional vocabulary of constitutionalism and rule of law.

A second distinctive aspect of tempering is that the concept lends itself less automatically, as 'limiting' lent itself to Hayek and many others, to the view that power is its foe, and weakening it its purpose. Indeed, an ambition to 'temper' power is consistent with acknowledging that among what is hoped for from constitutionalism and the rule of law are salutary forms of *strengthening* of the power to which it is applied. Tempered steel, after all is stronger, more fit for purpose, than iron or untempered steel; as Wikipedia informs us, the aim is 'to achieve greater toughness by decreasing the hardness of the alloy.'[40]

Applied to constitutionalism and the rule of law, then, tempering can suggest some judicious combination of mix, balance, moderation, self-knowledge, all contributing to particular and salutary sorts of strength. These suggestions need to be kept in mind, for the negative conception, the flint-edged realism of Shklar or other sceptics, is not the only way of viewing constitutionalism and the rule of law, and not on its own the best.

'Positive' Idealism

Jeremy Waldron has criticised views of constitutionalism according to which '[e]verything is seen through the lens of restraint and limitation', and has insisted on the empowering role and potential of constitutional provisions.[41] Constitutions, after all, *constitute* the elements of a polity, and *empower* particular institutions. They *distribute* power to some institutions and actors and not others, they establish fora for discussion and decision, 'so that public deliberation becomes a structured enterprise'.[42] All this crucial work is given short shrift by a perspective in which '[e]verything is seen through the lens of restraint and limitation'.[43]

Again, Stephen Holmes has long stressed the empowering consequences of constitutionalism and the rule of law; what, in contrast to the more

[40] As found on: https://en.wikipedia.org/wiki/Tempering_(metallurgy).
[41] J. Waldron, 'Constitutionalism: A Skeptical View', NYU School of Law, Public Law & Legal Theory Research Paper Series, No. 10-87 (2010), 25.
[42] *Ibid.*, 26. [43] *Ibid.*

common negative conception, he calls 'positive constitutionalism'.[44] Appropriately configured laws, on this view, provide 'enabling constraints'.[45] For the 'paradoxical insight' here, as Holmes describes it, is that

> Limited government is, or can be, more powerful than unlimited government. ... that constraints can be enabling, which is far from being a contradiction, lies at the heart of liberal constitutionalism ... By restricting the arbitrary powers of government officials, a liberal constitution can, under the right conditions, *increase* the state's capacity to focus on specific problems and mobilize collective resources for common purposes.[46]

On this view, like a swimmer (or a scholar) whose effective performance requires mastery of, and in a sense coming to be mastered by, techniques and disciplines that allow one to marshal and channel raw energy (or intelligence), so the ability to concentrate power, where and how it should be concentrated to serve good purposes, is enhanced by certain requirements, procedures and institutions which, among other things, redirect its movements so it doesn't splash around where and how it should not.

Or to use two other apt metaphorical variations from Holmes, one is that we should think of constitutional provisions and the shaping, channelling presence of the rule of law as constitutive, like the grammar of a language, rather than restrictive like, though he doesn't make this analogy, censorship. Without grammar we cannot speak, at least not in a way that communicates effectively with interlocutors. It disciplines what we can say comprehensibly but it doesn't thereby weaken our ability to communicate. On the contrary, it is a condition of it:

> The rules of grammar do not hinder but rather facilitate the ability to communicate, and that includes the ability to communicate surprising, unnerving, rude, unpopular, and even anti-constitutional ideas. It would obviously be inaccurate, therefore, to conceptualize such rules merely as don'ts, prohibitions, barriers, injunctions, no-trespass signs, or purely negative limitations on permissible behaviour. True, the rules of grammar

44 S. Holmes, *Passions and Constraint: on the Theory of Liberal Democracy* (University of Chicago Press, 1995), p. 120.

45 See D. Stark and L. Bruszt, *Postsocialist Pathways* (Cambridge University Press, 1998), pp. 166–88; M. Loughlin, *The Idea of Public Law* (Oxford University Press, 2003) and J. Elster, *Ulysses Unbound: Studies in Rationality, Precommitment, and Constraints* (Cambridge University Press, 2000).

46 Holmes, *Passions and Constraint*, xi.

introduce certain rigidities into ordinary language. But rigidities, for a variety of reasons, can be prodigiously enabling.[47]

Grammar is one thing, but constitutions in particular don't merely enable us to communicate, they also allot roles, responsibilities and powers among actors in the polity. And here too Holmes has a suggestive analogy:

> If we think of constitutional rules as scripts, rather than ropes . . . it is easier to understand why powerful actors, looking for protocols to facilitate rapid coordination, might be willing to incorporate them into their motivations as obligatory principles of conduct. They are not incapacitating but capacitating. They are not shackles making unwanted action impossible, but guidelines making wanted action feasible. Seen in this way, their binding power becomes more commonsensical than mysterious.[48]

These are not new discoveries. Thus Holmes traces the awareness of enabling constraints to Bodin in the sixteenth century. Montesquieu was well aware of them too. The whole of *The Spirit of the Laws* was bent to investigating the sources of moderation of government and recommending institutional ways to ensure it. He notes that, despite the horrors of despotism and the attractions of moderation, the world has seen many more despotic governments than well-ordered, moderate ones. He laments that but finds it unsurprising, because a moderate government is a much more complicated achievement. The language with which he makes the contrast is suggestive, for it is not a language of brute impediments:

> Despite men's love of liberty, despite their hatred of violence, most peoples are subjected to this type of government [despotism]. This is easy to understand. In order to form a moderate government, it is necessary to combine the several powers; to regulate, temper, and set them in motion; to give, as it were, ballast to one, in order to enable it to counterpoise the other. This is a masterpiece of legislation; rarely produced by hazard, and seldom attained by prudence. By contrast, a despotic government leaps to view, so to speak; it is uniform throughout; as only passions are needed to establish it, everyone is good enough for that.[49]

47 S. Holmes, 'Constitutions and Constitutionalism' in Michel Rosenfeld and András Sajó (eds.), *The Oxford Handbook of Comparative Constitutional Law* (Oxford University Press, 2012), p. 192.

48 *Ibid.*, p. 202.

49 C. L. de Secondat de Montesquieu, *The Spirit of the Laws*, A. M. Cohler (ed.) (Cambridge University Press, 1992), pp. 63. Cf. Craiutu, *A Virtue for Courageous Minds*, on 'the strong connection between moderation and institutional complexity, an idea that would resonate . . . with Montesquieu, Mounier, Necker, Mme de Staël, and Constant . . . classical authors praised the institutional framework of mixed government, not only

This is a language of difficult and complex balancing, tempering, regulating, not shackling and certainly not weakening. Indeed Montesquieu emphasised – with profound if counterintuitive insight – that although restrained government was not fearsome, as despotism was, it was in a crucial sense stronger than any despot could be, for

> A moderate government can, as much as it wants and without peril, relax its springs. It maintains itself by its laws, and even by its force. But when in despotic government the prince ceases for a moment to raise his arm, when he cannot instantly destroy those in the highest places, all is lost, for when the spring of the government, which is fear, no longer exists, the people no longer have a protector.[50]

Montesquieu died in 1755, thirty-four years before the French Revolution. Yet he understood that the French king's position was in effect weaker than that of the English monarch, notwithstanding that, as one author has observed, '[a]t every step the absolutist ambitions of the English Crown were thwarted: consent of Parliament was needed for taxes; consent of the law courts was needed for legal enforcement of alternative revenue sources; and, most important, consent of the gentry was needed for daily implementation of monopolies.'[51] Nevertheless, appearances were deceptive. As the same author explains,

> [L]egislation enacted by Parliament was usually implemented, whereas the will of the much stronger executive in France was less frequently carried out. A significant implementation gap existed under absolutism. . . . there were no legal limits on the French king's power or, by extension that of his ministers, yet time and time again his ministers succumbed to cabals within the court . . . Despite the legal limits on the Crown's power imposed by Parliament, the English king managed to maintain his position and policies. It seemed to many contemporaries that George III's ministers were more powerful and more likely to be obeyed than the unaccountable and theoretically stronger ministers of the French king.[52]

Not only was English government more effective than French, more able to raise taxes, more deeply embedded in society, but the English economy

because the latter blended various social interests and elements, allowing them to coexist harmoniously, but also because it made it extremely difficult for any group to impose its will over others and exercise arbitrary power.' (pp. 31–2).

50 C. Montesquieu, *The Spirit of the Laws*, p. 28.

51 H. L. Root, *Political Foundations of Markets in Old Regime France and England* (Berkeley, University of California Press, 1994), p. 156.

52 *Ibid.*, p. 214.

was more powerful than the French, and the people of England were freer than the people of France. This is not an accidental combination. And, though France had an apparently far more powerful system of centralised rule than England, the French *ancien regime* was swept aside in 1789, while the English system has survived with only evolutionary change since the seventeenth century. The French head of state had enormous discretionary power, which proved worthless when his own head was removed. The English kings, after matters were also brought to a head, as it were, over a century earlier, were forced to accede to legal limitations on their personal power and thereafter regularly died in bed.

Montesquieu's insight into the relative strengths of moderate and despotic governments was even more prophetic than this comparison between England and France suggests. The most dramatic recent evidence of it is the house-of-cards collapse of the Soviet Union and its dominions. This was one of the most despotic empires the world has known, and almost no one apart from Montesquieu predicted its collapse. But it was not the first occasion when apparently overwhelmingly powerful despotisms have wilted before forces which hardly seemed up to the task. Like the collapse of communism, the French and Russian Revolutions, the end of the Marcos regime, the fall of the Shah, all seemed overdetermined *after* the event. But they revealed that extraordinary fragility of despotisms which keeps taking us by surprise. It should not.[53] One last recent example might serve. Thus in the last moments of Yanukovych's rule in Ukraine:

> The absence of institutional checks on the presidency made the state-society standoff worse. Yanukovych used his free hand to rush through parliament a law that decreed new fines and even criminal penalties for various types of unsanctioned protests. This move too backfired, stoking tensions between police and demonstrators and helping to spread the protests well beyond Kyiv.
>
> Lack of institutional oversight also created a sense of impunity in law-enforcement ranks. Riot police used excessive force against anyone viewed as a potential protester and even resorted to deadly tactics in the final weeks of the confrontation. Undercover agents abducted protest participants, brutalizing or killing them to intimidate others. As for aboveboard efforts to prosecute demonstrators, these had no hope of legitimacy given the judicial system's notorious subordination to the president. With no impartial enforcement institutions, the legal order quickly disintegrated.[54]

[53] The last few paragraphs are drawn from my Australian Broadcasting Commission radio lectures (the Boyer lectures), M. Krygier, *Between Fear and Hope. Hybrid Thoughts on Public Values* (Sydney, ABC Books, 1997), pp. 112–13.

[54] S. Kudelia, 'The House that Yanukovich Built', *Journal of Democracy*, 25(3) (2014), 29.

generate a level and kind of *thoughtfulness* that Waldron has rightly argued is a benefit of both constitutionalism and the rule of law.[58]

One trouble with the view of constitutionalism and the rule of law as out to brake power *per se* is that it does not recognise the significant differences that exist between *kinds* of power. Thus the historical sociologist, Michael Mann, has distinguished between what he calls *despotic* power – 'the range of actions which the elite is empowered to undertake without routine, institutionalised negotiations with civil society' – and what he calls *infrastructural* power – 'the capacity of the state to actually penetrate society, and to implement logistically political decisions throughout the realm.'[59]

For the release and development of social and economic energies, as well as for political decency, it is infrastructural power that is crucial. Despotic states combine arbitrariness and lack of political or legal limits with chronic incapacity to mobilise social energies and make use of social potential. As a colleague of Mann's, John Hall, puts it, they sit like capstones atop the societies they dominate; they do not penetrate organically and effectively into the social structure. They dominate from above, but do little to contribute from within. Writing of the Chinese empire, for example, Hall writes that

> Politics played a crucial blocking role in Chinese history ... Those who have written about empires have tended to stress either strength or weakness. But *both* were present, and the paradox (for it is not a contradiction) of empires is that their strength, that is their monuments, their arbitrariness, their scorn for human life, hides, is based upon, and reflects social weakness. They are not able to deeply penetrate, change and mobilise the social order. Empires have ... strong blocking but weak enabling powers ... successful capstone government [is] incapable of generating a large sum of social energy.[60]

The connection between despotic strength and social weakness is not accidental. Though despots can repress effectively for a time, and

[58] See J. Waldron, 'Thoughtfulness and the Rule of Law', British Academy Law Lecture (2011) and Waldron, 'Constitutionalism: A Skeptical View'.

[59] M. Mann, 'The Autonomous Power of the State: Its Origins, Mechanisms and Resources' in M. Mann, *State, War and Capitalism* (Oxford: Blackwell, 1988), p. 32. See also M. Mann, *Sources of Social Power*, vol. 1 (Cambridge University Press, 1986), p. 477. Here, and more crisply, Mann contrasts 'power over civil society, that is, *despotism*' and 'the power to coordinate civil society, that is, *infrastructural power*'.

[60] J. A. Hall, *Powers and Liberties: The Causes and Consequences of the Rise of the West* (Berkeley: University of California Press, 1985), pp. 34–5, and for the contrast with organic governments, see pp. 133–41).

mobilise for limited specialised purposes such as war, they have proved very weak in the capacity to penetrate, mobilize, and facilitate energetic and resilient social forces. On the contrary, they typically seek to block them, and they stunt their development. In other terms, despotically strong states go along with weak societies. And this is centrally because of the arbitrariness and unpredictability with which they exercise power. These states are predatory and their societies are prey. They are not productive, and neither are their societies. Constitutionalism and the rule of law get in the way of despotic power, but they also channel, direct, facilitate and inform infrastructural strength. When they are understood to do both, real and ideal come together in salutary and mutually beneficial ways.

A somewhat paradoxical implication of these reflections is that negative constitutionalism, both as understood by those most committed to it and by those who think it must be traded against power in emergencies, does not merely slight positive ideals for the rule of law and constitutionalism. It is also unrealistic, since it inadequately captures the key significance of enabling constraints. And there is more.

Like the negative constitutionalists I have discussed, Philip Selznick also saw reduction of arbitrariness as the central point of the rule of law. He also viewed protection against the brute vices of unrestrained power as normatively prior to, though not necessarily more important than, more expansive moral aspirations. On the one hand, he understood the realistic appeal of the negative conception, and he often emphasised its importance. Thus, he agrees with those political realists who stress the importance of legality as a restraint on, and see the rule of law as a precious protection against abuse of, power.[61] But, he observes, that is not always and everywhere a problem of the same intensity and urgency. Moreover, Selznick makes a profound point which is often ignored in the thrust and counter-thrust between the fearful and the hopeful. For he observes that people, institutions, systems, communities, undergo what he calls 'moral development'.[62] At certain stages in the development of social institutions, for example, particularly formative stages, or when they are weak, or when assailed by strong forces hostile to them, certain values need strong support – because they are not yet established or institutionalised, or because they are at risk. All the more so, when there

[61] P. Selznick, *The Moral Commonwealth* (Berkeley: University of California Press, 1992), p. 174.

[62] See P. Nonet and P. Selznick, *Law and Society in Transition: Toward Responsive Law* (New Brunswick, NJ: Transaction Publishers, 2001), pp. 18–27.

are powerful forces which put them at risk. Such values must be secured and it is dangerous to compromise them. When, however, they are institutionally, socially, ideologically and in other ways relatively secure, the balance of emphasis in our moral ambitions can change. Striving towards aspirational ideals can more safely supplement the establishment and defence of realistic baselines. We can even take some risks. This is not because the baselines become less important, just that they are more firmly in place and risks are less risky. Where they are sufficiently secure we should be prepared to hazard more improvement, temper fear with hope, just as in more precarious circumstances we must temper hope with fear. The reverse, of course, also applies. Values which might be fruitful where institutions are strong, might be dangerous where they are weak or absent. Both conditions of survival and those of flourishing demand attention. Thus we must be alert to

> [T]he identification of reliable incentives and recurrent vulnerabilities. This leads readily to what we may call *baseline* morality – the idea that moral requirements should be closely tied to urgent problems.... A baseline morality is often the most we can aspire to; and it is always a precondition for further development.
>
> Nevertheless, we need not be content with limited aspirations. Once a baseline morality is secure, we can respond to opportunities for extending responsibility and enriching fellowship. The conditions of *survival* are easier to meet than those of *flourishing*, which are more complex and more fragile. It does not follow, however, that we should fail to treasure what is precarious or cease to strive for what is nobly conceived.[63]

There are no all-purpose bright line guides to the exact mix of fear and hope that our institutions should respect and reflect, no political and institutional recipes, stable and apt for every time and circumstance, which realism demands that we should follow without deviation, or idealism beckons us to pursue. Nor are there any useful fixed ideological positions which provide detailed solutions to whatever problems trouble us, particularly since these problems constantly change. Nor still a fixed range of preoccupations to be hammered, with the same tools, and always as insistently, whatever the circumstances. Rather, as Lord Keynes is alleged to have retorted on being accused of inconsistency, 'When the facts change, I change my mind. What do you do, sir?'

Arbitrariness, just to stay with that, comes in many kinds and degrees, and a successful legal-political order needs to attend to many things short

[63] Selznick, *The Moral Commonwealth*, p. 38.

of war, cruelty and fanaticism. One might also hope for more from rule of law constraints on the exercise of power than avoidance of such terrible forces. In well-established legal orders with strong traditions, institutions and professions, one can ask more of legal institutions than mere restraint on power, notwithstanding the preciousness of that. Rather,

> In contemporary discussions of the rule of law we find much that goes beyond the negative virtue of restraining official misconduct. . . . This thicker, more positive vision speaks to more than abuse of power. It responds to values that can be realized, not merely protected within a legal process. These include respect for the dignity, integrity, and moral equality of persons and groups. Thus understood, the rule of law enlarges horizons even as it conveys a message of restraint.[64]

Selznick is particularly insightful about the dynamic pressures that a legal order will tend to generate, both when it fails to satisfy subjects' expectations and when it succeeds. For unusual among writers on the rule of law, Selznick was a distinguished sociologist, and in part his objection to a purely limited conception of legality is that

> We cannot really separate the negative and positive aspects of the rule of law. Indeed it would be highly unsociological to try to do so, for we would then miss the moral and institutional dynamics which create demands for justice, and which induce rulers to accept accountability. . . . we should not reduce the rule of law to its most rudimentary forms.[65]

In this understanding, arbitrariness, and its antidotes constitutionalism and the rule of law, each takes on a larger meaning, attached to values to be vindicated, rather than simply to a set of institutions and practices imagined to guard them against threats. Arbitrariness is not found merely when a strict rule is overstepped but equally when law is 'inflexible, insensitive, or justified *only* by history or precedent'.[66] 'Going by the book' generates its own forms of arbitrariness, as anyone who has sought to deal with officious bureaucrats might testify.[67] To counteract such forms of arbitrariness, space needs to be made for a larger understanding of the contributions of constitutionalism and the rule of law, more 'idealistic', more open-ended and open to the complex realities of the world we seek uncertainly to navigate.

[64] P. Selznick, 'Legal Cultures and the Rule of Law'. In M. Krygier and A. Czarnota (eds.), *The Rule of Law after Communism* (Aldershot: Ashgate, 1999), p. 26.

[65] *Ibid.*, pp. 25–6. [66] *Ibid.*, p. 27.

[67] See E. Bardach and R. Kagan, *Going by the Book* (Philadelphia: Temple University Press, 1982).

Finally, as with most political values, constitutionalism and the rule of law are not the only games in town. If tensions occur between limiting the dangers of arbitrariness and using power to release aspirations, or between tempering power and other important values, or indeed between negative and positive aspects of such tempering itself, such tensions need to be examined and dealt with; sometimes mediated, softened; sometimes simply put up with, lived with. We do that with tensions all the time, as we do with those between realism and idealism, after all. We have few absolute and universal trumps in these games, and we should resist pressures to sacrifice something valuable – such as idealism – just because something else – realism, say – is valuable too.

3

Between the 'Real' and the 'Right': Explorations along the Institutional–Constitutional Frontier

PETER L. LINDSETH

Some Old Questions

How does a situation 'of fact' become one 'of law'? How, in other words, is the 'real' transformed into the 'right'? Conversely, how might conceptions of the 'right' that prevail in a particular community help to shape or reshape its social or political realities? How, in short, do the realms of 'real' and 'right' interact in a social or political order over time?

These admittedly abstract questions are as old (and as fundamental) as civilization itself, and I take them to be central concerns of this volume. When we inquire into the relationship between the real and the right, we are searching, at least initially, for an understanding of how a social fact evolves into something that is understood to exist by, under, or through law – however conceived, however aspirational, however even ironic – as in, say, 'the law of war'. The latter example is suggestive precisely because it lays bare the perhaps innately human desire to impose order on even violence and chaos. But then the dynamics of 'order out of chaos' may be the thread that runs through this entire process,[1] even as those dynamics are ultimately obscured, in the social and political domains at least, behind the institutional and legal constructions that we have built up over time.

These institutional and legal inheritances profoundly shape our present-day perspective, as well as the interaction between the real and the right going forward. As one historical sociologist has rightly observed, 'the world is always already institutionalized. Change unfolds on historically specific terrain'.[2] We cannot escape these inherited institutional and legal

[1] Cf. I. Prigogine and I. Stengers, *Order out of Chaos: Man's New Dialogue with Nature* (New York: Bantam Books, 1984).

[2] E. S. Clemens, 'Rereading Skowronek: A Precocious Theory of Institutional Change', *Social Science History*, 27 (2003), 446.

constructions. It is through them – and perhaps more importantly, through the cultural process of internalizing their seeming normative demands (whether explicitly or implicitly) – that we claim (hope) to live in a society governed by the 'rule of law' rather than by the whims of power and force.

This is a complex process, of course, and I do not pretend to offer a complete examination of it here. Rather, what I hope to offer are fragments of a theory of institutional (and by extension constitutional) change that might shed some light on the interplay between idealism and realism at the heart of this volume. After laying out some sources and influences for my own understanding of that interplay, I attempt to distil out elements of a theory in three primary dimensions – functional, political and cultural – while also introducing certain extensions and complications. From there, the discussion turns to a particular form of interaction between the 'real' and the 'right': the transformation of a set of 'institutions' into a robust 'constitution' for a political community. This transformation may be analogized to a kind of 'phase transition', to use the language of the natural sciences. Its key manifestation is the manner in which certain institutions attain a legitimacy to exercise not merely regulatory or normative power but also the power of compulsory mobilization, whether human (defence or policing) or fiscal (taxation, spending and borrowing). Legitimate compulsory mobilization, this discussion suggests, is a crucial element in the political metabolism of a community, converting social resources into work for public ends. It is the ultimate boundary – the Rubicon, if you will – between a merely 'institutional' regime as opposed to a robustly 'constitutional' order for a particular political community.

To illuminate the significance of this institutional-constitutional frontier, the chapter concludes with discussion of an historical example – the emergence and evolution of supranational governance in Europe over the last six and half decades. European governance is characterized by the migration of extensive regulatory and normative authority to supranational institutions. Nonetheless, it is also characterized by the retention of powers of legitimate compulsory mobilization (human and fiscal) in constitutional bodies at the national level. This distribution of power and legitimacy suggests that supranational governance in Europe – regardless of its obviously profound constitutional implications for the states and individuals that comprise it – should not be understood as autonomously 'constitutional' in its own right. Rather, European governance remains 'institutional' – or, as I have characterized it elsewhere, 'administrative' – relative to 'constitutional' bodies on the national level. This socio-institutional character (the 'real') defines the parameters for what European integration, in its current incarnation, can realistically achieve, and consequently also the legal character of the integration project (the 'right'). The EU's lack of autonomous constitutional legitimacy in the most robust sense – and hence the lack of autonomous powers of legitimate compulsory mobilization at the supranational level – helps to explain Europe's response to a series of recent crises, whether in the Eurozone, the influx of refugees or the response to terrorist threats.

Sources and Influences

Our point of entry into this discussion is an examination of the nature of institutional foundation and change. I begin, however, not with the burgeoning contemporary social science literature on the topic, no matter how important and rich that literature no doubt is.[3] My starting point is rather both older and a bit more obscure (at least to an English-language readership): the work of Maurice Hauriou (1856–1929), the *doyen de Toulouse* and the progenitor of the 'theory of the institution and the foundation'.[4]

Hauriou is recalled in France as perhaps the country's greatest administrative law scholar and a giant in the glory years of French public law under the Third Republic.[5] Because so little of his work has found its way

[3] See, e.g., J. G. March and J. P. Olsen, *Rediscovering Institutions: The Organizational Basis of Politics* (New York: Free Press, 1989); D. North, *Institutions, Institutional Change, and Economic Performance* (Cambridge University Press, 1990); E. Ostrom, *Governing the Commons: The Evolution of Institutions for Collective Action* (Cambridge University Press, 1990); S. Steinmo, et al. (eds.), *Structuring Politics: Historical Institutionalism in Comparative Analysis* (Cambridge University Press, 1992); P. A. Hall and R. C. R. Taylor, 'Political Science and the Three Institutionalisms', *Political Studies* 44(4) (1996), 936–57; A. Greif and D. Laitin, 'A Theory of Endogenous Institutional Change', *American Political Science Review* 98(4) (2004), 633–52; P. Pierson, *Politics in Time: History, Institutions, and Social Analysis* (Princeton University Press, 2004); J. Mahoney and K. Thelen (eds.), *Explaining Institutional Change: Ambiguity, Agency, and Power* (Cambridge University Press, 2009); M. Blyth et al. (eds.), *Evolution of Institutions, Special Issue of the Journal of Institutional Economics* (Cambridge University Press, 2011).

[4] M. Hauriou, 'La Théorie de l'institution et de la fondation', *Cahiers de la nouvelle journée*, 4 (1925), 2–45, as translated in A. Broderick (ed.), *The French Institutionalists: Maurice Hauriou, Georges Renard, Joseph T. Delos*, M. Welling (trans.) (Harvard University Press, 1970). Subsequent citations will be drawn from and paginated to the Broderick translation.

[5] Hauriou's *Précis de droit administratif* appeared in eleven editions between 1892 and 1927, his *Principes de droit public* appeared in two editions in 1910 and 1916, and his *Précis de*

into English (apart from old translations of excerpts and slivers here and there),[6] Hauriou has received relatively little attention in scholarly discussions in the English-speaking world. That is unfortunate. It was Hauriou, more clearly than any other theorist in my view, who articulated the 'special phenomenon of the institution [as] the transformation of an organization of fact into an organization of law, of the real into the right'.[7] In this way, the institution came to constitute, for Hauriou, 'the juridical basis of society and the state'.[8] And as we will see below, his theory of law also helps us understand the institutional-constitutional frontier as well as the role that law plays in the overall process of institutional and constitutional change.

My focus in this section will be on what Hauriou called 'institution-persons', or social bodies like states, corporations, associations, labour unions, etc.[9] Hauriou discerned three elements to their foundation: '(1) the idea of the work or enterprise to be realized in a social group; (2) the organized power put at service of this idea for its realization; (3) the manifestations of communion that occur within the social group with respect to the idea and its realization'.[10] This theory of institutional foundation and evolution thus focuses on the *interaction* of ideational, political and social factors rather than viewing any single factor as predominant.

In stressing this interaction, Hauriou was consciously staking out a position between two extremes he saw dominating the theoretical discourse of his time. At one end was the theory of *droit objectif* articulated by Léon Duguit, who emphasized social conditions in shaping the content of law and the direction of legal change. At the opposite extreme was what Hauriou characterized as the German notion of *Herrschaft*,

droit constitutionnel appeared in two editions in 1923 and 1929. Hauriou also regularly published analyses of decisions of the French Conseil d'État which were collected in three volumes as *Notes d'arrêts sur décisions du Conseil d'État et du Tribunal des conflits publiées au Recueil Sirey de 1892 à 1928* (1929).

6 See, e.g., Broderick, *The French Institutionalists*. More recently, see M. Hauriou, *Tradition in Social Science*, C. B. Gray (trans.) (Amsterdam: Rodopi, 2011), translating M. Hauriou, *La Science sociale traditionnelle* (1896).

7 M. Hauriou, 'An Interpretation of the Principles of the Public Law', *Harvard Law Review*, 31 (1918), 815. This article summarizes the argument set out in the 1916 edition of Hauriou's *Principes de droit public*.

8 Hauriou, 'La Théorie de l'institution et de la fondation', 93.

9 I will thus be leaving to one side 'institution-things', which Hauriou understood as juridical rules existing within society, such as property and contract, which borrow the power of sanction from social bodies but do not exist as social bodies themselves.

10 Hauriou, 'La Théorie de L'institution et de La Fondation', 100–1.

which emphasized political factors, in extremis armed force and violence (in Hauriou's gloss of *Herrschaft*, '[f]orce becomes law by success. Constituted law is an attack that has succeeded').[11] I take up Hauriou's critique of each position in turn, because each again helps us understand Hauriou's crucial insight: that institutional and legal change flows from the interaction of ideational, political and social factors rather than the predominance of any one factor alone.

Léon Duguit was Hauriou's principal interlocutor in France at the end of the nineteenth and beginning of the twentieth centuries. As a devoted follower of Durkheim, Duguit emphasized the predominance of 'objective' social forces in the creation of social 'solidarity', which Duguit deemed to be society's predominant *règle de droit*. Duguit largely dismissed the role of the individual and 'subjective' rights, which in his view were consequential only to the extent that they conformed to the *droit objectif*, which had clear primacy. This is one reason why Duguit had great influence on the development of functionalist legal theories in the early twentieth century[12] – i.e., the idea that law evolves as a function of objective social demand as well as the problems that society is seeking to solve at any given time. From this functionalist perspective, political will or power could play at most a secondary role in the process of institutional change, particularly as it related to the origins and contours of the state.[13]

Hauriou did not deny the role of social conditions or of functional demand in the process of social, political and legal change. Rather, his concern was the failure of Duguit's theory to account for agency: In Hauriou's view, 'the social milieu has only a force of inertia that finds expression in either a power of reinforcement of individual proposals when it approves them, or a power of opposition and reaction when it disapproves them; but of itself it has neither initiative nor power of creation'.[14] The 'social milieu', in other words, has no agency of its own, even if it no doubt created conditions that would shape human agency. For this reason, Hauriou found Duguit's social or functional objectivism to be 'excessive'.[15] He emphasized, rather, the historical

[11] Hauriou, 'An Interpretation of the Principles of the Public Law', 816.

[12] M. Loughlin, 'The Functionalist Style in Public Law', *University of Toronto Law Journal*, 55 (2005), 361–404.

[13] L. Duguit, *L'État, le droit objectif et la loi positive* (Paris: A. Fontemoing, 1901); L. Duguit, *Le Droit social, le droit individuel et la transformation de l'Etat* (Paris: F. Alcan, 1911).

[14] Hauriou, 'La Théorie de l'institution et de la fondation', 97.

[15] M. Hauriou, 'Les Deux Réalismes', *Récueil de Législation de Toulouse*, 1912, 1–10, as translated in Broderick, *The French Institutionalists*, p. 45. Subsequent citations will be paginated to the Broderick translation.

complexity of the relation between individualist and socializing tendencies in law and history:

> There has always been and there will always be something of the social function beside the individual right, something of the social institution beside contract, but also always something of the individual right beside the social function and something of the contractual beside the social institution. There is a duel of antagonistic forces here like that of the earth and the sea.[16]

Hauriou thus saw a dialectic of individual and social forces (interests/ideas and conditions/structures) in the process of institutional emergence and change. According to Hauriou, one of Duguit's principal failings was his failure to see that 'currents of ideas' could act as objective social facts (on this point, Hauriou admitted the influence of Fouillée's concept of *idée-forces*). Hauriou concluded:

> From the positive point of view, the question of the 'individual' and the 'social' proves to be reinscribed upon the current of ideas; some of them have individualist ends and others have social ends; both realize society and law. By their very opposition they keep each other in a certain state of balance. But this practical combination, while neutralizing certain of their effects, does not destroy either one of them; on the contrary, it utilizes both.[17]

But if ideas could have a social 'force' in this way, what then, in Hauriou's view, is the role of political power, particularly naked expressions of armed force and violence pure and simple? Here we must shift our focus to Hauriou's critique of *Herrschaft*, the other conceptual framework that Hauriou was arguing against in the construction of his own theory of institutional change.

Once again, in Hauriou's gloss of *Herrschaft*, '[f]orce becomes law by success. Constituted law is an attack that has succeeded'.[18] Hauriou, however, refused to equate law with a superior physical force. Rather, he argued that

> [if] an organization is created simply by force, . . . it then desires to live in peace. But to obtain a peaceful existence the new organization must obtain

[16] *Ibid.*, p. 46.

[17] *Ibid.*, p. 50. In his stress on the role of ideas and the individual in processes of social change, Hauriou drew from (and consciously took the side of) Gabriel Tarde in his ongoing debate with Durkheim. For more details on that debate, see M. Candea (ed.), *The Social after Gabriel Tarde: Debates and Assessments* (Routledge, 2010).

[18] Hauriou, 'An Interpretation of the Principles of the Public Law', 816.

> a pardon for its origin, must modify itself, must put itself in harmony with the conscience of jurisprudence. Peaceful existence is possible only when the demands of the law are satisfied. Until that is achieved the usurper must maintain an armed peace, and an armed peace is not a peaceful existence. So any organization derived from force becomes neither institutionalized nor legitimate save when law has beatified it. Nor does law beatify by reason of force alone.[19]

One might fairly ask, however: What is this 'law' that 'institutionalizes', 'legitimizes', 'beatifies' and/or legalizes by 'peaceful existence'? Hauriou insisted that he was not speaking of 'natural law', at least not of a sort that is identifiable *a priori*. Hauriou's institutionalizing and legitimizing 'law' is revealed socially and culturally, in the continuing process of historical development manifested in the balance of forces that society realizes in itself over time. This explains why – beyond the 'idea' and 'organized power' in service of that idea – Hauriou added the third element in the process of institutionalization: 'manifestations of communion that occur within the social group with respect to the idea and its realization'.[20] It is through these 'manifestations of communion' that a social group takes a kind of ownership of an organization of fact (whether created by political force or in response to functional demand). And it is through this process of internalization that a social legitimacy emerges, one that truly allows the 'real' to be viewed as 'right' for that particular community. The forms of law play a crucial role here, because, as Hauriou maintains, institutions are fundamentally both historical and legal constructions – they are 'born, live, and die' through acts of foundation, administration and/or dissolution that the community experiences, in a cultural sense, as having a specifically legal effect.[21]

If one senses religious overtones in some of Hauriou's terminology (e.g., 'beatify' or 'communion'), it is no coincidence. Beyond his committed liberalism, Hauriou regarded himself as a 'Catholic positivist' who, in effect, sought to accommodate the role of tradition in era of dramatic social change (see, e.g., his first major work entitled *La Science sociale traditionnelle* (1896); now available in translation).[22] But his theory of institutional foundation and change, despite its religious overtones, was not inherently conservative or traditionalist, even if his own personal preferences may have tended in that direction. His emphasis on the interplay of social, political and ideational factors has echoes in the

[19] *Ibid.* [20] Hauriou, 'La Théorie de l'institution et de la fondation', 100–1.
[21] *Ibid.*, 100. [22] Hauriou, *Tradition in Social Science.*

work of several later, distinctly non-conservative thinkers who stressed similar dynamics in their inquiries into the nature of historical change.

Consider, for example, Michel Foucault. Foucault found that there were 'manifold relations of power which permeate, characterize and constitute the social body', which depend on 'discourses of truth' in order to establish and maintain that power.[23] Likewise, Hauriou saw a multiplicity of law-giving powers in society, the institutionalization of which depended on the organization of 'power' that served to realize the 'idea' that animated (and in some sense defined) the life and contours of an institution.[24] Hauriou would have concurred with Foucault that one must 'conduct an *ascending* analysis of power, starting, that is, from its infinitesimal mechanisms, which each have their own history, their own trajectory . . . ' (emphasis in original).[25] Hauriou, in an analogous manner, argued that 'the sources of law most directly derived from government are subordinated to those hardly derived from that source at all'.[26] In some sense anticipating the recent insights of what has come to be known as 'legal pluralism',[27] Hauriou called this the 'decentralization' of law. From this perspective, custom was superior, not in any normative sense but in a positive or realist one: Constitutions, statutes, ordinances, decrees and all other manner of acts reflecting a subjective political will, need to contend with custom (not merely explicitly held ideas but also practices) in order to be 'legalized by peaceful existence'. Hauriou shared with Foucault the desire to understand these mechanisms *historically* and in an *ascending* fashion, from their most decentralized manifestations

[23] M. Foucault, *Power/Knowledge: Selected Interviews and Other Writings, 1972–1977* (New York: Pantheon Books, 1980), p. 93.

[24] Both concepts in turn resonate with modern-day sociological (or 'constructivist') theories that stress the role of 'logics of appropriateness' in shaping social actors' behaviour, as opposed to logics of interest-based calculation that rational-choice theories stress. J. G. March and J. P. Olsen, 'The Logic of Appropriateness', *Centre for European Studies, University of Oslo, ARENA Working Papers, WP 04/09*, 2009, available at http://www.arena.uio.no/publications/wp04_9.pdf. Vivien Schmidt has incorporated these constructivist elements into a broader theory of 'discursive institutionalism' that builds in part on Foucault. See V. A. Schmidt, 'Discursive Institutionalism: Scope, Dynamics, and Philosophical Underpinnings' in F. Fischer and H. Gottweis (eds.), *The Argumentative Turn Revisited: Public Policy as Communicative Practice* (Durham, NC: Duke University Press, 2012), p. 85.

[25] Foucault, *Power/Knowledge*, p. 99.

[26] Hauriou, 'An Interpretation of the Principles of the Public Law', 818.

[27] For a description and critique, see S. Douglas-Scott, 'Brave New World? The Challenges of Transnational Law and Legal Pluralism to Contemporary Legal Theory' in D. Schiff and R. Nobles (eds.), *Law, Society and Community: Socio-Legal Essays in Honour of Roger Cotterrell* (Fernham: Ashgate, 2014).

(for example, the 'infinitesimal' power of custom) rather than their more centralized forms (the state, constitutions, etc.). The key difference, of course, is that Hauriou did not share with Foucault the same critical ambition; rather, he sought to explain the deeply embedded power of tradition, not as domination, but as a manifestation of social acceptance and durability.

Consider also the historiographical theory of E. P. Thompson. According to Thompson, 'historical change eventuates . . . because changes in productive relationships are experienced in social and cultural life, refracted in men's ideas and their values, and argued through their actions, their choices and their beliefs'.[28] Given its Marxist underpinnings, Thompson's historiographical approach always included a historical-materialist focus on 'changes in productive relationships' – that is, on changes in the relationship of individuals or social groups to the ownership of the means of production. But Thompson was not exclusively concerned with material-structural change in an economic sense. Understanding the direction of history required, in his view, an understanding of how such change was '*experienced* in social and cultural life' (my emphasis), an approach that found clear expression in his masterwork, *The Making of the English Working Class* (1964). This sort of experience involved, for Thompson, two inter-related aspects: first, how material-structural changes are interpreted ('refracted') in the prevailing system of ideas and values; and second, how those interpretations motivate, or give meaning to, subsequent social and political action. To borrow from a more recent historical-institutionalist approach, 'individuals do not intervene in the world on the basis ad hoc generalizations distilled from randomly gathered information. Instead, complex sets of ideas, such as ideas about the workings of the economy, allow agents to order and intervene in the world by aligning agents' beliefs, desires, and goals'.[29]

This dialectical interplay between socio-economic conditions and the prevailing system of ideas and values (and more importantly how this interplay feeds into political agency) echoes Hauriou's intuition that 'the social milieu has only a force of inertia . . . but of itself it has neither initiative nor power of creation'. It is only through the mobilization of

[28] E. P. Thompson, 'History and Anthropology, Lecture Given at the Indian History Congress (Dec. 30, 1976), in E. P. Thompson, *Making History : Writings on History and Culture* (New York: Norton, 1994), p. 222.

[29] M. Blyth, *Great Transformations: Economic Ideas and Institutional Change in the Twentieth Century* (Cambridge University Press, 2002), p. 32.

ideas and cultural experience (values, conceptions of 'right') in *the realm of politics* that one locates 'initiative or power of creation'. It also here, however, that we locate the reciprocal influences that reshape cultural systems of interpretation as they interact with social/functional demand and political interest over time. As the cultural historian Sarah Hanley once succinctly put it:

> [T]he historical process [is] a renewable dialogue or cultural conversation, wherein history is culturally ordered by existing concepts, or schemes of meaning, at play in given times and places; and culture is historically ordered when schemes of meaning are revalued and revised as persons act and reenact them over time. One might regard this process of reordering as one that 'counterfeits culture'; that is, as a process that replicates the perceived original but at the same time (consciously or unconsciously) forges something quite new.[30]

This process of political-cultural interaction, I would submit, has a crucial role to play in illuminating the process of 'communion . . . within the social group' that Hauriou identified as the capstone of the process of institutional change.

Distillations, Extensions and Complications

It is time to take stock of where these theoretical fragments may be leading us. Distilled down to certain essentials, what might the basic elements of a theory of institutional emergence and change look like? How might they apply to the field of public law, the focus of our concern here?

We must begin with the proposition that 'the world is always already institutionalized'. As such, the process of institutional change always takes place against a background of existing institutions, some of which have attained the status of 'constitutional' bodies for particular communities (about which more in the next section). Historians of public law should focus on how changing *structures of public governance* (the 'real') have been 'experienced' in relation to ideas and values of legitimate government (the 'right'). Whether driven by functional demand or political interest, these changing structures of governance will never be perfectly congruent with prevailing understandings of legitimate governance inherited from the past. This inevitable disconnect between real and

[30] S. Hanley, 'Engendering the State: Family Formation and State-Building in Early Modern France', *French Historical Studies*, 16(1) (1989), 5–6.

right – sometimes great, sometimes small – provides the fuel for a Thompsonian politics 'through actions, choices, and beliefs'. The gap between socio-institutional reality and historically embedded conceptions of right need not necessarily lead to a breakdown in the system. The gap will, however, lead to a dialectic in which both structures of governance and understandings of a legitimate legal and political order are forced to adjust in the face of the reciprocal influences of the other.[31] In turn, the perceived disconnect between real and right inevitably influences subsequent political choices about how to structure the system of governance in the future.

In light of the theoretical fragments outlined in the prior section, one can view the process of institutional (and, by extension, constitutional) contestation and change as operating along three inter-related dimensions:

- the ***functional***, in which existing institutional structures are brought under pressure and even transformed as a consequence of objective social demands ('needs'), as well as by constraints imposed by the availability (or lack) of resources and technology
- the ***political***, in which actors with divergent interests struggle over the allocation of scarce institutional advantages and resources in responding to these functional pressures (whether in seeking to preserve existing advantages/resources or realize new ones)
- the ***cultural*** (in the sense that a historian like Thompson or Hanley uses the term), encompassing the ways in which competing notions of legitimacy (conceptions of 'right'), often legally expressed, are then mobilized by social and political actors either to justify or to resist changes in institutional and legal categories or structures[32]

Beyond these three primary dimensions, however, it is important to identify three secondary dimensions:

[31] Modern-day 'discursive institutionalists' also emphasize this sort of contestation in the process of institutional change. V. A. Schmidt, 'Taking Ideas and Discourse Seriously: Explaining Change through Discursive Institutionalism as the Fourth "New Institutionalism"', *European Political Science Review*, 2(1) (2010), 1–25.

[32] In admittedly speculative terms, these functional, political, and cultural dimensions could be said to correspond to what were once conceptualized as various 'wills' inherent in human psychology (i.e., the 'will to pleasure/avoidance of pain', the 'will to power' and the 'will to meaning'). Whether such a conceptual apparatus is helpful to our understanding remains to be explored and developed. Nonetheless, these categories point potentially to various means by which human beings, as both individual and social actors, process and respond to environmental stimuli/information, something essential to the process of institutional change.

- the ***interactive***, meaning that the three primary dimensions are constantly overlapping and influencing each other, and their separation above is in many respects simply an analytical heuristic
- the ***temporal***, meaning that the interaction of the three primary dimensions happens across time, thus necessitating a kind of 'thick' analysis in order to understand the process of institutional change in specifically historical terms
- the quest for ***settlement*** – in effect, 'order out of chaos' – in which actors seek a ***reconciliation*** between developments in the various dimensions in some roughly stable way; that is, they seek to satisfy functional and political demands while still recognizing the outcome from the perspective of persistent, though evolving, cultural conceptions of legitimacy

There is a temptation in recent historical-institutionalist literature in the social sciences to try to isolate 'independent variables' driving the process of change. These might be material or economic (which I associate primarily with the functional dimension), interest- or power-based (which I associate primarily with the political dimension), or ideational or social-psychological (which I associate primarily with the cultural dimension). However, the central intuition that one should draw from the theoretical fragments above is that the three primary dimensions of institutional change overlap and the causal relationship among them is varied and multidirectional. As a leading comparative policy historian rightly reminds us: 'Where a historical problem is big enough to matter, causation is invariably multiple, the factors intertwined and interdependent'.[33] The result is an inherently complex combinatorial dynamic, the understanding of which may demand more synthetic approaches drawing on the concepts and tools of 'complexity science', 'complexity theory' and 'complex adaptive systems' as they relate to socio-political phenomena.[34]

[33] D. T. Rodgers, *Atlantic Crossings: Social Politics in a Progressive Age* (Belknap Press of Harvard University Press, 1998), p. 200.

[34] These include (conceptually) open systems, interconnection, interdependence, nonlinearity, networks, adaptation, co-evolution, self-organization, feedback, emergence, etc., combined with (analytically) mathematical modelling and computer simulation via agent-based computational models. There is a potential connection between Hauriou's institutionalism and modern complexity theory, which may be found in Hauriou's attempt to draw on the lessons of thermodynamics for social analysis. See generally M. Hauriou, *Leçons sur le mouvement social: données à Toulouse en 1898* (Paris: Larose, 1899). Thermodynamics has of course been central to the development of modern complexity theory in the natural sciences. See, e.g., Prigogine and Stengers, *Order Out of Chaos*. For further background, see M. Mitchell, *Complexity: A Guided Tour* (OUP 2009).

Among materially inclined observers, functional demands, as well as the associated political interests to which they give rise, are often taken as the prime movers; from this perspective, 'social development' is 'juris-generative' even if 'seldom synchronized' with law.[35] However, it is important to remember that a functional concept like '[n]eed, to make the obvious point, is subjective, political, time-dependent, and cultural'.[36] How a particularly society views social and economic demands at any given moment will depend significantly on the system of interpretation that is then dominant, as well as how competing interests mobilize interpretative frameworks to serve their goals in political action. Moreover, a functional resource like 'property' can also operate to define 'interests' in the political dimension while also constituting an 'ideology' in the cultural dimension.[37] The same might be said of claims of 'interdependence' as a key driver in a complex process like European integration (interdependence may be less an objective fact than an ideological presupposition mobilized for strategic purposes).[38] Finally, 'legitimacy' – the seemingly quintessential *cultural* element of institutional change (as to both governing structures and legal rules) – can also be understood as a *functional* 'resource' that enables or constrains action in the *political* dimension.[39]

Consequently, if we could truly isolate changes in the functional dimension from the political or cultural dimensions (which arguably we cannot), then perhaps we would observe much smoother evolutionary development in legal and political institutions. Instead we find notorious 'stickiness', which arguably results from the same complex interplay of functional, political and cultural factors over time. Economic or social shifts in the functional dimension (e.g., the extension of markets beyond national borders) may, depending on the array of interests, trigger either

[35] C. F. Sabel and W. H. Simon, 'Epilogue: Accountability without Sovereignty' in G. de Búrca and J. Scott (eds.), *Law and New Governance in the EU and the US* (Oxford: Hart Publishing, 2006), p. 403.

[36] Rodgers, *Atlantic Crossings*, p. 199.

[37] See, e.g., *ibid.*, p. 200 (referring to 'accustomed rights of property' in the United States playing major roles as both 'interests and ideology' in the reception of European models of social policy in the late-nineteenth and early twentieth centuries).

[38] P. L. Lindseth, 'Interdependence, Political Will, and Morality: Banking Union Version', *EUtopialaw*, 20 December 2012, available at http://eutopialaw.com/2012/12/20/interdependence-political-will-and-morality-banking-union-version/; P. L. Lindseth, 'Thoughts on the Maduro Report: Saving the Euro through European Democratization?', *EUtopialaw*, 13 November 2012, available at http://eutopialaw.com/2012/11/13/1608/.

[39] P. L. Lindseth, *Power and Legitimacy: Reconciling Europe and the Nation-State* (Oxford University Press, 2010), p. 11.

support or resistance in the political dimension (e.g., the creation of, or opposition to, transnational forms of governance to regulate those markets). Moreover, this functional/political interaction will be subject to varying and potentially contradictory interpretations mobilized in the cultural dimension (e.g., theories of constitutionalism or democracy 'beyond the state', or invocations of 'sovereignty' to define the true locus of legitimate governance as 'national'). The line of causation will always be multidirectional, and there is no guarantee that new functional demands – or, for that matter, new arrays of political interests or even alternative conceptions of legitimacy that may emerge – will, in themselves, inevitably or inexorably lead to institutional change.

Indeed, if there is a bias in the system, it is arguably in favour of gradual change in the intermediate term, which will generally occur within the confines of a more enduring institutional 'settlement' rather than cause radical change leading to a new 'settlement' itself. The historical process, as noted above, often entails an effort to replicate a 'perceived original but at the same time (consciously or unconsciously) forges something quite new'.[40] Consequently, while we are not prisoners of inherited models and systems of interpretations – we do retain agency[41] – our natural inclination has been to seek to understand (i.e., 'to reconcile') corresponding shifts in structures of governance in terms of conceptions of legitimacy that are recognizable in historical and cultural, if still evolving, terms.[42]

This process of reconciliation inevitably acts as a drag on the process of institutional change, an example, perhaps, of what Bourdieu called 'hysteresis', specifically drawing from the natural sciences.[43] Dramatic moments of change – what specialists in the field today refer to as 'critical junctures'[44] – only arise when there is a rare confluence of functional, political, and

[40] Hanley, 'Engendering the State', 6.

[41] As the anthropologist Marshall Sahlins reminds us: 'For if there is always a past in the present, an *a priori* system of interpretation, there is also a "life which desires itself" (as Nietzsche says)'. M. Sahlins, *Islands of History* (University of Chicago Press, 1985), p. 152.

[42] Cf. P. L. Lindseth, 'Reconciling with the Past: John Willis and the Question of Judicial Review in Inter-War and Post-War England', *The University of Toronto Law Journal*, 55(3) (2005), 657–89.

[43] See generally C. Hardy, 'Hysteresis' in M. J. Grenfell (ed.), *Pierre Bourdieu: Key Concepts*, 2nd edn (London and New York: Routledge, 2014). The idea of hysteresis originated in the natural sciences to describe dynamic systems whose outputs are time-dependent on present and past inputs. The concept now has a wide range of applications across several scientific fields (notably physics) as well as engineering and economics. See generally A. Pokrovskii, *Systems with Hysteresis*, available at: http://euclid.ucc.ie/hysteresis/.

[44] See G. Capoccia, 'Critical Junctures and Institutional Change' in J. Mahoney and K. Thelen (eds.), *Advances in Comparative-Historical Analysis* (Cambridge University Press, 2015).

cultural shifts that radically undermine existing institutional settlements, thus overcoming this drag/hysteresis and thereby opening the way for genuinely new institutional configurations.

Phase Transition – from 'Institution' to 'Constitution' – and the Role ('Rule') of Law

The bias against radical institutional change is particularly manifest in the constitutional domain, a core focus of this volume. I am speaking here not of a 'constitution' in the merely formal sense as an act of positive law, i.e., a written document designated as such or an amendment thereof. Rather, I am speaking of a constitution in the most robust and substantive sense, something with strong socio-historical, socio-cultural and socio-political underpinnings within a particular community. Hauriou alluded to these underpinnings when he spoke of 'constitutional superlegality'; that is, 'a sort of constitutional legitimacy that occupies a place above even the written constitution'.[45] My colleague Rick Kay has staked out a similar position, arguing that what he calls 'constituent authority' – in effect, the ultimate socio-political, socio-cultural foundation of constitutional legitimacy in an ongoing sense – cannot be found merely in positive law.[46]

The transformation of a mere 'institution' into something genuinely 'constitutional' for a particular community – that is, the creation of a body or bodies capable of ruling legitimately and durably on the community's behalf – requires a special kind of transformation, something akin to a 'phase transition' from liquid to solid, to again borrow a notion from the natural sciences. In the democratic age in which we (hopefully) still find ourselves, this process is intimately tied to the historical emergence of a sense that a particular political community, as a collectivity, is '*entitled* to effective organs of political self-government'[47] through institutions that the community 'constitutes' for this purpose.

Crucial in this transition is collective historical memory, or the manner in which certain institutions are able to derive legitimacy from their popular

[45] N. Foulquier, 'Maurice Hauriou, Constitutionnaliste (1856–1929)', *Jus Politicum*, 2 (2009), 12–13, available at http://juspoliticum.com/IMG/pdf/JP2_Foulquier_Maurice_Hauriou.pdf, quoting M. Hauriou, *Précis de droit constitutionnel* (1st edn 1923), 296 [my translation].

[46] See R. S. Kay, 'Constituent Authority', *The American Journal of Comparative Law*, 59(3) (2011), 716 ('constituent authority cannot be legal authority').

[47] N. MacCormick, *Questioning Sovereignty: Law, State, and Nation in the European Commonwealth* (Oxford University Press, 1999), p. 173 (emphasis added).

association with the certain critical 'moments' in the community's past.[48] This democratic and constitutional self-consciousness – what we often call the sense of being a 'demos', 'people' or 'nation' – need not be grounded in exclusionary ethnic, religious or linguistic affinities nor does it preclude cooperation with other polities on the basis of reciprocity and interdependence. As Neil MacCormick has shown, this demos-consciousness can be 'civic' – based in shared ideals rather than ethnic, linguistic or religious affinities – although it still must be grounded in a 'historical' and indeed 'cultural' experience for that particular community.[49]

Through this special process of transformation – again, this 'phase transition' – mere institutions may gain a legitimacy not only to engage in regulatory actions of various kinds but also to exercise the core prerogatives of public power on a societal scale: the legitimate compulsory mobilization of resources, both human (policing, defence, i.e., coercion both internal and external) as well as fiscal (most importantly taxation, but also spending and borrowing). These compulsory mobilization powers, as well as the robust constitutional legitimacy that supports them, could be analogized to an 'emergent property' in a complex adaptive system (as 'consciousness' is an emergent property out of the biology of the human brain).[50] It is here that legitimacy makes itself felt not merely as a cultural conception of 'right' but truly as a functional resource that can be mobilized for political ends.[51]

Only certain kinds of institutions cross this threshold of legitimacy to overt societal mobilization, for good or ill.[52] Any regulatory system that ultimately requires a significant degree of mobilization in order to achieve its goals (nearly all do) must eventually attain constitutional legitimacy in its own right or find a way to borrow the capacities of

[48] See, e.g., P. L. Lindseth, 'Law, History, and Memory: "Republican Moments" and the Legitimacy of Constitutional Review in France', *Columbia Journal of European Law*, 3 (1997), 49–83.

[49] MacCormick, *Questioning Sovereignty*, pp. 169–74.

[50] That is, if we choose again to theorize in terms of complexity theory (see n. 34 above and accompanying text).

[51] See n. 39 and accompanying text.

[52] The prominent example, in the North Atlantic world, is the emergence of the elected assembly within the nation-state over the course of the nineteenth century. See n. 85 below and accompanying text. Tocqueville anticipated this development when he spoke of the process of 'centralization of government', particularly in elected assemblies, with the English Parliament being his paradigmatic example. A. de Tocqueville, *Democracy in America* (1835) (London: Longmans, 1889), pp. 64–7 (associating 'centralization of government' with the elected legislature, distinguishing it from decentralized 'local administration' in the United States).

bodies elsewhere that possess it. (This is the typical strategy, frankly, for administrative governance both 'within' and 'beyond the state', in which regulation ultimately relies on the mobilization powers of the state's 'constitutional' bodies – legislative, executive and judicial.)[53] The linkage between legitimate resource mobilization and effective regulation poses an unavoidable challenge to legal-pluralist theories that celebrate moving 'beyond constitutionalism' into a more pluralist realm as a means of effective transnational regulation.[54] A robust constitution must exist *at some level of governance* in order to achieve effective regulation, whether pluralist, transnational or otherwise.

The emergence of a robust constitution for a particular community – one capable of legitimate compulsory mobilization (human and fiscal) – necessarily stretches beyond law even if the realm of law serves as a key forum within which the deeper functional, political and cultural developments play themselves out. In this sense, the transition of a mere institution into a genuinely constitutional body for a particular community cannot be simply a formal process, the product of legal/institutional engineering by, say, an elite, however motivated. Without 'manifestations of communion within the social group' in a Hauriou sense, an elite's attempt at constitutional engineering will, at a minimum, be subject to ongoing contestation of a fundamental nature, at least if unaccompanied by the legitimacy needed to support the reallocation of compulsory mobilization powers.[55]

Moreover, even if such legitimacy were to exist within the cultural dimension, it does not automatically follow that constitutionally autonomous institutions will emerge. Rather, the cultural sense of entitlement to self-government must give rise to successful human agency, pursuing political interests in the face of functional demands/constraints. In other words, not all communities that see themselves as entitled to 'self'-government necessarily achieve it (for a contemporary example, think

[53] See, e.g., below nn. 93–98 and accompanying text (discussing the EU).

[54] MacCormick was arguably alluding to this challenge when he criticized pluralism for its inattention to 'societal insecurity that lie at the heart of Hobbes's vision of the human condition . . . The diffusionist [i.e., pluralist] picture is a happy one from many points of view, but its proponents must show that the Hobbesian problems can be handled even without strong central authorities, last-resort sovereigns for all purposes'. MacCormick, *Questioning Sovereignty*, p. 78. For an attempt to respond from a more strongly pluralist perspective, see N. Krisch, *Beyond Constitutionalism: The Pluralist Structure of Postnational Law* (OUP, 2012), p. 234ff.

[55] This is a concrete manifestation of what Hauriou termed the 'decentralization of law'. See above nn. 26–27 and accompanying text.

of the Kurds). Nor will political elites within a community that seek to achieve such 'self'-government durably achieve it against the oppositional mobilization of significant subgroups (think of the EU, as the subsequent sections discuss). Social actors within the community must possess the material and social resources (functionally) as well as the will or interest (politically) to realize the entitlement to 'self'-government not merely as a legal right (culturally) but also as an objective fact, against whatever functional, political, or cultural elements that may impede it.

It must be stressed, moreover, that even if this 'emergent property' of robust constitutional power and legitimacy is achieved at a particular point in history, its indefinite existence is not guaranteed. Constitutional legitimacy is, to borrow from Renan, a 'daily plebiscite'.[56] Just as institutions may be 'born, live, and die' (as Hauriou taught us), so too may 'constitutional' bodies, as well as the self-conscious political communities to which they correspond. This process of decay will also involve the complex interplay of functional, political and cultural factors over time. As with their emergence, the decay of constitutional institutions and their corresponding political communities will also stretch beyond formal legal processes, even if their transformation will no doubt find expression, at least in significant part, in the forms and processes of the law.

In this sense, the role (and 'rule') of law may be understood as a realm of functional, political, and cultural contestation in which constitutional institutions – indeed, legal institutions more generally – are 'born, live, and [perhaps even] die'. In this process of contestation, rather than marking seemingly clear lines between 'valid' and 'invalid' exercises of authority, the rule of law becomes more a system of 'resistance norms', operating 'as a "soft limit" which may be more or less yielding depending on the circumstances'.[57] The rule of law, moreover, should not be understood exclusively in relation to collective constitutionalism – in effect, 'sovereignty' writ large (which might itself be understood as a kind of emergent property). Sovereignty is in fact tripartite, involving constitutional, representative and individual elements.[58] Judicial power is best understood as an expression of the constitutional sovereign, in alignment with the individual sovereign; it does not belong to momentary possessors of representative

[56] E. Renan, 'What Is a Nation?' (1882), in G. Eley and R. G. Suny (eds.), *Becoming National: A Reader* (Oxford University Press, 1996).

[57] E. A. Young, 'Constitutional Avoidance, Resistance Norms, and the Preservation of Judicial Review', *Texas Law Review*, 78 (2000), 1594.

[58] Hauriou, 'An Interpretation of the Principles of the Public Law', 820–1.

sovereignty in the legislature or the executive. The latter may well control the centralized instruments of rulemaking or enforcement, but their legitimacy is subordinate to the decentralized constitutional legitimacy of the community itself, whose ultimate interest the judiciary should seek to vindicate, even if episodically and cautiously, by virtue of rendering justice in the particular case.[59]

Hence the importance that Hauriou assigns to the sovereignty of the individual within the nation-state, aligned with judicial power, as a necessary counterbalance to the more collective forms of sovereignty and their possession of powers of regulation and legitimate compulsory mobilization. '[T]he idea of sovereignty retained by the individual', Hauriou wrote, 'provides room for the two essential elements of a constitutional regime, individual liberty and the element of publicity'.[60] It is through such individual rights, as well as through transparency of public action, that private actors can both participate in 'the spontaneous collaboration for the public good' – notably through the legitimate mobilization of resources (human and fiscal) – and provide the necessary counterbalance to the pretences of public power wherever located.

European Integration and the Institutional-Constitutional Frontier

How might these theoretical fragments – along with the distillations, extensions, and complications described in the prior two sections – help us gain insight into an actual instance of institutional and constitutional change?

Consider the evolution of supranational governance in Europe from the post-war decades to the present.[61] Over the last six and half decades, EU public law has come to have a significant impact on legal relationships between and among institutions on both the supranational and national levels while also providing for a new patrimony of rights for private

[59] *Ibid.*, 819. [60] *Ibid.*, 820–1.

[61] Space does not allow a comprehensive review of how the theory applies to the European case; thus what follow are essentially highlights of arguments explored elsewhere. See Lindseth, *Power and Legitimacy*; P. L. Lindseth, 'The Eurozone Crisis, Institutional Change, and "Political Union"' in F. Allan, E. Carletti, and J. Gray (eds.), *Political, Fiscal, and Banking Union in the Eurozone?* (Philadelphia: Wharton Financial Institutions Press, 2013); P. L. Lindseth, 'Equilibrium, Demoi-cracy, and Delegation in the Crisis of European Integration', *German Law Journal*, 15(4) (2014), 529–67; P. L. Lindseth, 'Transatlantic Functionalism: New Deal Models and European Integration', *Critical Analysis of Law*, 2(1) (2015), 83–105.

parties in the process of European integration. Given these structural and rights-based dimensions, it is perhaps unsurprising that the EU legal order is often described in 'constitutional' terms, at least among European judges and their followers in the academy. Nonetheless, this conceptual vocabulary operates against the backdrop of a deeper socio-political, socio-cultural reality in which the locus of legitimate compulsory mobilization, for better or worse, has remained almost entirely national. How might the theory outlined above help us understand this reality?

We must begin by acknowledging that European integration represents a profound change in the nature of governance as measured by what came before it – the quasi-anarchic European state system. The catastrophic events of 1914–1945 certainly entailed the sort of confluence of functional, political, and cultural factors that could, in principle, radically undermine existing institutional and constitutional structures. And this confluence of factors did indeed open the way for new structures of public governance beyond the state in the immediate post-war years. Whether one viewed the situation in terms of the functional demands of reconstruction,[62] or in transcending the excesses of nationalism that were understandably viewed as responsible for the catastrophe,[63] the post-war political environment clearly offered fertile ground on which to cultivate supranational structures of governance in Europe. And indeed, after various fits and starts, both the functionalist argument (now often cast in terms of interdependence and the demands of international competition), along with the political-cultural ideal of European unity as a value in itself, were mobilized by the drafters of the Schuman Declaration of May 1950, most importantly Jean Monnet and his team, to kick-start the integration process as we know it today.

From the beginning, however, committed supranationalists understood the socio-political, socio-cultural challenge before them. Paul Reuter, the French law professor instrumental in writing the Schuman Plan for Monnet, placed a technocratic institution – the High Authority – at the heart of the integration project, and his reasons are telling. The creation of the High Authority (the future Commission) was, according to Reuter, 'in some sense a desperate solution' because, as he put it, there was 'neither a European parliament, nor government, nor people' on which to build an

[62] D. Mitrany, *A Working Peace System: An Argument for the Functional Development of International Organization* (London: National Peace Council, 1946).

[63] W. Lipgens, *Documents on the History of European Integration: Continental Plans for European Union 1939–1945* (Berlin: de Gruyter, 1985).

integrated polity or market; consequently, the purpose of supranational technocracy was 'to build Europe without Europeans' by 'address[ing] ourselves to independent personalities'.[64] By asking the member states to delegate significant normative authority to these 'independent personalities', the drafters sought to reduce the transaction costs of intergovernmental cooperation and to enhance the credibility of the member states' mutual treaty commitments among to each other. According to this 'pre-commitment' strategy of supranational delegation, the normative and regulatory decisions of these 'independent personalities' would then be binding upon national governments, parliaments and courts – a formula that has since been expanded to include not merely the normative and regulatory output of the Commission and EU legislature (Council and Parliament) but also that of the European Court of Justice and the European Central Bank, among others.

The marriage of the functional and political-cultural claims in support of integration would henceforth be the identifying characteristic of the most fervent advocates of supranational delegation in the European elite. Walter Hallstein, the lead German negotiator in the integration process in the 1950s and later the President of the European Commission in the 1960s, grounded his faith in Europe's federal destiny in a purportedly ever-expanding *Sachlogik*, or substantive logic, entailing functionalist 'spillover' of integration from one interdependent domain to the next.[65] Ernst Haas gave this faith an academic expression – via 'neofunctionalist' theory[66] – that would arguably become the guiding ideology of the Hallstein Commission.[67] The hope that the Commission would be the vanguard of an autonomous supranational regulatory system guiding the integration process would eventually be challenged, of course, by the reassertion of national executive prerogatives via the Council in the

[64] P. Reuter, *La Communauté européenne du charbon et de l'acier* (Paris: Librairie générale de droit et de jurisprudence, 1953), pp. 51–2.

[65] W. Hallstein, *Europe in the Making* (New York: Norton, 1972); R. Marjolin, *Architect of European Unity: Memoirs 1911–1986* (London: Weidenfeld and Nicholson, 1989), pp. 256–66; M. Schönwald, 'Walter Hallstein and the "Empty Chair" Crisis 1965/66' in W. Loth (ed.), *Crises and Compromises: The European Project 1963–1969* (Baden-Baden; Bruxelles: Nomos; Bruylant, 2001), p. 164.

[66] E. B. Haas, *The Uniting of Europe: Political, Social, and Economic Forces, 1950–1957* (Notre Dame, Ind.: University of Notre Dame Press, 2004) [originally Stanford University Press, 1958]; E. B. Haas, *Beyond the Nation-State: Functionalism and International Organization* (Stanford University Press, 1964).

[67] J. P. J. White, 'Theory Guiding Practice: The Neofunctionalists and the Hallstein EEC Commission', *Journal of European Integration History*, 9(1) (2003), 111–31.

Luxembourg Compromise and beyond.[68] This gave rise to the classic interplay between intergovernmentalism and neofunctionalism as dominant explanations of the integration process.

Despite the reassertion of intergovernmentalism, the marriage of ideological functionalism and European idealism was difficult to suppress. Rather, it found perhaps an even more hospitable home in the European Court of Justice – the body of 'independent personalities' *par excellence* – notably in the ECJ's major 'constitutionalizing' judgements of the 1960s and beyond.[69] Undergirding this extensive case law was a method of treaty interpretation – the so-called 'teleological method' – which was based on the idea that 'an ever closer union among the peoples of Europe' (as set out in the preamble to the Treaty of Rome of 1957) constituted the very purpose – the *telos* – of European integration. This was a classic instance of mobilizing a conception of 'right' in the cultural domain to justify political action in pursuit of institutional change. The judicial elite's overarching aim – its guiding 'idea' in a Hauriou sense – was the perceived need to promote the uniformity and autonomy of the supranational legal order.[70] The Court used the teleological approach (and the related doctrine of *effet utile*) to overcome textual obstacles, ambiguities or silences in the treaties to achieve the aims of integration as the judges understood them, looking to what they regarded as the 'spirit' and 'general scheme', and not just the 'wording' of the treaty.[71]

This approach also allowed the judges on the Court, by the 1980s, to conclude that the treaties amounted to a 'constitutional charter of a Community based on the rule of law',[72] in which the Court itself served as the ultimate legitimating mechanism. This was a crucial political pivot in the overarching process of contestation regarding the development of supranational governance in Europe. By establishing itself as a defender

[68] Lindseth, 'Transatlantic Functionalism'.

[69] A. M. Burley and W. Mattli, 'Europe Before the Court: A Political-Theory of Legal Integration', *International Organization*, 47(1) (1993), 41–76. Elements within the Commission's Legal Service were also crucial in the development of the Court's 'constitutionalizing' case-law: see, e.g., M. Rasmussen, 'Establishing a Constitutional Practice of European Law: The History of the Legal Service of the European Executive, 1952–65', *Contemporary European History* 21(3) (2012), 375–97.

[70] For a notable recent example, see Opinion 2/13 on EU Accession to the ECHR, 18 December 2014, available at http://curia.europa.eu/juris/document/document.jsf?docid=160882&doclang=EN.

[71] See Case 26/62, *Van Gend & Loos v. Nederlandse Administratie der Belastingen*, 1963 E.C.R. 1, at 12.

[72] Case 294/83, *Parti écologiste 'Les Verts' v. Parliament*, 1986 E.C.R. 1339, 1365 para. 23.

of a new patrimony of rights (generally market based) against national encroachments, the Court was able to draw on the perception that it was 'simply a continuation of the traditional role of European courts and, indeed, liberal courts everywhere: the protection of individual rights against the state'.[73] This discourse proved similarly empowering in the academy: Scholars could now assert that they were no longer operating within the traditional international law paradigm, with its questionable binding force; instead, they were now specialists in a new kind of genuinely 'constitutional' law, which offered considerably more normative traction, not to mention academic prestige.[74]

As crucial as this constitutional idealism proved to be, the fundamental lack of robust, autonomous constitutional legitimacy at the European level was hard to ignore, at least among observers who looked beyond the judicial into the political realms.[75] Robust constitutional legitimacy must be sociologically grounded in a broad-based (i.e., 'decentralized') perception that supranational institutions embody or express the identity of a new European demos to rule over and above those of member states. Here the dynamic interplay between the 'real' and the 'right' proved critical: The strongest indicia of the reluctance of the polycentric demoi of Europe to confer any genuine constitutional legitimacy on the EU was (and still is) to be found in the persistence of two enduring features of European public law: first, the EU's lack of any significant autonomous capacity to mobilize fiscal resources (apart from a supranational budget amounting to only one per cent of the aggregated member-state GDPs – only a limited portion of which derives from the EU's 'own resources'); and second, the near total absence of any autonomous capacity to mobilize human resources in policing or defence (apart from limited staff available for border-control support via Frontex as well as even more restricted policing and defence coordination via entities like Europol and the EDA). In this respect, the ECJ has acted as a 'pre-commitment' mechanism in an institutional apparatus whose function has been almost entirely normative and regulatory. The supranational 'constitutionalism' and 'rule of law' articulated by the Court, while seemingly pervasive in the eyes of lawyers

73 Burley and Mattli, 'Europe before the Court', 64.

74 Cf. T. Isiksel, 'Functional Constitutionalism in the European Union', EUSA Biannual Meeting, Boston, March 2015, available at https://eustudies.org/conference/papers/download/196, 5-6 (explaining the shift to a constitutional discourse in terms of 'epistemic empowerment' for scholars).

75 See, most famously, J. H. H. Weiler, 'The Community System: The Dual Character of Supranationalism', *Yearbook of European Law*, 1(1) (1982), 267–306.

and judges, have actually been quite 'weak' in its socio-political, socio-cultural reality.[76]

One obstacle to the emergence of an autonomous constitutional legitimacy for the EU has been the widespread perception of integration as a project by and for the elite. The principal beneficiaries of integration have been the educated and the socially mobile, exposing cleavages in European society that have proven quite challenging to manage politically.[77] Integration undoubtedly has its strong supporters – many of whom believe profoundly that an autonomous democratic constitutionalism at the supranational level is possible, starting with a legally engineered expansion of the powers of the European Parliament.[78] Nonetheless, for better or worse, the locus of democratic and constitutional legitimacy in Europe has remained 'national' – still a potent discourse in a Foucauldian sense, even if that discourse is not what it once was in the late-nineteenth century or, for that matter, the interwar period (thank goodness).

Indeed, the power of the national discourse persists even as the functional and political demands of interdependence and international competition have undoubtedly transformed European governance over the last sixty-five years. This national legitimacy may well be eroding from below in countries like Spain, Belgium or the UK, as a consequence of political and cultural developments pushing legitimacy even further downward to national sub-units. But these developments simply suggest that the national discourse remains potent enough to support a continuing sense of 'entitlement' to 'self'-government at a level *below* the EU, even as forms of supranational governance provide a conducive cocoon within which new forms of national autonomy might flourish.

In this sense, the true locus of self-government specifically 'of the people' remains, by and large, focused on national or even sub-national constitutional bodies rather than EU institutions, most importantly the European Parliament, which is always advanced as the great hope of European constitutionalists.[79] This is true even as vast amounts of

[76] Cf. P. L. Lindseth, '"Weak" Constitutionalism? Reflections on Comitology and Transnational Governance in the European Union', *Oxford Journal of Legal Studies*, 21(1) (2001), 145–63.

[77] See generally N. Fligstein, *Euroclash: The EU, European Identity, and the Future of Europe* (Oxford University Press, 2008).

[78] See, e.g., J. Habermas, 'Democracy, Solidarity and the European Crisis', speech at KU Leuven, 26 April 2013, available at http://www.kuleuven.be/communicatie/evenementen/evenementen/jurgen-habermas/en/democracy-solidarity-and-the-european-crisis.

[79] P. L. Lindseth, 'Of the People: Democracy, the Eurozone, and Lincoln's Threshold Criterion', *Berlin Journal*, 22 (2012), 4–7.

regulatory power have migrated to supranational institutions over the last six and a half decades, often for sound functional reasons (not least to ensure the credibility of national 'pre-commitments' to core goals of integration, such as free movement in its various manifestations). The EP undoubtedly provides a crucial measure of electoral accountability in the EU's regulatory system. Nonetheless, it has neither attained the status nor the powers of legitimate compulsory mobilization of a genuinely autonomous democratic and constitutional legislature representing a new, cohesive, 'self'-governing polity called 'Europe'.

The Contradictions of Supranational Governance in the EU

This disconnect at the heart of European integration – between supranational regulatory power, on the one hand, and national democratic and constitutional legitimacy, on the other – gives rise to a central feature of the public law of European integration that my work to date has attempted to highlight: the seemingly paradoxical combination of autonomy from, and yet dependence upon, national oversight mechanisms – executive, legislative and judicial – in the legitimation of the integration process.[80] These mechanisms are neither anomalous nor necessarily a sign of crisis in the European system.[81] Rather, they operate as means of 'mediated legitimacy' in a supranational regulatory system that, lacking autonomous democratic and constitutional legitimacy of its own, must borrow it from the national level.[82]

To fully understand this state of affairs, we must go back to the early years of the integration project and think more deeply about the functional, political and cultural reality at that time. Contra the federalist historiography of Walter Lipgens,[83] the magisterial work of Alan Milward taught us how the integration project was as much about the

[80] Lindseth, *Power and Legitimacy*. These mechanisms include, most importantly, collective oversight of the supranational policy process by national executives; judicial review by national high courts with respect to certain core democratic and constitutional commitments; and increasing recourse to national parliamentary scrutiny of supranational action, whether of particular national executives individually or of supranational bodies more broadly.

[81] Contra G. Majone, *Dilemmas of European Integration: The Ambiguities and Pitfalls of Integration by Stealth* (Oxford University Press, 2005), p. 64 (describing the imposition of national constraints on supranational autonomy as 'the symptom of a deeper crisis: a growing mistrust between the member states and the supranational institutions').

[82] See nn. 53–54 above and accompanying text.

[83] Lipgens, *Documents on the History of European Integration*.

'rescue' of the nation-state as the displacement of national sovereignty. 'This is not surprising', he continued,

> because in the long run of history there has surely never been a period when national government in Europe has exercised more effective power and more extensive control over its citizens than since the Second World War, nor one in which its ambitions expanded so rapidly. Its laws, officials, policemen, spies, statisticians, revenue collectors, and social workers have penetrated into a far wider range of human activities than they were earlier able or encouraged to do. If the states' executive power is less arbitrarily exercised than in earlier periods, which some would also dispute, it is still exercised remorselessly, frequently, in finer detail and in more directions than it was. This must be reconciled in theory and in history with the surrender of national sovereignty.[84]

There are, as Milward implies but does not explore, important linkages to be drawn between the development of the post-war administrative state and the shift of regulatory power to supranational bodies. Both depended on a combination of a seeming *fusion* of normative power in the national executive and a *diffusion* of power into a complex and far-reaching administrative sphere, one that operates at multiple levels within and beyond the state. Both, I would submit, were reflective of a conscious effort by major political actors to reinforce administrative governance – both national and supranational – by making it a more effective agent in the promotion of public welfare. This necessarily entailed the creation of an institutional apparatus separate from historically 'constituted' bodies of the state – legislative, executive and judicial – to collect taxes, refine legislative/treaty frameworks (through regulations and decisions), gather information and exercise other forms of enforcement power. We now call this institutional apparatus 'administrative governance' – not because it is somehow merely 'technical' – and certainly not because it is somehow not engaged in 'politics' (it clearly is). Rather, we call it 'administrative' because its legitimacy is derivative of, and ultimately mediated through, the 'constitutional' bodies of self-government located elsewhere, whether legislative, executive or judicial.

In the democratic age, the increasing separation of administrative governance from strongly legitimated constitutional bodies has a historical pedigree of its own, stretching back (at least) to the final third of the nineteenth century. Despite the 'remarkably resilient' constitutional settlements of the 1860s and 1870s (with elected national parliaments at their

[84] A. S. Milward, *The European Rescue of the Nation-State*, 2nd edn (London: Routledge, 2000).

core),[85] the European nation-state also confronted extraordinary, countervailing functional pressures to address a range of new regulatory challenges posed by urbanization, industrialization, and the globalization of markets in goods, capital and labour.[86] Over the final third of the nineteenth century, these pressures forced the historically constituted bodies of the nation-state to begin transferring regulatory authority outward and downward, into an increasingly complex, multi-layered administrative sphere comprised of sub-constitutional institutions of varying types.

This separation of regulatory power from democratic and constitutional legitimacy would be one of the identifying attributes of modern governance over the course of the twentieth century, eventually spilling outside the confines of the state itself. Under the new settlement that eventually emerged after 1945, traditional constitutional bodies retained crucial roles in defining the terms of compulsory mobilization of resources (human and fiscal). Nonetheless, these bodies often relinquished the exercise of regulatory powers *directly*, choosing instead to delegate these powers to administrative institutions, usually within but sometimes eventually beyond the state (as in European integration). Historically 'constituted' bodies retained roles primarily as *mechanisms of legitimation* – legislative, executive, and judicial – exercising various forms of oversight (if not direct control) over diffuse and fragmented administrative actors.[87] Over time, these mechanisms of mediated legitimation adjusted themselves to the functional demands of the integration project, emerging as crucial if often misunderstood dimensions of EU public law. National executive oversight of supranational action, first via the Council of Ministers and eventually also the European Council, provided the initial connection between supranational regulation and historically constituted representative government on the national level.[88] As supranational regulatory power expanded (notably from the 1980s onward), additional legitimating mechanisms became necessary, including national judicial oversight,[89] as well as increased national parliamentary scrutiny.[90] In this way, European public law has developed

[85] Cf. G. Eley, 'The Social Construction of Democracy in Germany, 1871–1933' in G. Reid Andrews and H. Chapman (eds.), *The Social Construction of Democracy, 1870–1990* (New York: New York University Press, 1995). p. 110 (referring to 'the constitutional frameworks fashioned [throughout Europe] in the 1860s' as 'remarkably resilient').

[86] Rodgers, *Atlantic Crossings*.

[87] P. L. Lindseth, 'The Paradox of Parliamentary Supremacy: Delegation, Democracy, and Dictatorship in Germany and France, 1920s–1950s', *Yale Law Journal*, 113(7) (2004), 1341–415; Lindseth, *Power and Legitimacy*.

[88] Lindseth, *Power and Legitimacy*, ch. 3. [89] *Ibid*., ch. 4. [90] *Ibid*., ch. 5.

oversight mechanisms and structural checks that, even if imperfectly, seek to do the work of 'reconciliation' not unlike similar mechanisms within the administrative state.[91]

Let me stress, however, that one should not necessarily be sanguine about the capacity of national constitutional bodies to effectively oversee, and therefore legitimize, Europeanized administrative governance. Given the reality of multiple constitutional principals in the European system, the technocratic agents in Brussels and Frankfurt (or juristocratic agents in Luxembourg for that matter) are entrenched to a degree not found in instances of purely national forms of administrative governance (this was, recalling Paul Reuter, arguably the very purpose of supranational delegation).[92] The fact of multiple national constitutional principals – and therefore of even more multiple 'veto players' – means that the political coordination needed to reverse supranational action is vastly more challenging than within a purely national administrative polity. This supranational entrenchment, combined with the overarching 'pre-commitment' function of supranational institutions (along with the ever-present capacity to mobilize functionalist and idealist arguments in favour of 'more Europe'), can give rise to a seeming *principal-agent inversion.* In these circumstances, supranational bodies appear to take on the character of principals in the integration process, supervising the conduct of member states as their agents. In the face of the otherwise extensive shift of normative and regulatory power to the EU level, all that remains to national institutions are the core constitutional powers of legitimate compulsory mobilization as the last true prerogatives of national 'self'-government.

Recent years have brought the consequences of these contradictions in European governance to the fore, not least in the Eurozone crisis but also (as of this writing in November 2015) the increasingly intense refugee crisis, combined with heightened terrorist violence. As one commentator pointed out in early fall 2015, whether we are speaking of the introduction of the common currency or the creation of the increasingly tenuous Schengen border-free zone, 'Europe embarked on highly symbolic projects before it had the tools to manage them properly'.[93] It lacked those tools precisely because the ultimate management of each project, on a micro level, called for autonomous capacities of legitimate compulsory

[91] Lindseth, 'The Paradox of Parliamentary Supremacy'; Lindseth, *Power and Legitimacy.*

[92] See above n. 64 and accompanying text.

[93] H. Dixon, 'Europe Just Isn't Ready: Similarities between Euro and Migrant Crises', *Reuters Breakingviews*, 14 September 2015, http://blogs.reuters.com/hugo-dixon/2015/09/14/refugee-and-euro-crises-share-features/.

mobilization.[94] The missing powers were both fiscal (taxing, spending and borrowing) and human (policing and defence), for which the EU not only lacks the power but also, more importantly, the legitimacy. The existence of supranational normative and regulatory power (the 'right'), no matter how extensive it might otherwise seemingly be, has simply not been enough to meet the demands of the profound socio-political, socio-economic challenges facing Europe (the 'real').

In short, both the Eurozone and the refugee crises, along with the increased threats of terrorist violence, have demonstrated once again the prescience of the warning of the Italian political theorist Stefano Bartolini in 2005: 'the risk of miscalculating the extent to which true legitimacy surrounds the European institutions and their decisions . . . may lead to the overestimating of the capacity of the EU to overcome major economic and security crises'.[95] In responding to both the Eurozone and refugee crises, the EU has been forced to rely on a strategy whereby all essential costs – political and economic – are borne internally, by the individual states, because that is where legitimate compulsory mobilization powers still reside. Moreover, to the extent that transnational coordination has been necessary, decision-making has been primarily national and intergovernmental rather than supranational (i.e., via the Commission and Court).[96] This has been true even as supranational surveillance of national actors has sometimes played an important role, consistent with the function of EU bodies as agents of the member states in overseeing certain policy 'pre-commitments' (e.g., to fiscal discipline in the Eurozone crisis, or in the enforcement of obligations under the Common European Asylum System in the refugee crisis).

The essential lesson here is that democratic and constitutional legitimacy, along with the concomitant powers of compulsory mobilization, are

[94] Cf. C. Thimann, 'The Microeconomic Dimensions of the Eurozone Crisis and Why European Politics Cannot Solve Them', *Journal of Economic Perspectives*, 29(3) (2015), 141–64.

[95] S. Bartolini, *Restructuring Europe: Centre Formation, System Building, and Political Structuring between the Nation State and the European Union* (Oxford University Press, 2005), p. 175.

[96] The primary exception has, of course, been the European Central Bank, but the ECB's sometimes 'heroic' role (e.g., in QE) has been driven by the incapacity of the EU and member states to mobilize fiscal resources on a coordinated, supranational scale commensurate with the demands of the Eurozone crisis. See generally P. L. Lindseth, 'Power and Legitimacy in the Eurozone: Can Integration and Democracy Be Reconciled?' in M. Adams, F. Fabbrini, and P. Larouche (eds.), *The Constitutionalization of European Budgetary Constraints* (Oxford: Hart Publishing, 2014).

indeed a functional resource and not merely a cultural phenomenon.[97] The creation of such legitimacy does not lend itself to straightforward legal or institutional engineering; rather, it is an 'emergent property' in a complex social and political system, and insofar as European integration is concerned, it has certainly not yet emerged on the supranational level. The continued locus of such robust legitimacy at the national level has had a direct bearing on the scope of power that can be successfully transferred to the EU institutions, whether in the Eurozone or refugee crises, or otherwise. As one observer rightly noted, there simply is 'a line in the sand beyond which only [national] governments can set priorities and act'.[98]

Concluding Thoughts

The various crises afflicting the EU these last several years have contributed to a more general atmosphere of disillusionment with the integration project, certainly among eurosceptics but also among erstwhile supporters. In a widely read 2011 essay exploring the 'political and legal culture of European integration', Joseph Weiler lamented what he saw as the depressing combination of legalism, technocracy and 'political messianism' that pervaded the integration project.[99] Supranational governance in Europe had never been 'particularly concerned with democracy (or, at inception, human rights). It sought its legitimacy in the nobility of its cause'.[100]

With this 'messianism' serving as an all-purpose excuse to pursue integration regardless of its legalistic or technocratic character, Weiler questioned whether the vaunted supranational 'rule of law' promoted by the Court of Justice in fact qualified as such. The Court's 'formalist, positivist and Kelsenian' conception of the rule of law failed, in Weiler's estimation, because it is 'not respectful of two conditions' in balance: 'rootedness in a democratic process of lawmaking and respectful of fundamental human rights'. Although the ECJ 'accepted the second of these conditions in an activist jurisprudence, beginning in 1969', it never

[97] See n. 39 above and accompanying text.

[98] J. Pisani-Ferry, 'Whose Economic Reform?', *Project Syndicate*, 30 July 2013, available at http://www.project-syndicate.org/commentary/the-purpose-and-strategy-of-structural-reofrm-by-jean-pisani-ferry.

[99] J. H. H. Weiler, 'The Political and Legal Culture of European Integration: An Exploratory Essay', *International Journal of Constitutional Law*, 9(3–4) (2011), 678–94.

[100] *Ibid.*, 689.

developed a jurisprudence to address the first.[101] Indeed, some observers who later developed Weiler's critique came to question whether the Court's conception of the rule of law is itself even all that concerned with human rights, focusing instead on the integrity of the internal market and the autonomy of the EU legal order.[102] The result is a purported 'justice deficit' in the EU.[103]

I highlight these critical voices in closing because they bring us back to certain key features of the theory of institutional and constitutional change that this essay seeks to advance. If change does indeed unfold 'on historically specific terrain', what does this suggest about the terrain in which supranational governance in Europe has developed? It suggests that the historic polycentricity of the European continent – most importantly in terms of the distribution of democratic and constitutional legitimacy, along with associated powers of compulsory mobilization (human and fiscal) – is a functional, political, cultural reality that has not been easily overcome in the integration process. Again the notion of 'hysteresis' may be appropriate here to describe a dynamic system whose outputs are time-dependent on present and past inputs, leading to institutional and constitutional lags despite functional and political pressures for change.[104] The 'real' in European integration has come back to bite the hoped-for construction of an autonomously 'constitutional' process of European integration, leading to a normative legal order (the 'right') of a vastly different character than what 'constitutional' label would suggest.

This has been true, in fact, despite strong functional and political claims to the seeming necessity of 'ever-closer union' in several different respects (interdependence, international competition, strategic coordination, etc.). These claims have been compelling enough to support the construction a highly technocratic and juristocratic normative and regulatory institutional apparatus. But the functional and even idealistic impetus behind integration has been insufficient to push the EU across the threshold of genuine democratic and constitutional legitimacy in a broader socio-political, socio-cultural sense. This

101 *Ibid.*, 691.

102 D. Kochenov, 'EU Law without the Rule of Law: Is the Veneration of Autonomy Worth It?', *Yearbook of European Law* (2015), 1–23.

103 D. Kochenov, G. de Búrca, and A. Williams, *Europe's Justice Deficit?* (London: Bloomsbury Publishing, 2015).

104 See above n. 43 and accompanying text.

explains Europe's repeated recourse 'to independent personalities'[105] – i.e., Europeanized elites, whether in the Commission or the Court, as well as, later, the European Central Bank – with all their advantages as well as limitations. The development of nationally mediated legitimacy in European integration is, from this perspective, an entirely understandable reaction to the EU's lack of democratic constitutional legitimacy of its own. It is the product of a dialectic between integration's persistent 'administrative character' and the underlying 'constitutionalist logic' posited by its legal elites, calling for uniformity and autonomy.[106] Nonetheless, despite this logic, European governance must borrow 'mediated legitimacy' from the national level in order to operate successfully, even within its primarily normative, regulatory domains.

There are limits, however, to this strategy of mediated legitimation – ones tied directly to the question of legitimate compulsory mobilization – which Europeans over the last two decades have unfortunately ignored at their peril. Whenever we talk about the legitimacy of European integration in its current incarnation, we must always ask the question 'legitimate for what?'[107] The scope and nature of the EU's legitimacy (merely 'institutional' and 'administrative' as opposed to robustly 'constitutional') has had a direct bearing on the legal authority that the EU possesses or is effectively able to exercise. The EU is clearly legitimate, at least in a mediated sense, when it acts as a vehicle to harmonize regulatory standards in service of the internal market across a whole range of substantive domains. Indeed, it may well also be legitimate, in certain circumstances, as a vehicle to enforce national precommitments to fiscal discipline, although here the traditional forms of mediated legitimacy may become more precarious (as the Greek case in the summer of 2015 increasingly demonstrated).

However, the EU is not (yet) sufficiently legitimate in its own right to exercise autonomous taxing, spending or borrowing power of any real macroeconomic or geopolitical significance, precisely because the EU does not (yet) possess the demos-legitimacy to support the exercise of such

105 Reuter, *La Communauté européenne*, p. 51.

106 P. L. Lindseth, 'Democratic Legitimacy and the Administrative Character of Supranationalism: The Example of the European Community', *Columbia Law Review*, 99(3) (1999), 735–8.

107 P. L. Lindseth, 'Author's Reply: "Outstripping", or the Question of "Legitimate for What?" in EU Governance', *European Constitutional Law Review (EuConst)*, 8(1) (2012), 153–64.

power. Nor, for that matter, is the EU apparently capable of imposing a workable collective solution to the refugee crisis (at least as of this writing); hence the significant erosion of the Schengen border-free system, including the temporary reimposition of national border controls in certain states. The rise in the terrorist threat, exemplified in the horrendous Paris attacks in November 2015, only seemed to exacerbate the situation.

How long such a situation can last, I cannot say. If experience is any indicator, the EU may well find a way to muddle through, albeit in a highly sub-optimal way that reflects the contradictions that flow from the odd mix of supranational regulatory power on the one hand with national powers of compulsory mobilization on the other. My historical-institutionalist instincts tell me that muddling through, without addressing the fundamental disconnect between regulatory power and democratic and constitutional legitimacy, is increasingly unsustainable where the EU seeks to undertake ever more ambitious projects like EMU or Schengen. At some point, Europeans will need to make a decision regarding their understanding of what democracy and constitutional 'self'-government are, as well as where they are located, particularly in the context of this increasingly ambitious integration agenda. An aspirational supranational 'constitutionalism' – no matter how appealing or empowering for supranational judges, lawyers and law professors – may no longer be viable in the face of persistent polycentric distribution of democratic and constitutional legitimacy at the national level.

Until Europeans show the necessary 'manifestations of communion' in the EU in a broader, decentralized, societal sense, the legitimacy (and hence legal authority) of supranational governance in Europe will likely remain mired on the merely institutional side of the institutional-constitutional frontier. Europeans must thus find a way to marshal the cultural legitimacy and political will needed to 'constitute' supranational bodies equal to the functional task of the developing integration agenda – notably ones possessing the necessary powers of legitimate compulsory mobilization – if not on the scale of all current member states, then perhaps among some significant subset. If this proves impossible, then a strategic retreat from the ambitious agenda may prove to be the only viable option. In fairness, any solution should require an equitable sharing of the agenda's unfortunate 'legacy costs' to date, which have been significant.[108] But more importantly, it should entail an unblinkered

[108] See Lindseth, 'Power and Legitimacy in the Eurozone'.

assessment of what a sub-'constitutional', 'institutional' (and hence 'administrative') process of European integration is realistically for. It will no doubt be a painful process, especially for the EU's judges, lawyers and law professors invested in the constitutional paradigm. But it will be a necessary one in order to develop a more sustainable model of integration going forward.

4

The Emergence of the Rule of Law in Western Constitutional History: Revising Traditional Narratives

RANDALL LESAFFER AND SHAVANA MUSA

Introduction

In June 1990, the representatives of the 35 States participating in the Conference on Cooperation and Security in Europe gathered in Copenhagen for what would turn out to become one of the most important stepping stones in the articulation of a new political and legal order for Europe at the end of the Cold War. At the conference, the US delegation, seconded by Canada and the UK, tabled a draft declaration on democracy, human rights and the rule of law. The Copenhagen Declaration,[1] which resulted from this, together with the Bonn Declaration on the market economy,[2] would become the backbone of the Charter of Paris for a New Europe of November 1990,[3] in which the order of the newly united Europe was laid out.

As Thomas Buergenthal, the international human rights lawyer, who was the main draftsman of the American submission, claimed, the Copenhagen Declaration was a veritable 'Democratic Manifesto'; the fullest statement to date of the Western political and legal system which thanks to the Western victory in the Cold War was now promoted to become the order of the whole of Europe. As Buergenthal well

[1] Organization for Security and Co-operation in Europe, 'Document of the Copenhagen Meeting of the Conference on the Human Dimension of the CSCE', 29 June 1990.

[2] Organization for Security and Co-operation in Europe, 'Document of the Bonn Conference on Economic Co-operation in Europe convened in accordance with the relevant provisions of the Concluding Document of the Vienna Meeting of the Conference on Security and Co-operation in Europe', 11 April 1990.

[3] Organization for Security and Co-operation in Europe, 'Charter of Paris for a New Europe', 21 November 1990.

understood, the Copenhagen Declaration's major historical significance lay in the fact that the text – which was underwritten by the Soviet Union and its former satellites – underscored the essential connectivity between human rights, the rule of law and pluralist democracy, based on the separation of power, representative democracy, free elections and an independent judiciary. Hereby, the Cold War 'agreement to disagree' that human rights could thrive outside the context of pluralist democracy was abandoned.

To Buergenthal, as to many others, including major political leaders such as George H. W. Bush, François Mitterrand or Helmut Kohl, and academics – most famously Francis Fukuyama – the triumph of the Western tripod of human rights, rule of law and pluralist democracy seemed to be the accomplishment of a long and gradual, but progressive evolution in European history. Buergenthal did not mince his words when he compared its historical significance to that of Westphalia.[4] With this, Buergenthal reflected an interpretation of history, which can safely be considered to be a part of the collective consciousness of constitutional and international lawyers today.[5] This mainstream interpretation of history amounts to a 'Whig interpretation of history'[6] in that it is straightforwardly teleological, progressive, liberal, and a winner's history: the winners being Protestant and Anglo-American. Its foundations were laid in the early eighteenth century, shortly after the Glorious Revolution is said to have made Britain into the first modern, parliamentary democracy. In this traditional narration, there are four major phases, which will form the basis of this chapter.

The Glorious Revolution in Britain of 1688–1689 forms the first step. It achieved the subjecting of King and government to law through the supremacy of Parliament over legislation and the means of power – weapons and taxes – and helped to further secure the control of the judiciary over the interpretation, application, and thus safeguarding of the law.

The second phase includes the American and French Revolutions a century later, whereby the English parliamentary system was exported to the old and new continents in a more radical form. Whereas the rule of law could be assured in Britain through the gradual evolution of the

[4] T. Buergenthal, 'Copenhagen: A Democratic Manifesto', *World Affairs*, 153 (1990), 5–8.

[5] R. C. van Caenegem, *An Historical Introduction to Western Constitutional Law* (Cambridge University Press, 1995).

[6] H. Butterfield, *The Whig Interpretation of History* (New York: W.W. Norton & Company, 1965).

constitution through customs and compromises between King and Parliament, in France and the United States this had to be done through revolution. The new settlement was laid down in a written constitution, to many political thinkers the embodiment of the social contract. The American and French Revolutions are also widely understood to have introduced two different forms of rule of law: one which guarantees the supremacy of the constitution through the right to constitutional review by the judiciary (the US model), and one which only guarantees the supremacy of the legislator over the executive through legislative judicial review (the French, or by extension European continental model). To both models, the separation of powers is central.

The third phase has been triggered by the moral bankruptcy of supreme state sovereignty and of the continental model during the 1930s and 1940s. This led to the gradual constitution of a higher, international juridical order – that of the international protection of human rights. This, fourthly, proved instrumental in the steady spread of constitutional review in countries of the continental model. Some historians, such as the American historian of human rights Samuel Moyn, collapse these two phases in one as they claim that the 'human rights revolution' only truly took place in the final phase of the Cold War, in the 1970s and 1980s.

Of course, this Anglo-American Whig interpretation of Western constitutional history has over the decades been constantly attacked and nuanced in detail as well as in synthetical studies by constitutional historians, political historians and historians of political thought. But as is so often the case with historical myths, they have been able to dent, but not fundamentally change the *communis opinio* nor to offer much in the way of an alternative grand narrative. While this chapter does not intend on putting forward its own revisionist history, it will tease out a few general ideas from existing revisionist historical readings in the hope of provoking some critical reflection on the dominant general outline.

This chapter will focus on these traditional narrations, as well as their subsequent revisions as to the emergence of the rules of law, mainly through the separation of powers. This chapter intends on providing a revisionist perspective to the traditional narration, which focuses on the gradual rise of parliamentary monarchy in England and then through revolution in the United States and France to achieve the rule of law by boxing in government through law and introducing the separation of powers.

Traditional Narrations about the Emergence of the Rule of Law

The English Story

As Schwoerer states, for 'almost three hundred years, the so-called Whig view of the Glorious Revolution prevailed, virtually unchallenged.'[7] The Glorious Revolution was the final moments in English history where the country was successfully invaded. Part and parcel of its extraordinary nature was the fact that the Dutch victor negotiated a compromise with Parliament to create a new constitutional settlement. Just as soon as the 1689 Bill of Rights was passed, it was the Whig party in power that took hold of the interpretation of the Revolution. This interpretation became crystallised in the notable work by David Hume on *A History of England*.[8]

According to the Whig interpretation, James II is portrayed in a negative light, in contrast to William III of Orange who is the saviour of England, freeing the country from the despotic hands of James II. Under Hume's interpretation, the Settlement following the Revolution did resolve all of the tensions that existed between King and Parliament and established a better system of government, overthrowing a king who had no 'regard and affection to the religion and constitution of his country'.[9] The parties passed a Convention which transferred the crown onto the Prince and Princess of Orange while the annexed Bill of Rights settled all points of dispute between the king, people and parliament. Never were the 'powers of royal prerogative (...) more narrowly circumscribed and more exactly defined, than in any former period of the English government'.[10]

Thomas Babington Macaulay followed on from Hume, as another writer providing the Whig interpretation of the Revolution, only this time going as far as stating that Parliament at the time agreed to 'assert the ancient rights and liberties of England',[11] in which no king could act

[7] L. G. Schwoerer (ed.), *The Revolution of 1688–1689: Changing Perspectives* (Cambridge University Press, 1992), p. 1; also see H. Hallam, *Constitutional History of England: From the Death of Henry VII to the Death of George II* (Cambridge University Press, 2011).

[8] D. Hume, *The History of England: From the Invasion of Julius Caesar to the Revolution in 1688*, new edn, 8 vols. (London: J. F. Dove, 1822).

[9] *Ibid.*, p. 348. [10] *Ibid.*, p. 355.

[11] T. B. Macaulay, *The History of England: From the Accession of James the Second*, 6 vols. (London: Macmillan & Co, 1913), p. 1300. For another Whig narrative, also see J. Tyrell, *Bibliotheca Politica: or an Enquiry into the Ancient Constitution of the English Government both in respect to the just extent of regal power, and the rights and liberties of the subject* (London: R. Baldwin, 1694).

without 'the consent of the representatives of the nation'.[12] Parliament was rightly victorious in the long enduring contest between King and Parliament. The Whig view of the Glorious Revolution meant that 'it was a triumph for the purity of constitutional law over an outrageous attempt at its perversion, a reaffirmation of the liberties of the English people',[13] of which James II was guilty of breaching.

In this sense, the aftermath of the Stuart era involved an alteration to the balance of power in England, placing constitutional limits onto the monarchy and transferring power to Parliament. The Bill of Rights 1689 contributed significantly to these constitutional developments and proclaimed several principles of freedom after the tumultuous period of revolution. Its essence was embedded in the principle that no government was above the law. William III and his wife Mary ascended to the throne, declaring their subjects' rights and freedoms. It was therefore after the Glorious Revolution, following centuries of tensions with the absolute state model in England that a system of constitutional and parliamentary government took shape. Whether this was a new model or an already-existing one has been the subject of much debate. One could argue the existence of preceding documents such as the Magna Carta and other similar liberty-inducing proclamations such as The Toleration Act of 1689, The Test Act of 1673 and the 1701 Act of Settlement as contributing to English constitutionalism.[14] These were all in one way or another declaring the intention that a Roman Catholic would never rule England. The constitutional restrictions asserted on the monarchy would never be formally codified, as continental counterparts would, but form part of all the documents aforementioned, in addition to unfolding through time via custom.[15]

The American Story

The United States of America was born out of a revolution of the thirteen British colonies on the Western seaboard of the North Atlantic.

[12] *Ibid.*, p. 1306.

[13] House of Commons Information Office, 'The Glorious Revolution', FS No. G4 Ed. 3. 4 August 2010, 4.

[14] R. C. van Caenegem, *An Historical Introduction to Western Constitutional Law* (Cambridge University Press, 1995), pp. 109–17.

[15] J. G. A. Pocock, 'The Significance of 1688: Some Reflections on Whig History' in R. Beddard (ed.), *The Revolutions of 1688* (Oxford: Clarendon Press, 1991); J. Miller, *The Glorious Revolution* (New York: Routledge, 2014), p. 25; C. E. Harrington, *The Whig Historians and the English Revolution* (Berkeley: University of California, 1953).

The constitutional process that stretched from the 1776 Declaration of Independence over the 1788 Constitution to the 1790 Bill of Rights marked a clean break with the institutions and governance system of the *ancient régime*. This most of all materialised in the rejection of the monarchy and of the class system, with its legal discrimination between different classes. It proclaimed the unity and equality of the people before the law.

In supporting their entitlement to rights under the common law, colonists used the work of various English lawyers, particularly the work of Sir Edward Coke (1552–1634). On this, it was Coke's view that the common law was far above the position of the monarch or Parliament, which remained important. Neither monarch nor Parliament could detract or infringe any of these common law rights. In aligning Coke's views, as 'the great fountain of Whig principles'[16] to the US Constitutional landscape, the common law was 'supreme', just as the American Constitution was the 'supreme Law of the Land'.[17] It was Coke's *Institutes of the Law of England* that would not only be the seminal legal works used in England, but the accepted works in America, at least until the late eighteenth century.[18]

One of the major constitutional products of the American Revolution is the mechanism of judicial review that guarantees the supremacy of the constitution. While the codified US constitution did not account for the right to constitutional review by the judiciary, it was thought as being implied by many commentators. This was the idea that the Constitution as the backbone of the American state structure was to have legislative adherence and it was the judiciary that would be suited to decide on this issue the best. Coke again made an enormous contribution to the idea of judicial review in the United States, especially from *Bonham's Case (1610)*. It was this case in which Lord Justice Coke writes that 'the common law will control Acts of Parliament, and sometimes adjudge them to be utterly void; for when an Act of Parliament is against common right and reason, or repugnant, or impossible to be performed, the common law will control it and adjudge such Act to be void.'[19]

[16] F. A. Hayek, *The Constitution of Liberty* (London: Routledge, 2014), p. 147.

[17] Article VI of the US Constitution available at: http://avalon.law.yale.edu/18th_century/art6.asp, accessed on 12 November 2015.

[18] E. Coke, *Institutes of the Laws of England*, 15th edn, 3 vols. (London: E. & R. Brooke, 1797).

[19] *Bonham's Case* (1610) 8 Co. Rep. at 118a, 77 Eng. Rep [652]. Since *Bonham*, there has been endless literature on the case and Coke's influence on the US constitutional

Following this case, Americans have continued to propound Coke's legal thinking and *Bonham's Case* as the leading authority for adopting judicial review of legislation into the American legal system. Even today, American judges refer to it as the 'fountainhead of the doctrine of judicial review'.[20] The first real instance of judicial review in the United States was in 1803 with the case of *Marbury v Madison* before the Supreme Court. This case provided the basis in which judicial review could be exercised and clarified the distinction between the executive and judicial forms of government.

Another general line of thought when it comes to US constitutional history is that the American Constitution was founded on the aim of placing limits on governmental action. This was the so-called federalist reasoning, quite notably stemming from Madisonian argumentation. Federalists believed that the post-revolutionary America was still experiencing 'excessive democracy', demonstrated by the unrestrained power of the state legislatures. This excessive power was deemed a threat to 'the common good of the union' and the sacred rights of individuals.[21] The traditional view is generally then based in the work of James Madison who saw the nature of the states as unalterable and the beauty of internal institutional safeguards as the key to protecting the virtues of the country as a whole, but also to protecting individual rights. The Constitution was created to limit state legislative power.[22] Commenting on the case of *McCulloch v. Maryland*,[23] Madison disputes the

> [H]igh sanction given to a latitude in expounding the Constitution which seemed to break down the landmarks intended by a specification of the Powers of Congress, and to substitute for a definite connection between

framework. See R. H. Helmholz, 'Bonham's Case, Judicial Review, and the Law of Nature', *Journal of Legal Analysis*, 1(1) (2009), 325–54; E. S. Corwin, 'The Establishment of Judicial Review', *Michigan Law Review*, 9 (1910), 102–25, 104; D. E. Edlin, *Judges and Unjust Laws: Common Law Constitutionalism and the Foundations of Judicial Review* (University of Michigan Press, 2008); W. Treanor, 'The Case of the Prisoners and the Origins of Judicial Review', *University of Pennsylvania Law Review*, 143 (1994), 491.

20 See the case of *US* v. *Davern* 970 F.2d 1490, 1509 (Sixth Circuit, 1992).

21 M. M. Edling, *A Revolution in Favor of Government: Origins of the US Constitution and the Making of the American State* (Oxford University Press, 2003), p. 4.

22 J. Madison, *The Federalist Papers: No. 10*, available at: http://avalon.law.yale.edu/18th_century/fed10.asp, accessed on 20 November 2015; J. Madison, *The Federalist Papers: No. 48*, available at: http://avalon.law.yale.edu/18th_century/fed48.asp, accessed on 20 November 2015.

23 *McCulloch* v. *Maryland* (1819) 17 US 4 Wheat 316.

> means and ends, a Legislative discretion as to the former to which no practical limit can be assigned.[24]

For Madison, this would mean the shifting of 'character at the will and according to the ingenuity of the Legislative Body' and therefore a great 'error in expounding the Constitution' could be found 'in the use made of the species of sovereignty implied in the nature of government'.[25] The Constitution could then not be interpreted to allow national government free unrestricted reign.[26] Scholars have therefore used the federalist stance, via the thought of James Madison to reason why the US Constitution ever came to be.

The French Story

Historically, the kings of France submitted laws to their *parlements* in order to register them. By doing this, the laws would be brought to the attention of the people and permit their enforceability within the jurisdiction of the respective *parlement.* In its simplest form, registration meant publishing the legislation through its public reading and legitimising it through a 'seal of approval'.[27] Absolutist theorists such as Jean Bodin and Cardin Le Bret viewed the legislative function of the *parlements* as simply declaring essentially what were the king's laws to the public. As Le Bret asserted, 'sovereignty was no more divisible than a geometric point'[28] and it was this that reflected the establishment view before the Revolution.

After the French Revolution, however, 'the Rousseaunian identification of legislation with the General Will and legislators with popular sovereignty was constitutionally enshrined.'[29] A much stricter separation of powers, delineating judicial power, was evident. In 1766, Louis XV had

24 Letter to Spencer Roane, 2 September 1819 in *Writings, Volume XIII*, 448; G. W. Carey, *In Defense of the Constitution*, revised and expanded edition (Indianapolis: Liberty Fund, 1995), available at: http://oll.libertyfund.org/titles/678, accessed on 19 November 2015.

25 *Ibid.*, 451–2.

26 *Ibid.* He also demonstrates this through his veto of the internal improvements bill of 1817.

27 J. J. Hurt, *Louis XIV and The Parlements: the Assertion of Royal Authority* (Manchester University Press, 2002), pp. 1–2.

28 *Ibid.*, p. 3; C. le Bret, *De La Souverainete du Roi in Les Oeuvres* (Paris, 1689), Bk. I, Ch. IX.

29 Article VI of the Declaration of the Rights of Man 1789, available at: http://avalon.law.yale.edu/18th_century/rightsof.asp, accessed on 10 November 2015; A. Stone Sweet, 'Why Europe Rejected American Judicial Review – and Why It May Not Matter', *Michigan Law Review*, 101 (2003), 2744–80, 2746.

refuted constitutional opinions present in the *parlements*, proclaiming his absolute sovereignty and owing no rationale for his demonstration of it. While the initial reaction to this was mild, over time provinces began vehemently arguing against this absolute royal authority in defence of their *parlements*.[30] The judiciary had the traditional role of guarding against absolutism, but had failed and become a symbol of conservative interests of the *ancien régime* in the eighteenth century, as reflected by class distinctions. With the stigma attached to a seemingly dishonest and unjust judiciary, along with the blurring of the lines between the various governmental functions, the revolutionary National Assembly eliminated the *Parlements* in 1789.

The traditional view is that in France, the rule of law had to be assured through revolution, just as in the United States of America. The French Revolution is understood to have introduced a new form of rule of law, one which guarantees the supremacy of the legislator over the executive through legislative judicial review, but does not provide for any judicial control over the legislator. French fundamental law was initially overthrown through processes in swift and sharp times of aggressive political evolution. This changed the entire basis of the French constitutional order, shedding the skin of the old and revealing a new rejuvenated one.

The traditional story of the French transformation begins in 1789. Here a 'bourgeois *Rechtsstaat*, with a constitutional and parliamentary monarchy'[31] was born. Following immense disagreements on governmental land tax proposals, royal absolutism, lack of freedom and inequality, and the consequential disputes that would occur as a result of the convocation of the Estates-General, the outvoted Third Estate and its allies from the other estates left the Estates-General and founded the National Assembly in July 1789. The Assembly regarded itself as the representative of the one nation, the entire people, not of one single or the whole of the estates. It was not until 1791, however, that the first written French Constitution would be effected, formalising sovereign rights by the people and using the 1789 Declaration of the Rights of Man as its preamble. The Revolution would ultimately leave the monarch as one of only constitutional standing, losing its sovereign authority in the process.

[30] M. P. Fitzsimmons, 'Sovereignty and Constitutional Power' in D. Andress (ed.), *The Oxford Handbook of the French Revolution* (Oxford University Press, 2015), pp. 201–17.

[31] Van Caenegem, *An Historical Introduction*, p. 174.

Many of the initial disputes were in opposition to judicial review and the monarchically driven laws by the *parlements*. As David states,

> The supreme courts of pre-revolutionary France, the *parlements*, made themselves very unpopular by opposing all reforms to the traditional legal system. Assiduous in their defense of an antiquated system based on the inequality of social classes and on self-serving premises, they failed in their ambition of becoming the nation's representatives. Nor did they succeed in really controlling government action or in imposing procedural rules upon it. Of their many ill-advised interferences in politics and government, people remember their opposition to those organizational reforms that the monarchy did attempt from time to time. Abolition of the *parlements* was one of the first acts of the French Revolution, on November 3, 1789.[32]

While many revolutionary events occurred after this already quite revolutionary change, it was clear that the *ancien régime* was dead and a new constitutional monarchy with a new national parliament, the *assemblée législative*, came alive. But this was not the end, as the second stage of the revolution came in 1792 with the *coup d'état* of the Jacobins. At the end of the Revolutionary and Napoleonic Wars in 1815, the Revolution had protected a Constitution, a national parliament and parity in law, or at least in reality attempted to do so. It is however Article 6 of the French Declaration of the Rights of Man and of the Citizen of 1789 that demonstrates the desire to view representative democracy as the backbone of a legitimate governmental system and the supremacy of the legislature.[33] It stated that the 'law is the expression of the general will. Every citizen has a right to participate personally, or through his representative, in its foundation.'[34] This traditional revolutionary view has continued to the present and resulted in the criticism of judicial review systems such as that in the United States, which have been viewed as 'gouvernement des juges'.[35] Excessive judicial power on the assessment of the constitutional law of a country would conflict with notions of democracy, parliamentary or otherwise.

[32] R. David, *French Law: Its Structure, Sources and Methodology*, Michael Kindred (trans.) (Baton Rouge: Louisiana State University Press, 1972), p. 23.

[33] See L. M. Aucoin, 'Judicial Review in France: Access of the Individual under French and European Community Law in the Aftermath of France's Rejection of Bicentennial Reform', *Boston College International and Comparative Law Review*, 15(2) (1992), 447; Article VI of the Declaration of the Rights of Man 1789, available at: http://avalon.law.yale.edu/18th_century/rightsof.asp, accessed on 16 November 2015.

[34] *Ibid.*

[35] Aucoin, 'Judicial Review in France', 447; M. M. Shapiro, 'Judicial Review in France', *Journal of Law and Politics*, 6 (1989), 531–48.

International Human Rights

In tracing the historical narrative of human rights, one often reads the Declaration of the International Rights of Man adopted in 1929 by the Institute of International Law in New York. This document placed human rights as a priority for the international community. It stated that the 'juridical conscience of the civilised world demands the recognition for the individual of rights preserved from all infringement on the part of the state'.[36] The narratives however placed a greater emphasis on the importance of the 1940s, when the World War propelled the idea of the international protection of human rights to the foreground.[37] The agenda was to imbed this idea through positive international law and sanction mechanisms, a century and a half after national equivalents were integrated in national constitutions.[38] While morality indeed played a role, the propaganda value of human rights is symptomatic of its strikingly aggressive thrust onto the international legal scene at the time when it did, or so traditional narratives have us believe. The 1942 Declarations by the United Nations read,

> Complete victory over [the] enemies is essential to defend life, liberty, independence and religious freedom, and to preserve human rights and justice in [our] own lands as well as in other lands.[39]

A snowball effect followed this proclamation of human rights, leading to it being used as a symbol of freedom and hope for inequalities and wrongs all around the world. More notable, then, is the birth of international human rights, often directly linked to the devastation that was caused by the Nazi regime and the Holocaust during World War II.[40] Human rights here were the cornerstone of why Nazi Germany had to be extinguished.

[36] Institut de Droit International, 'Preamble to the Declaration of the International Rights of Man', 12 October 1929, New York, taken from J. B. Scott, *Law, the State, and the International Community* (New York: The Lawbook Exchange 2002), pp. 420–1.

[37] See D. Shelton (ed.), *The Oxford Handbook of International Human Rights Law* (Oxford University Press, 2013); R. Burke, *Decolonization and the Evolution of International Human Rights* (University of Philadelphia Press, 2010).

[38] For example the 1689 Bill of Rights and 1791 French Constitution.

[39] Declaration by United Nations, Subscribing to the Principles of the Atlantic Charter, 1 January 1942 (Book Department, Army Information School, 1946).

[40] M. H. Randall, 'The History of International Human Rights Law' in R. Kolb and G. Gaggioli (eds.), *Research Handbook on Human Rights and Humanitarian Law* (Cheltenham: Edward Elgar, 2013), p. 15.

> Hundred of political, scholarly and religious organizations have, by their publications, appeals, manifestations and interventions, spread and impressed the idea that the protection of human rights should be part of the war aims of the Allied Powers, and that the future peace would not be complete if it would not consecrate the principle of international protection of human rights (. . .).[41]

While it is claimed that at the turn of the twentieth century, explicit human rights language was not rife in international affairs and diplomatic correspondence, the human rights discourse suggests that the specific linguistic nature of human rights entered the scene as a result of Allied propaganda against the German Axis powers during World War II.[42] Human rights allowed the justification of wartime aims and ensured peace and security within the international community in the future. In a sense, the human rights mission also allowed the cementing of politically different countries such as the Allied powers of the Soviet Union, the United States and Japan, against fascism. One example that helped promulgate the human rights mission was the Constitution of the Soviet Union in 1936, framing the discussions surrounding this issue after 1945.

At the end of World War II, a number of states had consented to the principles of the Atlantic Charter, composing members of the soon-to-be United Nations. For this reason 1945 is seen as the year of the international legal community. While it did not put forward a set of legally binding human rights principles, it did lead to the addition of human right-referring provisions and the inclusion of human rights in the UN Charter. The Preamble placed 'faith in the fundamental human rights, in the dignity and worth of the human person'.[43] These words were accepted by a whole manner of groups, including the church, unionists, feminist groups and Jewish groups. Human rights also filtered into freedom and nationalist movements, as well as global constitutional orders such as the Indonesian Constitution in 1945. Subsequently, the human

[41] See J. H. Burgers, 'The Road to San Francisco: The Revival of the Human Rights Idea in the Twentieth Century', *Human Rights Quarterly*, 14(4) (1992), 447–77, who quotes the French ex-minister and ex-delegate to the League of Nations.

[42] J. H. Quataert, *Advocating Dignity: Human Rights Mobilizations in Global Politics* (University of Pennsylvania Press, 2011), p. 41; R. Norman and S. Zaidi, *Human Rights at the UN: The Political History of Universal Justice* (Indiana University Press, 2008), p. 82; J. D. Skrentny, *The Minority Rights Revolution* (Harvard University Press, 2009), pp. 39–40.

[43] United Nations, 'Preamble to the UN Charter', available at: http://www.un.org/en/sections/un-charter/preamble/index.html, accessed on 15 November 2015.

rights project was instrumental in the steady spread of constitutional review in countries of the continental model.

European countries in particular adopted the centralised – or 'neoconstitutional'[44] – model of constitutional review in the post-war era. Although countries such as Austria, Spain and Lichtenstein had already established the review mechanism into their constitutional framework before World War II, it was only after 1945 that constitutional review extended significantly to other European states.[45] The increased presence of constitutional courts and review mechanisms has been portrayed as a reflection of the 'ideological change – a new and urgent concern for limited government after an era of authoritarianism – and structural inertia',[46] which allowed for the defence of constitutional and human rights.

An Attempt at Revision

Some of the key points from the aforementioned traditional narratives will now be highlighted from a revisionist perspective. What becomes clear is that while one cannot refute the significance of the traditional narratives completely in the history of constitutional law and order, one can neither deny that a more nuanced narrative deserves a place in constitutional history writing. The Whig interpretation of English constitutional history for one often sees the seventeenth century as an era giving way to the theory of the 'divine right of kings', to the right of rebellion and even popular participation in government. While many printed ideas on English constitutional history have served as the groundwork for the Whig history of 'an idyllic, almost teleological, appraisal of seventeenth-century England'[47] or even as 'a watershed in the development of the constitution and especially of the role of Parliament',[48] key cornerstones

[44] P. J. C. Ortiz, *EU Treaties and the Judicial Politics of National Courts: A Law and Politics Approach* (London: Routledge, 2015), p. 50.

[45] Hans Kelsen defends the constitutional review of legislation in his 'Judicial Review of Legislation: A Comparative Study of the Austrian and the American Constitution', *The Journal of Politics*, 4 (1942), 183; V. Ferreres Comella, 'The European Model of Constitutional Review of Legislation: Toward Decentralization?', *I.Con*, 2(3) (2004), 461; D. Rousseau, *La Justice Constitutionnelle En Europe* (Paris: Montchretien, 1998).

[46] H. J. Wiarda, *Comparative Politics: Western Europe and the United States: Foundations of Comparative Politics* (New York: Taylor & Francis, 2005), p. 86.

[47] *Ibid.*

[48] House of Commons, 'The Glorious Revolution' Factsheet G4 General Series, August 2010, available at: http://www.parliament.uk/documents/commons-information-office/g04.pdf, accessed on 19 October 2015.

of this Whig history such as the Act of Settlement 1701 or even the Bill of Rights 1689 did not necessarily establish the fundamental constitutional order that they often lead us to believe.

The Whig interpretation then deserves to be questioned, especially since the seventeenth-century clashes in England between free and mixed monarchy were in fact common in much of Europe, even if the outcome was rather different. All disputes hinged on the supposition of 'some pre-existing, binding legal framework that defined the proper role of king and Parliament'.[49] Even though the cause of the Revolution may not have been an allegiance to the constitution, but rather a safeguarding against religious subjugation, it was no less a constitutional revolution, where two objectives were at its heart: to eradicate the King, yet at the same time, to protect the constitution. The series of events that occurred were also never as foreseeable as they have been written to be. The tables of English constitutional order could have turned as quickly as they were first positioned. Even the smallest of changes in events could have led to an entirely different history. The nature of the Revolution is not as glorious as Whig narratives have led us to believe and consequently, these narratives have been placed under scrutiny.

Political agendas in the seventeenth century were embedded within a legal architecture, so much so that revolutions, developments in government and the changes in kingship were propounded using legal nomenclature. The role of law was dominant in legitimising and moulding the new government, even when it struck at the existing law and constitution with brutal force, more so in light of the fact that the actions of William of Orange and his wife Mary were unlawful in every sense of the English legal word. The only way the new government's illegality could be deemed lawful was paradoxically through a legal process. All unlawful actions would be entrenched in the law, as was indeed done during the Glorious Revolution of 1688. The constitution that was to come from the Revolution had to politically stand the test of faithfulness to the law, even though by getting to that test, it had in itself committed a constitutional infringement.[50]

While there are critical commentators who have attempted to negate the value of the Glorious Revolution as a constitutional event in history altogether, there are more balanced revisionist views that place the 1688 Revolution somewhere in the middle, as a more realistic account

49 R. S. Kay, *The Glorious Revolution and the Continuity of the Law* (Washington: The Catholic University of America Press, 2014), p. 20.

50 *Ibid.*

of how the revolution contributed to the evolution of the English constitution. The revisionist method can be approached in different ways, but it often involves embracing the proportionate uncertainties of political dimensions and ultimately assessing and exposing the core political narrative to other religious, social, cultural factors, as an embodiment of a number of constitutional contexts.[51] To a certain extent, there will always be a degree of reliance on the traditional narrative or other precursor revisionist refutations.

The Revolution affirmed the view that the Crown was not the only institution to govern the English political system. It was also not the defeat of James II and his rescue of England from royal absolutism that had legitimised William of Orange's place on the English throne. It was the Parliamentary procedures that followed and the eventual Bill of Rights that was enacted. Even though Mary was James II's daughter, it was the initiation by Parliament of William and Mary and not simple genealogy that would legally and constitutionally consecrate their new monarchical position.[52] The Bill of Rights was a legally binding document affirming their future reign. It also limited royal authority, which Parliament benefited from tremendously, thence later bolstering by passing a number of proceeding legislation to avoid a repeat of past Stuart absolutism. So while the revolution was not necessarily as glorious as Whig history portrays, it did facilitate the process of limiting monarchical power, allowing free press and inducing religious toleration via the Toleration Act 1689. However, while we see the Glorious Revolution in terms of a new regime, which introduced the *trias politica*, it was in fact the restoration of mixed government, harking back to a medieval idea that had been idealised in the contest against free monarchy since the days of James I. It also saw monarchy become almost elective, as the natural order was passed over and subjected to religion, as per Acts such as the Act of Settlement of 1701.

One thing revisionists and Whigs can however agree on is the sheer importance of the seventeenth century in concretising constitutional government in England and for the centuries after.[53] This undoubtedly extended to the influence of Britain on the constitutional affairs that would take place across the Atlantic in America. The institution comprising the tools for checks and balances spilled into American political ideas

[51] P. Lake, 'Narrowness Vindicated: Post-Revisionism and Life after the Death of Master Narratives' in J. F. Merritt (ed.), *The Political World of Thomas Wentworth Earl of Strafford 1621–1641* (Cambridge University Press, 1996), p. 270.

[52] Gordon, *Controlling the State*; Schwoerer, *The Revolution of 1688*.

[53] *Ibid.*

in a drastic way, as well as leading to the American government and the constitution. The American political system can then be seen as an altered form of the English, both fundamentally and institutionally.[54] The major difference was that there was no class distinction, with the idea of one people represented by the state, where Parliament was an organ, rather than the people representing itself in parliament, counterbalancing the king. Now the state was the people.

The ambition to box in government by subjecting it to the law is an old one, extending far back in time before the Glorious Revolution, with roots in the Early Middle Ages and even antiquity. But over time its purposes and effects have evolved. Today its two main purposes are to guarantee an equal treatment of citizens under the law and to protect the private sphere from the public domain by reigning in governmental power in relation to its citizens. For the sixteenth- or seventeenth-century gentlemen of the noble or urban elites who took up the fight against the spectre of 'free monarchy' in France, England, the Low Countries or Spain, its purposes would have been to guarantee the rights and privileges of each separate class – clergy, nobility and third estate – to protect the rights and jurisdiction of local and regional government against royal authority and to restrict the encroachment of royal government upon property to the utmost extent. To the gentleman living in the France of that arch-symbol of royal absolutism, Louis XIV, hearing Buergenthal cry the victory of the rule of law today would sound as an ultimate act of cynicism if he would then learn that the relative tax burden in France was now several times higher than it was under the Sun King.

Many historians have also stressed the fundamentally conservative, even reactionary character of the political programme of resistance by parliaments and estates against 'free' or 'absolutist' monarchy in the sixteenth and seventeenth centuries – which met with failure in countries like France or Spain and with success in England. They reacted against what they considered the violation of the balance between king and parliament, of their harmonious cooperation at the service of the common good. This conservatism is reflected in the doctrine of the separation of powers, and the works of its iconic proponents Locke and Montesquieu, which advocated a return to the dualist late-medieval construction of cooperation between the king and the estates. This reading is supported by the historical understanding of sixteenth- and

[54] *Ibid.*

seventeenth-century writers of constitutional law and history, such as François Hotman or Edward Coke, who founded their ideas of limited kingship on early medieval Germanic notions of elective kingship.

John Locke, for instance, was fundamentally concerned with a few key points. He wanted government that would not end in war. He wanted to end religious wars and 'a set of applied arts of governing appropriate to the early modern mercantile states in a balance of power system.'[55] His theory of government was written in the context of the seventeenth-century constitutional conflicts. Therefore, his theory related to the ambiguity surrounding the limits of royal power, which was ultimately attempting to infringe upon the sphere of rights. Parliament's financial control and power of impeachment gave it the means to intervene in governmental tasks. Ultimately, when one side impinged upon the other, there would be reactionary, or even retaliatory actions, which then resulted in additional impingements by the original impinging side. These ongoing frictions between parliament and government remained tense.

The disparity between jurisdiction and government was not reflective of the executive and the law. Medievally speaking, government was not simply the executive of the law. Jurisdiction's purpose at this time was also not to make the law, but instead to rule on ancient property rights stemming from common law. The medieval government did not need to impeach upon these rights in property. This changed as the modern era came along, when governmental issues and finances increased reflecting the evolving economic, social and most dominant, religious issues in society. The medieval government and jurisdiction then collided with each other continuously. A greater definition of power was required, which materialised following the 1688 revolution.

You could say that the elements of the separation of powers were already in place by the time Locke began his Two Treatises of Government.[56] While Locke's treatise became renowned for centuries as underpinning European constitutional order, it is undeniable that similar theories existed as apologies to revolution even previously to that.[57] Despite this he propounded a theory of the Free State based in

[55] J. Tully, 'Locke' in J. H. Burns, *The Cambridge History of Political Thought 1450–1700* (Cambridge University Press, 1994), p. 616.

[56] M. Vile, *Constitutionalism and the Separation of Powers* (Oxford: Clarendon Press, 1967).

[57] S. Ratnapala, 'John Locke's Doctrine of the Separation of Powers: A Re-Evaluation', *American Journal of Jurisprudence*, 38 (1993), 189–220.

the state of nature and natural rights away from the common law or any ancient constitutional basis. He avoided the direct references to the conflict between king and parliament and framed his theory on a broader political scale. Consequently, there was a greater degree of emphasis on the legislative body, unlike the previous emphasis on royal authority. Instead of calling for the abolition of the executive, Locke placed his focus on property and trusts. He certainly wanted a separation between legislative and executive, but he referred to the legislative as a supreme power, which has inevitably caused dissension among interpretations.[58] Nonetheless, Locke used the state of nature to analogise the various functions of the legislative and executive, including the judiciary. All bodies were subject to the law. Locke's legislative supremacy referred to the legislative as the body making the law and therefore supreme over the others, but not making it inconsistent with the separation of powers.

Charles Louis de Secondat, Baron Montesquieu is also famously known for his work on the separation of powers. His intention was to demonstrate that state laws were connected to the principles of its government and to the entire character and customs of a country.[59] He submitted three types of government: republican, monarchical and tyrannical and within each of these types of government articulated the allocation of power. In a republic, the power is with the people. Government in a republic could be divided into aristocracy, where the supreme power is only in part with the people and the same body holds the legislative and executive power. The republic could also be divided into the other category of a democracy, where full power is with the people.[60] The separation of powers was at odds however with the tyrannical form of government. In a monarchy, a single body would ascertain the laws. It was to the latter that Montesquieu placed the greatest amount of emphasis on checks and balances, especially with regard to the English constitutional landscape at that time.[61]

Indeed, the main inspiration for the opposition in the name of the 'people' – in the sense of the elite organised according to social class and represented in the estates or parliament – against 'free monarchy' was one of the protection of traditional privileges and of property against the progressive growth of royal power and tax. Today, most leading historians,

[58] J. Locke, *Two Treatises of Government*, in Peter Laslett (ed.), *Cambridge Texts in the History of Political Thought* (Cambridge University Press, 1988).

[59] C. de Secondat Montesquieu, *De l'Esprit des Lois* (Paris: Garnier, 1803), Bk. I, Ch. 3.

[60] *Ibid.* [61] *Ibid*; Vile, *Constitutionalism*.

albeit not all, look for the explanation for the rise of royal power in Early Modern Europe to the so-called 'military revolution'. The gunpowder revolution led to a dramatic rise in the size and cost of armed forces, whereby a process of bigger powers crowding out smaller powers as effective military players was triggered and whereby the build-up of the state as a war and tax machine commenced.

The elite-rebellions of the mid-sixteenth to mid-seventeenth centuries have also to be read as part of the slow adjustment to more fundamental and gradual shifts in constitutional conceptions that had already begun in the Late Middle Ages (from the eleventh and twelfth centuries onward). The most important paradigmatic shift concerns the relation between law and government. The traditional, medieval understanding of kingship was not of the king as lawmaker, as author of the law, but of the king as guardian of the law, of its correct application. Whereas royal legislation never disappeared during the Early and High Middle Ages, its major function was the confirmation and correction of – corrupted – law rather than its evolution, and it was considered to be the outcome of the harmonious cooperation between the king and the 'people'. As the head of the people's assembly, the king was also not acting as a judge in the modern sense but as the guardian of the correct application of the law, whereas the actual sentencing was left to the people or the bench of 'equals' of the parties in the trial (the king as 'judge in the old style').[62]

In this medieval setting, the law was not considered an instrument of government, but the expression of the customs of the community and existing order of society. The notion of law as custom also underpinned the dualist conception of the government as a cooperation between king and people. Finally, the traditional paradigm was deeply rooted in the dominant Christian, Augustinian ideology which saw law and order as the earthly, imperfect but not perfectible reflection of divine, heavenly order and was hence to be the immutable, stable concretisation of divine will and natural order, of divine and natural law. The early medieval thinkers did, however, not conceive of a formal hierarchy between divine, natural and human law, but of the total comprehension of the latter into the former. This is the legal expression of Ullmann's 'ordinatio ad unum'.[63] In the sixteenth and seventeenth centuries, political tensions arose where monarchs began to proclaim their 'absolute' positions as the

[62] A. Harding, *Medieval Law and the Foundations of the State* (Oxford University Press, 2002).

[63] W. Ullmann, *Medieval Foundations of Renaissance Humanism* (Cornell University Press, 1977).

supreme body not subject to any laws. This reflected the popularity among monarchs of Jean Bodin's theory of absolutism, where 'sovereignty is supreme power over citizens and subjects, unrestrained by the laws'.[64] Bodin's theory, however, did subject the monarch to the divine law. According to Bodin, everyone, including princes, was bound by divine law and natural law, as well as the fundamental laws of the realm.[65]

Under the influence of Roman imperial law and the onslaught of the example of papal monarchy, late-medieval and Renaissance kings started to promote themselves as authors of the law and shifted towards a more instrumental vision of law as a tool of governance. This led to the sharpening of doctrines about the relative powers of king and estates, to the articulation of contractual notions of kingship – leading to Catholic and Protestant resistance theories in the sixteenth century – and to an early form of rule of law whereby the king as lawgiver was subjected to higher, foundational norms of divine law, natural law, and constitutional law – as with Bodin. The latter subjection of the king to foundational norms was, even if no secular authority was recognised to effectively control the king, not without sanction as violations of natural and divine law weighed upon the conscience of the king and brought him within the remit of ecclesiastical courts, and far more importantly, the court of God at the end of times. The conception of the 'state' as a harmonious cooperation between king and people – as in the estates – for the 'common good', which had emerged in the twelfth to thirteenth centuries, still gave powerful support to the contractual notion of kingship.[66]

During the eleventh and twelfth centuries, the western legal tradition came as a result of the Papal Revolution.[67] With time, it led to a separation between the secular and ecclesiastical jurisdictions in order to allow the papacy to independently promulgate papal laws and establish its own judicial institutions. This was not the goal, but part of the instrumentarium to attain independent governance from secular power. The Church of Rome can then be viewed as a precursor to the

64 J. Bodin, *Six Books of the Commonwealth*, M. J. Tooley (trans.) (Oxford: Basil Blackwell, 1955).

65 W. A. Dunning, 'Jean Bodin on Sovereignty', *Political Science Quarterly*, 11(1) (1896), 94.

66 R. Lesaffer, *European Legal History* (Cambridge University Press, 2009); R. Lesaffer, '*De Opmars van de Wetgeving in de Continentale Juridische Traditie (11de-19de eeuw)*' in B. van Klink and W. Witteveen (Deventer: Tjeenk Willink, 2000) (Dutch).

67 H. J. Berman, *Law and Revolution: The Impact of the Protestant Reformations on the Western Legal Tradition, Volume II* (Harvard University Press, 2003), pp. 2–5.

modern state with its firm assertions of canon law. With the canon and secular law laying side by side, the legal plurality of these jurisdictions – including cooperation on one end and tension on the other – placed the law on a pedestal within a territory. The law was supreme. This eventual status made it supreme and autonomous over political authority. The King, and Pope, could make law, but not capriciously, and the king was bound by it too.[68]

Additionally, the power of king and government were seriously checked by the principle of '*iudicium parium*' (judgement by peers), the right of each class to be judged according to its own laws in its own courts by its peers – although the latter only truly applied to the elite of the three estates. This multiplied the diffusion of power and jurisdiction, which was already great because of the territorial dispersion of power. Legal plurality was highly complex. Clergy resorted to the canon lawyers and courts; feudal disputes amongst nobles were heard at feudal courts under feudal law and serfs had their seigniorial courts. This class distinction was perceived as being ordained by God and would last until the end of the eighteenth century.[69]

Between the midst of the sixteenth and the midst of the seventeenth centuries, however, Western Europe was marked by numerous rebellions against the rise of 'free monarchy'. The Reformation destroyed the role of ecclesiastical jurisdiction and in the longer haul led to a process of secularisation whereby the checking force of divine and natural law starkly diminished. This and the build-up of the fiscal and military royal state drove the resistance to more institutional solutions. By the early seventeenth century, in countries such as France and England, the elite-resistance centred on reaffirming the role of parliaments in legislation and taxation, ending in a successful claim to parliamentary supremacy in England and placing the guardianship over the law – its interpretation and application – in the hands of a 'sovereign' professional judiciary, independent from royal interference.

In the English seventeenth century, the notion of royal absolutism was being bludgeoned, almost to death. Initially this was done by the pro-aristocratic Calvinist movement and then by various classes who were victims to the dictatorial royal hands and bureaucracies. Revolution was rife at this time, as evidenced by the English Revolution of 1640; the civil war two years later; the 1649 Puritan Commonwealth; the Restoration

[68] Berman, *Law and Revolution*, p. 5.

[69] *Ibid.* Bishop Adalbero of Laon propounded this social and juridical principle.

from 1660 to 1688 and then the 1688 Glorious Revolution.[70] England, however, was not the only country experiencing revolution in the mid-seventeenth century; other European countries were also suffering from rebellions done in the name of anti-monarchy, such as the Dutch Revolt of 1566, the Fronde between 1648 and 1653 and the Catalan Rebellion between 1640 and 1659. While we have already stated that the 1688 revolution did not completely change the English legal system, but contributed significantly to its future development, these future developments included various legal concepts symbolic of English constitutional law. Common law courts began to usurp the power of other lesser courts such as the Chancery and Admiralty. The medieval High Court of Star Chamber and Court of High Commission were disestablished. English judges were also no longer the monarch's puppet, but given autonomy and life tenure. The independence extended to the jury who could not in turn be swayed by judges.

The constitutional compromise between King and Parliament, which came out of the Glorious Revolution in England was indeed the accomplishment of an inherently conservative programme to uphold class privilege in the face of royal power. The doctrine and reality of separation – and cooperation – of powers was in fact a new form of cooperation between king, peers and high clergy (House of Lords) and gentry and third estate (Commons, Common law courts). It was mainly framed in the language of 'mixed government', of government as a mixture of monarchy, aristocracy and democracy, which since (proto-) humanism had become the fashionable way of thinking about ideal government, with reference to Aristotle, Cicero, and the Roman Republic. Mixed government was the humanist remoulding of the medieval idea of dual government by king and people, or estates. This language played a crucial role in the formulation of the doctrine of the separation of powers.[71]

The major significance of the American and French constitutional revolutions at the end of the eighteenth century was then the shift from a class-based to a functional theory of the separation of powers. The rejection of juridical class distinction overhauled the historical legitimacy of parliaments. The American and French Revolutions allowed for the doctrine of

[70] Berman, *Law and Revolution*.

[71] R. Conant Moulton, *Separation of Powers, Mixed Government, and the Constitution* (University of Chicago, 1981); D. J Bederman, *The Classical Foundations of the American Constitution: Prevailing Wisdom* (Cambridge University Press, 2008); J. M. Blythe, *Ideal Government and the Mixed Constitution in the Middle Ages* (Princeton University Press, 2014).

the separation of powers to flourish in the palms of the anti-monarchists and challengers to aristocracy.[72] The replacements were various doctrines of 'popular sovereignty', which gave a new and actually far greater legitimacy to parliaments. Popular sovereignty united the state with the nation, and then the need to make the separation of powers to guard the nation against the state, as there was no inherent check through a real division of power. Whereas before the estates had just been one cog in the machine of state, representing just the organised part of the people and working together with the king towards the accomplishment of the common good, it now became the embodiment or representative of the whole nation and was sovereign over the whole machinery of state. The transfer of 'people' – as the organised elite – to 'nation' and the identification between nation, state and parliament in the long run forced a far greater assimilation between parliament and executive government than seventeenth or eighteenth century thinkers had envisioned. In fact, it also took away the main brake on the growth of state power – through taxation – and left 'judicial review' as the last man standing on the field against the growth of the state.

In France, revolution occurred to affirm democracy and the rights of man, as the 1789 Declaration states.[73] While the revolutionary intention was to eradicate aristocratic privileges and tyrannical monarchy, a legislative hand was democratically elected and a range of written constitutional documents were created to delineate the separation of powers. As Berman states, 'the executive was only to execute, and the judiciary was only to apply in individual cases, the law that the legislature alone had power to create'.[74] Where the English highlighted the judicial assessment of legal issues based in legal precedents, the French elucidated legal principles through the implementation of a series of laws. The earlier natural law was superseded by positivism, which gained even more ground in the nineteenth and following centuries.[75]

The American Revolutionary War was fought in the name of acquiring the same rights as those residing in the British Motherland. American colonists were beneficiaries to the English constitutional rights deriving from the English Bill of Rights or Magna Carta, to name a couple. Ironically, the Americans were besieged with the same royal absolutism as was previously fought against in England a century earlier. While there were aspirations to create a new constitutional order, the lure of the common law and historical precedents brought America back to the

[72] Vile, *Constitutionalism.* [73] The Declaration of the Rights of Man 1789.
[74] Berman, *Law and Revolution*, p. 11. [75] *Ibid.*

aristocratic foundations of the 1688 Revolution. At the same time however, a marriage of these English ideals was taking place with the French notions of democracy and the rights of man. Some commentators suggest that hybrid Anglo-French transplantation is reflected in the American Senate and House of Representatives, respectively.[76] In the United States of America, there was now a written constitution and a separation of powers closely resembling that fought for in the French Revolution. Quite new for any legal system at the time however was the introduction of judicial review on legislation and its conformity with the constitution.

France was of course never immune to judicial review, as we have read from traditional narratives. The *parlements'* relationship with the French King allowed them 'to examine all laws and decrees which [came to them] (...) to see that there [was] in them nothing contrary (...) to the fundamental laws of the realm'.[77] Frequently interfering in the functions of other state organs, the *parlements* were seen as abusing judicial power. It is predominantly because of these judicial interferences that the Revolutionary ideologies emphasised the invincibility of constitutional law and the strict separation of powers. It was the legislator as the symbol of popular sovereignty that would be best to secure essential rights.[78] Following the French Revolution however, there was a division in the Western constitutional trend, as the United States of America favoured older notions of subjecting the legislative and executive forms of government to the higher judicial authority who would interpret a supreme law. This supreme law was explicitly crystallised in the American constitution.

The traditional post-1945 human rights narrative, however, has also been subject to criticism and a revisionist approach by certain authors. Samuel Moyn is one such author who writes that the human rights project only emerged during the final stage of the Cold War in the 1970s and 1980s. According to critics such as Moyn, even in 1968, human rights were still tapping on the inner shell waiting to break out and therefore were never a reaction to Holocaustian atrocities. Human rights in fact surfaced in the

76 *Ibid.*, p. 15.

77 J. Flammermont and M. Tourneux (eds.), *Remontrances Du Parlement De Paris Au XVIIIe Siecle* (1888), p. 1; S. Cotta, *Montesquieu, la separation des pouvoirs et la Constitution federale des Erars-Unis, Revue Internationale D'histoire Politique et Constitutionnelle* (1951), 229, 234–5.

78 M. Cappelletti, 'Judicial Review in Comparative Perspective', *California Law Review*, 58(5) (1970), 1024–6.

1970s from somewhere beyond the ether. NGOs were virtually non-existent in the 1960s and it was not human rights, but other aspirations that flourished. These aspirations required a 'community at home, redeeming the United States from hollow consumerism, or "socialism with a human face" in the Soviet empire, or further liberation from a so-called neocolonialism in the third world.'[79] Human rights were not about freedom from the grasp of the evil colonial powers or self-determination of peoples. It was not the State that protected human rights, but humans that needed protection from the state.

Other critics go on to add that human rights transpired in the 1970s for many reasons. It first and foremost related to the desire for a European particularity away from an identity going hand in hand with the character of the 'Cold War'. There was also an apparent shift from the standard foreign policy nomenclature to one heavily personified by morality, especially after Vietnam, as well as the added dilemma of dealing with the postcolonial state. Finally, civil society began accepting Soviet and Eastern European opposition movements, adding to the affirmation of human rights. Human rights then began to spread and gain ground with the steady, but recognised work of organisations such as Amnesty International.[80] Human rights, as Moyn claims, became the 'last utopia' because other chimerical aims had failed. Human rights had superseded revolutionary nationalism. It had emerged to define the hopes of people in aid of a new idealistic notion of international law, away from the state itself.

The international protection of human rights also led to the rise of constitutional review in countries like Belgium and France. In focusing on the Belgian Constitution of 1831, adopted after the French model, one sees that it does not provide for constitutional control over legislation by the judiciary, but only for judicial review of governmental acts, where the Executive must conduct itself according to a constitutional act or legislative provision.[81] In 1971 the *Cour de Cassation*, however, ruled that there is judicial review over legislation, which violated international law with direct effect. The Court of Arbitration – founded in 1983 and later became the Constitutional Court – first started as a court to mediate the competences of the federal state and the different regions and communities. With time, it gained the right of constitutional review and

[79] S. Moyn, *The Last Utopia* (Harvard University Press, 2012), p. 3. [80] *Ibid.*, p. 4.

[81] Article 108 of the Constitution 1831. See also Article 159 of the Constitution, in which executive acts and decisions are subject to judicial review. For a good assessment of the Belgian Constitution, particularly on the principle of legality, see P. Popelier and K. Lemmens, *The Constitution of Belgium: A Contextual Analysis* (Hart Publishing, 2015), pp. 35–69.

individuals gained direct access, but at first only for the title in the constitution dealing with fundamental rights. Thus came an end to the absurdity that judges could refuse to apply legislation which clashed with international human right treaties, but not with constitutional rights.

Concluding Remarks

This chapter has focused on traditional narratives and revisionist approaches to these narratives, which deal with the emergence of the rule of law, mainly through the introduction of the separation of powers. The traditional narrative viewed the gradual rise of parliamentary monarchy in England and then revolution in the United States and France as achieving the rule of law through the separation of powers. Upon a broad assessment of the revisionisms to this traditional narrative, we have argued that the separation of powers was in fact just another way of boxing in government through law and happened at a time when the state was becoming stronger during the various revolutions, as a result of popular sovereignty. This was in contrast to the traditional narratives where it was little more than the affirmation of mixed monarchy, as per the Glorious Revolution.

The separation of powers also arrived at a time in the late eighteenth century when the abolition of classes and the unification of people and of state under the doctrine of popular sovereignty did in fact end the real 'separation of power'. This saw the real division of power transforming into a constitutional separation of powers. The subsequent emergence of international human rights then provided for a new allocation of power by adding a layer of authority and legal protection above the state. The world had realised that the separation of powers within the state had proven insufficient. All of these points indicate the more general need to consider revisionist approaches when embarking upon serious constitutional study, providing a more accurate understanding of how the rule of law and separation of powers came to be, as well as their relationship to one another in constitutional history.

PART II

The Rule of Law in Country-Specific Settings

Case Studies in Reconciling Realism and Idealism

5

Rule of Law, Democracy and Human Rights: The Paramountcy of Moderation

SUMIT BISARYA AND W. ELLIOT BULMER

> The spirit of moderation ought to be that of the legislator; the political good, like the moral good, is always found between two limits.
>
> (Montesquieu, Spirit of the Laws, Book 29, Ch. 1).

Introduction

The rule of law is an important and widespread constitutional ideal. The phrase 'rule of law' can be found in more than a hundred of the world's constitutions, often either in the preamble or in one of the first articles which defines the nature of the state.[1] The rule of law is praised and proclaimed, if not always upheld in practice, even in states that do not meet the minimum criteria for a functioning democracy. For example, the preamble of the Syria Constitution of 2012 provides that the Constitution is intended as 'the basis for the strengthening of the *rule of law*' (emphasis added), and Article 2 of the Vietnam Constitution (2013) states that 'the Socialist Republic of Vietnam State is a socialist *rule of law* State of the people, by the people and for the people' (emphasis added). Many more constitutions, even if they do not use the term explicitly, make implicit provision for the rule of law through such institutional structures as independent judiciaries, procedural rights and the separation of the powers.

Insofar as a constitution is a law – albeit a special type of law, with a particular authority, purpose and durability – constitutional government is necessarily predicated upon the rule of law. Government according to constitutional rules which limit, bind and compel rulers cannot take place unless there is a general respect for and adherence to impersonal

[1] Constitute Project, available at: www.constituteproject.org.

rules expressed in legal form. In the absence of the rule of law, constitutions are, at best, symbolic and aspirational political documents, and at worst, a cruel deceit.

If strictly and narrowly construed, the rule of law can exist, in John Locke's words, wherever there is a 'known and standing law', an 'impartial judge' and an 'efficient execution'[2]. Such a thin definition of the rule of law does not enquire very far into either the substantive content of the law or its provenance, origin or legitimacy. As such, the rule of law can be attractive to repressive or oligarchic regimes. It enables them to protect particular interests, in particular property rights, to encourage investment, and to share in the practical advantages of having known, regular, certain and impartial processes through which to govern, without presenting much of barrier to the use of legal authority for corrupt, repressive or anti-democratic ends. As will be seen below, in both Egypt and Tunisia before the Arab Spring, the rule of law was usually upheld, at least in the very narrow sense, insofar as rulers complied with the formulaic prescriptions of the law in the exercise of their powers.

However, as soon as we consider the teleological purposes of the rule of law, and ask 'What is the rule of law actually *for*?', it emerges that the rule of law is rarely pursued as an end in itself, but is valued for its contribution to other desired outcomes, such as good governance and the capacity of states to 'deliver the goods' in terms of public services and development outcomes.[3] According to the UNDP, the rule of law is instrumental for economic development, social and economic justice, preventing, mitigating and deterring conflict, crime and violence, strengthening accountability, reducing corruption, enhancing the fair allocation of services and protecting the environment and natural resources.[4]

If we see the rule of law in these terms, as an instrumental good that supports other public goods, then a narrow ideal of the rule of law cannot be pursued in isolation. If the rule of law is valued for its contribution to

[2] J. Locke, 'Second Treatise on Government' in J. Locke, *Two Treatises of Government* (Cambridge University Press, 1988).

[3] Indeed, in our current academic and professional culture, the connection between the rule of law and good government is so deeply engrained that it is almost axiomatic, and we struggle to remind ourselves that alternative conceptions of good government, which have resisted the cold impartiality of law and have emphasised instead the role of wise, personal, holistic judgement unfettered by abstract written rules, have also had a place in human societies – as evident, for example, in Plato's *Republic*.

[4] L.-A. Berg and D. Desai, 'Background Paper: Overview of on the Rule of Law and Sustainable Development for the Global Dialogue on Rule of Law and the Post-2015 Development Agenga', *UNDP*, 2013.

constitutionalism, clearly articulated this distinction between moderate and immoderate (or despotic) forms of government (Montesquieu n.d.). He regarded this distinction as more important than that between monarchies and republics, or between aristocratic and democratic states.[11] According to Montesquieu, the ruling councils of republics of that era (e.g. Venice, Genoa and Lucca) were as despotic as absolute monarchs because they concentrated all powers in their own hands, without moderation or restraint:

> Democratic and aristocratic states are not in their own nature free. Political liberty is to be found only in moderate governments; and even in these it is not always found. It is there only when there is no abuse of power. But constant experience shows us that every man invested with power is apt to abuse it, and to carry his authority as far as it will go.

In contrast to the 'despotic republic', Montesquieu and De Lolme (his fellow pre-revolutionary anglophile aristocratic liberal) favoured the 'moderated monarchy', for which England was the model. They believed moderated monarchies were better at sustaining liberty and at upholding the rule of law than both absolute monarchies and contemporary republics. According to Montesquieu, the political liberty found in England was based on moderation, and moderation was derived from the separation of the legislative, executive and judicial branches of government.

> When the legislative and executive powers are united in the same person, or in the same body of magistrates, there can be no liberty; because apprehensions may arise, lest the same monarch or senate should enact tyrannical laws, to execute them in a tyrannical manner. Again, there is no liberty, if the judiciary power be not separated from the legislative and executive. [...] There would be an end of everything, were the same man or the same body, whether of the nobles or of the people, to exercise those three powers, that of enacting laws, that of executing the public resolutions, and of trying the causes of individuals.

This observation became, in the hands of Montesquieu's followers, a prescriptive rule – a near-axiomatic maxim – of Western political thought. It is important to note, however, that neither Montesquieu nor his English predecessor John Locke invented this idea of the

[11] This was a breach with earlier political philosophy, stemming from the Italian renaissance, which had regarded the distinction between 'republics' and 'principalities' to be of primordial importance. See, for example, Q. Skinner, *Liberty before Liberalism* (Cambridge University Press, 1997); J. A. G. Pocock, *Machiavellian Moment* (Princeton University Press, 1975).

separation of the powers, or '*trias politica*'. Its origins lay in the medieval parliaments, which in many cases had gained control over matters of taxation and legislation.[12] A common feature of medieval parliamentarism was the representation of society through the 'estates of the realm' (typically, the nobility, clergy and burgesses, but in some cases also non-noble landowners and even universities). Representation was by orders, each with their own corporate identities, rights and privileges, rather than on the basis of universal and undifferentiated citizenship.

The separation of powers identified by Montesquieu was therefore closely interwoven with the idea of moderation, through a 'mixed' or 'balanced' constitution. This core doctrine of classical political thought, expressed by Aristotle[13] and Cicero,[14] and absorbed into Christian thought through Thomas Aquinas and through the political theorists of the Italian renaissance, including Bruni, Guicciardini and Machiavelli,[15] held that the good state (a *polity*, which was governed politically and for the common good) could be sustained only through a balanced mixture of the three 'simple' forms of government – by the one, the few and the many. The problem facing Aristotle and other classical writers on politics was that good monarchs became tyrants, aristocracies of genuine merit soon became oligarchies of wealth and privilege, and even rule by the people had a tendency to degenerate into mob rule – not the lawful rule of the whole community for the common good, but the arbitrary rule of the majority. By combining these forms of government, however, the advantages of each simple form could be enjoyed while mitigating, if not entirely avoiding, the corresponding disadvantages of each.[16]

In England, Scotland and the Netherlands, these medieval institutions – which elsewhere in Europe had atrophied in the early modern era – reasserted themselves under the impetus of the Reformation. Not only did the need to protect religion from state interference provide a material incentive for the resistance to arbitrary power, but the reformed political theology also provided a theoretical justification for the defence of the rights and privileges of parliaments and estates against the king. John

12 A. R. Myers, *Parliaments and Estates in Europe to 1789* (London: Thames & Hudson Ltd, 1975).
13 Aristotle, *Politics*, as translated by C. D. C. Reeve (Cambridge, MA: Hacket, 1988).
14 Cicero, *On the Republic*, as translated by D. Fott (New York: Cornell University Press, 2013).
15 Q. Skinner, *Foundations of Modern Political Thought (Vol. 1 The Renaissance)* (Cambridge University Press, 1979).
16 I. Honohan, *Civic Republicanism* (New York: Routledge, 2002).

Calvin, for example, referred to the best constitution as a balance of aristocratic and popular elements and noted with approval the role of parliaments as moderating institutions that were established in order to protect the common good by restricting, limiting and guiding rulers).[17]

By the middle of the seventeenth century, the idea that good government was a common enterprise of king, nobility and people, acting in concert but moderated by mutual checks and balances, was an essentially conservative one – as evidenced, for example, by *His Majesty's Answer to the Nineteen Propositions* (1642). At a time of deteriorating relationships between the Crown and Parliament in England, English Parliament had sought to establish control not only over budgets and legislation, but also over matters of war and peace and over executive appointments. To resist this attempt to curtail the royal prerogative, King Charles I did not rely on any divine right theory of monarchical absolutism (as advanced for example by Sir Robert Filmer)[18] nor on any secular theory of absolute sovereignty (such as that advanced by Thomas Hobbes), but instead on a notion of the mixed constitution that is rooted both in classical theories of moderation and in a defence of the historical moderating institutions of the medieval system of government.[19]

The *Answer* clearly shows how the mixture of monarchic, aristocratic and democratic estates was blended seamlessly with notions of checks and balances and with the doctrine of the separation of the powers in the official view of how the English system of government worked. Laws were 'jointly made by a King, by a House of Peers, and by a House of Commons chosen by the people, all having free votes and particular privileges'. The executive power was vested in the king, and included 'power of treaties, of war and peace, of making peers, of choosing officers and councillors for state, judges for law, commanders for forts and castles, giving commissions for raising men to make war abroad, or to prevent or provide against invasions or insurrections at home, benefit of confiscations, power of pardoning, and more of the like kind'. The Commons ('an excellent conserver of liberty, but never intended for any share in Government, or the choosing of them that should govern') was specifically

[17] J. Calvin, *Institutes of the Christian Religion (Book IV)*, 1536 Edition, as translated by F. L. Battles (Grand Rapids, MI: Wm. B. Eerdmans Publishing, 1995).

[18] Sir R. Filmer, *Patriarcha, or the Natural Power of Kings (1680)*, available at: http://oll.libertyfund.org/titles/221 (last accessed 22 December 2015).

[19] Charles I of England, *His Majesty's Answer to the Nineteen Propositions*, available at: http://www.yorku.ca/comninel/courses/3025pdf/Reply19Props.pdf (last accessed 22 December 2015).

invested with powers of impeachment and with the power of initiating taxation. The Lords ('an excellent screen and bank between the Prince and People, to assist each against any encroachments of the other') was entrusted, in its role as the final court of appeal, with 'a judicatory power'.[20] Whether or not the *Answer* accurately represents the working of the constitutional reality at the time, it nevertheless articulates an understanding of the constitutional order that looked remarkably similar to the system of separated powers outlined in many modern constitutions.

The *Answer*, it should be noted, was written half a century before the Glorious Revolution and the publication of John Locke's *Second Treatise on Government*, more than a century before Montesquieu's *Spirit of the Laws* and nearly a century and a half before *The Federalist Papers*. Moreover, these were not the views of radical reformers seeking to establish a new constitutional order with a novel idea for the separation of the power, but the views of an embattled king trying desperately to preserve the old order.

Yet that old order was cracking under the pressure of social, economic and technological change. It could not survive in the era of the stock exchange and the steam engine, the coffee house and the daily newspaper, the heliocentric solar system and the microscope. With its twin foundations of feudalism and Christendom eroded, the medieval society of orders and estates was finally swept away by the American and French revolutions. In its place arose notions of popular sovereignty and legally equal citizenship, as asserted by Tom Paine's *Common Sense*[21] and Abbé Sieyes' *What Is the Third Estate?*[22] Even if suffrage rights were still mostly restricted to property owners, the criterion for active citizenship was now wealth (which was portable, volatile, and increasingly gained through commercial or industrial activities) rather that order or estate. This created a problem. If the sociological conditions in which the moderated constitution so praised by Montesquieu had developed were no longer viable, how was moderation to be achieved, and despotism avoided?

In the United States, the first state constitutions of the revolutionary era were democratic by the standards of the time, but lacked moderating features.[23] They were characterised by the concentration of powers in the

20 *Ibid.*
21 T. Paine, *Common Sense* (1776) (Petersborough, ON: Dover Publications, 1997).
22 A. Sieyes, 'What Is the Third Estate?' (1789). Pdf available here: http://pages.uoregon.edu/dluebke/301ModernEurope/Sieyes3dEstate.pdf (last accessed 20 December 2015)
23 G. S. Wood, *The Radicalism of the American Revolution*, 2nd edn (New York: Random House, 1993).

hands of an elected legislature, sometimes unicameral and typically chosen by a broad suffrage for relatively short terms. Governors were in most cases elected annually or biennially by the legislatures.[24] This was seen as a betrayal of the principles of the Revolutionary War. As Thomas Jefferson wrote of the Constitution of Virginia:

> An elective despotism was not the government we fought for, but one which should not only be founded on true free principles, but in which the powers of government should be so divided and balanced among general bodies of magistracy, as that no one could transcend their legal limits without being effectually checked and restrained by the others.[25]

The Founding Fathers of the US Constitution attempted to restore moderation to a political system that acknowledged the principle of popular sovereignty and did not depend upon either hereditary monarchy or an order of nobility. This was achieved by five means.

The first means of promoting moderation was to vigorously reassert the doctrine of the separation of the powers. As James Madison expressed it in *The Federalist* (No. 47):

> The accumulation of all powers, legislative, executive, and judiciary, in the same hands, whether of one, a few, or many, and whether hereditary, self-appointed, or elective, may justly be pronounced the very definition of tyranny.[26]

The second was to establish a system of checks and balance that cut across the separation of the powers – for example, giving the president a veto over legislation, dividing the legislature into two Houses, giving the Senate authority to confirm cabinet appointments and the ratification of treaties, enabling Congress to impeach the President and so forth.

The third means of promoting moderation was federalism; although, in the US context, the starting assumption was not so much that state governments would act as moderating checks against the encroachment of the national government, but that the national government would restrain the democratic radicalism of the state governments, which – with policies such as debt relief and the debasement of currency – had seemed threatening to rich creditors.[27]

[24] *Ibid.*

[25] T. Jefferson, *Notes on the State of Virginia (1787)* (London: Penguin Classics, 1998), Q. XIII p. 2.

[26] A. Hamilton, J. Madison and J. Jay, *The Federalist Papers No. 47 (1787–8)* (London: Penguin Classics, 1987).

[27] Wood, *The Radicalism.*

The fourth technique for moderating power was filtering the popular vote through indirect elections to the Senate and presidency, a measure which was supposed to favour more mature and moderate judgement, and to give the advantage to the 'better sort' of people. The only part of the federal US government, as originally devised, to be directly elected was the House of Representatives. The use of staggered elections further moderated expressions of public opinion. Since no one could claim an unambiguous popular mandate that would not also be shared with other persons and institutions, authority was depersonalised through law.

Fifthly, the US Constitution was a rigid constitution with high thresholds for amendment. It soon acquired a bill of rights, placing substantial and procedural limits on power that would, after the *Marbury v. Madison* court decision, be judicially enforced.

Although we have recited these institutional features as they were concretely embodied in the text of the US Constitution, we are most interested, in terms of their contribution to the overall argument of this paper, in the work of Madison and his colleagues as applied political theorists, rather than as constitutional designers. Even if the US Constitution had never been ratified, and if *The Federalist* were a historical curiosity as obscure as King Charles' *Answer*, the response of Madison, Hamilton and Jay would still be of interest as a novel institutional response to the problem of combining moderation with democracy in a non-hierarchical society.

In France, meanwhile, the assertion of popular sovereignty through revolutionary upheaval resulted in the creation of a new, more effective, centralised, bureaucratic despotism, firstly in a republican and later in an imperial guise. This new 'totalitarian democracy' curtailed individual liberty, undermined the rule of law and crushed the free and civic way of life found in open societies.[28]

Following the restoration of the French monarchy, the *Constitutional Charter* of 1814 (*Charte Constitutionnelle*) created a system of moderation that looked back to the ideas of pre-revolutionary anglophile aristocratic liberal reformers such as Montesquieu. Like the US Constitution, the French *Charte* can be seen as a document of 'moderate reaction', reacting against an 'immoderate' democracy that had threatened the rule of law and property rights. The characteristics of the restoration regime included the vesting of executive power in a hereditary monarch and the

[28] J. Talmon, *Origins of Totalitarian Democracy*, 3rd edn (New York: W. W. Norton and Co, 1970).

sharing of legislative power between the king, the nobility and a representative assembly elected on a restricted property-based franchise.[29] Although both the monarchy and the peerage were restored, the *Charte* nevertheless represented an attempt to achieve moderation in a political system based on the equality of citizens before the law. Benjamin Constant, perhaps the most iconic French political thinker of the restoration period, recognised that the traditional hold of the monarchy and nobility over society was gone, that the bourgeois class was in the ascendency, and that both the legal equality of citizens and the ultimate sovereignty of the nation were irreversible.[30]

Explicitly borrowing from the English example, Constant envisaged a moderating role for the monarchy and the nobility, whose powers would restrain the excesses of popular government. He was also eager, however, to emphasise the importance of elective institutions, and of press freedom and ministerial responsibility as moderating institutions that would protect liberty and the rule of law. This is because, for Constant as for James Madison, liberty was not to be maintained by mere parchment barriers – that is, by formal constitutional guarantees of rights – but by the diffusion of political powers through moderating institutions that could provide mutual checks and balances:

> All the constitutions which have been given to France guaranteed the liberty of the individual, and yet, under the rule of these constitutions, it has been constantly violated. The fact is that a simple declaration is not sufficient; you need positive safeguards. You need bodies sufficiently powerful to be able to employ, in favour of the oppressed, the means of defence sanctioned by written law. Our present constitution is the only one that has created these safeguards and invested the intermediary bodies with adequate power. Freedom of the press, placed beyond attack thanks to trial by jury; the responsibility of ministers, and especially that of subordinates; and, finally, the existence of a large and independent representation; such are the bastions by which the freedom of the individual is surrounded today.[31]

Constant argued, moreover, that these moderating institutions, rather than weakening the government, actually strengthened and assisted it.

29 A. Cobban, *A History of Modern France (Vol. 2 – 1799–1945)* (London: Penguin, 1970); P. Campbell, *French Electoral Systems and Elections since 1789*, 2nd edn (London: Faber, 1965).

30 B. Fontana, *Constant: Political Writings* (Cambridge University Press, 1988).

31 B. Constant, *Principles of Politics Applicable to All Governments* (Indianapolis, IN: Liberty Fund, 2003).

Moderating institutions would provide advice, stimulate necessary action, prevent errors and thereby contribute overall to good government:

> Those institutions which act as barriers against power simultaneously support it. They guide it in its progress; they sustain its efforts; they moderate its excesses of violence and stimulate it in its moments of apathy. They rally around it the interests of the various classes. Even when it fights them, they impose upon it certain considerations which make its mistakes less dangerous. But when these institutions are destroyed, power, lacking anything to guide it, anything to contain it, begins to march haphazardly; its step becomes uneven and erratic. As it no longer follows a fixed rule, it now advances, now recoils, now becomes agitated, now restless; it never knows whether it is doing enough, or too much.[32]

Despotic states, precisely because they do not moderate the whims of rulers, behave erratically, unpredictably, inscrutably and foolishly. All contemporary democratic constitutions seek to guard against such despotism. As noted in the introduction to this volume, constitutionalism and the rule of law both seek to 'channel, discipline, constrain and inform [...] the exercise of power' (PG). This section has shown how central political moderation is to achieving these aims. However, the degree of moderation, and the means by which moderation is achieved, varies between constitutional models. These will be briefly discussed in the next section.

Mechanisms of Moderation in Contemporary Constitutions

Combining moderation with effective democracy requires constitutional designers to find the degree of moderation that is just right: a 'golden mean' that is sufficient to prevent tyranny, the abuse of power and ill-considered decision-making, but is not so great as to seriously undermine the efficiency and coherence of government or its responsibility to the people. At one extreme, the British system of government has been criticised for its immoderate concentration of power in the core executive, without effective checks and balances. This has led to haste, waste, confusion and rapid changes of direction and has thereby diminished the state's capacity to pursue sensible, sustained policies.[33] At the other extreme, there can be so many checks, balances and restraints that policy-making becomes unresponsive, the efficiency and coherence of government is

[32] Fontana, *Constant*, p. 133.
[33] A. King and I. Crewe, *The Blunders of our Governments* (London: One World, 2014).

undermined, and the responsibility to the people diluted. The US system of separated powers, for example, has been criticised for taking moderation too far, as the absence of clear lines of responsibility weakens democratic control over the government, incites political deadlock and makes it difficult to achieve change even when supported by a popular majority.[34] Excessive moderation can backfire, too; Presidents in some countries have even sought to overthrow, by anti-constitutional means, moderating restraints that appeared to them as irksome and unnecessary hindrances.[35]

Early democratic constitutions did not formally recognise the role of political parties. Indeed, until well into the nineteenth century political parties (which almost by definition represent a part, not the whole, of society) were often dismissed as 'factions' that were necessarily opposed to the common good. Now, however, it is recognised that the political parties are important moderating institutions in their own right, and that the party system will influence the overall degree of moderation in the polity, despite institutional design features. Each party typically forms a cohesive voting bloc, which aggregates preferences and coordinates policy choices across institutions, enabling members of different branches of government, or different levels of government, to act as one. Thus the US Constitution, despite all its institutional checks, may fail to restrain excessive concentrations of power in circumstances where presidency and the majority in both Houses of Congress are bound by party ties to a common agenda,[36] while a political system with relatively few institutional checks and balances, such as that of New Zealand, may in fact be moderated by the existence of a multi-party system in which parties have to share power in coalitions to hold office.[37]

Moreover, in modern democratic states, parties are the main instruments through which diverse segments of society (such as classes, regions, religions or ideologies) find expression in politics. The sharing of powers between parties at the parliamentary level reflects a degree of compromise or cooperation between the different societal segments that those parties represent. Whereas in the late eighteenth century, the standard answer to the question of how to achieve moderation in

[34] R. A. Dahl, *How Democratic Is the American Constitution*, 2nd edn (New Haven, CT: Yale University Press, 2004).

[35] J. J. Linz, 'The Perils of Presidentialism', *Journal of Democracy*, 1(1) (1990), 51–69.

[36] D. J. Levinson, R. H. Pildes, 'Separation of Parties, Not Powers', *Harvard Law Review* (2006), 2311.

[37] G. Palmer and M. Palmer, *Bridled Power: New Zealand's Constitution and Government* (Oxford University Press, 2004).

a democratic society was answered by institutional separation of the powers, by the beginning of the twenty-first century the sharing of power between parties was an attractive alternative option.

Perhaps the leading advocate of moderation in contemporary constitutional design is the Dutch-American political scientist Arend Lijphart. Although Lijphart never engages theoretically with the idea of moderation as such, it is strongly implicit in his model 'consensus democracy'. The essence of consensus democracy is that, in place of simple majority rule, there is 'rule by as many as possible',[38] thereby facilitating a more moderate government, in which deliberation and broad agreement are valued over rapid decision-making. Consensus democracies have many moderating features. These include institutional forms of moderation, including bicameral legislatures, judiciaries with the power of constitutional review, federalism or other forms of macro-decentralisation, rigid constitutions and a structured process of inclusive interest-group bargaining. However, the most important of these moderating, consensual features, for our purposes, are multi-party politics, proportional representation and power-sharing executives. Together, these ensure that parties can perform a moderating role, whether as coalition partners sharing in executive power, or as non-governmental parties whose support may nevertheless be necessary in key votes. In so-called 'majoritarian democracies', in contrast, there is usually a two-party system, with one party in government. This means that power is concentrated in the leader of the majority party.[39]

A sub-type of consensus democracy, which Lijphart identifies as 'consociational democracy', is characterised by formal power-sharing between different religious, ethnic or linguistic blocs. This model has been very influential as a way of securing peace, human rights and the rule of law (and even a semblance of democracy) in 'divided societies' prone to inter-communal conflict.[40] Notable examples include the tricephalous Constitution of Bosnia-Herzegovina, the dual executive in Northern Ireland, and the complex federalism of Belgium. Consociationalism has been criticised for entrenching social divisions, for promoting ascriptive voting, and for failing to address common problems faced by all segments of society. It denies the eighteenth century revolutionary concepts of equal

[38] A. Lijphart, *Patterns of Democracy* (New Haven, CT: Yale University Press, 1999), p. 4.
[39] *Ibid.*
[40] For a definition of divided society, see: S. Choudhry (ed.), *Constitutional Design for Divided Societies: Integration or Accommodation* (Oxford University Press, 2008), pp. 4–5.

citizenship and unified popular sovereignty, recalling an earlier form of mixed constitution – albeit with communal identity rather than estate being the basis of segmentation.[41]

Moderation may also be present through procedural rights for the 'Opposition' parties in Parliament or other political minorities. Unlike in a fully consociational system, this form of moderation is not, primarily, about power-sharing: oppositions moderate governments from without, unlike coalition partners who moderate from within. Secondly, the role of the opposition might not necessarily be to exercise a veto power that results in super-majority decision making. Rather, it might be to force deliberation, to encourage majorities to think again, to demand an enquiry, or to refer legislation to the court or to the people for an external decision. When there is clear support for a policy (which is not inconsistent with human rights or damaging to the basic institutions of the democratic state itself), then this form of moderation would allow a government supported by a majority in Parliament to act without undue restriction – provided there has been full opportunity for deliberation. Thirdly, the minorities concerned need not be ascriptive cultural minorities; they can be simply political minorities – those who have lost elections. The essence of this form of moderation is a give-and-take between the government and the opposition, with the government having the final say; this retains the principle of government accountability and overcomes some of the responsibility-diffusion problems associated with other forms of moderation, but still ensures that the opposition's voice be heard and that the government is required to justify its actions in the light of the opposition's criticisms.

There are around the world various ways of protecting and recognising the right of the political opposition to moderate government in this way. Back-and-forth between Prime Minister and Leader of the Opposition is associated with the physical geography of Westminster-style Parliaments, in which the two main parties (the system is predicated, in most cases, on the existence of two main parties, or at least two main coalition blocs) sit face-to-face. Most of the Westminster-derived constitutions, for

[41] Another kind of power-sharing (different in process, but similar in intended outcome) occurs in jurisdictions where double-majorities are used to elect presidents. In Kenya, for example, a president must win not only 50 per cent of the votes cast to be elected at the first round, but also at least 25 per cent of the votes in a majority of the counties. This provision, like preferential voting in the election of representatives, often termed as a means of integration as opposed to accommodation, is intended to moderate power by providing an incentive for candidates to reach out beyond their own ethnic constituency.

example, create the office of Leader of the Opposition and give the holder of that office certain procedural rights and privileges. In practice, many such countries also give the Leader of the Opposition certain resources that enable them to do their job of scrutinising the government and providing alternatives more effectively, such as a salary, office facilities and clerical support. The Leader of the Opposition may also be entitled to certain marks of status – a security detail, an official car and driver, the title of 'Right Honourable' rather than merely 'Honourable' member, and so forth. The procedural privileges of opposition leaders typically include the right to be consulted in the arrangement of the parliamentary timetable through 'the usual channels', the ability to schedule 'opposition day' debates where the Leader of the Opposition can choose the subject matter of discussion and the right to open the batting at Prime Minister's Questions. The Leader of the Opposition might also have a constitutionally guaranteed role, which is at least consultative and may extend to a formal or informal veto, in the appoint of certain public officials of a non-governmental nature, such as members of the Electoral Commission, Judicial Appointments Commission and so forth. Certain other procedural privileges may also be extended to Opposition members. For example, the Chair of the Public Accounts Committee may, by convention or by standing orders, have to be a member of the Opposition, and Opposition members may be entitled to a certain share of parliamentary committee seats.

Procedures that facilitate informed, constructive opposition are perhaps even more pronounced in some of the European democracies characterised by multi-party politics. Although there is no designated 'Leader of the Opposition', there may be procedural rules that apportion committee seats, or even committee convenorships, on the basis of proportionality, thereby ensuring that all sections of parliamentary opinion can be heard. There may also be means for the opposition to trigger an investigation. In terms of the legislative process, there may be mechanisms enabling the opposition party, or any substantial parliamentary minority, to delay the consideration of legislation for a certain period of time (thereby forcing broader and deeper debate) or to refer legislation to the constitutional court for a review of its constitutionality.

In some cases, such as Denmark and Latvia, parliamentary minorities can even force a referendum on legislation.[42] The decision rule remains

[42] W. E. Bulmer, 'Minority-Veto Referendums: An Alternative to Bicameralism', *Politics*, 31(3) (2011), 107–20.

a majoritarian one, since a majority of the votes cast in the referendum are decisive, so these rules allow the opposition to appeal from the governing majority in parliament to the popular majority outside. In practice, the main effect of such rules is to give the opposition a bargaining chip that they can use in order to convince the Government to consider their concerns with due gravity. The power of the minority-initiated referendum lies in its deterrent effect.

As the above survey has shown, moderation can be found in many institutional forms – whether in the separation of branches of government, federalism, proportional representation, consociational power-sharing or guaranteed procedural rights for the opposition. Its essence, however, it is always to be found in the existence of countervailing power – independent, legitimate sources of authority whose views must be taken into account and with whom rulers must consult and compromise.

In a democratic society, the people form an independent, legitimate authority, existing in a civil society outside the direct control of rulers, whose views must be taken into account and with whom rulers must – if they seek to win and retain power through regular competitive elections – consult and compromise. In this sense, political action, whether it takes place between the government and the people (through elections, referendums etc.), between different branches, institutions or levels of government or between government and opposition parties, always has moderating potential. The free articulation of opposing views, criticism, oversight and public competition for office in the electoral arena forces rulers to justify their actions in public and to seek the approval of others. The process of political government enables the reasoning behind decisions to be publicly aired and tested, and thereby erects political barriers in the path of arbitrary, capricious decision-making.[43]

On the other hand, where moderation is missing, and the political interplay of people and parties is restrained by fear, coercion or corrupt interests which establish vertical conduits of power, the rule of law – even in its narrowest and most formal sense – is unlikely to take hold. There will be no way to shine light upon breaches of legality and to challenge excesses. For this pragmatic reason, as well as for normative reasons of legitimacy, the rule of law requires open politics.

This defence of what might be termed 'political constitutionalism' has something in common with arguments of those scholars, such as Richard

[43] P. Pettit, *On the People's Terms: A Republican Theory and Model of Democracy* (Cambridge University Press, 2012).

Bellamy[44] and Paul Blokker,[45] who have expressed scepticism of 'legal constitutionalism'. It should not, however, be interpreted as a rejection of written constitutions and higher-law constitutional provisions as such. It is simply a reassertion of the fact that working constitutions are political and sociological documents as well as legal ones. They have to be read and understood, as well as written and applied, in their real political and sociological context. If a written constitution is to be more than an ineffective parchment barrier for the protection of individual rights, its function is above all to keep the channels of political action open, and to establish and protect the institutions of political government that will ensure that power is properly moderated.

Cases: Egypt and Tunisia

We now turn to an application of the concepts of political moderation as hitherto discussed to a pair of recent instances of constitution building, the 2014 Constitution of Tunisia and the 2014 Constitution of Egypt. For each, we offer an examination of the opportunities and challenges to political moderation under the existing constitutional framework with a view to examining whether rule of law, as an ideal, is reflected through the sociological operating reality of the Constitution. Specifically, with regards to the issues interrogated in Section II – do the new constitutions offer mechanisms for societal groups, including minorities, to express their views through organized politics? And, central to the theme of this chapter, for societal groups which are placed in charge of the decision-making apparatus of the State, do they still have tools and means to moderate the power of the majority?

The geographical proximity and contemporaneous nature of these two cases make them a compelling dyad for comparison, and there are certain similarities. These include shared origins of constitutional transition in the 'Arab Spring' citizen uprisings, a common 'drama'[46] in their contemporaneous and linked revolutions against authoritarianism, victory for previously banned political Islam parties in the first post-revolution elections in both countries and contentious debates over the role of Islam in public

[44] Bellamy, *Political Constitutionalism*.

[45] P. Blokker, *New Democracies in Crisis?: A Comparative Study of the Czech Republic, Hungary, Poland, Romania and Slovakia* (New York: Routledge, 2013).

[46] On the use of this term for a triggering event or circumstance for constitutional change, see R. Gargarella, *Latin American Constitutionalism 1810 – 2010* (Oxford University Press, 2013).

life during both constitutional negotiations. Both processes were also highly contemporaneous with revolutions occurring in January 2011, elections following soon thereafter and final constitutions promulgated in January 2014. Lastly, while the previous governments were overthrown in a surprisingly rapid revolution, the process to build a new government was similarly fraught in both countries with tension and violence: providing a vivid reminder of the words of John Adams that 'it is much easier to pull down a government, in such a conjuncture of affairs as we have seen, than to build up at such season as present'.[47]

But the similarities between the two cases should not be overstated. Demographically, Tunisia boasts a smaller and more homogenous population than Egypt, where Christian Copts make up almost 20 per cent of the citizenry. Regarding the nature of the previous regimes, that of Hosni Mubarak and his predecessors in Egypt was supported by a sizeable and strong armed forces, while in Tunisia the military was comparatively weak, both in terms of size and political clout. Importantly, the political landscape following the post-revolution elections resulted in a clear majority for the Freedom and Justice Party of the Islamic Brotherhood in Egypt, while in Tunisia no party was able to win a majority, resulting in a coalition of political Islam and secularist parties in government.[48] There are endless further distinguishing characteristics the more one examines the political and legal cultures of these two countries in detail, but there are also a host of similarities which make a comparison between the two transitions, and the resulting constitutions, compelling.

Egypt: Exclusionary Constitution Making: From Authoritarianism to Islamism and Back Again

Constitutional History and Context for Transition

It is beyond the scope of this paper to delve in too much detail into the constitutional history of Egypt,[49] but as with the study of all constitutional

[47] C. Bowen and C. Drinker, *Miracle at Philadelphia* (New York: Back Bay Books/Little Brown and Company, 1966), p. 3. Quoting letter from John Adams to James Warren, 1787.

[48] D. Pickard, 'Al-Nahda: Moderation and Compromise in Tunisia's Constitutional Bargain' in J. O. Frossini and F. Biagi (eds.), *Political and Constitutional Transitions in North Africa* (New York: Routledge Publishers, 2015).

[49] For a detailed history of the developments of constitutions in Egypt and the Arab World as a whole see N. Brown, *Constitutions in a Nonconstitutional World: Arab Basic Laws and the Prospects for Accountable Government* (State University of New York Press, 2012).

transitions it is important to note that the new Constitution, and the process through which it was formed, is influenced greatly by previous experience.

The first post-independence Constitution of 1923 established a constitutional monarchy with the King divested almost completely of executive powers which resided in a government responsible to parliament. However, the constitutional framework was never really given an opportunity to evolve into a mature political system. As with many post-colonial states, elections were dominated by the party which had fought for independence – in this case the Wafd party. This domination, coupled with the weak powers of the King and the absence of judicial review and strongly framed rights protections in the 1923 Constitution, gave the Wafd party unfettered control over the State, which resulted in the King resorting to extra-constitutional means to dismiss Wafd governments on at least two occasions.[50]

In 1952 a military coup overthrew the government and the monarchy, and in 1956 the new constitution was promulgated creating a presidential republic. Importantly in terms of our theme of political moderation, the constitution also created a one-party system led by Arab Socialist Union and President Abdel Gamel Nasser. The president was given broad legislative powers, and was able to dominate the legislature through his control of the only party. Selection of the President lacked any competitive element: the parliament nominated one candidate to be approved in a national referendum by the people.

A period of constitutional instability followed due to the creation and failure of the United Arab Republic, before President Anwar El-Sadat oversaw the promulgation of a new Constitution in 1971.

1971 Constitution

The 1971 Constitution was a document which 'gave with one hand, and took away with the other'.[51] It expanded the series of rights and freedoms, albeit still leaving significant loopholes, strengthened the judiciary through the creation of the Supreme Constitutional Court, but maintained a hyper-concentration of powers in the office of the President. Significantly, the process of choosing the President continued in the constrained manner of the 1956 document, ensuring there would be no candidates for President other than the incumbent. The only constraint

[50] *Ibid.*, pp 41–2. [51] *Ibid.*, p. 81.

on continuity of rule for the President – a two-term limit – was abolished in 1980.

Despite the strong repeated rhetoric from President Anwar Sadat explicitly claiming his regime was founded on the rule of law (*sayadat al-qanun*)[52] and the ending of a one-party state in the 1970s,[53] the operation of the 1971 Constitution provided little opportunity to moderate the power of the President.

Firstly, electoral competition was minimized. Due to the sprawling patronage network of the Arab Socialist Union and its successor, the National Democratic Party, as well as its increasingly close symbiosis with the military (see below), there were not significant secular parties allowed to form any kind of strong opposition. Significant abuses in parliamentary elections,[54] a porous set of political rights in the Constitution coupled with prolonged periods of states of emergency which allowed significant limitations to rights of assembly, association and speech,[55] and the Supreme Constitutional Court's 1990 decision to strike down a party list system as unconstitutional[56] combined as a perfect storm of conditions to prevent any moderating force emerging through competitive parliamentary elections.

Further, the regime ensured that there would be no opportunities for the Muslim Brotherhood to channel its organization and support into a legitimate political challenge to the ruling party's hegemony. Since its formation in the 1920s, the Muslim Brotherhood had been the best organized societal organization and most significant threat to complete political control by Egyptian leaders.[57] However, the law on political parties banned the formation of any parties on the basis of religion, thus preventing the development of a formal political power with the support and organization of the Muslim Brotherhood. When Muslim Brotherhood candidates were allowed to run as independents and won 88 out of 444 seats in the 2005 elections, the Constitution was soon amended

[52] T. Moustafa, *The Struggle for Constitutional Power: Law, Politics, and Economic Development in Egypt* (Cambridge University Press, 2007).

[53] K. Stilt, 'Constitutions in Authoritarian Regimes: The Egyptian Constitution of 1971' in T. Ginsburg and A. Simpser, *Constitutions in Authoritarian Regimes* (Cambridge University press, 2014), 111–37.

[54] Moustafa, *The Struggle for Constitutional Power.*

[55] T. Moustafa, 'Law and Courts in Authoritarian Regimes', *Annual Review of Law and Social Science*, 10 (2014), 281–99.

[56] Stilt, 'Constitutions in Authoritarian Regimes'.

[57] J. R. Bradley, *Inside Egypt: The land of the Pharoahs on the Brink of a Revolution* (New York: Palgrave Macmillan, 2008).

to prevent independence candidates from running, which meant the complete exclusion of Islamists from politics – and with them the views of a sizeable bloc of Egyptian society as the victory of the Muslim Brotherhood party in the first post-revolution elections showed.

Secondly, lest the legislature itself seek to exercise any moderating control over the President, a series of measures were in place to prevent this from happening. In addition to the almost-complete assurance that the President would never be faced with a legislature dominated by an opposition party through electoral manipulation and banning of political parties, in 1980 amendments to the Constitution created an upper house of Parliament, the Consultative Assembly, of whose membership one-third was to be appointed by the President. Approval from the Consultative Assembly was mandatory for constitutional amendments and organic laws, thus creating another opportunity for the President to forestall any attempts to moderate his power.

Thirdly, Egypt was governed under a state of 'endless emergency'[58] through which the Constitution armed the President with an extensive array of exceptional powers in a 'manner prescribed by law'. For the duration of the 1971 Constitution, and still today, that law was the 1958 Law Concerning the State of Emergency which provided for both a broad set of circumstances under which the powers could be invoked (including 'whenever public security or order are threatened' which may include war, natural disaster or 'internal disturbances'),[59] and an extensive set of tools to address such threats, such as restricting freedom of assembly and movement, confiscation of property, prior censorship and far-reaching exemptions from due process protections of the Criminal Procedure Code (Reza, 2007),[60] including through the creation of special State Security Courts.

The only check on the President's ability to invoke and maintain a state of emergency was the requirement that Parliament approve such a declaration, or extension. However, due to the domination of parliament through party control, this power was all but meaningless.

With regard to the civilian judiciary, both the Supreme Constitutional Court and the administrative court system became increasingly bold in deciding against the executive during the lifespan of the 1971 Constitution. With regard to the latter, it is likely that the administrative

[58] S. Reza, 'Endless Emergency: The Case of Egypt', *New Criminal Law Review*, 10 (2007), 532; Islamic Law and Law of the Muslim World Paper No. 08-11; Boston Univ. School of Law Working Paper No. 08-12; NYLS Legal Studies Research Paper No. 07/08-18.

[59] Law 162/1958 *Qanun bi Sha'n Halah al Tawaru* Art. 1.

[60] Reza, 'Endless Emergency'.

held until October 2015, enabling President Sisi to rule by fiat without even a weak Parliament to moderate his will until early 2016. Now that parliament is finally constituted, it is unlikely to act as any kind of moderating force on the President, as an alliance of parties loyal to Sisi have taken the vast majority of seats.[71]

The outlook is difficult to predict – after all there were few who predicted the fall of Mubarak before January 2011 – however, the ability of a political opposition in Egypt to first gather strength and numbers and to then exert any moderating force on the will of the majority is all but completely precluded under the current constitutional framework.

Tunisia: A Constitution of Moderation: Democracy through Compromise

We turn now to the case of Tunisia, beginning, as with Egypt, with a brief overview of constitutional history as it is relevant to our theme of political moderation.

Tunisia was home to the Arab world's first written national constitution, in 1861 when it formed part of the Ottoman Empire. Under the suzerainty of the Ottoman Empire, the Bey of Tunis ruled the country. Under the 1861 Constitution, there was to be a Grand Assembly – to which ministers were responsible and which could propose legislation, appoint and dismiss senior government officials, and control taxation, state spending and the size of the army.[72] However, any form of true constitutionalism – or political moderation – was encumbered by the fact that all Assembly members were directly appointed by the Bey himself.

Tunisia's first independence Constitution, following seven decades of French rule, came in 1959. The Constituent Assembly was dominated by the party of Habib Bourguiba, the Neo-Destour party, and created a strongly presidential, secular republic with Bourguiba clearly in mind as the first President. Rather than acting as a moderating force on the President, Parliament was a powerless appendage: the government was appointed by, and responsible to, the President, and Parliament was unable to impeach the President on any grounds; Parliament was out of session for six months of the year. When it was out of session, the

[71] www.egyptindependent.com/opinion/does-love-egypt-list-really-love-egypt (Last accessed January 15, 2015)

[72] M. P. Angrist, 'The Expression of Political Dissent in the Middle East: Turkish Democratization and Authoritarian Continuity in Tunisia' in *Comparative Studies in Society and History* (Cambridge University Press, 1999), pp. 730–57.

President could rule by decree, and when it was sitting, the President's legislative initiatives were to be given priority.

The role and emergence of the Neo-Destour (ND) party is critical to understanding the way in which political moderation worked (or did not work) under the 1959 Constitution. The ND party was the principal instigator – and subsequently negotiator – for independence from French rule, and as such it became the country's hegemonic legitimate political organization, with Bourguiba at its head.[73] When differences of opinion with regard to policy priorities or direction occurred, there was no threat of establishing a separate political party or seeking to challenge the ND from without, as only the Neo-Destour seemed to possess the necessary legitimacy to promote one's own political views: to be disassociated from the Party meant political death.[74]

Following independence, the country was under one-party rule, and the State and the Neo-Destour party operated as one entity – L'État Parti, with personnel interchanging between the party and the public administration at the will of the President – who headed both structures. In terms of moderating forces from the polity, there were three possible candidates with sufficient power to influence, or even compete for, public power: the business elite, trade unions and political Islam movements. As the focus of our chapter is on moderation through formal means of political engagement, we cover the business elite and trade unions only briefly here, before discussing in a bit more detail the role of political Islam movements.

Michele Penner Angrist[75] provides a nuanced view of how the business elites related with regard to regime and its leadership. In essence, her conclusions are two-fold: firstly, the Tunisian business elite was young, small and not a key constituency of Bourguiba's regime, which relied on peasants, civil service and organized labour for its support,[76] and therefore had minimal influence over the political leadership. And secondly, where differences did arise, disagreements were channelled through individualistic, informal channels *within* the party-state apparatus rather than through any demands for institutionalized access to decision-making power.

[73] *Ibid.*

[74] D. Vandewalle, 'Bourguiba, Charismatic Leadership and the Tunisian One Party System', *Middle East Journal*, 34 (1980), 152.

[75] Angrist, 'The Expression of Political Dissent'.

[76] E. Bellin. 2004. 'The Robustness of Authoritarianism in the Middle East: Exceptionalism in Comparative Perspective', *Comparative Politics*, 36(2) (2004), 138–57.

With regard to labour organizations, Tunisia's central labour union alliance, the Union Générale des Travailleurs Tunisiens (UGTT), has played a central role in the constitutional history of Tunisia, culminating most recently in the award of the Nobel Peace Prize for its role in developing consensus during the process of making the 2014 Constitution. During the fight for independence, UGTT had been a key ally of the ND in its struggle for political hegemony. In the early years of independence, the UGTT was co-opted into the government, with leaders such as Ahmed Ben Salah, UGTT secretary general, given key roles in government. This state of symbiosis lasted only for the first decade of independence, after which – in an environment of growing economic inequality and deteriorating work conditions – the UGTT membership gradually took on an increasingly oppositional stance towards the government, conducting a series of wildcat strikes in the late 1970s.[77] This was the start of a long history of opposition from the UGTT, which resulted in various attempts by the government to co-opt, repress or change the character of the union, which lasted until beyond the Jasmine Revolution of 2010–2011. For all this time, through use of the power to strike, the UGTT became a significant factor in seeking to force political moderation in the regime – the only 'structured and structuring force'[78] outside the ruling party.

The story of political Islam movements in Tunisia predates independence as various groups (including the Destour party from which the Neo-Destour party split) sought formal recognition of Islam within the legal and political identity of the State. However, for purposes of discussion of political moderation under the 1959 Constitution and beyond, we start in the early 1970s with the Islamic Tendency Movement (MTI). The MTI existed as a secret organization based on the writings of their leader, Racheed Ghannouchi, which advocated Islam-based solutions to Tunisia's problems as well as a liberal political system with free elections, political pluralism and peaceful alternation of power.[79]

Following the fall-out with the UGTT in the late 1970s, Bourguiba legalized political parties beyond ND in 1981, but continued the ban on the MTI, whose members were harassed and jailed throughout the rest of Bourguiba's rule. In 1987, then Prime Minister for just over a month,

[77] D. Vandewalle, 'From the New State to the New Era: Toward a Second Republic in Tunisia', *Middle East Journal*, 42(4) (1988).

[78] M.-S. Omri, 'No Ordinary Union: UGTT and the Tunisian Path to Revolution and Transition', *Workers of the World: International Journal on Strikes and Social Conflicts*, 1(7) (2013), 14–30.

[79] Pickard, 'Al-Nahda: Moderation'.

Zine El-Abidine Ben Ali declared Bourguiba incapacitated to exercise his duties as President and took over the office in line with the constitutional line of succession. He began his reign with moves towards a liberalization of politics, including the release of political prisoners – among whom were hundreds of MTI members. However, he refused the attempt of the MTI to register a political party named Al Nahda, affirming that no party could claim to represent Islam.[80] However, independent candidates were allowed to run in the parliamentary elections of 1989 – with those Al Nahda members winning 14.5 per cent of the vote but no seats due to the plurality-based electoral system. Al Nahda vastly outperformed the secular coalition (Movement of Democratic Socialists), leaving no doubt that the only serious political opposition was going to come from the Islamists.

This led to a complete shut-out of Al Nahda members from political life – between 1990 and 1992 an estimated 8,000 members were detained, and the leadership retreated into exile. As a potential moderating influence in politics, Al Nahda was no longer a force.

With Al Nahda out of the picture, Ben Ali and his party (newly renamed as Rassemblement Constitutionnel Démocratique) were able to control Tunisian politics without any form of political moderation. The electoral law was changed in 1994 to guarantee opposition presence in the legislature, and the requirement that Presidential candidates receive at least 30 supporting signatures from legislators was removed in 1999 – meaning that Ben Ali ran opposed for the first time. However, through a mixture of limiting political freedoms, a strong party patronage structure and the removal from politics of the one potentially serious competitor, Ben Ali never won less than 89 per cent of the vote, and the RCD – after the surprise in 1989 when Al Nahda was allowed to run its candidates as independents – never won less than 81 per cent of the seats in the legislature. The minimal opposition allowed to contest elections during this time was more another state resource utilized to bring the legitimating appearance of a multiparty democracy than a political representation of societal groups with a mandate and tools to moderate government decision making.

2014 Constitution

Following the overthrow of Ben Ali in the 2011 Jasmine Revolution, Al Nahda came back from the cold, and – with their underground

[80] *Ibid.*

organizational capabilities very much intact – won a plurality of seats in the Constituent Assembly elected to draft a new Constitution for Tunisia – taking 37 per cent of the vote, and 89 out of 217 seats, and then forming a governing 'Troika' government with two secular parties.

With no one party able to dictate its will on the Assembly, the constitution building processes – scheduled to last one year – stretched to three years with several crisis points which threatened to completely derail the process.[81] The eventual constitutional deal was arrived at through an informal forum outside the Assembly, a 'National Dialogue' brokered by four civil society organizations including the UGTT. In notable contrast to the Egyptian process, the deal that resulted from the National Dialogue brought with it broad-based support across political divides, reflected in a final vote which saw 200 of 216 delegates vote for the document.

The text of the 2014 Constitution reflects the compromise and negotiated consensus which eventually characterized the process through which it was drafted. In terms of the issues most contentious throughout the process, the secular parties were successful in ensuring a directly elected President, but the balance of powers in a semi-presidential system was more oriented towards a premier-presidential system, in keeping with Al Nahda's desire for a strong parliament. After much debate regarding how to characterize the relationship between religion and state, constructive ambiguity was employed in the drafting of Article 2, which describes Tunisia as a 'civil state' rather than a secular state or Islamic republic, with Article 1 stating that Tunisia is 'a free, independent, sovereign state, its religion is Islam ... ' (as per the previous Constitution) and there is no inclusion of a 'repugnancy' clause which would subject legislation to compliance with Islamic law or principles.

In addition to these contentious issues, the very structure of the political system is imbued with potential mechanisms for political moderation. Firstly, it should be noted that Article 35, on the right to form political parties, includes no restrictions on religious-based parties. Thus, a central societal pillar – those supporting political Islam – are able to channel their interests through politics.

Secondly, the electoral system – while left open in the Constitution – was decided in the electoral law passed just after the Constitution as list-PR, giving a better chance that smaller parties will have some say within parliament. This is very significant given Tunisia's recent electoral

[81] For a more detailed account of the constitution building process, see *Ibid.*

history, where the 1989 legislative elections – probably the most openly competitive in Tunisia's pre-revolution history – gave Al Nahda 14.5 per cent of the vote, but no seats under a plurality-based electoral system.

Thirdly, and perhaps most remarkably, Article 60 actually constitutionalizes the opposition. This does a few things. Firstly, it says that there *is* an opposition. Given that Tunisia spent much of its independent life under a one-party system, this is not insignificant. Secondly, it provides some key tools with which the political minority, the opposition, can moderate the power of the majority. These include chairing the finance committee, establishing and heading a committee of inquiry and (in Article 59) proportional representation on parliamentary committees.

Further, following the practice in France, political minorities within Parliament are given access to the Constitutional Court. Thirty legislators may send a bill to the Constitutional Court for review before it is promulgated (Article 120) and, similarly, 30 legislators may refer a declaration of a State of Emergency to the Constitutional Court any time after 30 days from the initial declaration for an examination of whether the emergency still exists.

Summarizing with regard to our theme of political moderation, the Tunisia Constitution provides mechanisms for the moderation of power through (a) providing opportunities that principal societal groups will have the opportunity to have their interests represented in the formal political sphere and (b) providing that even where a particular group manages to control the different political institutions, other groups will (i) be also present and (ii) will have certain tools to moderate, at least to some extent, the power of the majority in a manner which hinders the emergence of tyrannical rule.

Thus, in comparing the two cases of Egypt and Tunisia, it is apparent that previous constitutions in both countries maintained some formal adherence to a thin version of rule of law, but without any substantial forms of political moderation. In both countries the state apparatus was controlled by a party regime headed by a powerful presidency, and the channelling of contesting views and interests through politics was prevented through a mixture of banning of parties, limiting political freedoms and manipulation of electoral systems and their operation.

In terms of the new constitutional dispensations, our view is that while the Egyptian Constitution strongly asserts its rule of law objectives in the text, and contains strong formal guarantees for critical features of the rule of law – such as an independent judiciary, *nullem crimen sine lege* and other due process rights – it is the Tunisia Constitution that is more likely to lead to political moderation. We stress that this is not because of the institutional separation of powers, which sees a strong tilt towards presidentialism in the Egyptian Constitution, as compared with the more balanced powers in the Tunisia semi-presidential system, but rather because the Tunisia Constitution provides greater opportunities for sociological divides to negotiate their differences through politics thanks to a more inclusionary approach to political party and electoral system regulation (i.e. through not banning religious parties such as Al Nahda and a strongly proportional electoral system), and recognition of the importance of the role of a political opposition.

Conclusion

This book considers the contrast between the ideal and the real in constitutionalism and the rule of law. As noted in the introductory chapter, constitutions are often works of practical idealism. They seek to establish or to change a political and legal system in accordance with certain agreed ends that the supporters of the constitution deem to be good (the idealist element), while at the same time they seek to build upon, and to influence, the reality on the ground. This chapter has argued for the central role of political moderation as the real instrument through which constitutions can achieve ideal aims such as upholding the rule of law, democracy and human rights.

We have traced the evolution of political moderation, in relation to the aims of constitutionalism, from ancient origins, through medieval and early modern forms of representation, and the great constitutional revolutions of 1776 and 1789, to contemporary constitutional design practice. Our central tenet is that – without ignoring the contribution to political moderation of macro-level institutional structures such as the separation of the powers, rigid constitutionalism, or federalism, for example – political moderation is the foundation on which other ideals, such as the rule of law, human rights and democracy, are built. Political moderation can take many forms. Constitutions have sought to moderate powers in different ways – through different orders in society, through institutional separation, through multi-party systems, and through the role of the opposition. In all epochs, however, a consistent theme emerges, namely that constitutions should give expression to major social cleavages to enable ideas and interests to be contested through institutionalised, open and representative political processes. This may take the form of consensus decision making, with various blocs sharing power at the governmental level, but can also take the form of recognising oppositions and political minorities and empowering them to influence and therefore moderate the exercise of power. Whether this influence occurs through scrutiny and oversight, delay, participation in parliamentary committees or commissions of enquiry, the key notion is that those out of power can check – that is, can moderate – those in power.

We have interrogated two cases with regard to the principle of political moderation, the 2014 constitutions of Egypt and Tunisia. While we cannot generalise from two cases, particularly at such an early stage in the lives of these constitutions, we assert that a political reading of constitutions is called for in order to understand the potential dissonance between the formal 'paper constitution' and the real, living, constitution that actually determines the functioning of political society. The most important parts of the constitution, in reality, may not be those that define abstract ideals, rights or principles, but those that ensure the inclusion of parties representing the full spectrum of societal interests, that give the opposition a say over aspects of legislative process, or that enable political minorities to contest, delay or bring attention to, the decisions of the majority.

Thus, there is enduring value in Montesquieu's distinction between moderate and despotic forms of government. If we seek to establish the ideals of democracy, human rights and the rule of law, a constitution must provide for political moderation. In modern political societies, moderation includes not only the ability of formal institutions to check one another, but also the ability of societal groups – often through the intermediary of political parties – to oppose, contest and therefore moderate – each other's power.

While counselling against a narrowly legal or formalistic reading of constitutions, we are not saying that constitutions do not matter. Constitutions can and do constrain power. Neither, however, do we take the prescriptive and idealistic view that a mere constitutional text can by itself influence societal change in establishing the rule of law or other similar ideals. Rather, we see constitutions as devices that give political voice to social dynamics. They can enable contesting interests and ideals to freely interact in a political arena and it is this interaction that prevents the concentration of power and thereby moderates its exercise.

6

The Need for Realism: Ideals and Practice in Indonesia's Constitutional History

ADRIAAN BEDNER[1]

Introduction

When Indonesia proclaimed its independence in 1945 the nationalist elite shared three main ideals. They rejected colonialism, they aspired to national unity, and they pursued social and economic progress. These three ideals were common in most colonies on the verge of independence and they were exalted in speeches, proclamations and constitutions in Asia and Africa from the 1940s to the 1960s.[2] Yet they offered little practical guidance. Should independence be conquered by words or by force? Should the state have a federal or a unitary nature? Should economic development arrive in the form of a revolution or should it follow a capitalist or socialist path? Such existential questions led to fundamental debates in these almost-independent countries about 'second-order ideals' – ideals concerning the form and nature of the state. In many countries, including Indonesia, they eventually led to violence.

Constitutional debates and constitutional practices are a rich source for looking at first- and second-order political ideals and how they develop over time. They indicate how social relations and contestation over power and wealth are translated at the ideological level, and how in turn the resulting constitutions influence and shape social relations and contestation. While in the 1960s many political scientists still wondered whether constitutions matter, today there are probably as many 'constitutional political scientists' as there are constitutional lawyers.[3] The political

[1] The author wants to thank Jamie Davison and Jan Michiel Otto for their comments on a draft version of this article.

[2] See F. Heady, *Public Administration: A Comparative Perspective* (New York: Marcel Dekker, 1979), pp. 244–5.

[3] See on this issue the introduction to G. Sartori, *Comparative Constitutional Engineering: An Inquiry into Structures, Incentives, and Outcomes* (NYU Press, 1997).

scientists' 'realist' perspective considers constitutions in the first place as tools for the exercise of power by political elites and has little interest for the juridical subtleties espoused by constitutional lawyers. However, often this perspective falls short of explaining processes of constitution-making and constitutional policies. Not only may juridical subtleties be of considerable consequence, at times those who make constitutions may transcend their own interests. Liberating themselves from political strictures, they may take the discussion to another, more idealist level. Constitution-makers are not only 'pork-barrellers'; they are also part of intellectual traditions and they will be influenced by constitutional ideals from elsewhere. The nature of constitutional debate may, moreover, promote a form of self-consciousness that leads to a different balance between ideals and power politics, one that is usually absent in daily legislative practices in parliament. This, as we will see, has certainly been the case in Indonesia.

In this chapter my definition of ideals is the state of affairs people seek to realise in order to promote the common good. Realism refers not only to the awareness of these idealists that others involved in the process of constitution-making may primarily pursue private interests, but also that they may have different ideals and that compromises are required in order to proceed. The present chapter discusses how in Indonesia political ideals have been promoted, applied and led to compromise, both in constitutional debates and in the subsequent political and judicial practices based on them, from 1945 until the present. It will demonstrate how ideals may actually be nothing more than masquerades of vested interests, but how in many instances they are more than that. This has been particularly the case when constitution-makers try to redress past injustices and are aware of the responsibility they carry for preventing such injustices in the future.

The chapter starts with an introduction about the four major political/ideological currents of thought in Indonesia and the ideals they espouse. These four currents have been fairly constant over the years and offer an anchor for the ensuing discussion. The chapter then follows Indonesia's constitutional history, looking at how these ideological currents have shaped constitution-making efforts and how the results have been contested when they were implemented. As we will see, over time the most contentious issues have been freedom of religion, political liberties, and economic structures.

The chapter's point of departure is the 1945 Constitution, which was drafted under the Japanese occupation. It was in force during the Revolution, from 1945 to 1950, when by military and diplomatic means the Dutch attempted to restore their colonial empire. The next focus points are the Federal Constitution of 1949 and the Provisional Constitution of 1950. These were promulgated after the transfer of sovereignty by the Dutch to the new Republic. The chapter looks at the efforts to draft a new constitution during the second half of the 1950s, before turning once again to the 1945 Constitution – which was reinstated by President Soekarno in 1959 and remained in place during Soeharto's New Order regime. Only in 1999 was it amended for the first time. I will pay considerable attention to practices based on the 1945 Constitution under the Soekarno and the Soeharto regimes, but the emphasis of the chapter will be on the amendments of 1999–2002 and their aftermath.

Four Basic Ideologies

The tension between different ideals has been a constant in Indonesia's constitutional history. Never since the country became independent has one particular political current been able to fully impose its own vision upon the state – even if Soeharto's New Order came very close. Broadly speaking we can distinguish four political ideologies: liberalism, integralism, socialism and Islamism.[4] Indonesian liberalism can be distinguished by its relatively social-democratic outlook – as we will see, the emphasis Indonesian liberals place on collectivism and social justice is too strong for even a Rawlsian version of liberalism. Yet, human rights have always featured prominently in Indonesian liberal thought.

Integralism implies a view of the state which assumes a harmonious relation between state and society, as supposedly found in the Javanese village. State leaders, in this view, will by default pursue the common good, which in case of diverging views will be established through 'deliberation and consensus' (*musyawarah mufakat*). Integralism has its roots in German romantic thought and is ideologically close to fascism, in particular to the version promoted by the Japanese before and during World War II.[5] The link between integralism and authoritarianism is evident.

[4] D. Bourchier and V. Hadiz (eds.), *Indonesian Politics and Society: A Reader* (London and New York: Routledge, 2003), pp. 1–23.

[5] J. H. A. Logemann, *Nieuwe gegevens over het ontstaan van de Indonesische grondwet van 1945* [New data about the creation of the Indonesian constitution of 1945] (Amsterdam: NV Noord-Hollandsche Uitgevers Maatschappij, 1962). In an influential study published in 1994 Marsillam Simanjuntak has argued that Soepomo was mostly inspired by Hegelian

Socialism in Indonesia is a special case. It was highly influential until 1965, in particular in its communist version, but it lost its position as an admissible ideology in the aftermath of the failed coup in 1965. Under the Soeharto regime (1965–1998), communism and socialism were continuously vilified and the terms have remained 'contaminated' to the present day, communism in particular. Nonetheless, the state continued its involvement in the economy and introduced important social policies, while NGOs and the student movement kept alive socialist ideals.[6]

Probably the most difficult political label is Islam, because the political aspirations of Muslims are so diverse. Indonesia has always had its fair share of extremists pursuing a 'pure' Islamic state, but most of Indonesia's political Islam has been more concerned with the formal recognition of the Islamic character of the Indonesian state and the validity of Islamic family law for Indonesian Muslims. In any event, Islam as an ideology – or rather as a category of various ideologies – plays an important part in political and societal debates, and Islamic political discourse has gained prominence over the past 30 years.[7]

The relative influence of these four ideologies has shifted over time, but their proponents have almost always had to strike compromises. This is visible from Indonesia's four constitutions, even if they are profoundly different in their political, social and economic outlook. Changes were sometimes brought about by idealist reformers, and other times by elites seeking to extend their power. Still, all of them have had to operate within the strictures imposed by the balance of influence between proponents of these four diverging views about what constitutes the public good.

The 1945 Constitution

From 29 May to 17 July 1945, when Indonesia was still occupied by the Japanese army, the Indonesian nationalist elite started debates about

thought when he developed his ideas (M. Simanjuntak, *Pandangan negara integralistik: Sumber, unsur, dan riwayatnya dalam persiapan UUD 1945* [Reflections on the integralistic state: Its sources, elements, and history in the preparation of the 1945 Constitution] (Pustaka Utama Grafiti, 1994). Yet, there is a strong hint of Rousseau in it as well: as soon as the colonial state would be dismantled, the 'good citizen' would arise and a communalist society would become possible.

6 David Bourchier and Vedi Hadiz prefer the term 'radicalism' for the current representatives of the socialist tradition (Bourchier and Hadiz, *Indonesian Politics*, p. 9).

7 For an overview see A. Salim and A. Azra (eds.), *Shari'a and Politics in Modern Indonesia* (Institute of Southeast Asian Studies, 2003), introduction.

a constitution for an independent state.[8] The result was meant to sustain their claims to independence and nationhood. The participants were well aware of what was at stake: if they would fail, the struggle for independence would become even more difficult. Japan was losing the war and there was no doubt that the Dutch would try to regain their colony once Japan had been defeated. A constitution would give the new republic a legal basis and some of the formal legitimacy it would require in the eyes of the international community.

The debates took place under the auspices of the Japanese authorities, who did not, however, take an active part in them.[9] The majority of the participants were nationalists, with a 'modern' outlook. They had been trained at Dutch or Netherlands-Indies institutes of higher education, and several of them were renowned jurists. They were united in their wish to realise an independent Indonesia, but what this independent Indonesia should look like was less clear. All four ideological currents discussed above were represented, although communists (and several prominent socialists) were absent because of the Japanese repression.

The minutes of the constitutional debates contain a fascinating mixture of sometimes-grand rhetoric, historical consciousness, and a pervasive realism forced by the circumstances upon the participants.[10] Most of them considered the constitution they were drafting as a temporary document at best. It was to be replaced as soon as Indonesia's independence would have been consolidated, when a more inclusive drafting process could be conducted. Many ideological positions were spelled out, but in the end they seldom led to genuine debate, let alone to a new clause. As a result, the draft constitution itself to a large extent determined the final outcome.

The main author of this draft was Soepomo, a prominent legal scholar who under Dutch rule had been a professor at the Batavia Law School (*Rechtshogeschool*). In Soepomo's own words, what was to be created was

[8] The official name of the forum where these debates took place was the Investigating Body for Preparing Indonesia's Independence (*Badan Penyelidik Usaha Persiapan Kemerdekaan Indonesia*), see A. B. Kusuma and R. E. Elson, 'A Note on the Sources for the 1945 Constitutional Debates in Indonesia', *Bijdragen tot de taal-, land-en volkenkunde/Journal of the Humanities and Social Sciences of Southeast Asia*, 167.2–3 (2011), p. 196.

[9] One Japanese official was always present. He would never take part in the debates, but all results were reported to the Japanese command (Kusuma and Elson, 'A Note on the Sources', p. 204 f. 26.

[10] There is no English translation available. For the Indonesian transcript, see A. B. Kusuma. *Lahirnya Undang-undang Dasar 1945: Memuat salinan dokumen otentik Badan oentoek Menyelidiki Oesaha-2 Persiapan Kemerdekaan* (Depok: Badan Penerbit Fakultas Hukum Universitas Indonesia, 2004).

> ... a state which is united with all its people, which transcends all groups in every field. ... the state is nothing but the entire society or entire people of Indonesia, as an ordered, structured unity. ... There is no need to guarantee the fundamental rights and liberties of the individual against the state, because the state is not a power centre or political giant standing outside the environment of the individual man's freedom.[11]

At the state institutional level this integralistic ideology was translated into the establishment of the People's Consultative Assembly (*Majelis Permusyawaratan Rakyat*). This body was vested with the people's sovereignty, and consisted of parliament and representatives of 'social groups', a notion which was not further defined (Art. 2(1)). The president was to be elected by the People's Consultative Assembly (Art. 6(2)). The latter body also defined the General Guidelines for State Policy (*Garis Besar Haluan Negara*, Art. 3), which were to be implemented by the president. Apart from the Assembly, the institutional outline was not very special, with a President as head of state, an elected Parliament, a judiciary with a Supreme Court at the top, a national State Audit Body, and a few institutions of lesser importance. The powers of these bodies were not clearly defined, however, and the 1945 Constitution contained no guarantees for judicial independence.

Integralism was more conspicuous in the absence of an individual rights catalogue. Only freedom of religion was explicitly guaranteed (Art. 29), out of fear that otherwise non-Islamic regions of Indonesia would refuse to join the Republic. The single concession more liberally minded participants could wrest from the Committee concerned the freedom of expression and the freedom of assembly – these were to be regulated by act of parliament (Art. 28). Other individual rights were ultimately considered unnecessary.

One draft article received acclaim from all sides, but in particular from integralists and socialists. This Article 33 reads as follows:

(1) The economy shall be organized as a common endeavour based upon the principles of the family system.
(2) Sectors of production which are important for the country and affect the life of the people shall be under the powers of the State.
(3) The land, the waters and the natural resources within shall be under the powers of the State and shall be used to the greatest benefit of the people.

[11] H. Feith and L. Castles, *Indonesian Political Thinking 1945–1965* (Ithaca: Cornell University Press. 1970), p. 191.

This provision has continued to play an important role in Indonesian economic life until the present. That no one argued in defence of individual property rights reflects how the participants considered capitalism as one of the evils of colonialism, which should not receive any constitutional support.

The most fundamental debate conducted in the Committee did not concern the Constitution proper, but was about the basis of the state. The representatives of political Islam opposed the idea of secularism and argued that with its more than 80 per cent Muslim majority Indonesia should become an Islamic state. What they meant by this was unclear, but whatever it was, it was unacceptable to the other participants – Muslims and non-Muslims alike. Those who came from non-Muslim parts of Indonesia, such as Bali and North Sulawesi, threatened to withdraw their support for the new Republic. Nationalist leaders Soekarno and Hatta – the latter himself a pious Muslim – recognised this danger and also feared the influence of a constitutionally legitimised political Islam.

Pre-empting the imminent deadlock, Soekarno presented an alternative state ideology, the so-called *Pancasila* (Five Pillars). He explained that the procedures of 'deliberation and consensus[-making]' (*musyawarah mufakat*) already provided sufficient guarantee that the Muslim character of Indonesia would prevail, but he took this one step further: Indonesia should be based on the belief in God. This meant that every Indonesian 'can worship his God as he likes', but also that 'the state of Indonesia should be a state which has belief in God!'.[12]

The introduction of this principle into the preamble and Article 29 as the 'Belief in the Almighty God' (*Ketuhanan Yang Maha Esa*) has had far-reaching consequences, which we will come back to later. For one thing, this principle has been consistently interpreted as meaning that Indonesians cannot be atheists. None of the other pillars – that the state is based on 'A Just and Civilised Humanity', 'The Unity of Indonesia', 'A Society Led by Wise Policies Defined by Deliberation/Representation' and 'The Realisation of Social Justice for the Entire Indonesian Society' – has had a comparable influence.

Still, this was not enough for the representatives of political Islam. They forced an important concession from the Committee: seven words would be added to the preamble to establish that Islamic law (*sharia*) would apply to all Indonesian Muslims. These seven words have gone down in history as the 'Jakarta Charter'. Yet, when on 17 August 1945

[12] Feith and Castles, *Indonesian Political Thinking*, pp. 40–8.

Soekarno and Hatta declared Indonesia's independence and the Constitution came into force one day later, the Charter had disappeared from the text. Eventually the nationalists feared that it would continue to jeopardise the unity of Indonesia and would give too much power to political Islam; so at the last moment they decided to drop it. This 'treason' has cast a shadow over all constitutional debates conducted since.[13]

Even if the odds were against liberalism, one may still wonder why none of the participants made a stronger plea for individual political rights or mechanisms to control the state. As a matter of fact Muhammad Yamin did, but instead of suggesting amendments to the 'official' draft, Yamin presented a 'counter-draft'. This alternative was so different that, procedurally speaking, it could hardly be discussed together with the 'official' one. Most participants were of the conviction that once independence had been achieved a new constitution had to be made anyway, so they were less than enthusiastic about taking Yamin's draft to this level.[14]

The result of several weeks of deliberation was one of the shortest constitutions of all time.[15] Its 36 articles – including two of a transitional nature –reflected time constraints and the need for parties with profoundly different visions of the future state to attain a consensus. It contained hardly more than skeletal principles and lent itself to very different interpretations. This soon became evident, for only two months after it came into force the presidential system was replaced by a parliamentary one with a prime minister – a system that certainly had never been intended by the drafters, but that nonetheless could function without violating the letter of the constitution.[16]

The 1945 Constitution and its legislative history laid out a blueprint for all the constitutional debates that would follow. The same issues would surface time and again and require new compromises. And in some respects the Constitution was quite outspoken. Indonesia was to be a unitary, religious polity with an important role for the state in the

[13] S. Butt and T. Lindsey, *The Constitution of Indonesia: A Contextual Analysis* (Oxford: Hart Publishing, 2012), pp. 228–9.

[14] Kusuma and Elson suggest that at the time of his speech to the Committee Yamin had not even actually written the draft. They also refer to Yamin's 'shady reputation', which certainly will not have worked to his advantage (Kusuma and Elson, 'A Note on the Sources', pp. 204–5).

[15] Butt and Lindsey. *The Constitution of Indonesia*, p. 2.

[16] P. J. Drooglever. 'The Genesis of the Indonesian Constitution of 1949', *Bijdragen tot de Taal-, Land-en Volkenkunde*, 153 (1997), pp. 68–9.

economy. Political freedoms were ignored, and democracy was far from guaranteed. Integralist ideals had prevailed.

A final note is that no matter how much the drafters tried to establish a truly Indonesian constitution, the debates demonstrate how well aware many participants were of constitutional theories in the rest of the world. The language they used was Indonesian, but to clarify their ideas they would also use Dutch, German, French and sometimes English. Apparently there was no need for a translation. References were made to a whole range of philosophers, politicians, and social scientists, from Marx to Renan, and from Bentham to Jean Jaurès. This was a generation of intellectuals who were well versed in Western political philosophy and who tried hard to strike a balance between the 'East' and the 'West', between the new Indonesia and the powers that had colonised it. The ideals they espoused were neither parochial nor a basket of badly understood quotes. This makes the result even more disappointing.

The Constitutions of 1949 and 1950

From 1945 to 1950 the Dutch waged a war against the Republic to restore their power. The new state was moreover under attack from rival Indonesian groups and had to confront a communist uprising in Madiun in 1948. As a result the 1945 Constitution could hardly be brought fully into practice. The Republican leaders were well aware that their chances of success to a large extent depended on the international pressure they could bring to bear upon the Dutch. To this end, they had to convince the United States that an independent Indonesia would become a liberal democracy. When in early 1949 negotiations between the Republic, the Dutch and the representatives of the non-Republican Indonesian territories resumed, it was decided that the Indonesians would have to agree on a provisional constitution by themselves. Its outlines were drawn during a conference in Yogya and it was finalised in the Netherlands before the Round Table Conference in December 1949. Just as had happened four years earlier, external pressure forced the Indonesian drafters to come up with a document in a very short time.[17]

The new political conditions resulted in an entirely different document than the 1945 Constitution. The 1949 Constitution contained a blueprint

[17] Drooglever, 'The Genesis', pp. 78–81. Drooglever mentions that an active part was played by Soepomo, Hatta, Yamin and Anak Gde Agung (the latter represented the non-Republican Indonesian territories).

for a liberal, democratic state, with a comprehensive list of civil and political rights, a number of socio-economic rights (with much attention for labour and labour conditions), a fully elected parliament and guarantees for an independent judiciary. Integralistic elements were absent, and references to the involvement of the state in the economy were replaced by the guarantee of property rights (Art. 25 and 26). Furthermore, Indonesia was to become a federal state instead of a unitary one.

While the differences are overwhelming, there were continuities. First, the *Pancasila* ideology as the basis for the state was maintained, even if in abbreviated form. The typical Indonesian compromise of a religious state without a state religion thus became a consistent feature of the state order, just as the emphasis on nation-building and economic development. Another similarity was its presumed temporary nature. The 1949 Constitution included a section which held that a constitutional assembly (the 'Konstituante') was to be elected as soon as possible to finally create a genuinely national, Indonesian constitution.

That ideals did matter became evident when within half a year Indonesia abolished the federal articles in its constitution. The Indonesian nationalists had first and foremost struggled for a unitary state. This had been the basis of the whole enterprise, which started in 1928 with the so-called 'Oath of the Youth' (*Sumpah Pemuda*) and the proclamation of the belief in 'one motherland, one nation and one language'. Nation-building was and is of the utmost importance in a state as diverse as Indonesia, and a Dutch-promoted federal state was deemed incompatible with this pursuit.[18] Yet, the rest of the 1949 Constitution remained in place and it was under this Constitution[19] that Indonesia elected a new parliament as well as the Constitutional Assembly in 1955.

The Constitutional Assembly and the Return to the 1945 Constitution

The Constitutional Assembly in the end never adopted a new constitution, but its debates from 1955 to 1959 are important to understanding Indonesian constitutional thinking. For the first time the constitution-making process reflected a truly democratic process and the drafters were not confronted by the external pressure and time constraints their

[18] Of course there were also practical reasons to do away with the federal structure, but it is beyond doubt that ideological considerations were key to this decision.

[19] Its official name is the 'Provisional Constitution' (*Undang-Undang Dasar Sementara*).

predecessors faced. That their efforts in the end were in vain for a long time impeded any new efforts at constitution-making.

According to the authoritarian regimes of Soekarno (1959–1966) and Soeharto (1966–1998) the Constitutional Assembly failed because political divisions caused it to become deadlocked. This view resonates with the decline of democracy during the 1950s, caused by increasing ideological divisions between the different parties and in particular a growing antagonism between the communists on the left and modernist Islam on the right.[20] Their respective ideals on what development should bring were diametrically opposed. Under Soeharto this negative perspective became the standard argument for dismissing any suggestion at constitutional amendment.

This changed by the publication of a study written by a prominent critic of the Soeharto regime, human rights lawyer Adnan Buyung Nasution. His 1992 dissertation demonstrated that the political divisions led to much debate, but that in the end agreement on virtually all topics of importance prevailed – both regarding the institutional design of the state and human rights. If the Constituent Assembly would have had its way, Indonesia would have continued to be a liberal democracy, more decentralised than it was at the time and with a long list of social-economic rights added. Apparently, the ideal which had initially been imposed from the outside had a lot of traction after all.[21] Only a single issue proved divisive: the question whether the seven words of the Jakarta Charter should be added to the Preamble or not.[22]

In the end the Constituent Assembly came under the same time pressure as its predecessors. The political divisions that could be resolved at the more abstract level of constitutional principles in daily politics led to an increasingly unstable government. President Soekarno had long been frustrated by the political bickering and was eager to expand his limited, ceremonial function. The rapid deterioration of the economic situation and armed rebellions aimed at secession in West Sumatra and South Sulawesi added to the political instability. In this situation the one political actor which had been excluded from the constitutional process

[20] See generally H. Feith, *The Decline of Constitutional Democracy in Indonesia* (Ithaca: Cornell University Press, 1962).

[21] Of particular interest is the constructive attitude of the PKI, the Indonesian Communist Party.

[22] A. B. Nasution, *The Aspiration for Constitutional Government in Indonesia: A Socio-Legal Study of the Indonesian Konstituante, 1956–1959* (Pustaka Sinar Harapan, 1992), pp. 388–401.

made the difference: the army seized the opportunity to push the country towards an authoritarian system diametrically opposed to the one agreed upon by the Constituent Assembly. In the end, with the army's support President Soekarno unilaterally reintroduced the 1945 Constitution in 1959.[23]

Authoritarianism Rules: The 1945 Constitution from 1959 to 1998

The flexibility of the 1945 Constitution is evident from the fact that the two completely different regimes of Soekarno and Soeharto both operated under it. The main difference is that under Soekarno its socialist features played an important role, whereas Soeharto's New Order released its integralistic potential to the full. This is epitomised in the different images these two presidents promoted of themselves: Soekarno as the daring 'older brother' and Soeharto as the benevolent 'father of the nation'.[24]

The absence of constitutional checks and balances came to play a key role in both regimes. Under Soekarno the separation of powers went completely overboard and the judiciary even became formally subject to the president. Soeharto acted in a more subtle but ultimately more damaging way, by his constantly emphasising the integralistic roots of the Constitution. This helped him gain complete control over the People's Consultative Assembly and to legitimise the dominance of the executive over the other branches of government. A number of legal scholars provided the underpinning of this constitutional interpretation.[25] The *Pancasila* acquired a central role in education and in public discourse in order to support two central objectives of the regime: to disempower political Islam and what remained of the political left, and to guarantee the centralised nature of the state and the role of the military in it.[26]

The absence of any guarantees for civil and political rights served both regimes likewise. As already stated above, freedom of expression and

[23] D. S. Lev, *The Transition to Guided Democracy: Indonesian Politics, 1957–1959* (Equinox Publishing, 2009).

[24] This is evident from the common references to them as 'Bung Karno' and 'Pak Harto'.

[25] Best-known is Padmo Wahyono, see for instance P. Wahyono, *Sistem hukum nasional dalam negara hukum pancasila* [The national legal system in the state under the Pancasila rule of law] (Universitas Indonesia, 1983).

[26] M. Morfit. 'Pancasila: The Indonesian state ideology according to the New Order government', *Asian Survey*, 21.8 (1981), 838–51.

freedom of association were to be further regulated by statute. Soekarno interpreted this as a mandate to use the law to completely abolish freedom of the press. Once again, Soeharto took a more subtle approach. Through a system of censorship in combination with licensing requirements, press freedom was severely curtailed. When the system came under challenge from the judiciary, the regime used its control over the Supreme Court to restore the status quo.[27]

As to the freedom of association, Soekarno abolished the Islamic party that was most critical of his politics, but the other parties were at least allowed to continue to exist – even if no more elections took place and MPs were appointed from the party lists by the president. By contrast, Soeharto used his emergency legislative powers to overhaul the party landscape. What was left of the PKI and other leftist parties after the 1965–1966 massacres was prohibited.[28] The remaining parties were forced to merge into one 'nationalist' and one 'Islamic' party. At the same time the new Golkar party was established, which together with the seats reserved for the military secured the regime a safe majority in parliament. No party activities were allowed at the grassroots level, except for a three-weeks' campaigning period just before elections. In practice, Golkar was allowed much more leeway than its two competitors and it consistently translated its advantage into landslide victories. Limitations on freedom of association were extended to NGOs and other civil society organisations. As from 1985, all Indonesian organisations were forced to subscribe to the *Pancasila* as their ideological basis. Organisations considered too critical of the regime were disbanded. The ultimate aim was the complete depoliticisation of society – the ultimate integralistic ideal.[29]

Freedom of religion was severely curtailed under Soeharto. Although Article 29 of the 1945 Constitution explicitly guarantees freedom of religion, as long as it is in line with the 'belief in the One and Almighty God', the Blasphemy Law (1/PNPS/1965) limited the number of religions recognised by the state to six only: Islam, Catholicism, Protestantism, Hinduism,

[27] H. P. Wiratraman, *Press Freedom, Law and Politics in Indonesia: A Socio-Legal Study* (Leiden University Press, 2014), chapters 3.4 and 4.

[28] After a failed coup attempt on 30 September 1965, the military seized control, blamed the communists and organised one of the largest mass-murders in Southeast Asia, killing an estimated half-million citizens (see, for instance, R. Cribb. 'Genocide in Indonesia, 1965–1966' *Journal of Genocide Research* 3.2 (2001), 219–39).

[29] H. Crouch, 'Patrimonialism and Military Rule in Indonesia', *World Politics*, 31.04 (1979), pp. 571–87.

Buddhism and Confucianism. This measure targeted the many adherents of mystic and animist beliefs. It was also anti-communist and pro-Islam, as it forced many who did not consider themselves as 'full' Muslims to register as such.[30] In 1967 the government also excluded Confucianism from the list of official religions in an attempt to impose the assimilation of Chinese Indonesians.[31]

The role of religion was further stimulated by the Marriage Law of 1974, but this time against the wishes of the regime. According to Article 2 marriages are valid when they have been concluded 'in accordance with the rites of the religions of each of the partners'. The second paragraph stipulates that marriages must be registered, but the law is silent on the question whether an unregistered marriage may also be valid. This was the start of a long and confusing process to establish whether there can be anything like a civil marriage in Indonesia.

Originally the Soeharto government never intended to reinforce the religious basis of marriage. Before 1974 marriage was largely unregulated and marriage practice was quite diverse. Only few Indonesians took the effort to register their marriage, and for those who so wished the civil registry provided an alternative to a religious marriage. This lack of state control jeopardised women's rights and for many years the women's movement promoted the promulgation of a national marriage law. In its pursuit of nation-building and an all-encompassing state, the Soeharto regime adopted this idea and proposed a system of secular marriage, together with serious limitations on age and on male prerogative with regard to divorce and polygamy. However, the proposal met with serious opposition from the Islamic party in parliament and demonstrations by conservative Muslim organisations. The bill would have passed a vote in parliament, but in the end the government struck a compromise: equal divorce rights and the limitations on polygamy remained but the secular basis of marriage was replaced.

That the ideal of a secular marriage was no longer viable became clear after a few years, when the government and the judiciary started to interpret Article 2 as meaning that a religiously valid marriage should become liable for state recognition. Simultaneously the government limited the options for alternative marriage arrangements by the civil registry. Religiously mixed marriages could no longer be concluded by the civil registry, but even simple registration of mixed marriages that

[30] In the classic work of Geertz, this group is labelled as *abangan*.

[31] S. Butt and T. Lindsey, *The Constitution of Indonesia*, pp. 241–2.

were valid according to the rules of the religions of one the prospective spouses became difficult.[32] The same applied to marriages between adherents to non-registered religions. While these developments did not lead to complete state control over marriages, since many marriages remained unregistered, it did mean that freedom of religion guaranteed by the state as originally intended by the 1945 Constitution became even more illusory.[33]

One of the few generally agreed ideals in the 1945 Constitution concerned the involvement of the state in the economy. Yet, the interpretation of the relevant Article 33 changed considerably from the Soekarno to the Soeharto regime. The former intended to establish a semi-socialist system where the means of production were held by the state. An important step was the nationalisation of Dutch possessions in Indonesia from 1956–1959, which provided the Indonesian state with a wealth of plantations, factories, trade enterprises, etc.[34] Special state enterprises were established to manage these assets – many of them controlled by the military. They were not particularly effective in stimulating the economy, however, which at the end of Soekarno's regime was in a ruinous state.[35]

A central law to implement Article 33 was the Basic Agrarian Law 5/1960 (BAL), adopted under Soekarno. It stipulated that all land not held in private ownership was state land, which could be encumbered with use rights for a certain period of time. Private ownership was interpreted in a very restricted way, excluding collective ownership rights which were still commonly found throughout the archipelago. Although the preamble to the law asserted that it presented a clean break from the past, in fact it continued the colonial land policy. The main difference was that the law largely removed the colonial protection of communal land rights against the state, as the new law made it much more difficult for

[32] This applies in particular to marriages between Muslims and Christians. In most versions of Islam a marriage between a Muslim man and a Christian woman is allowed if the children are educated as Muslims. However, the Muslim Civil Registry sends those who wish to register any marriage involving a Christian to the Civil Registry, while the Civil Registry argues that it is not allowed to register a Muslim marriage.

[33] M. Cammack, A. Bedner, M. Cammack and S. van Huis. 'Democracy, Human Rights, and Islamic Family Law in Post-Soeharto Indonesia', *New Middle Eastern Studies*, 5 (2015), available at: http://www.brismes.ac.uk/nmes/archives/1413.

[34] This programme was carried out under the Constitution of 1950, flaunting its guarantees on property protection.

[35] A. Booth, *The Indonesian Economy in the Nineteenth and Twentieth Centuries: A History of Missed Opportunities* (Houndsmill: Palgrave MacMillan, 1998), pp. 63–9.

local communities to be recognised as '*adat* law communities'.[36] In fact the BAL tried to establish a western land rights system with a dominant role for the state. This would be the way forward to nation-building and economic development.

The Soeharto regime embarked on a successful programme of economic liberalisation to attract foreign capital. New laws were enacted to allow investments into mining and forestry, and rural development emphasised the opportunities for peasants to determine themselves what crops they wished to grow. However, the government never relinquished the old ideals of a state-led economy and continued to play an active role in the economy. Crucial sectors such as oil and gas, water, electricity, and telecommunication remained in the hands of the state. In other sectors, good relations with the government were key to successful entrepreneurship. From the 1970s to at least the 2000s this 'developmental state' was the dominant model in East and Southeast Asia.[37] It certainly was in line with the 1945 Constitution and ideologically the Soeharto regime aligned its economic policy with the *Pancasila* ideology. Economic success thus became linked to the political repression legitimised by the same ideal, and to the integralistic ideal originally at the basis of the 1945 Constitution.

The economic policy also led to serious mismanagement. This became most immediately visible in the land acquisition processes related to developmental projects. Over time the type of projects deemed to be 'in the public interest' expanded from public infrastructure such as roads and hospitals to include hotels, golf courses and shopping malls. The unwillingness of the government to pay proper compensation to those expropriated and the evident violation of expropriation procedures further contributed to the image of a government that was more concerned with lining its own pockets than with development. When those losing their land offered resistance the military was always ready to intervene on behalf of 'development'.[38]

[36] In its introduction the law actually said that Indonesia was one large *adat* community and that therefore the state held the right to avail for all Indonesians. In certain provisions, however, such as Article 5, it becomes clear that this is not the single definition of the *adat* right to avail.

[37] K. Jayasuriya (ed.), *Law, Capitalism and Power in Asia* (London and New York: Routledge, 1999), p. 2, p. 17.

[38] The poster child for unfair expropriation became the Kedung Ombo case, where hundreds of farmers lost their land to an artificial lake project. The case contained all the ingredients of a typical expropriation case, but because of its scale and the relentless opposition of a number of farmers it drew an unusual amount of attention (A. Rumansara, J. A. Fox, and

The BAL's limitation of *adat* rights was implemented in an increasingly strict manner. The state usurped virtually limitless powers to allocate land for logging, mining, and the development of plantations. For forest-dwelling peoples the consequences were dire. As time moved on, the possibility to move further away into the forest became limited, and as a result many eventually moved into nature reserves – insofar as these had not fallen prey to logging and mining as well.[39]

The main problem with the integralistic state model was its reliance on patron-client relationships. These increasingly dominated the political economy and led to excessive abuse. State enterprises were confided to Soeharto's cronies and children, who seldom operated for public benefit.[40] Logging and mining are sectors where short-term interests tend to be dominant already, but the patron-client structure reinforced this tendency as it removed any controls from the system.[41] At the end of the Soeharto era the ideals of the *Pancasila* ideology sounded entirely hollow, as all could see the massive corruption and cronyism that characterised the regime.

The Post-Soeharto Constitutional Amendments: From Authoritarianism to Democracy and Rule of Law

When in 1997 Indonesia was struck by the Asian financial crisis, the integralistic model had reached its limits. Dissatisfaction with the regime was widespread. Yet, there seemed to be not much of an alternative and at the start of the crisis few foresaw that this could mean the end of an era. However, once Soeharto stepped down in May 1998 the situation quickly changed. The new Habibie government introduced new laws which

L. D. Brown, 'Indonesia: The Struggle of the People of Kedung Ombo' in A. Rumansara, J. A. Fox, and L. D. Brown, *The Struggle for Accountability: The World Bank, NGOs, and Grassroots Movements* (Cambridge, Massachusetts and London: The MIT press, 1998), pp. 123–49).

39 See for instance J. McCarthy, *The Fourth Circle: A Political Ecology of Sumatra's Rainforest Frontier* (Stanford University Press, 2006).

40 Already during the 1970s Soeharto's fellow military officer Ibnu Sutowo almost pushed the national oil company Pertamina into bankruptcy by taking excessive risks and by extracting large amounts of public funds from it for political purposes. See A. Goldstone, 'What Was the Pertamina crisis?', *Southeast Asian Affairs,* (1977), 122–32.

41 The most extreme example is the logging sector where Soeharto favourite Bob Hasan forced companies to sell its plywood under the production price in order to conquer the Japanese market. The effect was a net loss for Indonesian entrepreneurs and the state at the same time (C. M. Barr, 'Bob Hasan, the Rise of APKINDO, and the Shifting Dynamics of Control in Indonesia's Timber Sector', *Indonesia*, 65 (1998), pp. 1–36.

limited the influence of the military, promoted a sweeping decentralisation programme, codified human rights, lifted the prohibitions on political parties and prepared for free elections. In 1999 Indonesia elected a parliament with a truly democratic legitimacy. As it turned out, this would provide a basis for a complete reassessment of the foundations of Indonesia and what kind of state it should be.

It was far from obvious that the constitution would be changed. The Indonesian 1945 Constitution had been the basis for a more or less democratic government from November 1945 to December 1949, and the Habibie government had adopted its liberalising laws without constitutional conflict. Moreover, even if the *Pancasila* had lost much of its appeal, many feared that a new constitution would get caught in the same deadlock over the foundation of the state as in 1959.

In the end these objections lost out against the importance most activists and politicians attached to having a constitution with guarantees for democracy and checks on power. The constitutional drafters preferred to call the process one of amendment and indeed the result is still being referred to as the 1945 Constitution, with its inherent historical symbolism. The amendment process was unique in the way it was conducted. It took four years – with each year a session of the Peoples' Consultative Assembly to adopt a number of new provisions. In between these sessions the Assembly's committee charged with the drafting could work quietly to test what would work and what would not. As a result some amendments were later undone, when ideas about the form of the state moved into another direction.[42] Another result was that many of the changes went largely unnoticed. Certainly, outside Indonesia few seemed to be aware that these were the new foundations of the Indonesian polity.[43] But what was most important was that the quiet and protracted debates allowed those involved to reconsider their positions and to adopt more of a long-term vision on what kind of state they wished and how it could be best guaranteed. I will now discuss the main results, one by one.

[42] The clearest example of this concerns the President's position. While the second amendment seemed to lead Indonesia towards a semi-presidential or even a parliamentary system, in the end the opinions swung around towards a truly presidential system. See D. L. Horowitz, *Constitutional Change and Democracy in Indonesia* (Cambridge University Press, 2013), pp. 109–23.

[43] In 2002 the National Democratic Institute published a report with the title 'The Fundamental Changes that Nobody Noticed: The MPR Annual Session, November 2001' (Last accessed September 5, 2015, at http://ndi.org/files/1378_id_gov_112002.pdf.

Basis of the State

Aware of its sensitivity, the Reform Committee relegated the decision on the basis for the state to the final session of the amendment process. Those who expected a heated debate were proved wrong: two conservative Islamic parties did propose to add the seven words of the Jakarta Charter to the Preamble, but an overwhelming majority voted against it. The fear of secession that led the Nationalist leaders to drop the Charter in 1945 was still present, but there was also a willingness to compromise.[44] Indonesia thus retained its character as a religious, but not an Islamic state. The emphasis on Indonesia's unitary nature and continued nation-building remained. These ideals of Indonesia's founders were thus preserved.

Sovereignty and State Model

While the Preamble was maintained in its entirety, the first Article of the amended constitution constitutes a clear break away from the authoritarian past. The new clauses 2 and 3 hold that 'sovereignty is in the hands of the people' instead of 'vested in the People's Consultative Assembly' and that 'Indonesia is a state under the rule of law'. The new ideal is a liberal-democratic state, in which there is no place for appointed representatives or overriding powers for the government over other state branches.[45]

This ideal has been translated into a set of institutions completely different from their predecessors. The democratic nature of the People's Constitutional Assembly itself is guaranteed by the removal of all appointed members from its ranks. The Assembly consists of two-thirds of parliament and one-third of representatives of the provinces and districts, all of them elected (Art. 2(1)). The only task left for the People's Constitutional Assembly is to amend the constitution and to install the president and the vice-president. Elections are organised and supervised by an independent Election Commission whose decisions can

[44] Horowitz, *Constitutional Change*, p. 264.

[45] During the reign of Soeharto some constitutional law scholars developed a constitutional theory which argued that Indonesia did not know any separation of powers, but that state power was concentrated in the People's Consultative Assembly. The President acted on behalf of the People's Consultative Assembly and delegated certain tasks to other state branches, such as Parliament and the Judiciary (see Wahyono, *Sistem hukum nasional dalam negara hukum pancasila*). This made it even more urgent for the reformers to remove the legal basis for such an interpretation.

be appealed to the new Constitutional Court (Art. 24 C(1)). After an initial move towards a semi-presidential system, the reformers in the end opted for a directly elected president who is not accountable to parliament.[46] The People's Consultative Assembly stripped itself of the power to 'impeach' the President on political grounds. It can only dismiss the President if the Constitutional Court has found him or her guilty of a serious crime. This is a rare example of a political body giving up its own power in pursuit of the long-term objective of political stability.[47] As an indispensible requirement for the rule of law, the independence of the judiciary is now guaranteed in Articles 24 and 24A.

The Constitution establishes several 'guardian' institutions, which are meant to ensure accountability of the government and the judiciary. The already-existing State Auditing Body saw its independence confirmed (Art. 23E, 23 F and 23G). The Constitutional Court (Art. 24 C), the Election Committee (Art. 22E(5)), and the Judicial Commission (Art. 24B) are entirely new. The Constitutional Court is arguably the most important among these institutions. Following in the footsteps of South Korea and Thailand, Indonesia created a judicial body designed specifically to make sure that Parliament does not exceed its constitutional limitations. The intention to prevent the usurpation of power by one state branch is reflected in the procedure for appointment of constitutional judges, with the President, Parliament and the Supreme Court each nominating three for this position.

Other guardian institutions were established outside the constitutional framework, such as the National Human Rights Commission, the Anti-Corruption Commission and the Ombudsman. Forty years of authoritarian

[46] This decision was not easily reached – for a long time it seemed that direct elections for the president was a bridge too far. That in the end the major factions all agreed to this change was partly due to an understanding that an unstable presidency would destabilise the nation, and perhaps also because the staunchest opponent, the PDI-P, may have become convinced that its leader Megawati would win the next elections (Horowitz, *Constitutional Change*, pp. 113–20). Another point which merits attention is that on the basis of Art. 20(2) the president has complete veto power. Formally, therefore, the powers of the president under this constitution have been augmented rather than reduced (for a different interpretation see Butt and Lindsey, *The Constitution of Indonesia*, p. 32), except for the fact that a president can never run for a third term (Art. 7).

[47] This was even more remarkable given the involvement of the People's Consultative Assembly in the 'impeachment' of President Abdurrahman Wahid in 2001. Many expected the Assembly to translate the political events into a semi-presidentialist system, but apparently they acknowledged the dangers inherent in a continued blurring of boundaries between the different branches (Horowitz, *Constitutional Change*, pp. 108–13).

rule based on integralistic and (under Soekarno) socialist ideals inspired the reformers with an overriding concern for checks and balances.

Civil and Political Rights

One of the most conspicuous changes to the constitution was the incorporation of a comprehensive set of human rights. The inclusion of civil and political rights provides another indication of the extent to which integralism had been compromised by the Soeharto regime. By inserting these, Indonesia undeniably moved away from the 1945 Constitution's collectivism to a more liberal model. Still, some provisions continue to reflect the importance attached to collectivist ideals and a strong state. The most important one is that according to Art. 28 J(2), the human rights listed in the Constitution can be circumscribed by acts of Parliament

> to guarantee the recognition and respect for the rights and freedoms of others and to satisfy justified demands in accordance with moral considerations, religious values, security, and public order in a democratic society.

It is the second part of the definition, and then in particular the 'moral considerations' and 'religious values', which are reminiscent of the Soeharto regime's policies. We will later see how this provision has indeed been used in a similar way by subsequent governments.

While the 'liberal' majority in the People's Consultative Assembly conceded to introduce this limitation, it made sure that certain basic freedoms could not be jeopardised. Thus, Art. 28I(2) holds that

> The right to life, the right not to be tortured, the right to freedom of thought and conscience, the right to practise religion, the right not to be enslaved, the right to be recognised as an individual before the law, and the right to not be prosecuted on a legal basis of retrospective application are human rights that cannot be circumscribed under any circumstances.

As we will later see, this provision has failed to provide the degree of protection it suggests to offer.

Other articles contain specific limitations that are reminiscent of integralistic ideology. Thus, Art. 28 C(2) only provides protection to those who want to champion their rights collectively 'in order to develop society, the people and the state'.

Some rights are important, because they seem to fly in the face of broadly supported legal and social norms. Thus, Art. 28B(1) gives the right to all persons to 'establish a family and to have offspring within a valid marriage'. This provision seems hard to combine with the abolition of civil marriages described earlier, as well as with the international obligation of Indonesia to ensure protection of children born outside wedlock. Another example is Art. 28I(3), which guarantees 'respect for the cultural identity and rights of traditional communities in harmony with the changes in time and civilisation'. The conditions of the second limb reflect the continued preference for modernisation rather than for protecting 'old-fashioned' ways of living.

There are a few idiosyncratic rights whose inclusion can only be understood in the particular Indonesian context. An important one is Art. 28D(1), which holds that every person has a right to 'legal recognition, guarantees, protection and certainty . . .'. This provision implicitly denunciates the way the Soeharto regime operated, and more particularly how the courts lost their legitimacy. Similarly, Art. 28D(3) holds that every citizen has 'the right to equal opportunity in government'. The intention seems to guarantee equal opportunity to become a government employee. Likewise, Art. 28H(4), which guarantees the right to property, is an indictment of the Soeharto regime's practice of expropriation rather than a turn towards a capitalist economy.

Altogether, the importance of these rights can hardly be overestimated. They indicate the constitutional legislator's aspiration to establish a liberal-democratic state with checks and balances, and they prove the new ascendancy of the liberal/socio-democratic over the integralistic, socialist and political Islamic ideals.

Socio-Economic Rights and the Role of the State in the Economy

The amended Constitution contains a broad range of socio-economic rights and thus continues the support for a developmental state. The inclusion of the rights to education (Art. 31(1)), health services and a clean environment (Art.28H(1)), and social security (Art. 28H(3) and 34(2)) put a serious duty on the government to provide services to its citizens.

Here it should be recognised that Soeharto had considerably expanded social welfare. The measures ranged from the provision of agricultural training and fertiliser to the establishment of a system of first-line health care centres and making available contraceptives. These services were, however, always formulated in terms of the benignity of the state – and of 'Father Soeharto' in particular. They thus contributed to the family metaphor for the ruler and the people implied in the integralistic ideal. The new provisions in the Constitution, by contrast, formulate the aspiration to social welfare in terms of rights. In the case of education this goes so far as to require the state to use at least 20 per cent of its budget for education (Art. 31(4)). Their orientation is thus entirely different.

The original articles about the role of the state in the economy remained in place, including Article 33, which gave the state ownership over natural resources. This did not go without saying, as its abuse by the Soeharto regime had created much resentment. Yet many critics feared that its abolition would pave the way for a neo-liberal economy that would be even more detrimental to the poor and disadvantaged. In the end the following particle was added:

> The national economy is run on the basis of economic democracy based on the principles of co-operation, fair efficiency, sustainability, environmental consciousness, independence, and preserving the balance between progress and national economic unity.

Just as with some of the articles discussed above, it is difficult to understand this provision without any knowledge of earlier practices. Its intention is unmistakably to prevent abuse of power by the state when it comes to economic policies.

Decentralisation

Sweeping measures under the Habibie government immediately after Soeharto stepped down included the decentralisation of state powers and tasks to the districts.[48] Inspired by the fear that certain provinces wished to secede, the new Law on Decentralisation abolished the top-down system of government and the parallel military structure and replaced it with a system where most government tasks were implemented by the districts. The new system met resistance from the military and others who held vested interests in the centralised mode of government. Their main argument was that decentralisation violated the principle of the unitary state. To reinforce their argument, opponents drew parallels between the decentralisation programme and the attempts of the Dutch to turn Indonesia into a federal state.[49]

[48] See for instance B. Smith, 'The Origins of Regional Autonomy in Indonesia: Experts and the Marketing of Political Interests', *Journal of East Asian Studies*, (2008), pp. 211–34.
[49] Horowitz, *Constitutional Change*, pp. 58–9.

This explains why regional autonomy did receive a constitutional basis, but few true guarantees. Article 18 only determines that 'regional governments implement the widest autonomy, excepting government matters that have been determined by acts of parliament as falling within the authority of the central government'. Article 18A(2) adds that 'the relations regarding finances, public services, and the use of natural and other resources between the central and the regional government are regulated and implemented in a fair and harmonious manner on the basis of an act of parliament'. Some reformers wished to put into place a structural mechanism to ensure that these provisions would be properly implemented. This led to the establishment of the Regional Representative Council, which forms part of the People's Consultative Assembly. This Council is entitled to present and discuss bills in Parliament regarding any topic of regional autonomy. However, its members have no right to vote. Regional autonomy thus acquires a place in the amended Constitution, but without any solid guarantees.

From Ideals to Practice: The Amended Constitution in Reality

The 1999–2002 amendments to the Indonesian constitution were a watershed in the way the state should be structured, in how it should govern, and in how it relates to society. As the reforms meant such a profound break with the past, their implementation was likely to run against vested interests and practices. This would make it difficult to realise the liberal-democratic state under the rule of law the drafters envisaged. Yet, the process resulting in these amendments was one of extensive negotiations involving all the important parties. Horowitz has pointed to a unique propensity of the Indonesian amendment process, which is that it only started after free elections were held. Usually it is the other way round: following the demise of a regime a new constitution is adopted first and only then are elections organised. The People's Consultative Assembly thus enjoyed a degree of legitimacy that constitutional drafters in similar situations seldom have.[50] This arguably improved the prospects for effective implementation.

And indeed, at first sight the constitution is successful. Indonesia is a functioning democracy with free elections, an active constitutional court, a vocal press, a vibrant civil society, an increasingly well-organised labour

[50] *Ibid.*, pp. 4–5.

movement and an expanding social welfare system. In addition to the Constitutional Court, the National Human Rights Commission, the Anti-Corruption Committee and the Ombudsman promote government accountability. If we stay at the surface, Indonesia's transition from an authoritarian state based on an ideology of integralism to a liberal democracy could hardly have been more successful.

Yet, if we look closer at the various features of the amendments discussed above, the picture is more mixed. In this section I will look at the main problems standing in the way of realising a liberal democracy under the rule of law[51] and assess to what extent they are ideological or rather structural in nature.

Democracy

In recent years the democratic nature of the elections has been increasingly criticised. The political party system has become self-serving and ideological differences between parties are small. Most parties for instance support a similar model of economic development. That the Yudhoyono government (2004–2014) shrank from slashing the fuel subsidies his successor Joko Widodo abolished is not informed by any ideology but rather by the question of whether the government is sufficiently popular to get away with it. The degree to which parties are opportunistic can also be shown from the finding that most so-called 'sharia bylaws' in districts have been enacted by district heads with a 'secular' party background.[52]

Campaigns have become extremely expensive, to the extent that in many regions there is only one candidate running for governor or district head.[53] So-called 'money-politics' have become widespread, with voters expecting to be given money in exchange for their support. This has made candidates dependent on businesses to fund their campaigns, and such 'debts' have to be satisfied in the form of government contracts and other

[51] On this issue, see J. Davidson, 'Dilemmas of Democratic Consolidation in Indonesia', *The Pacific Review*, 22.3 (2009), 293–310.

[52] R. Bush, 'Regional Sharia Regulations in Indonesia: Anomaly or Symptom?' in G. Fealy and S. White (eds.), *Expressing Islam: Religious Life and Politics in Indonesia* (Singapore: Institute of Southeast Asian Studies, 2008), pp. 174–91.

[53] BBC Indonesia, *Risiko di balik calon tunggal pilkada* [The risk behind a single candidate for the regional head elections], 3 August 2015, Last accessed September 5, 2015, at http://bbc.com/indonesia/berita_indonesia/2015/08/150803_indonesia_politik_pilkada_surabaya.

favours later on.[54] A few mayors as well as the current president are exceptions to this rule and have managed to get elected primarily on the promise of effective and clean government. However, a recent change in the Election Law has made it even more difficult for independent candidates, as they need to gather 10 per cent of all the voters' signatures in a district to be allowed to run for office.[55]

The national parliament in particular has been criticised widely for being dysfunctional and corrupt. MPs reportedly spend most of their time outside parliament, some of them paying a brief visit to this institution in order to collect their presence fee. While targets for legislative output are not excessively high, they are never met. In 2014, for instance, Parliament passed a total of 193 laws on a target of 284.[56] No wonder that the legitimacy of the institution has dropped to an unprecedented ebb. This is a worrying development, as it tends to undermine the belief in democracy as a system.

This experience indicates that the constitutional choice for a presidential system was wise. Combined with the Indonesian culture of adopting acts of parliament that are extremely broad in scope and leave all the details to be regulated by the executive,[57] the government can still move forward. Apart from this, one cannot blame the Constitution for the present situation; in the end, constitutional rules are a resource for political forces: they cannot enforce themselves.

If we take democracy in a broader sense, the situation is less bleak. Even if freedom of expression is sometimes under pressure (see below) to politicians, civil society is now a factor to be counted with.[58] NGOs constantly question government policies and champion interests ranging from women's rights to environmental quality to anti-corruption. Many of them have good relations with government officials and manage to

[54] See for instance M. Mietzner, 'Party Financing in Post-Soeharto Indonesia: between State Subsidies and Political Corruption', *Contemporary Southeast Asia: A Journal of International and Strategic Affairs*, 29.2 (2007), 238–63.

[55] The Jakarta Post, 'Indie Candidates Say Goodbye to Elections', 13 June 2015. On my last trip to Indonesia (August 2015) I noticed that the campaign to gather signatures for the incumbent independent governor of Jakarta, Ahok, had started already, while the elections were still two years away.

[56] A. B. Azed. 'Observing the Indonesian House of Representatives's Performance', *Indonesia Law Review*, 4.2 (2014), 150.

[57] A. Bedner. 'Amalgamating Environmental Law in Indonesia' in J. Arnscheidt, B. van Rooij and J. M. Otto (eds.), *Lawmaking for Development. Explorations into the Theory and Practice of International Legislative Projects* (Leiden University Press, 2008), pp. 171–98.

[58] For example M. Mietzner, 'Indonesia's Democratic Stagnation: Anti-Reformist Elites and Resilient Civil Society', *Democratization*, 19.2 (2012), 209–29.

influence policies and legislation. The role of television, the press and social media are equally important and are at least a constant source of pressure on the government and parliament to account for their actions.[59] Politically, Indonesia has never before been such an open society.

Judiciary and Guardian Institutions

With the deterioration of political accountability and the rise of self-serving politics, the role of the judiciary and guardian institutions has been of growing importance. The problem is that the judiciary finally acquired constitutional guarantees for its independence at a time when it had become corrupt and ineffective.[60] The new guarantees therefore make judicial reform even more difficult than it already had been without them. This tension has become visible in a number of conflicts between the Supreme Court and the Judicial Commission, when the latter's effort to review court judgements in search for corruption was halted by the Supreme Court. According to the Court this constituted unacceptable interference, a view corroborated by the Constitutional Court when it had to decide the matter.[61]

Nonetheless, some reforms have been implemented and the Supreme Court now includes a number of well-qualified, non-corrupt judges. In cases where there is much public attention, judges will be careful to prevent allegations of partiality and the Supreme Court has passed a number of courageous judgements vindicating the rights of disadvantaged groups.[62]

That the judiciary cannot provide the degree of legal certainty one would wish for can therefore not be reduced to the Constitution. Years of

[59] K. Hamayotsu 'The Limits of Civil Society in Democratic Indonesia: Media Freedom and Religious Intolerance', *Journal of Contemporary Asia*, 43.4 (2013): 658–77.

[60] S. Pompe, *The Indonesian Supreme Court: A Study of Institutional Collapse* (Southeast Asia Program: Cornell University, 2005); A. Bedner, *Administrative Courts in Indonesia: A Socio-Legal Study* (Kluwer Law International, 2001).

[61] S. Butt, 'The Constitutional Court's decision in the dispute between the Supreme Court and the Judicial Commission: Banishing Judicial Accountability?' in A. MacIntyre and R. McLeod (eds.), *Democracy and the Promise of Good Governance* (Institute of South East Asian Studies, 2009), pp. 178–200.

[62] A good example is a 2011 judgement in which it argued that former political prisoners' citizen's rights were to be fully restored (see A. Bedner, 'Citizenship Restored Communism Continues to Be a Taboo in Indonesia, but "Former Communists" Have Finally Regained Their Rights', *Inside Indonesia* (2015, http://www.insideindonesia.org/citizenship-restored).

authoritarian rule have undermined the rule of law. The low quality of legislation, the unavailability of case law and doctrine of good quality, the problems with legal education, the incredible complexity of the Indonesian legal system, the backlog of the Supreme Court which forces its judges to decide some ten cases a day,[63] and the culture of corruption which has become engrained in the day-to-day practices of the courts all contribute to this lack of legal certainty.[64] The Constitution cannot do more than provide a basis for change.

There is one exception to this rule. Insulated from the problems plaguing the judiciary in general, the Constitutional Court has become a major success story. In developing its own interpretations and precedents, it has borrowed from foreign constitutional jurisprudence and managed to give teeth to many of the human rights clauses discussed above. It has moreover played a stabilising role in the political system by effectively resolving many election disputes. The Court has managed to do so by immediately demonstrating its independence in the first cases that were brought before it.[65]

The Court has thus more than any other judicial institution protected the political and civil rights of Indonesians. Unfortunately, in so doing it has become politicised itself. The academics and NGO-activists serving on the Court during the first 10 years of its existence have now been largely replaced with politicians. How dangerous this development is became evident when in June 2014 the Chairman of the Constitutional Court, Akil Mochtar, was convicted to life imprisonment for accepting bribes worth US$ 4.7 million in electoral disputes.[66] Through its appointment procedure, the Court ultimately remains dependent on the President, Parliament and the Supreme Court.

[63] Interview with Supreme Court Judge Irfan Fachruddin, August 2015.

[64] See for instance A. Bedner, 'Indonesian Legal Scholarship and Jurisprudence as an Obstacle for Transplanting Legal Institutions', *Hague Journal on the Rule of Law*, 5.02 (2013), 253–73.

[65] To give one example, once again in the field of citizens' rights, in 2003 the Court invalidated a provision in the Election Law which barred ex-political prisoners from running for political office. See generally S. Butt, 'Indonesia's Constitutional Court: Conservative Activist or Strategic Operator' in B. Dressel, *The Judicialization of Politics in Asia* (London and New York: Routledge, 2012), p. 116; M. Mietzner, 'Political Conflict Resolution and Democratic Consolidation in Indonesia: The Role of the Constitutional Court', *Journal of East Asian Studies*, 10.3 (2010), 397–424.

[66] In June 2014 he was convicted to life imprisonment (The Jakarta Post, 'Historic Sentence for Akil', 1 July 2014).

The same applies to another novel institution of outstanding performance, the Anti-Corruption Commission (ACC).[67] Although lacking a constitutional basis, the ACC is part of the range of guardian institutions introduced by the same liberal reforms that produced the constitutional amendments. Over the years the ACC has become the symbol of the fight against corruption, getting convictions of district heads, governors, MPs, former ministers and – as mentioned above – a chairman of the Constitutional Court. Inevitably the ACC has become the target of the same groups that resist the existence of an independent Constitutional Court. When in 2014–2015 the ACC increasingly focused its attention on the top brass of the police, the latter retaliated by arresting three of the five ACC-members on charges of fraud. At the time of writing the selection procedure for the ACC is ongoing and fears abound that Parliament will use its powers of appointment to further emasculate the ACC. Once again, the interdependence between state institutions makes it difficult for individual ones to stay immune from politics.

Human Rights

Although human rights reports indicate that breaches of human rights are still common,[68] the situation overall is much better than it was before the amendments. The human rights catalogue now included in the Constitution makes it easier for activists to demand the government to account for violations. It is beyond the scope of this chapter to go into each and every human right, but I will offer a few general observations.

The basic rights to life, freedom from torture and fair trial all present problems. This is caused in part by their having been insufficiently translated into legislation and in part by the difficulty of changing the attitude of the police and other key state actors. The important role that vigilante-like organisations play in security matters further jeopardises these rights. On the other hand, the National Human Rights Commission has played an active role in addressing such violations,[69] and the

[67] See generally S. Butt, *Corruption and Law in Indonesia* (New York: Routledge, 2011) and S. A. Schütte, 'Against the Odds: Anti-Corruption Reform in Indonesia', *Public Administration and Development*, 32.1, (2012), 38–48.

[68] See at http://amnesty.org/en/countries/asia-and-the-pacific/indonesia/report-indonesia/ and http://hrw.org/world-report/2015/country-chapters/indonesia.

[69] For an overview see K. M. P. Setiawan, *Promoting Human Rights: National Human Rights Commissions in Indonesia and Malaysia* (Leiden University Press, 2013).

Constitutional Court has consistently annulled legal provisions that violate these rights.[70]

Probably the most positive change in human rights protection concerns the freedom of association. This is evident from Indonesia's vibrant civil society, but also from the development of trade unions. Severely repressed under the Soeharto regime, trade unions have grown rapidly in number and influence, and one of them has entered the field of politics by mounting candidates for regional parliaments.[71]

Press freedom is more of a problem. The notorious 'hate sowing' and the 'lèse majesté' articles have been annulled by the Constitutional Court, but equally repressive provisions are still in place. Some of them have been challenged before the Constitutional Court as well, but in these cases the Court judged that if used with circumspection they remained within the constitutional limits.[72] Lower courts have often wrongly applied the rules in the Press Law (40/1999), deciding cases against editors and journalists which they should have referred to the Press Council instead. The Supreme Court has consistently overturned such judgements, but their case law is frequently disregarded. Equally worrying is the use of violence against journalists, which seldom leads to an adequate reaction by the state.[73]

As noticed earlier, the most controversial right in Indonesia concerns freedom of religion, and it will be of little surprise that its contestation has continued after the constitutional amendments. In fact, very little has changed. Already-existing prohibitions against proselytising have remained in place. Another controversial issue are so-called 'sharia bylaws' which were passed by district and provincial governments in many parts of Indonesia. Some of them are limited to dress codes, but others contain prohibitions against women moving around freely at night, or they require prospective marriage partners to be able to recite the Quran. Such bylaws can be contested before the Supreme Court, but so far this seems a merely theoretical option.[74]

[70] Butt and Lindsey, *The Constitution of Indonesia*, pp. 205–16. The authors are critical of the Court's failure to offer a clear standard by using the concept of rule of law for this purpose without properly describing what they mean by it (p. 218).

[71] S. Tjandra, *The Development of Labour Law in Indonesia* (Leiden University Press, 2016).

[72] Butt and Lindsey, *The Constitution of Indonesia*, pp. 196–202.

[73] See H. Wiratraman, *Press Freedom in Indonesia: A Socio-Legal Study* (Leiden University Press, 2014).

[74] See N. Parsons and M. Mietzner, 'Sharia By-Laws in Indonesia: A Legal and Political Analysis', *Australian Journal of Asian Law*, 11.2 (2009), 190–217. The authors argue that such challenges would be unlikely to succeed.

In another case the Constitutional Court upheld the provisions in the Marriage Law that put strict conditions on polygamous marriage. That it allowed the Parliament to limit such rights was not in itself surprising, but the way in which it did so was: the Court engaged extensively in Islamic religious interpretation in order to find that the contested provisions were valid. This indicates how the state increasingly imposes its own interpretations of Islamic law on Indonesian society – or rather, the interpretations of one side of the Islamic establishment. When this happens in the form of new legislation, there seems not to be much of a problem, but one may wonder whether it is a good idea for a constitutional court to engage in an interpretive competition with scholars of Islamic jurisprudence.[75]

These are but a few examples of a trend which endangers religious freedom. Over the past years the government has often been unwilling to act against Islamic hard-liners imposing their opinions on social life. This has resulted in problems for Christians seeking to get building permits for churches, or even seeking their continued use of already existing churches. The effects have been harshest, however, for those who consider themselves to be Muslims, but who are labelled as heretics by representatives of the conservative Muslim establishment. The result has been violence and persecution of Ahmadiyah and Shia Muslims, with the government unwilling or afraid to intervene.[76]

This issue also came to the fore in the challenge to the Blasphemy Law (1/PNPS/1965) in the Constitutional Court. According to the plaintiffs, the limitation of official religions to only six went flatly against the freedom of religion. They moreover denounced the prohibition to publicly voice religious interpretations or perform rituals that deviate from the basic tenets of one of these six religions (Art. 1), the authority of the President to disband any organisation found to do so, and the stipulation that any act that can be interpreted as 'dishonouring' one of these religions is punishable.

The Court rejected the claim (with one dissenting opinion). It found that the Blasphemy Law did not intend to limit the freedom of religion, but by contrast tried to protect the freedom of religion of the adherents of the six official religions, and that it only wished to make sure that people

[75] Bedner, Cammack and Van Huis, 'Democracy, Human Rights, and Islamic Family Law in Post-Soeharto Indonesia'.

[76] For an overview see the Human rights Watch report 'In Religion's Name: Abuses against Religious Minorities in Indonesia', available at http://hrw.org/report/2013/02/28/religions-name/abuses-against-religious-minorities-indonesia.

would not create tensions within communities. With its emphasis on community and community values, this judgement is a clear return to an integralistic position. The Court even expressly stated that in this respect the Indonesian state under the rule of law differs from Western rule of law. The judgement puts beyond doubt that the limitation of Article 28H(2) needs to be taken seriously: claims based on human rights must 'satisfy justified demands in accordance with moral considerations, religious values, security, and public order in a democratic society'.[77]

Economy

Under President Susilo Bambang Yudhoyono, Indonesia continued liberalising its economy. While most of the measures remained well within the limits of the Constitution, the privatisation of key state assets such as the national water company and the national electricity company incurred serious criticism. Eventually, leftist NGOs challenged these measures before the Constitutional Court. In both cases the Court went quite far in supporting the socialist ideas incorporated in Article 33 of the Constitution. Although the judges did not reject any private investment in such vital sectors, they made clear that ultimately the state should remain in control of them. Such control can be regulatory, but leaving everything completely to market forces goes too far. In the case of the Electricity Law (20/2002), this led the Court to annul the entire law.[78]

Of all the cases decided by the Constitutional Court, those concerning the Water Law (7/2004) are the most revealing. This statute sought to secure private foreign investment for the drinking water sector and was challenged twice, immediately after its enactment in 2004 and then again in 2015. At first the Constitutional Court rejected the claims that the Water Law violated the requirement for state control. The Court did emphasise the government's responsibility for Indonesians' access to clean drinking water, however, and formulated a number of principles that should be honoured by the government in its implementation of the law. The challenge brought in 2013 argued that the government had

[77] For a more elaborate discussion of the Blasphemy case, see Butt and Lindsey, *The Constitution of Indonesia*, pp. 234–46. See also the Amnesty International report 'Prosecuting Beliefs: Indonesia's Blasphemy Laws', available at http://amnesty.org/en/documents/ASA21/018/2014/en/.

[78] Butt and Lindsey, *The Constitution of Indonesia*, pp. 255–6. In this case the government subverted the judgement by reproducing the rules from the Electricity Law in a government regulation, which the Constitutional Court cannot review.

failed to take such measures and that therefore the Water Law should be annulled after all. An assessment of implementing regulations led the Court to the conclusion that this was indeed the case. As a result, nine years of implementing regulations and contracts concluded on their basis are now dangling.[79]

Conclusion

Indonesia's constitutional history can be characterised as a constant moving between the ideological visions associated with integralism, liberalism, socialism and political Islam. For many years, the integralistic ideal was dominant, and although it has been replaced almost completely by the ideal of a liberal democracy, in practice it continues to be influential. At the same time we have seen how, in their implementation, these ideals have often become the masks for private political and monetary interests instead of vehicles to promote the common good.

This is not surprising. The ideals of a constitution need to be realised by state structures which are formed over the years and cannot be changed overnight. Law itself is predicated upon the functioning of a set of interdependent institutions – judiciary, universities, the bar, public prosecutors police. Forty years of authoritarian rule have undermined all of these institutions, and rebuilding them is a difficult task. The same applies to the political party system, which is still coloured by the 'lack of politics' associated with the integralistic model. Presently, political parties in particular represent private interests rather than ideological positions.

The Indonesian case shows how important ideals are, but also how they need institutional underpinning. It is the range of newly established guardian institutions which has been pre-eminent in guaranteeing more freedom to citizens. The Constitutional Court has been important, but so have the National Human Rights Commission, the Anti-Corruption Commission, the Judicial Commission and the Ombudsman. These provide the bridge between civil society and the state that parties fail to present. But without the liberal ideal inherent in the catalogue of human rights, it would be impossible for them to operate effectively. Freedom of expression in particular has been key to the liberalising developments in Indonesia.

[79] Indonesian Law Digest, issue 402, 10/4/2015 (Hukumonline).

These liberal ideas are widely supported. Although with the passing of time a growing number of Indonesians are becoming nostalgic about the Soeharto regime and the stability it offered, they generally enjoy their free press and the new opportunities they have. The integralistic ideology is seldom heard of and only lingers in ceremonies commemorating the defeat of the Dutch during the Revolution or in the failed coup of 1965.

There are two exceptions to liberalism's pre-eminence. When it comes to religion, the *Pancasila* is generally regarded as the only protection against the Islamisation of the state instead of the liberal ideal of a secular state. It is true that at the constitutional level political Islam has consistently failed in imposing its ideals of an Islamic state and Islamic family law for all Muslims. Yet, it has been quite successful in pushing its agenda at the level of lower legislation. The question is no longer whether state law of an Islamic nature defines much of public life, but rather what this Islamic nature implies. We have seen that the Constitutional Court has been hesitant to annul such legislation. The consequence is that much of the debate about women's rights, for instance, is now couched in religious terms rather than in the opposition between the secular and the religious.

The other exception is the interference of the state with the economy. The continued involvement of the state in major sectors and the willingness of the Constitutional Court to actually put limits to liberalisation of certain sectors guarantees that the socialist ideal is not fully lost.

Finally, I would like to make a few remarks on the process of constitution-making in Indonesia, and what this has meant for its outcome. The first is that Indonesia's present constitution is the single one that resulted from a process where the lawmakers were not under time pressure. The way in which the process was conducted has proven to be of exceptional importance for its outcome. It stimulated the constitution-makers to take a long-term view instead of focusing on short-term interests. This was possible because the amendment process started *after* elections had been held rather than *before* them, but also because the process lasted for almost four years. As ordinary politics continued during this entire period, the constitutional legislators could react to certain events and make adjustments accordingly, For instance, after having reduced the powers of the president in the first amendment, they reinforced them when they saw from the crisis of Abdurrahman Wahid's presidency what kind of instability may result from a semi-presidential or parliamentary system.

The lack of public attention to the process also allowed the legislators to take a more detached view and to more quietly conduct the politics inevitably involved in constitution-making. This is remarkable because most of the members of the People's Consultative Assembly were also members of parliament, and in this capacity they were confronted on a daily basis with 'short-term politics' in the limelight of public attention. The availability of sufficient time available for careful preparation and negotiation of the proposed amendments certainly expedited this detachedness. The lead was taken by one commission, whose chair, Jakob Tobing, was a well-respected and experienced politician. Under his leadership the commission somehow managed to create the degree of solidarity required to bring the process to a successful result.[80]

There was, to be sure, pressure on the process: failure was a possibility. Without this sense of urgency the process might have ended in endless bickering. As the large majority of the participants did not want to return to the 1945 Constitution, the odds in favour of constitutional change were high. In short, the Indonesian constitution-making process was unique in several ways, although some of its lessons might be of relevance to other countries as well.

The second note concerns ideals: it is striking that when Indonesia's constitution-makers got the opportunity, they opted for a liberal vision of the state. There are several factors that explain this. It was a response to the repressiveness and the cronyism of the integralistic Soeharto administration – even if many of those involved in the constitution-making had been part and parcel of that regime. Yet, a strong feeling that the restoration of order and the state's legitimacy required a clean break with the past contributed to this tendency. The need for Indonesia to restore investor and donor confidence to overcome the economic crisis also promoted a liberal model.

Nonetheless, I would argue that another important cause was indeed the nature of the constitution-making process.

It assisted constitution-makers in transcending their own views and interests and in opting for a liberal-democratic ideal. In fact this was the only ideal that had not become tainted over time. By opting for a presidential system those promoting democracy could also rebuke the criticism that democracy had failed in the 1950s, as they did not reinstall the parliamentary regime. Even Soeharto's New Order had given up its full-scale rejection of human rights as a western invention after the 1994 Vienna World Conference on Human Rights. Moreover, there was a

80 A. Ellis, 'Constitutional Reform in Indonesia: A Retrospective', *International Institute for Democracy and Electoral Assistance* (2005), 6.

precedent, as under Habibie the parliament had already enacted a Human Rights Law. The adoption of a human rights catalogue was therefore a step rather than a jump. The inclusion of socio-economic rights, moreover, emphasised the political side of liberalism and bears evidence of a commitment to social justice which runs as a red thread from Indonesia's independence to the present.

More puzzling is the constitutional restoration of judicial independence and the establishment of a range of guardian institutions. To me there seems to be only a single explanation: in the end the constitutional legislators were truly committed to a liberal state. And, once again, there is a precedent: in a similarly 'detached' process in the 1950s the Constitutional Assembly likewise created a largely liberal constitution – even if communists, integralists and others were far better represented at that time. This does not mean that the turn to a liberal-democratic state is the only plausible outcome in case of a well-considered process. Yet, in the particular Indonesian contexts of the late 1950s and 1999–2002 integralism, Islam and socialism were not viable options.

This chapter cannot end on this positive note. A good constitution always means the start of another process. The challenge now in Indonesia is to make sure that those implementing the liberal democratic ideal laid down in the constitution transcend their own interests as well. This has become increasingly difficult in view of the developments in Indonesia's political system which promote clientelism and money politics.[81] The guardian institutions entrenched in the new state system do resist this tendency, but they run a serious risk of being subverted by their opponents. Whether this means that in the end the liberal democratic ideal will lose its legitimacy is uncertain. But it is clear that the present practices do undermine the ideal that was so carefully crafted.

[81] See, e.g., E. Aspinall and M. Sukmajati (eds.), *Electoral Dynamics in Indonesia: Money Politics, Patronage and Clientelism at the Grassroots* (Singapore, NUS Press, 2016).

7

Constitutionalism à la Rwandaise

NICK HULS

Introduction

In this chapter, I analyse the Constitution of Rwanda, a small African country that experienced a devastating genocide in 1994. For the theoretical underpinning of my analysis I use illiberal state building, a concept that is explained in the first paragraph. Next, I will describe the political history of Rwanda, its constitutions and the differences they did (not) make until 1994. I continue with a brief description of the situation after the end of the genocide until 4 June 2003, the date that Rwanda's 'homegrown' Constitution came into force. In the third part of this paper, I start with some salient provisions and analyse and criticize the Constitution, which was amended by the end of 2015. After this, I will give an overview of the main external criticism, i.e. from the international community and from academics. I continue with an appraisal of the illiberal state building project that is going on in Rwanda, including the country's relationship with the rest of the world. Finally, I suggest how a legal complex approach could bridge the gap between the paper ideals in the Rwandan Constitution and their incomplete realization.

Liberal, Postliberal and Illiberal State-Building

The international debates about constitutionalism have been dominated for a long time by the ideals of the American liberal legal tradition as a victory over dictatorship.[1] According to Mark Tushnet, '[l]egal scholars and political theorists interested in constitutionalism as a normative concept tend to dichotomize the subject'.[2] There is liberal constitutionalism of the sort familiar in the modern West, with core commitments to

[1] B. Ackerman, *The Future of Liberal Revolution* (New Haven: Yale University Press, 1994).
[2] M. Tushnet, 'Authoritarian Constitutionalism', *Cornell Law Review*, 100 (2015), 391, at 394.

human rights and self-governance implemented by means of varying institutional devices, and there is authoritarianism, rejecting human rights entirely and governed by unrestrained power-holders'. I will show that this dichotomy is too simple for a good understanding of Rwanda.

For a long time the American constitutional debates were of a liberal (in the sense of 'progressive') character. Most scholars argued that the US Constitution is a living document that must be interpreted in the context of the needs of modern society. In the 1960s and 1970s the Warren Court delivered many progressive decisions in the area of civil rights and defendants' rights.

Since the 1980, when the political Zeitgeist in the United States changed, a more conservative movement of lawyers[3] and the constitutional doctrine of 'original intent' came to the fore. In this view, the Constitution must be interpreted in accordance with the opinions of the Founding Fathers. Since then constitutional debates in academia and in the Supreme Court have become extremely politicized and polarized.[4] A liberal constitution does not contain a clear policy agenda.

When South Africa faced the end of Apartheid in the 1990s, the negotiations between the liberation movement and the National Party led to a constitution with a political program. It gave the government and the Constitutional Court a mandate to leave the white racist past behind and guide the country towards a democratic, participatory and egalitarian society. The progressive ideals that were formulated in the South African Constitution led critical legal scholars like Karl Klare,[5] who over a long period of time had criticized the individual liberal character of the US Constitution, to speak of a *post-liberal* Constitution and of transformative constitutionalism, i.e. a constitution with a progressive agenda.

After the fall of the Berlin Wall in 1989 many observers hoped for a 'second liberation' of Africa, a 'new crop' of African leaders, the possibility of an African renaissance and a 'new world order'.[6] In reality, ethnic aspirations broke to the surface in many countries where they were

[3] S. M. Teles, *The Rise of the Conservative Legal Movement: The Battle for Control of the Law* (Princeton and Oxford: Princeton University Press, 2008).

[4] M. V. Tushnet, *Red, White and Blue. A Critical Analysis of Constitutional Law*, 2nd edn (Lawrence: University Press of Kansas, 2015).

[5] K. Klare, 'Legal Culture and Transformative Constitutionalism', *SAJHR*, 14 (1998), 146–88.

[6] B. Kagoro, 'The Paradox of Alien Knowledge, Narrative and Praxis: Transitional Justice and the Politics of Agenda Setting in Africa' in M. C. Okello et al. (eds.), *Where Law Meets Reality. Forging African Transitional Justice* (Capetown: Pambakuzea Press, 2012), p. 22ff.

previously suppressed. The liberalization of that time exacerbated class, ethnic, gender, generational and racial tensions. Some key ingredients for the development of a liberal democracy were clearly missing outside of South Africa.

In a 2013 paper Jones, Soares and Verhoeven argued that today African states are usually categorized as either developing in the direction of liberal democracies, as failed states or as self-serving dictatorships.[7] The authors found that Rwanda – and some other states[8] – did not fit in any of these categories. They developed a new political and economic model, the so-called illiberal state, with the following characteristics:

- The leader is strong man, a freedom fighter raised from the role of a terrorist to the role of head of state.
- As president, he is also the commander-in-chief of the army.
- The dominant political party has left-wing/socialist ideological roots,[9] but once in power, it opens up the country to the global economy.
- The policies of the ruling party have a solid support of the population.
- In their international relations they are good friends of the West but they develop an independent position vis-à-vis their allies and donors.

I will argue that an illiberal state prism is helpful in explaining the situation of Rwanda as an African country that has chosen its own path for the future.[10] The ideal of the present rulers is not limited government but – on the contrary – a strong-performing state that provides basic services for its people. The aims of the ruling elites are managerial, and they care less about civil liberties, press freedom or competitive politics that might undermine their policies.

However, this does not imply that Rwanda is not at all committed to rule-of-law principles. Because the country wants to be open to the global economy it offers a conducive legal system. Under the aegis of the World Bank, Rwanda has modernized its commercial laws to facilitate a safe investment climate. The commercial dispute resolution systems (courts

[7] W. Jones, R. S. de Oliveira and H. Verhoeven, '*Africa's Illiberal State-Builders*', Working Paper series nr. 89, Refugee Studies Centre, University of Oxford (2013).

[8] The other countries are Sudan, Angola and Ethiopia.

[9] G. Piccolino, 'Winning Wars, Building (Illiberal) Peace? The Rise (and Possible Fall) of a Victor's Peace in Rwanda and Sri Lanka', *Third World Quarterly*, 36(9) (2015), at 1778: 'The RPF has been deeply shaped by ideas of Western and Marxist-Leninist origin about the state, economic development and the transformative mission of political elites'.

[10] A discussion that started with the article of F. Zakaria, 'The Rise of Illiberal Democracy', *Foreign Affairs*, November/December (1997).

and arbitration) work pretty well and also render judgements against the government of Rwanda in commercial matters.

Furthermore, Rwanda wants to play a role in the United Nations, and the President has signed many human rights treaties. The country reports regularly to the Monitoring Groups of the UN in Geneva and promises there to perform better in the future.

In its wish to adjudicate genocide suspects in Rwanda after the International Criminal Tribunal for Rwanda (ICTR) closed down, the country has adapted its criminal legal system in order to meet the international standards.

So the government of Rwanda shows at least some sensitivity to the rule of law and human rights. I will argue that this (admittedly lukewarm) attitude might offer an opening for critical debate and progressive lawyering within the country.

A History of the Rwandan Political Community

Rwanda is a small country, about the size of Belgium, a former colonizer. Unlike many other African countries, Rwanda has a long tradition of a strong central court, probably since 1400. Kings of several dynasties ruled the territory that was acquired via many wars over time. The King, called 'Umwani', possessed political, military and legal (legislative, executive judicial and administrative) powers in the pre-colonial state.[11] So it can be argued that illiberalism has historical traces in Rwanda.

Of old, the Rwandan territory was inhabited by three groups: Hutus, Tutsi and Twa. Traditionally the Hutu majority of around 80 per cent were peasants, the Tutsi minority of 15 per cent were herders, while the Twa counted for about 1 per cent and were mainly bush people.[12] The three groups are of different descent, but they all speak the same language: Kinyarwanda.

There is debate among scholars whether the three categories refer mainly to race, ethnicity, social status or power. There are some external characteristics that differentiate Tutsi from Hutus – such as height, a sharp nose, lighter skin – but after generations of intermarriage between the two groups, these distinctions have blurred. A child becomes a Hutu

[11] J. Vansina, *Antecedents to Modern Rwanda: The Nyiginya Kingdom* (Kampala: Fountain Publishers, 2003).

[12] The Twa are a rather isolated part of the Rwandan population, with little political influence. In present-day Rwanda they are recognized by the government as a vulnerable group, but they play no role in the constitutional issues that are discussed in this paper.

or a Tutsi depending on the background of the father.[13] Hence, in a traditionally polygamous society like Rwanda, one mother could have Hutu and Tutsi children from different men.

But the Hutu–Tutsi divide had also a social and an economic dimension. As one's wealth was determined by the amount of cows that one possessed, the Tutsi herders with big cattle herds were seen as rich. But a Hutu who acquired cows could be 'promoted' to Tutsi status and – reversely – a Tutsi could become a Hutu when he lost his cows.

The Kings were all Tutsi, and before colonialism the Tutsi were clearly the politically and economically dominant group in Rwanda.

During the Berlin Conference of 1890, the European powers decided that Germany would take control over Rwanda and Burundi. The Germans left the existing institutions largely intact, the so-called 'indirect rule' form of colonization.[14]

After World War I, the Versailles Peace Treaty of 1919 assigned Rwanda and Burundi to Belgium, a move that was confirmed by a Mandate of the League of Nations in 1923. The Belgians ruled their territories in the Great Lakes District via a Governor General. The Belgian Parliament and King promulgated the applicable laws.

The Belgians also governed Rwanda via indirect rule: They left the existing power structure intact and ruled the country via the King and the Tutsi-led command structure. The Belgian state and the Catholic Church strengthened the Tutsi domination through an exclusive system of education.

When it became clear during the democratization wave of the 1960s that in a popular vote in Rwanda the Hutu would easily get the majority, Belgium changed its politics radically and started to favour and support the Hutu. The former privileges were from then on granted to the other ethnic group. As a control mechanism, the Belgians had introduced identity cards in which the Hutu/Tutsi identity of the cardholder was determined.

After World War II, the United Nations stimulated the movement towards self-governance and independence. During the so-called social revolution in 1959, the Hutu majority took political power in the country and the monarchy was abolished. The Tutsi part of the population was

[13] M. Mamdani, *When Victims Become Killers. Colonialism, Nativism and the Genocide in Rwanda* (Kampala: Fountain Publishers, 2002), ch. 2

[14] M. Mamdani, *Citizen and Subject. Contemporary Africa and the Legacy of Late Colonialism* (Kampala: Fountain Publishers 1996), pp. 16–17 and ch. 3.

discriminated against and harassed systematically and many of them were killed or had to flee the country.

On 1 July 1962 Rwanda gained independence as a separate state, without having a constitution.

The First Republic (1962–1978)

In 24 November 1962 the first Rwandan Constitution came into force. Article 1 declared Rwanda a democratic, social and sovereign republic. The Constitution has been praised for its complete list of the human rights defined in the Universal Declaration of Human rights. There were no references made to ethnicity. Freedom of religion and expression were recognized, and communist activities and propaganda were prohibited.

Although lip service was paid to political pluralism, President Kayibanda quickly established a single-party system and during the elections in August 1963, he won 98 per cent of the votes. In reality this regime simply replaced the Tutsi domination of the colonial times with a Hutu domination.

In May 1973, the Constitution was amended to allow the President to be elected for an indefinite term, while the economy would be oriented to the principles of democratic socialism.

The Second Republic (1973–1994)

Soon thereafter, on 5 July 1973 General Habyarimana took over the Presidency through a military coup d'état. The new regime instituted a one-party system in which every Rwandan was a party member. The second Constitution became effective on 20 December 1978 after an affirmative popular vote of 99 per cent. The Habyarimana government introduced discriminatory quota systems for schools, universities and government services.

In the 1990s the Habyarimana regime began to lose its grip on the country because of internal political problems between the North and the South, and also because of the civil war that the Tutsi in exile had started, led by the military branch of the Rwandan Patriotic Front (RPF).

In the following years, the tensions in the country grew. Under the new Constitution of 1991 a multi-party system and press freedom were introduced. This was a short period of political liberalization in Rwanda, which ironically paved the way to the genocide.[15] On August 18 1992, the

[15] Piccolino, 'Winning Wars, Building (Illiberal) Peace', 1779.

international community brokered a Peace Accord that was signed in Arusha. It aimed at a fusion of the armies, a transitional government and the prospect of democratic elections.

The Genocide (April 6 until July 17, 1994)

The situation exploded when the plane of President Habyarimana was shot down on 6 April 1994, an event that was immediately followed by a genocide that lasted 100 days.

The international community was not ready to intervene and the UNAMIR Peace-Keeping Unit under the command of Romeo Daillaire was not allowed to fight against the Interahamwe and other death squads.[16]

To make things worse, the French intervened at the end of the genocide with Operation Turquoise, which provide a safe haven for the old government troops that had been trained by the French army before.

The RPF officially put an end to the genocide on 17 July by its own force and took control over the country.

The RPF-Dominated Government (July 1994–Present)

During the first ten years after the genocide, the Rwandan state apparatus had to be reconstructed from scratch. The new government made security and economic development its top priorities. The justice sector was non-existent because there were hardly any lawyers left or available.

The prisons were overcrowded with genocide suspects waiting for a trial.[17] The courts were filled with judges who had not even a bachelor degree in law, and the bar was very small, with many advocates who were inexperienced.

The RPF pledged loyalty to the Arusha Peace Agreement and the 1991 Constitution, which included power sharing in the context of a broad-based transitional government, the establishment of the rule of law and the promise that the armed forces were open to all Rwandans. Political parties that had participated in the genocide were forbidden. There was the general proviso that all of this was subject to 'amendments made necessary by the tragic situation of the country'.[18]

[16] R. Dallaire, *Shake Hands with the Devil: The Failure of Humanity in Rwanda* (London: Arrow Books, 2003).

[17] C. Tertsakian, *Le chateau; The Lives of Prisoners in Rwanda* (London: Arves, 2008).

[18] T. Mulisa, 'The Republic of Rwanda: Commentary' in R. Wolfrum, R. Grote and C. M. Fombad, *Constitutions of the World* (Oxford University Press, 2015), p. 12.

Between 1994 and 2003 the legal basis of the Rwandan government consisted of a set of documents that combined President Habyarimana's 1991 Constitution, the Arusha Peace Agreement, the RPF Declaration and the agreement of political parties, which together formed the Fundamental Law.[19] The government of Rwanda extended the transition period – which was scheduled for 22 months – several times until 2003.

After the genocide, the RPF dominated the political field, although some appearances were kept up. In the words of Filip Reyntjens '[u]nder the labels of "power sharing" and "national unity", which are necessary for international consumption, one discovers a constitutional order allowing the victorious military party to pull the strings'.[20]

For almost ten years the government lacked a solid constitutional basis.[21]

Drafting the Constitution

As required by the Arusha Accords, a constitutional commission was set up in 2000 to draft a new permanent constitution that would adhere to a set of fundamental principles including equitable power sharing and democracy.

The Legal and Judicial and Constitutional Drafting Commission designed a 'home-grown' constitution that was tailored to Rwanda's specific needs. The Commission rejected offers of help from the international community, apart from financial support.[22]

In 2002 the Commission sent thousands of assistants to the countryside with a list of sixty questions with constitutional issues, such as land and marriage. The questionnaires were stored in a database and the data were summarized in a booklet for feedback.

After two months of drafting, the Commission organized a seminar about a Draft that was attended by 800 persons, including some experts from abroad. After some amendments by the transitional Parliament,

[19] *Ibid.*, p. 31.

[20] F. Reyntjens, 'Constitution Making in Situations of Extreme Crisis: The Case of Rwanda and Burundi', *Journal of African Law*, 40(2) (1996), 238.

[21] See for this period the chapter on Rwanda by J. M. Kamatali in J. Oloka-Onyango (ed.), *Constitutionalism in Africa: Creating Opportunities, Facing Challenges* (Kampala: Fountain Publishers, 2001).

[22] P. Y. Ankut, 'The Role of Constitution-Building Processes in Democratization. Case Study Rwanda', IDEA, at: http://idea.int and W. Gasamagera, 'The Constitution Making Process in Rwanda: Lessons to Be Learned', paper presented at the Global Forum for Reinventing Government, Vienna (2007).

a Referendum was held on 26 May 2003 and the Constitution received a support from 93 per cent of the population.

The Constitution of 2003 as Amended in 2015

The Constitution of 2003 was preceded by a Preamble with twelve considerations, while the Constitution itself had 202 articles. This Constitution is the starting point of Rwanda's efforts to build a *Rechtsstaat.*

In 2015 the leadership of the RPF decided that President Kagame's job would not be finished in 2017, the end of his second constitutional term. Hence, a campaign was launched to convince the population that a third term was necessary. The major other political parties supported this strategy, which was aimed to give the outside world the impression that the population begged President Kagame to lead the country for many more years.

On 8 October 2015 the Rwandan Supreme Court had dismissed a constitutional claim of the Green Party that Article 101 of the 2003 Constitution stands in the way of a third term. The Court argued that the people of Rwanda could decide for themselves how they are governed.

On November 17 the Senate approved a new version of the Constitution. The amendments regarded many more issues than only the third term. No time was wasted: on 18 December 2015 the new Constitution received the support of 98 per cent of the population in a referendum.[23]

Hutu–Tutsi in the Constitution

The third section of the new Preamble reads as follows:

> CONSCIOUS of the genocide committed against Tutsi that decimated more than a million sons and daughters of Rwanda, and conscious of the tragic history of our country...

This consideration speaks of the genocide against the Tutsi. Apart from being mentioned here, the Hutu–Tutsi divide has disappeared from the public and legal discourse. With the departure from the ethnic policies of the past, the post-genocide government aimed to overcome the problems that the identity cards and racial quota had caused in the past.

[23] Published in the Official Gazette Nr Special of 24/12/2015.

April is Rwanda's month of mourning, in which the genocide is commemorated, and that is the only time of the year that one could hear the word Tutsi. I have no doubt that the genocide was planned and executed against the Tutsi part of the population and that the slaughter was prepared and guided by Hutu extremists. But I consider 'against the Tutsi' an unfortunate addendum, because many Hutu also lost their lives in that very period.

Some Key Articles of the Constitution

Article 4 defines the Rwandan state as an independent, sovereign, democratic, social and secular Republic, and Article 10 contains the fundamental principles of the Constitution.

1 *prevention and punishment of the crime of genocide,* ***fighting*** *against denial and revisionism of genocide as well as* ***eradication*** *of genocide ideology and all its manifestations*
2 ***eradication of*** *discrimination and divisionism based on ethnicity, region or on any other ground as well as promotion of national unity*

The words that I highlighted in boldface type sound like a declaration of war. The Constitution is a pamphlet under the battle cry 'Never again genocide'. I only found a similar hawkish text in the preamble to the Portuguese Constitution, where the 'fight against fascism' is proclaimed.[24]

The RPF liberated the country by putting an end to the genocide. Divisionism and genocide ideology are seen as the main contributing forces behind the 1994 genocide, and therefore must be vigorously oppressed. The laws based on these principles are heavily criticized because they are so broadly formulated that they also function as a vehicles to stifle free speech and political opposition.[25]

3 *equitable power sharing*

This principle is elaborated in Article 62, Section 2: 'The President of the Republic and the Speaker of the Chamber of Deputies shall not belong to the same political organization', and Section 3: 'No political party can hold more than half of the Cabinet posts'.

[24] P. B. Cliteur and W. Voermans, *Preambules* (Alphen aan de Rijn: Kluwer, 2009), p. 78.
[25] Y.-O. (Nani) Jansen, 'Denying Genocide or Denying Free Speech? A Case Study of the Application of Rwanda's Genocide Denial Laws', *Northwestern Journal of International Human Rights*, 12(2) (2014), 191–213.

4 *building a State governed by the rule of law, a pluralistic democratic Government, equality of all Rwandans and between men and women which is affirmed by women occupying at least thirty per cent (30%) of positions in decision-making organs*

Women's organizations participated actively in the drafting process and they were able to secure some important victories. The Constitution aimed to liberate women from their historical and cultural submissive position. Section 4 of Article 10 guarantees them at least 30 per cent of the seats in public institutions. Many Rwandan households were headed by widows and single mothers after the genocide. Therefore this legal emancipation of women, among others in land and inheritance rights, was also a matter of necessity.[26]

5 *building a State committed to promoting social welfare and establishing appropriate mechanisms for equal opportunity to social justice*
6 *constant quest for solutions through dialogue and consensus*

Here we see a key concept of the political ideology of the RPF, an outright rejection of competitive politics. The language of the Constitution is consociational,[27] like the Arusha Peace Agreements, while in reality there is clear political dominance of the RPF.[28]

The fourth chapter of the Constitution contains many human rights provisions in Articles 12 to 40. The long list looks impressive, but because most of the articles have claw-back clauses and self-limitations,[29] practice is in reality rather restrictive. From the beginning there has been a lot of criticism on the limitations of human rights in Rwanda.[30]

Article 41 stipulates that the promotion of human rights is a responsibility of the state that is particularly exercised via the National Commission for Human Rights, and Article 42 says that the judiciary is the guardian of human rights and freedoms.

A typical Rwandan element of the Constitution is its emphasis on duties of the citizens (Article 48, Section 2). A well-known example is

[26] C. Braeckman, *Rwanda. Milles collines, mille douleurs* (Bruxelles: Editions Nevicata, 2014), p. 51.
[27] A. Lijphart, *Thinking about Democracy. Power Sharing and Majority Rule in Theory and Practice* (New York: Routledge, 2008), Part II *Consociational and Consensus Democracy.*
[28] R. Lemarchand, 'Consociationalism and Power Sharing in Africa: Rwanda, Burundi and the DRC', *African Affairs*, 106/422 (2006), 1–20.
[29] T. Mulisa, 'The Republic of Rwanda', p. 15, see also article 41 of the Constitution.
[30] P. Uvin, 'Rwanda's Draft Constitution: Some Personal Reflections', 14 February 2003 at: http:/opjdr.org/constitution.

Umuganda: on the last Saturday morning of the month, Rwandans have to engage in community work.

Article 57: Political organizations are prohibited from basing themselves on race, ethnic group, tribe, lineage, region, sex, religion or any other division which may lead to discrimination.

This article aims among others to prevent the establishment of a political party along ethnic (majority) lines.

Article 59: The National Consultative Forum of Political Organizations brings together political organizations for the purposes of political dialogue, and building consensus and national cohesion.

This Forum is meant to be the place where the political parties discuss the issues at hand and iron out their differences. Supporters of this model praise the consociational character of the Forum. Critics argue that via this Forum the RPF can impose its will on the other parties behind closed doors.

All political parties participate in the Forum, including the recently registered Green Party, the tiny opposition party without a seat in Parliament. Other oppositional parties like the Rwanda National Congress and FDU operate in the diaspora.

The Legislature

Legislative power is vested in a Parliament consisting of two chambers, the Chamber of Deputies and the Senate.

Deputies are elected by a direct universal suffrage through a secret ballot from a final list of names using the system of proportional representation (Article 75, Section 1). A deputy is supposed to represent the whole nation (Article 65, Section 1), but when he is expelled from his political party, he automatically loses his seat. This implies a strict party discipline.

Parliament has the final say in legislative matters and it can overrule a Presidential veto by a majority of two-thirds in the case of ordinary laws and three-quarters in the case of organic laws (Article 106, Section 3).

Only the Chamber of Deputies can cast a no-confidence vote against a member of the Cabinet. In 2000 the chairman of the Chamber of Deputies, Joseph Sebarenzi, tried to defend the law that gave Parliament oversight of the executive branch, but when he failed to convince Kagame, he had to flee the country.[31]

[31] J. Sebaranzi, *God Sleeps in Rwanda. A Personal Journey of Transformation* (Oxford: One World Publications, 2009).

Article 95 says that the Constitution is at the top of the hierarchy of legal instruments. International treaties must be domesticated in Rwandan law. If a treaty is in conflict with the Constitution, the latter prevails until the Constitution has been changed (Article 170).

The Executive

The President of the Republic is the Head of State.

Article 101 says: *The President of the Republic is elected for a five (5) year term. He or she may be re-elected once.*

However, for the incumbent president Kagame, the new Article 172 says:

> The President of the Republic in office at the time this revised Constitution comes into force continues to serve the term of office for which he was elected. Without prejudice to Article 101 of this Constitution, considering the petitions submitted by Rwandans that preceded the coming into force of this revised Constitution, which were informed by the particular challenges of Rwanda's tragic history and the choice made to overcome them, the progress so far achieved and the desire to lay a firm foundation for sustainable development, a seven (7) year presidential term of office is established and shall follow the completion of the term of office referred to in the first paragraph of this Article. The provisions of Article 101 of this Constitution shall take effect after the seven (7) year term of office referred to in the second paragraph of this Article

This article implies that Kagame not only got his third term of seven years, but that he is also allowed to run for another two terms of 5 year thereafter.

Changing the Head of State from time to time is part of Western liberal constitutional thought, as it is a classical weapon against despotism. The US government and other Western countries are not in favour of constitutional changes that allow incumbent African presidents to stay in power. Samantha Powers, the US Ambassador to the United Nations, and a staunch supporter of the Rwandan government, criticized this move to secure extra terms for Kagame. During a press conference on 2 December 2015 she suggested 'parliamentary manœuvering'.[32] In that period, Federica Mogherini, the High Representative of the EU for Foreign

[32] See www.Afrikareporter.com, December 3, David Matovu, 'Rwanda: *Kagame Says US to Back Off, as Third Term Rift Deepens*'.

Affairs and Security Policy, pointed at Article 23 Sub 5 of the African Charter of Democracy, Elections and Government:[33]

State Parties agree that the use of, inter alia, the following illegal means of accessing or maintaining power constitute an unconstitutional change of government and shall draw appropriate sanctions by the Union:

5. Any amendment or revision of the constitution or legal instruments, which is an infringement on the principles of democratic change of government.

Burundi, the so-called false twin of Rwanda, is facing international sanctions after President Pierre Nkurunziza was sworn in for a contested third term in October 2014. In 2016 President Kabila of DRC is preparing a third term for himself. The presidents Robert Mugabe of Zimbabwe and Yoweri Museveni of Uganda are examples of freedom fighters who liberated their countries, and consider themselves as irreplaceable.

So the project of a third term has actually resulted in three more terms (one extension of seven years and two new terms of five years). If Paul Kagame wishes, he can remain in office until 2034.

The President determines who is nominated as a member of the Cabinet. He picks candidates from all the political parties. The RPF occupies not more than half of the cabinet posts.

The Judiciary

The 2003 Constitution reformed the judiciary considerably. Until 1992 the President of the republic was also the head of the judiciary administrative services, with power to appoint or remove judges.[34]

Originally Rwanda opted for the French cassation system. The Supreme Court was only competent for procedural matters, which led to long-lasting lawsuits and a lot of uncertainty. The 2003 Constitution allowed the Supreme Court to decide cases on the merits and also on the facts.[35] Article 144 of that Constitution introduced the principle of precedent by declaring Supreme Court decisions binding on all parties concerned, including judicial officers.

The system of judicial review was also changed in 2003. Before, the Council of State could exercise *a priori* review, i.e. it could declare a draft law unconstitutional before the draft was enacted as law. Under the 2003

[33] See The East African, 4 December 2015 at http://www.theeastafrican.com.

[34] *Ibid.*, p. 13.

[35] S. Rugege, 'Adopting a New Constitution Was Crucial for National Reconciliation', 17 October 2014, at http://www.verfassungsblog.de.

Constitution, this approach was replaced by *a posteriori* review. If a constitutional issue is raised, the court must refer the case to the Supreme Court.

The President and Vice-President of the Supreme Court are appointed by the President for a not-renewable term of eight years. The President and Vice-President of the High Court and the Commercial High Court are appointed for a period of five years, renewable once. All the other judges are appointed by the High Council of the judiciary. This Council is chaired by the Chief Justice. Only four out of the thirty-two members are appointed from outside the judiciary: the Ombudsman, the President of the national Human Rights Commission and two deans of law schools. The bar and civil society are not represented.

According to Sam Rugege, the current Chief Justice, the Rwandan judiciary is *de jure* independent. The *de facto* independence is harder to establish. He points that the earlier practice that judges had to report to local authorities at the provincial and district levels has been abolished because of a history of attempts to influence judicial decisions. Rugege expressed some concern about the financial autonomy of the judiciary.[36]

The Chief Justice also chairs the Inspectorate of the Courts, the institution that is responsible for the quality of judicial decisions, the education of legal personnel, etc.

Power Relations

The Rwandan model is clearly a presidential system with much power vested in the presidency. For Paul Kagame there is not much difference between leading an army and leading the country. He governs his country with an iron fist and hence Rwanda is governed in a hierarchical and top-down manner. Security of the state is the number-one priority of the President, who is also the Commander-in-Chief of the army and the Head of the Secret Service (SSF).[37]

The Government of Rwanda is praised for its ability to formulate concrete goals for the future[38] and its capacity to actually deliver public services. This sets Rwanda apart from its neighbours.

Since 1994, the RPF has won every election with landslides. Almost all other political parties agree most of the times with almost all of the RPF

[36] S. Rugege, 'Judicial Independence in', *Global Business & Development Law Journal*, 19 (2007), 411–25.

[37] Kagame was also the former head of intelligence in Museveni's army that toppled Obote.

[38] Vision 2020, see the website http://rsb.gov.rw.

policies. The Constitution has some articles that prevent one-party rule, but in practice the RPF is very dominant. The party is well organized at all levels of government and has a firm grip on the citizens.

The President has a clear presence in the legislative sphere.[39] Also, members of the Cabinet can ask to take the floor in Parliament and they can be questioned by its members. Only the Chamber of Deputies can initiate a motion of no confidence in a certain minister.

The President may request Parliament to reconsider a certain law, but his veto can be overruled by a substantive majority vote.

The President has the power to call for a referendum on a certain law (Article 107) and he also has the authority to exercise mercy (Article 109).

Almost all legislation is prepared by the executive, i.e. within the Ministry that is responsible for the underlying policy of the law. Before a draft law is sent to the Cabinet, the Rwandan Law Reform Commission checks the law on legal and linguistic issues.

Separation of Powers?

The Constitution aims at a clear-cut separation of powers. Article 98 Section 2 stipulates that the President is the defender of the Constitution. In the 2003 version he was mentioned as the 'guardian'. It is not clear how this section relates to Article 44, which states that the judiciary is the guardian of rights and freedoms.

Article 96 of the 2003 Constitution stipulated that the authentic interpretation of Laws shall be done by both chambers of Parliament acting jointly after the Supreme Court has given an opinion on the matter. Tom Mulisa criticized this article and argued that it was hard to reconcile a real commitment to human rights if Parliament has the final say in the interpretation of laws.[40] He stated that the legislative organs possess neither the knowledge of human rights jurisprudence nor the effective remedies for breach of these rights.

The new Article 96 takes a step forward where it says that 'authentic interpretation of laws is done by the Supreme Court'. I assume that this new article is also a confirmation of the situation that the Supreme Court is a constitutional court. Article 144 of the 2003 Constitution stipulated that the Supreme Court is the highest court in the country . . . and that its decisions shall be binding on all parties concerned whether organs of the

[39] Mulisa, 'The Republic of Rwanda', p. 22 for some examples.
[40] Mulisa, 'The Republic of Rwanda', *ibid.*, p. 29.

state, public officials, civilians, military, judicial officers or private individuals.

This article – which has been skipped by the 2015 amendments – implied that the Supreme Court is a constitutional court. In only a few cases did the Court declare a law unconstitutional. The best-known example is the striking-down of the Article in the Criminal Code that formulated a tougher punishment for women than for men in case of adultery.[41]

Freedom of Press

Given the malicious role that the media – and especially the radio – played in the genocide,[42] the government has a firm grip on the media. There are no oppositional newspapers or radio programs. The tone of the national media reports is mainly constructive. This sets Rwanda apart from neighbouring countries like Uganda, Kenya and Tanzania, where the Presidents and their governments are openly criticized in the media with a rigor and intensity that is not conceivable in Rwanda.

There is no direct prohibition or permanent censorship of foreign media, although from time to time a foreign news agency is banned, Recently the Kinyarwanda banned the BBC after the international broadcast of the video recording of *Rwanda's Untold Story* on 1 October 2014.

External Criticism

The International Community

The US State Department issues yearly Human rights reports on every country in the world. The 2014 Report on Rwanda, published in May 2015,[43] offers an overview of the concerns of the international community. I summarize the relevant aspects for this analysis.

The state security forces (SSF) operate in a way that is insufficiently checked by the judiciary. Cruel, inhuman or degrading treatment or punishment of prisoners is forbidden in the Constitution, but government

[41] The Morurunkwere Case of 11 January 2008, cited by Mulisa, 'The Republic of Rwanda', p. 15.

[42] A. Thompson (ed.), *The Media and the Rwanda Genocide* (Kampala: Fountain Press, 2007).

[43] US State Department, Bureau of Democracy, Human Rights and Labor, *Human Rights Reports 2014: Rwanda.*

action against abuses is rare. Several political opponents remain in prison after many years. Press freedom is limited and sometimes journalists are harassed. The strict regulation of the elections and the emphasis on harmony make it hard for opposition parties to participate freely in fair elections. In practice, the preventive control of the Rwanda Governance Board is a big hurdle for new parties attempting to enter the political arena.

As a result of these and other shortcomings, Rwanda does not qualify for financial support by the US Millennium Challenge Corporation. Rwanda does not have a prominent place on the scorecards of institutes that measure civil liberties (Freedom House), political rights (Freedom House) and voice and accountability (World Bank Institute).

Academic Criticism

I have not found any positive academic comment on the Rwandan Constitution. Most observers consider it a mere instrument in the hands of the RPF-led government to give the world – especially the donor community – the impression that Rwanda is adhering to liberal political values.

The most vocal and comprehensive critic is Filip Reyntjens,[44] who argues that Paul Kagame is a dictator, that Rwanda applies a form of victor's justice and that the judiciary is not at all an independent third branch.

Reyntjens sees many similarities between the style of leadership by Kagame and those of the King and the presidents Kayibanda and Habyarimana. He also points at the landslide victories that both Kagame and his two predecessors won in fake or rigged elections.

By 'victor's justice', the critics mean that the RPF crimes during and after the genocide, both in Rwanda and in the Democratic Republic of Congo (DRC), have been left unpunished. The Government of Rwanda urged the withdrawal of Prosecutor Carla del Ponte when it became clear that she wanted to prosecute RPF crimes for the ICTR. Until now the well-documented critical report of the Group of Experts about RPF crimes in the refugee camps in DRC has not led to serious legal steps from the international community or the DRC.

The analysis of the critics is that Rwanda has been very successful in exploiting the guilt feelings of the international community because of its

[44] F. Reyntjens, *Political Governance in Post Genocide Rwanda* (New York: Cambridge University Press, 2013).

non-intervention in 1994. As a result, they argue, there is a kind of double standard justice in Rwanda and impunity for the crimes that the Tutsi-led army committed against Hutus. The trial of Victoire Ingabire and the arrest of her attorney are presented as evidence that the Rwandan judiciary is not independent. Critics often warn of a new cycle of violence in Rwanda,[45] and they call the country a sleeping volcano.

Evaluating the Rwandan Illiberal Model

It is clear that a cleavage exists between the human rights ideals formulated in the Rwandan Constitution and their actual realization.

A Poor Human Rights Record

There are many practices in the country that do not qualify as a genuine adherence to the rule of law principles. In terms of freedom of the press and allowing room for legitimate dissent, Rwanda performs poorly.

I can only agree with the critique against the violent actions against political opponents and the harassment of journalists and other critics. The military background of the RPF leadership and its background in the Ugandan secret service and intelligence organizations have led to a political psychology full of paranoia and chronic distrust of the world outside the liberation movement. These are the direct products of years of underground operations before coming to power and explain much of otherwise seemingly overblown actions.[46] It is obvious that Rwanda is not the kind of liberal democracy that some donors pretend to see. The position of the Presidency is overwhelmingly strong and the countervailing powers in the public domain and in civil society are weak. There is indeed continuity between the former regimes and the present government in terms of top-down governance and a submissive electorate.[47]

Also, today it requires a lot of courage to stand up in public against the authorities. Rwanda is not going through a process of transitional justice

[45] See for instance T. Longman, 'Limitations to Political Reform: The Undemocratic Nature of Transition in Rwanda' in S. Straus and L. Waldorff, *Remaking Rwanda; State Building and Human Rights after Mass Violence* (Madison: Wisconsin University Press, 2011), p. 43.

[46] Jones et al., 'Africa's Illiberal State-Builders', 7.

[47] J. M. Kamatali, 'Following Orders in Rwanda', *The New York Times*, 4 April 2014 and C. Braeckman, *Rwanda mille collines, mille douleurs* (Primento, 2014), p. 50.

in which a liberal government is replacing a former authoritarian regime. Rwanda wants to become like Singapore, a country that, according to Mark Tushnet, has opted for a stable form of authoritarian constitutionalism.[48]

However, I cannot concur with the critics that Rwanda is heading towards a new round of violence, let alone a new civil war or genocide.

First, this is due to the strong presence of the police, the army and the secret service in everyday life. This form of physical control is combined with a form of political control. President Kagame and the RPF are winning the hearts and minds of the Rwandans – including the Hutu majority – via sensitization programs, strict media control and image-building of a President who can solve each and every problem.

Second, the present government also has legitimacy in the eyes of many Rwandans because it performs quite well in terms of security, health, education and physical infrastructure. It helps that the government is tough on corruption, also inside the civil service and the police. Furthermore the Rwandan economy is modernizing and growing. These achievements are quite rare in the Great Lakes Region and Kagame c.s. deserve full credit for this.

Third, there are many political systems without term limits. There might be good arguments that Kagame's job is not finished, and that he is presently the only person that is able to control both the political and military forces in the country. On the other hand, it is not without risk that there is no second-in-command in the RPF elite. What will happen if the President dies? Rwanda needs strong institutions and not only the strong personality of its leader.

'Never Again'

The Rwandan government is determined to restore a country that was plunged into the abyss of genocide in which a majority group was exhorted to kill all the minority neighbours in broad daylight. The victors are in charge now and they have banned the Hutu–Tutsi dichotomy from the public discourse.

At first glance it seems to open the door for equality before the law. Non-ethnic policies are a clear break from the heinous quota politics of

[48] M. Tushnet, 'Authoritarian Constitutionalism', *Cornell Law Review*, 100 (2015), 391 and also G. Silverstein, 'Singapore's Constitutionalism: A Model, But of What Sort?', *Cornell Law Review Online*, 23 (2015), who quotes the former leader of Singapore Lee who said in 1992, 'A country must first have economic development, then democracy will follow'.

the Habyarimana regime. It is laudable that vacancies for government jobs are filled on the basis of merits.

But the proclaimed irrelevance of the Hutu–Tutsi dichotomy denies part of the identity of the Rwandans, who know from each other who is Hutu and who is Tutsi. It is clear to insiders that Tutsi dominate the political and business classes.[49] The shift towards the mandatory use of English in education, for instance, clearly favoured the Tutsi who grew up in Uganda. It is nearly impossible for a Hutu to file a discrimination complaint against the government or an employer, because one is not allowed to define oneself in that category.

But we cannot ignore the reality of Rwandan politics. How could the new government in 1994 adhere to a majoritarian form of democracy in the aftermath of a genocide in which the majority almost completely eradicated the minority? The fight against genocide ideology and divisionism was and is a serious business, which should not be underestimated.

The *Forces Democratiques de liberation du Rwanda* (FDLR), composed of a group of genocidaires that wants to topple the regime in Kigali by force, is operating not too far from the borders. Grenade attacks take place regularly on Rwandan soil. Many leaders of the genocide who were convicted by the ICTR showed no remorse. This can be seen as a sign that the genocide ideology is still alive in some circles (probably also inside Rwanda).

Rwanda's obsession with security issues and its vigilant oppression of ethnic discourse can be explained and – to a certain extent – also be justified by its recent past and the damage that racist discourse has caused in the country. Rwanda lives under the threat of a counter-majoritarian danger that requires serious consideration.

Illiberal Liberators

The illiberal state model is a local invention and not imposed on Rwanda by colonial or international powers. The illiberal prism enables us to analyse the attempts of former illegal liberators to build a strong and modern state after they have seized power and have become legitimate leaders. The ruling elite has won popular support by providing security, economic progress and a performing state that is tough on corruption and delivers education, health and infrastructure. Rwanda still is one of

[49] D. Booth and F. Golooba-Mutebi, 'Developmental Patrimonialism? The Case of Rwanda', *African Affairs*, 111/444 (2012), 379–404.

the poorest countries in the world, but many Rwandans have been alleviated from poverty. Unlike in some neighbouring countries, the Rwandan government shows that donors' money is well spent and is not channelled to Swiss bank accounts.

The government of Rwanda has described its goals very clearly in Vision 2020. This blueprint is an expression of a technocratic 'hypermodernity' in which Rwanda's economy is transformed from subsistence farming into a services and IT hub, which includes a massive migration of the population from the countryside and the hills to the cities.

Performance contracts (*imihigo*) are used at all levels of the administration, which leads to a considerable bureaucracy. In its exaggeration it results sometimes in a new kind of Stalinism. Unrealistic and undesirably high production targets, such as a 100 per cent conviction rate by the prosecution, lead to all kinds of strategic behaviour and shadow boxing.

The Rwandan government wants to hold every Rwandan accountable, but Bert Ingelaere has demonstrated that this does not mean that leaders are accountable vis-à-vis the citizens, but on the contrary, citizens must report to their leaders about their behaviour.[50]

Furthermore the government stimulates patriotism and self-reliance as part of their nation-building efforts.

The fast forward movements of the country coincide with the re-evaluation of some traditional Rwandan values. One of the most striking examples was the reinvention of the old grassroots dispute resolution system *Gacaca* to handle the massive amount of genocide cases.[51] The objective of these courts of lay judges was truth finding, the speeding up of genocide trials, contributing to the national unity and reconciliation process and demonstrating the capacity of Rwanda to resolve its own problems. In a period of ten years almost 2 million cases were handled.[52]

Gacaca was heavily criticized by human rights organizations,[53] but some academics came to a positive evaluation.[54] Another form of justice

[50] B. Ingelaere, 'The Ruler's Drum and the People's Shout: Accountabliity and Representation on Rwanda's Hill', in Straus and Waldorf (eds.), *Remaking Rwanda*, pp. 87–97.

[51] F. Reyntjens, 'Le gacaca ou la justice du gazon au Rwanda', *Politique Africaine*, 40 (1990), 31–41.

[52] National Service of *Gacaca* Courts, Summary of the Report presented at the closing of Gacaca courts activities, Kigali (2012).

[53] Human Rights Watch, *Justice Compromised. The Legacy of Rwanda's Community-Based* Gacaca *Courts* (New York: Human Rights Watch, 2011).

[54] P. Clark, *The* Gacaca *Courts, Post-Genocide Justice and Reconciliation in Rwanda: Justice without Lawyers* (New York: Cambridge University Press, 2010).

without lawyers has been introduced since 2006 for ordinary conflicts among citizens. Rwandans must first present their case before a local committee of *Abunzi* before they can go to court. These mediators are volunteers, but their work has a legal status and they are quite successful in keeping cases away from the court system. The Abunzi are elected by members of the local community and their activities have been evaluated.[55]

The liberators are not interested in establishing procedures that have the possibility of bringing the defeated enemies back in power. In lieu of adversarial or competitive politics the illiberal liberators prefer the image of consensus politics so they can control the political process behind closed doors.

The device of strong legal institutions that could restrain government was not a priority of the founders of the illiberal state. Some of the restrictions of the Arusha Peace Accords were respected, but the RPF was successful in extending the transition period until 2003, so in the meantime it could lay the foundations for a state of their own design.

Like South Africa, Rwanda is a 'dominant party democracy'.[56] Well-prepared and controlled elections without any meaningful opposition invariably result in landslide victories by the RPF and serve to legitimize the political status quo, led by a very strong President.

A Security State

The RPA, led by Paul Kagame, was the military branch of the RPF that fought the liberation war and put an end to the genocide. The well-trained and organized military played an important role in the reconstruction of post-genocide Rwanda. The 'struggle' remains part of the political psychology of the liberators, including the belief in violence as a legitimate means of escaping from political impasse, and chronic mistrust of 'the enemy'.[57]

55 See M. Mutisi, 'Local Conflict Resolution in Rwanda: The Case of Abunzi Mediators' in M. Mutisi and K. Sansculotte-Greenidge (eds.), *Integrating Traditional and Modern Conflict Resolution: Experiences from Selected Cases in Eastern and the Horn of Africa*, Africa Dialogue Monograph series 2/2012, ACCORD, Durban, South Africa, ch. 2, and RCN Justice & Democratie, R. de Witte and A-A. Pohu, 'Mediation in Rwanda: Conceptions and Realities of Abunzi Justice (2011–2014)', *Proximity Justice in Rwanda*, Vol. 3 (2015).

56 See the chapter by De Vos in this volume.

57 In Jones et al., 'Africa's Illiberal State-Builders', 8; compare the friend-enemy distinction in C. Schmitt, *The Concept of the Political* (1932), Dutch translation: (Amsterdam: Boom/Parresia, 2001).

The Rwandan army under the leadership of General James Kabarebe was instrumental in toppling Mobutu.[58] Here the Rwandan Defence Forces (RDF) earned their nickname 'soldiers without borders'. Rwanda became involved in several peace-keeping operations in regional trouble spots where donors have a key strategic interest, but are reluctant to deploy soldiers themselves: 'African solutions for African problems'.[59] The FDLR in the Kivus is a real external threat to Rwanda's security as its political goal is to overthrow Kagame c.s., and also via its grenade attacks within the borders of Rwanda.

So the army is an important political force in Rwanda. The military is under the control of the RPF and Kagame is the Commander-in-Chief. From time to time military defectors who were close to His Excellency have had to flee the country, and they often join the ranks of the diaspora opposition, the Rwandan National Congress.

One of the delicate tasks of the Rwandan leadership is to integrate the military into society and curb the threat of a military coup. Some older generals might feel that their role as liberator is not well appreciated any more.

Part of the International Community

One of the wake-up calls of Paul Kagame to his fellow Rwandans is that they are not living in isolation on their hill, but that Rwanda is part of the global community. The country has opened itself for foreign investors and is proud to be one of the most attractive countries in which to do business. The country is small, landlocked and not endowed with many natural resources, so the government has deliberately chosen to become a member of some supranational organizations.

The EAC and the Commonwealth

For economic reasons Rwanda has opened itself to the East. Together with Burundi, in 2009 the country joined the East African Community (EAC), which then consisted of Tanzania, Kenya and Uganda, three former English colonies. The EAC mirrors itself to the European Union, as its wants to become one single market without internal borders. There are

[58] G. Prunier, *From Genocide to Continental War. The 'Congolese' Conflict and the Crisis of Contemporary Africa* (London: Hurst, 2011), ch. 6.

[59] J. Fisher and D. M. Anderson, 'Authoritarianism and the Securization of Development in Africa', *International Affairs*, 91 (2015), 131–51.

heated political debates about mutual recognition, tax harmonization, one currency and approximation of laws. The EAC is still in its infancy because it is not easy for the five heads of state to give up part of their sovereignty. For Rwanda the EAC promises one much bigger market and direct access to the sea.

Rwanda also gained access to the Commonwealth, although it is not a former British colony. Rwanda is also in the process of embracing the common law tradition, as it is the preferred legal regime of the international business community. But because the basics of the legal system are laid down by Belgium, a civil law country, Rwanda's legal situation has become a cocktail of civil and common law elements with the addition of some flavours of local legal values. As a result Rwanda has a hybrid legal system.

The African Union

Rwanda is also a member of the African Union, a 'Panafrican' organization,[60] which sometimes plays a political role in solving local conflicts. Rwanda has sent troops to South Sudan as part of the peacekeeping mission of the African Union. And when Rwanda was competing in 2012 for a seat in the Security Council of the UN, it received the backing of all the members of the African Union.

The United Nations

Rwanda has developed a double-bind relationship with the United Nations. During the genocide, Rwanda had a seat in the Security Council and the Habyarimana regime did everything to downplay the seriousness of the situation in the country.

After the genocide, the new government held the UN responsible for its lack of intervention, despite the clear signals from Romeo Dallaire, the UNAMIR commander on the ground. The genocide in Rwanda became a black page on the CV of Kofi Anan, who was responsible for UN peacekeeping operations in 1994.

Another point of contention was the venue for the ICTR, the International Criminal Tribunal for Rwanda. The UN did not want to situate this high-profile court in Rwanda, in fear of partial justice and lack

[60] A. Y. Abdulqawi, 'Pan-Africanism and International law', *The Hague Academy of International Law*, AIL Pocket, (2014), ch. 4.

of security. Rwanda wanted ownership of the legal procedures about the crimes that were committed on its territory. At the end of the day, Rwanda was the only country that voted against Arusha, Tanzania as the place of residence of the ICTR. In the years that followed, Rwanda put a lot of effort into criticizing and discrediting the Tribunal and often refused to cooperate with the ICTR in hearing Rwandan witnesses.

The third conflict between Rwanda and the UN arose from the investigations into alleged war crimes by Rwandan soldiers in the DRC in the period after the genocide. Several reports of experts documented large-scale atrocities and mass graves with hundreds of thousands of Hutus, allegedly committed by Rwandan soldiers in the refugee camps in the Kivus. In a highly politicized context – the double-genocide theory – the Rwandan diplomacy has been successful to date in preventing high-ranking members of the Rwandan government from being brought to justice.

The same holds true for the Group of Experts that in 2012 and 2013 investigated the role of Rwanda in supporting M23, a Tutsi rebel group that for a short period of time conquered the city of Goma in North Kivu. Rwanda challenged the integrity of the Chairman of the committee. Apart from some temporary suspension of donor money, the report did not lead to political sanctions against Kigali.

M23 was disarmed by the Congolese army and UN troops in December 2013 and one of its former leaders, Bosco Ntaganda, will probably be on trial in 2016 before the ICC in The Hague. It will be interesting to hear what he has to tell the Court about his ties with the regime in Kigali.

Rwanda is a signatory of most of the treaties of the UN and its affiliated organizations. The country reports regularly about the implementation of its obligations under these treaties. Rwanda also hosts convicted war criminals from Sierra Leone, and shows the international community that Mpanga prison meets the high international standards.

Many African countries are questioning the legitimacy of the ICC, which African leaders recently started to describe as an arena for a white witch-hunt, because only African leaders appear there. Leaders of powerful states like the United States, Russia and China and their client states cannot be required to appear in The Hague for their alleged war crimes. The status of international law as an effective mechanism in the fight against impunity for war crimes and crimes against humanity is heavily debated, because of its selective application.

But as long as Africa does not offer 'African solutions for the African problem of impunity', the criticism is at least half-hearted, because Africa has a tradition of mass violence and cruelties that should not last forever. Filip Reyntjens writes that Paul Kagame is 'probably the worst war criminal in office today'.[61]

But the international human rights community cannot turn a blind eye to the reverse effects that ICC procedures have on the stability in the region, as the Kenyatta/Rutto case clearly shows. These leaders were elected in 2012, during which the issue of their role in the 1997 post-election violence was openly debated. Obviously, there are no easy answers in these delicate instances where justice and politics clash.

Rwanda wants to play a role at the highest levels in the international community. So winning a seat in the Security Council in 2012 and the prestige that is attached to it was a big victory for Kigali. Its critics maintained that from this strategic position Rwanda could block any direct action by the UN against its activities in the DRC.

Rwanda is a very poor country and is heavily dependent on foreign aid. About half of the public budget comes from international donors. Because the internal national opposition is very weak, many commentators argue that the international donor community must use donor money as a lever to move in the direction of a true democracy. Until now the Government of Rwanda has been remarkably successful in resisting these attempts.

The Rwandan government is very clever in exploiting the guilt feelings of the superpowers, who did nothing during the genocide and therefore do not have the legitimacy now to criticize the present government.

In Conclusion

Most discussions about Rwanda are extremely polarized. There is wide gap between the self-congratulations of the Rwandan government, its supporters and donors on the one hand,[62] and the foreign academic critics and Rwandans in the Oppositional Diaspora on the other hand.[63]

[61] Reyntjens, *Political Governance*, p. 254

[62] See P. Crisafulli and A. Redmond, *Rwanda, Inc.; How a Devastated Nation Became an Economic Model for the Developing World* (New York: Palgrave McMillan, 2012) and P. D. Habumuremyi, a former Prime Minister, *Rwanda: Building a Model Nation State* (Bogota: American University of Nigeria, 2013).

[63] G. Gahima, *Transitional Justice in Rwanda: Accountability for Atrocities* (Abingdon: Routledge, 2012) a former Rwandan top legal official, and for academic criticism, see the contributions in Straus and Waldorf, *Remaking Rwanda*.

The defenders of the regime are eager to point at the progress that is being made in terms of the abolition of the death penalty, the successes of *Gacaca*, the full package of human rights treaties and the improvements of the performance of the institutions in the justice sector. The opposing camp is convinced that all these actions are deliberate manipulations of Kagame c.s. to hide the dismal human rights situation on the ground in order to guarantee that the donor monies keep pouring in.

Both extreme positions are untenable, and I try to situate myself somewhere in the middle as a 'critical friend'. It simply is not true that Rwanda is already a fully fledged *Rechtsstaat*, and neither can it be maintained seriously that Paul Kagame is a traditional dictator who is only interested in oppressing the majority of the Rwandan population for his own benefit.

Rwanda lacks a strong democratic and constitutional tradition. The present government is not chosen by the Rwandan demos, but became rulers after they won a civil war. The political elites rule a population that is to a large extent poor and illiterate. The government sensitizes the population to adhere to values that the elite groups think are important. They educate large segments of the population and teach them how they must change their behaviour in order to realize the goals of Vision 2020. Unfortunately this blueprint of Rwanda's future does not contain a reference to the Constitution or the rule of law.

The priorities of the country are clearly – and for good reasons – of a material nature: reducing poverty through economic growth and making sure that the security of the state and its citizens is guaranteed. Illiberal peace-building sacrifices individual freedoms, but can in some cases secure negative peace in the form of stability and abatement of armed violence.[64]

I agree with Omar Mcdoom that an important new step in the development of Rwanda would be the opening of political space,[65] especially for legitimate dissent. In the present political climate, criticism, especially in sensitive ethnic issues, is too easily discredited and labelled as divisionism or genocide ideology.[66] Combined with a strict media law, the policies of the prohibition of ethnic identification in the public sphere

[64] Piccolino, 'Winning Wars, Building (Illiberal) Peace', 1781.

[65] O. S. McDoom, 'Rwanda's Exit Pathway from Violence: A Strategic Assessment', working paper, World Development Report: Background Case Study, 62054, available at: http://eprints.lse.ac.uk/36291/.

[66] Kinyarwanda language seems to have no word for positive criticism.

run the risk of creating resentment in the Hutu part of the population if they have no avenues to voice their grievances.

The international community can help by urging the Democratic Republic of Congo and MONUSCO to neutralize the armed remnants of the FDLR in the Kivu. It is crucial that this external military threat to Rwanda's security cease to exist. That might convince the Rwandan leadership to loosen the strict and restrictive security measures and open the constitutional space[67] for more political freedom.

The Role of Lawyers in an Illiberal State

I would like to conclude with a suggestion of how lawyers can help to give meaning and societal impact to the many rights of the Rwandan Constitution. The Rwandan legal community must emancipate itself from the classical Belgian civil law tradition in which judges just apply the laws that the politicians have made. In that vision the law is an instrument in the hands of the executive and legislative branches.

The transitional justice paradigm with its optimistic worldview that post-conflict societies have a tendency to move in a democratic and liberal direction is not very helpful in terms of increasing understand of the legal development of Rwanda.[68] I have found inspiration in the 'legal complex'[69] approach that has been applied in some third-world countries.

I advocate for an active role for lawyers and legal professions and institutions to create more room for dissent and critique inside Rwanda's illiberal state. This approach departs from the technocratic legal development rhetoric, and builds upon the tradition of lawyers with a public calling. Motivated lawyers can use the legal arena as a forum where the struggle for a moderate state and political freedoms for the citizens can be discussed in public. In my valedictory lecture at Erasmus School of Law I argued earlier that this approach is viable for Rwanda.[70]

[67] See G. Silverstein, 'Globalization and the Rule of Law: A Machine that Runs by Itself?' *International Journal of Constitutional Law*, 1 (2003), at 442 for the background of this concept.

[68] P. Clark and Z. D. Kaufman (eds.), *After Genocide. Transitional Justice, Post-Conflict Reconstruction and Reconciliation in Rwanda and Beyond* (London: Hurst & Company, 2008).

[69] T. Halliday, L. Karpik and M. Feely (eds.), *Fighting for Political Freedom. Comparative Studies of the Legal Complex and Political Liberalism* (Portland: Hart, 2007), ch. 1.

[70] N. Huls, *Rwanda: een rechtsstaat in de mist. Een rechtssociologische analyse* (The Hague: Boom juridische Uitgevers, 2015) (Dutch).

In the fast-changing modern world, the role of courts has become more oriented towards the needs of society. Highest courts in particular are partners in the creation of a strong and effective legal order in which the rights of citizens are protected AGAINST the state and especially state actors like the secret service and the police.[71]

The Rwandan Constitution is a text that meets the international standards. The President has signed many treaties that aim to strengthen the rule of law and human rights in Rwanda. At the international level, the state has pledged to guarantee the full package of legal protection of its citizens. But that is only a first step towards making the ideals of the laws and treaties into a living reality inside Rwanda.

It would be good if the Constitution did not remain a sleeping beauty, but instead gained political prominence and salience and got a place in Rwanda's guide for the future. The Rwandan Constitution is a young document that has not yet resulted in a lively constitutional culture or debate. This can be partly explained by a lack of a vibrant constitutional tradition in which the other two branches of government are taught that their actions are restricted by the power of the highest court. Traditionally the executive, be it the King or President Habyarimana, did not see itself as bound by judicial decisions.

Article 96 of the amended Constitution stipulates that the Supreme Court has the final say in the interpretation and application of the Constitution. This opens the door for courageous advocates and judges to challenge government practices that do not meet rule of law and human rights principles. Article 3, Section 2 is clear: *Any law, decision or act contrary to the Constitution is without effect.*

The Supreme Court is well placed to lead the public discourse in the direction that it has the final say in the meaning of the law and the Constitution. The executive must be taught that a restriction of their powers is in the interest of the Rwandan citizens. This lesson will not be swallowed easily by the RPF-leadership, and the realization of this task requires skilful and authoritative judicial leadership.[72]

Furthermore, the members of the Rwanda Bar Association must advocate for more room for aggressive lawyering in constitutional cases that challenge government actions to the court. The RBA seems to be too

[71] A. Friedman, 'Kagame's Rwanda: Can an Authoritarian Development Model Be Squared with Democracy and Human Rights?', *Oregon Review of Human Rights*, 14 (2012), 272.

[72] N. Huls, 'Introduction: From Legitimacy to Leadership', in N. Huls, M. Adams and J. Bomhoff (eds.), *The Legitimacy of Highest Courts' Rulings. Judicial Deliberations and Beyond* (The Hague: T.M.C. Asser Press, 2009), p. 28ff.

closely linked to the government and does not claim an adversarial position for its members.

A self-assured bar is necessary to contribute to a vibrant constitutional culture in Rwanda. Independent advocates who are not afraid to challenge unconstitutional government practices in court are a much-needed driving factor. The Rwandan Bar Association can learn a lot from the Ugandan, Kenyan and Tanzanian Law Societies that are not afraid to advocate aggressively against their governments, when human rights are at stake. These umbrella organizations must protect their members from government interference and also explain the role of the advocate to the general public. A lawyer who vigorously defends a suspect in a criminal case is not obstructing the course of justice, but protects his client against the state.

Legal academia is also a vital part of the legal complex, where it is a breeding place for critical and independent thinking. The legal education in Rwanda still suffers from the formalistic Belgian civil law heritage. The step towards a more open and policy-oriented curriculum has not yet been made in full. Therefore is it necessary that the law faculty of the University of Rwanda develop critical courses on public interest litigation and constitutional law. The future generations of law graduates must gain knowledge and skills to use the law for the effective protection of human rights. Professionally and critically educated lawyers can assist citizens in their struggle for more political freedom. The many human rights that are mentioned in the Rwandan Constitution are waiting to be activated and implemented.

8

Between Promise and Practice: Constitutionalism in South Africa More Than Twenty Years after the Advent of Democracy

PIERRE DE VOS

Introduction

When South Africa became a democracy in 1994 I was a young lecturer eager to learn more about the new Constitution.[1] At the time I truly believed that the newly adopted Constitution would change *everything*, by which I mean that I believed that judges of the Constitutional Court would interpret and apply the provisions of the Constitution in a manner that would help to alter the political culture (facilitating a move towards a more open, transparent and democratically accountable government) and would transform South African into a more equal and caring society in which the human dignity of all would be respected and protected. Unaware that a newly established Constitutional Court in a transitional society with a dominant governing party would face challenges regarding its institutional security – its capacity to resist real or threatened attacks on its independence[2] – and that such a Court may pragmatically choose to show a certain deference to the elected branches of government in order to try and protect its institutional security, I imagined that the Court would play a decisive role in the radical transformation of South Africa into a flourishing, and more egalitarian, democracy. I also contended at the time that law was an instrument of power and that power, in the Foucauldian sense, was productive: it contributed to the

[1] Constitution of the Republic of South Africa, Act 200 of 1993, which was an 'interim' Constitution replaced by the 'final' Constitution in 1996 (The Constitution of the Republic of South Africa, 1996).

[2] T. Roux, 'Principle and Pragmatism on the Constitutional Court of South Africa', *International Journal on Constitutional Law*, 7 (2009), 109.

production of reality.[3] Following this insight, I argued that a Constitution – interpreted and applied by an independent and progressive Constitutional Court – would be a powerful tool through which a set of norms would be produced which would have both disciplining and emancipatory possibilities. A Constitution, I argued, not only sets out the legal rules according to which a country must be governed, but also creates a normative framework, which helps to shape the way in which democratic politics function.[4] A successful democratic Constitution does not only create institutions (legislatures, executives and a judiciary) which operate openly and democratically and provide for a system in which each institution checks the exercise of power by the other, it also helps to establish a democratic culture which enables these institutions to operate optimally and to not be captured and hollowed out.

Twenty years later much has changed in South Africa and the lives of most ordinary citizens are indeed better than under the racist, oppressive, authoritarian rule of the apartheid regime. Yet, it is not clear that the norms contained in the Constitution have had the decisive salutary effect on the manner in which democratic politics are conducted in South Africa. The Constitutional Court is, arguably, not as institutionally secure as it should be and its impact on South African life is perhaps less decisive than I had imagined it would be. There remains a gap between the establishment of a different, more people-centred, more transparent, responsive, and more accountable, type of politics promised by the Constitution and the manner in which political contestation actually happens in South Africa. The electoral dominance of the former liberation movement,[5] the electoral system of pure proportional representation which strengthens party leaders vis-à-vis elected

[3] M. Foucault, *Discipline and Punish: The Birth of the Prison* (New York: Pantheon, 1977), p. 194; P. de Vos, 'The Constitution Made Us Queer: The Sexual Orientation Clause in the South African Constitution and the Emergence of Gay and Lesbian Identity', in D. Herman and C. Stychin (eds.), *Sexuality in the Legal Arena* (London: Athlone Press, 2000), p. 199.

[4] De Vos, 'The Constitution', pp. 199–200.

[5] The governing ANC has won every single national election held since the advent of democracy with an overwhelming mandate. In 1994 it obtained 62.65 per cent of the votes, in 1999 66.35 per cent, in 2004 69.69 per cent, in 2009 65.90 per cent, and in 2014 62.15 per cent of the votes. See S. Issacharoff, *Fragile Democracies: Contested Power in the Era of Constitutional Courts* (Cambridge University Press, 2015), pp. 246, 255. However, in the 2016 local government election the ANC's electoral support dropped sharply and the party obtained only 53.91 per cent of the total votes cast. See Independent Electoral Commission Results Dashboard accessed on 10 September 2016 at https://www.elections.org.za/LGEDashBoard2016.

representatives,[6] the initial demobilisation or co-optation of civil society groups and the centralising impulses of the dominant party have all been identified as factors which have inhibited the deepening of democracy.[7] Moreover, the political system and culture have not been entirely successful in producing the more egalitarian society in which the human dignity of all South Africans are equally respected and protected. In this chapter, I describe the transformative nature of the 1996 Constitution and the normative framework contained in it, point out the challenges created for the Constitutional Court in its interpretation and enforcement of the constitutional norms, show how the promise of the Constitution has not been met and conclude with some tentative suggestions about why I believe this has been the case and how it could be addressed.

South Africa's 1996 Constitution: Establishing a Transformative Vision

South Africa's 1996 Constitution, adopted by the Constitutional Assembly in 1996, creates a sovereign democratic state founded on the values of human dignity and the advancement of equality, non-racialism and non-sexism, the supremacy of the Constitution, the rule of law, universal adult suffrage and a multiparty system of democracy in which free and fair elections are held regularly with the aim of establishing a system of accountability, responsiveness and openness.[8] It is thus avowedly a document with a strong normative content. The Constitutional Court has said that it is a values-based Constitution,

[6] R. M. Mattes, 'South Africa: Democracy without the People?', *Journal of Democracy*, 13(2002), 22–36; P. de Vos and W. Freedman (eds.), *South African Constitutional Law in Context* (Oxford University Press, 2014), pp. 66–7.

[7] P. Heller, 'Moving the State: The Politics of Democratic Decentralization in Kerala, South Africa, and Porto Alegre', *Politics and Society*, 29 (2001), 134.

[8] Section 1 reads:

> 'The Republic of South Africa is one, sovereign, democratic state founded on the following values:
> (a) Human dignity, the achievement of equality and the advancement of human rights and freedoms.
> (b) Non-racialism and non-sexism.
> (c) Supremacy of the constitution and the rule of law.
> (d) Universal adult suffrage, a national common voters roll, regular elections and a multi-party system of democratic government, to ensure accountability, responsiveness and openness'.

which, like the German Constitution, contains 'an objective, normative value system'.[9] The adoption of the text has been described as a 'constitutional revolution'.[10] Parliamentary sovereignty has been replaced by constitutional sovereignty and the Constitution is now the supreme law of the Republic and law or conduct inconsistent with it is invalid, and the obligations imposed by it must be fulfilled (section 2). It contains a detailed Bill of Rights that sets out a list of civil, political, social and economic rights and that places both a negative and a positive obligation on the state and – in some cases – a further obligation on private individuals and institutions, to respect, protect, promote and fulfil the rights in this Bill of Rights (section 7(2)).

The Constitution was written in response to the social, economic and political history of South Africa and is often described as a transformative Constitution,[11] a document committed to social, political, legal and economic *transformation* of the country and its political and legal culture. The transformative nature of the South African Constitution has been confirmed in several judgements of the Constitutional Court.[12]

9 *Carmichele v Minister of Safety and Security* (CCT 48/00) [2001] ZACC 22; 2001 (4) SA 938 (CC); 2001 (10) BCLR 995 (CC) (16 August 2001) para. 54. In the *Carmichelle* case the Court quoted German Federal Constitutional Court as follows:

> The jurisprudence of the Federal Constitutional Court is consistently to the effect that the basic right norms contain not only defensive subjective rights for the individual but embody at the same time an objective value system which, as a fundamental constitutional value for all areas of the law, acts as a guiding principle and stimulus for the legislature, executive and judiciary.

See, *BVerfGE* 39, 1 at 41. See also *Du Plessis and Others* v *De Klerk and Another* [1996] ZACC 10; 1996 (3) SA 850 (CC); 1996 (5) BCLR 658 (CC) at para. 94.

10 L. W. H., 'The Legal Nature of the South African Constitutional Revolution', *New Zealand Law Review*, 4 (2004), 633.

11 D. Davis and K. Klare 'Transformative Constitutionalism and the Common and Customary Law', *South African Journal on Human Rights*, 26 (2010), 403; K. Klare, 'Legal Culture and Transformative Constitutionalism', *South African Journal on Human Rights*, 14 (1998), 146; A. Chaskalson, 'The Third Bram Fischer Lecture: Human Dignity as a Foundational Value of Our Constitutional Order', *South African Journal on Human Rights*, 16 (2000), 193; P. Langa, 'Transformative Constitutionalism', *Stellenbosch Law Review*, 17(2006), 35; D. Moseneke, 'Transformative Constitutionalism: Its Implications for the Law of Contract', *Stellenbosch Law Review*, 20 (2009), 3; M. Pieterse, 'What Do We Mean When We Talk about Transformative Constitutionalism?', *South African Public Law*, 20 (2005), 155.

12 *Mkontwana* v *Nelson Mandela Metropolitan Municipality* 2005 (2) BCLR 150 (CC) para. 81; *Soobramoney* v *Minister of Health* (KwaZulu-Natal) 1997 (12) BCLR 1696 (CC) para. 8; *Investigating Directorate: Serious Economic Offenses* v *Hyundai Motor Distributors (Pty) Ltd: In re: Hyundai Motor Distributors (Pty) Ltd* v *Smit NO* 2000 (10) BCLR 1079 (CC) para. 21. South African constitutionalism thus attempts to transform society *from* one

Exactly how the end product of this metamorphosis should look and when, if ever, it will be achieved must necessarily remain uncertain and dependent on the outcomes of this continuous interaction, but should simultaneously not be conceived as so vague as to preclude meaningful and deliberate participation in the process.[13] Unlike traditional liberal constitutions which are said to authorise, regulate and check the exercise of public power, but supposedly allow voters and politicians to decide in which direction a society will move and at what pace that movement will occur, the South African Constitution is said to contain a commitment to creating a society that would look fundamentally different from the one that existed at the time when the Constitution was being drafted. When interpreting the text of the Constitution it is therefore necessary to look both backward and forward. There was a need to look backwards at the history of South Africa and to ask what negative aspects of our past this document aimed to address and to transform, to what extent the transformation was required and at what pace. At the same time, the document also signals a tentativeness, suggesting that it is a permanent work-in-progress, always looking forward, always subject to revision and improvement to try to achieve the society envisaged by the Constitution.[14]

This vision of the transformative nature of the Constitution is at least partly derived from the text of the Constitution itself, a text which acknowledges that the new dispensation arose in a particular historical context and requires an acknowledgement of the effects of past and ongoing injustice. The notion that the Constitution is a transformative document is also captured by referring to it as a 'postliberal' document because, so it is said, while the Constitution contains many provisions that mirror provisions in other constitutions in liberal democracies (such as the

deeply divided by the legacy of a racist and unequal past, *into* one based on democracy, social justice, equality, dignity and freedom (Davis 1999, p 44; *S* v *Makwanyane and Another* (CCT3/94) [1995] ZACC 3; 1995 (6) BCLR 665; 1995 (3) SA 391; [1996] 2 CHRLD 164; 1995 (2) SACR 1 (6 June 1995) para. 262.

[13] H. Botha and J. van der Walt, 'Democracy and Rights in South Africa: Beyond a Constitutional Culture of Justification', *Constellations*, 7 (2000), 341–62.

[14] See particularly Articles 1, 7. The Constitution's historically situated character has been recognized in several Constitutional Court judgements. See, for example, *Azanian People's Organization* v *President of the RSA* 1996 (8) BCLR 1015 (CC) para. 50 ('constitutional journey from the shame of the past to the promise of the future'); para. 42 ('[w]hat the Constitution seeks to do is to facilitate the transition to a new democratic order'). See also P. de Vos, 'A Bridge Too Far? History as Context in the Interpretation of the South African Constitution', *South African Journal on Human Rights*, 17 (2001), 1–33.

US Constitution), it also departs from liberalism as it envisages a move towards an 'empowered' model of democracy.[15] The transformative or 'postliberal' nature of the South African Constitution manifests itself with reference to several unique characteristics of the document which were first highlighted by Karl Klare: it is social, redistributive, caring, positive, at least partly horizontal, participatory, multicultural and self-conscious about its historical setting and transformative role and mission.[16]

Between Promise and Practice: One-Party Dominance and the Limits of Constitutionalism

South Africa's constitutional experiment has not (yet) fully delivered on its promise. South Africa remains a deeply inegalitarian society.[17] Despite the rapid creation of a new middle class, an underclass of citizens with little education and often no prospect of employment remains trapped in a spiral of poverty. Respect for diversity, openness and transparency is not always apparent among citizens or in the actions or attitudes of organs of state.[18] The political culture tends to the secretive.[19] Accountability of those who exercise power is not particularly effective and efforts to hold those who exercise public power accountable sometimes lead to severe tensions in the system.[20] The system of checks and

[15] Klare, 'Legal Culture', 152. [16] *Ibid.*, 153–6.

[17] B. Ozler and J. G. M. Hoogeveen, 'Not separate, not equal: Poverty and inequality in post-apartheid South Africa', William Davidson Institute Working paper No. 739 (2005).

[18] In 2008 and 2015 xenophobic attacks on foreigners swept across South Africa. Gay men and lesbians are also often attacked because of their sexual orientation. Racist incidences occur frequently and are regularly reported in the media.

[19] In 2014 Parliament adopted the Protection of State Information Bill (not yet signed by the president), which has been severely criticized as it is being seen as an attempt to clamp down on the free flow of information and to shield the state from scrutiny, especially in cases of corruption. See G. Bizos and W. Kerfoot 'Legal Resources Centre, Constitutional Litigation Unit, Submission on Bill B6-2010 Protection of State Information Bill on behalf of People Against Suffering, Suppression, Oppression and Poverty, February 17 2012', accessed on 3 October 2015 at http://constitutionallyspeaking.co.za/bizos-kerfoot-lrc-submission-on-secrecy-bill/.

[20] The manner in which the executive and the governing party has responded to a Report by the Public Protector (South Africa's version of an Ombudsman) on the unjustified spending of R250 million (20 million Euros) on the renovation of President Jacob Zuma's private house is a case in point. The investigation was stymied and after it was published politicians launched personal attacks on the Public Protector and attempted to discredit her findings. See P. de Vos, 'Nkandla: Zuma's convoluted series of Houdini moves' accessed on 3 September 2014 at http://constitutionallyspeaking.co.za/nkandla-zumas-convoluted-series-of-houdini-moves/; and P. de Vos, 'Nkandla scandal: attacking Public Protector must be seen as admission of wrongdoing', accessed on

balances – both horizontal and vertical – are not as effective as intended by the drafters of the Constitution. The democratically representative constitutional institutions – national and provincial legislatures and executives – are dominated by the members of one political party and there tends to be a conflation between the dominant party (the ANC) and the state. At the time of writing there does not seem to be the potential (at least in the foreseeable future) of an 'alternation of elites'. There is also a tendency among leaders of the dominant party to conflate the political organization/party and state.[21]

There are many reasons – relating to the history of South Africa and the political culture in South Africa – why the constitutional institutions do not operate optimally, why the constitutional norms have not been firmly entrenched, and why the forms of democratic politics that emerged after the end of apartheid rule are not as open, accountable and responsive as envisaged by the norms embodied in the Constitution. In this section I explore some of these reasons, arguing that constitutional design, coupled with – until recently – the complete electoral dominance of the governing party, the precarious institutional position of the Constitutional Court has made it more difficult to transform democratic politics in the way envisaged by the norms embodied in the Constitution.

South Africa's constitutional democracy was established to replace the deeply authoritarian and secretive apartheid system in the wake of a long liberation struggle in which the liberation movement had to contend with the attacks and infiltration by the apartheid state. The culture within the ANC which now governs the country was therefore by necessity secretive and characterised by a form of 'democratic centralism'.[22] Some of these 'habits' that were prevalent in the entirely abnormal political space before 1994 have not entirely disappeared.

Political parties play a decisive role in the South African system of government, firstly, because of the nature of the electoral system currently in operation in South Africa and, secondly, because of the dominant position of former liberation movements in current politics. It would be impossible to come to grips with the manner in which the

3 September 2014 at http://constitutionallyspeaking.co.za/nkandla-scandal-attacking-public-protector-must-be-seen-as-admission-of-wrongdoing/.

21 R. Suttner, 'Democratic Transition and Consolidation in South Africa: The Advice of "the Experts"', *Current Sociology*, 52 (2004), 767; T. Lodge, 'The ANC and the Development of Party Politics in Modern South Africa', *The Journal of Modern African Studies*, 42 (2004), 190.

22 Mattes, 'South Africa'.

various provisions of the Constitution operate and the challenges faced in establishing a fully normative form of constitutionalism without understanding – in broad terms – the South African political landscape. The ANC has won every national election in South Africa since the advent of democracy. In 1999 it increased its support to 66.3 per cent of the total vote and in 2004 this further increased to 69.7 per cent of the vote. Its closest competitor has been the Democratic Alliance, who won only 9.56 per cent of the votes in 1999 and 12.37 in 2004. The ANC has enjoyed electoral dominance and continues to win free and fair elections with all other parties lagging far behind. Such a system in which one political party continuously wins overwhelming electoral victories in free and fair elections is often referred to as a '*dominant-party democracy*'.[23] Issacharoff – writing before nationwide student protests rocked the country in the second half of 2015, arguably presenting the first real challenge to the authority and legitimacy of the governing ANC since its election in 1994 – wrote that

> In South Africa today there is simply no escaping the fact that the ANC is now the established and dominant political force in the country and, thus

[23] S. Choudhry, 'He Had a Mandate: The South African Constitutional Court and the African National Congress in a Dominant Party Democracy', *Constitutional Court Review*, 2 (2009); Issacharoff, *Fragile Democracies*. Whether South Africa can indeed be characterised in this manner has been the subject of intense debate. See R. Southall, 'The South African Elections of 1994: The Remaking of a Dominant-Party State', *Journal of Modern African Studies*, 32 (1994), 629; H. Giliomee, 'South Africa's Emerging Dominant-Party Regime', *Journal of Democracy*, 94 (1998), 128; R. Southall, 'The Centralization and Fragmentation of South Africa's Dominant Party System' *African Affairs*, 97 (1998), 443; S. Friedman, 'No Easy Stroll to Dominance: Party Dominance, Opposition and Civil Society in South Africa', in H. Giliomee and C. Simkins (eds.), *The Awkward Embrace: One Party Domination and Democracy* (Amsterdam: Harwood Academic Publishers, 1999), p. 97; R. Southall, 'Opposition in South Africa: Issues and Problems', *Democratization*, 8 (2001), 1; H. Giliomee, J. Myburgh and L. Schlemmer, 'Dominant Party Rule, Opposition Parties and Minorities in South Africa', *Democratization*, 8 (2001), 161; R. Southall, 'Conclusion: Emergent Perspectives on Opposition in South Africa', *Democratization*, 8 (2001), 275; R. Alence, 'South Africa after Apartheid: The First Decade' *Journal of Democracy*, 15(3) (2004), 78; T. Lodge, 'The ANC and the Development of Party Politics in Modern South Africa', *Journal of Modern African Studies*, 42 (2004), 189; J. Hamill, 'The Elephant and the Mice: Election 2004 and the Future of Opposition Politics in South Africa', *The Round Table: The Commonwealth Journal of International Affairs*, 93 (2004), 691; R. Southall, 'The "Dominant Party Debate" in South Africa', *Afrika Spectrum*, 40 (2005), 61; R. Suttner, 'Party Dominance Theory: Of What Value?', *Politikon*, 33 (2006), 277; A. Handley, C. Murray and R. Simeon, 'Learning to Lose, Learning to Win: Government and Opposition in South Africa's Transition to Democracy', in E. Friedman and J. Wong (eds.), *Political Transitions in Dominant Party Systems: Learning to Lose* (New York: Routledge, 2008), p. 191.

> far, faces no significant political opposition. As is often the case when electoral competition recedes, the dominant party becomes the centre for all political and economic dealings with the government, and an incestuous breed of self-serving politics starts to take hold.[24]

Although this description is disputed, it is important to note that the electoral dominance of one political party has the potential to influence the manner in which various constitutional structures in a democracy operate. Advocates of the dominant-party thesis argue that the dominant status of one political party in a democracy has the tendency to erode the checks on the power of the executive created by a democratic but supreme Constitution. Legislative oversight over the executive in Parliament may be stymied and opposition parties may be marginalised where one political party dominates the legislature. There is also a danger that a dominant party may 'capture' various independent institutions – including the judiciary and other bodies like the Prosecuting Authority, the Police Service and other corruption-busting bodies – by deploying its members to these institutions to remove effective checks on the exercise of power by the government. In a one-party dominant democracy, so they argue, the formal mechanisms through which power is exercised become hollowed out while the separation between the political party and the state breaks down. This essentially shifts the centre where real decisions are made from the formal constitutional structures – the Presidency and the Cabinet on the one hand and the legislature on the other – to the decision-making body of the governing party. In such a system, they argue, the leadership of the dominant party makes all important decisions, which are then merely formally endorsed by the constitutional structures. This process is characterised by a blurring of the boundary between party and state. This has the effect of reducing the likely formation of independent groups from within civil society that are autonomous from the ruling party. It is also characterised by possible abuse of office and arbitrary decision making. This undermines the integrity of democratic institutions, particularly that of the legislature and its ability to check the executive. But political dominance by one party for an extended period of time also places 'inordinate pressure on any top court unable to carve out space for judicial independence amid political uncertainty'.[25] This is because parties who are secure in the knowledge that they will not lose elections are more likely to confront the judicial authority head-on. Courts acquire at least some of their

[24] Issacharroff, *Fragile Democracies*, p. 255. [25] *Ibid*., p. 254.

legitimacy and institutional security from political parties who understand that they may have to turn to courts when they are not in power. A confident dominant party may well 'jettison the hazy political legitimacy conferred by judicial independence, for the hard and fast claims to power from leveraging its electoral mandate'.[26] It is exactly at this point that the top court sits in a constitutional democracy, precariously placed to safeguard its legitimacy while also protecting the democratic space within which it must remain possible for non-dominant political actors to play a significant role.[27]

If this is true, it will influence the manner in which the legislature, the executive, the judiciary and other constitutional institutions operate, as the dominant party will have a disproportionate influence on these institutions, thus posing difficulties for their effective operation. I contend that the electoral dominance of one political party in South Africa for the first 22 years of democracy has had a significant effect on governance, not because of the dominance of the party *per se* but because that dominance is amplified by other factors which have a tendency to weaken constitutional structures, procedural safeguards, independent bodies and mechanisms of checks and balances. These factors are set out below. I also contend that the dominance of the ANC places the Constitutional Court in a difficult position. It needs to protect the democratic space without overreaching. If it overreaches it will become easier for the dominant party to hollow out the court by packing it with judges aligned to the party or to reduce the powers of the court to ensure it is no longer able to check the exercise of power by the other branches of government.

There are factors peculiar to South Africa that exacerbate the challenge posed by one-party dominance for a constitutional democracy as set out above. South African constitutional democracy is founded on a multi-party system of government. However, unlike the electoral system in place in the United Kingdom and in South Africa before 1994 (based on geographical voting constituencies), the present electoral system for electing members of the National Assembly and of the provincial legislatures must 'result, in general, in proportional representation'. This means a person who intends to vote in national or provincial elections must vote for a political party registered for the purpose of contesting the elections and not for a candidate. It is the registered party that nominates candidates for the election on regional and national party lists. Political

[26] *Ibid.*, p. 255. [27] Choudhry, 'He Had a Mandate'.

parties are therefore indispensable conduits for the enjoyment of the right to vote in elections. If a person chooses to become a member of a political party and wants to take part in its internal elections, that person has a right to do so in accordance with the rules of that party. The exercise of the right is protected not only against external interference but also against interference arising from within the party. Although it is left largely to political parties themselves to regulate how they deal with internal elections, political parties may not adopt constitutions which are inconsistent with the right of citizens to join political parties and to participate in their activities. This means that the constitution of a political party that limits or extinguishes the rights of members of that party freely and fairly to take part in its internal elections could be declared invalid by a court as being in breach of section 19 of the Bill of Rights.[28]

Be that as it may, in practical terms political parties and their leaders hold enormous power over elected members of the various legislatures and executives in South Africa. There are five interrelated reasons for this:

> [*] First, South Africa inherited our system of parliamentary government from Britain. In this system the support of the majority party in parliament is required to form the executive.[29] Thus, the executive requires the continued support of the majority of members of the legislature to survive. This provides a strong incentive to members of the legislature to 'toe the party line', regardless of any differences an individual member of the legislature may have with the decisions or actions of the political party leadership. If members of the governing party fail to respect party discipline and vote with opposition parties and against the majority party, and the government lose a vote in parliament, this can erode the democratic legitimacy of the government and can ultimately lead to the fall of that government.
>
> [*] Second, the country also inherited the convention of strict party discipline from the Westminster system associated with the system of parliamentary government.[30] This convention – which places severe restrictions on individual members of Parliament to disobey party leaders when they engage in legislative or executive action – applied in pre-democratic South Africa in the Westminster Parliament as well as the tri-cameral

[28] *Ramakatsa and Others* v *Magashule and Others* (CCT 109/12) [2012] ZACC 31; 2013 (2) BCLR 202 (CC) (18 December 2012) para. 74.

[29] See sections 86, 89 and especially 102.

[30] J. L. Hiebert, 'Constitutional Experimentation: Rethinking How a Bill of Rights Functions', in T. Ginsburg and R. Dixon (eds.), *Comparative Constitutional Law* (Cheltenham: Edward Elgar Publishing Ltd, 2011), p. 307.

Parliament. When the new democratic system replaced the old system, the convention of strict party discipline was retained.

[*] Third, the internal culture of South African political parties places great emphasis on internal party discipline. This type of internal culture values and rewards party members who demonstrate loyalty to the party and the decisions democratically arrived at by that party. It also values respect for the leadership of the party and rewards those who display such respect.[31] At its most extreme, such a culture can be said to be one of democratic centralism. This allows internal party debate on an issue until the party has made a decision on that issue, after which no debate is generally allowed.

[*] Fourth, the electoral system in South Africa assists party leaders to enforce strict discipline among members of the legislature. This is because members of the legislature depend on the support of their various political parties to get elected to the legislature and can also easily be removed from the legislature by their respective political parties. Accordingly, members of the legislature are, to some extent, beholden to the leadership of their respective political parties and to the party machinery to retain their positions. This means that the members of the legislature are not free to act as they see fit in fulfilling their various duties as members of Parliament.

[*] Fifth, because a pure proportional representation electoral system is in place for election to the National Assembly and provincial legislatures[32] and because members of the National Council of Provinces (NCOP) (the second house of the national legislature) are selected based on their party membership,[33] representative democracy[34] is wholly dependent on political parties for its realisation. No person can serve in the national or any of the provincial legislatures without being a member of a political party and without having been chosen or selected by that political party to represent the interests of the political party in the respective legislatures.[35]

[31] The disciplinary case lodged against former ANC Youth League leader, Julius Malema and his ultimate expulsion from the ANC illustrates the governing party's insistence on party discipline. See 'ANC statement on the National Disciplinary Committee of appeal today', accessed on 8 January 2013 at http://www.anc.org.za/show.php?id=9363.

[32] Section 46(1)(d) affirms that the National Assembly consists of members elected in terms of an electoral system that 'results, in general, in proportional representation', while section 105(1)(d) contains an identical provision regarding provincial legislatures.

[33] Constitution of the Republic of South Africa, 1996, section 61.

[34] As the Constitutional Court explained in *Doctors for Life International* v *Speaker of the National Assembly and Others* (CCT12/05) [2006] ZACC 11; 2006 (12) BCLR 1399 (CC); 2006 (6) SA 416 (CC) (17 August 2006) at para. 115: Representative democracy entails free and fair election through which citizens vote for public representatives while participatory democracy requires citizens to take part in the governance of the country.

[35] See *Majola* v *The President* (48541/2010) [2012] ZAGPJHC 236 (30 October 2012) where the South Gauteng High Court rejected a challenge to the constitutionality of section 57A read with Schedule 1A of the Electoral Act No. 73 of 1998 because of an alleged

> This is because at national and provincial level political parties – and not individual candidates – contest elections and voters cast their ballots for the political party of their choice.[36] Voters have no direct say on who appears on the electoral lists of political parties, on the order in which names are to appear on these electoral lists or on the order according to which candidates who appear on individual party lists will be dispatched to the various legislatures according to the percentage of votes garnered by that specific political party.[37] Moreover, the President – in whom the executive authority of the Republic is vested (section 85(1)) – is formally elected by the members of the National Assembly (section 86(1)) while the various Premiers – in whom executive authority of a province is vested (section 125(1)) – are formally elected by the various provincial legislatures (section 128(1)). In theory, this means that the members of the majority party in the National Assembly and in the various provincial legislatures determine who will serve as the President and as the various Premiers. In practice, it is the extra-parliamentary leadership of the majority party in each legislature that determines who serve as President and as the various Premiers and then instruct their elected representatives to vote for the agreed upon candidate.

All these factors have a tendency to 'hollow out' formal constitutional structures and displace real power to political party structures. While decisions are formally made in the appropriate constitutional structures (the various legislatures and executives for example), there is a strong pull to have these decisions dictated by the extra-constitutional structures in the form of the top leadership of the governing party. In South Africa this can be called the Luthuli House effect (as the headquarters of the governing party is situated at Luthuli House in Johannesburg). The Luthuli House effect obviously weakens constitutional structures as well as the system of checks and balances. Although power is formally distributed both vertically and horizontally, the question is whether 'real' power does not in fact reside in Luthuli House. If it does, several of the constitutional provisions and safeguards (including the system of checks and balances) cannot operate effectively. Moreover, partly because of the constitutional design which affirms the dominant position of political parties within the

inconsistency between these provisions and section 19(3)(b) of the Constitution. For a critical discussion of the judgement, see L. Wolf, 'The Right to Stand as an Independent Candidate in National and Provincial Elections: Majola v The President', *South African Journal on Human Rights*, 30 (2014), 159–82.

36 *Ramakatsa and Others* v *Magashule and Others (CCT 109/12) [2012] ZACC 31; 2013 (2) BCLR 202 (CC) (18 December 2012)* at para. 66. See also part 3 of the Electoral Act 73 of 1998 (Electoral Act).

37 The Electoral Act 73 of 1998 confirms that parties wishing to contest national or provincial elections can only do so if they are registered and if they have submitted prescribed lists of candidates. See section 26 and 27 of Electoral Act.

constitutional system and partly because of the electoral popularity of the governing party and its dominant position in South African democracy, the provisions in the Constitution aimed at establishing a radically different normative framework within which democratic political contestation should take place have been less effective than expected. At least, these have been less effective than this writer expected at the time when the 1996 Constitution was adopted.

The question arises as to whether the Constitutional Court can counter these tendencies. Could it safeguard its institutional security while playing a decisive role in checking the exercise of power by constitutional institutions controlled by the dominant party? Clearly, if the Constitutional Court vigorously and expansively interprets its powers and the provisions in the Constitution in an attempt to check the excesses associated with one-party dominance as Choudhry suggests it should do,[38] it will bring the Court in direct conflict with the governing party, which, as I have pointed out, is electorally dominant and unlikely to lose an election in the foreseeable future, and may incentivise the party to pack the court with more pliable judges or to seek to amend the Constitution to diminish the powers of the Court. Alternatively, it may also lead to a situation in which the decisions of the court are ignored or not fully implemented.

Entrenching Democracy in a One-Party Dominant System: The Role of the Constitutional Court

The Position of the Constitutional Court and the Appointment of Judges

A supreme Constitution – especially one as expansive as the South African Constitution – will always create tension between the political branches of the state and the judiciary. The Constitution contains a promise that the state will protect traditional civil and political rights, including the rights whose protection is a prerequisite for the flourishing of democratic contestation. It also contains the promise that the state will progressively provide access to several social and economic rights, including the right to housing, health care, food and water. It further imposes limits on the exercise of power by the two democratic branches of government. The Constitutional Court is called upon to play a pivotal role in realising these promises. As Klug points out, 'the South African

[38] Choudhry, 'He Had a Mandate'.

Constitutional Court has been called upon to address issues and to face challenges that would be considered extraordinary for any judiciary'.[39] It would be surprising if these powers did not lead to contestation. During the first 10 years of the democracy the Court 'enjoyed something of a honeymoon regarding acceptance of its institutional role'.[40] But during the presidency of Thabo Mbeki the Court for the first time faced challenges to its institutional position, particularly in the build-up to the celebrated *Treatment Action Campaign* case. Health Minister Manto Tshabalala-Msimang stated on national television that she would not stand by the Constitutional Court's decision were it to go the same way as the preceding High Court judgement – against government – although the remark was quickly retracted.[41] However, criticism of the Court and outright attacks on the Court by leaders of the governing party (inside and outside government) gained momentum during the presidency of Jacob Zuma. On 1 September 2011, Ngaoko Ramathlodi, at the time the Deputy Minister of Correctional Services and a member of both the ANC's National Executive Committee and the Judicial Service Commission, wrote an opinion piece in which he charged that

> Apartheid forces sought to and succeeded in retaining white domination under a black government. This they achieved by emptying the legislature and executive of real political power ... We ... have a Constitution that reflects the great compromise, a compromise tilted heavily in favour of forces against change ... [T]he black majority enjoys empty political power while forces against change reign supreme in the economy, judiciary, public opinion and civil society.[42]

Ramathlodi argued that 'forces against change' used the judiciary to undermine the will of the majority as represented by the ANC. In an address to a conference on access to Justice, President Jacob Zuma also complained about the role played by the judiciary, remarking that

[39] H. Klug, *The Constitution of South Africa: A Contextual Analysis* (Oxford: Hart Publishing, 2010), p. 1.

[40] T. Roux, *The Politics of Principle: The First South African Constitutional Court, 1995–2005* (Cambridge University Press, 2013), pp. 167–77.

[41] *Ibid.*, p. 298; Democratic Governance Rights Unit (DGRU), *Has the South African Constitutional Court Over-Reached? A Study of the Court's Application of the Separation of Powers Doctrine between 2009 and 2013*, accessed on 27 October 2015 at http://www.dgru.uct.ac.za/sites/default/files/image_tool/images/103/Separation%20of%20Powers%20Draft%20August%202014.pdf, 5.

[42] N. Ramathlodi, 'ANC's Fatal Concessions', *The Times*, 1 September 2011, accessed on 27 October 2015 at http://www.timeslive.co.za/opinion/commentary/2011/09/01/the-big-read-anc-s-fatal-concessions.

> Political disputes resulting from the exercise of powers that have been constitutionally conferred on the ruling party through a popular vote must not be subverted, simply because those who disagree with the ruling party politically, and who cannot win the popular vote during elections, feel other arms of the State are avenues to help them co-govern the country. . . . Political battles must be fought on political platforms.[43]

As Issacharoff points out,[44] these attacks alert us to the precarious position of the Constitutional Court and its limited power to narrow the gap between the promises contained in the Constitution and practice because in 'repeated engagements with entrenched political power, a confrontational judiciary is at grave risk of emerging as the loser'.[45]

I contend that the Constitutional Court has attempted to deal with this matter in two distinct ways. First, it has developed a comprehensive body of jurisprudence aimed at promoting the transformative promise of the Constitution. Given South Africa's history of racial exclusion and economic exploitation the pursuit of transformative goals enjoys broad support from the majority of South Africa's citizens. The argument is that in considering the relationship between legal legitimacy of a court, public support for that court, and the institutional security of that court, one can assume that 'institutional security typically follows from public support'.[46] The vigorous pursuit of transformative goals will, at least in theory, enhance the institutional security of the Constitutional Court as it will enhance public support for it. Although social surveys suggest that the Constitutional Court does not enjoy overwhelming public support.[47] I would argue at the very least that the Court's popularity would have been much lower (especially among black South Africans) and its institutional security thus far more precarious had it not embraced the transformative vision in the Constitution.

Second, I contend that in some of its recent judgements the Constitutional Court tentatively and pragmatically began to grapple with the effects of

[43] M. Monare, 'ANC's contempt for the judiciary cause for alarm', *Mail & Guardian* 26 June 2015 accessed on 26 October 2015 at http://mg.co.za/article/2015-06-25-ancs-contempt-for-the-judiciary-cause-for-alarm.

[44] Issacharoff, *Fragile Democracies*, p. 264. [45] *Ibid.*

[46] Roux, 'Principle and Pragmatism', p. 110.

[47] J. L. Gibson and G. A. Caldeira, 'Defenders of Democracy?: Legitimacy, Popular Acceptance, and the South African Constitutional Court', *Journal of Politics*, 65 (2003); J. L. Gibson, 'The Evolving Legitimacy of the South African Constitutional Court', in A. du Bois F. du Bois (eds.), *Justice and Reconciliation in Post-Apartheid South Africa* (Cambridge University Press, 2008).

one-party dominance and with its role in countering the effects of such dominance. In 2009, Sujit Choudhry criticised the Court for failing to develop a 'robust conception of dominant-party democracy'.[48] He pointed out that in several cases in which the Court had been asked to confront this issue, it 'dismissed the relevance of ANC domination to the constitutional challenge'.[49] This, he argued, reflected 'the Court's inadequate understanding of the concept of a dominant-party democracy, its pathologies, the pressure it puts on what is otherwise a formally liberal democratic system because of the lack of alternation of power between political parties, and how this pressure is generating constitutional challenges'.[50] As Issacharoff points out, in recent cases a new constitutional jurisprudence is emerging 'to address the threats to democratic governance'.[51] Although he is critical of the Court's lack of a robust theory of constitutional protection of democracy against democratic manipulation,[52] I nevertheless contend that recent judgements suggest that the Court is beginning to grapple with this question, taking tentative and pragmatic steps to protect democracy while, at the same time avoiding a head-on confrontation with the dominant party.

In the next section I turn to specific examples of the two ways in which the court has attempted to solidify its institutional security while attempting to narrow the gap between promise and practice. But before I proceed to do so, I turn to the legal provisions in the Constitution that formally safeguard the institutional independence of the judiciary in general and the Constitutional Court in particular. Although it must be clear from the preceding paragraphs that I do not contend that these mechanisms insulate the Court entirely from direct attack by a dominant political party, I would argue that it provides at least some formal protection for the Courts against attack by powerful political forces.

Section 165(2) of the Constitution formally affirms that the 'courts are independent and subject only to the Constitution and the law, which they must apply impartially and without fear, favour or prejudice'. Section 164(3) prohibits any 'person or organ of state' from interfering with the functioning of the courts, while section 165(4) affirms that '[a]n order or decision issued by a court binds all persons to whom and organs of state to which it applies'. Judges enjoy security of tenure (section 176(1)-(2)) and the salaries, allowances and benefits of judges may not be reduced' (section 176(3)). Moreover, judges may be removed from

[48] Choudhry, 'He Had a Mandate', 5. [49] *Ibid.* [50] *Ibid.*
[51] Issacharoff, *Fragile Democracies*, p. 256. [52] *Ibid.*, p. 260.

office only if the Judicial Service Commission finds that the judge suffers from an incapacity, is grossly incompetent or is guilty of gross misconduct; and the National Assembly calls for that judge to be removed, by a resolution adopted with a supporting vote of at least two-thirds of its members (section 177). No judge has ever been removed from office in South Africa. However, the independence and impartiality of judges are not only secured by these provisions that safeguard the institutional independence of judges. Where an overbearing executive uses its power to appoint intellectually incurious judges or judges perceived to be loyal to the dominant political party, the independence and impartiality of the judiciary could also be eroded over time.

It is for this reason that the appointment of judges – especially Constitutional Court judges – elicits much interest in the media and elsewhere in South Africa. If the judiciary is packed with talentless, intellectually uninquisitive judges with little empathy for the plight of the vulnerable and economically and socially marginalised in society, if it is packed with judges overeager to please the powerful and the well-connected in both the political and the economic spheres, the progressive constitutional project will be fundamentally threatened. If the decisions of the courts are not obeyed and if their orders are not effectively implemented the 'bite' of the Constitution will disappear and it will become largely a semantic document. In the South African context this means that it is important to examine the role played by the Judicial Service Commission (JSC) in the appointment of judges and to ask whether there has indeed been an attempt to pack the judiciary with individuals who will neither be impartial nor progressive in interpreting and applying the Constitution. The JSC nominates all judges for the various High Courts as well as all ordinary judges of the Supreme Court of Appeal (SCA). Moreover, it plays a pivotal role in the appointment of ordinary Constitutional Court judges as it has to nominate three more candidates than there are vacancies on the Constitutional Court, allowing the President to select one of the nominees for appointment (section 174).

The JSC – with 23 members almost equally divided between politicians and political appointees on the one hand and judges, lawyers and other representatives of the legal profession on the other – was designed to prevent party political considerations from trumping all others in the appointment of judges while not insulating the appointment of judges entirely from political considerations.[53] I contend that it is important for

[53] De Vos and Freedman (eds.), *South African Constitutional Law*, p. 231.

politicians to play *some* (but not a decisive) role in the appointment of judges to ensure the survival of a legitimate but independent judiciary. This is so because in a constitutional democracy like South Africa judges who enforce an expansive and supreme Constitution would be particularly vulnerable to attack by politicians when the decisions of the judges have far-reaching political consequences. As I argued above, in a one-party dominant democracy in 'repeated engagements with entrenched political power, a confrontational judiciary is at grave risk of emerging as the loser'. The institutional security of the judiciary is best safeguarded by pragmatic judges who are prepared to enforce the provisions of the Constitution against the politically dominant legislature and executive but also appropriately deferent to avoid, as far as possible, a head-on confrontation with the democratically representative branches of government. This circumspection is particularly important in the South African context in which until 1994 the majority was denied any say in the governance of the country.

Although the JSC is subject to much criticism, I contend that at least some of the criticism is unfounded. This is so because some of the criticism is based on a mistaken understanding of the exact nature of the function performed by the JSC when it appoints judges and the failure to appreciate the political 'cover' provided for judges by the JSC. Some critics of the JSC appear to believe that any political influence on its work represents a fundamental attack on the independence and impartiality of the judiciary. On the other hand, some members of the JSC seem to labour under the misconception that any criticism of the JSC is illegitimate. The truth lies somewhere between these two extreme positions. If we acknowledge, as we must, that judges in a constitutional democracy make decisions with potentially far-reaching political consequences and that the values, beliefs and political views of judges play some role in how they will decide some of the more difficult and contentious cases, we cannot avoid the fact that being a judge is not an entirely apolitical activity.

Although judges may not be seen to choose sides in partisan political disputes and must interpret the Constitution in accordance with its text and the precedent of the Constitutional Court, this still leaves them with a wide discretion in many difficult cases and this discretion will be exercised partly with reference to their judicial philosophy, world view, experience and ideological commitments. It would therefore be naïve to pretend that politics – with a small 'p' – does not play a role in constitutional adjudication. By involving politicians in the appointment of judges through the JSC and by ensuring the appointment of judges that will, over time, make the judiciary look more like the general population in terms of race and gender (but also in terms of sexual orientation, class, rural representation, language and the like), I would argue that the Constitution provides political cover to judges to do their job. It potentially also helps to prevent the appointment of judges whose views about the world and the role of law in regulating the world are completely out of kilter with the norms embodied in the Constitution and/or with the broad values of the majority of citizens. Of course, there is a potential tension between the norms embodied in the Constitution and the beliefs of many voters, who often harbour the most reactionary views on how to treat criminals or marginalised and vulnerable groups in society. Once appointed, judges will often try to navigate the waters between upholding the high principles of the Constitution while pragmatically trying not to alienate the overwhelming majority of voters and the political elites. The South African Constitutional Court has been extremely skilful in navigating these waters.[54] Roux argues that unlike other constitutional courts in new democracies, the South African Constitutional Court has not always needed to heed or to court public opinion in order to safeguard its institutional security because

> [T]he ANC political elite has shielded the Court from the political repercussions of its most unpopular decisions, allowing it to build its legal legitimacy through principled decision making in several important cases. In return, the CCSA has been careful to manage its relationship with the political branches, retreating from principle where such compromises were in the long-term interests of the constitutional project. In this way, a mutually beneficial relationship has developed between the CCSA and the ANC government, with the CCSA's reputation for legally credible decision making lending considerable legitimacy to the ANC's social transformation policies, and the ANC government's continued respect for, and obedience to, the CCSA's decisions helping to cement the CCSA's reputation as one of the most successful of the post-1990 constitutional courts.[55]

In the following section I explore this thesis further. However, I amend it slightly by arguing that the Court *has sometimes* courted public opinion while at other times courting the opinion of the dominant ANC, by handing down judgements that advanced the progressive transformative vision contained in the Constitution. In some cases (the death penalty case, gay rights cases, and cases on race and redress) the Court directly or

[54] Roux, 'Principle and Pragmatism'; Roux, *The Politics of Principle*.
[55] Roux, 'Principle and Pragmatism', p. 138.

indirectly courted the dominant party. In other cases (the social and economic rights cases as well as the racial redress cases) the Court directly or indirectly courted public opinion.

The Transformative Reach of the Constitution: A Partial Success

As stated above, the creation of a new constitutional order of 1996 aimed to create an entirely new set of rules in terms of which the country would be governed. But it set out to do more than that: it also aimed to establish an 'objective normative value system' within which political contestation was to take place. The question that must arise is whether these goals have been met. In this section I argue that the Constitution has been partly successful. I claim that it would be a mistake to say that the South African Constitution has not had any effect or impact on South African society and on the governance of the country and that the Constitution is thus no more than a semantic exercise in window dressing. Far from it. Because the Constitution is supreme, because its provisions are enforced by an independent judiciary and because the orders of the courts are largely obeyed and carried out by the other branches of government, it has (in certain areas) had a major impact, both on the protection of the human rights of everyone and on the quality of the governance and the functioning of the other branches of government. It would be very difficult – perhaps impossible – to demonstrate that the set of norms contained in the Constitution has had a decisive influence on the manner in which political contestation occurs in South Africa. It is easier to demonstrate that the judgements of the Constitutional Court have been decisive and that the jurisprudence of this court has had a major impact on the respect for human rights and on the quality of governance. In this section I aim to do so by highlighting the outcome in selected cases.

In the first case ever heard by the Constitutional Court in 1995, it declared the death penalty – which had still formally been legally sanctioned – unconstitutional.[56] Despite the fact that a majority of South Africans support the death penalty it has been illegal ever since. The judgement provided both a tangible and a symbolic affirmation of a new respect for human life and for the dignity of citizens. This commitment was tested on the afternoon of 16 August 2012 when members of a contingent of the South African Police Service, from an elite special unit

[56] See *S* v. *Makwanyane and Another* (CCT3/94) [1995] ZACC 3; 1995 (6) BCLR 665; 1995 (3) SA 391; [1996] 2 CHRLD 164; 1995 (2) SACR 1 (6 June 1995).

(McMichael 2012),[57] opened fire with submachine guns on a group of striking miners. Thirty-four miners were killed, and at least 78 were wounded. The incident was the single most lethal use of force by South African security forces against civilians since the Sharpeville massacre during the apartheid era. However, telling was the swift and robust response from civil society and from the government, who immediately set up an independent judicial commission of inquiry to investigate the killings.

The 1996 Constitution was the first in the world to contain an explicit, directly judicially enforceable prohibition against discrimination on the basis of sexual orientation (section 9(3)).[58] In a long line of cases the Constitutional Court declared invalid several forms of discrimination against gay men and lesbians invalid.[59] This culminated in the decision to extend marriage rights to same-sex couples, *Minister of Home Affairs and Another* v. *Fourie and Another*.[60] However, these dramatic legal changes have not yet led to a dramatic change in the attitudes of ordinary citizens towards same-sex love. A 2008 study surveying social attitudes in South Africa revealed that despite the legal gains, the number of respondents in South Africa who indicated their belief that 'homosexuality' is 'always wrong' only declined marginally from 84 per cent in 2003 to 82 per cent in 2007.[61] A Pew Research Centre survey (asking a different research

[57] C. McMichael, 'The South African Police Service and the Public Order War', *Think Africa Press*, 3 September 2012.

[58] Section 9(3) of the Constitution of the Republic of South Africa, 1996, states; 'The state may not unfairly discriminate directly or indirectly against anyone on one or more grounds, including race, gender, sex, pregnancy, marital status, ethnic or social origin, colour, sexual orientation, age, disability, religion, conscience, belief, culture, language and birth.'

[59] See *National Coalition for Gay and Lesbian Equality and Another* v. *Minister of Justice and Others* 1998 (12) BCLR 1517 (CC); *Satchwell* v. *President of the Republic of South Africa and Another* [2002] ZACC 18; 2002 (6) SA 1 (CC); 2002 (9) BCLR 986 (CC); *J and Another* v. *Director General, Department of Home Affairs and Others* [2003] ZACC 3; 2003 (5) SA 621 (CC); 2003 (5) BCLR 463 (CC); *Du Toit and Another* v. *Minister of Welfare and Population Development and Others (Lesbian and Gay Equality Project as amicus curiae)* [2002] ZACC 20; 2003 (2) SA 198 (CC); 2002 (10) BCLR 1006 (CC); *Gory* v. *Kolver NO and Others* (CCT28/06) [2006] ZACC 20; 2007 (4) SA 97 (CC); 2007 (3) BCLR 249 (CC) (23 November 2006).

[60] CCT 60/04) [2005] ZACC 19; 2006 (3) BCLR 355 (CC); 2006 (1) SA 524 (CC) (1 December 2005).

[61] B. Roberts and V. Reddy, 'Pride and Prejudice: Public Attitudes towards Homosexuality', *HSRC Review*, 6(4) (2008), 9, available at http://www.hsrc.ac.za/HSRC_Review_Article-121.phtml accessed on 2 July 2015; J. C. Mubangizi and B. K. Twinomugisha, 'Protecting the Right to Freedom of Sexual Orientation: What Can Uganda Learn from South Africa?' *Stellenbosch Law Review*, 22 (2011), 339.

question) published in 2013 found that 61 per cent of South Africans surveyed believed that 'homosexuality' should never be accepted, with little change from previous years.[62] However, the situation may be more complex than these surveys suggest. A 2016 survey conducted by the Other Foundation found that while 72 per cent of respondents believed same-sex sexual activity was morally wrong, 51 per cent believe that gay South Africans should have the same human rights as all other citizens.[63]

The social and economic rights jurisprudence of the Constitutional Court has had a major impact on the government's policy towards providing treatment for people living with HIV by giving effect to the right of access to health care (section 27(1)(a)).[64] When litigation was launched the government was resisting the provision of anti-retroviral drugs to people living with HIV, but after the Court ordered the government to roll out a programme of anti-retroviral treatment for all HIV-positive pregnant mothers to prevent mother-to-child transmission of HIV, the government attitude changed dramatically and today a comprehensive programme is in place to provide all HIV-positive individuals with access to effective treatment. The campaign led by the Treatment Action Campaign (TAC), was only partly reliant on judicial intervention. While approaching the courts and invoking the right of access to health care protected in section 27 of the Constitution, the TAC also used the political space created by the Constitution to mobilise community support, thus placing pressure on the government to change its stance.[65] The case is a textbook example of the potential salutary effect of the Constitution on political culture and practice. The TAC used the space created by the Constitution to engage in a different kind of politics which succeeded in holding the elected government accountable in ways that would almost certainly not have been possible had it relied merely on the electoral process.

The jurisprudence of the Constitutional Court has also had a major impact on giving effect to the right of access to housing (section 26(1))

[62] Pew Research Centre, 'Global Views on Homosexuality', 15 April 2014, available at http://www.pewglobal.org/2014/04/15/global-morality/table/homosexuality/ accessed on 20 June 2015.

[63] The Other Foundation "Progressive Prudes"(2016) accessed at http://theotherfoundation.org/learning/ on 12 September 2016.

[64] See *Minister of Health and Others* v *Treatment Action Campaign and Others (No 2)* (CCT8/02) [2002] ZACC 15; 2002 (5) SA 721; 2002 (10) BCLR 1033 (5 July 2002).

[65] S. L. Robins, *From Revolution to Rights in South Africa: Social Movements, NGOs and Popular Politics after Apartheid* (Scotsville: University of KwaZulu-Natal Press, 2010), pp. 117–19.

and the prohibition on the eviction of anyone from their home, or have their home demolished, without an order of court made after considering all the relevant circumstances. No legislation may permit arbitrary evictions (section 26(3)). In the landmark case of *Government of the RSA and Others v. Grootboom and Others*,[66] the Constitutional Court found that there was a positive obligation on the state to take reasonable steps, within its available resources, progressively to realise the right of access to housing. The innovative aspect of the judgement centres on the use of a reasonableness standard by the court in order to give some 'bite' to the right without threatening the court's institutional legitimacy by interfering too drastically in the policy decisions of the government. The Court said that it would judge the reasonability of the steps taken to pursue the achievement of the right to housing by determining whether there was a comprehensive policy, encompassing all three tiers of government, to realise the right of access to housing progressively (para. 41). What would be required was for the state to act in order to achieve the intended result according to comprehensive policies and programmes that are reasonable both in their conception and implementation (para. 42). To determine whether such measures were reasonable, it would be necessary to consider housing problems in their social, economic and historical context and to consider the capacity of institutions responsible for implementing the programme. The programme had to be 'balanced and flexible'. A programme 'that excludes a significant segment of society cannot be said to be reasonable' (para. 43). More pertinently, those whose needs are the most urgent and whose ability to enjoy all rights were most in peril, could not be ignored by the measures aimed at achieving the realisation of the goal. Where measures, though statistically successful, fail to respond to those most desperate, they may not pass the test of reasonability (para. 44). The Court also affirmed the need for the government to take immediately steps to facilitate access to adequate housing progressively. The state had a duty to move expeditiously and effectively towards that goal. Any deliberate retrogressive measures in that regard would require the most careful consideration and would need to be fully justified by reference to the totality of the rights provided in the Bill of Rights (para. 45). The Court found that the failure of the government policy to take account of the needs of those who have been left destitute because they are homeless rendered the policy unreasonable and hence unconstitutional. However, the judgement was only a partial success as it

[66] 2000 11 BCLR 1169 (CC).

did not require the government to provide houses for the litigants in the case or for others similarly situated. When Mrs Irene Grootboom, the main litigant in the case, died in 2008, she was penniless and was still living in a shack. This revived criticism of the social and economic rights jurisprudence of the Constitutional Court and its focus on 'reasonable action' by the state.[67] However, it would be simplistic to conclude that the judgement – and subsequent judgements on the right to housing – achieved nothing. The judgement led to the government revising its housing policy to bring it in line with the judgement. It has thus had 'a direct material impact on many people's lives – perhaps many millions of lives'.[68] This judgement, and subsequent Constitutional Court jurisprudence on social and economic rights illustrate the efforts of the Constitutional Court to perform a precarious balancing act on social and economic rights and transformation. On the one hand, it is acutely aware of its institutional weakness and the dangers posed by attacks on its legitimacy and authority from the members of the democratically elected branches of government for 'interfering' with policy decisions of the elected branches of government (in the subsequent section I point out that this concern about political criticism was not unfounded). On the other hand the Court attempts to give some meaningful content to the social and economic rights contained in the Constitution, with the hope that 'rights-directed litigation can improve the conditions of a considerable group of socially vulnerable people, in ways that would not have eventuated without rights'.[69] In a public lecture one of the judges of the Constitutional Court, Justice Edwin Cameron (who was not a member of the Constitutional Court when it handed down *Grootboom*) was anxious to point out that decisions such as that handed down in *Grootboom* 'show how rights-claims can be practically translated into material improvements to people's lives'.

Finally, the Constitutional Court's equality jurisprudence dealing with the permissible scope of redress measures (called 'affirmative action' measures in the United States) to correct the effects of past (and arguably

[67] E. Cameron, 'What you can do with rights', The Fourth Leslie Scarman Lecture Middle Temple Hall, London Wednesday 25 January 2012, accessed on 3 October 2015 at http://www.lawcom.gov.uk/wp-content/uploads/2015/05/Scarman_2012_Justice_Cameron_What_you_can_do_with_rights.pdf, para. 29–30; C. A. Wertman, 'There's No Place like Home: Access to Housing for All South Africans', *Brooklyn Journal of International Law*, 40 (2015), 729.

[68] Cameron, 'What you can do', para. 32; S. Liebenberg, *Socio-Economic Rights – adjudication under a transformative constitution* (Cape Town: Juta Law, 2010), p. 58.

[69] *Ibid.*, para. 40.

ongoing) discrimination on the basis of race and gender, has also struck a careful balance between the interests of those who previously benefited from racial and gender discrimination on the one hand, and those who can potentially benefit from the redress measures. Section 9(3) of the South African Constitution prohibits both direct and indirect 'unfair discrimination ... against anyone on one or more grounds, including race, gender, sex, pregnancy, marital status, ethnic or social origin, colour, sexual orientation, age, disability, religion, conscience, belief, culture, language and birth'. However, section 9(2) explicitly provides for redress measures making clear that – unlike the US anti-discrimination approach – the South African equality jurisprudence must be understood as rejecting the notion that corrective measures are a deviation from, or invasive of, the right to equality guaranteed by the Constitution.[70] In *Minister of Finance* v. *Van Heerden*,[71] the Constitutional Court held that redress measures are not 'reverse discrimination' or 'positive discrimination' but are rather integral to the reach of equality protection under the South African Constitution (para. 30). Although it has been suggested that the court's judgement is largely deferential to government measures aimed at correcting the effects of past or ongoing racial discrimination[72] and that the court might require little more than an application of a rationality standard when measuring whether such programmes comply with the Constitution,[73] I would contend that a careful reading of the majority judgement in the *Van Heerden* case indicates that the Constitutional Court understands section 9(2) of the Constitution as imposing substantial constitutional limits on redress programmes. Thus, according to the Constitutional Court, any programme or policy aimed at addressing the effects of past (and continuing) racial discrimination has to meet at least three requirements contained in section 9(2) before it would be considered to be constitutionally permissible. The first question is whether the programme of redress is designed to protect and

[70] For a helpful discussion of the differences between the South African and US approaches to 'affirmative action' see K. C. Naff and O. Dupper, 'Footprints through the Courts: Comparing Judicial Responses to Affirmative Action Litigation in South Africa and the United States', *International Journal of Comparative Labour Law and Industrial Relations*, 25 (2009), 157–190.

[71] 2004 (11) BCLR 1125 (CC).

[72] C. Albertyn and B. Goldblatt, 'Equality' in S. Woolman et al (eds.), *Constitutional Law of South Africa*, 2nd edn, Cape Town: Juta & Company Ltd, 2007 pp. 29–40; J. L. Pretorius, 'Fairness in Transformation: A Critique of the Constitutional Court's Affirmative Action Jurisprudence', *South African Journal of Human Rights*, 26 (2010), 549–57.

[73] Pretorius, 'Fairness in Transformation', 561–6.

advance a disadvantaged group. This question requires a determination of whether the overwhelming majority of members of the favoured class are persons designated as disadvantaged by unfair exclusion (para. 40). The second requirement for a valid restitutionary programme is that the measure must be 'designed to protect or advance' those disadvantaged by unfair discrimination. What is required, however, is that the measures 'must be reasonably capable of attaining the desired outcome' of addressing the effects of past and ongoing racial discrimination and racism. If the remedial measures are arbitrary, capricious or display naked preference they could hardly be said to be designed to achieve the constitutionally permissible goal (para. 41). The third requirement for a valid remedial programme is probably the most difficult and complex to comprehend and apply. It requires a value judgement on the part of the presiding officer, a judgement that would have to be made in the light of all the circumstances, including the apartheid history of the country. According to the court, remedial measures can only be constitutionally valid if, thirdly, such a measure 'promotes the achievement of equality' in the long term. On the one hand, it 'must be accepted that the achievement of this goal may often come at a price for those who were previously advantaged (para. 44).[74] On the other hand, 'it is also clear that the long-term goal of our society is a non-racial, non-sexist society in which each person will be recognised and treated as a human being of equal worth and dignity'. Thus, a redress measure 'should not constitute an abuse of power or impose such substantial and undue harm on those excluded from its benefits that our long-term constitutional goal would be threatened' (para. 44).

The jurisprudence of the Constitutional Court aimed at advancing the transformative vision of the Constitution is important for the constitutional project because at its best it will contribute to the material improvement of the lives of many South Africans. Court judgements on their own cannot effect the social and economic transformation of society and cannot create a more egalitarian system. Yet, it can contribute to the achievement of this goal by goading the elected government into action, while requiring that government to balance the economic and social interests of various groups when doing so. Through this jurisprudence the court, at its best, can thus help to speed up the creation of a more

[74] This reflects the statement first made by the Constitutional Court in *Bato Star Fishing (Pty) Ltd* v. *The Minister of Environmental Affairs and Tourism and Others* 2004 (7) BCLR 687 (CC) para. 76, to the effect that: 'The measures that bring about transformation will inevitably affect some members of the society adversely, particularly those coming from the previously advantaged communities'.

egalitarian society while at the same time imposing discipline on the government and providing at least a degree of protection for politically vulnerable groups who previously benefited from the apartheid system. If the court manages this process well, it could help contribute to its own legitimacy and authority of the court in the eyes of ordinary citizens. In section 3.4 I point out why it is important for the survival of the court and for the project of entrenching constitutional democracy, that the court retains a degree of legitimacy and authority.

The Constitutional Court and the Protection of Democracy

Commentators have criticised some of the early decisions of the Constitutional Court – including the *New National Party* case dealing with the requirement that only voters in possession of green bar-coded ID books could register and vote in elections and the *UDM* case dealing with floor crossing – for the rather narrow and formalistic view they espoused of democracy.[75] In *UDM*, for example, where the Constitutional Court had to decide whether to invalidate floor-crossing provisions that protected larger parties from floor crossing of their MPs but exposed smaller parties to poaching of MPs by larger parties by imposing requirement that at least 10 per cent of the MPs of a party had to cross the floor for the crossing to be legally valid, the Court adopted a formalistic approach to democracy, stating that

> The rights entrenched under section 19 are directed to elections, to voting and to participation in political activities. Between elections, however, voters have no control over the conduct of their representatives. They cannot dictate to them how they must vote in Parliament, nor do they have any legal right to insist that they conduct themselves or refrain from conducting themselves in a particular manner.[76]

As Theunis Roux argued, the argument advanced by the Constitutional Court here seems misplaced in relation to section 19(1) of the Bill of Rights. After all, the right to participate in the activities of a political party may not only be meaningfully exercised at election time and is clearly capable of being violated in between elections.[77]

[75] T. Roux, 'Democracy' in Woolman et al. (eds.), *Constitutional Law*, pp. 10–11.

[76] *United Democratic Movement* v. *President of the Republic of South Africa and Others*, at para. 49.

[77] Roux, 'Democracy', para. 49.

In *Ramakatsa and Others v. Magashule and Others,*[78] the Court arguable adopted a more robust approach to protecting the democratic right of citizens to take part in the political process.[79] In the case – heard in the run-up to the elective conference of the governing ANC at Mangaung in December 2012 – the appellants, acting in their personal interests and also in the interests of a class of persons made up by members of the ANC and voters resident in the Free State, sought an order setting aside the Provincial Conference of the ANC held earlier that year at Parys as well as the decisions taken there (para. 59). The majority of the court held that the appellants' constitutional right to participate in the activities of the ANC – as guaranteed by section 19(1)(b) of the Bill of Rights – was breached as a result of a number of irregularities that occurred before the challenged conference was held (para. 60). The judgement confirmed the pivotal role that political parties play in the South African constitutional democracy as 'elections are contested by political parties' and it is 'these parties which determine lists of candidates who get elected to legislative bodies' (para. 66). The Court seemed to be sympathetic to the theory that intra-party democracy represents a virtuous circle, linking ordinary citizens to government, benefiting the parties that adopt it, and more generally contributing to the stability and legitimacy of the democracies in which these parties compete for power.[80] The Court linked participation in political parties and the realisation of the right to vote, affirming that political rights are not limited to the right to vote in an election but extend to participation in political activities – including the activities of political parties – in between elections. It is unclear what form the Constitutional Court envisages such participation to take and to what extent the participation must be meaningful and capable of influencing both the policies of the party and the selection of its candidates for public office or its office bearers. The closest the *Ramakatsa* judgement comes to explain what the content of this right might be and to what degree this might impose a duty on political parties to ensure at least certain forms of intra-party democracy in their organisation is where the majority concludes that the implication of section 19(1) of the Bill of Rights is that the 'constitutions and rules of political parties must be

[78] CCT 109/12) [2012] ZACC 31; 2013 (2) BCLR 202 (CC) (18 December 2012)

[79] Issacharoff, *Fragile Democracies*, p. 256.

[80] S. Scarrow, *Political Parties and Democracy in Theoretical and Practical Perspectives: Implementing Intra-Party Democracy* (Washington: The National Democratic Institute, 2005), p. 3.

consistent with the Constitution which is our supreme law' (para. 72). Yet, the Court carefully avoided a direct confrontation with the dominant party. The majority of judges in the case thus suggested that political parties should, at the very least, have some margin of appreciation (although they do not use that term) in determining how they wish to regulate how members of the political party should exercise the right to participate in the activities of their party as '[t]hese activities are internal matters of each political party' and parties are therefore 'best placed to determine how members would participate in internal activities' (para. 73).

The Constitutional Court has also in recent judgements signalled that it would be prepared to protect the right of opposition parties to take part in the activities of the legislature in a meaningful manner in the Ambrosini and Mazibuko judgements. Given the dominant electoral position of the governing party and its overwhelming legitimacy in society because of the central role it played in the struggle against apartheid, there would be few electoral consequences for the majority party if it limited the ability of opposition parties to mobilise support and to take part in democratic processes in Parliament. It is for this reason that the line of decisions by the Constitutional Court safeguarding the role of opposition parties in Parliament is significant. The Constitutional Court confirmed that opposition party members have a right to prepare and introduce legislation for a vote in Parliament and that it was not only the government or the governing party who had such a right.[81] It also confirmed that the rules of the national legislature must allow opposition parties to introduce motions of no confidence in the President of the country.[82] As such motions provide opposition parties with a platform to raise concerns with the leadership of the government and to publicise their criticisms of the leadership to a wider audience, the judgement helped to protect a formal space for political contestation.

Despite the major impact of Constitutional Court judgements on various aspects of governance and on the enjoyment of human rights, the system of governance and the concomitant checks and balances built into that system by the Constitution has not been an unqualified success.

[81] *Oriani-Ambrosini, MP* v. *Sisulu, MP Speaker of the National Assembly*, CCT 16/12 [2012] ZACC 27; 2012 (6) SA 588 (CC); 2013 (1) BCLR 14 (CC) (9 October 2012).

[82] *Mazibuko* v. *Sisulu and Another*, CCT 115/12) [2013] ZACC 28; 2013 (6) SA 249 (CC); 2013 (11) BCLR 1297 (CC) (27 August 2013).

Conclusion

In this chapter I explored the gap between the promise and the practice of South African constitutionalism. I highlighted the effectiveness of the judiciary – especially the Constitutional Court – in enforcing several aspects of the Constitution and suggested that the Court is able to do so because of its principled but pragmatic engagement with the provisions of the Constitution. However, I noted that the dominance of the ANC in government as well as other factors relating to internal party culture and the electoral system have a tendency to shift power from formal constitutional structures to party structures. The decisions of party structures are not open to much scrutiny or oversight. The Constitution avowedly aimed at establishing an 'objective normative value system' within which political contestation was supposed to operate. But because of the weaknesses in the electoral system and the electoral dominance of the governing party these provisions have been less effective than anticipated.

9

Idealism and Realism in Israeli Constitutional Law

ADAM SHINAR

Introduction

This chapter investigates three distinct, though interrelated, questions. First, what do the concepts of idealism and realism mean in the context of constitutional law? Second, what can the Israeli constitutional regime teach us, if anything, about the supposed gap between idealism and realism? Third, should a constitutional system work towards bridging the ideal and the real? The common intuition is that the gap between idealism and realism, however those terms are understood, should be bridged. If the real does not meet the ideal, then the real should be revised to make it adhere more closely to the ideal. The chapter will critically examine this proposition, at least in the Israeli context, but hopefully provide some more general insights. Throughout the chapter, I make two overarching claims. One is that the categories of idealism and realism, though seemingly intuitive, turn out to be quite complicated to disentangle. The second claim is that the existence of a gap between the ideal and the real, though seemingly problematic at first blush, might have, on closer examination, limited normative significance.

Accordingly, the chapter proceeds as follows. The second part, immediately following the introduction, takes a close look at the concepts of idealism and realism as categories of analysis for constitutional law. It suggests that both concepts cannot be understood without paying attention to two dimensions. The first dimension focuses on the constitutional agent – whose idealism counts? The second dimension is temporal. Assessing the gap between idealism and realism requires determining at least two points in time, evaluating one against the other. But when studying a constitutional system, determining whose ideals, what ideals, and which reference points, prove to be quite difficult.

Mindful of the problems of idealism and realism, and armed with a provisional definition of each, the third part examines three areas of Israel's constitutional structure: constitution-making, rights protection, and institutional image. For each area, I discuss the ideal and the real, and especially the gap between the two. Regarding constitution-making, I show how today's constitutional settlement looks very different from the one that was envisioned by the framers' of Israel's Declaration of Independence. My main argument, however, is that much of the difference lies in form rather than substance. Regarding rights protection, I show how Israel's judiciary took it upon itself to protect individual rights when the legislature stalled. Here too I argue that despite a seeming gap between idealism and realism, much of the difference lies in the form of protection rather than its substance. Regarding institutional image, I demonstrate how the Supreme Court seeks to transmit to its foreign audiences an image of a progressive rights protecting court by deciding which decisions to translate into English. I then point to a gap between the translated and non-translated decisions dealing with the same or similar issues. Examination of the translated decisions together with the non-translated decisions reveals a more complicated and messier picture than the Court would like to convey.

What, then, are the normative implications that follow from my analysis? The fourth part revisits the concepts of idealism and realism in light of the three areas examined in the third part of this chapter. In line with the theoretical objections to idealism and realism as categories of analysis for constitutional law, my conclusion is that at least with respect to the Israeli case study, these categories do not generate a robust normative judgement. The gap between idealism and realism, though inevitable, is not in itself a reason to commend or reject a constitutional arrangement. Moreover, examining a constitutional arrangement through the idealism-realism dichotomy may actually obscure an evaluation of the arrangement itself. When it comes to constitution-making and rights protection, the categories of idealism and realism thus tell us very little about the desirability of the arrangements themselves. Things are different, however, when we come to institutional image. Here, I believe, the categories of idealism and realism can do more meaningful work, as they are helpful in exposing the motivations of institutional actors. Still, even here the categories do not generate anything close to a clear pronouncement.

Problematizing Idealism and Realism

At first blush, idealism and realism may seem intuitive, easy-to-grasp concepts.[1] My purpose here, however, is to problematize both, especially in the context of constitutional law in general, and Israeli constitutional law in particular. Building on the work of John Rawls, I distinguish between ideal and non-ideal theory.[2] Ideal theory sketches the principles (ideal principles) that it assumes people will comply with. It idealizes the state of affairs by assuming-away extant conditions such as social strife, law breaking or scarcity of resources. In that sense, it posits favourable social conditions, those that are necessary for the working of the idealizing conditions and for fostering cooperation among people. Ideal theory thus serves as a type of blueprint. It sets a vision, a goal of what society should be striving for. Non-ideal theory, then, can only be understood in reference to ideal theory. Once we have outlined the ideal principles, we can figure out, by outlining non-ideal principles, how best to revise our political practices so that they will direct us towards the ideal, given our less-than-perfect conditions.[3]

For Rawls, the ideal and non-ideal roughly correlate with our intuitive understanding of idealism and realism. Our constitutional ideals are, presumably, those we had in mind when we sat down to write the constitution. But the act of writing, the existence of political disagreements, and the internal and external conflicts and tensions that beset political life may have gotten us away from whatever notion of the 'ideal' we had at the outset. Often, then, constitutional interpreters, especially courts, are working at the gap between idealism and realism, trying to bridge the two.

A case in point is the theory of Originalism. Despite the various strands and approaches,[4] Originalism broadly stands for the idea that a constitution should be interpreted according to the understandings that prevailed at the time of its framing and ratification – that is, before it actually came

1 At least in the colloquial sense. Of course, there are disciplines, for example international relations, where these concepts have specific meanings. Those will not be my concern here. For elaboration, see R. M. A. Crawford, *Idealism and Realism in International Relations: Beyond the Discipline* (New York: Routledge, 2000).

2 J. Rawls, *A Theory of Justice* (Oxford University Press, 1971); J. Rawls, *The Law of Peoples* (Harvard University Press, 1999).

3 For discussion of Rawls's concepts of ideal and non-ideal theory, see M. Phillips, 'Reflections on the Transition from Ideal to Non-Ideal Theory', *Noûs*, 19 (1985), 551.

4 For an overview, see L. B. Solum, 'What Is Originalism? The Evolution of Contemporary Originalist Theory' in G. Huscroft and B. W. Miller (eds.), *The Challenge of Originalism: Theories of Constitutional Interpretation* (Cambridge University Press, 2011), p. 12.

into practice.[5] One justification, which is also the most popular, is that only Originalism justifies judicial review.[6] Rather than inserting their own subjective beliefs, judges defer to those that informed the constitutional text. Since judges are mostly unelected and unaccountable, only this 'objective' examination democratically grounds their authority to review the output of a democratically elected branch.[7] Thus when judges strike down legislation, they are not acting as a super-legislature, but are instead subjecting legislation to the considered principles of 'The People', as embodied in the constitutional text, structure, and history.

But Originalism also tries to do something else. A constitution, at the time of its framing, is, in a sense, the 'ideal'. It is the place where those who were to embark on a new experiment in governance placed their hopes and aspirations. A constitution is thus a vision for a new political regime, a vision which purports to enable co-existence and collaboration and to secure the goods of community while maintaining law and order and protecting individual rights. Over time, due to political, social, and economic developments, the constitution comes to mean different things than it perhaps meant during its framing. Thus a divide grows between what is considered the ideal and the real. Originalists are busy at restoring (restoring is a key word here) the ideal by narrowing the perceived gap between the ideal and the real. In Rawlsian terms, Originalists are devising non-ideal principles to help us reach the ideal.[8] Originalism is thus one way of understanding (and attempting to bridge) the gap between idealism and realism. It is simply what happens during the period from enactment to practice.

To be sure, this is not the only way to conceptualize idealism and realism. It is not necessary to view them as distinct points in time. One could, for example, think of idealism as an always-ongoing practice of critique and contestation against the 'constitution-in-practice', what is

[5] Of course, the central question is 'whose intentions'. Some originalists (increasingly few) examine the 'original intent' of those who wrote the Constitution. New originalists, by contrast, examine the original public meaning of the Constitution, that is, how the words and provisions were understood by the public at the time of their drafting and ratification.

[6] See e.g. A. Scalia, *A Matter of Interpretation: Federal Courts and the Law* (Princeton University Press, 1998); A. Scalia, 'Originalism: The Lesser Evil', *U. Cincinnati Law Review*, 57 (1988), 849.

[7] To be clear, these are the standard tropes in support of originalism. There are many solid critiques of originalism both on theoretical and practical grounds. For an overview, see M. N. Berman, 'Originalism Is Bunk', *New York University Law Review*, 84 (2009), 1.

[8] One of the differences between Rawls and Originalists is the temporal dimension, which is strong in Originalism but not explicit or central to Rawls.

sometimes called 'living constitutionalism'.[9] People draw on ideals, some of which were already present at the founding moment, in order to shape the constitution towards their desired vision. This, according to some, is what gives life (and legitimacy) to a constitution – its ability to confer meaning through the political and interpretive activities of subsequent generations.[10]

Competing schools of constitutional theory understand 'idealism' and 'realism' in different ways, and thus will adopt different proposals and strategies for bridging idealism and realism. For the purpose of this chapter, however, I will start by considering idealism and realism as points along a temporal dimension. This is not because I think Originalism is superior to living constitutionalism, but rather because the temporal dimension offers a key to understanding the development of Israeli constitutional law as a process of constitutionalism-in-the-making. On my conceptualization, the first point is the time of the framing, when the constitution is at the level of ideas and values, the level of imagination, as a blueprint for the desired future real. Once the constitution is put into writing, is implemented by political agents, and is enforced by courts and other entities, it almost inevitably changes. It has moved into the domain of constitutional realism. To be clear, in principle, the constitution as practiced may not differ from the constitution as idealized, though in all likelihood it will, simply because of the ever-changing background against which it operates. On this view, the domain of idealism differs from the domain of realism mainly on the axis of time.

This account, though seemingly simple because it has a definite starting point and a spectrum against which to measure compliance with that starting point, actually proves to be more complicated than it first seems. Here are three difficulties that problematize the basic concepts of idealism and realism. I note them here because I want to acknowledge them and bracket them, not because I purport to have a definitive solution to these complications.

The first problem when thinking about idealism is, whose idealism counts? For Rawls it was easy because his theory of justice – his ideal

[9] See D. A. Strauss, *The Living Constitution* (Oxford University Press, 2010).

[10] Although displaying vastly different positions, such an approach to constitutional contestation and the 'ideal' can be found in L. M. Seidman, *Our Unsettled Constitution: A New Defense of Judicial Review* (Yale University Press, 2001) and J. M. Balkin, *Constitutional Redemption: Political Faith in an Unjust World* (Harvard University Press, 2011); J. M. Balkin, *Living Originalism* (Harvard University Press, 2014).

theory – was *his*. But constitutions are rarely, if ever, the product of a single author. They are the effort of a collective, where each member has distinct beliefs, interests, ideals, and values that they want actualized.[11] In order to identify the content of the ideal constitution, then, we have to trace it to ideals that were present at the time of its framing, but then whose ideals do we turn to? Such an exercise is futile, as it is impossible to divine the intent of a collective body, and it is almost impossible to determine which person's ideals are causally connected to the finished text. At most, we can decipher various constitutional idealisms. Yet once we achieve that, we are faced with the problem of constitutional realism. Against which idealism should we measure the extant situation on the ground? We need both a starting point and an end point, but if we don't know which idealism counts, it will be difficult to decide on the starting point that is crucial for determining progression or regression.

But perhaps I am being too literal. Constitutional idealism is not necessarily what someone wanted, but rather what should an ideal constitution, properly understood, include. Framing the issue in this way turns the inquiry from a sociological-empirical one (What did people think and want?) to a normative-philosophical one (What should the ideal constitution look like?). Yet here, too, we quickly run into difficulties that are by now familiar. The problem now is not empirical disagreement or divining collective intent, but instead theoretical disagreement over what, exactly, constitutes the ideal constitution. One possible reply is that such an ideal does not exist, since every constitutional arrangement should be tailored to the particular circumstances in which it is adopted, so at most we have constitutional idealism that is local and particular. Yet limiting the scope of idealism to particular circumstances does not relieve us of contestation, since we merely reproduce the theoretical disagreement, though perhaps on a smaller scale. Importantly, the problem of theoretical disagreement has implications for the legitimacy of the attempt to bridge idealism and realism, or, in Rawlsian terms, devising non-ideal principles to reach the ideal. If the problem of theoretical disagreement over constitutional ideals is pervasive, then any bridging activity will be questionable and suspect, because we lack second-order principles on the basis of which to decide between competing conceptions of constitutional ideals.

[11] Cf. K. A. Shepsle, 'Congress Is a "They," not an "It": Legislative Intent as Oxymoron', *International Review of Law & Economics*, 12 (1992), 239; N. Rao, 'Public Choice and International Law Compliance: The Executive Branch Is a "They" not an "It"', *Minnesota Law Review*, 96 (2011), 194.

The second difficulty has to do with our notion of realism, and constitutional realism in particular. The idea underlying the distinction between constitutional idealism and constitutional realism is one of comparison. We compare what ought to have been (the ideal constitution) to what we have in practice. But just like the disagreements we encounter at the stage of idealism, similar problems surface at the stage of evaluating the extant constitutional landscape. Not only do we disagree about the proper interpretation of constitutional provisions, we often fail to reach agreement about what courts have said in their decisions. Many decisions, especially in constitutional law, are ambiguous and open to interpretation, and generate uncertainty over their future application. This leads to disagreements both over what the law 'is' and how the law might develop.[12] Importantly, many of these disagreements are reasonable and are partly the result of the constitutional materials themselves, in addition to the biases, interests, and values of commentators, jurists and scholars. Thus, taking constitutional realism seriously means acknowledging that at a certain point there will be deep disagreement about the state of the law as practiced. While this problem is familiar, the consequence is that it will be difficult to compare the distance between idealism and realism.

Finally, the third difficulty I wish to highlight has to do with temporality. Under the version of idealism and realism proposed here, evaluating the gap between idealism and realism entails consideration of two points in time. Choosing the end points, however, proves to be tricky. Consider, for example, the state of Israeli constitutional law. As will be discussed momentarily, Israeli constitutional law is a work in progress. Elsewhere I have called the process of Israeli constitution-making 'accidental', in that it has developed in a piecemeal fashion, without a clear trajectory or intention.[13] When Israel was established, the Declaration of Independence called for a constitution, but a political compromise that was reached shortly thereafter determined that the constitution will be broken into laws that will be enacted separately.[14] Since then, twelve basic

[12] For example, consider the constitutionality of affirmative action programs in higher education in the United States. Conflicting decisions make discerning the holding difficult, while lower courts struggle to properly apply the standard of review (see, e.g., *Fisher v. University of Texas*, 133 S.Ct. 2411 (2013); *Fisher v. University of Texas*, 758 F.3d 633 (5th Cir. 2014)).

[13] A. Shinar, 'Accidental Constitutionalism: The Political Foundations and Implications of Israeli Constitution-Making', in D. Galligan and M. Versteeg (eds.), *The Social and Political Foundations of Constitutions* (Cambridge University Press, 2013), p. 207.

[14] The reasons for this compromise remain contested. For an overview, see *ibid.*, pp. 210–12.

laws have been enacted dealing with the structure of government, the budget, lands, and individual rights, although many argue that essential rights and provisions are still missing.[15] Given this partial constitution, how are we to evaluate the gap between idealism and realism? If we take the present as our end point, it is unclear whether the Israeli constitution has met the ideal of a complete written constitution announced during its establishment.[16] But perhaps if we look at the overall trajectory, Israel is moving towards meeting the blueprint announced at its founding and the disagreement will revolve around the pace of such movement. The more general point is that it is difficult to adjudicate such a dispute, precisely because its resolution turns on contestable assumptions and factual analysis. This is further complicated by the need to determine temporal points before the comparison between the ideal and the real can be undertaken.

The preceding three problems call into question the utility of idealism and realism as descriptive and normative categories of analysis. In the pages that follow, however, I will nevertheless embrace this terminology as a placeholder for multiple meanings. For the purpose of this chapter, constitutional idealism will stand for two ideas. One is the prevailing ideas that have dominated the Israeli constitution-making process from its inception until the present day. The second meaning of idealism has to do with the image governmental institutions want to project in relation to their constitutional commitments. In particular, part of this chapter will discuss the institutional image of Israel's Supreme Court, Israel's final and authoritative constitutional interpreter.[17] The image the Court wants to maintain is, I believe, a type of constitutional idealism. Correlatively, my investigation of constitutional realism will focus on how the twin conceptions of idealism hold up to criticism. In the end, a gap between the ideal and the real is inevitable. But on the normative front, such gaps are not necessarily undesirable or problematic. The chapter will therefore end with a discussion of the normative implications of the descriptive gap.

[15] Some, though increasingly few, argue that despite the basic laws, Israel still lacks a constitution at all. See R. Gavison, 'The Constitutional Revolution: A Reality or a Self-Fulfilling Prophecy?', *Mishpatim*, 28 (1997), 21, 31 (Hebrew).

[16] As I argued above, opinions will differ because both the ideal and the real are contested and open to interpretation.

[17] On the *de facto* supremacy of the Israeli Supreme Court, see O. Aronson, 'Why Hasn't the Knesset Abolished Basic Law: Human Dignity and Liberty? Status Quo as Countermajoritarian Difficulty', *Tel Aviv University Law Review*, 37(2016). 509 (Hebrew).

Idealism and Realism in Israeli Constitutional Law – Three Axes

This part examines three aspects of Israeli constitutional law where I believe the gaps between the ideal and the real are identifiable, sharp, and normatively interesting. The first subpart discusses the process of Israeli constitution making. It provides a brief overview of how Israel came to have a type of written constitution, and it contrasts the present day result with the intentions of those who embarked upon that process. My claim is that Israeli constitutional law has proceeded in a direction that attempts to come close to realizing the vision of the founding generation, but that this process happened in a way that the latter could not have imagined. The second subpart examines the protection of substantive rights in Israeli constitutional law and how the level of protection changed over time. Here the claim is similar to that in the first subpart: over time the constitutional regime accommodated more and more rights claims. However, those came about through expansive judicial interpretation instead of a decisive legislative or constituent move. Finally, the third subpart turns from constitutional structure and rights protection to institutional image. Here I examine the way in which the Supreme Court, the ultimate constitutional interpreter, chooses to shape its institutional image to audiences abroad through the decision of which opinions to translate. Unlike in the first two subparts, where the Court has often played the role of a progressive agent, my claim is that when it comes to transmitting an institutional image, the court carefully crafts an image of a court concerned with individual rights while downplaying crucial complexities that are visible mostly to the informed domestic audience. Thus the last subpart addresses a different aspect of the idealist–realist divide. Idealism will be conceptualized as the 'ideal' image the Court is interested in transmitting, whereas 'realism' will be the Court's activity *in toto.*

Constitution Making

Ideally, Israel was to have a constitution at its inception. Before its establishment in 1948, soon after the British Mandate over Palestine ended, there were already at least eight different drafts for a constitution, and several more were added during the year of independence.[18] Indeed, the

[18] See Past Constitutional Drafts, available at: http://huka.gov.il/wiki/index.php/%D7%94%D7%A6%D7%A2%D7%95%D7%AA_%D7%97%D7%95%D7%A7%D7%94_%D7%91%D7%A2%D7%91%D7%A8 (Hebrew).

Declaration of Independence stated that the Constituent Assembly shall draft a constitution no later than 1 October 1948.[19] The plan for a written constitution, however, did not materialize. Elsewhere I have elaborated on the reasons for constitutional paralysis during the first years of Israel's independence.[20] While those reasons remain contested, they are less important here. The bottom line is that, for a mix of political, demographic, and ideological reasons, Israel failed to enact a constitution during its early years. Instead, a political compromise, known as the 'Harari Resolution', was reached. Its purpose was to break up the constitution-making process into small parts so that each constitutional arrangement would be reached separately, over time, and in the end be compiled into one constitution.[21]

Although the Harari Resolution became Israel's constitution-making method, it differed significantly from the vision expressed in the Declaration of Independence. First, constitutionalization would now be protracted, incrementalist, and piecemeal. This allowed for greater flexibility, as the constitution can be tailored to extant circumstances in real time.[22] However, leaving things undecided can potentially generate a more long-term constitutional paralysis.[23] Often, constitutions are enacted during times of great political upheaval, which assists in facilitating their passage.[24] Barring such a constitutional moment, the process can become more belaboured and subject to problems of political

[19] See Declaration of Independence, Official Gazette, 14 May 1948, 1. 1 L.S.I. 3 (1948). See also A. Rubinstein and B. Medina, *The Constitutional Law of Israel*, 6th edn, 2 vols. (Schoken, Jerusalem and Tel Aviv, 2005), vol. I, p. 35 (Hebrew).

[20] For a discussion of the various reasons leading to constitutional paralysis, see Shinar, 'Accidental Constitutionalism'; G. Sapir, *Constitutional Revolution in Israel: Past, Present and Future* (Bar Ilan and Haifa University Presses, 2010), pp. 29–40 (Hebrew).

[21] 5 Knesset Records 1743 (1950). The Resolution provided that 'The First Knesset (Israel's parliament – A.S.) charges the Constitution, Law, and Justice Committee to prepare a draft constitution. The constitution will be comprised of chapters, in a way that each will be a fundamental law unto itself. The chapters will be brought before the Knesset, if the committee finishes its work, and all the chapters together will become the constitution of the state.'

[22] True, there is always the possibility of a constitutional amendment, but many constitutions are entrenched in ways that make amendment difficult.

[23] But see J. Segev, 'Who Needs a Constitution? In Defense of the Non-Decision Constitution-Making Tactic in Israel', *Albany Law Review*, 70 (2007), 409, 420; H. Lerner, *Making Constitutions in Deeply Divided Societies* (Cambridge University Press, 2011) (arguing that in deeply divided societies, such as Israel, an incrementalist approach is preferable).

[24] See J. Elster, 'Forces and Mechanisms in the Constitution-Making Process', *Duke Law Journal*, 45 (1995), 364, 370.

will.[25] Indeed, as will be discussed below, the subsequent developments in Israel reflect such difficulties.

The second difference between the intention pronounced in the Declaration and the Harari Resolution is that the task of writing the constitution shifted from a constituent assembly to the ordinary legislature. Thus the political compromise also resulted in changing the identity of the constitutional designer. We have no way of knowing what a constituent assembly would have done, because the first (and only) assembly that was elected by a popular vote quickly changed its designation to a regularly constituted parliament, the Israeli Knesset.[26] Since then, the legislature has enacted twelve constitutional chapters, known as Basic Laws, without ever convening a constituent assembly. But, depending on the way the legislature and a constituent assembly are elected, it is reasonable to assume that they would have reached different results. A constituent assembly whose members are not up for re-election is likely to behave differently than legislators who, all things being equal, are interested in keeping their seat.[27]

Having dispensed with the idea of creating one document written by a constituent assembly, the Knesset began enacting basic laws, each dealing with a distinct aspect of governance. But because these laws were the result of the Harari Resolution, and because the prevailing sense was that only in the future they would become a part of the constitution, the basic laws were considered no different than ordinary legislation. Their normative status was not superior to that of any other law, most of them were not entrenched, and the Supreme Court did not treat them differently – in terms of interpretation or superiority – than any other law.[28] Similarly, the

[25] For the idea of a constitutional moment, see B. Ackerman, *We the People: Foundations* (Cambridge, Harvard University Press, 1991).

[26] See §1 Transition Law-1949 ('The legislature shall be called the "Knesset". The constituent assembly shall be called the "First Knesset". A delegate of the constituent assembly shall be called "Member of the Knesset"').

[27] For the idea that the desire to be reelected affects political behaviour, see, e.g., R. K. Weaver, 'The Politics of Blame Avoidance', *Journal of Public Policy*, 6 (1986), 371; G. Biglaiser and C. Mezzetti, 'Politicians' Decision Making with Re-Election Concerns', *Journal of Public Economics*, 66 (1997), 425.

[28] H.C. 148/73 *Kaniel v. Minister of Justice* [1973] IsrSC 27(1) 795; C.A. 107/73 Negev – Automobile Service Station v. State of Israel [1974] IsrSC 27(1) 640. *But see* H.C. 98/69 *Bergman v. Minister of Finance* [1969] IsrSC 23(1) 693 (establishing judicial review only when the Knesset violates an entrenched provision of a basic law. In effect, this only applied to election laws that impacted the equality of elections and which were passed without the stipulated requisite majority of 61 MKs).

public reaction to the enactment of the basic laws, for the most part,[29] was indifferent.

Indeed, at least and up until 1995, very few believed Israel had a written constitution, as opposed to a material constitution.[30] The question, then, is how, from a situation where very few, if any, believed Israel had a constitution, did Israel arrive at the present situation, where there is a consensus, at least among all the government branches and the scholarly community, that Israel has a written constitution?

The answer is that the incrementalist constitutional project that was initiated by the Knesset, according to the plan outlined in the Harari Resolution, has been almost completely displaced by the Supreme Court, which assumed centre stage starting from 1995, by declaring a 'constitutional revolution'.[31] It was the Court, not the legislature, which elevated the basic laws to a constitutional status. The reasons for this power shift are complex and contested, but several reasons are traditionally offered.

First, up until 1992, all the basic laws addressed structural issues: the way elections are to be held, the composition of the government, the powers of the judiciary, the principles regarding the state budget, the management of state lands, the status of the military, and so forth. Most of these basic laws were not contentious and they enjoyed a broad political consensus. Importantly, none of the basic laws protected individual rights.[32] This changed in 1992, when the Knesset passed two basic laws: Basic Law: Freedom of Occupation, and Basic Law: Human Dignity and Liberty.[33] The first protected the freedom to choose one's occupation. The second, and more important of the two, protected human dignity, life, liberty, property, privacy and freedom of movement.

[29] A notable exception was the rewriting of the Basic Law: The Government that changed the way the Prime Minister is elected. The law generated much controversy and was soon changed back. However, the public debates surrounding the law had more to do with its content than its supposed constitutional status.

[30] See A. L Bendor, 'The Purpose of the Israeli Constitution', in G. Sapir, D. Barak-Erez and A. Barak (eds.), *Israeli Constitutional Law in the Making* (Oxford, Hart Publishing, 2013), p. 41. Even to this day, there are a few holdouts. See Gavison, 'Constitutional Revolution', 31.

[31] Constitutional revolution was the phrase coined by the former President of the Supreme Court, Aharon Barak, who was also the principal author of the United Bank Hamizarachi decision.

[32] An exception is section 4(a) of Basic Law: The Knesset, protecting the equality of elections.

[33] The story behind the passage of these basic laws goes beyond the scope of this chapter. For elaboration, see Shinar, 'Accidental Constitutionalism'.

Placing individual rights under the basic law regime opened up the possibility, in theory, for judicial review of primary legislation.[34]

The passage of the two basic laws enabled – indeed motivated – legal challenges to legislation that, it was argued, violated the protected rights. The new basic laws gave courts, especially the Supreme Court,[35] a textual authorization for the exercise of judicial review.[36]

Textual authorization, however, was not the only reason the Court took up the task of consolidating the Israeli constitutional project when it gave the basic laws supreme status over every other type of legislation. Indeed, even before the passage of the 1992 basic laws there were hints the Court would be willing to strike down legislation that conflicted with the basic values of the legal system.[37] A second, equally important reason for the power shift was that the political climate was amenable to such a move by the judiciary at the expense of the legislature.[38] Although the decisive moment came in 1995, with the Court's decision in *United Mizrahi Bank*,[39] which held that the basic laws are superior to ordinary legislation and that the way to enforce the new constitution would be through judicial review, the seeds of which were planted much earlier. They resulted both from a growing ideological commitment to constitutionalism and from a political impasse that blocked a legislative consensus over the proper constitutional arrangement.[40]

[34] It should be noted that before the passage of these basic laws the Supreme Court had no difficulty invalidating secondary legislation (rules, regulations and administrative decisions) based on a theory of a judicial bill of rights, See e.g. H.C. 73/53 *Kol Ha'am v. Minister of Interior* [1953] IsrSC 7(2) 871.

[35] The Israeli Supreme Court sits as both a court appeals and as a high court of justice. In the latter capacity, the Court sits as a court of first instance in most constitutional and administrative matters. See Y. Sagy, 'For the Administration of Justice: On the Establishment of the High Court of Justice of Israel', *Tel Aviv University Law Review*, 28 (2004), 225 (Hebrew).

[36] It should be noted that the 1992 basic laws protected certain rights and stated that no laws may infringe upon these rights unless they met the requirements of a limitations clause, essentially a proportionality formula. Yet nowhere did the basic laws say that it was the function of *courts* to decide whether laws violate the basic law, and nowhere did the basic laws say that courts have the authority to strike down statutes.

[37] See H.C. 149/89 *Laor v. Speaker of the Knesset* [1990] IsrSC 44(3) 529.

[38] In an earlier piece, I referred to this phenomenon as 'judicial constitution making'. See Shinar, 'Accidental Constitutionalism', 214.

[39] C. A. 6821/93 *United Mizrachi Bank v. Migdal Cooperative Village* [1995] IsrSC 49(4) 221.

[40] The Israeli commitment to constitutionalism was part of the global trend towards constitutionalism after the end of World War II. See R. Hirschl, 'The Strategic Foundations of Constitutions', in D. Galligan and M. Versteeg (eds.), *The Social and Political Foundations of Constitutions* (Cambridge University Press, 2013), p. 157 (describing such theories as ideational theories).

The political impasse stemmed from growing fragmentation in Israeli politics. For the first thirty years since Israel's independence, the centre-left labour party (Mapai) dominated Israeli politics. The change came with the 1977 elections, which, for the first time, gave the right wing Likud party a convincing majority. Ever since then, the left-right split has become more pronounced. And indeed, although, since the 1990s, Israel's right wing parties controlled the political agenda, though neither party's control was ever complete. In order to govern, both right and left wing parties needed to enter coalitions with parties that had different, often sectarian agendas. This made consensus difficult, especially over heated ideological issues like individual rights and the relationship between religion and state.

The political fragmentation reflected growing polarization in the general population. Demographic changes in the Jewish community, increasing political consciousness of Mizrahi Jews, immigration waves from the former Soviet Union, tensions between religious and secular Jews, a growing minority of Israeli Palestinians, plus the ongoing occupation of the Palestinian Territories made governance difficult. Public trust in political institutions decreased, and calls to pass a written constitution became more frequent. Several legislators and think tanks heeded the call and began working on various proposals to enact a comprehensive constitution. Yet those attempts failed precisely because of the impasse and polarization that they attempted to overcome.

In this contested landscape, the Supreme Court, which enjoyed very high levels of public trust,[41] began to assert a more dominant position. Starting in the 1980s, it significantly relaxed its justiciability and standing requirements, essentially allowing almost everyone to come forward claiming that the rule of law has been breached.[42] NGOs, human rights organizations, and even legislators who were exasperated with the often-deadlocked political process thus turned to the Court attempting to vindicate their claims. For its part, the Court was more than happy to entertain these petitions, and signalled so to potential litigants.[43]

[41] See generally M. Mautner, *Law and the Culture of Israel* (Oxford University Press, 2011); A. Meydani, *The Israeli Supreme Court and the Human Rights Revolution: Courts as Agenda Setters* (Cambridge University Press, 2011).

[42] H.C. 910/86 *Resler v. Minister of Defense* [1988] IsrSC 42(2) 441.

[43] Ran Hirschl has argued that judicial aggrandizement in Israel is the result of political and cultural elites' (mainly the Ashkenazi secular bourgeoisie) gradual loss of political power. In an attempt to salvage some of their influence, these embattled hegemons turned to the courts in order to preserve some of the power they felt they were losing. See R. Hirschl, 'The Political Origins of Judicial Empowerment through Constitutionalization: Lessons

Although constitutional review only appeared on the scene in 1995, it was preceded by years of robust administrative adjudication, examining whether administrative acts were 'reasonable' or 'proportional' to the harm they inflicted on judicially created rights.[44]

The transition to a full-fledged constitutional democracy came not with a legislative or constituent act, but in a judicial decision – *United Mizrahi Bank*.[45] In that case, Israel's version of *Marbury v. Madison*,[46] the Court declared that the basic laws are a constitution, even if the Knesset had still not finished writing all the basic laws. Subsequent cases affirmed that all basic laws (not just the two from 1992) are superior to ordinary legislation, that they can be amended only by new basic laws, and that the Court has the power to strike down laws that do not meet the limitations clauses and proportionality formula to which all rights violations are subject. In the years since, the Court has regularly, though not frequently, struck down laws and provisions that violated protections provided in the basic laws, especially the two basic laws enacted in 1992.

For the purpose of this chapter, what matters is that the gap between idealism and realism was bridged, though in a way that was different from what most of the 'idealists' believed was necessary. Although there is still a question whether the ideal was the promise of a constitution in the Declaration of Independence or the political compromise reached in the Harari Resolution, there can be no argument that neither path came to fruition. There was no constituent assembly that passed an entire constitution; and despite passing twelve basic laws, many aspects of governance had still not been attended to by the legislature.[47]

from Israel's Constitutional Revolution', *Comparative Politics*, 33 (2001), 315, 326; and see more generally R. Hirschl, *Towards Juristocracy: The Origins and Consequences of the New Constitutionalism* (Harvard University Press, 2004). Elsewhere I argued that Hirschl's thesis ignores developments in Israel that had little to do with loss of power by former hegemons. See Shinar, 'Accidental Constitutionalism', p. 222.

44 Shinar, 'Accidental Constitutionalism', pp. 215–16 (collecting judicial decisions attesting this trend). For example, freedom of speech, religion, equality and occupation, were all recognized by the Court years before they were constitutionalized. True, laws that violated these rights were not subject to judicial review, but secondary legislation could not violate these rights without explicit authorization by the legislature to do so.

45 C.A. 6821/93 *United Mizrachi Bank v. Migdal Cooperative Village* [1995] IsrSC 49(4) 221.

46 5 U.S. 137 (1803).

47 To name just a few, several basic laws were proposed but never passed. See, e.g., Basic Law: Legislation (determining how laws are to be made and establishing the courts' power of judicial review); Basic Law: Freedom of Speech and Assembly; Basic Law: Social and Economic Rights.

In a move criticized by commentators, legislators and the parts of the media, the Court stepped into the vacuum created by the legislature. Despite frequent protestations and attempts to curb the Court's power of judicial review by the legislature, the Court persisted and the attempts failed.[48] For now, I merely wish to note the gap between idealism and realism, and how that gap can nevertheless be closed or narrowed in way that was not envisioned when the ideal was put forward. In the fourth section of this chapter I will discuss the normative implications of such a move: 'Does it matter how the gap is bridged or should we only consider that it was bridged in fact?'

Protection of Individual Rights

Similarly to the process of constitution making that put the judiciary at the centre stage of the constitutional project, the task of protecting individual rights was also taken up by the judiciary, even before 1995, when the *United Bank Hamizrachi* case was decided.

Recall that the Declaration of Independence called for a written constitution. Similarly, it stated that rights such as conscience, equality, and religion would be protected in the new state, and that it will adhere to the principles in the U.N. Universal Declaration of Human Rights. Absent a constitutional text, however, it was unclear how such rights would be safeguarded, especially since the Knesset enacted few statutes for their protection. Still, there was a felt need to protect individual rights. In lieu of a written constitution, the Court developed a judicial bill of rights based on Israel's professed status as a democracy committed to the rule of law. This bill of rights derived from case law and amounted to a corpus of judicially created rights that had no constitutional grounding, other than being announced by the Court. Accordingly, this 'judicial bill of rights' could not protect against statutory infringements, but it did protect individuals against infringements traced to secondary legislation such as regulations, rules, policy guidelines and administrative decisions, i.e., infringements by the executive branch. In this way, the Court managed to protect a wide array of rights such as free speech, equality, due process, religion, and the freedom to pursue an occupation.[49] Until 1995, all infringements by the executive branch were subject to this judicial bill

[48] For a discussion and explanation of this phenomenon, See Aronson, 'Why Hasn't the Knesset'.

[49] See, e.g., H.C. 73/53 *Kol Ha'am v. Minister of Interior* [1953] IsrSC 7 871 (recognizing the right to free speech); H.C. 1/49 *Bejerano v. Minister of Police* [1949] IsrSC 2(1) 80.

of rights. Secondary legislation could violate a recognized individual right only if the primary legislator expressly authorized the violation. Otherwise, this was a simple case of *ultra vires*.[50] This move was closely connected with the idea of the rule of law, which, absent a written constitution, was viewed by the Court as the most important limiting device of partisan politics.[51]

1995, however, was not only a watershed moment for constitutionalism generally, it was also a crucial point for rights protections. Up until 1995 the Court protected individual rights against some infringements, but the legislature had the last word and could authorize the executive to engage in rights violations.[52] The constitutional revolution of 1995 changed all that. Elevating the basic laws to constitutional status meant that the rights protected by the Basic Law: Human Dignity and Liberty and Basic Law: Freedom of Occupation now limited the Legislature itself. It would no longer do, then, to expressly authorize rights violations, since those too would be subject to the Basic Law's requirement of proper purpose and proportionality.

But there was also a second, perhaps unintended consequence of the constitutional revolution. The constitutionalization of the basic laws and the growing involvement of the Court in the process of constitution-making generated a backlash in the legislature. The backlash took two forms. First, numerous (largely unsuccessful) court curbing attempts.[53] Second, an almost complete legislative disengagement from constitutional law, resulting in a cessation of basic law legislation.[54] In the vacuum that was created, the Court expanded, through constitutional

50 D. Dorner, 'Does Israel Have a Constitution?', *Saint Louis University Law Journal*, 43 (1999), 1325, 1327.

51 M. Edelman, *Courts, Politics, and Culture in Israel* (University of Virginia Press, 1994) p. 33.

52 It should be noted that this authority did have limits grounded in administrative law doctrines such as reasonableness and proportionality. See e.g. H.C. 6163/92 *Eisenberg v. Minister of Construction and Housing* [1993] IsrSC 47(2) 229; H.C. 3477/95 *Ben Atiya v. Minister of Education* [1996] IsrSC 49(5) 1.

53 See Aronson, 'Why Hasn't the Knesset', 17.

54 See Gavison, 'Constitutional Revolution', 137 (arguing that the constitutional project has come to a halt in the legislature because legislators feel cheated and do not trust the court). Two exceptions are worth mentioning. One was the enactment of a basic law that allowed the government to pass a bi-yearly budget. The second was a basic law requiring a referendum before the approval of an agreement relinquishing control of territory held by Israel. Significantly, these two basic laws did not change the general contours of the constitutional regime nor did they seek to protect additional rights not included in previous basic laws.

interpretation, the scope of the individual rights included in Basic Law: Human Dignity and Liberty. In particular, it interpreted the right to dignity as including many other rights not contained in the Basic Law, including those that were intentionally left out by the Knesset such as free speech[55] and equality.[56,57] The Court also expanded somewhat the scope of socio-economic rights. Although several attempts to include social rights in the basic laws failed,[58] the Court held that a right to dignity includes a right to a minimal standard of living.[59] Moreover, commentators have also argued that the right to dignity includes the right to an education, health, an adequate standard of living and the right to a clean environment.[60] Those have yet to be constitutionalized, but, of course, the Israeli constitution is a work in progress.

The expansion of the Basic Law to include additional rights, though controversial,[61] was probably inevitable. Before 1995, when the status of the basic laws was similar to ordinary legislation, all rights were on equal footing: individual rights were recognized by the Court; they constrained the executive, and could be overridden by the legislature. But the elevation of the Basic Laws meant that now some rights counted more than others.[62] Strict construction of Basic Law: Human Dignity and Liberty would mean that dignity, property, and privacy were protected, but rights such as speech, equality and religion were relegated to a lesser status. This artificial division was, in the view of most judges, untenable. As a result, the rights to liberty and dignity were soon expanded to cover additional rights that could be derived from human dignity. For example, according to several judges, to be discriminated meant to be humiliated, and when

55 H.C. 10203/03 *'Hamifkad Haleumi' v. Attorney General* [2008] IsrSC 62(4) 715.

56 H.C. 6427/02 *Movement for the Quality of Government in Israel v. the Knesset* [2006] IsrSC 61(1) 619.

57 See generally, H. Sommer, 'The Non-Enumerated Rights: on the Scope of the Constitutional Revolution', *Mishpatim*, 28 (1997), 257 (Hebrew).

58 See, e.g., proposed Basic Law: Social Rights (P/3783/18) (12 December 2011) (listing previous attempts to constitutionalize social and economic rights).

59 H.C. 366/03 *Association for the Commitment to Peace and Social Justice v. Minister of Finance* [2005] IsrSC 60(3) 464.

60 See T. Hostovsky Brandes, 'Human Dignity as a Central Pillar in Constitutional Rights Jurisprudence in Israel: Definitions and Parameters' in G. Sapir, D. Barak-Erez and A. Barak (eds.), *Israeli Constitutional Law in the Making* (Oxford, Hart Publishing, 2013), p. 270. On the right to health, see A. Gross, In Search of the Right to Health in Israeli Constitutional Law', in G. Sapir, D. Barak-Erez and A. Barak (eds.), *Israeli Constitutional Law in the Making* (Oxford: Hart Publishing, 2013), p. 311.

61 The move was criticized by several Israeli scholars. See Sommer, 'Non-Enumerated Rights'.

62 Sapir, *Constitutional Revolution*, p. 107.

a person is humiliated her dignity is harmed.[63] When a person is not allowed to speak her mind, her autonomy and right to realize her goals are harmed, and thus her right to liberty and dignity is violated.[64] Dignity, then, became a general right that serves the foundation for most other individual rights, and perhaps some social and economic rights.

In conclusion, we can see that the process of protecting individual rights happened in more or less the same way as did the process of constitution making. Initially, or ideally, it was the legislature's task to fashion a bill of rights, in the spirit of the Declaration of Independence or the Harari Resolution. For reasons that are by now familiar, the constitutional project was halted when the Court entered the fray. Unlike the constitution-making process however, the Court had already created a judicial bill of rights before the constitutional revolution. From there, it was but a short leap to ground the non-enumerated constitutional rights in the general right to dignity. Thus the framers' intention has seemingly been fulfilled, yet not in the precise way they envisioned. As with the constitution-making process, I will address the potential normative implications of this move in the fourth section of this chapter.

Institutional Image

The first two axes discussed the familiar constitutional issues of constitution making and the protection of individual rights along the idealism-realism spectrum. I want to move now to a far less-explored terrain – the way in which Israel's highest constitutional authority – the Supreme Court – chooses to construct its image.

As is often claimed and acknowledged, courts, having neither the power of the purse nor the sword,[65] rely on their legitimacy in order to secure compliance with their decisions. That legitimacy can be normative – that is, derived from courts' adherence to principles of legitimacy under a particular theory of justice – or it can be sociological – that is, derived

[63] H. C. 4541/94 *Miller v. Minister of Security* [1995] IsrSC 49(4) 94. Deducing equality from humiliation was only an interim position, held by a few judges. The accepted position now is that equality can be directly deduced from dignity. See H.C. 1113/99 *Adala v. Minister of Religion* [2000] IsrSC 54(2) 154.

[64] See e.g. H.C. 10203/03 *'Hamifkad Haleumi' v. Attorney General* [2008] IsrSC 62(4) 715; H.C. 5239/11 *Avneri v. The Knesset* [2015] IsrSC (unpublished).

[65] The Federalist No. 78 (Alexander Hamilton).

from the empirical fact that people, for whatever reason, happen to find their decisions acceptable.[66]

Courts, however, no longer play on their own 'turf'. The act of judging has, in a sense, been internationalized. As Anne-Marie Slaughter argues, adjudication has been globalized; judges and courts interact with each other beyond national borders to form a global community of courts.[67] This global conversation means that there are 'important new audiences for judicial output, and judiciaries may earn prestige through citation by courts of other countries'.[68] This phenomenon, called 'transnational judicial dialogue', usually refers to two types of judicial activities. First, judges directly interact with judges from other countries in conferences and judicial delegations. Second, judges cite decisions from other countries to support their own decisions.[69] Although citations of foreign decisions is not new nor are the meetings between judges from different countries, there has been a relative surge in the study and conceptualization of these judicial networks, which have been facilitated by the increasing ease of transnational communication.[70]

Partly as a result of this process of increasing interaction, the Israeli Supreme Court has managed to secure a prestigious place among

[66] On the different meanings of legitimacy in the judicial context, see R. H. Fallon, Jr., 'Legitimacy and the Constitution', *Harvard Law Review*, 118 (2005), 1787; O. Bassok, 'The Sociological-Legitimacy Difficulty', *Journal of Law & Politics*, 26 (2011), 239.

[67] A. Slaughter, 'Judicial Globalization', *Virginian Journal of International Law*, 40 (2000), 1103; A. Slaughter, 'A Global Community of Courts', *Harvard International Law Journal*, 44 (2003), 191.

[68] T. Ginsburg and N. Garoupa, 'Judicial Audiences and Reputation: Perspectives from Comparative Law', *Columbia Journal of Transnational Law*, 47 (2009), 451.

[69] The reasons for cross-citation are multiple. As one scholar argues, they are not necessarily a means for communication, but can also be used for strategic reasons. See E. Voeten, 'Borrowing and Nonborrowing among International Courts', *Journal of Legal Studies*, 39 (2010), 547.

[70] See, e.g., E. Benvenisti and G. W. Downs, 'National Courts, Domestic Democracy, and the Evolution of International Law: A Rejoinder to N. Lavranos, J. Katz Cogan and T. Ginsburg', *European Journal of International Law*, 20 (2010), 1027; A. Wiener and P. Liste, 'Lost without Translations? Cross-Referencing and a New Global Community of Courts', *Indiana Journal of Global Legal Studies*, 21 (2014), 263; D. S. Law, 'Generic Constitutional Law', *Minnesota Law Review*, 89 (2004), 652, 653–7; M. Gelter and M. M. Siems, 'Citations to Foreign Courts – Illegitimate and Superfluous, or Unavoidable? Evidence from Europe', *American Journal of Comparative Law*, 62 (2014), 35; A. Shinar and A. Su, 'Religious Law as Foreign Law in Constitutional Interpretation', *International Journal of Constitutional Law*, 11 (2013), 74; O. Frishman, 'Should Courts Fear Transnational Engagement?', *Vanderbilt Journal of Transnational Law*, 49 (2016), 56.

courts.[71] For example, the US federal courts, although stingy with their overall citations of foreign courts, cite the Israeli Supreme Court as frequently as they do the European Court of Human Rights, the High Court of Australia, and the Supreme Court of India.[72]

Increasing citations of Israeli law are also a consequence of the Court having decided many cases resulting from the occupation of the Palestinian Territories (OPT), which have been under Israeli military rule since 1967. By extending the Supreme Court's jurisdiction to military acts in the OPT, the Court is probably the only domestic court in the world routinely deciding cases involving international humanitarian law and the law of occupation. In the post-9/11 era, many countries and scholars have thus turned to Israel to study how the Court addresses state actions designed to combat terrorism.[73]

In its quest to become influential, the Israeli Supreme Court itself has translated its major decisions into English so that they can be studied and used by other courts. In particular, the Court has embarked on a project of translating especially those decisions having to do with combating terrorism. On its English website, for example, one can find a special box titled 'Judgments of the Israeli Supreme Court: Fighting Terrorism within the Law.'[74] The same decisions also appear on the website of Israel's Ministry of Foreign Affairs.[75]

The subtext of these publications is clear. By singling out those decisions having to do with terrorism, the Court signals that these decisions are important, that they are a reflection, a good exemplar, of the Court's work, and that it hopes that people from other countries, who do not know Hebrew, will now be able to learn from the Court and perhaps apply these decisions in similar contexts abroad. Put differently, these

[71] See, e.g., C. L'Heureux-Dubè, 'The Importance of Dialogue: Globalization and the National Impact of the Rehnquist Court', *Tulsa Law Review*, 34 (1998), 15; D. A. Farber, 'The Supreme Court, the Law of Nations, and Citations of Foreign Law: The Lessons of History', *California Law Review*, 95 (2007), 1335.

[72] D. Zaring, 'The Use of Foreign Decisions by Federal Courts: An Empirical Analysis', *Journal of Empirical Legal Studies*, 3 (2006), 297, 325.

[73] See, e.g., Farber, 'The Supreme Court', 1363; R. Murphy and A. J. Radsan, 'Due Process and Targeted Killing of Terrorists, *Cardozo Law Review* 31 (2009), 405; P. Gaeta, 'May Necessity Be Available as a Defence for Torture in the Interrogation of Suspected Terrorists?', *Journal of International Criminal Justice*, 2 (2004), 785; S. J. Schulhofer, 'Checks and Balances in Wartime: American, British and Israeli Experiences', *Michigan Law Review*, 102 (2004), 1906.

[74] Available at: http://elyon1.court.gov.il/verdictssearch/EnglishVerdictsSearch.aspx.

[75] Available at: http://mfa.gov.il/mfa/aboutisrael/state/law/pages/fighting%20terrorism%20within%20the%20law%202-jan-2005.aspx.

decisions are one of the ways in which the Court presents an institutional image to other courts, judges, policymakers, scholars, and laypeople.

At the same time, the Court, like any other institution, is constrained in the amount of decisions it can translate. The Court issues hundreds of decisions every year. Given that there are finite resources and a finite number of translators, not every decision can be translated. Thus the Court inevitably must choose what foreign audiences see. It is thus an active participant in the shaping of its image.

For the purpose of this chapter, I will treat the cases that the Supreme Court decides to translate as the 'ideal'. They represent, in the eyes of the Court, the best, most important decisions that the Court issues. Since judges handpick the decisions that get translated, it is reasonable to assume that they choose those that they are especially proud of and think worthy of foreign eyes.[76]

An examination of all 284 translated decisions that appear on the Court's website goes beyond the scope of this chapter. Instead, I have decided to examine the decisions that comprise the collection 'Judgments of the Israeli Supreme Court: Fighting Terrorism within the Law'. The collection, totalling 27 decisions, provides a window into the Court's activity vis-à-vis the OPT and Israel's attempts to combat what it perceives as security threats. Where applicable, I have also looked at the larger database of general translations, which contains decisions dealing with similar security related issues that are not included in the special collection.

My aim in investigating these decisions is not only to see what the Court has decided to translate, but what it has decided *not* to translate. As I argued above, the decision to translate a particular case is part of how the Court selects to presents itself to non-domestic audiences, how it constructs its image. Because the decisions are written in Hebrew, and because most, though not all, of the scholarly literature on Israeli case law is in Hebrew, translated decisions are among the most important primary sources for understanding the jurisprudence of the Court.

However, as I will argue below, reading the translated Israeli case law may provide a skewed image of what the Court does on a daily basis.

[76] In the past, each judge could decide which of his or her decisions would be translated. The cases would then go into a queue. In 2014, Yeshiva University's Cardozo Law School has embarked upon a project, called Versa, to translate Israeli Supreme Court decisions based on the recommendations of an academic advisory board, of which this author is a member. The new project will most likely replace the Court's selection mechanism. Until now, relatively few decisions have been translated by the new project. The project is available at http://versa.cardozo.yu.edu/.

Indeed, I will be arguing that there is a gap between the idealistic image the Court is interested in conveying – that of a liberal, relatively progressive, rights-conscious court – and that of a court that may not live up to the ideals it purports to hold in its translated decision. The 'real', then, is far messier and complicated than the 'ideal'.

In order to make this argument, made here in abbreviated form,[77] I will examine two issues that have been subject to extensive litigation before the Supreme Court: Torture and the Separation Wall. For each issue I will examine the case or cases that were translated, and juxtapose them with untranslated cases dealing with the same issues. This juxtaposition, I will argue, reveals the selective nature of the decision to translate, leading to the argument that there is a gap between the 'ideal' court and the 'real' court, a gap that is rendered visible only when comparing translated and non-translated decisions. This gap, in turn, manages to sustain the image of the ideal alongside the more complicated reality of the Court's routine docket, a reality which often detracts from the ideal image the Court seeks to maintain.

Torture

In its seminal 1999 decision,[78] the Court held that the Israeli Security Authority (ISA) does not have the legal authority to apply physical pressure on the people it subjects to interrogations. Physical pressure, sometimes amounting to torture, was often applied in ISA interrogations, with the justification being that it is necessary to prevent terrorist attacks, for example in 'ticking bomb' scenarios. However, the Court ruled that necessity can be, at most, a defense to criminal charges but not ex-ante authorization to commit torture, which the interrogators did not have under Israeli law. Physical pressure, therefore, was *ultra vires*. In its conclusion, the Court stated

> An investigator who employs these methods exceeds his authority. His responsibility shall be fixed according to law. His potential criminal liability shall be examined in the context of the 'necessity defense.' Provided the conditions of the defense are met by the circumstances of the case, the investigator may find refuge under its wings. Just as the

[77] This argument is part of more comprehensive research in its early stages. See A. Shinar, 'Comparative Debiasing' (unpublished work in progress, on file with author).

[78] H.C. 5100/94 *Public Committee Against Torture v. State of Israel* [1999] IsrSC 53(4) 817, translation available at http://elyon1.court.gov.il/Files_ENG/94/000/051/A09/94051000.A09.htm.

> existence of the 'necessity defense' does not bestow authority, the lack of authority does not negate the applicability of the necessity defense or of other defenses from criminal liability. The Attorney-General can establish guidelines regarding circumstances in which investigators shall not stand trial, if they claim to have acted from 'necessity'.[79]

The decision was a watershed. The fact that it came from Israel, a country embroiled in conflict from its inception, suggested that countries can combat terrorism without giving up on their international legal commitments and moral values. Inside Israel, the decision forced the ISA to change its policies. Unintended perhaps by the Court, the ISA, together with the Attorney General, seized on the Court's closing in *obiter dictum* suggesting that guidelines be established, and put together internal procedures determining when the necessity defense would be recognized.[80] Thus even though the amount of torture decreased overall, torture took on an administrative form through the management of 'exceptional situations' that could provide legal cover to interrogators who apply physical pressure.[81]

Today, the procedure for investigating complaints of subjects who claim they were tortured is not done through the police, but through a special functionary in the Ministry of Justice who decides, after reviewing the complaint, whether an investigation by the Department of Police Investigations (an office in charge of investigating complaints against police officers) should be opened.[82] A petition challenging this procedure, demanding that the police investigate every complaint of torture, was rejected by the Supreme Court.[83]

The Court's 1999 decision seemingly announces a flat ban on torture, and this is the way the decision was communicated internationally. For the most part this was the way scholars understood the decision.[84] Yet the post-1999 reality looks very different from the one case the Court decided to translate to its foreign audience.

79 *Ibid.*, para. 38.

80 The guidelines have been published as an appendix in E. Rubinstein, 'Security and the Law: Trends', *Hapraklit*, 34 (1999), 409 (Hebrew).

81 See I. Mann and O. Shatz, 'The Necessity Procedure: Laws of Torture in Israel and Beyond, 1987–2009', *Unbound*, 6 (2010), 59.

82 It should be noted that until 2013 the person in charge of investigating complaints was a functionary inside the GSS. This raised claims of partiality and bias. In 2013 the position was moved to the Ministry of Justice.

83 H.C. 1265/11 *Public Committee against Torture v. Attorney General* [2012] IsrSC (unpublished).

84 Mann and Shatz, 'The Necessity Procedure'.

According to data compiled by the Public Committee Against Torture, between 2001 and 2010, more than 700 complaints have been filed against ISA interrogators alleging torture in interrogations, without the opening of a single criminal investigation. All the complaints were summarily rejected by the special functionary in the ISA in charge of handling such complaints (the position was later moved to within the Ministry of Justice).[85] This grim reality was also noted by the Supreme Court in its decision upholding the procedure for inquiries, but only to say that individual complaints should be treated according to the guidelines the Court sanctioned.[86]

The Court's seminal decision prohibiting torture generated numerous petitions. Most of the petitions challenged decisions to close cases of complaints and not initiate criminal charges. All of these petitions were summarily rejected by the Court, usually in one- or two-page decisions, for various procedural reasons.[87] None of the decisions was translated. A lengthier decision, the one upholding the State's procedure for investigating complaints, was also not translated.

Thus the ideal is of a strongly worded decision complying with international human rights norms and human dignity. This is the image transmitted to foreigners. But the reality is more complicated. Torture has decreased, but it has not disappeared. The police do not investigate charges of torture by those interrogated by the ISA. Hundreds of complaints (today probably close to a thousand) have been filed with the Ministry of Justice (and before that with the ISA), yet not a single one has generated criminal charges, let alone a conviction. Petitions challenging the State's decision to close cases of complaints alleging torture are summarily and briefly dismissed, without ever being translated. Yet all the while, the public image of the Court, based on its 1999 decision (the only one to be translated), has remained relatively untarnished. In fact, the Court's rightfully seminal decision has elevated its status and contributed to its positioning as a key judicial institution in the global context.

85 See Public Committee against Torture, Still Unjustifiable: Periodic Update: January 2012 (2012) (Hebrew).

86 H.C. 1265/11, supra note 83, at para 3 (Vogelman, J., concurring).

87 See e.g. H.C. 11447/04 *Center for the Defense of the Individual v. Attorney General* [2005] IsrSC (unpublished); H.C. 7987/11 *Center for the Defense of the Individual v. Ministry of Justice* [2012] IsrSC (unpublished); H.C. 7273/12 *Mujrabi v. Attorney General* [2014] IsrSC (unpublished).

Separation Wall

As a result of the second intifada that began in late 2000, with Palestinian terrorist attacks occurring inside Israel, Israel began constructing a wall in the West Bank with the aim of limiting the movement of Palestinians into Israel.[88] Instead of constructing the Wall along the Green Line (the 1949 armistice line between Israel and Jordan), parts of the Wall were erected on private Palestinian land, for which the military commander issued seizure decrees. Many of the decrees were challenged by Palestinian individuals and municipalities, and quickly made their way to the Supreme Court, which heard dozens of 'wall cases'.

The construction of the wall between Israel and Palestine, and the fact that significant parts of the wall (around 85 per cent) were built inside the West Bank, provoked extensive controversy, both in Israel and the international community. The first legal pronouncement, the *Beit Sourik* case,[89] came from Israel's Supreme Court. In that case, the Court held that the military government has the authority to construct the wall, yet it found that portions of the challenged route were disproportionate in that the harm to the petitioners' rights was not justified by the security benefits. It therefore ordered the military to reroute those parts.

Soon after the decision, the ICJ rendered its own advisory opinion on the construction of the wall in the OPT.[90] The ICJ was not convinced there was a security need for the wall, given that Israel controls the territory and that attacks came from areas under its control. Consequently, it decided that Israel has no authority to construct a wall on Palestinian Territory under the circumstances. Responding to the ICJ, the Israeli Supreme Court, in the *Mara'abe* case,[91] accepted the ICJ's legal framework, but held that it did not possess all the necessary information that was before the Court, which accounts for the divergent outcomes. Unlike the ICJ, the Court wrote that the wall has to be examined in 'segments' and that each segment would be subject to the requirements of

[88] Much controversy surrounds the name of the Separation Wall. The translation from Hebrew is 'fence', and sometimes the word 'barrier' is used. To an extent this is true, because parts of the barrier are not a wall, but rather fences or other means of separation. However much of the barrier is indeed a tall concrete wall, and the international community, in the ICJ advisory opinion, has used them same term, which I use here as well.

[89] H.C. 2056/04 *Beit Sourik Village Council v. Government of Israel* [2004] IsrSC 58(5) 807.

[90] Legal Consequences of the Construction of a Wall in the Occupied Palestinian Territory, Advisory Opinion (Int'l Ct. Justice 9 July 2004), 43 ILM 1009 (2004).

[91] H.C 7957/04 *Mara'abe v. Prime Minister of Israel* [2005] IsrSC 60(2) 477.

proportionality, as opposed to striking down the entire wall as a whole. Applying the framework adopted in the earlier *Beit Sourik* case, the Court struck down the wall that surrounded the settlement of Alfei Menashe, stating that the military should have considered alternative routes that would have achieved a similar security benefit while inflicting less harm on Palestinians.

Two more decisions are worth mentioning, for reasons that will soon become clear. The first is the *Bil'in* case.[92] In this case, petitioners challenged the construction of the wall on lands belonging to the village of Bil'in. In a move familiar from *Mara'be* the Court held the military must seek alternative routes, as the same security benefits the military seeks can be achieved by planning an alternative route that entails less harm to Palestinians' rights. Specifically, the planned route was topographically inferior and the Court was not convinced that a different route, one that would have a lesser impact on Palestinians' rights to property and movement, would entail sacrificing the military's need for security for Israelis.[93] The second decision is the *Dhahiriya* case.[94] In this case, petitioners challenged seizure decrees that served to build a very low concrete barrier on their lands,[95] ostensibly for security purposes. Similar to the other cases discussed, the Court held that the goal of security can be achieved through less restrictive means. The Court ordered the military to dismantle the low concrete barrier and replace it with a metal barrier, so that Palestinians' livestock may be able to pass under the railing. The same security benefits, the Court determined, can be achieved either by using concrete or metal railings, but Palestinians' lives would be considerably eased by the latter option.

Each of the decisions just discussed addresses a different segment of the wall. Each involved different parties. Some of the legal issues were shared by all four cases, though some were not. But there is one thing that connects all these decisions. These are the decisions the Court chose to translate.[96] To be sure, all are important decisions, and *Beit Sourik* and *Mara'abe* are even seminal cases that outline the basic framework for

[92] H.C. 8414/05 *Yassin v. Government of Israel* [2007] IsrSC 62(2) 822.

[93] In addition, the Court held that the route failed the third sub-test of proportionality – there was no proportionate relationship between the security benefits and the harm to Palestinians' rights and lives.

[94] H.C. 1748/06 *Mayor of Ad-Dhahiriya v. IDF Commander in the West Bank* [2006] IsrSC (unpublished).

[95] The height of the barrier was 82 centimetres long. See *ibid.*, para. 3.

[96] Three of the decisions are found in the Court's special 'terrorism' compilation and one can be found in the general decision database in English.

adjudicating these disputes. Still, it is interesting that all the decisions that were translated are decisions that struck down parts of the wall. Decisions that upheld segments of the wall, even in key parts such as Jerusalem that have a tremendous impact on those affected by the wall,[97] or the decision that upholds the 'permit regime' for Palestinians who live in areas that lie west of the wall and border on Israel,[98] have not been translated. Of course, the reasons why other decisions were not translated are not available. It could be that other decisions were not deemed as important from a jurisprudential perspective.[99] It could be that other decisions merely applied the framework that was established in the cases that were translated. And perhaps other considerations such as budget and translation resources were also present. Yet the fact remains that out of about 150 cases that were litigated before the Court,[100] only a select few, those that portray the Court in a favourable light, were translated for the benefit of non-Hebrew speakers. The reality, however, is that although a few petitions were accepted, the vast majority of petitions were denied.[101] Those who wish to learn about the wall through the Court's translated cases will only get a partial and quite incomplete picture.

[97] See H.C. 4289/05 *Beer Nabalah Local Council v. Government of Israel* [2006] IsrSC (unpublished).

[98] H.C. 9961/03 *Center for the Defense of the Individual v. Government of Israel* [2011] IsrSC (unpublished). This is especially noteworthy since the decision's scope encompasses vast areas, it took the Court about eight years to render a decision, and the decision itself holds some fifty pages. A translated version of the decision cannot be found in the general database either.

[99] This can definitely be said about *Beit Sourik* and *Mara'be*, but from a jurisprudential perspective, it's not clear what makes *Bil'in* or *Dhahiriya* unique.

[100] This figure is based on the latest update provided by the Ministry of Defense on its website dedicated to the wall: http://securityfence.mod.gov.il/Pages/Heb/hadashot.htm #news76. The data is correct for 14 August 2007. It is likely that the overall number is not much higher since most of the decrees seizing land were issued and litigated in the early stages of building the wall, starting in 2002.

[101] See e.g. H.C. 2942/05 *Mantzur v. State of Israel* [2006] IsrSC (unpublished) (challenging the wall in areas known as the 'fingers of Ariel'); H.C. 426/05 *Bidu Village Council v. Government of Israel* [2006] IsrSC (unpublished) (challenging the wall in northwest Jerusalem); H.C. 1348/05 *Mayor of Salfit v. State of Israel* [2006] IsrSC (unpublished) (challenging the wall around the city of Ariel); H.C. 2645/04 *Nasser v. Prime Minister* [2007] IsrSC (unpublished) (challenging the wall north of the city of Modi'in Ilit); H.C. 4289/05 *Beer Nabalah Local Council v. Government of Israel* [2006] IsrSC (unpublished) (challenging the wall surrounding Jerusalem); H.C. 4825/04 *Aliyan v. Prime Minister* [2006] IsrSC (unpublished) (challenging the wall near the villages of Shukba and Budrus); H.C. 10202/06 *City of Dhahiriya v. Military Commander in the West Bank* [2012] IsrSC (unpublished) (challenging the wall near the settlement of Eshkolot); H.C. 9961/03 *Center for the Defense of the Individual v. Government of Israel* [2011] IsrSC (unpublished) (challenging the 'permit regime' in areas in the OPT west of the wall).

Similar to the torture cases, the Court presents an image of a progressive institution, one that is sensitive to the violation of rights of people under military occupation, and one that is ready to confront the security establishment even in times of exigency, something very few courts are willing to do.[102] To be clear, my argument is not that this is a false image. Instead, my argument is that the positive image the Court conveys to its *international* audience is but an aspect of the total image the Court projects, which is only available if one reads both the translated and non-translated decisions.

The Idealism-Realism Gap Revisited

The foregoing analysis discussed three axes where there is a discernible gap between idealism and realism in Israeli constitutional law. The *first* gap addressed the issue of constitution-making. The constitution-making process degenerated from a promise of a full-fledged written constitution in the Declaration of Independence, to a political compromise by the legislature to split up the constitution into chapters that will make up the constitution in the future, and finally, to a constitutional 'revolution' by the Supreme Court that took the existing basic laws and declared them a fully operative constitution. The *second* gap addressed the issue of rights protection. Although the Declaration of Independence promised a constitution and the protection of rights, for many years rights were protected only by the Supreme Court, which relied on a judicially created bill of rights. Particular individual rights were included in two basic laws as late as 1992, but it was only in 1995 that the Court held that those rights can be used to strike down ordinary legislation. Since then, the Court has relied on these basic laws to further develop the constitutional protection of rights by reading into certain rights, particularly the right to dignity, additional rights that were not explicitly included in the basic laws. The *third* gap discussed the Court's institutional image. Unlike the first two gaps, which implicated traditional legal materials, the third gap addressed the way the Court might be

[102] Courts are relatively weak institutions in times of crisis. See, e.g., O. Gross, '"Once More unto the Breach": The Systemic Failure of Applying the European Convention on Human Rights to Entrenched Emergencies', *Yale Journal of International Law*, 23 (1998), 437; L. Epstein, D. E. Ho, G. King and J. A. Segal, 'The Supreme Court during Crisis: How War Affects Only Non-War Cases', *New York University Law Review*, 80 (2005), 1; E. A. Posner and A. Vermeule, 'Emergencies and Democratic Failure', *Virginia Law Review*, 92 (2006), 1091.

perceived by the audiences whom it tries to influence by looking at the decisions it decided to translate into English.

Although the idealism–realism gaps address different issues and themes, the common thread is that all view the Supreme Court as a political player vis-à-vis the legislature, the executive and foreign audiences. On the view presented here, the Court is, among other things, engaged in a competition for power, influence and policy.[103] By asserting a more forceful position, and given the relative weakness of other branches, the Supreme Court has managed to become an agenda-setter in Israel in a way that was likely not foreseen by those who laid the foundations of Israel's constitutional infrastructure. And while the ascendance of the Supreme Court and its expansive interpretation of constitutional rights engendered fierce criticism inside Israel,[104] the political and bureaucratic establishment has also been quick to showcase the Court's progressive decisions in order to fend off international criticism alleging human rights violations. Thus, for example, Prime Minister Netanyahu praised the Supreme Court as a beacon for the democratic world.[105] And the state, in its reports to the ICCPR Human Rights Committee, regularly invokes decisions by the Supreme Court to defend its human rights record, sometimes to the point of irony. For example, the Supreme Court has found constitutional rights to free speech and equality in the enumerated right to dignity,[106] even though both were intentionally left out of the constitutional settlement of 1992.[107] Although the Court's move was contentious domestically, in its reports to the UN Human

[103] For this view of courts, see generally attitudinalist and neo-institutional literature. In the Israeli context, see, e.g., Y. Dotan, 'Judicial Accountability in Israel: The High Court of Justice and the Phenomenon of Judicial Hyperactivism', *Israel Affairs*, 8 (2002), 87.

[104] For a description of some of the attempts to amend the Basic Law and to cut back on the Court's power of judicial review, see Aronson, 'Why Hasn't the Knesset'; Shinar, 'Accidental Constitutionalism'.

[105] See, e.g., Speech of Prime Minister Benjamin Netanyahu at the swearing in ceremony of Supreme Court President Grunis (2 March 2012): 'I believe that Israel serves as a role model to the entire world regarding the way in which these rights [individual and minority rights on the one hand, and national security concerns on the other – A.S.] can be balanced. From the day the State of Israel was established, and during the past several years, under your leadership Justice Beinisch [the Court's previous president – A.S.], the court has defended the rights of individuals while providing the State with the means to defend itself. This is a great accomplishment for the State of Israel, but I believe it is a greater accomplishment for the democratic world – the fact that Israel serves as a role model, I would even venture to say "a textbook solution" to a problem that is complex and cannot be resolved by textbooks, but rather by the life experiences and wisdom of the justices.' Speech available at http://www.israelgateway.co.il/articles/3469/.

[106] See text accompanying notes 55–56.

[107] See Sommer, 'Non-Enumerated Rights'.

Rights Committee, Israel regularly cites judicial decisions that reference equality and free speech as constitutional principles in order to respond to charges of rights violations.[108]

The ways in which the idealism-realism gap has played out in Israeli constitutional law give rise to two questions. First, is a gap inevitable? Second, is a gap a problem? And relatedly, might it be desirable?

The Inevitability of a Gap

As discussed in the first two parts of this chapter, the gap between the ideal and the real is inevitable. The temporal dimension that separates enactment from practice means that, in addition to the difficulty of identifying the 'ideal' and the 'real', the people and institutions that framed the constitution will not be those that will interpret and apply the constitution. This is also true regarding the Court's institutional image. Even if the Court were to translate all of its decisions, it would still not have complete control over its image, since that is also determined by non-judicial actors. To be sure, the inevitability of a gap takes place even if one considers idealism and realism not as temporal points but as the practice of constituting values and ideals into the interpretation of the constitution. If a constitution is a site of political contestation, then that contestation puts forward ideals that are not fully implemented in the constitution as applied. On this view, a constitution is always becoming something, and not limited to being.

Given its inevitability, the mere existence of a gap between the ideal and the real is not especially noteworthy. The more interesting questions

[108] See e.g. UNCHR 'Fourth Periodic Reports of States Parties Due in 2013: Israel' (14 October 2013) UN Doc CCPR/C/ISR/4 § 264 ('Just as the Israeli legislature crafts and adopts both new laws and administrative measures to ensure that government agencies adhere to the principle of equality and do not engage in any discriminatory act or practice, the country's independent judiciary serves to interpret, guide, and enforce these measures. The Supreme Court has, on several occasions, reiterated the notion that equality is a constitutional right, derived from the Basic Law: Human Dignity and Liberty, and that maintaining human dignity also prohibits discrimination' (footnotes omitted); UNCHR 'Consideration of reports submitted by States parties under article 40 of the Covenant: Third Periodic Report of Israel' (20 January 2011) UN Doc CCPR/C/SR.2717 § 14 ('Israeli courts had continued to play a crucial role in anchoring and promoting human rights throughout Israeli society. The Supreme Court . . . ensured that all the branches of Government and the private sector operated in accordance with the law. Moreover, in its decisions, the Supreme Court had further established and protected basic rights such as the right to freedom of speech, the right to strike, the right to associate and, especially, the right to full equality, as fundamental values in Israel.').

are whether such gaps are problematic or can they be, counterintuitively, desirable?

Is a Gap a Problem?

That a gap between the ideal and the real is inevitable does not mean it is not a problem. Inevitable things can be problematic (think of a meteor rushing towards earth). Yet given the dynamics of constitutional law, the existence of a gap, in and of itself, does not seem problematic. If there are problems, they would have to do with the particular nature of the gap and its contents. For example, legitimacy concerns may arise if the gap between ideal and praxis is too wide. If, for example, the ideal is the vision of the framers, and courts are perceived by the political branches and the public to be departing too much from that vision, this may invite attempts to rein in on their power.[109] Thus instead of discussing the problems that such gaps raise generally, the remainder of this chapter will turn to examining the normative aspects of the particular gaps identified above.

The gaps having to do with constitution-making and rights protection both concern a particular feature in Israeli constitutional law – the ascendance of the Court and the paralysis of the legislature in making constitutional law. Paradoxically, this feature has enabled the Court to bring the constitutional vision closer to the promise entailed in the Declaration of Independence and the Harari Resolution. Both documents envisioned a fully written constitution, but the legislature, for reasons discussed above,[110] has stalled.

To an important extent, the constitutional vision has already been realized: the basic laws are superior to ordinary legislation; constitutional review is a stable feature of Israeli constitutional law; central rights (speech, equality, association, religion) have been deduced from the right to dignity enshrined in the basic law. The difference, then, is not in the content of the constitutional arrangement (though there are

[109] As indeed happened in Israel due to the Court's expansive interpretation of Basic Law: Human Dignity and Liberty and its assertion of constitutional review powers. See Aronson, 'Why Hasn't the Knesset'.

[110] I have also discussed the reasons for the constitutional paralysis elsewhere. See Shinar, 'Accidental Constitutionalism'. The ascendancy of the Court over the political branches is also evidenced by the rise of elected representatives who turn to the court instead of using ordinary political channels. See Y. Dotan and M. Hofnung, 'Legal Defeats – Political Wins: Why Do Elected Representatives Go to Court?', *Comparative Political Studies*, 38 (2005), 75.

important differences between ideal and praxis),[111] but rather in the way the constitutional vision has been implemented. Specifically, the implementing agent is the Supreme Court rather than the legislature or a constituent assembly.[112]

Thus the question is whether the change in the agent's institutional identity matters in any meaningful sense, even if the end result is not that far from what was imagined. For example, does the fact that it was the Court that declared and operationalized the transition to a constitutional system affect the legitimacy of the transition? Will court-initiated changes be harder to justify and maintain than changes that have a more democratic provenance?

While a normative theory of legitimacy might be wary of such moves,[113] in previous research I have argued that at least in Israel, normative contestations about the role of the Supreme Court have obscured how the Israeli constitutional structure has produced arrangements that are both stable and similar to those of countries whose constitution originated in more 'democratic' processes. Normative concerns about the instability that would result from a court-initiated transition simply did not materialize. Indeed, the deviation from the plans detailed in the Declaration and the Harari Resolution have had relatively little impact on the day-to-day manageability and workability of the constitutional structure that came about instead. This calls into question the assumption that there is a necessary relationship between a polity's constitution-making process and the particular features that process generates.[114]

I am hesitant to suggest, however, that bridging the gap through the judiciary had *no* effect on the adoption and acceptance of Israel's constitutional structure. It may very well be that, had the legislature delivered on

[111] I do not mean to suggest that the constitutional scheme is by any means complete. Important aspects are still missing from the constitutional landscape. For example, the demarcation of religion and state, the status of the Arab minority, the formal entrenchment of judicial review, and central aspects of the legislative process, still need to be worked out and ideally enacted.

[112] After *Bank Hamizrachi* case, the dominant approach to constitution-making in Israel holds that the Knesset can function under two hats: as a legislature and as a constituent assembly. See Rubinstein and Medina, *The Constitutional Law.*

[113] For example, Ruth Gavison has argued that because the status of the constitutional regime was brought about by judicial fiat, this would undermine the legitimacy of the constitutional arrangements and generate instability. See R. Gavison, 'Legislatures and the Quest for a Constitution: The Case of Israel', *Review of Constitutional Studies*, 11 (2006), 345–6, 394.

[114] See generally Shinar, 'Accidental Constitutionalism'.

the promise entailed in the Declaration or the Harari Resolution, the constitution would have garnered more legitimacy, at least initially. It may well be that the *pace* of constitutional change would have been different had the legislature been more involved, and it is likely that there would have been fewer court-curbing attempts had the push for a full-fledged constitution come from the legislature. Indeed, the Court has suffered legitimacy costs for its decision to push forward on the constitutional project.[115] Prior to the constitutional revolution, the Court was perceived as a neutral, apolitical, and professional institution.[116] Its judges, chosen by a nine-member committee where politicians are the minority, were highly regarded lower court judges, elite lawyers, or established law professors.[117] Once the Court spearheaded the constitutional transition, it lost, to some degree, its professional and apolitical image. Constitutional adjudication has embroiled the Court in political disputes, and consequently its judgements are often portrayed in popular discourse as aligning with the views of a particular political camp, usually the left. For those who wish the Court to remain 'outside politics', this may be regrettable. On the other hand, there is a price to pay for recognizing that the Court is part of a political structure. Acknowledging the relationship between law and politics suggests a more nuanced and complicated view of the legal enterprise, which is also more 'real'.

In conclusion, although a legislature-led constitutional transition would have looked differently than a judicially led transition, it seems that overall the process by which the idealism–realism gap has been bridged mattered less than the result of the bridging itself. Put differently, what mattered was having a constitution and a more robust protection of individual rights. Whether that would be done by the Court or the legislature proved to be of secondary importance. True, initially there was concern and even resistance among the political establishment and parts of the scholarly community. Over time, however, the resistance subsided. In a process that lasted less than a decade since *Bank Hamizrachi* was decided, the new constitutional structure has been consolidated, accepted, and defended by most segments of Israeli society.

[115] See Y. Hadar, 'Israeli Public Trust in Institutions of Government over the Past Decade', 63 *Parliament* (Israel Democracy Institute, 2009) (Hebrew); Revital Hovel, 'New Research: The Public Is Losing Trust in the Law Enforcement System', *Haaretz* 4 August 2013 (Hebrew).

[116] See G. Barzilai, E. Yuchtman-Yaar, Z. Segal, *The Israeli Supreme Court and the Israeli Public* (Papyrus, Tel Aviv University, 1994) (Hebrew).

[117] *See* §4 Basic-Law: Adjudication.

Things are more complicated, however, when we examine the gap in the Court's institutional image. When it comes to constitution-making and rights protection, we can detect a relatively clear point of departure, and, it seems to me, a widespread consensus that even if the Court's move was normatively problematic, there has been a *de facto* acceptance of the new situation by the relevant political actors. Indeed, commentators are no longer debating the legitimacy of the constitutional revolution, but rather discussing its details and future implementation. By contrast, the gap between the way the Court presumably wants to portray itself to foreign audience and the way it is perceived by its domestic audience is much more difficult to gauge. It might require comparative public opinion polls, whose results will differ considerably depending on the population being asked (laypeople, minorities, lawyers, scholars, etc.). To the best of my knowledge, no such comparative polls were taken nor is there anything close to consensus on the image of the Court. Indeed, although there is abundant literature on the Court, there is a paucity of material dealing specifically with its image.[118]

This is why I focused on translations of decisions, which, for the reasons discussed above, is a reliable metric for what the Court (or its individual judges) considers its legacy. Examining the gap between the decisions that were translated and those that addressed the same or similar issue but were not translated revealed a problematic picture. In the two areas that were examined, the Court presents a partial picture of its activity, usually the cases that the judges believe are more important, but are also the ones likely to portray it in a favourable light among civil libertarians. To be sure, the distortion cannot be complete, since there are Israeli commentators who write about the non-translated cases. Still, the idea–real gap allows the Court to present itself as something that it is not, and whether that image is mitigated by *other* actors seems inapposite.

To be clear, I am not suggesting that the Court intends to promote a distorted picture of its activity. Judges decide to translate the cases they believe are important, courageous, and interesting. These cases often happen to be the 'big name' cases that generate long, important decisions that often go against the state's interests. It is only natural that such cases be translated and that more run-of-the-mill, mundane cases are neglected. Yet this neglect has consequences for the Court's

[118] For such an attempt, though by now dated, see Barzilai, Yuchtman-Yaar, Segal, *The Israeli Supreme Court*.

reputation: it improves it because outside readers will not necessarily get the whole picture. Moreover, selective translations may allow the state apparatus (not the Court) to present itself abroad as setting a particular standard when it comes to human rights when the reality is more complicated.

It is possible, however, that the gap also has beneficial consequences. Perhaps the gap serves as a 'feedback loop' that the judicial system can use for self-correction by adjusting its output, given the image it maintains. For instance, perhaps the progressive image that the Court holds up to foreign audiences will cause it to try to live up to that image in all its decisions (those that are translated and not translated). The more important the Court's international image and reputation becomes to the judges, the more likely such a feedback loop will be to motivate judicial decision-making.

Conclusion

This chapter has sought to show that although idealism and realism are possible categories of analysis for the study of constitutional law, their utility is limited, sometimes to the point of simply noting that there is a gap, but without any attendant normative baggage. In itself, the idealism–realism divide does not tell us much about the desirability of particular constitutional arrangements, unless one attributes normative power to temporal arguments.[119] Moreover, problems of defining an ideal and the real mean that disagreements over first principles might obscure the evaluation of the arrangements themselves.

The chapter demonstrated this general argument by using Israeli constitutional law as a case study. There is little doubt that the process of Israeli constitution-making departed from the 'ideal' plan set out in the Declaration of Independence and the Harari Resolution, but this departure tells us little about whether the arrangements in place today are desirable in any meaningful sense. To be clear, nothing prevents that evaluation, but it will not depend on the existence of a gap. Indeed, early

[119] For constitutional interpretation, the gap between the ideal and the real has normative significance. As I discussed with respect to Originalism in the first section of this chapter, Originalists argue that judges should adhere to the original intent or meaning of constitutional provisions. Even if one does not accept Originalists' claims, few doubt that things such as original intent and meaning are not important, even if they are not dispositive. This chapter however is not concerned with constitutional interpretation, but with evaluating a constitutional system generally.

arguments that the gap undermined the legitimacy of the constitutional transition have fallen by the wayside.

Although the idealism–realism gap has limited utility in evaluating a constitutional system, it might have some value in understanding the motivations of institutional actors, as the translations case study sought to demonstrate. Institutions craft their image by carefully choosing which features to place in the forefront. Less desirable features are cast aside, downplayed, ignored or silenced. Thus there will almost always be a gap between what an institution wants to project and the less-visible aspects of its activity. This gap, then, is meaningful for evaluating both the reputation the institution wishes to achieve and the possible motivations of its central actors. Yet here too, the existence of a gap does not necessarily translate into a particular normative assessment. Gaps can be problematic because they operate to conceal unpleasant, though important, information. On the other hand, there is a possibility, however unlikely, that some gaps will operate as positive feedback loops, incentivizing institutional improvement.

10

Idealism and Realism in Chinese Constitutional Theory and Practice

FENG LIN*

Introduction

The tension between idealism and realism in Chinese constitutional law is most likely one of the most obvious ones, if not the most obvious one, in all different kinds of constitutional systems in the world. This chapter is a case study on China which examines the tension as well as interaction between idealism and realism in both Chinese constitutional theory and practice. It analyses the issue from several different perspectives. Firstly, it examines the tension between idealism and realism from a temporal dimension, i.e., Chinese constitutional history. The discussion of the historical constitutional development in China, especially in contemporary China, shows that the tension between idealism and realism existed in China from the very moment when China attempted to enact its first constitution in 1908. That tension continued when the Communist Party of China (CPC) came into power and enacted its first Constitution in 1954 and continues even now under the current Constitution.

Secondly, it discusses the tension between idealism and realism in contemporary Chinese constitutional practice. Three examples are chosen for detailed discussion. One is electoral law versus electoral practice, with the discussion demonstrating that on the one hand the written electoral law represents idealism while electoral practice in China represents realism. That had been the case with idealism and realism in Chinese constitutional practice until a new dimension was added by the debate on the justiciability of the Chinese Constitution, which will be the second example to be discussed. The Supreme People's Court

* The author would like to thank Ms. Pinky Choy, research fellow at the Centre for Chinese and Comparative Law of the School of Law of City University of Hong Kong, for helping him to complete many footnotes in this paper.

(SPC) in China got itself involved voluntarily by issuing its judicial opinion on the justiciability of the Chinese Constitution in the *Qi Yuling* Case.[1] That judicial opinion actually led to serious scholarly debate on the justiciability of the Chinese Constitution. While the SPC had the intention to create a Chinese *Marbury v. Madison*,[2] it eventually withdrew that judicial opinion several years later. That can be interpreted as an example where realism prevailed over idealism. The related third example is the debate over a suitable mechanism for constitutional supervision in China. While there are many well-established constitutional supervision models in the world from which China may learn, the most recent proposal by a group of leading constitutional scholars to the Central Government is to establish a special committee under the National People's Congress (NPC)[3] to conduct constitutional supervision. It indicates their support that China should start from something which is suitable to Chinese reality and its unique constitutional structure. The last two examples reveal two different kinds of tension. One is the tension between judicial activism and the CPC's conservatism in maintaining the status quo. The other is the tension between transplantation of foreign models and Chinese domestic reality. In addition, the three examples also demonstrate the interaction between the forces behind both idealism and realism.

Thirdly, it discusses the tension between idealism and realism in contemporary Chinese constitutional theory. Modern Chinese constitutional theory, like any other legal theories in China, started from the end of 1970s. Chinese scholars have transferred relatively quickly from their endorsement of the orthodox Marxist class struggle theory of law in 1980s to general acceptance of Western rule of law and constitutionalism in 1990s. The tension between written constitutional norms and constitutional reality has led some Chinese scholars to challenge the suitability of Western theory for China. Among all alternatives, two stand out: one is socialist constitutional theory, the other, political constitutional theory. The emergence of these alternative domestic constitutional theories serves as evidence that some Chinese scholars have realized that

[1] For the facts of this case, see K. Shen (translated by Y. Liu), 'Is It the Beginning of the Era of the Rule of the Constitution? Reinterpreting China's "First Constitutional Case"', *Pacific Rim Law & Policy Journal*, 12(1) (2003), 199–232.

[2] *Marbury v. Madison*, 5 U.S. 137 (1803). In this case, the US Supreme Court confirmed that it has the authority to interpret the US Constitution and conduct constitutional review.

[3] The NPC together with its Standing Committee (NPCSC) constitute the Chinese Parliament.

normative constitutional theory represents only the idealism, but not the reality in China and that they have attempted to create theories which actually represent and match Chinese constitutional reality.

The chapter concludes by summarizing the reasons behind various examples of tension and interaction between idealism and realism in Chinese constitutional theory and practice. As far as tension is concerned, it argues that the main reason is lack of political will from those in power. As far as interaction is concerned, various people and institutions have made their efforts to close the gap between idealism and realism, including legal scholars, legislature, judiciary, and lawyers, especially rights-defending lawyers. The interaction has gone sometimes more in favour of idealism, though most of the time is against it. That is understandable given that the ruling political party, i.e., the CPC, is in strong possession of its ruling position and still lacks the political will to move towards full endorsement of constitutionalism. However, this chapter argues that, given that more and more people from different sectors of society have become more rights-conscious, particularly with not only individuals but several legal institutions such as the legislature, the judiciary and the legal profession in favour of idealism, the trend is definitely tipped towards idealism though the process may take a longer time.

Tension between Idealism and Realism in Chinese Constitutional History

When the necessity to enact a constitution was first conceived, the purpose was to save the governance of the Qing dynasty with a written constitution, rather than out of belief in the intrinsic value of constitutionalism.[4] The Qing Government drafted the Outline of the Imperial Constitution (Outline) in 1908,[5] which was modelled on the Japanese Meiji Constitution.[6] Apart from nine articles on citizens' rights

[4] See Y. Wang, *Zhongguo Xiandai Xianzheng Yundong Shi* [The History of Constitutionalism in Modern China] (Beijing: People's Press, 1996), p. 3. See also C. Xu (ed.), *Zhongguo Xianfa* [Chinese Constitutional Law] (Beijing: People's University Press, 2010), p. 61.

[5] It is also translated as 'Outline of Constitution by Imperial Order', or 'Outline of Imperial Constitution', or 'the Principles of the Constitution'. The proposal was not constitutional itself and therefore had no legal effect. For the details and the full text of the Outline, see X. Ying, *Jindai Zhongguo Xianzheng Shi* [The History of Modern Constitutionalism in China] (Shanghai: Shanghai People's Press, 1997), pp. 54, 275–6.

[6] For the full text of the Japanese Meiji Constitution, see 'The Constitution of the Empire of Japan (1889)', https://history.hanover.edu/texts/1889con.html (last accessed 13 January 2016).

and obligations, it also contained fourteen articles which codify the power of the emperor. It states that the emperor shall rule the Qing Empire forever and his power is sovereign and inviolable. He has supreme executive, legislative, judicial and military powers subject to no checks and balances.[7] The purpose of the Outline is to legitimize imperial ruling rather than to limit the sovereign power of the emperor. Three years later, on 3 November 1911, the Qing Government issued the Imperial Constitution, under pressure from uprising militants. In contrast to the Outline, the Imperial Constitution actually limited the authority of the emperor by providing that powers of the emperor and his succession shall be prescribed and governed by the Constitution, the Constitution shall be drafted and passed by a special constitution-making body, and any constitutional amendments could only be proposed by the Parliament.[8] The Imperial Constitution had the spirit of controlling governmental power. But the Qing dynasty and the Imperial Constitution were soon put to its end by the Nationalist Party when the latter established its interim government in Nanjing on 1 January 1912.[9] Hence, enactment of the Imperial Constitution had no implication at all that the late Qing Government had any respect for constitutionalism. There was, therefore, a tension between idealism, reflected in the Imperial Constitution, and realism, that the late Qing Government only had the intention to prolong its ruling status through a written constitution.

The CPC enacted an interim constitution when it took full control of China in 1949,[10] and its first Constitution in 1954 through the NPC. The 1954 Constitution was very similar to the 1936 Constitution of the former Soviet Union in terms of its structure, general principles, state structure, and the basic rights and obligations of the citizens.[11] On the one hand, it contained some essential democratic constitutional

[7] See the 14 articles on the emperor's power in the Outline of Imperial Constitution. Ying, *The History of Modern Constitutionalism*, pp. 275–6.

[8] The Imperial Constitution only has 19 articles and was modelled upon the Sovereign Charter in the United Kingdom. For details and full text of the Imperial Constitution, see Ying, *The History of Modern Constitutionalism in China*, pp. 96–104; Q. Zhang, *The Constitution of China: A Contextual Analysis* (Oxford: Hart Publishing Ltd., 2012), pp. 13–4, 276–7.

[9] Zhang, *The Constitution of China*, pp. 13–4.

[10] It was called the Common Program. See, Z. Wen, *Gongheguo Xianzheng Lichen* [The History of Constitutionalism of the People's Republic of China] (Zhenzhou: Henan People's Press, 1994), pp. 1–17.

[11] Wen, *The History of Constitutionalism*, p. 55.

principles such as sovereignty of the people, basic rights of citizens, and so on. On the other hand, it provided the leadership of the CPC, socialism, proletarian dictatorship, and adherence to Marxist ideology in the preamble, established the people's congress system, and established democratic centralism as the organizational principle for all constitutional organs.[12] The 1954 Constitution was not properly implemented due to a series of political movements starting from 1956,[13] during which basic rights and rule of law were completely ignored. The 1954 Constitution at most represented the idealism the CPC intended to achieve.

The second Constitution was enacted in 1975, which was near the end of the Cultural Revolution (1966–1976). In comparison with the 1954 Constitution, it put leadership of the CPC in the text of the Constitution and stated that the CPC exercises the core leadership over all Chinese people.[14] The objective of the 1975 Constitution was to consolidate the so-called 'achievements' of the Cultural Revolution. I have argued elsewhere that the best lesson the 1975 Constitution taught Chinese people is how a constitution might be utilized to negate and eliminate the implementation of constitutionalism.[15] The third Constitution was enacted in 1978, just two years after the Cultural Revolution. It still had the marks of the Cultural Revolution, especially the insistence on class struggle, and it failed to address many issues such as the role of the private economy, the stability and authority of constitutional amendment and so on.[16]

The 1982 Constitution is the fourth and current Constitution and was later amended in 1988, 1993, 1999 and 2004.[17] The 1988 amendments include two articles. One adds a new paragraph to Article 11, which reads: '[t]he State permits the private sector of the economy to exist and

[12] For the full text of the 1954 Constitution, see 'Zhonghua Renmin Gongheguo Xianfa (1954 Nian)' [Constitution of the People's Republic of China], http://www.npc.gov.cn/wxzl/wxzl/2000–12/26/content_4264.htm (last accessed 14 January 2016).

[13] Wen, *The History of Constitutionalism*, pp. 58–94.

[14] Article 2, 1975 Constitution.

[15] F. Lin, 'Modern Constitutional Development in China' in P. Costa and D. Zolo (eds.), *The Rule of Law: History, Theory and Criticism* (Dordrecht: Springer, 2007), p. 637.

[16] Wen, *The History of Constitutionalism*, pp. 120–42.

[17] For the full text of the 1982 Constitution, see 'Zhonghua Renmin Gongheguo Xianfa' [Constitution of the People's Republic of China], http://news.xinhuanet.com/ziliao/2004-09/16/content_1990063.htm (last accessed 14 January 2016); for the subsequent amendments to the 1982 Constitution, see 'Xianxing (Di Si Bu) Xianfa de Jici Xiugai' [Several Amendments to the Existing (The Fourth) Constitution], http://news.xinhuanet.com/ziliao/2004-02/18/content_1319796.htm (last accessed 14 January 2016).

develop within the limits prescribed by law. The private sector of the economy is a complement to the socialist public economy. The state protects the lawful rights and interests of the private sector of the economy, and exercises guidance, supervision and control over the private sector of the economy'.[18] The other amends the fourth paragraph of Article 10 as '[n]o organization or individual may appropriate, buy, sell or otherwise engage in the transfer of land by unlawful means. The right to the use of land may be transferred according to law'.[19]

The background for the 1988 amendments was that China started economic reform in Shenzhen with the intention to attract foreign investment. Chinese companies offered to use the land they possessed as their contribution to joint ventures. But state ownership of land and socialist public economy as stated in the 1982 Constitution became constitutional obstacles to attracting foreign investment, though both the Chinese Government and companies had gone ahead to establish some joint ventures before the 1988 constitutional amendments were adopted.[20] The 1988 constitutional amendments legitimized the existence of private economy and the transfer of land-use rights.

The 1993 amendments include nine articles. The spirit underlying the amendments is to build socialism with Chinese characteristics. Among the nine articles, six are related to different aspects of a so-called 'socialist market economy with Chinese characteristics', as the CPC had made it clear that economic development was its primary task. From a theoretical perspective, the CPC had realized that it might take China a much longer time to achieve socialism as described by Marx. It therefore introduced an ambiguous concept of socialism with Chinese characteristics, which in reality is capitalism.[21]

The 1999 amendments include six articles, of which three are concerned with the establishment of a market economy with Chinese characteristics by giving the private economy equal status with the state-owned public economy and legitimizing other means of allocation. The most important article is the one incorporating the rule of law. As of its amendment in 1999, paragraph 1 of Article 5 provides that: '[t]he People's Republic of China governs the country according to law and makes it a socialist

[18] 'Several Amendments to the Existing (The Fourth) Constitution'. [19] *Ibid.*

[20] 'Dujia Jiedu: Sici Xiuxian Licheng' [Exclusive Interpretation: Process of the Four Constitutional Amendments], http://big5.china.com.cn/news/zhuanti/shzytsfl/2011-02/22/content_21974283.htm (last accessed 16 January 2016).

[21] For a detailed discussion, see F. Lin, *Constitutional Law in China* (Hong Kong: Sweet & Maxwell Asia, 2000), p. 18.

country under rule of law'. That amendment reveals a formal commitment by the CPC to the adoption of rule of law principles in China. It is however only a wish, because it is common understanding that China is not a rule-of-law state yet.[22] Those amendments concerning market economy and private economy, however, merely confirm and legitimize the practice which had already been in existence. The 2004 amendments include ten articles, of which the two on the protection of private rights and property and on the protection of human rights are the most important.[23] The new paragraph 3 added to Article 33 states: '[t]he State respects and preserves human rights'. The incorporation of a general principle on human rights protection has been hailed as a great achievement.[24]

As I have noted elsewhere,[25] the inclusion of Marxism means that the Constitution must reflect the characteristics of Marxist constitutional jurisprudence about state and law. The amendments made to the 1982 Constitution prove that Chinese constitutional practice is fully consistent with Marxist theory. Its Constitution devotes much space to the economic system. As the Chinese economy is undergoing a fundamental reform, the Constitution unavoidably presents obstacles, and therefore needs to be amended from time to time. Frequent constitutional amendments have shown that unauthorized economic activities had been carried out before the relevant amendments were made. That is why some scholars have proposed the concept of benign constitutional violation and argued that such benign constitutional violations as the introduction of foreign private investment and transfer of land-use rights before 1988 constitutional amendments is unavoidable and should therefore be tolerated.[26]

If we focus on constitutional principles/values, a country claiming that it has achieved constitutionalism has to show that it has embodied and also practiced the following principles/values: (i) limited government through constitution, (ii) rule of law and (iii) protection of fundamental

[22] See for example, L. C. Backer, 'The Rule of Law, The Chinese Communist Party, and Ideological Campaigns: *Sange Daibiao* (The "Three Representatives"), Socialist Rule of Law, and Modern Chinese Constitutionalism', *Journal of Transnational Law & Contemporary Problems*, 16(1) (forthcoming 2016), 29–102.

[23] 'Several Amendments to the Existing (The Fourth) Constitution'.

[24] See for example, D. Cai, 'Social Transformation and the Development of Constitutionalism' in D. Cai and C. Wang (eds.), *China's Journey Toward the Rule of Law: Legal Reform, 1978–2008* (Leiden, Boston, Mass.: Brill, 2010), p. 59.

[25] Lin, 'Modern Constitutional Development in China', pp. 639–40.

[26] T. Hao, 'Lun Liangxing Weixian' [Analysis of Benign Violation of Constitution], *Faxue Yanjiu* [CASS Journal of Law], No. 4 of 1996, 89–91.

rights, especially political rights.[27] The above examination of the 1982 Constitution, together with its subsequent amendments, shows that China has expressly adopted the rule of law principle and protection of fundamental rights. In addition, Chapter Two of the 1982 Constitution lists many other fundamental rights which should be protected, and those rights are very similar to those covered under the International Covenant on Civil and Political Rights (ICCPR) and the International Covenant on Economic, Social and Cultural Rights (ICESCR).[28] Furthermore, Chapter 3 of the 1982 Constitution sets out the powers and obligations of various constitutional organs, including the legislature (both national and local), executive, and judicial organs.[29] That means those constitutional organs have to exercise their powers within the limits set by the 1982 Constitution. Hence, the three essential values of constitutionalism have been incorporated into the 1982 Constitution.

It is, however, common knowledge that just because a country has a written constitution, that does not mean that it has achieved constitutionalism. The incorporation of those essential constitutional values into the 1982 Constitution does not mean China has achieved constitutionalism. At most, the Constitution represents the ideals which China aims to achieve. The reality may be quite different. In fact, one prominent Chinese constitutional scholar opines that the Chinese Constitution is dead because of a lack of implementation,[30] while the orthodox view held by the majority of Chinese and foreign scholars is that Chinese Constitution represents a political manifesto and needs to be implemented through specific national legislation.[31]

We can see from the above discussion that when the very first modern constitutional document in China was drafted in 1908, its purpose was to prolong the ruling position of the Qing dynasty rather than out of respect for constitutionalism. Though the Imperial Constitution contained provisions to limit government power, its promulgation was under the

[27] See, for example, R. S. Kay, 'American Constitutionalism' in L. Alexander (ed.), *Constitutionalism: Philosophical Foundations* (Cambridge University Press, 1998), pp. 16–63.

[28] Chapter 2, 1982 Constitution. [29] Lin, *Constitutional Law in China.*

[30] Q. Zhang, 'A Constitution without Constitutionalism? The Paths of Constitutional Developments in China', http://www.sef.hku.hk/aslea2011/private/paper/43.%20 Zhang_Qianfan_full_paper.pdf (last accessed 14 January 2016). See also, Lin, *Constitutional Law in China.*

[31] See for example, Zhang, *The Constitution of China*, pp. 65 and 85; T. Kellogg, 'Constitutionalism with Chinese Characteristics? Constitutional Development and Civil Litigation in China', *International Journal of Constitutional Law*, 7(2) (2009), 217.

pressure of militants instead of out of the genuine intention of the late Qing Government. So the tension between idealism and realism existed from the very beginning of Chinese modern constitutional history.

After the CPC came into power in Mainland China, its constitutional history reveals that the primary objective of the CPC has been to maintain its ruling position rather than to promote constitutionalism. The CPC's ideology of Marxism has determined that the Chinese Constitution is at most a blueprint for the future rather than the current norms with binding force for the purpose of limiting government power. That is the root cause of tension between the written Constitution and political reality in China.

Tension between Idealism and Realism in Contemporary Chinese Constitutional Practice

Though there are no constitutional cases decided by Chinese courts,[32] there exist numerous events and practices involving constitutional issues. In the next section, we will choose three specific constitutional practice/events – electoral practice, the debate on the justiciability of the Chinese Constitution, and the debate over suitable constitutional supervision mechanism for China – as a basis for discussion of the tension between idealism and realism in contemporary Chinese constitutional practice.

Electoral Law and Practice

China's electoral system is composed of three elements: (i) the electoral system of grassroots autonomous organizations such as village residents' committees; (ii) the electoral system of the people's congresses at all levels; and (iii) the electoral system of officials of governmental organs at all levels.[33] What's chosen for discussion here is the electoral system of

[32] Several cases decided by Chinese courts have been called constitutional cases by some Chinese scholars. The *Qi Yuling* Case is one of them. But they are not real constitutional cases. For example, *Qi Yuling* is actually a civil case.

[33] For the details about these elections, see Cunmin Weiyuanhui Zuzhifa [Organic Law of the Villagers' Committees]; Quanguo Renmin Daibiao Dahui he Difang Geji Renmin Daibiao Dahui Xuanjufa [Election Law for the National People's Congress and Local People's Congresses at All Levels] (hereafter 'Election Law'); and Difang Geji Renmin Daibiao Dahui he Difang Geji Renmin Zhengfu Zuzhifa [Organization Law of the People's Republic of China for Local People's Congresses at All Levels and Local People's Governments at All Levels]. See also, F. Lin, 'Electoral Reform in China: Its

people's congresses under the Electoral Law on the National People's Congress and All Local People's Congresses (Electoral Law).

Before taking over power in Mainland China, the CPC stated publicly that it would organize democratic elections once it would come into power.[34] But after coming into power in 1949, the CPC came to the view that there would be great difficulty in practicing direct democracy in a country which was poor, undeveloped, and populous. Different senior officials of the CPC had expressed similar views on various occasions. The justifications can be summarized as follows:[35] (1) the population in China was too large for direct election; (2) the population of peasants was too large to ensure equality between workers and peasants, because most deputies to the people's congresses would be peasants if direct elections were implemented; (3) the education level of Chinese citizens was too low and many were illiterate, making it difficult to have secret-ballot voting; (4) China did not have enough experience in elections and the masses did not have good understanding of elections and were not enthusiastic about elections; (5) the CPC emphasized the substance of elections rather than formal procedures. But practice under the above conditions would make elections a formality, without substance, because people's votes would not be genuine votes. It is clear that the CPC was not willing to introduce direct elections during the early period of its rule. That is why, when the first Electoral Law was enacted in 1953, it limited direct elections to township people's congresses, while prescribing indirect election for all of the other four higher levels of people's congresses.[36]

After the Cultural Revolution, the CPC realized the necessity to reform its political system and electoral system. The direct reason for the reform is that some senior leaders of the CPC were of the view that the expansion of direct elections and the democratization of the electoral system would put the mass in direct control of county people's congresses, and in indirect control of provincial congresses as well as the NPC. In so doing, Chinese people could participate in administration as well as be

Context, Recent Development, and Future', Civic Exchange (January 2006) (On file with the author).

34 See *Mao Zedong Xuanji (Hedingben)* [Selected Works of Mao Zedong (combined version)] (Renmin Press, 1968), pp. 969–70, quoted from D. Cai, 'Zhongguo Xuanju Zhidu de Lishi he Xianzhuang' [The History and Current Situation of China's Electoral System] in D. Cai (ed.), *Zhongguo Xuanju Zhuangkuang de Baogao* [Report on the Situation of Election in China] (Beijing: Law Press, 2002), pp. 2–3.

35 See Cai, 'The History and Current Situation', p. 4.

36 For the main contents of the 1953 Election Law, see Cai, 'The History and Current Situation', pp. 4–6.

in charge of the country's future. Furthermore, some senior officials also expressed the view that the reform of the electoral system would involve fundamental measures to prevent the re-occurrence of such a tragedy as the Cultural Revolution.[37] Hence, the CPC had the genuine intention to develop a democratic electoral system in the end of 1970s. A new Electoral Law was enacted by the NPC on 1 July 1979, which extended direct elections to county/district-level people's congress.[38]

When the CPC held its 13th National Assembly in 1987, the Working Report delivered by the Secretary-General of the Central Committee of the CPC contained the following on the electoral system of the people's congresses:

> In recent years, the degree of democracy in election in China is increasing. But the electoral system is still not yet satisfactory and existing statutory provisions have not been implemented fully and effectively. In the future, we should fully respect the will of voters and ensure that voters have the freedom to vote. We should insist on the principle that the number of candidates should be more than positions available, improve the methods for the nomination of candidates, and the methods to introduce candidates. Practice has proved that rigid statutory provision on the ratio of candidates of different backgrounds is against the freedom of voters to express their own wills through election. In order to ensure that candidates represent different interests, methods other than geographical election can be introduced, including functional constituencies or any other feasible methods.[39]

The above quotation indicates that the CPC had already formed some opinions on how to reform the electoral system. But after the June Fourth Incident in 1989,[40] the political environment in China became relatively tense. As a result, reform stopped when the election was held in 1990.

[37] Z. Peng, 'Guanyu Quanguo Xuanju Shidian Gongzuo de Jidian Yijian' [Several Opinions on National Election Work on Trial] in Z. Peng, *Lun Xin Shiqi de Shehui Zhuyi Minzhu yu Fazhi Jianshe* [On the Establishment of Socialist Democracy and Legal System in New Era] (Beijing: Central Literature Press, 1989), pp. 38–43; see also Z. Peng, 'Difang Renda Changweihui de Gongzuo' [The Work of the Standing Committees of Local People's Congresses] in Z. Peng, *On the Establishment of Socialist Democracy and Legal System in New Era*, pp. 56–8; quoted from Cai, 'The History and Current Situation', pp. 10–11.

[38] The 1979 Electoral Law has since been amended five times; in 1982, 1986, 1995, 2004, 2010 and 2015, respectively.

[39] Z. Zhao, 'Yanzhe You Zhongguo Tesi de Shehui Zhuyi Daolu Qianjin' [Marching Alone the Socialist Road with Chinese Characteristics], Part V, http://cpc.people.com.cn/GB/64162/64168/64566/65447/4526368.html (last accessed 14 January 2016).

[40] In April 1989, while mourning the death of Hu Yaobang – a high ranking Chinese official who has been regarded as a pro-reformist, many students in China started to demonstrate and stage protests, demanding the Chinese government to carry out democratic reform

China's political environment became more liberal after 1992. That is why in the later amendments to the 1979 Electoral Law (including 2004, 2010 and 2015) some progress has been made in making the Electoral Law more ideal. For example, the 2004 amendments made it possible again for candidates to meet voters[41] and the 2010 amendments finally achieved the objective of equality between rural and urban votes and improved communications between candidates and voters.[42]

If we focus our attention on the relevant statutory provisions on direct election in the Electoral Law, it is fair to say that the main principles available in electoral legislation in other democratic countries such as the principles of universality, equality, direct election, and secret ballot are all there. The Electoral Law is developing towards the direction of an ideal electoral law similar in many aspects to those in democratic countries.[43]

Electoral Practice

Electoral practice has, however, presented another picture. As early as in 1980, when direct election was first held for district/county people's congresses, in Beijing alone around 100 students participated in the election and eight of them were elected as deputies of Haidian District People's Congress.[44] Since a detailed discussion of electoral practices is

and eradicate corruption. Their protests eventually developed into a large-scale student movement. They occupied the Tiananmen Square. Such a mass movement shocked the senior officials and senior CPC members who feared that the movement would shake the autocratic rule of the CPC. In order to disperse the crowd, in the early morning of 4 June 1989, the People's Liberation Army was ordered to clear up the Tiananmen Square. As a result, many died in this incident. For a detailed account of this Incident, see for example, P. J. Cunningham, *Tiananmen Moon: Inside the Chinese Student Uprising of 1989* (Lanham, MD: Rowman & Littlefield Publishers, 2009); C. Feng, *Liu Si Riji: Guangchang Shang de Gongheguo* [June Fourth Diary: The Republic in the Square] (Taipei: Free Culture Press, 2009). Feng was one of the student leaders of the student movement in the June Fourth Incident.

41 See the amendments to the Election Law in 2004, http://www.people.com.cn/GB/14576/28320/39838/39842/2947930.html (last accessed 14 January 2016).

42 See the Amendment to the Election Law in 2010, http://www.gov.cn/flfg/2010-03/14/content_1555450.htm (last accessed 14 January 2016).

43 Albert Chen has opined that you can hardly see any different between Chinese Electoral Law and Western ones. See, A. Chen, *An Introduction to the Legal System of the People's Republic of China* (Hong Kong: Lexis/Nexis, 2011), p. 99.

44 Y. Wang, '2003 Gongmin Quanli Nian' [2003 The Year of Citizens' Rights], *Xinwen Zhoukan* [China Newsweek], No. 47 of 2003, 20–1. See also, L. Luo, 'Shui Shi Shoupi Duli Jingxuanren?' [Who Are the First Batch of Independent Candidates?], *Nanfang Zhoumo* [Southern Weekends], 12 June 2003; quoted from S. Zou, J. Tang, and W. Huang, '2003 Nian Renda Daibiao Jingxuan de Qunti Xiaoying: Beijing yu Shenzhen Bijiao'

beyond the scope of this paper, I will instead choose two cases for discussion here.

The first case is about Mr Yao Lifa, who started in 1987 to participate in the election of Qianjiang Municipal People's Congress as an independent candidate.[45] In 1998, there were only two independent candidates, of whom Yao was one. When he had participated in the election for the fourth consecutive time, he was finally elected as a deputy. Yao's success in election indicates that the organs of both the CPC and people's governments have shown their tolerance of and even implied consent towards ordinary citizens standing for election of local people's congresses. It has also shown that two important factors which have caused citizens to voluntarily join election competition are their interests and rights' conscience.[46] This has been supported by other scholars' research.[47]

During his term of five years as a deputy, Yao put forward 187 recommendations/bills to supervise the government. His existence had, however, given some local officials a headache.[48] In 2003, the subsequent election year, Yao participated again together with 31 independent candidates, and was nominated as a candidate. Since there were more candidates than the statutory maximum, the process of repeated consultation and deliberation was held. As a result, most of them were screened out and only two of them became formal candidates. In the election, the two independent candidates and some other formal candidates got less than 50 per cent of votes from voters participating in the election. According to the Electoral Law, they should therefore participate as formal candidates in a by-election to be held. But the township

[The Collective Effect of 2003 Election of Delegates to the People's Congresses: A Comparison of Beijing and Shenzhen], *Makesi Zhuyi yu Xianshi* [Marxism and Reality], vol. 2 of 2004, 36.

45 For the facts of Yao Lifa's case, see Y. Sun, 'Independent Candidates in Mainland China: Origin, Development, and Implications for China's Democratization', *Asian Survey*, 53(2) (2013), 245–6.

46 E. Rosenthal, 'Far from Beijing, a Semblance of Democracy', *The New York Times*, 8 March 2002, A3.

47 Zou, Tang and Huang, 'The Collective Effect'; see also, Z. Wang and D. Ma, 'Participation and Competition: Innovations in Cadre Election and Selection in China's Townships', *Journal of Contemporary China*, 24(94) (2015), 298–314.

48 J. Hu, 'Luoxuan Renda Daibiao Shangjing Dijiao Shensu: Ti Renmin Shuohua Releshui?' [A Formal Delegate Who Lost Election Went to Beijing to Submit His Petition: What's Wrong with Speaking on Behalf of People?], *Xin Jing Bao* [The Beijing News], 13 January 2004, http://news.sina.com.cn/c/2004-01-13/02211569429s.shtml (last accessed 14 January 2016).

election organization committee did not organize the by-election on the grounds that those candidates had no intention to participate in another election and had given up their rights to participate in a by-election. The end result is that none of the 32 independent candidates got elected.[49] After the election, Yao together with some voters were of the view that their rights to vote and to stand for election had been infringed, and therefore petitioned the standing committee of Qianjiang Municipal People's Congress and some other governmental organs to address the issue. Yao also brought a legal action to a local court, which refused to accept his case. Yao further wrote a petition letter to the Standing Committee of the NPC (NPCSC) requesting that it start a special investigation procedure to investigate the problems.[50] But no organization, including the NPCSC, has ever investigated or dealt with Yao's petition. Thereafter, he has never succeeded in winning any election. What happened to Yao has also happened to many other independent candidates in people's congress election in China.[51] Yao's failure in all later elections proves that the procedure to determine formal candidates in existing electoral system can be used by election organizers to exclude those preliminary candidates they do not like so that such candidates will not become formal candidates.

The second case is a serious electoral corruption case which happened in Hengyang City, Hunan Province, at the end of 2012.[52] It was reported that at the first meeting of the People's Congress of Hengyang City held between 28 December 2012 and 3 January 2013, 527 deputies attended the meeting and elected 76 out of 93 candidates to be deputies

[49] F. Li, 'Cong Qianjiang Renda Xuanju Shijian Kan Zhongguo Jiceng Minzhu de Fazhan' [Analysis of the Development of Chinese Grassroots Democracy through the People's Congress Election Event in Qianjiang], *Renda Yanjiu* [People's Congress Studying], No. 4 of 2004, 24–8.

[50] *Ibid.*

[51] Sun, 'Independent Candidates in Mainland China'; see also, J. He, 'Independent Candidates in China's Local People's Congress: A Typology' in K. J. O'Brien and S. Zhao (eds.), *Grassroots Election in China* (New York: Routledge, 2011), Chapter 16; F. Lin, 'Renda Xuanju Zhidu de Xianzhuang Ji Qi Weilai' [Current Situation of People's Congress Election System and Its Future], *Fazhi Luncong* [The Rule of Law Forum], 24(3) (2009), 18–29; Zhang, *The Constitution of China*, pp. 250–8.

[52] This incident has been chosen as a special event in addition to the ten most influential constitutional events in 2013. L. Zheng, 'Tebie Shijian: Hengyang Renda Daibiao Huixuan Shijian' [Special Incident: The Case of Bribery in the Election of Deputies of Hengyang People' Congress] in J. Hu (ed.), *2013 Zhongguo Shida Xianfa Shili Pingxi* [Analysis of the Top Ten Constitutional Cases in China in 2013] (Beijing: Law Press, 2015), pp. 1–14.

of Hunan Provincial People's Congress. Later, it was revealed that 56 elected deputies spent 110 million RMB as corruption money to bribe the voters, i.e., the deputies to the People's Congress of Hengyang City, and relevant working staff in order to get elected. Meanwhile 518 deputies to the People's Congress of Hengyang City and 68 working staff received either money or gifts from the candidates. A similar large-scale electoral corruption happened in Nanyun City, Sichuan Province, involving 477 individuals.[53] Actually, it has been noted by various scholars and media that corruption is a widespread problem in electoral practices in China.[54]

Though Yao was an independent candidate, as far as the whole country is concerned the number and percentage of persons who stand for election upon their own initiative is still very low, and the percentage of such candidates who finally get elected as deputies is even lower.[55] Furthermore, undue influence was imposed to persuade those independent candidates not to participate in the election, and various obstacles have been created in some cases to make it difficult for such candidates get elected.[56] Up to now, election is still confirmative rather than competitive in the majority of township and county people's congresses in China.[57] The tension is therefore shown between the Electoral Law, as reflecting idealism, and electoral practice, as reflecting realism. The corruption cases reflect another aspect of such tension, i.e., tension between the idealism pursued under the Electoral Law and the realism that substantial numbers of people do not take seriously the Electoral Law, which includes legal punishments for corruption, and are willing to violate the law for the purpose of getting elected.

[53] 'Sichuan Yancha Nanchong Lapiao Huixuan An' [Sichuan Seriously Investigate into the Case of Buying Votes and Election Bribery in Nanchong], http://society.people.com.cn/n/2015/0916/c136657-27589272.html (last accessed 14 January 2016).

[54] See for example, R. Levy, 'Village Elections, Transparency, and Anti-Corruption: Henan and Guangdong Provinces' in E. J. Perry and M. Goldman (eds.), *Grassroots Political Reform in Contemporary China* (London: Harvard University Press, 2007), Chapter 2; J. J. Kennedy, 'The Price of Democracy: Vote Buying and Village Elections in China', *Asian Politics & Policy*, 2(4) (2010), 617–31; Zhang, *The Constitution of China*, pp. 250–8.

[55] Lin, 'Current Situation of People's Congress Election'.

[56] *Ibid.*; He, 'Independent Candidates'.

[57] This has been confirmed by the author's field trip in 2005 and recent scholarly writings on electoral practice in China. See, Lin, 'Current Situation of People's Congress Election'; Lin, 'Electoral Reform in China'; Zhang, *The Constitution of China*, pp. 250–8.

Debate on the Justiciability of the Chinese Constitution

The debate on the justiciability of the Chinese Constitution started with the publication of the SPC's judicial opinion issued in the *Qi Yuling* Case.[58] The case has been widely discussed by both Chinese constitutional scholars and those foreign scholars specializing in Chinese law,[59] and can be summarized as follows: In 1990, Qi Yuling and Chen Xiaoqi were classmates at the Eighth Middle School in Tengzhou, Shandong Province. They took the pre-selection middle-level training school examination. Qi passed the exam while Chen failed. Qi sat the subsequent uniform examination and achieved scores good enough for admission. Jining Municipality School of Commerce of Shandong Province made her an offer but her letter of acceptance was stolen by Chen who used it to get into Jining Municipality School of Commerce and later graduated. Thereafter, Chen got employed, still using Qi's name.[60] Qi found out about the identity theft a few years later. She filed a civil suit in Zaozhuang Municipality Intermediate People's Court of Shandong Province. She claimed that Chen, together with other defendants, jointly committed identity theft, thus violating her rights to her name, to receive education, and other relevant rights and interests, and sought relevant remedies.

Qi's identity theft claim was on solid ground as Chen's actions had violated Qi's right to her identity under the General Principles of Civil Law.[61] What is controversial is Qi's claim for damages on the ground that Chen had violated her constitutional right to education. The Shandong Provincial Higher People's Court heard the case on appeal. Being uncertain about whether it could deal with Qi's claim of her constitutional right in a civil case, the Higher People's Court sought guidance from the SPC. The SPC issued its reply as follows:

> We have received your court's Request for Instructions Concerning the Dispute Involving Rights in a Person's Name between Qi Yuling and Chen Xiaoqi, Chen Kezheng, Jining Municipality School of Commerce of Shandong Province, Tengzhou Municipality No. 8 High School of Shandong Province and Tengzhou Municipal Education Commission of Shandong Province. After study, we hold, on the basis of the facts in this case, that Chen Xiaoqi and others have violated the fundamental right to receive education enjoyed by Qi Yuling in accordance with the provisions

58 Shen, 'Is It the Beginning of the Era'.

59 See for example, *ibid.*; Kellogg, 'Constitutionalism with Chinese Characteristics', 215–46.

60 Shen, 'Is It the Beginning of the Era'.

61 Article 99, Minfa Tongze [General Principles of Civil Law].

> of the Constitution by means of violating rights to a person's name. Because this violation has resulted in actual damages, commensurate civil liability arises. Reply is hereby given.[62]

The SPC's intervention led to an explosion of academic debate. The *Qi Yuling* Case provided a much-needed opportunity for discussion of a wide range of constitutional issues, of which one is the justiciability of the Chinese Constitution, and another of which is whether Chinese courts are suitable organs to conduct constitutional supervision. Discussion here will focus on the first issue, while the second issue will be examined in the next section.

In an article, former Justice Huang Songyou from the SPC stated that the intention of the SPC in issuing its Reply in the *Qi Yuling* Case was to create a *Marbury v. Madison* in China.[63] Chinese scholars' views are sharply divided on whether the Chinese Constitution is justiciable. Professor Wang Lei and Professor Wang Zhenmin are two strong advocates for a justiciable Constitution. Their essential arguments can be summarized as follows. No statutory provisions can be found in any legislation that the Constitution cannot be applied to by courts in specific cases. Even if the SPC had expressed the view that the Constitution should not be relied on in specific cases, which they denied to be the case, that would not constitute an obstacle for the courts to apply the Constitution in specific cases. This is because the SPC cannot do anything in violation of the Constitution and national law, which contain no such restriction.[64]

Many other scholars are of the view that Chinese Constitution is not justiciable. Their arguments can be summarized as follows. Firstly, the *Qi*

[62] 'Guanyu yi Qinfan Xingmingquan de Shouduan Qinfan Xianfa Baohu de Gongmin Shou Jiaoyu Quanli Shifo Chengdan Minshi Zeren de Pifu' [Reply Concerning Whether Civil Liability Arises When the Constitutionally Protected Fundamental Right of Citizens to Receive Education Is Violated by Means of Violating Rights to a Person's Name], cited and translated in Shen, 'Is It the Beginning of the Era', 204.

[63] S. Huang, 'Xianfa Sifahua Ji Qi Yiyi – Cong Zuigao Renmin Fayuan Jintian de Yige "Pifu" Tanqi' [Judicialization of the Constitution and Its Implication – Opening the Talk with a Reply Issued by the Supreme People's Court Today], *Renmin Fayuan Bao* [People's Court Daily], 13 August 2001.

[64] Q. Zhang, 'Woguo Fayuan Shifou Keyi Shixian' [Can the Chinese Courts Interpret the Constitution], *Faxue* [Law Science], No. 4 of 2009, 39–42; L. Hai, 'Zai Xianxing Tizhi Xia Fayuan Reng Ying Jianjie Shiyong Xianfa' [Courts Should Still Indirectly Apply the Constitution under the Existing System], *Faxue* [Law Science], No. 4 of 2009, 42–5; L. Wang, *Xianfa de Sifahua* [Judicialization of the Constitution] (Beijing: China University of Political Science and Law Press, 2000), pp. 19–21; Z. Wang, 'Woguo Xianfa Kefou Jinru Susong' [Can the Chinese Constitution Be Applied in Litigation], *Fashang Yanjiu* [Studies in Law and Business], No. 5 of 1999, 28–36.

Yuling Case is an ordinary civil case rather than a constitutional case because a typical constitutional case will involve the exercise of public power by one party to the case. Secondly, the Chinese Constitution gives constitutional supervision power to the NPC and NPCSC instead of to the courts.[65] A constitutional amendment is needed in order to authorize courts to exercise such power. Thirdly, court's exercise of constitutional supervision power is a violation of the people's congress system, under which the NPC and NPCSC are supreme.[66]

All those Chinese scholars in favour of justiciability of the Chinese Constitution are aware of the arguments against them. The reason for their support of justiciability has been expressed vividly by Professor Jiang Mingan. According to him, the Chinese Constitution has been packed away and put on a high shelf for decades. The Constitution was considered a 'restricted area' by courts and judges because some constitutional rights are sensitive. The right to education involved in the *Qi Yuling* Case is not a sensitive right and was relatively easy to handle. It is therefore an appropriate case for the SPC to use to make a breakthrough in application of the Constitution in trying cases.[67] The *Qi Yuling* Case has also been hailed by rights-defending lawyers. For them, it is essential that Chinese courts be able to apply the Constitution to try cases. If the right to education can be applied by courts, there is hope that courts will apply civil and political rights provisions in trying cases.[68]

The *Qi Yuling* Case has given hope to judges, scholars, and rights-defending lawyers that the ideal picture as presented by the written Constitution can be achieved in reality through judicial application of the Constitution. As far as the SPC is concerned, it wants to become the pioneer or breakthrough point for achieving rule of law in China. The SPC is fully aware of the fact that there is not much hope for

[65] For details about constitutional supervision, see next section of this paper.

[66] Z. Tong, 'Xianfa Sifa Shiyong Yanjiu Zhong de Jige Wenti' [Various Problems in Research on Usability of the Constitution], *Xianfa Yanjiu* [Studies on Constitutionalism], (2002), 271–84, quoted in Kellogg, 'Constitutionalism with Chinese Characteristics?', 232.

[67] G. Guo, 'Xianfa Sifahua Sirentan' [Four Peoples Discussing Judicialization of the Constitution], *Nanfang Zhoumo* [Southern Weekends], 14 September 2001, http://www.people.com.cn/BIG5/shehui/46/20010914/560852.html (last accessed 15 January 2016).

[68] *Ibid.*; see also, T. E. Kellogg, 'The Constitution in the Courtroom: Constitutional Development and Civil Litigation in China' in M. Y. K. Woo and M. E. Gallagher (eds.), *Chinese Justice: Civil Dispute Resolution in Contemporary China* (Cambridge: Cambridge University Press, 2011), p. 363; C. X. Lin, 'A Quiet Revolution: An Overview of China's Judicial Reform', *Asian-Pacific Law & Policy Journal*, 4(2) (Summer 2003), 270–4.

achieving rule of law if the Constitution can be ignored and cannot be implemented in practice.

But despite the efforts of the SPC, many scholars and also rights-defending lawyers, the SPC made an announcement in 2008 to repeal its Reply in the *Qi Yuling* Case on the ground that the Reply has stopped being applicable.[69] If that is the proper justification, there was no need for the SPC to have issued its Reply at the first place because the case was a civil instead of a constitutional case. It is therefore logical to suspect that its repeal was for other reasons, of which the most likely was that the SPC has either realized or been told that it is not appropriate for it to issue such a reply with the intention to apply the Constitution.

Though the repeal of the Reply by the SPC evidences that reality has prevailed over idealism, the *Qi Yuling* Case is still very important in that through this case a constitutional institution, i.e., the SPC, which was and is still under the leadership of the CPC, started to take the leadership in promoting idealistic constitutionalism in China and bridging the gap between idealism and realism.

Debate on a Suitable Constitutional Review Mechanism

As mentioned above, another constitutional issue brought up by the *Qi Yuling* Case is whether courts are proper organ for conducting constitutional supervision in China.[70] In fact, constitutional supervision mechanism has been a hot topic for Chinese constitutional law scholars since 1981, when discussion and debate were held for the enactment of the 1982 Constitution.[71] The drafting committee was actually in favour of the idea of the establishment of a constitutional committee to conduct

[69] 'Zuigao Renmin Fayuan Guanyu Feizhi 2007 Niandi Yiqian Fabu de Youguan Sifa Jieshi (Di Qi Pi) de Jueding' [Decision of the Supreme People's Court on Abolishing Judicial Interpretations Issued Prior to 2007 (Seventh Batch)], http://old.chinacourt.org/html/article/200812/24/337161.shtml (last accessed 15 January 2016).

[70] Shen, 'Is It the Beginning of the Era'; R. J. Morris, 'China's Marbury: Qi Yuling v. Chen Xiaoqi – The Once and Future Trial of Both Education and Constitutionalization', *Tsinghua China Law Review*, 2(2) (2010), 273–316.

[71] See H. He, 'Lun Xianfa Jiandu' [On Constitutional Supervision], *Wuhan Daxue Xuebao (Renmin Kexue Ban)* [Wuhan University Journal (Humanity Sciences)], No. 1 of 1982, 3–9; Z. Zhang and S. Tie, 'Lun Xianfa de Shishi' [On the Implementation of Constitution] in Y. Zhang (ed.), *Xianfa Lunwenji (Xubian)* [Collection of Essays on Constitutional Law (Continued)] (Beijing: Mass Press, 1982), pp. 283–98; Xu (ed.), *Chinese Constitutional Law*, pp. 46–53.

constitutional supervision.[72] It eventually gave up because of the difficulty of defining the legal status and the authority of such a committee and because of China's lack of necessary deliberation and experience in this aspect.[73]

The 1982 Constitution has mainly followed the approach as laid down in the 1954 and 1978 Constitutions, i.e., to grant the authority of constitutional supervision to the supreme organ of state power – the NPC and NPCSC. In comparison with the mechanism under the 1954 Constitution, the 1982 Constitution has revised the constitutional supervision mechanism in following aspects. Apart from the NPC,[74] it adds the NPCSC as the organ to conduct constitutional supervision.[75] The 1982 Constitution has expanded the authorities of the NPCSC.[76] In order to prevent the occurrence of any inappropriate act of the NPCSC in the exercise of its expanded authorities, it also adds another check and balance by providing that the NPC has the authority to alter or annul any inappropriate decisions of the NPCSC.[77] This ensures that the NPC still enjoys the supreme authority in China and can supervise any activities of the NPCSC, including its activities in constitutional supervision. The 1982 Constitution provides that the NPC may establish various special committees. They have been assigned the task to assist the NPC and the NPCSC in conducting constitutional supervision. Such assignment is specifically stated in the Organic Law of the National People's Congress, which provides that the special committees have to perform the following function:

> [t]o examine and submit reports on items received from the NPCSC which are considered to be in contravention of the Constitution or the law, namely: administrative regulations, decisions and orders issued by the State Council; orders, instructions and regulations issued by the ministries and commissions under the State Council; regulations and resolutions issued locally by the people's congresses of the provinces, autonomous regions, and municipalities directly under the Central Government and

72 Y. Chen, *Minzhu Xianzheng Xincao: Xianfa Jiandu de Lilun yu Shijian* [New Trends of Democratic Constitutionalism: Theory and Practice of Constitutional Supervision] (Beijing: People's Press, 1988), p. 257.

73 L. Liu, 'Luelun Xianfa Jiandu' [A Brief Discussion of Constitutional Supervision], *Shehui Kexue* [Journal of Social Sciences], No. 3 of 1981, 106–8; Hu (ed.), *Analysis of the Top Ten Constitutional Cases in China in 2013*, p. 200.

74 Article 62(2), 1982 Constitution. 75 Article 67(1), 1982 Constitution.

76 The NPCSC has been granted the authority to make laws and to interpret the Constitution and national laws.

77 Article 62(11), 1982 Constitution.

> their standing committees; and decisions, orders and regulations issued by the people's governments of the provinces, autonomous regions, and municipalities directly under the Central Government.[78]

Though the constitutional supervision mechanism under the 1982 Constitution is more detailed and better structured than before, the actual performance of the NPC and NPCSC in the area of constitutional supervision has not been satisfactory. In practice, there do exist unconstitutional activities. The *Sun Zhigang* Case is one of many examples.[79] But neither the NPC nor the NPCSC has formally annulled or repealed any laws, administrative regulations, local legislation and local rules.[80]

That has led Chinese scholars to explore alternative constitutional supervision models. Five different models have been put forward. One is to establish a constitutional court, basing on the model of the Constitutional Court in Germany or Constitutional Committee in France.[81] Another approach is to set up a constitutional committee under the NPC to conduct constitutional supervision. As to the constitutional status of the constitutional committee within China's legal system, scholars held different views. Some suggest that it should have the same status as the NPCSC. Some argue that it should be a special committee of the NPC, similar to the other special committees of the NPC. Some say that it should be a working organ of the NPC, similar to the Legislative Affairs Commission of the NPCSC at the moment.[82] A third approach is to grant the constitutional supervision authority to the people's procuratorates. The fourth is to establish limited constitutional litigation system by granting the authority to the courts. The fifth is to mix the advantages of the three main constitutional

[78] Article 37(3), 1982 Organic Law of the National People's Congress.

[79] For the facts of this case, see Zhang, *The Constitution of China*, pp. 75–81; K. J. Hand, 'Using Law for a Righteous Purpose: The Sun Zhigang Incident and Evolving Forms of Citizen Action in the People's Republic of China', *Columbia Journal of Transnational Law*, 45(1) 2006, 114–47.

[80] It has been argued that 'The Decision of the Standing Committee of the NPC on the Treatment of the Laws Previously in Force in Hong Kong in Accordance with Article 160 of the Basic Law of the Hong Kong Special Administrative Region of the People's Republic of China', adopted by the Standing Committee of the NPC on 23 February 1997, amounts to a constitutional supervision activity. For the full text of the Decision, see http://www.basiclaw.gov.hk/en/basiclawtext/images/basiclawtext_doc16.pdf (last accessed 15 January 2016).

[81] Professor Xu Chongde was the leading scholar supporting this approach. See also, Cheng, *New Trends of Democratic Constitutionalism*.

[82] Legislative Affairs Commission is the working unit for the NPCSC. Its primary function is to draft national legislation. All legal draftsmen are civil servants.

supervision models in the world to create a new type of constitutional supervision mechanism which best suits China's reality and needs.[83]

The constitutional supervision mechanism adopted by a specific country is influenced by the historical and cultural tradition, the political system and the legal structure of the country concerned. In the case of China, its political system is the people's congress system, which implements democratic centralism. Under such a system, the NPC and NPCSC are the supreme organs of state power. They exercise not only legislative power but also leadership and supervision authority over other state organs. The difficulty for China in transplanting either the American or German or French model is not about whether those models are good or bad. Instead, the main difficulty is that the theoretical basis for those models does not exist in China because Chinese constitutional law follows a completely different constitutional theory, which believes in the supreme power of the NPC and NPCSC and categorically denies the necessity of separation of powers.[84]

The 2000 Legislation Law has provided more details to the constitutional supervision mechanism under the 1982 Constitution.[85] In particular, there is a requirement that the NPCSC must give a legislative interpretation if a request comes from a specified constitutional organ.[86] But it has not changed the fact that the primary authority and obligation to conduct both legal and constitutional review of other sources of law still rest with the NPC and NPCSC. With the gradual development of its segmented constitutional supervision mechanism,[87] there is little chance that China will follow any of the major models in the world. Instead, China will most likely develop a unique kind of constitutional supervision mechanism of its own.

Though the existing constitutional supervision mechanism under the 1982 Constitution and the 2000 Legislation Law still has some structural problems,[88] the mechanism can be put into operation if there exists a political will. In 2015 a group of leading scholars made a proposal to

[83] Lin, *Constitutional Law in China*. [84] *Ibid.*, p. 62.

[85] For the full text of the Legislation Law, see http://english1.english.gov.cn/laws/2005-08/20/content_29724.htm (last accessed 15 January 2016).

[86] Article 43, Legislation Law.

[87] Under Chinese Constitution and Legislation Law, constitutional supervision power is granted to various constitutional organs, including the NPC, the NPCSC, the State Council, some local people's congresses and their standing committees, and also some local people's governments. For details, see Articles 88, 90 and 91 of the Legislation Law.

[88] See for example, Zhang, *The Constitution of China*, pp. 93–6; Lin, *Constitutional Law in China*, pp. 299–301.

the Central Government advocating again for the establishment of a special constitutional supervision committee under the NPC to be in charge of constitutional supervision in China. The reason they have done so is that they have been approached by some senior officials of the CPC.[89] It is unclear yet whether that is an indication that the CPC is planning to create an effective constitutional supervision mechanism. The four sets of constitutional amendments to the 1982 Constitution were made almost every five years. Now about 12 years have passed since the last constitutional amendments in 2004. There is a possibility that the CPC is actively preparing the next set of constitutional amendments. The past practice has been that every set of constitutional amendments was initiated by the CPC. Only when they were endorsed by the CPC would they be submitted to the NPC for consideration.[90] If it is true that the CPC is considering the introduction of a special committee to conduct constitutional review in China, that can be seen as its positive response to the request to implement and enforce the Constitution in China. That will be a very positive interaction between the forces behind idealism and realism in China.

Tension between Idealism and Realism in Contemporary Chinese Constitutional Theory

Modern Chinese constitutional theory, like other legal theories in China, started in the 1980s when Chinese scholars generally believed in the orthodox Marxist class-struggle theory of law. They believed that the Constitution, like any other laws, was the result of class struggle and reflected the will of ruling class, i.e., the working class led by the CPC in China, rather than any universal values or principles.[91] But the majority of Chinese constitutional scholars transferred relatively quickly from that approach to acceptance of some essential components of Western understanding of the rule of law and constitutionalism in 1990s. For example, Professor Xu Chongde has defined the Constitution as 'the fundamental law of the state stipulating the fundamental systems of tasks of the state,

[89] Information was provided to the author by two scholars involved in the process.

[90] That has been argued by some Chinese constitutional scholars as a constitutional convention in China. Zhang, *The Constitution of China*, p. 58.

[91] Q. Gao, 'Geming, Gaige yu Xianzhi: "82 Xianfa" Ji Qi Yanjin Luoji' [Revolution, Reform and Constitutional System: 1982 Constitution and the Logic of Its Evolution] in Q. Gao, *Zhengzhi Xianfaxue Gangyao* [Outline of Political Constitutionalism] (Beijing: Central Compilation & Translation Press, 2014).

reflecting the balance of political forces of different classes and guaranteeing the basic rights of individuals'.[92] Though the class nature is still maintained, the essential nature of constitutional supremacy and protection of fundamental rights have been accepted.

Normative Constitutional Theory

While it is beyond the scope of this paper to discuss comprehensively all constitutional theories in China, it suffices for the purpose of this paper to discuss three of them to show how the tension between constitutional idealism and realism has influenced the development of Chinese constitutional theories. Nowadays, the majority of Chinese constitutional scholars adhere to what is generally called normative constitutionalism in Western countries.[93] Within normative constitutional theory, two more specific schools are worthy of noting: one is called 'normative constitutional theory', the other 'constitutional interpretation theory'.[94]

Normative constitutional theory was first advocated by Professor Lin Laifan in 2001.[95] According to him, constitutional law research should focus on constitutional norms including constitutional text, other constitutional legislation, and constitutional cases.[96] While acknowledging the necessity and importance of studying other elements of constitutional phenomena such as constitutional theory, constitutional system and constitutional relationship, he argues that constitutional law research should focus on constitutional norms and formulate a theory or theories on constitutional norms. In addition, he opines that after establishing the status of constitutional norms in constitutional study, normative

92 Xu (ed.), *Chinese Constitutional Law*, p. 19.

93 L. Lin, *Cong Xianfa Guifan Dao Guifan Xianfa: Guifan Xianfaxue de Yizhong Qianyan* [From Constitutional Norm to the Theory of Normative Constitution: A Preface to the Theory of Normative Constitution] (Beijing: Law Press, 2001); Q. Gao, 'Zhengzhi Xianfaxue de Xingqi yu Shanbian' [The Rise and Evolution of Political Constitutionalism] in Gao, *Outline of Political Constitutionalism*.

94 X. Liu, 'Guifan Xian yu Guifan Xianfaxue: Zhongguo Xianfaxue Zhu Liupai Tanxi' [Normative Constitution and the Theory of Normative Constitution: Analysis of Various Schools of Constitutional Thoughts in China], *Ershiyi Shiji Shuang Yuekan* [Twenty-First Century Bimonthly], No. 4 of 2015, 75–91; D. Han, L. Lin and L. Zheng, 'Xianfa Jieshixue yu Guifan Xianfaxue de Duihua' [A Dialogue between Constitutional Interpretation Theory and Normative Constitutional Theory], *Zhejiang Xuekan* [Zhejiang Academic Journal], No. 2 of 2008, 34–143.

95 He mainly studied law in Japan and has not received formal legal education in Mainland China.

96 Lin, *From Constitutional Norm to the Theory of Normative Constitution*, p. 1 of Preface.

constitutional theory should promote a normative view of the constitution, as defined by Karl Loewenstein.[97] Scholars believing in normative constitutional theory mainly argue that Chinese constitutional law should aim at developing itself towards Western constitutionalism's focus on researching constitutional norms, legislation, and enabling constitutional supervision, ideally by an independent organ, be it constitutional court or ordinary court.[98]

Professor Han Dayuan is the leading advocate for constitutional interpretation theory.[99] He has advocated for years that constitutional research in China should be based on the constitutional document and its interpretation. According to him,[100] constitutional interpretation theory arises against the background that Chinese constitutional law is too political and lacks independence from politics. As a result, the aims of constitutional interpretation theory are to ensure that the text of the Chinese Constitution is taken seriously, to maintain the legal nature of the Constitution rather than its political aspect (and to turn the political constitution into a legal constitution), and to sever the natural connection between politics and law in Chinese constitutional law. In doing so, it expects to maintain the independence of constitutional law from politics and to change the study of constitutional law from political logic to legal logic so as to shift research focus to constitutional phenomena and logic.[101]

Professor Han recognizes the tension between constitutional norms contained in Chinese Constitution and the reality. He opines that the way to handle this is the greatest challenge facing Chinese constitutional law

[97] *Ibid.*, p. 8 of Preface, referring to K. Loewenstein, 'Reflections on the Value of Constitutions in Our Revolutionary Age' in A. J. Zurcher (ed.), *Constitutions and Constitutional Trends after World War II: An Examination of Significant Aspects of Postwar Public Law with Particular Reference to the New Constitutions of Western Europe* (New York University Press, 1951), Chapter 11.

[98] Lin, *From Constitutional Norm to the Theory of Normative Constitution.*

[99] Han, Lin and Zheng, 'A Dialogue between Constitutional Interpretation Theory and Normative Constitutional Theory'. Han is the present chairman of Chinese Constitutional Scholars' Association and Dean of the School of Law of Renmin University of China.

[100] D. Han, 'Renzhen Duidai Zhongguo Xianfa Wenben' [Treating the Text of Chinese Constitution Seriously], *Qinghua Faxue* [Tsinghua University Law Journal], No. 6 of 2012, 5–18; D. Han, 'Zai Xianfa Jieshixue Shang Xunzhao Daan' [Finding the Answer from Constitutional Interpretation Theory], http://www.aisixiang.com/data/60054.html (last accessed 15 January 2016).

[101] Han, 'Finding the Answer from Constitutional Interpretation Theory'.

and scholars. According to him, the biggest lesson China has learned in the 30 years after the enactment of the 1982 Constitution is that too much concession has been made to political power and reality at the price of ignoring the existence and value of constitutional text. The basic position of constitutional interpretation theory is to adhere consistently to the value of constitutional norms contained in the constitutional text. Even though constitutional norms are conservative, they should be stuck to in order to maintain constitutional order of the country.[102]

On the other hand, he argues that constitutional interpretation theory has an important role to play in removing the tension between idealism and realism, between constitutional norms and political reality. The way to achieve this objective is to apply constitutional interpretation techniques and methods as far as possible to reconcile constitutional norms and political reality. He acknowledges that there is a limit beyond which constitutional interpretation methods cannot help. By then, only constitutional amendment can achieve the objective of consistency between constitutional norms and political reality. Without any constitutional amendments, constitutional norms have to be adhered to.[103]

Despite the efforts of these scholars advocating normative constitutionalism, the reality in China is that constitutional norms are often ignored. In fact, many economic reforms in the first three decades of reform since 1978 were carried out in clear violation of constitutional norms.[104] Some of the current reforms including judicial reform have also been criticized for their violation of the existing Constitution.[105] It is therefore common knowledge not only to legal scholars but also to the general public that the Chinese Constitution is not really a piece of

[102] *Ibid.* [103] *Ibid.*

[104] Liu, 'Normative Constitution and the Theory of Normative Constitution'; D. Chen, 'You Fuqiang Dao Ziyou: Zhongguo Xianfa de Jiezhi Quxiang yu Sifahua de Kenengxing' [From Wealthy to Freedom: The Value Orientation and Possibility of Judicialization of the Chinese Constitution], http://article.chinalawinfo.com/ArticleHtml/Article_30336.shtml (last accessed 17 January 2016); D. Han, 'Lun Xianfa Guifan yu Shehui Xianshi de Chongtu' [On the Conflicts between Constitutional Norms and Social Reality], *Zhongguo Faxue* [Chinese Legal Science], 3–16.

[105] See for example, L. Su, 'Sifa Gaige Luoji de Yanjiu – Ping Zuigao Fayuan de Yinjiu Cizhi Guiding' [Study on the Logic of Judicial Reform – Commenting on the Rule on Resign for Admitting Responsibility of the Supreme People's Court], *Zhanlue yu Guanli* [Strategy and Management], No. 1 of 2002, 27–37; Han, 'On the Conflicts between Constitutional Norms and Social Reality'; H. Zheng, 'Lun Sifa Tizhi Gaige Beijing Xia de Xianfa Xiugai Wenti' [On the Issue of Constitutional Amendment in the Context of Judicial System Reform], http://www.lwlm.com/guojiafaxianfa/201512/804003.htm (last accessed 17 January 2016).

enforceable legislation. Against this background, some scholars have challenged normative constitutional theory by searching out and putting forward alternative theories, among which two stand out. One is socialist constitutional theory, the other political constitutional theory.

Socialist Constitutional Theory

Like scholars in favour of normative constitutional theory, advocates of socialist constitutional theory also have differences in what they specifically support.[106] In essence, they have put forward several arguments. First, socialism and constitutionalism are not repugnant to each other. Instead, they are consistent with each other and a socialist country such as China can have constitutionalism.[107] Second, the Chinese Constitution is a socialist constitution, which is different from capitalist constitutions. The differences which have been identified include the class nature of the state, the ruling position of the CPC, and democratic centralism as an organization principle for all constitutional organs.[108] Third, the essence of socialist constitutionalism is to acknowledge the constitutional legitimacy of governance by the CPC while at the same time having clear legal provisions on the scope of power enjoyed by the CPC and the procedural rules on exercise of power by the CPC.[109]

Nowadays, class nature is of less and less importance in China in both theory and practice. The purpose of the principle of democratic centralism is primarily to strengthen the governing capacity of the CPC. The essential difference between socialist constitutional theory and normative constitutional theory seems to be the unchallengeable ruling position of the CPC in China. Apart from that, the advocates of socialist constitutionalism accept Western constitutionalism. It is therefore fair to say that their approach tries to combine acceptance of political reality with Western constitutionalism. Its actual intention is to persuade the CPC to endorse constitutionalism in China.

106 Professor Zhiwei Tong is one of the leading scholars among them. Z. Tong, 'Liqing Xianzheng yu Shehui Zhuyi Guanxi de Jiben Xiansuo' [Clarifying the Basic Clues on the Relationship between Constitutionalism and Socialism], *Faxue Pinglun* [Law Review], No. 5 of 2015, 22–30.

107 Q. Qin and H. Ye, 'Lun Shehui Zhuyi Xianzheng' [On Socialist Constitutional Theory], http://article.chinalawinfo.com:81/article_print.asp?articleid=23845 (last accessed 16 January 2016).

108 *Ibid.*; Tong, 'Clarifying the Basic Clues'.

109 Tong, 'Clarifying the Basic Clues'.

Political Constitutional Theory

Political constitutional theory was first advocated by Professor Chen Duanhong from Peking University Law School in 2008.[110] Ever since, many other scholars have joined him, although some support his methodology but not all of his arguments.[111] Political constitutional theory has criticized normative constitutional theory in China as hypocritical and useless because normative constitutional theory neither reflects political reality nor is capable of resolving existing constitutional issues in China.[112]

In their view, the Chinese Constitution can hardly be regarded in a Western normative sense as effective, as most rights provisions stay on paper only, have not been implemented and do not have judicial guarantee. The Chinese Constitution can be described as decorative in a normative sense. Nevertheless, China has had a written Constitution for years and the 1982 Constitution has already been there for 34 years. There is a constitutional system in China of which some mechanisms have been effectively implemented.[113] Further, the Chinese political system has been functioning effectively in the last three decades. It can even be said that Chinese political system has been quite forceful in maintaining political order, keeping the country and society integrated, and developing its economy rapidly.[114]

The concern of political constitutional theory is neither normative interpretation of Chinese constitutional text nor direct application of ideological slogans of a political nature nor judicialization of the Chinese Constitution. Political constitutional theory regards 'political constitution' as the core question for Chinese constitutional law. It treats the norms of political order as a constitution, tries to reveal the true picture of the Constitution under the leadership of the CPC, and discusses its future constitutional reform.[115] It goes direct to the structure of the Chinese Constitution, constitution-making authority, and the constitutional spirit that lies thereunder.[116] Hence, political nature becomes the core concept of political constitutional theory, and so is the relationship between politics and the Constitution, the norms of Chinese politics and

[110] D. Chen, 'Lun Xianfa Zuowei Guojia de Genbenfa yu Gaojifa' [On the Constitution as a Country's Fundamental Law and Higher Law], *Zhongwai Faxue* [Peking University Law Journal], 20(4) (2008), 485–511.

[111] Another leading scholar on political constitutional theory is Gao Quanxi. See, Gao, 'The Rise and Evolution'.

[112] *Ibid.* [113] *Ibid.* [114] *Ibid.* [115] *Ibid.* [116] *Ibid.*

Chinese political system, the relationship between the Constitution and the norms of existing political system and its operation. Accordingly, legislative authority, instead of judicial authority, becomes the core issue of political constitutional theory. People, revolution and constitution-making, instead of judges, judiciary and rights, have become main concepts for study.[117]

Political constitutional theory believes the central theme of the existing political system in China lies in the Preamble of the Chinese Constitution and in the unified structure of the CPC and the state. Hence, research on Chinese constitutional law should start from the Preamble of the Constitution, and from the real structure of the constitutional system,[118] because the Preamble reveals the political nature of the Chinese Constitution. As to the exact meaning of 'political nature', different political constitutional theorists hold different views. Chen suggests that there are five fundamental constitutional norms in China, including leadership of the CPC, socialism, democratic centralism, modernization, and protection of fundamental rights. He opines that China mainly relies on political mechanisms instead of legal mechanisms to implement the Constitution.[119]

But Gao Quanxi criticizes Chen by stating that his theory blindly endorses political reality. In Gao's view, constitutional law is not politics; it is in essence about normative limits on political powers. Political constitutional theory should still acknowledge the normative value of a political constitution, i.e., the legitimacy of the Constitution. Further, he argues that constitutional law has another dimension: it has political authorization as its basis. To put it in another way, in answering the question of origin of a constitution, constitutional law must face politics and cannot be severed from politics. A constitution is the result of politics, or the result of people's exercise of constitution-making authority. Without original political authorization, there will not be a constitution.[120]

According to Gao, mainstream constitutional theories[121] in China are only valid and useful in normal circumstances under which constitutionalism has been realized. In contrast, political constitutional theory is concerned with the political nature of constitution-making under

[117] *Ibid.* [118] *Ibid.*

[119] Chen, 'On the Constitution as a Country's Fundamental Law and Higher Law'; Liu, 'Normative Constitution and the Theory of Normative Constitution'.

[120] Gao, 'The Rise and Evolution'.

[121] They refer to normative constitutional theories discussed above and some other schools thereof which have not been discussed in this chapter.

abnormal circumstances, i.e., where China is now.[122] Hence, Gao in essence suggests that the Chinese Constitution is a political constitution which is a transitional constitution. The function of the existing political constitution in China is to gradually establish and realize the value of normative rules, and its ultimate goal is to turn revolutionary politics[123] into constitutional politics, to create constitutional norms internally to limit the CPC's own powers, and eventually to lead China into a country with constitutionalism.[124]

Conclusion

This chapter has discussed the tension as well as interaction between idealism and realism in Chinese constitutional theory and practice from modern Chinese constitutional history, three examples of constitutional practice, and three competing constitutional theories. The discussion proves that the tension between idealism and realism is a constant theme in every aspect of Chinese constitutional law, from history, to practice, to theory. Further, the tension is multi-dimensional. The first is the most commonly observed tension between constitutional norms and political reality dominated by the political will of those in power. The second is tension between judicial activism and the CPC's conservatism in maintaining the status quo. The third is the tension between transplantation of foreign models and Chinese domestic reality. As far as tension is concerned, it argues that one of the reasons is the lack of political will. While being the main reason, it is not the only one. China's unique constitutional system and structure is another one.

As far as interaction is concerned, various people and institutions have made their efforts to close the gap between idealism and realism, including legal scholars, legislature, judiciary, lawyers (especially rights-defending lawyers), and ordinary citizens like Yao Lifa. What is of particularly symbolic value is judicial activism as shown by the SPC in the *Qi Yuling* Case. On the one hand, judges have been trained to believe in idealism. On the other, the realization of idealism will also benefit the judiciary and judges by enhancing its importance and legal status. The Reply by the SPC in the *Qi Yuling* Case was eventually repealed by the SPC itself, possibly for the reason that the SPC is of the view that it should not take such leadership in closing the gap between idealism and

[122] Gao, 'The Rise and Evolution'.

[123] That is how the CPC came into power in 1949.

[124] Gao, 'The Rise and Evolution'.

realism in Chinese constitutional law and practice. That would be a decision based on its judgement of the political environment in China. Once the political environment changes, there is every reason to believe that the Chinese judiciary, especially the SPC, will make another effort in achieving constitutionalism in China.

The second group consists of legal scholars, as they are always working to achieve idealistic rule of law and constitutionalism in China. That is normal because in most countries, scholars are always at forefront for achieving constitutionalism. The third is the legislature. That is somewhat unique in China because among all constitutional institutions, the legislature is, comparatively speaking, a weak legal institution because the NPCSC consists of essentially senior officials who have retired from the CPC organizations, the executive branch, and so on. The realization of idealistic constitutionalism will help to enhance its status in comparison with the other legal institutions, especially the executive and the CPC. The fourth group consists of lawyers and other legal professionals, especially rights-defending lawyers. They play a key role in raising rights-consciousness by creating rights-based, if not constitutional, cases and defending the rights of those ordinary citizens involved therein. The fifth group consists of ordinary citizens like Yao Lifa who have, due to various reasons, become rights-conscious and have stood up for their rights. With the growing of the number of this group, a civil society will gradually form. That will be an enormous force for closing the gap between idealism and realism.

All of them have made efforts to close the gap between idealism and realism in the past four decades. However, not much progress has been made so far. Even though the CPC's recent policy has made it clear that it intends to achieve rule of law in China, its practice in controlling scholarly speeches and lawyers defending human rights has made people doubt whether its policy reflects the genuine intention of the CPC. This paper argues that that is not really a new phenomenon as the CPC has always been in such a paradoxical position since it came into power in China. On the one hand, it has realized that rule of law and constitutionalism is the international trend and is demanded by the Chinese people. Rule of law and constitutionalism will also give legitimacy to its ruling position. On the other, its intention to keep its ruling position in China has been consistent and never changed. The CPC must understand that the realization of idealistic rule of law and constitutionalism will inevitably end perpetual rule by the CPC in China. In order to further close the gap between idealism and realism, various interest groups mentioned above need to work together continuously. Their efforts have forced the CPC to respond to their demand for constitutionalism, and will continue to do so. In addition, if the CPC has the courage to lead the nation to realize constitutionalism and rule of law, as the Nationalist Party did in Taiwan several decades ago, the process of bridging the gap between idealism and realism in China can be shortened enormously.

The interaction among different forces has gone sometimes more in favour of idealism, though most of the time is against it. That is understandable given that the CPC is in strong hold of its ruling position and still lacks the political will to move more quickly towards idealism. However, the author of this paper argues that given that more and more people from different sectors of society have become more rights-conscious, particularly with not only individuals but several legal institutions such as the legislature, the judiciary and the legal profession in favour of idealism, the trend is definitely tipped towards idealism, although the process may take a relatively longer time.

11

Realism and Idealism in the Italian Constitutional Culture

JÖRG LUTHER

Introduction

This chapter explores what impact idealism and realism have on Italian constitutional law, both with regard to constitution-making and constitutional review. This is a new question, new at least to the extent that Italian constitutional lawyers do not frequently use these concepts. They do have normative ideas of what a good constitution should entail and a minimum of morals in constitutionalism, which implies a trend towards idealism. Furthermore, they have views on what is the effective state of the constitution, which is a claim for realism. Simplifying, we could say that idealists consider the human world as generated and driven by principles or values and faiths produced in human reasoning and conscience. Realists, on the other side, hold that there is an objective existence generated and conditioned by place, time and anthropological, social or economic necessity, quite independent from (or contrary to) subjective ideologies. When dealing with constitutional law and politics, lawyers and politicians are always working with both, the ideal and the real. The bridging happens when political and legal ideas get 'realized' in positive law and justice and when political and legal facts get 'idealized' in good order(s) and values, customs and conventions.

If idealism and realism are potentially competing and conflicting, their relationship might differ from time to time and from country to country, and even from one constitution to a subsequent one. Universal ideals coexist with particular realities, ideal symmetries in rights with real asymmetries in powers. If the written constitution is a good and 'living' one, both are optimized; if it is by no means realized or if it just idealizes a reality of a power without common ideals, there is a lack of constitutionalism.

The international dialogue helps us understand whether the idealism/realism divide matters for the still-existing national differences in constitutionalism and constitutional cultures. This chapter can of course offer only some insight into the circulation of constitutional ideas and in the particular constitutional identity of Italy.

There have been more realist and more idealist moments in the Italian path to constitutionalism and, therefore, a country study has to be very much aware of history and narrative. In order to focus the Italian case, we need first to remember the long traditions of idealism and realism in national history and to measure their impact on political and legal philosophy. In a second step, we look at the constitutional history of Italy and the concept of constitutionalism as a learning process. The ideals of the Constitution of the post-war Italian Republic aimed to learn from that history but were only gradually and partially realized. For the present, the most relevant question is how realism and idealism matter for the reforms of the Italian Constitution. The role of constitutional judges in the ongoing reform procedure in this regard will be highlighted. The conclusions cannot offer an exhaustive assessment of the quality of constitutional culture in Italy. From a comparative point of view, one should avoid any rating and prefer a principle of plural constitutionalism that promotes dialogues. Even in moments of crisis, the constitutional state needs both idealism and realism, but has to avoid the tendency of the former to degenerate into hypocrisy and the latter into cynicism.

The general idea advanced in this chapter is that Italian constitutionalism is a process of common learning for a sustainable living constitution, a European legal and political culture that bridges ideals and reality through good theories and practices. The culture seems to work well in the courts, but suffers when it comes to constitutional reforms under expectations of international markets.

Traditions of Realism and Idealism in Italian History

Italian constitutional culture today has to face a general context of multiple crises that mean that new realism might be more the spirit of the time.[1] There is a long tradition of realism preceding even the idealism of the late nation-state building and constitutionalism in nineteenth century. Realism is the older European concept that juxtaposed dialectics 'in things' to dialectics 'in voice' A starting point could be found in Plato's failure to overcome the Sicilian tyranny and in the sceptical opposition of the real,

[1] M. Ferraris, *Manifesto del nuovo realismo* (Bari: Laterza, 2012).

corrupted human power to the ideal divine justice offered in the late Roman Empire by Augustine, a prominent source of Catholic political realism.[2] This realism erased the republican ideals of Cicero's *potestas in populo, auctoritas in senatu*, the so-called ancient constitutionalism. They were surrogated by ideals of Christian justice and Christian Republicanism that inspired the realist's Aquina's teaching that positive law derived from natural and divine law through determinations or conclusions based on human *participatio luminis Dei*. The same ideals inspired the Pontifical State, but also the new orders of monks and of universities where the Roman concept of law as *'res sanctissima'* was defended against the practices of jurisprudence as *scientia lucrative*.[3]

New ideals opposed to medieval tyranny were promoted by humanism during the Renaissance. They framed concepts of human dignity and good government, with local autonomy, national spirit and universal monarchy. At that time, realism became a strong ideology of political empowerment and hegemony for the Italian model of urbanized culture and economy.[4] Being useful for the limitation of divine power, it was adopted as an official doctrine under the French king Louis XI in 1474. The autonomy of political prudence from moral conscience was the new *'ragion di stato'* developed by Guicciardini and Machiavelli in Florence and Giovanni Botero in Venice as a privileged view on common good.[5] The political realism of Machiavelli asked to look empirically at political life in republics and monarchies in order to draw reasonable conclusions for government and commerce, taking into account both the reality of evil and the virtues of political freedom.[6] From the end of the republic

[2] Augustine, *De civitate Dei contra Paganos* (ca. 426), IV, 4: 'Remota itaque iustitia, quid sunt regna nisi magna latrocinia? quia et latrocinia quid sunt nisi parva regna? Manus et ipsa hominum est, imperio principis regitur, pacto societatis astringitur, placiti lege praeda dividitur.' P. Portinaro, *Realismo politico* (Roma: Laterza, 1999), p. 37f. The author holds that the 'realism of the poor' is founded in Matthew 10, 16: 'I am sending you out like sheep among wolves. Therefore be as shrewd as snakes and as innocent as doves.'

[3] Quoted by M. Bellomo, *Saggio sull'università* (Roma: Cigno Galileo Galilei, 1996), p. 20ff.

[4] See F. Braudel, *Le Modèle Italien* (Paris: Arthaud, 1989).

[5] F. Guicciardini, 'Del reggimento di Firenze' (1525), in: *Opere* (Milano: Rizzoli, 1942), II, p. 666: 'ragione degli stati'; G. Botero, *Ragion di Stato* (Venezia: Gioliti, 1589).

[6] N. Machiavelli, *Il Principe* (1513), Chapter XV: '(. . .) it appears to me more appropriate to follow up the real truth of the matter than the imagination of it; for many have pictured republics and principalities which in fact have never been known or seen, because how one lives is so far distant from how one ought to live, that he who neglects what is done for what ought to be done, sooner effects his ruin than his preservation; for a man who wishes to act entirely up to his professions of virtue soon meets with what destroys him among so much that is evil.'

of Florence until the first modern written constitutions, the Italian peninsula was politically more and more regionalized and divided in autocratic (Pontifical State, Savoy, Venice, Genoa) or dependent states under the Holy Empire, Austrian, Spanish or French hegemony (Sicily, Sardinia, Lombardy). Meanwhile the legal absolutism of these early states was contrasted by natural-law-based ideas and practices anticipating constitutionalism:[7] the enlightenment promoted the idealization of the Roman Empire and Renaissance and stimulated the '*Risorgimento*'. This movement for a voluntary nation-state building process could not be realized through the national constitutional assembly invoked by Mazzini, but the ideals of civilization (*incivilimento*) survived the hope for constitutional revolutions. When in 1861 the Kingdom of Sardinia transformed itself by way of plebiscites into the Kingdom of Italy, the Albertinian Statute of 1848 became a flexible constitution of the whole Italy and the concept of constitutionalism entered into the public debate as a new argument of legitimacy.[8]

While the nation-state has thus been an idealistic project, the concept of idealism as such appeared in Italian legal culture only at the beginning of the twentieth century, when the new state was already declared to be in crisis by the realism of the new political scientists and the Italian school of legal positivism. Meanwhile natural law philosophers[9] and Hegelians[10] upheld older traditions, the new Italian

[7] G. Gorla, 'Iura Naturalia sunt Immutabilia' in A. Pizzorusso (ed.), *Italian Studies in Law* (Dordrecht: Nijhoff 1992), p. 55ss.; A. Trampus, *Storia del costituzionalismo italiano nell'età dei lumi* (Roma: Laterza, 2009).

[8] *Esame degli stati civilizzati del mondo dal quale resta statisticamente dimostrata la preponderanza che l'elemento nazionale ed il costituzionalismo vanno sempre più acquistando* . . . (Torino: Paravia, 1860); V. Sansonetti, *Significato della Magna Carta d'Inghilterra nella storia del costituzionalismo europeo* (Napoli: Vaglio, 1863); V. Ballerini, *Il costituzionalismo di re Vittorio Emanuele* (Pavia: Bizzoni, 1878). In France and Germany earlier C. Pecqueur, *Théorie nouvelle d'économie sociale et politique* (Paris: Capelle, 1842), p. 95; K. H. Scheidler, *Paränetische Propädeutik der Rechtsphilosophie* (Jena: Cröker, 1842).

[9] See A. Rosmini, *Filosofia del diritto*, 2 vol. (1841–3); G. del Vecchio, *Il sentimento giuridico* (1902), *I presupposti filosofici della nozione del diritto* (1905), *Il concetto del diritto* (1906), *Il concetto della natura e il principio del diritto* (1908), *Sui principi generali del diritto* (1921), G. Capograssi, *Saggio sullo Stato* (1918), *Riflessioni sull'autorità e la sua crisi* (1921), *La nuova democrazia diretta* (1922), *Analisi dell'esperienza comune* (1930), *Il problema della scienza del diritto* (1937), *Studi sull'esperienza giuridica* (1939).

[10] G. Fassò, *La filosofia del diritto dell'Ottocento e del Novecento* (Bologna: Mulino 1988), p. 292 quotes I. Petrone, *La filosofia del diritto al lume dell'idealismo critico* (1896), *Il diritto nel mondo dello spirito* (1910); G. Solari, *La scuola del diritto naturale nelle dottrine etico-giuridiche dei secoli XVII e XVIII* (1904); A. Ravà, *Il diritto come norma tecnica*

idealism of Benedetto Croce[11] and Giovanni Gentile,[12] both ministers for public school in the last liberal and the first fascist government, reduced the law to volitions in the realm of economy (Croce), and to the so-called 'ethical state' as an idealization of force and power (Gentile).[13]

It is in this general philosophical and historical context that the passions of armed '*Resistenza*' against Germany and the '*Repubblica Sociale Italiana*' (1943) inspired a second national '*Risorgimento*' in the Constituent Assembly. The liberation from the cynical fascism united forces and ideas of socialists, Catholics and others, even liberals. The Catholics renounced to the confessional character of the state, the left renounced to revolution and both opted for a constitutional promise of social justice. A long-rigid Constitution of the Republic, articulated in 'Fundamental Principles', a detailed rights catalogue and a rationalized parliamentary form of government with constitutional review was agreed. We could call this the moderated optimistic 'original idealism' of the founding fathers of the Republic.

The constitution of the new Republic suffered ideological clashes and vetoes in the name of realism against its implementation in the post-war reconstruction era, and also when the signing parties could not survive the so-called 'transition' after 1989. In short, the Italian Constitution was written in a moment of idealism, but its implementation was always moderated by a more realist political and legal culture. The Republic favoured a more sceptical legal positivism (*giuspositivismo*), but traditional natural law school (*giusnaturalismo*) survived and new schools of legal realism (*giusrealismo*) grew.[14] Today a more postmodern

(1911), *Lo Stato come organismo etico* (1914); F. Battaglia, *Diritto e filosofia della pratica* (1931); W. Cesarini Sforza, *Il concetto del diritto e la giurisprudenza integrale* (1931); G. Calogero, *Saggi di etica e di teoria del diritto* (1947).

[11] *Estetica come scienza della espressione e linguistica generale* (1902), *Logica come scienza del concetto puro* (1905), *Filosofia della pratica* (1909), *Teoria e storia della storiografia* (1915/17).

[12] *La riforma della dialettica hegeliana* (1913); *I problemi della scolastica e il pensiero italiano* (1913); *Sommario di pedagogia* (1913/14), *Teoria generale dello spirito come atto puro* (1916); *I fondamenti della filosofia del diritto* (1916); *Le origini della filosofia contemporanea in Italia* (1917/23), *Sistema di logica* (1917/23).

[13] B. Mussolini, *Fascismo; Dottrina, Enciclopedia Treccani* (1932): State as 'the conscience and universal will of man in his historical existence'; 'true reality of the individual'; 'synthesis and unity of any value'; 'universal ethical will, creator of the law', 'ethical reality'. at http://www.treccani.it/enciclopedia/fascismo_(Enciclopedia-Italiana)/.

[14] See L. Ferrajoli, *La cultura giuridica nell'Italia del Novecento* (Roma: Laterza, 1999); G. Fassò, *Storia della filosofia del diritto*, I–III, ed. C. Faralli (Roma: Laterza 2001); E. Pattaro (ed.), *A treatise of legal philosophy and general jurisprudence*, vol. 12 (Dordrecht: Springer, 2015); M. Barberis, *Giuristi e filosofi* (Bologna, 2011). The new American and Scandinavian realism

constitutional culture has to face a *Zeitgeist* that is tending towards realism since Parliament, based no more on proportional representation, is allowed to change the constitution by absolute majority and with a confirmative referendum.

Constitutional History and Constitutionalism as a Learning Process

Over the last decade, Italian legal philosophy has proposed a concept of '*neocostituzionalismo*' to describe the institutional practices of the constitutional state as a model that can be used for apologetic and critical purposes. It is based on: (a) a minimal connection between law and moral customs embodied by supreme constitutional principles and values; (b) a pragmatic view on balancing and reasonableness in law-making, and (c) a moderate optimism in formal rationality of interpretation.[15]

If we compare this concept with the classical ideal of a constitution (as a way of guaranteeing rights and the separation of powers) with the traditional notion of '*costituzionalismo*' of the nineteenth century, a key difference between the two is that it is no longer primarily used for purposes of constitution-making, but for the implementation of the constitution, which means for the interpretation and realization of the constitution by elites of politicians, judges and administrators. The older concept designed the now-established qualities of entrenched constitutions, whereas the newer one looks at constitutional justice and at the ongoing dynamics of constitutionalization of state and society. Secondly, if we use the idealism–realism divide, classical constitutionalism seems to be closer to prescriptive idealism and to promote the idealization of the work of founding fathers. Meanwhile, neo-constitutionalism seems to be more open to descriptive realism and to idealization of existing practices of lawmakers and judges. Thirdly, modern constitutionalism was originally linked to nation-state

in authors like G. Tarello, R. Guastini, E. Pattaro was preceded by the older French 'legal realism': V.E. Orlando, 'Leone Duguit e la scuola del realismo giuridico' (1929), in: *Diritto pubblico generale*, Milano: Giuffrè 1954, 73ff. References to Machiavelli, German Legal Historism, ethnological jurisprudence and sociology in U. Forti, *Il realismo nel diritto pubblico, a proposito di un libro recente*, Camerino: Savini, 1903, p. 13ff.

15 See M. Barberis, *Manuale di filosofia del diritto* (Torino: Giappichelli, 2011), p. 33ff.; M. Dogliani, '(Neo)costituzionalismo: un'altra rinascita del diritto naturale?' (2010), at http://costituzionalismo.it/articoli/357/; L. Ferrajoli, *La democrazia attraverso i diritti: il costituzionalismo garantista come modello teorico e come progetto politico* (Roma: Laterza, 2013).

building, but after World War II and 1989, the new (global or multilevel) constitutionalism is extended to supra-, inter- and transnational ideals like the 'constitutionalization' of the European Union, the defence of human rights in transnational orders or a cooperative pluralism of national and international legal orders.[16]

The concept of constitutionalism is in a learning process. If we look at the constitutional history of Italy from a comparative perspective, the learning can be found already in the idealism of the constitutional thoughts of the Enlightenment that inspired constitutional projects of the Grand Duke of Tuscany (1787). When Napoleon adapted the French model of Constitution to local traditions beginning with the first constitutional articles of Bologna (1796), he learned from the Italian Constitution of Corsica in 1755, but did not offer sufficient guarantees to the Church. Giuseppe Compagnoni, first teacher of constitutional law in Ferrara, opposed a more realistic political concept of constitution to the idealistic French one: 'Constitution in politics is just that certain and stable way a people exists and governs itself with'.[17] Another famous realist metaphor emphasized that Italy was not France: '[t]he constitutions are like clothes: it is necessary that any individual, any age of the individual has its own and if you want to give the same to others, it will vest badly.'[18]

After the Congress of Vienna, Gian Domenico Romagnosi defined the concept of a 'constitution' as a fundamental law 'by which a government shall now and in future proceed to administer the state', and 'by which a people imposes to those who govern in order to protect itself against despotism'.[19] The more revolutionary constitutions of 1821, 1831 and

[16] H. Vorländer, 'Die Verfassung vor, nach, über und unter dem Staat' in: H. Lindemann et al., *Erzählungen vom Konstitutionalismus* (Baden-Baden, 2012), p. 25ff.

[17] I. Mereu, *La rivoluzione liberale di Giuseppe Compagnoni* (1799) (Milano: Buccinasco, 1989), p. 31. Compagnoni is considered the author of the flag 'tricolore' that symbolizes the values of the French revolution and hope or (in the codes of masonry) the nature as a source of rights and richness.

[18] V. Cuoco, *Saggio storico sulla rivoluzione napoletana del 1799* (1801) (Bari: Laterza, 1913), p. 218, for the Constitution of Rome see idem, *Platone in Italia* (Bari: Laterza, 1928), I, p. 233.

[19] G. Romagnosi, *La scienza delle costituzioni* (Torino, 1848). Similarly the economist P. Rossi, *Cours de droit constitutionnel* (Paris: Guillaumin, 1866): '*Car ce serait une grande et funeste erreur que d'imaginer que le mécanisme constitutionnel peut se suffire à lui-même, que ta machine, après avoir reçu la première impulsion, peut fonctionner toute seule, qu'on peut ne pas tenir compte des penchants et des passions de l'homme, ne pas demander le concours des volontés. (. . .) La constitution d'un État, dans le sens général, est l'ensemble des lois qui président à son organisation; dans un sens plus restreint, c'est la loi des peuples*

1848, however, failed under the reactions of the Holy Alliance: liberal constitutionalism, federalist approaches to unification and the idea of a constituent assembly were rejected by the clergy.[20]

After 1848, the only way towards constitutionalism was the transformation of the *'Statuto Albertino'* of the 'Italian' Kingdom of Sardinia/ Piedmont in a 'constitutional statute' for the unified Kingdom of Italy (1861). The principle of nationality justified unification under international law[21] and the ideals of constitutionalism were used as a narrative that helped to balance monarchy with parliamentary government and individual rights with national duties.[22] In his lectures on constitutional law, Gaetano Mosca remembered the British 'model of all modern constitutions' as an attractive concept of a 'great modern state governed under a regime of public discussion'.[23] In the light of this political ideal, the political class used the constitution as a 'living instrument' that puts and holds together all institutions, an 'organism of laws and fundamental and essential rules that confer to the State and to its government its characteristic form and limits in order to avoid any not indispensable interference' into society.[24]

The *Statuto* of 1848 was adapted through interpretative conventions to general principles of a 'constitutional government', a highly 'civilized' form of state with a monarchy that accepted the principle of legality of administration as the core principle, equivalent to the rule of law.[25] The new civil (1865) and criminal code (1889) and the new administrative justice section within the Council of State (1889) formed ideally a liberal, but vigorous and active state that was mainly based on the will of legislators, assisted by academic lawyers. The new national school of public law promoted a legal positivism based on a realist *'principio*

libres, le pacte qui garantit les droits et les libertés de chacun. L'organisation sociale est le but, l'organisation politique, le moyen.'

20 *Encyclica Mirari Vos* (1832): 'Experience shows, even from earliest times, that cities renowned for wealth, dominion, and glory perished as a result of this single evil, namely immoderate freedom of opinion, license of free speech, and desire for novelty.'

21 P. S. Mancini, *Della Nazionalità come fondamento del dritto delle genti* (Torino: Botta, 1851).

22 G. Mazzini, *I doveri dell'uomo* (Genova: Dagnino, 1851).

23 G. Mosca, *Appunti di diritto costituzionale* (Milano: Sel, 1912), p. 57. Cf. C. Caristia, *L' analisi odierna del costituzionalismo* (Torino: Bocca, 1908).

24 G. Arangio Ruiz, *Istituzioni e leggi costituenti* (Milano: Vallardi, 1892), p. 9.

25 U. Allegretti, *Storia costituzionale italiana* (Bologna: Mulino, 2014); M. Fioravanti, *Costituzionalismo. Percorsi della storia e tendenze attuali* (Bari: Laterza, 2009); P. Costa, 'Lo Stato di diritto: un'introduzione storica' in P. Costa, D. Zolo (eds.), *Lo Stato di diritto*, Milano: Feltrinelli 2002, p. 89ff.

giuridico' (principle of law) whereby public lawyers had to deal, 'not with the best, but with the existing state, not with sovereignty of an idea, but with sovereignty of constituted powers, not with rights of man, but with legal protection of the sphere of the individual, thus liberty being conceived no more as a mere potentiality, but as an effective activity.'[26] '*Stato di diritto*', a literal translation of the German term *Rechtsstaat*, meant just a state with administrative judges.[27]

Interpretative realism was further strengthened when the later president of the Council of State, Santi Romano, promoted a new institutionalism and denied any legal value to the concepts such as constitution, constituent power, popular sovereignty and parliamentarism. Studying the 'instauration by way of fact of a constitutional order' (1901), he focused on the *coup d'état*, popular revolutions and interventions of foreign states in order to assert the legitimacy of any state and government that effectively exists.[28] Necessity produced by social forces became the highest 'source of law' that regenerated sovereignty in crisis. At the end of World War I, his theory of the plurality of 'legal orders' depicted the state as an aggregation of partial orders and institutions; he even considered the mafia as a legal order.[29]

The authoritarian fascist regime understood itself as respecting legality and the formal concepts of the rule of law,[30] but did not create a new constitution and even eliminated constitutionalism from the vocabulary of the fascist party. Constantino Mortati offered a new realist concept of constitution in a material sense, embracing the political forces and ideas

[26] V. E. Orlando, 'I criteri tecnici per la ricostruzione del diritto pubblico'(1889), in *Diritto pubblico generale* (Milano: Giuffré, 1954), p. 20f. Cf. A. Sandulli, *Costruire lo Stato* (Milano: Giuffré, 2009), p. 49ss.

[27] O. Ranelletti, *Principii di diritto amministrativo* (Napoli: Pierro 1912), I, 142: 'when the State subjects itself to the law and ensures respect even on its own behalf through specific institutions it is a "stato di diritto"'. Cf. M. Ruini, *La distinzione tra società e Stato e la teoria dello Stato di diritto* (Roma: Unione cooperativa editrice, 1905).

[28] S. Romano, 'L'instaurazione di fatto di un ordinamento costituzionale e sua legittimazione' (1901), in: idem, *Scritti minori* (Milano: Giuffré, 1990), p. 131ff. See also E. Lombardo Pellegrino, *Il diritto di necessità nel costituzionalismo giuridico* (Roma: Associazione per lo studio del diritto pubblico italiano, 1903).

[29] S. Romano, *L'ordinamento giuridico* (Pisa: Spoerri, 1918), p. 111. Cf. A. Catania, 'Carl Schmitt e Santi Romano' in *Il diritto tra forza e consenso* (Napoli: ESI, 1987), p. 150ff; M. La Torre, *Norme, istituzioni, valori* (Bari: Laterza 1999), p. 120ff.

[30] Cf. S. Panunzio, *Lo Stato di diritto* (Città di Castello: Solco, 1921), p. 15; C. Costamagna, 'Lo Stato corporativo quale Stato di diritto' in *Diritto del lavoro* (1928, I, p. 397ss.; C. Caristia, 'Ventura e avventure di una formola: Rechtsstaat' in *Rivista di diritto pubblico* (1934), I, p. 388ss; F. Battaglia, 'Stato etico e Stato di diritto' in *Rivista internazionale di filosofia del diritto* (1937), p. 237ff.

of the fascist party as an organ and the basis of the state.[31] On the other hand, the resistance groups that opposed the occupying German forces and the Italian Fascist puppet regime of the Italian Social Republic (1943) produced new constitutional ideals, including a new European federalism. At the end, Romano acknowledged the victory of the principles of 'constitutionalism' with British and even Roman roots; principles 'implied in the existence of the State, of its structure and concrete attitudes'.[32] Nevertheless, the founding fathers and parties of the new republican constitution learned that the flexible statute could no more be restored, and looked at changing European ideals of constitutionalism.

The Constitution of the Post-War Italian Republic: Gradually Realized Ideals with Partial Gaps

'Constitutionalism' was not a slogan of the founding fathers, but rather a common spirit that has been synthesized especially in the narrow popular sovereignty clause of the first of the aforementioned twelve 'fundamental principles' of the Constitution: '[s]overeignty belongs to the people that exercises it in the forms and within the limits of the Constitution'. A preliminary version of that clause had been discussed more significantly in view of the need for a '*stato di diritto*'.[33] The adopted sovereignty clause expressed an original basic consensus on the interpretation of constitutional history: the failure of monarchy and the success of multiparty Resistenza, the founding myth for a new *Risorgimento*.

Over the long run of the Republic the more liberal colours and the irenic nature of the western model of constitutionalism have been changed into a specific Italian model of a 'thick' social or societal constitutionalism. The following elements of the new 'constitutional state' absorbed the older concepts of legality and *stato di diritto*.[34]

[31] C. Mortati, *La costituzione in senso materiale* (1940) (Milano: Giuffré, 1998). V. Crisafulli, 'Costituzione' in *Enciclopedia del novecento* (1976), p. 1030 distinguishes three concepts: texture, fundamental and conditioning norms and institutes, socio-political or socio-economical structure of the community.

[32] S. Romano, *Principii di diritto costituzionale generale* (Milano: Giuffrè, 1945), p. 134. Cf. C. Pinelli, *La Costituzione di Santi Romano e i primi maestri dell'età repubblicana* (2012), at http://.rivistaaic.it.

[33] M. Ruini quoted by R. Bin, 'Stato di diritto' in *Enciclopedia del diritto* (Annali IV, Milano: Giuffré 2011), p. 1149ff.

[34] G. Zagrebelsky, *Il diritto mite* (Torino: Einaudi, 1991).

(1) A long texture enshrining secular fundamental principles and values with commitments to substantial equality (art. 3), labour (art. 4) and culture (art. 6–9) and a long catalogue of social, cultural and political fundamental rights.
(2) A multi-party democracy (art. 1, 49) coloured by plebiscitary elements, especially a referendum for the abrogation of legislative acts (art. 75) and for constitutional amendments (art. 138).
(3) A specific constitutional protection of independence and partial self-administration of the judiciary, including public prosecutors, the separation of administration and judiciary from politics and procedural rights (art. 24, 101ff.).
(4) A differentiated regionalism with regional powers of legislation as an alternative to federalism and centralization, and as a guarantee against secessionism (art. 5, 114ff.).
(5) A sort of rule of international law with commitments for protection of human rights, foreigners, peace and limitations of sovereignty (art. 2, 10, 11, 52).
(6) A Constitutional court for constitutional review of legislation promoted by other jurisdictions and for specific litigation between state powers or between state and regions and a mechanism of constitutional revision that promotes bipartisan agreements in Parliament, otherwise leaves the last word to the people (art. 134ff.).

The realism of constitutional lawyers was less relevant for the constitution writers than for the implementation and interpretation of the Constitution of 1947. The fundamental principles and rights of the new long and entrenched constitution could be read as general clauses of law and as general policies agreed through a historical compromise that has been criticized over time. They were recognized as legally binding, but their implementation in legislation, administration and jurisdiction was a long – still-ongoing – struggle with realist and idealist moments and positions. The implementation of the Constitution produced a political pacification of the country and gradually realized most ideals, but the fundamental principles are still prone to specific old and new gaps between ideals and social, economical and political realities:

(1) The principle of labour for all and the realization of social rights are today being threatened by the financial and economic crisis, meanwhile post-secular cultural conflicts are no longer governed by the party of Christian Democracy.

(2) Multi-party representative democracy at all levels has been challenged by party fragmentation, unstable coalition governments, media concentration, corruption and an imperfect bipolarization through electoral reforms, adopting limited first-past-the-post rules and promoting direct election of mayors and regional governors.
(3) The principle of legality is being challenged by conflicts between judges and politicians on corruption and juristocracy, as well as by inefficient justice and by lacks of quality and equality in legislation.
(4) National unity has being challenged by asymmetries between a rich north and a poor south and clashes between regionalism and localism, with new ideals of asymmetric federalism and old customs of centralism
(5) The principle of internationalism has been challenged first by the loss of colonies and the conflicts between East and West, later by the rights-based counter-limits on the international limitations of sovereignty and the risk of new hegemonies within Europe.
(6) The political force of the constitution has been weakened by the dissolution or transformation of the founding parties and the electoral reforms allowed governments to search popular consent for non-bipartisan constitutional reform.

What happened to the original idealism of the founding fathers in the judicial and political interpretation and implementation of the constitution as a fundamental law? If one looks at the performance of the Constitution assessed in the official celebrations, the first three decades were focusing on the necessity and difficulty of implementation, while the following three decades were focusing on symptoms of constitutional crisis and the need for constitutional reform.[35] Meanwhile the performance of the Constitution during the first decades has been considered positive as far as fundamental rights chapters were concerned; the reform debate in the following decades delegitimized the chapters related to powers but could not build a consensus on a constitutional reform.

Interpreters of the Constitution can, in line with this, be divided in political or judicial activists of idealism and supporters of realism. The former criticized the lack of implementation and backed the idealism by extensive interpretations *magis ut valeat*, the latter criticized the founding myth and backed realism through the opposite interpretation, considering constitutional norms as almost flexible, open and elastic.[36]

[35] E. Cheli, *Nata per unire* (Bologna: Mulino 2012), p. 29ff.
[36] M. Dogliani, *Interpretazioni della costituzione* (Milano: Angeli 1982), p. 65ff.

Nevertheless, over the decades a real popular constitutional culture has been developed by civic education in public schools, debates in newspapers and television, and even through political conflicts and litigation on issues of fundamental rights and duties.

If we go back to the Cold War in the 1950s of the last century, an anti-Communist '*conventio ad excludendum* – a convention that aimed to exclude communists from government – ' deleted the envisaged social and institutional reforms, including the establishment of the Constitutional Court (1956). Even political studies of comparative constitutionalism favoured on the one hand a critical distance from the new social ideals of the constitution,[37] and on the other hand the gradual implementation of constitutional review.[38] The implementation of referendum and regionalism, civil and social rights guarantees in the 1970s favoured finally a political culture of agreements between majority and oppositions, the so-called 'consociativism' with the (now-) 'euro-communists' toleration of a government of 'national unity' against terrorism (1976–78). At that time a new generation of judges embraced the original idealism of the constitution when promoting questions of constitutional review, making interpretation of law in the light of the Constitution and electing two-thirds of the members of the High Council of Judiciary that decides recruitment, career and discipline.

Over the last decades the Constitutional Court has presented its own mission devoted mainly to the protection of fundamental rights, but in the Court's practice of judicial minimalism, the interpretation of the Constitution is subsidiary to the interpretation of legislation and to the practice and conventions of the other powers. The general human rights clause[39] allowed only in a very few cases the discovery of 'new' fundamental rights.[40] The Court was criticized for being more than a negative legislator when it adopted a wide range of sophisticated decision formulas in order to get the wordings and meanings of the legislation compatible with the Constitution, including so-called 'manipulative

[37] G. Maranini, *Crisi del costituzionalismo e antinomie della Costituzione* (Firenze: Vallecchi, 1953).

[38] M. Calamandrei, *Costituzionalismo e pragmatismo come principi ideali della storia americana* (Milano: Giuffré, 1958).

[39] Article 2 Constitution: 'The Republic recognizes and guarantees the inviolable rights of the person, both as an individual and in the social groups where human personality is expressed, and demands the performance of the non-derogable fundamental duties of political, economic, and social solidarity.'

[40] Decision n. 217/1988 (right to housing); 138/2010; 170/2014 (same-sex marriages).

decisions'. A decision by the Constitutional Court can even declare laws unconstitutional if they neglect a constitutional principle that the legislator has to transform into rules, but that could even be implemented by the other judges if the legislator does not act.[41] The legislature has not always respected recommendations of the court, especially with regard to media pluralism,[42] but the constitutional judgements have over time generally been accepted by judiciary and legislature even without specific enforcement instruments. On the other hand, the Court itself declares inadmissible questions interfering with the legislator's discretion.

Learning how to bridge judicial idealism and political realism, the Court occasionally highlights 'values' incorporated into constitutional and/or legal norms and even constitutional conventions and customs. The most frequently uttered mantra and bridging method is a pragmatic call to avoid 'unreasonableness', and, more recently, to 'proportionality'.[43] Reasonableness allows comparison of the ideas of the legislators and the founding fathers with legal and constitutional facts. The Court has recognized that even changing social conscience matters, for example in cases regarding the ideal of gender equality.[44]

The Court has finally been involved in an increasing number of conflicts between the central state and the regions or between political and judicial powers. Since the latter are often linked to real conflicts of powers, for example when bioethical questions or the costs of social rights are at stake,[45] the constitutional judges always look for equilibrium. Sometimes, the constitutional judges refer even to the rule of law as a general legal principle shared with the supranational and

41 Cf. V. Barsotti et al., Italian Constitutional Justice in Global Context, Oxford University Press 2016, for the ideals see G. Zagrebelsky, *Principi e voti* (Torino: Einaudi, 2005); *La legge e la sua giustizia* (Bologna: Mulino, 2008).

42 Decision n. 420/1994 (private television).

43 R. Bin, 'Il fatto nel diritto costituzionale', July 2015, at http://www.robertobin.it/ARTICOLI/Catanzaro2014.pdf.

44 Decision n. 128/1968.

45 For example, decision n. 85/2013 upheld a governmental emergency decree enabling 'facilities of strategic national interest' to continue to operate notwithstanding the judicial seizure of assets and applying *de facto* only to the ILVA steelworks in Taranto. Facing a problem of equilibrium between the protection of the right to health protection and the right to work on the one hand and between political and judicial power on the other, the Court defended administrative decisions taken in the form of a law legislative that excluded access to an administrative court and affected the execution of the decision of seizure taken by the judge when prosecuting crimes under environmental law.

international level in the fight against terrorism, organized crime and corruption.[46]

The concept of constitutionalism was rediscovered in the 1980s when the constitutional reform of the form of state and of the form of government entered into the political agenda and when the debates on neo-constitutionalism echoed those on judicial constitutionalism in the United States. The new association of constitutional law professors named themselves '*costituzionalisti*' (1985), adopting a denomination used already by political scientists.[47] In the 1990s, the electoral reform opened a period of transition that ended the life of most of the old, and opened to new, political parties.[48] '*Tangentopoli*', or the judicial fight against corruption in politics, called for more morals and ethics but also undermined the trust in institutions. The reality of corruption demanded strengthening of the ideals of constitutionalism and an increase in constitutional guarantees. Furthermore, new risks of populism, a concentration of economic, cultural and political powers and increasing undemocratic supra- and international powers needed to be faced. Realism supported the demand for constitutional reform, but radical pessimism was sometimes even directed against ideals of the Constitution, including social justice and separation of powers. In 2003 a new periodical, named '*Costituzionalismo.it*', was founded with the mission to defend the *acquis* of political and legal civilization,[49] and common confidence in the 'normative force of constitutions and in the ability of constitutionalism to become a sort of 'higher' law in the path of history'.[50] On the battleground of constitutional reform, realism has made progress and constitutionalists risk even to lose self-confidence.[51]

46 R. Bin, *Lo Stato di diritto* (Bologna: Mulino, 2004); J. Luther, 'L'uso dei principi nella giurisprudenza costituzionale' in S. Staiano (ed.), *Giurisprudenza costituzionale e principi fondamentali* (Torino: Giappichelli, 2006), p. 969ff.

47 First G. Miglio, *Una Repubblica migliore per gli Italiani (verso una nuova Costituzione* (Milano: Giuffré, 1983).

48 First A. Di Giovine, *Verso un costituzionalismo della diseguaglianza*? (Milano: Teti, 1996); A. Barbera, G. Zanetti (eds.), *Le basi filosofiche del costituzionalismo* (Roma: Laterza, 1997); P. Ridola, *Diritti di libertà e costituzionalismo* (Torino: Giappichelli, 1997); G. Volpe, *Il costituzionalismo del novecento* (Roma: Laterza, 2000). Last P. Ciarlo, *Il costituzionalismo dopo le costituzioni* (Nola: L'arca, 2013); G. Azzariti, *Il costituzionalismo moderno può sopravvivere*? (Roma: Laterza, 2013).

49 G. Ferrara, 'Le ragioni di una rivista nuova', February 2003, at http://www.costituzionalismo.it/articoli/84/: 'institutions to guarantee and consolidate the acquis of civilisation obtained and adequate for the development of freedoms and equality'.

50 G. Azzariti, 'Le ragioni di un nuovo impegno', July 2003, at http://www.costituzionalismo.it/articoli/111/: 'Legal Science exploded'.

51 G. Zagrebelsky, ‚Die Verfassungslehrer', *Jahrbuch des öffentlichen Rechts* 61.2013, p. 1ff.

The Slow Path of Constitutional Reform: Lacks of Idealism and Realism

The final chapter of the Constitution deals with the heart of the practices of new constitutionalism: the 'guarantees of the Constitution' offered by the Constitutional Court and the constitutional amendment procedure with a facultative constitutional referendum ('revision'). Both guarantees are needed for filling the gaps between the ideal and the real in the constitutional order. From the point of view of the constitution, the constitutional judges should be the conservers, whereas the politicians and the people should be the innovators of the ideals and of their realization. However, both have to maintain and adapt the constitutional order to changing realities. The older a constitution is, the more the reality can influence the interpretations of the ideals for purposes of efficiency. Reformers can bring in new ideals or bring back old ideals and adapt norms to changing realities or to unchanging traditions. Constitution revisers among politicians as well as constitutional judges need inspiration from ideals and reality, but they are not empowered to destroy either the contra-factual normative force of constitutional law or the real support and consensus the Constitution as a whole enjoys in society.

If we look at the historical ideal and the reality thereof, one could say that generally the judges as well as the reformers of the Constitution have contributed to bridging idealism and realism, but in Italy the judicial bridge seems to have had the better fortune.[52] European scholars of constitutionalism hold that a modern constitution is always amenable to reform, but the Italian Constitution has a tradition neither of frequent reforms nor of successful ones.

The common mantra of most Italian reformers is that the fundamental principles and rights need no total restyling, just more efficient protection – including a constitutional prohibition of the death penalty and concrete due process rules inspired by ECHR – and a better machinery of politics. In the last three decades several bicameral committees have made proposals to strengthen an unstable executive power and to rationalize a bicameralism being ironically named 'perfect' since it is based on two elected chambers with almost identical powers. Whereas the reform of the constitution's provisions on the form of government and on the judiciary were highly controversial, the

[52] See *inter alia* L. Elia, *Costituzione, partiti, istituzioni* (Bologna: Mulino 2009), p. 363ff.

commissions built a bipartisan consensus to strengthen regionalism and to change a bicameralism which was perceived, from a comparative point of view, rather as an Italian exception in the world of constitutionalism.[53]

The referendum for a (mainly) majoritarian electoral system in the 1990s weakened the Constitution, because the government can now more easily muster an absolute majority in Parliament for its own projects of constitutional reform and try to win a confirmative referendum. The Parliament preferred bipartisan reforms and adopted controversial constitutional legislation on *ad hoc* bicameral procedures for a more organic reform, but all these procedures ended with the legislatures. In order to strengthen the rule of law, some reforms on immunities and amnesties have been enacted, but they were unable to end the struggle between the political class and the judges. In 1999, direct election of regional governors was prescribed and in 2001 the Prodi government obtained a thin majority in a constitutional referendum for a reform of the chapter dealing with regionalism. The reform increased the powers of regions, namely through a general clause for all legislative competences not conferred to the central state and a principle inspired to fiscal federalism, but prospected further constitutional reform and detailed enabling laws that have not been completed. In 2006 in an attempt by Berlusconi, then Prime Minister, to get more power for his office, a federal senate and a reform of the judiciary and the Constitutional Court were proposed and subsequently rejected by the people.

Civil society appears increasingly less invested in the endless debates over mostly undecided or non-implemented constitutional reforms. Notwithstanding this popular fatigue, subsequent governments declared constitutional reform part of the structural reforms needed for financial and economic consolidation. Already in 2011 a letter from the former and new presidents of the European Central Bank to the Italian government recommended a balanced budget amendment to the Constitution.[54] A document by the Minister of

[53] See J. Luther, P. Passaglia, R. Tarchi (eds.), *A World of Second Chambers* (Milano: Giuffré, 2006) and J. Luther, 'The Institution of the Italian Senate under Reform: Sacrifice or Self-Reflection?' in H.-J. Blanke et al. (eds.), *Common European Legal Thinking* (Berlin: Springer, 2015), p. 477 ff.

[54] 'A constitutional reform would be appropriate in order to get more binding the rules of budget', see A. Simoncini, 'Back to "Flexible" Constitutions? The Impact of Financial Crisis and the Decline of the European Constitutionalism', August 2011, at http://www.ijpl.eu/assets/files/pdf/2013_volume_2/5.Simoncini.pdf.

Finance of February 2014 stated furthermore: 'In June 2013, the Government inaugurated a program of constitutional reforms to streamline governance. The proposals under discussion aim to modernize the electoral law, the form of government and Parliament'.[55]

The strongest input for constitutional reform came from the President of the Republic. When the new Parliament failed to elect his successor, the president accepted a second term under the condition that a new government of 'large agreements between left and right' would carry out a special mission of constitutional and electoral reform.[56] Experts nominated prior to the re-election prepared guidelines.[57] A committee of constitutional lawyers and politicians created by the new government headed by Letta recommended a reform of bicameralism and regionalism, but did not reach a consensus either on the abolition of the Senate or on a transformation hypothesis, and offered only key elements for electoral reform.[58] The Renzi government finally presented a bill for a broader constitutional reform.[59] Key objectives were

[55] http://www.dt.tesoro.it/export/sites/sitodt/modules/documenti_it/analisi_progamma zione/analisi_programmazione_economico/Nota_riforme_in_inglese_febbraio_2014-final.pdf.

[56] Discourse in Parliament, April 2013, at http://www.quirinale.it/elementi/Continua.aspx?tipo=Discorso&key=2700: 'Recent years have seen a failure to provide satisfactory solutions to well-founded needs and urgent calls for institutional reform and a renewal of politics and of the parties, in a situation that became interwoven with an acute financial crisis, a grave recession, and growing social malaise. . . . What little success was achieved in terms of adjustments and innovation to reduce the operational costs of our Institutions and increase transparency and morality in public life was easily ignored or undervalued. And dissatisfaction with and protest against politics, the parties, the Parliament, were easily (but also heedlessly) fuelled and magnified by deleterious opinion campaigns, by one-sided, indiscriminate and unilateral representations of the world of politicians and of the organizations and institutions in which they act. . . . Unforgivable was the failure to reform the electoral law of 2005. Just a few days ago, Prof. Gallo, President of the Constitutional Court, was obliged to point out that the Court's recommendation to review, in particular, the provisions concerning the attribution of a "majority bonus", without the minimum threshold of votes or seats having been reached, had been ignored. . . . No less unforgivable is the failure to make any headway on the reforms – limited and targeted as they were – pertaining to the second part of the Constitution, reforms that took such effort to agree on and yet which never managed to break the taboo of "equal bicameralism".' See M. Gorlani and N. Maccabiani, *Il bis di Napolitano* (Gussago: Bibliofabbrica, 2013).

[57] http://www.leggioggi.it/wp-content/uploads/2013/04/2013-04-12_relazione_finale.pdf (L. Violante, V. Onida, G. Quagliariello, M. Mauri).

[58] www.governo.it/DIE/attivita/pubblicazioni/Per%20una%20democrazia%20migliore.pdf.

[59] The reform proposal was approved with modifications by the Senate in August 2014, further modified by the Chamber of Deputies on March 2015 and the Senate in October 2015 but needs still at least three votes. Cf. G. Della Cananea, L. Violini,

(1) reforming the constitutional reform of 2001 in order to strengthen again the powers of the central state and to abolish any concurring legislation of the state and the region[60]
(2) repealing the constitutional guarantees of provinces (except Bozen/Trento) to allow their abolition
(3) strengthening the powers of government in Parliament through (a) abolition of the confidence vote of the Senate, (b) reduction of Senate powers over legislation and budget, (c) a preferential treatment for governmental proposals in law-making procedures, (d) a higher quorum for popular law-making petitions (from 50.000 to 150.000) and (e) unenforceable promises envisioning a constitutional reform to create means of participative democracy and stronger guarantees to parliamentary minorities and opposition in the standing orders
(4) reducing the number of senators from about 320 to 100, elected by regional councils, to lower the cost of politics and transform the Senate of the Republic into a representation of 'territorial institutions' that participates to some extent in the legislative procedures, evaluates the performance of public administrations and the impact of EU law on the territories and elects two of fifteen constitutional judges
(5) lifting the majority for the parliamentary election of the President from absolute to three-fifths
(6) abolishing the anachronistic 'National Council for Economy and Labour' as representation of social categories

The most controversial aspect was whether the senators should be elected directly by the people or indirectly by regional councils. A compromise agreed upon election by regional councils 'in conformity to the choices expressed by the voters on behalf of the candidates for the councils in the elections for their renewal'. The final referendum is expected for summer 2016, but no prophecies can be made. For optimists, the outcome will be more institutional efficiency through a stronger government and better legislation. For pessimists, both scenarios – popular ratification as well as the failure of the reform – could weaken the basic consensus regarding the Constitution.

R. Bifulco and others in *Italian Journal of Public Law*, 6(1) (2014); F. Rigano (ed.), *La Costituzione in officina* (Pavia University Press 2013).

60 Inspired by the abolition of the German *Rahmengesetzgebung*.

Of course, constitutionalism has been invoked to defend or criticize the quality of the project. The defenders are optimistic and combine realism with a minimum of idealism. They hold that the people's right to choose their rulers would be better protected and their preference for local government honoured. Vertical and horizontal separation within the legislative power would be rationalized through the new formula of 'territorial representation' as a compensation for the loss of legislative powers of the regions. The constitutional reform would correct the previous reform errors and save the original ideals, relying on alternatives already discussed in the Constituent Assembly. The opponents among politicians and constitutionalists are pessimistic and call for more respect for the original idealism of the Constitution. They object to a risk of majoritarian tyranny in the governmental method and in the power-concentrating substance of the reform and argue that territorial representation would just serve the personalization of politics and strengthen the power of political parties. The reform would advantage the bigger parties more than the less-developed territories. Constitutional reform would make new errors by weakening the regions and the parliament and ratify the will of the new political class to set aside the old ideas of the constitution, the basis of social cohesion and confidence in politics. The next steps could be the abolition of regional governments and of the self-administration of the judiciary.

From a constitutionalist point of view the people's decision in the referendum will be not easy. Any call on 'popular constitutionalism' or the will of the people to change or conserve the constitution could risk the appearance of an act of hypocrisy on the part of politicians. So what should be the role and the responsibility of the constitutional lawyers as advisers of the people? They could defend the ideals of constitutionalism against any cynical form of realism, allowing the governmental majority to make rules in its own interest, and at the same time be realists, even when it comes to their own limits. There are cognitive limits to the type of objections that can be voiced against constitutional reform, as the real impact of constitutional rules tends to be hard to know. The devil is well known to dwell even in the details of the constitutional rules that concretize the ideals of the rule of law and democracy.

Looking at separation of powers and rule of law, the second Chamber would be no longer conceived as a strong guarantee against the tyranny of the majority. One could wonder whether from that point of view Italy is lowering the existing standard of constitutionalism. Idealists could object that the reform promotes a rule of politics at the expense of the rule of law. There is of course a reason for getting more efficiency and speed in legislation and more cohesion in government majorities. But why should the people no longer be allowed to choose a second body of controllers? And why is it wrong to have different majorities in both chambers to force parties into coalitions? Realists could add other objections. For example, senators should simultaneously work as regional counsellors or mayors, with fewer immunities than Deputies and stronger governmental control on regional policies and finances. Furthermore, even with a reduced veto power of the Senate, the law-making procedures will get further differentiated and more complicated (see above, under sub 3c).

Voters in the constitutional referendum will also be asked to accept a weakened right to legislative initiative and to renounce the power to directly elect senators. The senators, even those nominated by the President of the Republic, will no longer represent the nation, but merely the 'territorial institutions'. The purpose here is not the invention of some form of Italian federalism, but just a discursive defence of 'autonomous' governments. This ideal does not take into account the reality of the political landscape. The bigger political parties represented in Parliament could exclude smaller minorities from representation of territories when deciding on the legal details of indirect election 'in conformity to the choices expressed by the voters' at regional elections. Unlike the Austrian model, regional councils are elected with a strong majority bonus for the governor, and unlike the German model, the senators would have no responsibility towards these councils.

If the real objective of the governmental constitutional reform is to get more authority and powers over Parliament and even vis-á-vis the EU and the international community, that does not however justify the prophecy of an authoritarian involution from parliamentary democracy towards a strong prime-minister or presidential regime with fewer checks and balances. The fears are related principally to the already-adopted electoral reform for the Chamber of Deputies, the law n. 52/2015 (so-*Italicum*) that renders parliamentary democracy even more majoritarian and is based on an indirect election of the President of the Council of Ministers through the prevision of a majority for the party list that takes 40 per cent of the votes at the first round or wins a second ballot. But this electoral reform could be declared (partially) unconstitutional or abrogated through referendum (see next section). The risks of populism and personalization of power cannot be denied, but the actual impact on the political landscape cannot yet be assessed and a clear and present danger for democracy cannot be proven.

One critical question is whether the diminished democratic legitimacy of the new Senate affects the democratic legitimacy of the *pouvoir constituant constitué*, the remaining power to co-decide and to veto constitutional legislation. The Constitution was enacted by a referendum that opted for republicanism and by a vote for a national constituent assembly dominated by political parties, most of which do not exist anymore. The new parties have the right to change the Constitution by democratic procedures. From their point of view the new Senate of the Republic could start even an (often evocated) Second Republic, ending the long transition since the 1990s of the previous century. Now the senators would no longer have full responsibility for legislation and government, but could still be veto players in constitutional politics in the name of their 'territories'. Should senators who do not respond to the people nor to elected regional councils but mostly to bigger political parties really get a veto power on further constitutional reforms of the judiciary, and even on direct election of the President or on the fundamental principles and rights catalogues? Although the people today actually still hold the final say on such a constitutional reform, tomorrow a senate with little democratic legitimacy could have the final say. The right of the people to change the constitution, a right that may include the right to correct an unsuccessful constitutional reform or the geography of an inefficient regionalism designed into the Constitution, would get less protection.

Last but not least, realism demands that one look at the undeniable fact of reform fatigue of the people that have now been for more than one generation involved in reform debates. The fatigue could prevent the people from actually reading what they are asked to ratify. The decision on the reform could become just a matter of confidence in the government. If there is no quorum, the people could abstain and hand over the constitutional reform to the supporters or opponents of the existing governmental majority. On the other hand the people could support the promises of minor 'costs of politics' by cutting seats, but it could even reject the reform as a self-interested project of the political class that promotes the 'rule of politics'. The success as well as the failure of the reform decided with thin majorities in a condition of reform fatigue could have a negative impact on the basic consensus for the reformed or unreformed constitution.

Italy to some extent still harbours a constitutional patriotism, because people still love and support their Republican Constitution. The reform discourse has to maintain a sufficient level of idealism, and that includes a minimum of civic passion, hope and desire among the people, as well as a realism that does not reduce constitutionalism to an elitist ideology of the past. If the political class ignores the people's reform fatigue, there might be a double lack of both idealism and realism.

How Do Constitutional Judges Deal with Constitutional Reforms?

Already in 1988 the Constitutional Court decided that constitutional reforms – unlike Lateran Treaties, international treaties and EU law – must respect the supreme principles of the Constitution, including effective fundamental rights protection.[61] It has not yet declared unconstitutional a constitutional reform approved by referendum, but the case law on the enacted reforms looks at the original ideals and makes quite creative interpretations on the new articles.

The Court has never been allowed to be heard in parliamentary proceedings, but performs a cooperative role of indirectly 'participating observer', even when constitutional reform is pending in Parliament. The annual speech of the Constitutional Court President of January 2014 recalled the 'tortuous judicial activism' that the last organic constitutional reform of 2001 faced. He made a sort of implicit endorsement of the ongoing constitutional reform, but demanded a simplification of the legislative competences and an institution where the frequent conflicts between the state and the regions could be resolved by political means. The speech invoked 'balance of powers' as a key ideal of constitutionalism, considering the 'constitutional equilibrium' even an 'existential reason' of pluralistic democracy: 'It is not the Court itself that has to design the specific form of the strictly necessary reform steps; on this occasion I limit myself to acknowledge a general problem of imbalance of the Italian regional system that the Court hardly tries to remedy in single cases, with the necessary episodic nature of its judicial sentences.'[62]

[61] Decision n. 1146/1988.

[62] 'By force of experience of a long and tortuous constitutional jurisprudence – prior and subsequent to the reform of 2001 – we have to stress out two needs that are complementary each other: on the one hand a strong simplification of the criteria of distribution of competences is unavoidable, on the other hand institutional opportunities for a confrontation need to be strengthened in order to return to politics as more appropriate means for governing conflicts between the centre and the periphery, without expecting adjustments and repairs from the judge of the legislation'. www.cortecostituzionale.it/documenti/relazioni_annuali/Silvestri_20140227.pdf.

In 2015 the presidential speech maintained the support for the reform process, notwithstanding statistics showing a clear decrease of litigation between the state and the regions.[63] At a seminar organized by the Court, the President concluded the narration of the case law on the constitutional reform of 2001 with a clear warning message related to the text already approved in first lecture by both Chambers: '[t]he risk is that expressions in the reform bill like 'general and common articles' for exclusive legislative competences of the state and 'as far as of regional interest' for those of the Regions could foster conflict in the relationship between the State and the Regions and produce new constitutional litigation.'[64]

The support and endorsement of the reform is not disinterested, because the reform also has an impact on the structure and the functions of the Constitutional Court. Five out of fifteen judges are elected by a joint session of the Chambers with at least a three-fifths majority, another five by the supreme ordinary and administrative courts, and five are chosen by the President of the Republic. The Chamber of Deputies rejected the proposal that its 630 members would elect three and the 100 members of the Senate two constitutional judges. The Senate decided to insist on this provision, but the reduced democratic legitimacy of the Senate – and of the President of the Republic elected by both Chambers – could diminish even the limited input-legitimacy of the Court.

Furthermore, the reform project grants direct access to the Constitutional Court prior to the promulgation of electoral laws on the initiative of one-third of the members of each Chamber. The Constitutional Court would become a sort of *Conseil constitutionnel* just for that category of cases. In an oral response to journalists the President of the Court voiced criticism that the impact on the political relevance of constitutional justice had not been sufficiently reflected.[65]

This choice of the reformers seems to be first of all a reaction to the decision n. 1/2014 of the Constitutional Court that declared the existing electoral laws unconstitutional. The decision struck down two elements of the electoral laws of the bicameral Parliament, namely the so-called

63 www.cortecostituzionale.it/documenti/interventi_presidente/R2015_Criscuolo.pdf.

64 www.cortecostituzionale.it/documenti/convegni_seminari/AperturaCriscuolo.pdf. Cf. the Court's seminar of 2013 on the constitutional reform of 2012: www.cortecostituzionale.it/documenti/convegni_seminari/AperturaBilancioSilvestri2.pdf.

65 www.ansa.it/sito/notizie/politica/2015/03/12/consulta-criscuolo-corte-garante-di-diritti-inviolabili_6302445a-4034-4328-a674-521bdf4666bc.html.

'majority bonus' (*premio di maggioranza)* and the rule that admitted only fixed lists (*liste bloccate*) for elections in large constituencies that express a plurality of seats. The first mechanism gave a majority of seats to the party or to the coalition of parties that received the most votes on the national level for the Chamber of Deputies and on the regional level, split in each of the twenty regional constituencies for the Senate. When no minimum share of votes is fixed and the mechanisms are differentiated, the premium cannot ensure stable and homogeneous majorities in both Chambers and violates substantial equality of the vote. The second rule prevented voters from voting for personal preferences, thus bound by the ranking of the list decided by the respective political party. The decision was anticipated by various *obiter dicta*, but has been criticized as (1) contrary to prior judgements and principles that declared similar questions inadmissible political questions, (2) making explicit referral to German constitutional case law related to a proportionality system, (3) manipulating the existing electoral laws and restricting to much the discretion of the legislator and (4) making an *obiter dictum* that the existing Parliament need not be dissolved. The decision seemed to urge for electoral reform and to make implicit referral to the discussions on electoral reform made in the governmental committee on constitutional reform.

The constitutional reform process has not been stopped by dissolution of the Parliament, but the opposition argued that the Parliament, elected under an unconstitutional electoral law with a majority representing less than a third of the voters in one Chamber and a thin incongruent majority in the other, did not have sufficient legitimacy for passing a great constitutional reform. In any case, the constitutional reform process has been slowed down by the aforesaid electoral reform law n. 52/2015 (so-called *Italicum*), approved together with a question of confidence that allowed all amendments to be set aside.[66] The combination of a new quorum of 40 per cent for the majority bonus at the first ballot and no quorum for the second ballot restricted the two major party

[66] The territory will be divided into 100 constituencies electing proportionally from 3 to 9 deputies. For each constituency, the parties designate a list of candidates with a 'head of list' that can run in up to 10 constituencies. At the first round, electors vote for a single party and its head of the list and express up to two additional preference votes for other candidates of the same list. The party that takes a majority of at least 40 per cent of valid votes obtains 340 seats (55 per cent). If no party passes the threshold a ballot between the two major parties at national level will decide even without a minimum consensus at the first round. The remaining 277 seats are allocated proportionally to all parties that reach at least 3 per cent of votes at the national level, respecting the number of preferences.

lists. This mechanism could allow a leader of a party that leads with less than 25 per cent at the first ballot and wins with the same votes at the second ballot 55 per cent of the seats to prevail. The voters could no longer force parties to enter into a grand coalition. The vote of preference being limited only for a second or third choice, most members of the one-chamber Parliament would be designated by the party and not by the electorate. The law n. 52/2015 will not enter into force until 2016, but procedures for constitutional review and for an abrogation through referendum have already been started. When deciding on the new questions and on the admissibility of the referendum, the Constitutional Court will be asked not only to strike down the reform, but even to re-open the political process of constitutional reform.

Other hard cases for the Constitutional Court had a direct impact on constitutional reform. The decision n. 230 of 2013 held that the government could not use an emergency decree for any organic reform of provinces in order to anticipate the decision of the Parliament to abolish them and to erase provinces from the constitutional infrastructure.[67] Decision n. 118 of 2015 declared unconstitutional a regional law of Veneto that provided for some referendum on independence and autonomy for the region, because the region interfered with 'fundamental choices at the constitutional level'.[68]

Perhaps the hardest case concerned a conflict of powers was initiated by the President of the Republic against the public prosecutor of Palermo in order to obtain the immediate destruction of phone tabs of its conversations in a criminal investigation regarding negotiations of ministers with mafia.[69] The Court pointed out that, by way of fact, the functions of the President of the Republic are premised on informal contacts and networking, which would be entirely thwarted if any of his communications became public. The necessity of confidentiality was recognized as a source of a new implicit constitutional rule derived merely from the position and role of the Head of State as the 'supreme guarantor of the

[67] Decision n. 230/2013. Cf. even decision n. 50/2015.

[68] Decision n. 175/2015, http://www.cortecostituzionale.it/documenti/download/doc/recent_judgments/S118_2015_en.pdf.

[69] Decision n. 1/2013, www.cortecostituzionale.it/documenti/download/doc/recent_judgments/S001_2013_en.pdf: 'it was not for the Palermo public prosecutor at the Tribunale di Palermo to assess the pertinence of the telephone tapes of conversations of the President of the Republic ordered in relation to criminal procedure no. 11609/08', nor 'to refrain from requesting the judge to order the immediate destruction of the documentation relating to the telephone taps indicated . . .' without any 'hearing at which the parties are entitled to make representations'.

equilibrium between the branches of state'.[70] The Court supported a sort of presidential *'ragion di Stato'* that may override even the rule of law if 'interests relating to supreme principles of constitutional law are not sacrificed'.[71] As an exception, the protection of life and personal freedom and the safeguarding of the constitutional integrity of the institutions should always be ensured by judicial authority. This decision ratified the *de facto* presidentialism and idealized the President of the Republic as the 'supreme guarantor of the equilibrium between the branches of state', like an angel that protects the republic in times of multiple crises. This decision even contributed to the president's decision to accept re-election only under the condition that a constitutional reform would be realized. Whatever the constitutional reform will be, as long as the supreme political watchman maintains the equilibrium, the Constitution and the ideal of equilibrium will be hold safe.

The Court and the Presidency, so it seems, are good neighbours. The existence of a political guarantor facilitates the judicial maintenance of the constitution. The President of the Republic is the President of the High Judiciary Council, with two-thirds of members elected by the judiciary, and the Constitutional Court is a judge of conflicts between political and judicial powers, with one-third of members elected by the supreme ordinary and administrative courts. Both are needed for the equilibrium between politics and judiciary. The election of these organs is highly sensitive and even interdependent. The new President of the Republic had already been elected as a constitutional judge before taking on the presidential office and is now obliged to urge the Parliament to elect new constitutional judges.

From an idealist point of view the president's political constitutionalism promotes more the reform of the legal framework of powers;

[70] 'The failure to provide for authorisations similar to those in place for members of Parliament and ministers, along with the fact that constitutional law does not impose state limitations for categories of offence, cannot result in the paradoxical consequence that the communications of the President of the Republic should enjoy less protection . . . On the contrary, it must lead to the more consistent conclusion that the Constitution's silence on this point is an expression of the mandatory status . . . of the rule that the President's communications must remain confidential. This mandatory status results from the position and role of the Head of State within the Italian constitutional system and cannot be inferred from a specific and explicit rule, since there is no provision that identifies an institutional figure competent to authorise exceptions to that prerogative. Therefore, it is not a lacuna, but on the contrary the logical prerequisite under constitutional law of the inviolable status of the communications of the supreme guarantor of the equilibrium between the branches of state.'

[71] Decision n. 238/2014.

meanwhile the Court's judicial constitutionalism promotes more the adaptation of the legal framework of rights. *Jurisdictio* and *gubernaculum* remain divided, but cooperate for common ideals of constitutionalism. From a more realistic point of view the president is a moderator of politics, the Constitutional Court a moderator of the judiciary. Both are needed in order to moderate political and judicial powers. That might explain why the constitutional reform does not even try to resolve the existing tensions between political and judicial powers. It might also explain why the reformers of the Constitution normally prefer not to enter into a constitutional reform of fundamental rights, but to leave their development both to legislators and judges. The reform will not substantially increase the powers of the Constitutional court and President, but will impact their democratic legitimacy. A Court with judges elected by the new Senate could become more sensitive to territorial autonomies, and a president elected by a supermajority of three-fifths could stand more above the parties. Both are optimistic ideas, but might lack realism if we look at the past presidential elections and the present reluctance of Parliament to elect three new constitutional judges.[72]

A Constitutional Culture under International Stress

As we have seen, the Italian Constitution reflects a high level of idealism, including social justice in the principles of constitutionalism and rule of law. The Italian culture has an even longer tradition of realism tempered by that idealism. Moments of idealism in Renaissance, *Risorgimento* and *Resistenza* inspired the framers of the 1947 Constitution, moments of realism in unification, post-war reconstruction, and post-1989-inspired constitutional case law and politics in practice.

Being often invoked, but rarely explained, the constitutional ideals of this 'social constitutionalism' played a limited, but not secondary, role in political and legal practice. The Constitution did not promise a revolution and a perfect system of planned welfare, but granted social, cultural and political rights and over time it has increased social justice and allowed some progress in society. The historical conversation between idealism and realism has been made in all constitutional bodies and in the public sphere of a real, existing popular constitutional culture. The people can have direct access to legislators, abrogate laws through

[72] In November 2015, the 28th scrutiny failed for the first of them.

referendum and decide over constitutional reforms that lack large parliamentary consensus, but they have no direct access to the constitutional court.

The guarantees of constitutional justice and constitutional reform are specific bridges between idealism and realism created within the constitution. The judges' bridging seems to have had more success in Italy than the politics of constitutional reform. The case law of the Constitutional Court maintained the original idealism tempered with the realism of reasonableness and prefers always the interpretation of the legislation to an interpretation of the Constitution. Less tempered was the case law of the regular judiciary, where moments of initial passivism have been followed by more frequent moments of activism. The judicial use of reasonableness and proportionality and of supreme constitutional principles and values can be defined as the key aspects of the normative concept of '*neocostituzionalismo*'.

Nevertheless, the text of the Constitution is getting older, but constitutional reforms have been less frequent and less successful than electoral reforms. The enacted reform laws have been inspired by non-ideal populism (1993) and presidentialism (1999), unrealistic federalism (2001) and an unrealistic fiscal compact (2012). The ongoing constitutional reform has been supported by the Court and can be read as a realist correction of the ideals of strong regionalism and symmetrical bicameralism, but it has also been perceived as an idealization of a strong '*gouverne-mentalité,*' the opposite of liberal constitutionalism. The consequences of the reform fatigue are uncertain, as well as the reform impact on the basic consensus of the Constitution that is still supported by a popular culture of constitutional patriotism.

Nevertheless, the future of the Italian constitutional culture depends not only on the Italian people, but also on the international context. The pluralist constitutionalism in Europe offers opportunities for comparative dialogues and interaction, but even for mechanisms of interference. The case law of the European Court of Human Rights in Strasbourg and of the European Court of Justice in Luxembourg, the opinions of the Venice Commission and further European or international mechanisms of rights watching offer data bases for the concretization of normative ideals and for the real performance of the constitutional culture. An intensive dialogue with the European courts and institutions is focusing on constitutional ideals as elements of constitutional identity and 'counter-limits' for the limitation of democratic sovereignty, as well as on margins of appreciation regarding national realities and needs. The Council of Europe's work on prisons, length of judicial proceedings and expropriations shows the shadows of reality.[73] On the other hand, the Constitutional Court opposed 'counterlimits' to the transfer of sovereignty rights and decided that even the International Court of Justice violated the right of access to justice, opposing a more idealistic national view on international customary law of state immunity in the name of the rule of law.[74]

Looking at the World Justice Project indicators,[75] the Italian rule of law concept might add ideals of social justice, such as rights to health care and schooling, and ideals of peace through international law. The country has a highly independent judiciary, a valuable public health system and an advanced international law culture, but suffers from corruption, organized crime, regulatory enforcement deficits and unreasonable delays of justice. The existing indicators still do not yet measure with sufficient precision the realization of social rights or the relevance of territorial asymmetries.

Looking furthermore at the democratic elements of constitutionalism, the ideals of popular sovereignty, pluralism of confessions, trade unions, political parties and mass media and a rationalized parliamentary form of government have been challenged by real trends to populism, confessionalism, neocorporatism, partitocracy, media-concentration, instable governments and – last but not least – a severe debt crisis. The Democracy Index, compiled by the *Economist*, of 2014 qualified Italy as an 'imperfect democracy'.[76] The history of referendums, electoral reforms, primaries and new parties in the last decades, and the political life of the civil society at the local level could be seen as evidence of some progress in Italian democracy. However other developments such as the spread crisis that conditioned the building of a government of the ex-EU commissioner Mario Monti, the increasing abstention of citizens from elections and politics, the increasing number of foreign population excluded from vote and the worst corruption perception index in EU and Western Europe point to a possible increase of the gap between the ideal principles and the actual practice of democracy in Italy and Europe.

[73] Cf. decision n. 278/2013 (unreasonably rigid, a law that rendered irreversible for 100 years the choice to remain anonymous made by a biological mother whose child had been adopted); 162/2014 (unconstitutional prohibition of heterologous artificial insemination for infertile couples); 49/2015 (binding force only for consolidated interpretations of ECHR).

[74] Decision n. 238/2014.

[75] See the contribution by Ginsburg and Versteeg in this volume.

[76] 29th position: www.eiu.com/public/topical_report.aspx?campaignid=Democracy0115.

The discussion of the above outlined 'balance sheets' of the rule of law and democracy might help to find new bridges between the ideal and the real, but the aforesaid indicators do not yet measure the impact of supranational and international governance, for the Italian example especially on social rights protection or on parliamentary democracy. The surviving Italian ideal of European federalism (art. 11, 117 Const.) has to face an increasing loss of confidence in the respect of rule of law and democracy in the European Union, especially in the Union's capacity to rule on the banking system or the migration policies.

If we look at European and international governance, there is on the other hand a risk that the aforesaid indicators, rankings and peer-review could just be used for a 'rating' of constitutions, far from any real decision-making and law enforcement power of citizens. At the present moment of the economic and financial crisis, the troika of European Commission, European Central Bank and International Monetary Fund notoriously promoted structural reforms of labour, public administration, justice and tax issues. They imply 'institutional reforms' and reforms of the written formal or unwritten material Constitution and generate neoliberal reservations against any ideal of social justice. A paper of JP Morgan from 2013 shows how economic powers already use an informal 'rating' of European constitutions.[77] The neoliberal efficiency ideals of the markets favour strong executives, strong central states relative to the regions, less constitutional protection of social rights, consensus building systems with less clientelism and less political protest movements. But the less-sovereign the state's debts are, the more financial power can be used for pushing such neoliberal institutional reforms.

The lenience of constitutionalism, founded on the virtues of mitigation of powers and peaceful struggle for rights, comes therefore under the stress of the markets. The diversification of constitutional cultures is threatened actually more by the clichés of economists than by the

[77] 'The political systems in the periphery were established in the aftermath of dictatorship, and were defined by that experience. Constitutions tend to show a strong socialist influence, reflecting the political strength that left wing parties gained after the defeat of fascism. Political systems around the periphery typically display several of the following features: weak executives; weak central states relative to regions; constitutional protection of labour rights; consensus building systems which foster political clientelism; and the right to protest if unwelcome changes are made to the political status quo. The shortcomings of this political legacy have been revealed by the crisis. ... The key test in the coming year will be in Italy, where the new government clearly has an opportunity to engage in meaningful political reform.' http://culturaliberta.files.wordpress.com/2013/06/jpm-the-euro-area-adjustment-about-halfway-there.pdf.

findings of constitutional economics that 'political factors are much more important than economic factors' and 'domestic rather than international influences appear to be the dominant ones'.[78] The European constitutional culture should end neither in the cynical realism of a supermarket of constitutions nor in a hypocritical idealism that ignores the multiple crises of the Union. It should instead aim to temper the ideals of 'political union' and 'global constitutionalism' and to strengthen the separation of the political from economic and cultural powers upholding a basic consensus even in divided societies like the Italian and European.

[78] B. Hayo, S. Voigt, Determinants of Constitutional Change: Why Do Countries Change Their Form of Government? (2010), p. 33, http://ssrn.com/abstract=1562553 or http://dx.doi.org/10.2139/ssrn.1562553

12

Constitutional Culture in the Netherlands: A Sober Affair

MAURICE ADAMS AND GERHARD VAN DER SCHYFF

Introduction

Political Power and the Governmental Process, by Karl Loewenstein, is one of those rare pieces of twentieth-century European scholarship that explicitly calls to attention the practical significance of constitutions. Writing in the 1950s, Loewenstein was interested in 'the concordance of the reality of the power process with the norms of the constitution'.[1] An ideal constitution, according to him, is one where the norms of a constitution are faithfully observed: its norms govern the political process, or the power process adjusts itself to the norms. Loewenstein calls such a situation 'normative constitutionalism' and compares it to a tailor-made suit. This he distinguishes from 'nominal constitutionalism' where the desired fit of the 'suit' has yet to be achieved, and 'semantic constitutionalism' where the constitution is meaningless in practice, such as under juntas.[2]

Loewenstein also noted the lack of attention for the dynamics that was conducive for the achievement of normative constitutionalism and was very aware of the fact that a constitution does not operate automatically once it has been adopted. 'To be a living constitution, that is, lived up to in practice by power holders and power addressees, a constitution requires a national climate conducive to its realization.'[3] Such a statement provokes

[1] K. Loewenstein, *Political Power and the Governmental Process* (Chicago/London: The University of Chicago Press, 1957 (2nd edition 1965)), pp. 147–8.

[2] There are of course many other (overlapping) constitutional typologies possible. E.g. on the basis of author: Plato, Aristotle, Cicero, Montesquieu, Hobbes, Rousseau, Bryce, Wheare, Strong, Azkin, etc. Or by period: Antique, medieval, Modern, etc. Or by political ideology: liberal, Marxist, etc. Or by physical appearance: long or short, with or without preamble, with or without judicial constitutional review, uni- or multi-documentary. Or by forms of state: federal, centralised or decentralised, etc.

[3] Loewenstein, *Political Power*, p. 148.

questions about the dynamics between constitutional law and socio-political practice, or between the formal and material validity of a constitution. Loewenstein, a Jewish émigré from Nazi Germany who became an American citizen,[4] was troubled by these questions, and was in his days one of the few scholars who called for more systematic attention for them.[5]

In this chapter we want to discuss this theme in the context of Dutch constitutional culture.[6] What role, if any, does the Dutch Constitution play in channelling and/or constraining the political state of affairs? And is the Dutch Constitution capable of governing the dynamics of the political power process? These questions are highly relevant, since constitutions are considered to be the ultimate means of building and sustaining a just and stable politico-institutional order.

A terminological note is apt here. In this chapter we use 'Constitution' as referring to the actual Dutch document known as such. As Martin Krygier notes in his chapter to this volume, a constitution is about the way public power is constituted; it has to do with the legal architecture and frame of a polity (institutional design, foundations and structure), as well as the character of its major institutions and their occupants, their relations among themselves and with the subjects of power.[7] Constitutional*ism*, then, refers to the way *the exercise* of such power is constituted, made up.[8] As Krygier also notes, if a constitution is to

[4] Loewenstein was trained as both a lawyer and a political scientist. For an intellectual biography, see M. Lang, *Karl Loewenstein. Transatlantischer Denker der Politik* (Stuttgart: Franz Steiner Verlag, 2007) (German).

[5] To be sure, today there is more attention than ever before for the types of – interdisciplinary – questions Loewenstein posed. The work of for example T. Ginsburg c.s. is relevant here. See his *The Endurance of National Constitutions* (Cambridge University Press, 2009) (together with Z. Elkins and J. Melton). But this doesn't preclude the fact that, in European academic circles at least, a specifically legal approach still seems dominant. See A. von Bogdandy, 'Comparative Constitutional Law: A Contested Domain' in M. Rosenfeld and A. Sajo (eds.), *The Oxford Handbook of Comparative Constitutional Law* (Oxford University Press, 2012), p. 28.

[6] Loewenstein, as we saw, talks about a 'climate' in this context.

[7] For the purposes of this chapter this also encompasses the rule of law, which for us encompasses fundamental rights, judicial review, the separation of powers, as well as a variety of governance structures. Cf. M. D. McCubbins, D. B. Rodriguez and B. R. Weingast, 'The Rule of Law Unplugged', *Emory Law Journal*, 59 (2010), 1455. We thus use a substantive conception of the rule of law. On the distinction between formal and substantive conceptions, see B. Z. Tamanaha, *On the Rule of Law. History, Politics, Theory* (Cambridge University Press, 2004), pp. 91–113.

[8] See Chapter 2 in this volume.

contribute to constitutional*ism*, it must be implemented and be effective in the institutions and practices of the political order. That implies that the constitutional culture must be conducive to constitutionalism. The phrase 'constitutional culture' here refers to the agglomeration of beliefs and attitudes that the people, judges, lawyers and the state hold towards the Constitution and constitutional law in general.[9]

Some Institutional Facts

The Netherlands is a small, unitary country with some 17 million inhabitants. It is highly affluent and densely populated, and also a (mainly) ceremonial monarchy.[10] The Netherlands has traditionally, and for a long time already, been a country of minorities, especially in religious and political terms (albeit with hardly any linguistic minorities). This also shows in electoral results, as no political party has ever been able to succeed in winning a parliamentary majority since the introduction of universal suffrage in 1917.[11]

Parliament, which consists of two Chambers, is situated in The Hague. The so-called Second Chamber or lower house consists of 150 members, who are elected once every four years – if there are no new elections as a result of government collapse – through a system of proportional representation. The First Chamber or upper house, also informally called the Senate, consists of 75 members who are elected every 4 years by the members of the provincial councils (i.e. 12 councils with 564 members in total, accounting for 12 provinces). Its election, however, does not coincide with elections for the lower house. The position of Senator is a part-time one of – formally at least – one day a week, with no parliamentary assistance. Its members come from all sectors of society.

[9] See K. Y. L. Tan, *The Constitution of Singapore. A Contextual Analysis* (Oxford: Hart Publishing, 2015), p. 58. A more general definition refers to the network of understandings and practices that structure a specific constitutional culture. See R. Siegel, 'Text in Context: Gender and Constitution from a Social Movement Perspective', *University of Pennsylvania Law Review*, 150 (2001), 303. Cf. Nelken, who understands the term legal culture, in its most general sense, as one way of describing relatively stable patterns of legally oriented social behaviour and attitudes. D. Nelken, 'Defining and Using the Concept of Legal Culture' in E. Örücü and D. Nelken (eds.), *Comparative Law. A Handbook* (Oxford: Hart Publishing, 2007), p. 113.

[10] A useful and detailed overview about Dutch political history and its institutional shape can be found in R. Andeweg and G. A. Irwin, *Governance and Politics of the Netherlands* (Basingstoke: Palgrave Macmillan, 2014).

[11] *Ibid.*, pp. 22–3.

Although having more or less the same powers of governmental oversight as the lower house, the upper house has no right of legislative initiative or even amendment, but it nevertheless has to approve legislation accepted by the lower house. It can only fully or partially accept or reject this legislation, making for a rather intricate and complicated relation between the lower and upper houses. Constitutional convention has it that the upper house is supposed to focus on technical issues of legislative quality (*chambre de réflexion*), but once in a while it behaves more politically. Its existence and legitimacy has been a matter of debate over the years, especially when it contradicts the lower house on what are understood to be 'political' decisions, which are considered by some to be the prerogative of the lower house.[12]

Next to being a monarchy, the Netherlands is a parliamentary democracy, which means that the existence of the government is dependent upon a majority in parliament (especially the lower house).

Dutch constitutionalism could be described as being a rich tapestry of customs and documents.[13] Two national documents nevertheless stand out in this regard. On the one hand, there is the *Charter of the Kingdom of the Netherlands* (1954), and on the other hand, we find the *Constitution of the Kingdom of the Netherlands* (the first version dating back to 1815, but with its last major revision in 1983). Of the two, the Charter is the less known, but higher in terms of legal hierarchy nonetheless. The Charter regulates the relationship between the countries forming the Kingdom, namely the Netherlands, Aruba, Curaçao and (Dutch) Saint Martin (the latter three islands being situated in the Caribbean), stating them to be equal partners. The Dutch Constitution itself however, is only applicable to the Netherlands and foresees a decentralised unitary state. When we in this chapter refer to Dutch constitutionalism or the Dutch Constitution, it is with this document in mind.

A Sober Affair

The casual observer might be excused for thinking that the written Constitution of the Netherlands belongs to the same category as its

[12] On this M. Adams, 'De nieuwe Belgische Senaat en het wetgevingsproces: kamer van reflectie of doublure? Enkele beschouwingen in het licht van de Nederlandse situatie', *RegelMaat. Tijdschrift voor Wetgevingsvraagstukken* (1996), 230 (Dutch).

[13] G. van der Schyff, *Judicial Review of Legislation: A Comparative Study of the United Kingdom, the Netherlands and South Africa* (Dordrecht: Springer, 2010), p. 23 (on which this paragraph is partly based).

United States or German counterparts. However, this would be to exaggerate the importance of codifying a constitutional system in a single document which is then entrenched to protect it from later legislative whim.

Instead the Constitution of the Netherlands might have more in common with its unwritten British neighbour than one might expect; it is in any case difficult to imagine the Dutch Constitution as an apex document containing the system's *Grundnorm* from which all else is to be deduced. This is because the Dutch Constitution is not intended as the beginning and end of rule of law values and constitutional culture in the Netherlands, similar to section 2 of the Constitution of South Africa that makes its superiority and all-encompassing role in that order more than clear by stating that

> This Constitution is the supreme law of the Republic; law or conduct inconsistent with it is invalid, and the obligations imposed by it must be fulfilled.

Instead the Dutch Constitution creates an incomplete constitutional framework to be further developed by parliamentary legislative or non-legislative means.[14] In this sense the Constitution allows the political process great freedom in developing and regulating constitutional law, as is the case in the United Kingdom where a sovereign parliament is not hindered by a codified constitutional document aimed to curtail a potentially rampant parliament. As a matter of fact, to say that the Constitution 'creates' a system in the Netherlands might be an overstatement in some respects, as opinion may differ on whether the legislature owes its competence to the Constitution or whether its legislative function exists independently of the two-hundred-year-old document. This is because it may be argued that article 81 of the Constitution establishes the legislature as comprising the government and the States General while endowing it with law-making powers; conversely, though, it may be argued that the Constitution simply recognises the legislature and provides for its specific procedure. Depending on one's view, the difference between the Dutch

[14] See also the foreword to J. R. Stellinga, *De Grondwet systematisch gerangschikt* (Zwolle: Tjeenk Willink, 1950) (Dutch). Further on this, e.g. M. C. Burkens, H. R. B. M. Kummeling, B. P. Vermeulen and R. J. G. M. Widdershoven, *Beginselen van de democratische rechtsstaat*, 7th edn (Kluwer: Alphen aan den Rijn, 2012), p. 76 (Dutch) support the view that the Constitution creates a general competence to legislate, while W. J. M. Voermans, *Toedeling van bevoegdheid* (The Hague: Boom Juridische Uitgevers, 2004) (Dutch) notes and criticises the difference of opinion in this regard.

Constitution and its British neighbour might be smaller than between the Dutch Constitution and its German neighbour.

The Dutch Constitution, one can safely say, is one of sober ambition as far as its own worth is concerned. Although the document begins with a bill of rights as is commonplace among many modern constitutions and even incorporates socio-economic rights, a number of remarks may be made. The range of rights does not include those to a fair trial; the right to life is also absent unless one deploys interpretative vigour when it comes to article 114, which provides that capital punishment may not be imposed. Conspicuous by its absence is also a general right to property or ownership; instead, article 14(1) allows expropriation but only upon compensation having been paid in accordance with an act of parliament.

This latter construction is also typical of the scheme that applies to the limitation of rights. While many declarations of rights focus on the extent to which a right may be limited, providing for instance that rights may only be limited insofar as reason or necessity demands, as in the case of the South African bill of rights or the European Convention on Human Rights, the Dutch Constitution focusses on the agent capable of limiting a given guarantee. Invariably, that agent is the legislature that is allowed to limit a right in an act of parliament or by means of delegating the relevant authority.[15] The effect is to place the centre of decision-making outside the Constitution when it comes to limiting rights, instead of providing a shield with which to fend off interferences with the scopes of rights; the Dutch Constitution puts its faith in the wisdom of the legislature when it comes to deciding sensitive matters such as the conditions under which rights should be protected. Placing the gravity of decision-making outside the Constitution is even more in evidence when the structure of socio-economic rights is considered. For instance, article 22(1) provides that the 'authorities shall take steps to promote the health of the population'. This is not the language of enforceable subjective rights, but that of reminding the political institutions of what is expected of them in exercising their powers.

A close look at many of the rights in the Constitution also reveals that they are presented not as principles, but as rules. Rules might be clear and succinct in that they either apply or not, but principles allow more terrain to be constitutionalised.[16] The rule-like nature of especially the civil and

[15] See, e.g., art. 8 of the Constitution: 'The right of association shall be recognised. This right may be restricted by Act of Parliament in the interest of public order.'

[16] The distinction is of course made prominently by Dworkin. See R. Dworkin, *Taking Rights Seriously* (Cambridge, MA: Harvard University Press, 1977), pp. 22–8.

political rights becomes apparent when the first two sub-provisions of article 7 are read:

1. No one shall require prior permission to publish thoughts or opinions through the press, without prejudice to the responsibility of every person under the law.
2. Rules concerning radio and television shall be laid down by Act of Parliament. There shall be no prior supervision of the content of a radio or television broadcast.

Article 7 guarantees not so much the principle of 'free expression' as it regulates various forms of communication. Even if one would want to focus on the principle underlying the provision, subsection 4 limits the scope of its application by excluding commercial advertising from constitutional protection.[17] Casting rights as rules essentially reduces the reach of the Constitution and serves to emphasise its reluctance as a source of norms that extends to every nook and cranny of society.

The sober nature of the Constitution is not only apparent in the context of fundamental rights, but also goes to the heart of the country's political process. The fact that the Netherlands is a parliamentary system that allows governments and their members to be relieved of their posts through parliamentary motions of no-confidence is not a direct product of the Constitution. The cardinal rule that government is subject to parliamentary confidence is an unwritten rule of constitutional law dating from the nineteenth century when parliament flexed its muscle in controlling the king's ministers, such as by refusing to pass budgets.[18] All the Constitution had to state on the matter was to say that ministers and not the king would be responsible for acts of government, while remaining silent on the matter to whom ministers had to be accountable.[19]

Far from dictating the form of government as in Germany, for example, the Constitution provides very little on how governments are to be formed and the conditions under which they may exercise office.

[17] Art. 7(4) of the Constitution reads: 'The preceding paragraphs do not apply to commercial advertising.'

[18] See further L. Dragtra, N. S. Efhymiou, A. W. Hins and R. de Lange, *Beginselen van het Nederlandse Staatsrecht*, 17th edn (Deventer: Kluwer, 2012), pp. 100–6 (Dutch); Burkens et al., *Beginselen*, p. 249; E. M. H. Hirsch Ballin and E. Y. van Vugt, 'De transformatie van de bevoegdheid tot ontbinding van het parlement' in E. Witjens, V. van Bogaert and Bollen (eds.), *E Hofi Di Ley* (The Hague: Boom, 2014), pp. 113–15 (Dutch).

[19] Art. 42(2) of the Constitution.

Constitutional innovation or change is rather the product of political practice, as became apparent again when the lower house of parliament decided to exclude the king from the process of forming a new government.[20] Previously the king appointed an *informateur* to explore the possibilities in constructing a new coalition, as no single party ever attains an absolute majority. On the advice of this mediator the king would appoint a *formateur* who would choose ministers and who usually becomes the new prime minister. Yet since the general election of 2012, the lower house decides by itself who should investigate and negotiate the political landscape in forming a new cabinet. As this process is not codified in the Constitution or in an act of parliament, it is essentially a question of pure political will as evidenced by the fact that the change was affected by simply amending the lower house's standing orders.[21]

Furthermore, there is little appetite in the Netherlands to change the culture of timidity where the Constitution is concerned. While the Constitution has certainly been developed since its inception, for example though the addition and expansion of a catalogue of rights, it remains debateable whether the document is the font of rule of law values and constitutional culture in the country. For example, calls to modernise the dated provisions of article 7 on a free press, most recently again in 2010 by the State Commission on the Constitution, have fallen on deaf ears.[22] Eliminating the provision's reference to specific forms of communication and focussing it on the protection of all communication and information irrespective of mode have come to nothing. By still concentrating its efforts on regulating the printed press, the digital age has hardly arrived as far as the Dutch Constitution is concerned.

More importantly than updating the Constitution in such respects, the government also let the opportunity pass to include a comprehensive value provision in the Constitution itself in lieu of a preamble, as suggested by the Commission in its report. The Commission suggested to refer to the country as a 'democratic *rechtsstaat*', to require the state to promote and protect core values such as human dignity and to base the exercise of public power on the Constitution and legislation. The then-government, though, had little appetite to inject the Constitution with a value-laden provision that would have counterbalanced the document's preoccupation with rules and procedures. Instead a later government

20 Burkens et al., *Beginselen*, p. 243.

21 Art. 139(a)-(b) of the Standing Orders of the Second Chamber of 22 June 1993. See also Parliamentary Papers II 2011–2012, 32 759, no. 6.

22 W. Thomassen, Rapport Staatscommissie Grondwet, 2010, pp. 70–1 (Dutch).

agreed, only after quite some political pressure, to include a watered-down value provision in the Constitution. Importantly though, the proposal still has to withstand the difficult and unpredictable process of constitutional amendment in order to be adopted.[23] Also, there is no word whatsoever in the Constitution about the European Union. The Dutch Constitution as such, we might conclude, is rather uninspiring.[24]

Constitutional Silence

The Constitution is not only a rather sober document, but its role in everyday political and constitutional life is more limited than that of some other constitutions, so much so that in some respects one might even speak of a 'constitutional silence'[25] or a lack of constitutional discourse. Although the Constitution is the highest national norm apart from the overarching Charter, one might be forgiven for thinking that it was just an ordinary law at times.[26] This conclusion can be based on the use of the Constitution during parliamentary debates, as well as its enforceability before, or lack thereof in, the country's courts.

Turning first to parliamentary debate, Hirsch Ballin noted that members of parliament make little use of the Constitution in debating each other on current issues.[27] His survey of lower house debates in 2013 showed that the Constitution was only mentioned when amendments to the document were discussed, the topic of European monetary union had to be considered and the criminal liability of the government featured on the agenda.[28] When a member of the house asked whether the Constitution was contravened when local councils circumvented statutory provisions on charging for care, the responsible secretary of state did not respond.[29] And when a member of government did refer to the Constitution, such as reference to article 15 of the Constitution and article 5 of the European Convention on Human Rights by the minister responsible for justice (in a debate on expanding the grounds for

[23] See Parliamentary Papers II 2011–2012, 31 570, no. 20; Parliamentary Papers II 2013–2014, 31 570, no. 24.

[24] About this G. van der Tang, 'Een Grondwet voor de politieke samenleving' in *De Grondwet herzien, 25 jaar later*, pp. 91, 94 (Dutch).

[25] E. M. H. Hirsch Ballin, *De Grondwet in Politiek en Samenleving* (Boom Lemma: The Hague, 2013), p. 9 (Dutch).

[26] On the hierarchy of norms, see Burkens et al., p. 91.

[27] Hirsch Ballin, *De Grondwet*, p. 9.

[28] See also *ibid.*, pp. 9–12 for the examples discussed here.

[29] Parliamentary Proceedings II, 13 January 2013, p. 40-5-33.

detention without trial), the Chamber did not engage in debate on the provisions.[30] Interestingly, a member of parliament referred to the written Constitution in embellishing his argument that it was parliament's duty to hold government accountable.[31] This member was obviously not aware that in the Netherlands this seminal aspect of parliamentary governance is not regulated as such in the Constitution but is the product of political practice as recognised by unwritten constitution law, as discussed above. Not only does this example illustrate the sober nature of the Constitution, but it also shows the lack of knowledge about constitutional fundamentals when it comes to parliamentarians.

The sober nature of the Constitution is probably only part of the reason for its absence from political debate. For instance, Hirsch Ballin argues that the Constitution can definitely play a role in the debate on the extent to which the legislature has to respect the courts' discretion in sentencing matters. In his analysis he points to a number of provisions from the Constitution, such as articles 15 and 16 on deprivation of liberty according to law and article 113(1), which attributes the settling of criminal cases to the courts' jurisdiction.[32] From these provisions he deduces that the Constitution implies a separation of powers in criminal matters between the legislative and judicial branches, more in particular a certain political detachment in deciding such cases. The separation of powers, he concludes, is a device with which to protect the individual against public power, in this case the will of legislative majorities. Hirsch Ballin's analysis shows that the Constitution can indeed be used to further political debate, but that Dutch constitutional culture is in effect unable to speak coherently about its Constitution and norms. As a result it is also not able to *ipso facto* sustain itself.[33]

Enforcing the Constitution through the Judiciary?

The fact that the Constitution is not part and parcel of the politician's everyday lexicon or discourse is probably as much to be ascribed to the Constitution's lack of enforcement mechanisms, especially in the form of

30 Parliamentary Proceedings II, 12 June 2013, p. 94–13-96.
31 Parliamentary Proceedings II, 17 January 2013, p. 4–13-10.
32 Hirsch Ballin, *De Grondwet*, p. 12.
33 See also on this failure of constitutional discourse M. E. Brandon, 'Constitutionalism and Constitutional Failure' in S. A. Barber and R. P. George (eds.), *Constitutional Politics. Essay on Constitution Making, Maintenance, and Change* (Princeton University Press, 2001), pp. 298–313.

judicial constitutional review, as it is to a political culture that is disinterested in its provisions (or maybe the former should be seen as an expression of the latter). Indeed, not only politicians, but judges, too, are well-placed to apply constitutions. The expansion of judicial power since World War II has meant that in many if not most countries, acts of parliament are generally subject to judicial review.[34] Constitutional law is increasingly treated less as a special branch of law that falls outside the scope of judicial enquiry and more as enforceable law. Even in a jurisdiction without a codified constitution such as the United Kingdom, some members of the judiciary have warned that, were parliament to violate basic constitutional fundamentals, such as abolishing the courts' control function in its entirety, the courts might use the common law to refuse such a move any legal force.[35] In other words, the constitutional function of the common law might be revived to counter a parliament intent on abusing its sovereign position in the legal order.[36]

Constitutional law in the Netherlands occupies a very different position in this regard. Whereas constitutional relationships might be somewhat fuzzy in the United Kingdom, thereby leaving the back door open for the common law to save the day in the event of a constitutional crisis of the magnitude described above, the Constitution of the Netherlands is quite clear on the role of the courts in matters of constitutional application. Uncertainty about the place of the courts in the institutional arrangement was taken away in 1848 when a bar on constitutional review was inserted. In its current guise as article 120, the provision holds that the 'constitutionality of Acts of Parliament and treaties shall not be reviewed by the courts'. The effect is to enforce a strict separation of powers. Although the Constitution is the highest national norm, it may not be used to judicially test acts of parliament, or treaties for that matter.[37]

[34] See generally C. N. Tate and T. Vallinder (eds.), *The Global Expansion of Judicial Power* (New York University Press, 1995); W. Sadurski, *Rights Before Courts: A Study of Constitutional Courts in Postcommunist States of Central and Eastern Europe* (Dordrecht, Springer, 2005); T. Ginsburg, *Judicial Review in New Democracies: Constitutional Courts in Asian Cases* (Cambridge University Press, 2003); S. Gloppen, R. Gargarella, E. Sklaar (eds.), *Democratization and the Judiciary. The Accountability Function of Courts in New Democracies* (London: Frank Cass, 2004).

[35] *Jackson v. Her Majesty's Attorney General* [2005] UKHL 56, para. 102, 159.

[36] See G. van der Schyff, 'Exploring the Parameters of Lawmaking: Lessons from the United Kingdom' in M. de Visser and W. J. Witteveen (eds.), *The Jurisprudence of Aharon Barak: Views from Europe* (Nijmegen: Wolf Legal Publishers, 2011), p. 125.

[37] See M. Adams and G. van der Schyff, 'Constitutional Review by the Judiciary in the Netherlands: A Matter of Politics, Democracy or Compensating Strategy?', *Zeitschrift für ausländisches öffentliches Recht und Völkerrecht*, 66 (2006), 399.

The provision has stood the test of time by withstanding numerous calls and attempts to abolish it, or to reduce its reach. The Cals/Donner State Commission advised in the 1960s that the bar be lifted in respect of civil and political rights, but to no avail.[38] The bar also survived the grand constitutional revision of 1983, albeit with different wording. In the early 1990s the government of the day declared its intent to modify the ban, an intention which the Supreme Court supported when asked for its advice in the matter.[39] But governments come and go while the bar remains, it seems. More recently the National Convention, a body appointed to consider ways to bring the political process closer to the people, recommended in its report in 2006 that the bar be lifted in respect of civil and political rights and that a constitutional court be established to carry out any review.[40] Again the proposals were not acted on, as was the case for the advice of the State Commission in 2010 that the bar be reconsidered.[41]

To date, the most concrete proposal for reform concerns a constitutional amendment tabled in 2002 by a then-member of the opposition (the 'Halsema' proposal or bill, after the member of the parliamentary opposition). The bill advocates the lifting of the bar in the case of what it terms 'enforceable rights'.[42] Reference to the list of exempted rights quickly establishes that exempted rights amount to civil and political rights, while it is to remain in effect for socio-economic rights as well as all other provisions of the Constitution, such as the legislative process, for instance.[43]

Amending the Constitution is no easy affair, though. A bill first has to be accepted by a simple majority in both houses of the States General, and before it can be read for a second time the lower house of parliament must have been re-elected.[44] The idea is that the voters must have the opportunity to express themselves on any constitutional amendments before a second reading may take place. Importantly also, a bill wishing to amend the Constitution must attain a two-thirds majority in its second

38 J. L. M. Th. Cals and A. M. Donner, *Tweede Rapport van de Staatscommissie van advies inzake de Grondwet en de Kieswet*, The Hague, 1969 (Dutch).

39 *Nota inzake rechterlijke toetsing*, 1991. For the Court's advice, see 7 *NJCM-bulletin* 1992, 243 (Dutch).

40 R. J. Hoekstra, *Hart voor de publieke zaak: aanbevelingen van de Nationale Conventie voor de 21e eeuw* (The Hague, National Convention, 2006) (Dutch).

41 For the government's negative reaction, see Parliamentary Papers II 2011–2012, 31 570, no. 20.

42 Parliamentary Papers II, 2001–2002, 28, 331, no. 2; 2002–2003, 28, 331, no. 9.

43 Parliamentary Papers II, 2002–2003, 28, 331, nos. 9, pp. 18–19.

44 For the procedure, see art. 137 of the Constitution.

reading in order to successfully amend the Constitution. The effect of this drawn-out process is that the Constitution is particularly rigid, especially as general elections usually deliver a different composition of the lower house and new political objectives with that. Although even more than one general election has taken place since its first reading, the Halsema bill is only now being read for a second time, as its supporters have been wary to initiate the second reading because the political climate might not be amenable to the bill passing the tough two-thirds majority. The most recent parliamentary debate on the bill took place on 5 March 2015, while the further legislative course is still to be decided.[45] This long duration between the tabling and second reading of the bill points not only to the hesitance of those wanting the amendment to pass, but also to the lack of appetite among politicians to allow the courts a greater say in shaping the constitutional culture through interpretation and application of enshrined fundamental rights. The fact that the bill stresses that the function of constitutional review would be a supplementary one and is in no way intended to replace political initiative and legislative control over the Constitution has seemingly fallen on deaf ears.[46]

Applying International Law

An analysis of the protection of rule of law values and the constitutional culture in the Netherlands is not simply a straightforward choice between the legitimacy of elected representatives as opposed to unelected judges as the guardians of the Constitution. The debate takes an unexpected turn when one considers that although acts of parliament are not subject to constitutional review by the courts, they are subject to treaty review to determine whether they violate international law, most commonly in the form of treaties concerned with fundamental rights such as the European Convention on Human Rights.[47] Treaty review is a consequence of the country's monist legal order that makes no distinction between national and international law in deciding what amounts to applicable law in the Netherlands. The scope of review becomes even broader when European Union law is added to the equation, as the monist nature of that legal order requires that domestic judges must refuse to apply any national

[45] See the Diary of the Second Chamber of 11 December 2015.

[46] Parliamentary Proceedings II, 2002–2003, 28, 331, no. 9, p. 14.

[47] Burkens et al., *Beginselen*, pp. 353–6, 361–7; N. S. Efthymiou and J. C. de Wit, 'The Role of Dutch Courts in the Protection of Fundamental Rights', *Utrecht Law Review*, 9 (2013), 75.

norms that conflict with any primary or secondary norms of European law independent of what national law may rule on the issue.[48]

Whereas EU monism might be considered a necessary feature of belonging to the Union, the judicial application of other sources of international law is a matter of national constitutional law. In this latter regard the sober character of the Constitution comes to the fore once again. Monism as such is not a principle created by the Constitution, but is a rule of unwritten constitutional law as recognised by the courts.[49] Although the principle is somewhat modified by the Constitution in articles 93 and 94, its source is extraneous to the document. The function of the Constitution is to limit the applicability of international law, other than EU law of course, given its autonomous operation, by requiring that courts may only apply binding international law. This requirement has been interpreted to exclude socio-economic rights from judicial application, instead favouring civil and political rights, and to limit the courts to applying written international law as opposed to custom.[50] This situation would obviously not apply to the protection of the Charter of Fundamental Rights of the EU, which is not governed by national constitutional law, thereby opening up another avenue of rights protection.

When comparing treaty review with the Halsema bill, the similarities are not mere coincidence. The bill was purposely designed to emulate treaty review in order to lower political resistance to accepting constitutional review by upsetting the *status quo* as little as possible. The Halsema bill therefore restricted its review to civil and political rights and intended for review to be conducted by all judges (and not just with a single or specialised apex court), as is the case with treaty review in the Netherlands. While this type of decentralised constitutional review might seem to be of little comfort to jittery politicians, a centralised and purpose-designed constitutional court was judged by some as a greater threat to the dominant position of political institutions, as such a court would speak with one voice, while a multitude of judges applying the Constitution in diverse ways would not pose a unified challenge.[51] These design concessions failed to convince doubters of constitutional review and have clearly not had much effect to date. Similarly, the breach in the inviolability of acts of parliament occasioned

[48] Art. 267 TFEU; CJEU *Costa v. ENEL* [1964] ECR 585 (6/64).

[49] HR 3 March 1919, *NJ* 1919, p. 371 (*Grenstractaat Aken*) (Dutch).

[50] Burkens et al., *Beginselen*, pp. 362–5.

[51] C. A. J. M. Kortmann, 'Advies van prof. mr. C. A. J. M. Kortmann', *NJCM-Bulletin*, 17 (1992), 305–6 (Dutch).

by treaty review has not convinced legislators to increase the range of norms with which to review acts of parliament and again shows the reluctance to shift the gravity of political decision-making from the legislature to the judiciary more than is absolutely necessary.

Based on the reluctance to take the plunge and introduce the constitutional review of acts of parliament, however careful and measured that plunge may be, one might be tempted to argue that treaty review compensates constitutional review, thereby obviating the need for the latter.[52] While this argument is certainly true to a certain extent as the Constitution protects rights that can also be found in various treaties, such as rights to freedom of religion and expression, to name but two common examples, it fails when a right such as that to education is considered. The right to education in article 23 of the Constitution is specifically tailored to the situation in the Netherlands, as its eight subsections will attest. The same can be said of the privacy protection offered in article 10, leading to the conclusion that the Constitution is not simply a copy of international law and vice versa. Moreover, the Constitution is not limited to protecting fundamental rights, as the document also regulates the legislative process, for instance. Articles 81 to 88 explain the legislative process by detailing the stages that a bill has to follow before it can be enacted as valid law. While treaty review goes some way in embellishing rule of law values in the Netherlands, the fact remains that international law can never supplant the Constitution, even though the latter may be a somewhat sober document and not exactly exuberant in its ambitions.

Having said all this, developing or establishing a constitutional culture of course demands more than simply agreeing to conduct judicial review, whether it be with regard to constitutional or treaty review. For instance, while treaty review indeed is a feature with a long track record in the Netherlands, its more recent exercise has been marked by reluctance on the part of the courts. Although there have been periods of what might be termed judicial activism when legislation was actively taken to task and measured for compatibility with binding international law, such as the review of family laws in the 1980s, courts in the Netherlands are generally careful to exercise their powers of treaty review.[53] The case of Salah

[52] See also the inaugural lecture by R. de Lange, *Concurrerende rechtsvorming* (Ars Aequi Libri: Nijmegen, 1999) (Dutch).

[53] See also J. Uzman, T. Barkhuysen and M. L. van Emmerik, 'The Dutch Supreme Court: A Reluctant Positive Legislator' in A. R. Brewer-Carías (ed.), *Constitutional Courts as Positive Legislators: A Comparative Law Study* (Cambridge University Press, 2011), p. 645.

Sheekh, a failed asylum seeker from Somalia, presents a good example. The applicant complained that the possibility of his expulsion to Somalia would threaten his article 3 right in the European Convention on Human Rights not to be 'subjected to torture or to inhuman or degrading treatment or punishment'.[54] This, he argued, would be his fate as a member of the minority Reer Hamaar community, because his expulsion to the relative safety of northern Somalia where he had no family or clan members to protect him would make him vulnerable and probably result in him having to live in a camp for internally displaced persons.[55] In contesting the application, the government contended that the applicant had failed to exhaust all available domestic remedies, as required in article 35(1) of the Convention, before he approached the European Court of Human Rights for relief.[56] This was the case, the government averred, because the applicant had not lodged a further appeal with the Administrative Jurisdiction Division of the Council of State, as that court was the highest appellate instance in the matter.

To the amazement of the Dutch establishment, the Strasbourg Court ruled that the requirement in article 35 had not been breached. The bench then proceeded to review the merits of the application before ruling that his expulsion to Somalia would indeed violate article 3 of the Convention.[57] The Court found that the position of the Council of State in this matter was so predictable as to warrant the Council being bypassed altogether.[58] The effect was to reprimand the Council of State, if not in so many words, for a judicial line that was formalistic to the extent that the court's adjudicative function amounted to little more than a formulaic approach in deciding the merits of a case such as that of Salah Seekh's. This is all the more reiterated by the Court finding a violation of article 3, as a closer inspection of the available facts deemed the safe areas to be particularly unsafe for someone in the position of the applicant.[59] In other words, not only did the Strasbourg Court bypass the national court hierarchy in a somewhat spectacular fashion, but it also made it

[54] ECtHR, *Salah Sheekh v. The Netherlands* of 11 January 2007, para. 114, 128.

[55] *Salah Sheekh v. The Netherlands*, para. 128.

[56] *Salah Sheekh v. The Netherlands*, para. 119.

[57] *Salah Sheekh v. The Netherlands*, para. 147; capturing the establishment's amazement at the decision F. Jensma, 'Hof Europa dwingt ander asielbeleid af', *NRC* 24 May 2007, for this newspaper article see: http://vorige.nrc.nl/binnenland/article1800486.ece/Hof_Europa_dwingt_ander_asielbeleid_af (Dutch).

[58] *Salah Sheekh v. The Netherlands*, para. 123.

[59] *Salah Sheekh v. The Netherlands*, para. 149.

patently clear that the highest court's judgement would have been so unsympathetic to the situation as to violate a core right of the Convention.

To its credit the government of the day responded quickly by adjusting its asylum policy to meet the requirements as set out in the *Salah Sheekh* case.[60] However, this does not address the cultural and institutional issue of constitutional checks and balances when it comes to realising constitutional and rule of law values in the Netherlands. Although the *Salah Sheekh* case might not be evident of everyday adjudication in the Netherlands, it does pose the question whether the courts are not too reticent in adjudicating sensitive matters such as asylum practice and policy. Treaty review might exist, but its exercise must not be allowed to fade into the sunset if it is to fulfil any role in helping to maintain the rule of law.

In gauging the country's rule of law culture, it is therefore somewhat concerning then that a member of parliament tabled a proposal in 2012 to prohibit the courts from reviewing the compatibility of acts of parliament with binding international law.[61] Whereas the previously discussed Halsema bill wants to introduce constitutional review along the lines of treaty review, the Taverne bill wants to abolish treaty review along the lines of the bar on constitutional review. The bill argues that norms of international law are vague and should therefore be interpreted by the legislature because of its greater democratic legitimacy than that of appointed judges.[62] Were the Taverne bill to succeed in amending the Constitution – a slim prospect, one imagines, given the legislative hurdles it would have to pass – it would make the country's constitutional culture more dependent on external stimuli, as in *Salah Sheekh*, than on domestic impulses.[63] It is therefore encouraging that the Council of State, which gives advice on bills apart from acting as one of the country's highest courts, has severely criticised the proposal for, among other reasons, not showing why the courts are to be denied the power of review.[64]

[60] Parliamentary Papers II 2006–2007, 29 344 and 30 800 VI, no. 64.

[61] Parliamentary Papers II 2011–2012, 33 359 (R 1986), nos. 2, 6.

[62] Parliamentary Papers II 2011–2012, 33 359 (R 1986), no. 6, p. 6–7, 10.

[63] The fact that the Member of Parliament responsible for the bill, Joost Taverne, later tabled a bill relying on the current role of the judiciary, instead of its exclusion, in applying international law confirms the slim chance of the proposed amendment succeeding. According to the new bill, which is not aimed at amending the Constitution, judges can only apply international law after parliament's express instead of implied consent in approving a new treaty. The effect would be to increase parliamentary oversight instead of sidelining the constitutional function of the judiciary. See Parliamentary Papers II 2014–2015, 34 158 (R 2048), nos. 2, 5.

[64] Parliamentary Papers II 2011–2012, 33 359 (R 1986), no. 4.

In addition the Council for the Judiciary, which advises on matters that affect the courts, warned that the bill would seriously affect the quality of the *Rechtsstaat* by not recognising that the courts complement the legislature instead of vying with the legislature.[65] In other words, both the legislature and the courts are necessary to ensure the quality of legislation, and not just one or the other.[66]

Evaluation and Explanation

On the basis of the above we can typify the Dutch Constitution more as a general guide to the exercise of political power, as opposed to a collection of robust guarantees in the service of rule-of-law values. The Netherlands is marked by a rather sober or moderate constitutional culture, and by a strong distance between constitution and politics. As one author had it, 'It is virtually impossible to find any politician in The Hague [the seat of Parliament] who would want to win or lose a political debate on the ground that a certain topic would be contravening the Dutch Constitution.'[67] As a result, there are very few people, apart from those who belong to the inner circle of constitutional specialists, who consider themselves as the 'guardians of the constitution'. The Dutch Constitution does not function as a strong normative document[68]; it is rather

65 Para. 3.2 of the letter from the Council for the Judiciary of 17 May 2013 addressed to the chair of the lower house of parliament. For the letter, see http://www.rechtspraak.nl/Organisatie/Raad-Voor-De-Rechtspraak/Wetgevingsadvisering/Wetgevingsadviezen2013/2013-15-Advies-Taverne.pdf (Dutch).

66 It can be added that the Dutch policy response to critical recommendations of international human rights bodies is generally defensive and sometimes borders on complete denial. See J. Krommendijk, 'Dutch Denial? The Response to Recommendations of International Human Rights Bodies' in *The Netherlands Yearbook of International Law* (Heidelberg/New York/Dordrecht/London: Springer, 2015) and J. Krommendijk, *The Domestic Impact and Effectiveness of the Process of State Reporting under UN Human Rights Treaties in the Netherlands, New Zealand and Finland. Paper Pushing or Policy Prompting?* (Antwerp: Intersentia, 2014).

67 L. F. M. Besselink, 'Constitutionele klimatologie', *Nederlands Juristenblad* (1998), 212 (Dutch). On constitutional culture see also G. F. M. van der Tang, *Grondwet en grondwetsidee* (Arnhem: Gouda Quint 1998), pp. 373–5 (Dutch); M. Adams, 'Constitutional and Socio-Political Dynamics in the Netherlands and Belgium' in H. Glaser (ed.), *Norms, Interests, and Values. Conflict and Consent in the Basic Constitutional Order* (Baden Baden: Nomos Verlag, 2015), pp. 89–129.

68 The expression of its normativity differs essentially from that of neighbouring Belgium for instance, especially in the realm of the relations between the different constituent parts of the Belgian federation. See M. Adams, 'Disabling Constitutionalism', *International Journal of Constitutional Law*, 12 (2014), 279–302.

a codification of political practice than the other way round.[69] All this might not necessarily be considered a problem. Because since the Netherlands is generally regarded as a tolerant and democratic nation, the Dutch might as well praise themselves for such a situation.

So how can this constitutional culture be explained? And what are its implications? Arend Lijphart's political theory could well offer an explanation for the specific institutional configuration of the Dutch politico-constitutional system, and also for the behaviour of the actors shaping this. Lijphart has termed his theory 'consociational democracy'.[70] It means 'government by elite cartel to turn a democracy with a fragmented political culture into a stable democracy'.[71]

A consociational democracy, as is clear from the definition just cited, is most often found in societies that are strongly divided. While it was generally assumed that political stability was beyond reach for such societies, Lijphart demonstrated that political *in*stability is not a predestined terminus for fragmented or even disunited societies. The potentially destabilising effects of division are on the contrary likely to prompt established political actors to search for pragmatic ways to deal with societal cleavages. Alternative methods of political accommodation, contrary to regular majoritarian politics, are thus explored, and the different segments in society actively strive for cooperation, consensus and stability: they seek to find each other and to cherish common ground as much as possible. As a result, differences between (ruling) groups are not politicised or exaggerated and a substantial number of the political leaders cooperate in governing the country, thus neutralising destabilising tendencies. This also should prevent major political groups from becoming estranged from the political system. As a result, although political decision-making in consociational democracies is strongly affected by the interplay of past and present political and other tensions, in practice, so the theory goes, it operates in a way that defuses these tensions and encourages compromise.

The hallmarks of a consociational democracy are broad government coalitions, political proportionality (in elections and representative

[69] As the Dutch scholar J. van der Hoeven already in 1958 observed, in his seminal *De plaats van de grondwet in het constitutionele recht* (Zwolle: Tjeenk Willink, 1958) (Dutch).

[70] On this, see in particular his *The Politics of Accommodation. Pluralism and Democracy in the Netherlands* (Berkeley: University of California Press, 1968); *Democracy in Plural Societies: A Comparative Exploration* (New Haven: Yale University Press, 1977); and *Democracies: Patterns of Majoritarian and Consensus Government in Twenty-One Countries* (New Haven: Yale University Press, 1984).

[71] A. Lijphart, 'Consociational Democracy', *World Politics*, 21 (1969), 216.

bodies, but also in advisory bodies, the civil service, etc.), mutual rights of veto in political decision-making, and 'pillarisation'. *Pillarisation* is a term that describes the vertical organisation of a society along traditional ideological, religious, and/or politico-economic divides. Pillarised societies are divided in several smaller segments, or pillars, according to different religions or (mainly socio-economic) ideologies. Each of these pillars has its own social institutions (broadcast companies, newspapers, schools and universities, sports clubs, mutual sickness funds, etc.) and resources, with each group retaining autonomy of how to use them. As the political scientist Van Schendelen observed, 'In the pillarized society the cleavages between the . . . main social grouping were such that "the common government" could handle only a few issues and usually only in a procedural way, leaving as much substantial decision-making as possible to the pillars themselves.'[72]

The Netherlands played an important part in the development of Lijphart's views and theories. In the past the country was deeply ideologically divided between liberals and socialists, and between Catholics and Protestants. According to Lijphart, Dutch society from the 1960s onwards was a classic example of both a pillarised society and a consociational democracy.[73] Through the pillars, societal tensions were contained, as it were, and potential problems were resolved by means decision-making among the elites of these pillars. Due to the complicated nature of the process of reaching political compromises, the political elite mostly made decisions behind closed doors. Transparency was no hallmark of consociational democracy.

What is important to note here is that, although the Dutch pillars have crumbled as religious divisions have weakened and large groups of society have become emancipated, elite compromise still remains a key theme and operational device in Dutch political decision-making.[74] Indeed, Dutch society and its institutions often still avail themselves of

72 M. van Schendelen, 'The Netherlands: From Low to High Politicisation' in M. van Schendelen and R. J. Jackson (eds.), *The Politicisation of Business in Western Europe* (London: Croom Helm, 1987), p. 65.

73 And he considered Belgium to be 'the most thorough example of a consociational democracy'. A. Lijphart, 'The Belgian Example of Cultural Coexistence in Comparative Perspective' in A. Lijphart (ed.), *Conflict and Coexistence in Belgium. The Dynamics of a Culturally Divided Society* (Berkeley: Institute of International Studies, 1981), p. 1. See also A. Lijphart, *Democracy in Plural Societie: A Comparative Exploration* (New Haven: Yale University Press, 1977), pp. 223–38.

74 R. Hague and M. Harrop, *Comparative Government and Politics* (Basingstoke: Palgrave MacMillan, 2007), p. 115.

channels other than constitutional and rule-of-law discourse to deal with social or political conflicts and interests, including the protection of fundamental rights. But whereas previously societal problems were solved within the so-called pillars, today pivotal organisations dealing with these problems include, next to parliament, the Council of State, the Social and Economic Council, the Auditor's Office, the Scientific Council for Government Policy, the High Council of the Judiciary, Ombudspersons, and other public advisory, controlling or decision-making bodies.[75]

In line with Lijphart's reasoning, it could then well be argued that the renowned late-twentieth-century Dutch 'polder model' is an offshoot of consociational democracy. The phrase 'polder model' has uncertain origins, but is mostly used to describe the typically Dutch version of consensus politics developed in the 1980s and 1990s in socio-economic affairs.[76] The term, referring to the typical Dutch 'polders',[77] is shorthand for an institutionalised form of cooperation and consensus-seeking between political actors, social partners and other societal organisations. The term was, however, also quickly adopted in other situations of pragmatic consensus decision-making by elites in the face of diversity and plurality. So, following the gradual dissolution of the old 'pillarised' way of organising Dutch society, the Dutch system of political decision-making found new, distinctly non-judicial and non-legal ways to avoid potential bottlenecks in political decision-making processes.

If this were a correct evaluation, it would not be unfair to state that the Dutch are constitutionally relativistic and sometimes even maybe negligent, but one might be led to believe that this is not a problem, given the country's perceived democratic maturity. 'Blessed is the country that has such a firm democratic order, that the Constitution can be safely

[75] The Council of State for example *advises*, next to being the highest administrative court, on the legislative quality (including the constitutionality) of pending bills.

[76] J. J. Woldendorp, *The Polder Model: From Disease to Miracle? Dutch Neo-Corporatism 1965–2000* (Amsterdam: Thela, 2005), p. 28.

[77] A polder refers to a piece of land won from the water and enclosed by embankments such as dykes. Although not typically Dutch, polders are usually associated with the country's landscape. The analogy is according to many used for the Dutch way of political decision-making, where since the Middle Ages, different communities living in the same polder had to cooperate with one another to prevent flooding and disaster for all, even when they were at odds with each other. So the potentially destabilising effects of conflict paradoxically prompted the political actors to search for pragmatic ways to cooperate and to deal with the potentially disastrous effects of flooding.

ignored!', one might be tempted to remark.[78] And in any case, under such conditions, a weak constitutional culture could be considered advantageous, because it at least does not act as an obstacle for the smooth – non-legal – facilitation and absorption of economic, social and cultural developments.

The question for us of course is whether or not this last evaluation is correct, and if the relativistic Dutch constitutional culture is still fitting for contemporary society. The composition of Dutch society has in any case been changing significantly through immigration in the last few decades, especially as a result of the arrival of new ethnic and religious minorities, Muslims in particular.[79] This presents the country with pressing issues surrounding integration, even more so since many immigrants belong to disadvantaged groups. The pressures were amplified for instance by the murders of the politician Pim Fortuyn in 2002 and of public commentator Theo van Gogh in 2004. Social divisions are in any case deepening, but the traditional pillars are not there anymore to even out potential societal tensions. The rise of the populist, anti-elitist right and left is strong and seems to be enduring, there have been multiple calls for more-direct democracy,[80] and political competition seems to intensify with no guaranteed voters available anymore, as was the case in the era of pillarisation. The dominant political configuration is nevertheless still elitist and operates within the consociational tradition. There is a lot of criticism of this situation though, because it hampers institutional and constitutional reform. In this sense, consensus government in a *de*pillarised society might even breed populism and anti-democratic and anti-establishment tendencies.[81] As it develops, the typical Dutch elitist way of political decision-making can thus harden or rigidify pre-existing group differences,[82] with political instability as the result. In the Netherlands, constitutional relativism – which as we have argued might be understood as an offshoot of elitist decision-making – nevertheless still prevails, even though it is a constitutional relativism in an unstable political culture.

[78] W. J. Witteveen, 'Hoe instructief moet de Grondwet zijn?', *Socialisme en Democratie*, 11 (2008), 54 (Dutch).

[79] On this see Andeweg and Irwin, *Governance*, p. 49ff. [80] *Ibid.*, p. 51.

[81] *Ibid.*, p. 286.

[82] R. Pildes, 'The Legal Structure of Democracy' in K. Whittington, R. Keleman and G. Kaldeira (eds.), *The Oxford Handbook of Law and Politics* (Oxford University Press, 2008), p. 333.

Two Proposals

We have seen that the Netherlands cannot be classified as marked by a well-developed constitutional and rule-of-law culture. As a result the Dutch Constitution does not play a prominent role in channelling and/or constraining the political process. If we believe this to be a problematic situation, this provokes the question, 'To what extent could or should consensus government be supplemented or replaced by a more fully developed constitutional culture, in order to enable political stability and diffuse societal tensions?' Can a constitution fulfil such an enabling function? Here we will present two proposals based on the preceding analysis. The first represents a bottom-up approach, and the second a top-down approach, the idea also being that they facilitate each other.

To begin with the last question, according to Stephen Holmes, a constitution can indeed assume an enabling role. A constitution can help create or facilitate the very *demos* which governs itself through the constitutional regime, a situation he calls 'positive constitutionalism'.[83] In this sense a state can use its constitutional powers to achieve cooperation and support, and use a constitution to construct power and guide it 'towards socially desirable ends, and prevent social chaos and private oppression, immobilism, unaccountability, instability, and the ignorance and stupidity of politicians'.[84] As Choudhry has it, 'Concrete experiences of shared decision-making within the framework of the rule of law, and without resource to force or fraud, can serve as the germ of a nascent sense of political community.' It can 'constitute a *demos* by encoding and projecting a certain vision of political community with the view of altering the very self-understanding of citizens'.[85]

At the same time, in a complex democracy any important public policy is likely to create disagreement, and inevitably such disagreement will advance some interests and values while threatening others. This will of course also have an impact on the perceived legitimacy of such choices.[86]

[83] S. Holmes, *Passions and Constraint. On the Theory of Liberal Democracy* (University of Chicago Press, 1995), pp. xi–xiii, 5–7, 161–4.

[84] *Ibid.*, p. 51.

[85] S. Choudhry, 'Bridging Comparative Politics and Comparative Constitutional Law: Constitutional Design in Divided Societies' in S. Choudhry (ed.), *Constitutional Design for Divided Societies. Integration or Accommodation?* (Oxford University Press, 2008), p. 6.

[86] W. F. Murphy, *Constitutional Democracy. Creating and Maintaining a Just Political Order* (Baltimore: The Johns Hopkins University Press, 2007), pp. 332–3.

This is what Sunstein calls 'deliberative trouble',[87] and such a situation is unavoidably part and parcel of any society which is prepared to call itself democratic. What is, however, important to note here is that this political disagreement can be heightened, simply by virtue of the fact that like-minded people mostly, and sometimes even exclusively, talk *to one another*. As a result they are likely to end up thinking a more extreme version of what they thought before; social fragmentation will be the result, a situation which has to be avoided but which today is very much amplified by new technologies such as the Internet.

This brings us to our first proposal. The Dutch 'official' relativistic constitutional culture is not surprisingly mirrored in the lack of knowledge of the Constitution among the general public.[88] A constitution can nevertheless provide us with a common language which makes it possible to communicate and debate about the – constitutionally warranted – values that seem to be constitutive for a polity.[89] That could enhance or steer the process of reason-giving, 'ensuring something like a "republic of reasons"'.[90] A necessary, albeit not sufficient, condition for a healthy constitutional culture, where reason-giving is prime, is thus the development of a more engendered form of *constitutional literacy.*[91] Constitutional literacy reminds us of the concept of cultural literacy as it was coined by E. D. Hirsch.[92] Hirsch states that in order to be able to communicate in a meaningful way with each other, people have to be able to rest or rely upon a minimal common body of knowledge. For this, more than just knowledge of words and facts is necessary; a shared contextual knowledge and culture is also important. 'The complex undertakings of modern life depend on the cooperation of many people with different specialties in different places. Where communications fail, so do the undertakings. (That is the moral of the story of the Tower of

[87] C. R. Sunstein, *Designing Democracy. What Constitutions Do* (Oxford University Press, 2001), pp. 239–43.

[88] See B. Oomen, 'Constitutioneel bewustzijn in Nederland: van Burgerzin, burgerschap en de onzichtbare Grondwet', *Recht der Werkelijkheid*, 30 (2009), 55 (Dutch). Only 15 per cent of the respondents to a questionnaire about constitutional knowledge thought they knew the Dutch constitution reasonably well or even good. See in the context of human rights also B. Oomen, *Rights for Others: The Slow Home-Coming of Human Rights in the Netherlands* (Cambridge University Press, 2013).

[89] We are not talking about detailed constitutional knowledge here.

[90] Sunstein, *Designing*, p. 239.

[91] On this M. Adams, 'Constitutionele geletterdheid voor de democratische rechtsstaat', *Nederlands Juristenblad*, 88 (2013), 1110 (Dutch).

[92] E. D. Hirsch, *Cultural Literacy. What Every American Needs to Know* (New York: First Vintage Books, 1988).

Babel).'[93] Hirsch emphasises that too big an information dissymmetry or imbalance can result in a certain service not being present at all anymore. 'Ultimately our aim should be to attain literacy at a very high level, to achieve not only greater economic prosperity but also greater social justice and more effective democracy.'[94] There is hardly any reason to believe that this would not be true of constitutionalism too, which is all the more reason to make more work of constitutional literacy.

A stable polity also needs institutions that can efficiently settle controversies.[95] Not, that is, just controversies among citizens or groups of citizens, but also between officials and private citizens. And by 'settling', here we mean dealing with constitutional questions according to official procedures that most officials as well as most politically aware and active citizens will, most of the time, consider legitimate.[96] Returning to the institutional dimension of the Dutch constitutional fabric, what is clear from the analysis in this chapter is that in the Netherlands there are hardly any 'after the fact' constitutional warranties in the system of checks and balances. With the exception of treaty review, which is subject to the courts' reticence, nearly all constitutional checks are situated *before* legislation is approved (and mostly in an advisory sense), leaving the constitutional system almost completely dependent on political majority rule.[97] We submit, and this is our second proposal, that the introduction of judicial constitutional review in the Netherlands might be one way of facilitating an enabling or capacitating dimension to Dutch constitutionalism. In this vein, Sunstein rightly stresses that the creative use of judicial power in terms of judicial constitutional review can be used to energise a democracy.[98] But under the condition that it is indeed not just looked at as a system of 'blocking' government by having just one competence – i.e. simply and unequivocally striking down legislation – but that it can also be used as a means to start a constitutional dialogue, leaving ground for the legislature to act upon questions that a constitution

[93] *Ibid.*, p. 2. [94] *Ibid.* [95] Murphy, *Constitutional Democracy*, p. 333.

[96] This of course also provokes questions about *what* it is these institutions should interpet: the text of the Constitution, or the broad constitutional order? And also questions about *how* what is to be interpreted should be interpreted. See Murphy, *Constitutional Democracy*, p. 333.

[97] See also A. Brenninkmeijer, 'Stresstest rechtsstaat Nederland', *Nederlands Juristenblad* (2015), 1046 (Dutch). Brenninkmeijer talks about 'complete systemic failure'.

[98] Sunstein, *Designing*, p. 241.

poses. In this way it is able to find a balanced middle ground between a parliamentary type of democracy on the one hand and a constitutionally entrenched democracy on the other; a supplement, in other words, to the Dutch political system. Therefore, one road ahead might be to come up with an institutional design that also provides the opportunity to stimulate a dialogue[99] between the legislature and the judiciary on the content of the Constitution.[100] Inspiration can for example be found in Canada. The Canadian Charter of Rights and Freedoms states in section 33 (also known as the 'notwithstanding clause') that 'Parliament or the legislature of a province may expressly declare in an Act of Parliament or of the legislature, as the case may be, that the Act or a provision thereof shall operate notwithstanding a provision included in . . . this Charter'. The clause can be used to negate for a limited (but through re-adoption renewable) period of time any federal or provincial judicial review by overriding the rights enunciated in the Charter. A declaration to that extent should be included in the law, specifying which rights have been overridden. Such a declaration lapses after five years or a lesser time, as specified in the clause. In effect, this means that parliament or the provincial legislature can restrict the applicability of certain sections of the Charter dealing with fundamental freedoms, as for example expression, religion, the press, or due process and equal protection. Section 33 is, as former Canadian Supreme Court Justice Frank Iacobucci has said, 'a vivid reminder of Canada's parliamentary tradition, that sovereignty resides . . . in Parliament and the provincial legislatures and that parliamentary supremacy is not yet a matter of pure historical interest'.[101] Although hardly used, a main attraction of

[99] The dialogical metaphor was first used by P. W. Hogg and A. Bushell, 'The Charter Dialogue between Courts and Legislatures', *Osgoode Hall Law Journal*, 35 (1997), 75. There exists a wealth of literature on this topic. A prominent believer in this type of dialogue is K. Roach, *The Supreme Court on Trial: Judicial Activism or Democratic Dialogue* (Toronto: Irwin Law, 2001). Critical of the democratic potential of such an arrangement, is L. B. Tremblay, 'The Legitimacy of Judicial Review: The Limits of Dialogue between Courts and Legislatures', *International Journal of Constitutional Law*, 3 (2005), 617.

[100] Another example might be the situation in the United Kingdom under the Human Rights Act. See e.g. J. Jowell, 'Judicial deference: servility, civility or institutional capacity?', *Public Law*, (2003), 592; R. Clayton, 'Judicial Deference and "Democratic Dialogue": The Legitimacy of Judicial Intervention under the Human Rights Act 1988', *Public Law*, (2004), 33. And, most prominently, A. Sathanapally, *Beyond Disagreement. Open Remedies in Human Rights Adjudication* (Oxford University Press, 2012).

[101] F. Iacobucci, 'Judicial Review by the Supreme Court of Canada under the Canadian Charter of Rights and Freedoms' in D. M. Beatty (ed.), *Human Rights and Judicial Review. A Comparative Perspective* (Dordrecht: Martinus Nijhoff, 1994), p. 106.

the provision is that it forces politicians to accept the responsibility that comes with the use of section 33 and give reasons for such a limitation of rights.[102] The provision can thus engender democratic public and parliamentary debate on the constitutional issues at stake.

All this of course raises concrete – prominently including empirical – questions of a constitution's normative and practical value. Under what conditions does a constitution make a difference in real life in a specific jurisdiction, in other words? the answers to these questions are necessarily a combination of general insights about constitutional compliance and development, in combination with informed estimations about how these insights match highly contingent local conditions. As a result, the answers are not clear-cut, and there does not seem to exist an objective or ideal set of rules for matching a people and their situation with a set of institutions.[103] But whatever the case may be, there is one general insight we are willing to pose here, namely that democratic politics without constitutionalism is troublesome; in the long run no democracy can survive such a state of affairs.[104] Societal instability indeed comes with an array of negative consequences, the possibility of violence being one of them. The inability of the Dutch Constitution to sufficiently govern the dynamics of the political power process and its insufficient role in forging a polity can therefore be understood as a warning of the demise of the state's possibilities to effectively act as the agent of its citizens' well-being. In such conditions, the Constitution runs the risk of falling prey to deliberate political manipulation.

Rounding Up

'A constitution is what power holders and power addressees make of it in practical application', Loewenstein wrote.[105] That of course is a true. It is nevertheless important to be aware of the fact that constitutionalism and

[102] Cf. A. S. Butler, 'Judicial Review, Human Rights and Democracy' in G. Huscroft and P. Rishwort (eds.), *Litigating Rights. Perspectives from Domestic and International Law* (Oxford: Hart Publishing, 2002), p. 69.

[103] See D. S. Lutz, *Principles of Constitutional Design* (Cambridge University Press, 2006), p. ix. Loewenstein too discards the idea of trying to devise a 'perfect theoretical constitution', instead claiming that 'an ideal constitution has never existed, and will never exist'. See: Loewenstein, *Political Power*, p. 151.

[104] Cf. H. van Gunsteren, 'Het staatsrecht in de politiek', *Nederlands Juristenblad* (2010), 1111.

[105] Loewenstein, *Political power*, p. 148.

rule-of-law values, concepts which are supposed to have authority through constitutions, cannot fly on autopilot. They need maintenance and active direction, so as to create a conducive constitutional culture. Constitutions, and courts, might in this process be seen as the indispensable oxygen to keep the flame of liberty alive.[106] The demise of the old pillars, that constituted society in the Netherlands and formed the basis of its governance and the key to its political stability, might therefore alert one to the need to develop a stronger constitutional culture and to help fill the vacuum left by the dissolution of the old power structures.

[106] Cf. R. Dworkin, 'What Is Democracy?' in G. A. Tóth (ed.), *Constitution for a Disunited Nation. On Hungary's 2011 Fundamental Law* (Budapest/New York: Central European University Press, 2012), pp. 33–4.

13

Illiberal Rule of Law? Changing Features of Hungarian Constitutionalism

GÁBOR ATTILA TÓTH*

Introduction

Law rules in modern societies. A great many scholarly descriptions follow the Hobbesian view that law is a fruit of human civilization.[1] Law as a system of rules[2] or a practice of authoritative institutions to mediate people's interests[3] can be considered an invention of human culture, one that allows communities to regulate social relations efficiently and effectively.[4]

Descriptive observations and normative claims support the standard belief that constitutions are necessary and distinguished parts of contemporary legal systems. Almost every country in the world accepts Tocqueville's claim that the term 'constitution' refers to the highest set of written legal rules.[5] Although constitutions vary immensely in terms of their content, they typically frame institutional design, i.e. powers of the legislative, executive and judicial branches and other crucial domestic organizations; determine the authoritative sources of law; set out fundamental civil and political rights of inhabitants; and – last, but by no means least – settle some integrative principles and symbols of the state and society.

* The author thanks Maurice Adams, Dimitry Kochenov, Kriszta Kovács, Martin Krygier, Jonathan Tomkin and Mila Versteeg for their valuable comments and suggestions.

1 T. Hobbes, *Leviathan*, R. Tuck (ed.) (Cambridge University Press, 1996), p. 89.

2 H. L. A. Hart, *The Concept of Law*, P. A. Bulloch and J. Raz (eds.), 2nd edn (Oxford: Clarendon Press, 1994), pp. 102–10.

3 J. Raz, *The Authority of Law, Essays on Law and Morality* (Oxford: Clarendon Press, 1994), pp. 37–9

4 S. J. Shapiro, *Legality* (Cambridge, MA/London: The Belknap Press of Harvard University Press, 2011), p. 36.

5 A. de Tocqueville, *Democracy in America* (London/New York: Penguin Books, 2003), p. 130.

Evolving legal systems and especially constitutional transformations have received widespread scholarly attention.[6] One of the countries currently in focus is Hungary. Since 2010 the Hungarian government, backed by a two-thirds parliamentary majority, has been altering the whole legal system, most importantly the constitutional structure. The basic elements of the previous Constitution were promulgated in October 1989, on the thirty-third anniversary of the 1956 revolution, two weeks before the fall of the Berlin Wall. The new Constitution (called the Fundamental Law) was promulgated on April 2011, Easter Monday, on the first anniversary of the 2010 parliamentary elections, which qualified the winning party to reshape the constitutional system.

The new Hungarian constitutional reality based upon the Fundamental Law has provoked many descriptive analyses from and normative debate among specialists in Hungarian and comparative law and politics. Although, on the face of it, the Fundamental Law upholds rule of law, primary status of human rights, and parliamentary architecture with constitutional constraints, the way the text was drafted as well as the content of the text itself are highly controversial, not to mention the frequent subsequent modifications.

Some scholars argue that the determining factor is legal continuity: since the former legal order remained valid, and a democratically elected parliament adopted the Fundamental Law in conformity with the old Constitution's two-thirds rule, the new system is both legal and legitimate.[7] According to many opposing views, however, this has nothing to do with the formally continuous legality because the Fundamental Law and its subsequent amendments are in conflict with the basic normative features of constitutional legitimacy.[8]

While most analysts agree that regardless of legal continuity, we have been witnessing a course of model change in Hungarian constitutionalism,

[6] See e.g. B. Ackerman, *We the People, Volume 2: Transformations* (Harvard, MA/London: The Belknap Press of Harvard University Press, 1998); R. G. Teitel, *Transitional Justice* (Oxford University Press, 2000); J. Kis, 'Between Reform and Revolution', *East European Politics & Societies*, 12(2) (1998), 300–83; L. E. Miller (ed.), *Framing the State in Times of Transition: Case Studies in Constitution Making* (Washington: US Institute of Peace, 2010).

[7] A. Jakab, P. Sonnevend, 'Kontinuität mit Mängeln: Das neue ungarische Grundgesetz', *Zeitschrift für ausländisches öffentliches Recht und Völkerrecht*, 72 (2012), 79–102.

[8] M. Bánkuti, G. Halmai, K. L. Scheppele, 'Hungary's Illiberal Turn: Disabling the Constitution', *The Journal of Democracy*, 23 (2013), 138–46; G. A. Tóth (ed.), *Constitution for a Disunited Nation: On Hungary 2011 Fundamental Law* (Budapest, New York: Central University Press, 2012).

they draw remarkably different conclusions. On the one hand, the new system receives favourable reviews because reportedly the Fundamental Law and its governmental enforcement replace judicial supremacy with parliamentary sovereignty. The representative government of Hungary gives the majority of people what they want instead of the former rule of 'juristocracy', i.e. the counter-majoritarian activity, indeed, time-to-time zealotry, of the unelected Constitutional Court.[9] On the other hand, several critics warn that the aim behind the Fundamental Law is to safeguard and promote the interests of a particular political force and its constituency, without constitutional checks and balances. What is more, several constitutional or statutory provisions are framed in a manner suggesting that they either do not reach the level of protection required by international human rights conventions, or require conduct that is incompatible with the principles and individual rights listed in those instruments.[10]

Political theorists also face difficulties when they attempt to label the new Hungarian constitutional system. In formal terms it still belongs to constitutional democracies, but according to various views the Hungarian democracy is majoritarian rather than consensual, populist instead of elitist, nationalist as opposed to cosmopolitan, religious and not neutral. In sum, it is based upon realist considerations in place of idealist theories. Jan-Werner Müller, a prominent observer of the Hungarian transformation, applies the term 'illiberal democracy'[11] to Hungary because political power is based upon repetitive elections, but the power-holders systematically violate the freedoms of the people they represent. More than this, Hungarian Prime Minister Viktor Orbán has proudly announced his government's break with liberal democracy.[12] The late Ronald Dworkin, however, would argue that what we are experiencing is not democratic at all. The unrestrained majoritarian decision-making 'has set the country on a road to the ruin of democracy

[9] See generally M. Tushnet, *Taking the Constitution Away from the Courts* (Princeton University Press, 1999); R. Hirschl, *Towards Juristocracy: The Origins and Consequences of the New Constitutionalism* (Cambridge, MA: Harvard University Press, 2007).

[10] J. McBride, 'Trees in the Wood: The Fundamental Law and the European Court of Human Rights' in Tóth (ed.), *Constitution*, pp. 359–70.

[11] F. Zakaria, 'The Rise of Illiberal Democracy', *Foreign Affairs*, 76 (1997), 6, 22–43.

[12] J-W. Müller, 'Eastern Europe Goes South: Disappearing Democracy in the EU's Newest Members', *Foreign Affairs*, 93, 2 (2014), 22–43. J-W. Müller, 'Moscow's Trojan Horse: In Europe's Ideological War, Hungary Picks Putinism', *Foreign Affairs*, 6 August 2014. www.foreignaffairs.com/articles/141825/jan-werner-mueller/moscows-trojan-horse (Accessed 31 August 2015).

because it has subverted the most basic principles that would entitle the community to claim that it's a partnership of self-government.'[13]

In this piece I examine the Hungarian constitutional transformation from a different perspective. I put the concept of 'rule of law' into the main focus for a better understanding of the nature of the Hungarian regime-changes and the competing scholarly positions. First, I summarize briefly the story of the rise and fall of the legal system based upon the 1989 Constitution and the emergence of a new regime founded by the 2011 Fundamental Law. The contrast between the two legal systems raises the normative question whether the new regime represents an alternative conception of rule of law or goes beyond this notion. So as to provide an answer to this question, the second part describes two rival traditions of rule of law, which I call Lockean (rule of law by a limited government) and Hobbesian (rule of law by a sovereign government) conceptions. The Lockean tradition became influential during the development of the 1989 system. The Hobbesian conception, which is a historical predecessor of Locke's ideas, turned out to be arguably a powerful justificatory idea of the 2011 Fundamental Law. In the third part, however, I argue that the new Hungarian constitutional system is not a step to an alternative, equally valid rule-of-law conception. The Hobbesian tradition may open the way to gradual liberal and democratic advancements with substantive rule of law guarantees. In contrast, the Fundamental Law and its amendments lead to an authoritarian regime, where rule of law is a purely formalistic concept. Hungary is ruled, of course, by law. But descriptive analysis and normative claims support the same conclusion: this kind of law is neither a fruitful product of the society nor a limit on arbitrary governmental activity.

The Emergence of Two Different Constitutional Systems

The 1989 Constitution: 'Revolution under the Rule of Law'

After World War II, Stalinist dictatorships prevailed in Eastern Europe. In 1949 the communist-dominated Hungarian Parliament adopted a constitution – the first charter constitution to enter into force in the country – which closely followed the Soviet Stalinist Constitution of

[13] R. Dworkin, 'What Is Democracy?' in Tóth (ed.), *Constitution*, p. 33.

1936. The regime based on legal and extra-legal repression occurred mainly in its first years and after the failure of the 1956 Revolution. Although the political system became gradually more consolidated, rule of law and constitutionalism were alien to the soft dictatorship, and the numerous constitutional changes that occurred during the communist period made little difference in this regard.

Like other communist constitutions, the provisions of the 1949 Constitution served purely ideological purposes; in other words, as a semantic constitution it was a political declaration and was never intended to serve as normative guidance in the actual use of political power, which was determined by the interests and whims of the Communist Party leadership. Formally, Hungary was considered to be a parliamentary system; in reality, however, the Communist Party made all crucial decisions and most of these decisions were transposed into law through constitutional organs (Parliament, Presidium, or Council of Ministers). Officially, the judicial system enjoyed personal and institutional independence, but many sources reveal that the Communist Party interfered constantly and harshly in the administration of justice. The 1949 Constitution recognized certain fundamental rights, but only to the extent that these rights served the interests of the workers. The formal constitutional system did not intend to provide genuine protection of fundamental rights at all, since the 1949 Constitution could not be invoked in court.

The historical turning point for the transformation from authoritarian regime to democracy was the autumn of 1989. The single-party system collapsed through a series of negotiations and compromises between the old regime and the democratic opposition. In formal terms, the 1989 Constitution was a mere modification of the 1949 Constitution. In substantive terms, however, the 1989 political transition breathed new life into the Hungarian Constitution. Since the models of the reshaped Constitution were international human rights instruments, as well as the more recent Western constitutions, it was written in the language of modern constitutionalism.[14]

The 1989-born democracy can be characterized by the main institutions of constitutionalism: free and fair elections, representative government, a parliamentary system, an independent judiciary, ombudspersons

[14] In more detail, see G. A. Tóth, 'Hungary' in L. Besselink, P. Bovend'Eert, H. Broeksteeg, R. de Lange and W. Voermans (eds.), *Constitutional Law of the EU Member States* (Deventer: Kluwer, 2014), pp. 775–9.

to guard fundamental rights, and a Constitutional Court to review the laws for their constitutionality. According to two of the ground-breaking principles, the Republic of Hungary 'shall be an independent, democratic State under the rule of law' and 'shall recognize the inviolable and inalienable fundamental human rights; respecting and protecting these rights are primary obligations of the State.'

Like other post-communist Eastern European democracies, Hungary followed Western European traditions in establishing an adapted parliamentary system instead of importing a United States presidential architecture.[15] The Hungarian Constitution copied the German Chancellor-led system, including a weak president elected by the parliamentary representatives. A 1990 constitutional amendment made it clear that the Prime Minister heads the executive and the Government is the supreme body of that branch, responsible to Parliament. Judicial protection of the Constitution was also closer to the centralized German model than to the US judicial review.[16] This meant that the Constitutional Court was institutionally separated from the ordinary court system and had unique, *erga omnes* constitutional interpretative authority. One of the main reasons for this was that the transition was characterized by a deep mistrust of the judiciary among the new elites and the masses, as it was considered to be a means of oppression from the previous regime.[17]

Under the 1989 constitutional system, the broadest competence of the Hungarian Constitutional Court was the abstract constitutional review of legal rules, when there was no case or controversy. Anyone was entitled to bring an action without limitation; there were no deadlines to be observed nor was the applicant required to show any impact or other legally protected interest (*actio popularis*).[18] In the first two decades the great majority of the proceedings fell in this category.

The Constitutional Court seemed to be the most important institutional guarantee of constitutionalism, on account of its decisions favouring

[15] L. Garlicki, 'Democracy and International Influences' in G. Nolte (ed.), *European and U.S. Constitutionalism* (Cambridge University Press, 2005), p. 264.

[16] From theoretical and critical point of view see, W. Sadurski, *Rights before Courts: A Study of Constitutional Courts in Post-Communist States of Central and Eastern Europe* (Dordrecht: Springer, 2005). See also H. Schwartz, *The Struggle for Constitutional Justice in Post-Communist Europe* (University of Chicago Press, 2000).

[17] A. Sajó, 'Contemporary Problems of the Judiciary in Hungary' in *The Social Role of the Legal Profession* (International Centre for Comparative Law and Politics, University of Tokyo, 1993).

[18] L. Sólyom and G. Brunner, *Constitutional Judiciary in a New Democracy: The Hungarian Constitutional Court* (Ann Arbor: The University of Michigan Press, 2000), p. 81.

human rights and principles of the rule of law.[19] The Court established a Rawlsian conception of state neutrality, and declared a broad protection of freedom of conscience (*Churches Case I*).[20] It adopted the Dworkinian conception of equal dignity and affirmative action (*Family Protection Case*).[21] With the help of the proportionality principle, and the *allgemeine Handlungsfreiheit* imported from Strasbourg and Karlsruhe, as well as the *clear and present danger* scrutiny derived from the US constitutional adjudication, the Court protected fundamental rights effectively (*General Personality Right Case*,[22] *Hate Speech Case I*).[23] The decision on the abolition of the death penalty (*Capital Punishment Case*),[24] the argument for which was based upon human dignity, served as an example for the Ukrainian, Lithuanian, Albanian and South-African Constitutional Courts.[25]

The substantive protection of constitutionalism was based upon the Constitutional Court's considerations on rule of law, including supremacy of the law, legal certainty, prohibition of *ex post facto* law and arbitrariness. In its landmark decision on the retroactive punishment of several crimes committed during the former non-democratic regime, the Constitutional Court famously stated the following in the *Retroactive Political Legislation Case I*:

> The change of system has been carried out on the basis of legality. The principle of legality imposes on the state governed by the rule of law the requirement that legal regulations regarding the legal system itself should be realized fully. The politically revolutionary changes adopted by the Constitution and all the new fundamental laws were enacted, in full

[19] C. Dupré, *Importing the Law in Post-Communist Transitions: The Hungarian Constitutional Court and the Right to Human Dignity* (Portland: Hart Publishing, 2003); S. Zifcak, 'Hungary's Remarkable, Radical, Constitutional Court', *Journal of Constitutional Law in Eastern and Central Europe*, 1(3) (1996), 1–56.

[20] Judgment 4/1993 HCC. J. Rawls, *A Theory of Justice* (Cambridge, MA: The Belknap Press of Harvard University Press, 1971).

[21] Judgment 9/1990 HCC. R. Dworkin, *Sovereign Virtue, the Theory and Practice of Equality* (Cambridge, MA: Harvard University Press, 2000). The Court determined the abstract principle of dignity in a Kantian way. However, the interpretive practice of the Court was also influenced by an alternative conception of the Second Vatican Council, a progressive but non-secular Catholic view. See also, G. A. Tóth, 'Unequal Protection: Historical Churches and Roma People in the Hungarian Constitutional Jurisprudence', *Acta Juridica Hungarica*, 51, 2 (2010), 122–35.

[22] Judgment 8/1990 HCC. [23] Judgment 30/1992 HCC. [24] Judgment 23/1990 HCC.

[25] *The State v. T. Makwanyane and M. Mchunu*, CCT/3/94, Judgment of 6 June 1995. See also V. Vaicaitis, 'The Constitutional Court of the Republic of Lithuania and the Death Penalty', *Review of Central and East European Law*, 1 (2000).

> compliance with the old legal system's procedural laws on legislation, thereby gaining their binding force. . . .
>
> A fundamental principle of the rule of law is legal certainty. Legal certainty demands, among others, the protection of vested rights, non-interference with legal relations already executed or concluded and limiting the possibility to modify existing long-term legal relations. . . .
>
> [T]he basic guarantees of the rule of law cannot be set aside by reference to historical situations and the state governed by the rule of law is a requirement of justice. A state governed by the rule of law cannot be created by undermining the rule of law.
>
> The Constitutional Court cannot ignore history since it has to fulfill its task embedded in history. The Constitutional Court is the repository of the paradox of the 'revolution under the rule of law': in the process of the peaceful transition, beginning with the new Constitution, the Constitutional Court must, within its competences, in all cases unconditionally guarantee the conformity of the legislative power with the Constitution.[26]

As a consequence, a peaceful, coordinated political transition resulted in the revolutionary outcomes embedded in the 1989 Constitution: a pluralist society replaced the dominance of communist ideology; democratic institutions replaced an authoritarian regime; and the judiciary changed from a tool of the ruling party to the implementer of rule-of-law requirements.

The Failures of the 1989 Constitutional System

Although Hungary set up what looks like a path to a mature democracy, the country faced from the beginning serious legal and extra-legal difficulties. First of all, it was the only nation in the region that did not adopt an entirely new constitution after the fall of Communism. The 1989 roundtables were meant to regulate the transition from the old regime to a new one, but they did not actually have a mandate for constitution making. They had neither the formal authorization to make law for the old regime nor the popular authorization to make law for the new regime. The roundtables therefore understood their task to be limited to facilitating the run-up to free, competitive elections, and were determined to leave it to an elected assembly to give a constitution to the new regime.

[26] Judgment 11/1992 HCC. See Sólyom and Brunner, *Constitutional Judiciary*, p. 214. G. A. Tóth, 'The Bitter Pills of Political Transition' in A. Jakab, P. Takács, A. Tatham (eds.), *The Transformation of the Hungarian Legal Order 1985–2005* (Alphen aan de Rijn: Kluwer Law International, 2007), pp. 281–6.

In order for their decisions to come into legal effect, those decisions needed to be sent for enactment to the old legislature.

Consequently, the roundtables were exceptional bodies having the capacity to start a coordinated process of constitutional change, but leaving the completion of the process to an assembly with the democratic mandate they were lacking.[27] János Kis has characterized the constitution-making profile of the 'revolution under the rule of law' as consisting of two stages. In the first stage, a roundtable agreement determines the ground rules of preparing and holding free elections. The second stage takes place when a body of freely elected representatives adopts, in the sovereign people's name, a new constitution.[28] Unlike the other post-communist countries, however, Hungary omitted the second step, as it did not adopt a formally new constitution prior to 2011.

This failure may seem unexpected because compared to those of other European states, the 1989 Hungarian Constitution was easy to amend. Despite the fact that the Constitution could not be modified or amended by the ordinary law-making procedure according to a simple majority rule, it was regarded as relatively flexible rather than rigid, in the sense that it did not render any provision or principle un-amendable, and it required only the votes of two-thirds of members of the one-chamber legislative body. Neither a referendum nor any other form of ratification (e.g., approval by the subsequent parliament) was required for the adoption of a new constitution or a constitutional amendment. The two-thirds parliamentary majority could not only modify the Constitution and several crucial acts, but also elect the President of the Republic, the Supreme Court Chief Justice, the members of the Constitutional Court, and ombudspersons.

[27] J. Kis, 'Introduction: From the 1989 Constitution to the 2011 Fundamental Law' in Tóth (ed.), *Constitution*, pp. 1–23. Kis characterizes the coordinated transition as an interruption of legitimacy, but continuity of legality. Kis, 'Between Reform and Revolution', p. 317. See also a critical reflection of the legitimacy of the 1989 Constitution, A. Arato, 'Dilemmas Arising from the Power to Create Constitutions in Eastern Europe' in M. Rosenfeld (ed.), *Constitutionalism, Difference, Identity, and Legitimacy* (Durham: Duke University Press, 1994), pp. 165–94.

[28] In the aftermath of the Polish Round Table Agreement, the old constitution was amended in April 1989, and the first democratic parliament then reshaped the relations between the legislative and executive branches of the state ('Small Constitution'). The reformed constitution was finally replaced in 1997 by a completely new constitution for Poland. The old constitution of Czechoslovakia was also amended in 1989. The Charter of Fundamental Rights and Basic Freedoms was incorporated in 1991. After the dissolution of the federal state, the Czech Republic and the Slovak Republic each adopted a new constitution in 1992. In Bulgaria and Romania, the second step was made in 1991.

As a further factor, a party could secure two-thirds of the parliamentary seats with a little more than 50 per cent of the votes, because Hungary had a mixed – majoritarian and proportionate – electoral system with single-member districts, county lists and a compensatory list. This kind of disproportionality enhanced the flexibility of the Constitution.

Prior to 2010, there was only one period, between 1994 and 1998, when the Government was supported by two-thirds of the seats in Parliament. During that period, Hungary made an attempt to bring the post-communist constitution-making process to a conclusion. Even though on a number of issues the then-ruling parties failed to seek the consent of the opposition regarding certain acts requiring a two-thirds majority, the governing coalition also expressed some willingness to co-operate with the opposition in constitution-making. They modified the procedural guarantees of the Constitution to the effect that Parliament should decide by a four-fifths majority in the preparatory process on the cornerstones of the new Constitution.

However, the talks in the constitution-making process collapsed in 1997 because of the hostile political environment and the divergent constitutional conceptions (the very same year Poland enacted its new constitution). The ideas of the rival political parties – even within the ruling coalition – regarding the legal frameworks of the political community were diffuse enough to prevent a consensus on a brand new constitution. This is why, although the 1989 Constitution was amended several times (e.g., to empower Hungary to join NATO and the European Union), the country did not accomplish the symbolic mission: it failed to adopt a constitution, which would have demonstrated a successful completion of the democratic transition.[29]

This lack of a new constitution increased the responsibilities of the Constitutional Court as the ultimate interpreter of fundamental rights, and the most crucial constitutional check on the powers of Parliament. The activism of the Constitutional Court seems undeniable. However, after the starting three or four years of its jurisdiction, the Court became much more self-restrained.[30] Moreover, the Constitutional Court had

[29] A. Arato, 'Post-Sovereign Constitution-Making in Hungary: After Success, Partial Failure, and Now What?', *South African Journal on Human Rights: Constitution-Making as a Learning Process*, 1, 26 (2010), 19–44. A. Arato, 'The Constitution-Making Endgame in Hungary', *East European Constitutional Review*, 5, 4 (1996), 31–9.

[30] Bruce Ackerman foresaw this. B. Ackerman, *The Future of Liberal Revolution* (New Haven, CT: Yale University Press, 1992), p. 110.

a Janus-faced constitutional adjudicatory role, especially when it was not able to escape from intolerant social attitudes or inappropriate political expectations. The Court, for example, never clashed with the legislature in order to support women's rights, and despite several petitions, the problems relating to the exclusion and discrimination of Roma remained absolutely hidden.[31] Between 2006 and 2010, the Court, activist again, almost paralysed the legislature by declaring an unprecedented number of newly adopted acts unconstitutional and void. During this period the Head of the State also vetoed as many acts as his predecessors did in the previous one-and-a-half decades. As an apparent result, citizens witnessed a 'checked and balanced' constitutional system, which did not work at all.

Last but not least, there were serious social and political tensions at work under the surface of the failed legal system. The political left and right were involved in a cold civil war with each other, and could not cooperate in partnership under and for a shared constitution.[32] They not only saw each other as competitors in the contest for an election victory but also as enemies who were detrimental to national existence and progress. A poor tradition of democratic political conventions, weakness of civil society, imperfections of public education, and other sociological factors all made the constitutional balance fragile. In other words, political reality threatened seriously the fulfilment of constitutional ideas.

The 2011 Fundamental Law: 'Revolution in the Polling Booth'

The two-thirds rule and the disproportionate electoral structure began working in 2010. In the parliamentary election, the then-opposition party Fidesz won a landslide majority of 68 per cent of the seats with 53 per cent of the votes. It was a majority sufficiently large to amend the Constitution or rewrite it totally.

During the election, the necessity of a new constitution was not on the agenda. However, very soon after the 2010 elections the new Prime Minister announced that he would provide a brand new constitution for the nation. As a first step, Parliament adopted a proclamation statement of national co-operation,[33] and a governmental ordinance was

[31] Tóth, 'Unequal Protection', 122–35.

[32] On partnership theory of democracy, see R. Dworkin, *Is Democracy Possible Here? Principles for a Political Debate* (Princeton University Press, 2006), pp. 131–47.

[33] 1/2010. (VI. 16.) Proclamation of the Parliament.

published which made it compulsory for the proclamation to be prominently displayed in governmental buildings. The proclamation declares,

> [A]fter 46 years of occupation, and 20 confused years of transition, Hungary has regained the right and power of self-determination, . . . In spring 2010, the Hungarian nation gathered its strength once again, and brought about a successful revolution in the polling booth. Parliament declares that it recognizes and will respect this constitutional revolution. . . . Parliament declares that in April's election a new social contract was born. . . . The pillars of our common future will be work, home, family, health and order.[34]

The election results opened the way for a flow of constitutional changes.[35] In the first one-and-a-half years of its term, the ruling party adopted a range of amendments to the 1989 Constitution regulating *inter alia* the representative bodies, judiciary and civil liberties.

First, the governing party used its two-thirds vote to remove the constitutional rule requiring a four-fifths vote to approve the cornerstones of the new Constitution.[36] The Parliament also adopted a symbolic constitutional amendment to reduce the number of subsequent parliamentary deputies. Hungary had until then a 386-seat parliament, while under the new rules the number of Members of Parliament 'shall not exceed 200'. Other acts also reduced the number of local government representatives, modified the substantive and procedural statutory rules of the elections, and significantly reshaped the boundaries of the electoral constituencies. In order to speed up court proceedings and to achieve 'law and order' in society, a new constitutional provision was adopted. According to this, court secretaries (lawyers without a judicial appointment) might rule on cases within the competence of local courts, including, among others, cases concerning the detention of those committing minor offenses. This meant that court secretaries had the competence to rule on deprivation of personal liberty.

The new Parliament also changed the regulation of the Constitutional Court. It reformed the nomination and election process in order for the parliamentary majority alone to choose candidates. It enlarged the

[34] 1140/2010. (VII. 2.) Resolution of the Government.

[35] For a detailed analysis, see K. Kovács and G. A. Tóth, 'Hungary's Constitutional Transformation', *European Constitutional Law Review*, 7 (2011), 183–203.

[36] Arato argues that this provision was unchangeable: one cannot change by two-thirds what only four-fifths can change. A. Arato, *Orban's (Counter) Revolution of the Voting Booth and How It Was Made Possible*, http://comparativeconstitutions.org/2011/04/arato-orbans-counter-revolution-of.html. (Accessed 31 August 2015).

Court's membership from eleven to fifteen, adding up to four justices to the bench (in sum, due to vacancies seven new justices were elected within one year). It limited the competence of the Court by banning the annulment of unconstitutional tax and financial measures.[37]

The two-thirds parliamentary majority adopted new constitutional provisions on freedom of expression and media. Prevention of information monopolies and structural pluralism of the media were no longer constitutional requirements.[38] The amendment established a powerful Media Authority and gave competence for its Head to issue decrees that are binding on everyone, and to supervise and sanction the content of the broadcast media, print and Internet outlets. The Prime Minister appointed the Head of the Authority for a term of nine years.[39]

Consequently, the Parliament suspended key constitutional checks on legislation and facilitated a constitution-drafting process that could proceed without opposition involvement. In this way the constitutional changes were only the first steps in a larger development. Most of the constitutional amendments in fact served a temporary goal.

The modifications to the 1989 Constitution and drafting of a new one went side by side. Donning the mantle of '2010 revolution in the polling booth', the ruling coalition started to work on a new constitution. It argued that the period of post-communist transformation should draw to a close, and for this reason Hungary needed a new constitution. Prime Minister Viktor Orbán personally established an advisory council and named its members, who were to elaborate a draft. In addition, the Parliament set up a special parliamentary ad-hoc committee to develop the regulatory frameworks of the new Constitution. Although at the outset all the parliamentary parties were represented in this committee, the opposition quit immediately after the Constitutional Court's competence was seen to be curbed. Within a couple of months, the remaining

[37] Venice Commission, Opinion No. 614/2011, para. 10.

[38] For a critical evaluation, see Council of Europe, Committee of Ministers, Recommendation on media pluralism and diversity of media content, Rec (2007) 2, https://wcd.coe.int/wcd/ViewDoc.jsp?id=1089699. (Accessed 31 August 2015).

[39] For a critical evaluation, see Organization for Security and Co-operation in Europe Office of the Representative on Freedom of the Media, *Analysis and Assessment of a Package of Hungarian Legislation and Draft Legislation on Media and Telecommunications*, September 2010, http://www.osce.org/files/documents/1/3/71218.pdf. Council of Europe, Commissioner for Human Rights, *Opinion of the Commissioner for Human Rights on Hungary's media legislation in light of Council of Europe standards on freedom of the media*, CommDH (2011)10, https://wcd.coe.int/wcd/ViewDoc.jsp?id=1751289 (Accessed 31 August 2015).

committee had completed its preparatory task and published the Regulatory Framework of the Constitution of Hungary. Subsequently, Parliament discussed this regulatory framework and decided that the document was no longer seen as determining the direction of framing the Constitution, but served as material in support of the deputies' constitution-making work.[40] Finally, instead of working together with the parliamentary committee, the ruling coalition set up a three-member panel of politicians to draft the text of the new Constitution.

To lend the constitution-writing process legitimacy, a National Consultation Body was set up with the aim of sending a questionnaire to every citizen of Hungary. This questionnaire was composed of twelve issues, including the relation between fundamental rights and obligations; the restriction of the public debt; the role of the family, public order, labour and health; the need for extra votes for mothers as a proxy for their children; the ban on levying taxes on the expenses related to child rearing; the protection of future generations; the conditions of public procurement; the unity of Hungarians across frontiers; the protection of natural diversity and national treasures; the protection of land and water; the need to include the sentencing to life imprisonment into the Constitution; and the obligation for a person to testify before a Parliamentary Commission if summoned. According to unaudited data, approximately 900,000 citizens filled in and sent back questionnaires. (About 10 million inhabitants live in Hungary.) The answers were in the middle of being processed when the draft new Constitution was submitted to Parliament.

The draft text of the new Fundamental Law was released in March 2011. The parliamentary agenda ensured five days for the plenary debate about the concept, and four days about the details, meaning nine days from start to finish. The date of promulgation (April 25) was chosen to identify the Fundamental Law with the first anniversary of the election victory. It entered into force on 1 January 2012.

In addition, based on the authorization from the Fundamental Law, Parliament enacted the Transitional Provisions of the Fundamental Law, which consisted not only of transitory norms but also of retrospective paragraphs and substantive amendments to the Fundamental Law. Parliament also adopted five separate amendments to the Fundamental Law between 2012 and 2014, which changed about 20 per cent of the

[40] 9/2011. (III. 9.) Resolution of the Parliament.

original text, including significant parts of the basic constitutional values, individual rights, and competences of state organs.

Besides the permanent transformation of the constitutional system, the parliamentary activity significantly reshaped the whole legal system, for example in adopting a new Civil Code and Penal Code. The Head of the State, who was elected by the parliamentary majority in the summer of 2010, promulgated 319 acts in the first eighteen months of the term, without practicing his veto power. Both the legislative activity and the presidential passivity appear to be unprecedented in contemporary Hungarian constitutionalism. Moreover, the packed and limited Constitutional Court proved to be incapable of controlling or balancing the government-led parliamentary machinery.

In sum, several factors had challenged the constitutional stability established in 1989. Among some plausible explanations we find the failure to adopt a formally new constitution, undue flexibility of the 1989 Constitution, shortage of democratic traditions, and a hostile political climate. As a result, exceptionally in the region, the political system of the Fundamental Law arguably represents the 'winner-takes-all' concept of democracy and rule of law. From a procedural perspective, while the rival parties agreed upon the 1989 constitutional modifications, the 2011 Fundamental Law lacks political consensus and compromises. Substantially, the 1989 Constitution was based on robust principles of rule of law and constitutionalism. The Fundamental law, which also echoes that 'Hungary shall be an independent, democratic State under the rule of law', however, requires further investigation to understand the current nature of rule of law in Hungary.

Two Rival Traditions of Rule of Law

Both the 1989 Constitution and the 2011 Fundamental Law specify in formal words that Hungary shall be a state under the rule of law. Does this mean that despite the numerous changes to the constitutional system, the domain of rule of law was untouched? This depends on what we mean by the rule of law.

The fundamental concept of rule law receives divergent definitions in legal theory as well as in international and national laws. However, as a report from the Venice Commission argues, there is now a core meaning of the rule of law and the elements contained within it.[41]

[41] Venice Commission, *Report on the Rule of Law*, No. 512/2009, para. 34–35.

A definition by Tom Bingham covers some essential elements of rule of law as follows:

> [A]ll persons and authorities within the state, whether public or private, should be bound by and entitled to the benefit of laws publicly made, taking effect (generally) in the future, and publicly administered in the courts.[42]

As the Venice Commission emphasizes, the definitive elements of the rule of law are not only formal but also substantial. They are: legality, including a transparent, accountable and democratic process for enacting law; legal certainty; prohibition of arbitrariness; access to justice before independent and impartial courts, including judicial review of administrative acts; respect for human rights; non-discrimination and equality before the law.[43] Alternatively, Jeremy Waldron distinguishes formalistic, substantial, and prominently, procedural elements of the rule of law.[44]

From these perspectives, rule of law seems a precondition for democracy, constitutionalism and human rights. Rule of law means no less than that the autonomy and dignity of the individual citizen are treated as ultimate legal values.[45] As the European Court of Human Rights underlines in the case of *Stafford versus United Kingdom*, the rule of law is a concept inherent in all articles of the Convention.[46] In other words, procedural and substantive elements of rule of law are equally essential to limit public powers.

Protection against cruel, oppressive, unreasonable use of governmental power is considered the core meaning of constitutionalism. US Supreme Court Justice Louis Brandeis pointed out that constitutional guarantees of limited governments are not present to promote efficiency, but to prevent autocracy and arbitrary power.[47] However, a well-functioning legal system

42 T. Bingham, *The Rule of Law* (London: Penguin Books, 2010), p. 8.

43 Venice Commission, para. 41.

44 J. Waldron, 'The Rule of Law and the Importance of Procedure', *NYU School of Law, Public Law Research Paper*, No. 17-73. Waldron also puts emphasis on the role of people organized in political institutions in upholding the rule of law. J. Waldron, 'Public Rule of Law', *NYU School of Law, Public Law and Legal Theory Research Paper*, No. 14-41.

45 T. R. S. Allan, *Constitutional Justice: A Liberal Theory of the Rule of Law* (Oxford University Press, 2003), pp. vi, 301–15.

46 *Stafford v. United Kingdom*, Judgment of 28 May 2002, para. 63.

47 *Myers v. United States*, 272 U.S. 52, 293 (1926). On reasons that arbitrary power is unacceptable, see M. Krygier, 'Four Puzzles about the Rule of Law: Why, What, Where? And Who Cares?' in J. E. Fleming (ed.), *Getting to the Rule of Law* (New York University Press, 2011), pp. 78–81.

requires not only institutional limits of power, but also effectiveness. Without rule-of-law principles such as legal certainty, foreseeability, or prohibition of arbitrariness, legal systems cannot realize democratic, constitutional objectives.

The one-time debate between the *Federalists* and *Antifederalists* may remind us that constitutional architecture aims at restrained but efficient government. Hannah Arendt argues that what the founders of the federal American Constitution 'were afraid of in practice was not power but impotence', because of, on the one hand, the experiences of the defects and paralysis of the Confederacy and, on the other hand, the view of Montesquieu that republican government was effective only in relatively small territories. Hence 'the true objective of the Constitution was not to limit power but to create more power, actually to establish and duly constitute an entirely new power center, destined to compensate the confederate republic'.[48] In sum, the inspiring principles of the US Constitution were the dualism between liberty and efficiency; a strong yet still limited union.

This two-fold character of constitutionalism goes back to two rival traditions of rule of law originating from Thomas Hobbes and John Locke. We can learn from Hobbes why an effective civil government of a country is needed, and from Locke what fundamental rights are. I call the former conception 'rule of law by a sovereign government', the latter 'rule of law by a limited government'. The Lockean view became influential in Hungary during the development of the 1989 system. The Hobbesian approach turned out to be arguably a powerful justificatory idea of the 2011 Fundamental Law.

Rule of Law by a Limited Government: The Lockean Tradition

The *annus mirabilis*, the year 1989, proved that the spirit of liberty still lives in the hearts of East-Central European men and women. Roughly speaking, Hungarian opposition movements echoed John Locke's view that human beings are 'by nature all free, equal, and independent, no one can be put out of this estate and subjected to the political power of another without his own consent.'[49] Everybody seemed to agree with

[48] H. Arendt, *On Revolution* (London/New York: Penguin Books, 1990), pp. 153–4.

[49] J. Locke, 'The Second Treatise' in *Two Treatises of Government and a Letter Concerning Toleration*, I. Shapiro ed. (New Haven/London: Yale University Press, 2003), p. 141, para. 95.

the Lockean belief that, on the one hand, no one is born to rule, or to be ruled, and on the other hand, the right to life, liberty, and property belong to all. Some of the political players followed the classical natural law theory by referring to God, while others, who did not share this religious view, appealed to equal dignity as the highest humanistic principle.[50]

The country had not, of course, been in a state of nature with perfect freedom and equality; on the contrary, political society had suffered under a single-party political oppression. This is why the people of Hungary sought an institutional order wherein the legislative and executive powers do not violate systematically, but maintain and promote individual rights. Moreover, it was a common claim that legal disorder, namely the arbitrary administration and adjudication of law according to the demands of the ruling party, should be replaced by a legal system under the procedural and substantive guaranties of rule of law. Locke, again, was found to be a teacher of the rule of law by a limited government:

> [T]he legislative or supreme authority cannot assume to itself a power to rule by extemporary, arbitrary decrees, but is bound to dispense justice, and to decide the rights of the subject by promulgated, standing laws, and known authorized judges.[51]

As a consequence, the 1989 constitutional transformation can be described in accordance with Lockean guidelines. The Constitution was to be based upon 'the inviolable and inalienable fundamental human rights. The respect and protection of these rights is a primary obligation of the State.'[52] This meant that the Constitution contained enforceable legal provisions rather than a collection of mere good wishes. Its purpose was seen as limiting the authority of state power. It recognized and protected judicial independence and established a Constitutional Court to limit the legislature. Since members of the legislature had been selected through periodically held free and fair elections, the ultimate power remained in the hands of the people.

As Locke, or Montesquieu, the other inventor of the notion of limited government, might have said, legitimate political institutions

[50] The most influential normative theory for the 1980's democratic opposition had its roots in Kantian philosophy. See in samizdat, J. Kis, *Vannak-e emberi jogaink?* (Budapest: AB Független Kiadó, 1985) and J. Kis, *L'égale dignité : essai sur les fondements des droits de l'homme* (Paris: Seuil, 1989).

[51] *Ibid.* p. 160, para. 136. [52] Article 8(1).

were meant to create certain foreseeable legal rules or serve as checks upon abuse of law-making authority.[53]

Rule of Law by a Sovereign Government: The Hobbesian Tradition

The rather agreeable story of post-communist constitutional transformation in Hungary has been spoiled gradually.[54] Poor democratic traditions, weakness of civil society, and imperfection of legal institutions all made the constitutional system vulnerable.

During the period of decline, observers of Hungarian politics and law might have witnessed a cold civil war, paralysed legal institutions, and distrust for the old constitution. Several pieces of empirical research reveal that an overwhelming sector of Hungarian society distrusted legal institutions such as the Parliament, courts, and governmental administrative bodies. According to a comparative survey two decades after the fall of the Wall, 77 per cent of Hungarians were dissatisfied with the way democracy was working in the country. The approval of change from a single-party system to democracy had decreased by 18 per cent.[55]

Finally, the cold civil war between the political left and right ended in a landslide election victory for the latter, paving the way for a total transformation of the legal system that resulted in the adoption of the 2011 Fundamental Law and its amendments.

The cold civil war and the anarchy-like state (*bellum omnium contra omnes*) restored to life a Hobbesian view of constitutionalism. Thomas Hobbes, whom Locke seemed to be arguing with, believed that a strong central authority is needed in order to triumph over the evils of disorder.[56] As Hobbes might have said, the governing person or body (the *Sovereign*) can be empowered by a social contract that will afford people a life other than what was available to them in the previous period.

[53] J. Dunn, 'What Is Living and What Is Dead in the Political Theory of John Locke?' in Dunn, *Interpreting Political Responsibility* (Cambridge: Polity Press, 1990), p. 24.

[54] For reconsidering the regional developments between the collapse of communism and the enlargement of the European Union from the point of view of the rule of law and constitutionalism, see A. Czarnota, M. Krygier, W. Sadurski (eds.), *Rethinking the Rule of Law after Communism* (Budapest: Central European University Press, 2005).

[55] *Two Decades after the Wall's Fall: End of Communism Cheered but Now with More Reservations*, The Pew Global Attitudes Project, Washington: Pew Research Centre, 2009. www.pewglobal.org/files/2009/11/Pew-Global-Attitudes-2009-Pulse-of-Europe-Report-Nov-2-1030am-NOT-EMBARGOED.pdf (accessed 31 August 2015).

[56] T. Hobbes, *Leviathan*, XXX. 3.

To ensure escape from legal disorder, people should renounce their rights and establish an effective law enforcement system headed by the Sovereign, who enforces whatever rules and restrictions it wishes.

From a Hobbesian perspective, in the Hungarian legal system the two-thirds parliamentary majority is led by a person in charge, that is, the party leader and prime minister is the highest legal power, i.e. the Sovereign. Since the majority of voters gave this entity the authority to enact laws, everybody should obey the imposed regulations, regardless of disrespected individual interests or moral rights.

Hobbes, in the manner of any magnificent thinker, is highly complex. There is a path from Hobbes to liberal theorists and modern rule of law. It is a way that leads, first, from a sovereign King to a sovereign Parliament, then, to a limited parliamentarianism, firmly established by Albert Dicey[57] and developing in the contemporary jurisprudence.[58] The Hobbesian tradition, however, as an interpretation by Carl Schmitt reveals, may be a justificatory idea for authoritarian legal systems, which prefer not only efficient but also arbitrary central government to individual liberties.[59] Now the question is as follows: 'Which way is Hungary going?'[60]

57 Dicey argues that the rule of law, which forms a fundamental principle of the constitution, has three meanings: In the first place, the absolute supremacy of regular law as opposed to the influence of arbitrary power. It means, second, equality before the law, or the equal subjection of all classes to the ordinary law of the land administered by the ordinary courts. The rule of law, lastly, expresses that the laws of the constitution are not the source but the consequence of the rights of individuals, as defined and enforced by the courts. A. V. Dicey, *Introduction to the Study of the Law of the Constitution*, R. E. Michener (ed.) (Indianapolis: Liberty Fund, 1982), pp. 145–53.

58 For a substantive interpretation of the idea of the rule of law, see J. Jowell, 'The Rule of Law and Its Underlying Values' in J. Jowell and D. Oliver (eds.), *The Changing Constitution* (Oxford University Press, 2011), pp. 11–34. For a critical approach to Dicey's idea, see E. Barend, *An Introduction to Constitutional Law* (Oxford University Press, 1998). See also J. Goldsworthy, *The Sovereignty of Parliament: History and Philosophy* (Oxford University Press, 1999).

59 C. Schmitt, *Der Leviathan in der Staatslehre des Thomas Hobbes: Sinn und Fehlschlag eines politischen Symbols* (Köln: Klett-Cotta, 1995). M. J. Oakeshott, *Hobbes on Civil Association* (Oxford: Blackwell, 1975).

60 Some would rather understand the Hungarian state of affairs as Rousseauian. See in general, J. L. Talmon, *The Origins of Totalitartain Democracy* (London: First Sphere Books, 1970). In my view, neither *volonté general* nor *volonté de tous* is helpful to justify the system under the Fundamental Law. To be sure, the two-thirds parliamentary majority, first, is not backed by the majority of citizens allowed to vote; second, has been manipulating the voting rules and gerrymanders the voting districts; and third, fears referendum.

Features of an Illiberal Constitutional System

I noted earlier that the new Hungarian legal system arguably represents an 'illiberal' or 'winner-takes-all' concept of democracy and rule of law.[61] Now I examine briefly four aspects of the Fundamental Law: secularity, popular sovereignty, retroactive legislation, and judicial review. Some requirements deriving from rival traditions of rule of law may offer a reconsideration of the main characteristics of the system.

Secularity

From Hobbes it is clear that modern states are secular innovations of human culture. In other words, the rule of law means rule of *secular law*.[62] The Rawlsian principle of state neutrality has its home in the liberal tradition,[63] but can also be regarded as a remote descendant of Hobbes' notion of the secular sovereign.

The Fundamental Law, in contrast, does not follow the ideas of secular state and religious neutrality, but has its foundations in religious considerations. The text of the Preamble (called the 'National Creed') places special emphasis on values such as family, nation, loyalty, faith and love, and is dominated by religious references. It was written in the spirit not just of Christianity but specifically of the Catholic faith. This is what the reference to Saint Stephen and the Holy Crown implies: 'We are proud that one thousand years ago, our King Saint Stephen established the Hungarian State on solid foundations and led our country to become part of Christian Europe' and 'we acknowledge the nation-preserving role of the Christian faith'. The text explicitly mentions 'the Holy Crown, which embodies the constitutional continuity of the state and the unity of the nation' and the historical constitution. In this way, the Fundamental Law not only recalls the historical role of Christianity in founding the Hungarian State, but also expresses that present Hungarian constitutionalism is based upon the

[61] According to the conception of compromise, democracy is simply majority rule, based on the principle 'One person, one vote'. J. Elster, *Constitutionalism and Democracy* (Cambridge University Press, 1988) p. 1. Here I follow a rival conception of democracy. J. Kis, *Constitutional Democracy* (Budapest/New York: Central European University Press, 2003), pp. 183–94.

[62] Hobbes, *Leviathan,* p. 376. However, as opposed to subsequent liberal thinkers, Hobbes held that people must submit to the absolute supremacy of the sovereign government in both secular and religious matters.

[63] J. Kis, 'State Neutrality' in M. Rosenfeld and A. Sajó, *The Oxford Handbook of Comparative Constitutional Law* (Oxford University Press, 2012), p. 318.

traditional Christian faith.[64] Consequently it breaks with the solution applied in the 1989 Constitution, which remained neutral as to competing moral convictions, worldviews and interests.

The Preamble, while giving preference to the thousand-year-old Christian tradition, expresses that 'we value the various religious traditions of our county'. The choice of words displays its model of tolerance, under which the various worldviews do not have equal status, although following them is not impeded by prohibition and persecution. It is however significant that the tolerance thus declared only extends to the various 'religious traditions', but does not apply to the more recently established branches of religion, or to those that are new to Hungary, or to non-religious convictions of conscience.

The proponents of the new system repeatedly mentioned the Polish Constitution as a model of the Fundamental Law. Indeed it is well known that the Polish Constitution refers to Christianity. In a European context, these are rare and controversial references. However, the social facts and constitutional norms in Hungary are different from those in Poland. Hungarian citizens are divided by ethical, political, and religious disagreements. According to a recent poll, 44 per cent of Hungarians answered that they believed there is a God, 31 per cent answered that they believed there is some sort of spirit or life force and 19 per cent identified themselves as atheists. Meanwhile, while more than half of the population belongs to the Roman Catholic Church, and 20 per cent of the citizens are Protestant, only 10 per cent are churchgoers and follow religious norms. In contrast to Hungary, Poland remains one of the most religious countries in Europe, where 89 per cent of the population belongs to the Roman Catholic Church, and more than half goes to church.[65]

In spite of this, the Polish Constitution treats believers and nonbelievers as equals. The Polish text refers to: 'those who believe in God as the source of truth, justice, good and beauty, as well as those not sharing such faith but respecting those universal values as arising from other sources, equal in rights and obligations' and: 'our culture is rooted in the Christian heritage of the Nation and in universal human values'.[66] In contrast to the Polish constitution, however, the Hungarian

[64] S. Radnóti, 'A Sacred Symbol in a Secular Country: The Holy Crown', in Tóth (ed.), *Constitution*, pp. 85–110.

[65] Tóth, 'Hungary', pp. 778–80.

[66] B. Banaszak, 'The Republic of Poland' in Besselink, Bovend'Eert, Broeksteeg, de Lange, Voermans (eds.), *Constitutional Law*, pp. 1249, 1295.

Fundamental Law does not mention the role of universal secular values or those who respect such values. In this way, it does not simply remember the historical role of Christianity in founding the Hungarian State, but expresses that the Hungarian constitutionalism present is based upon traditional Christian faith.

Consequently, the main difference between the Polish and Hungarian legal systems is that the latter identifies itself with the moral and political foundations of the faith. It does not merely approve of the worldview, religion, practices and cultural heritage of a portion of the country's citizens, but also states a position regarding the question as to which worldview and perception of life is true and correct, thereby according lower status to rival doctrines and cultural practices.[67]

Popular Sovereignty

Hobbes, Locke, and modern political philosophy identify members of political society with people who are subjects of the same legal system. Today the concept of popular sovereignty means that the source of public – political and legal – powers is the people. The constitutional categories of '*We the people*', '*Le peuple français*', '*Das deutsche Volk*' represent this notion.

The Hungarian legal system, however, insists that its subjects are all ethnic Hungarians regardless of their habitual residence and effective link to the state. The Preamble of the Fundamental Law rewrites the category of '*We the people*'. The 1989 Constitution identified the 'people' with those citizens who reside in the country and who are the subjects of the legal rights and obligations. In contrast to this, the Fundamental Law expresses that there is 'one single Hungarian nation that belongs together' and it consists of all ethnic Hungarians regardless of their habitual residence or the centre of their interests. It follows from its provisions that 'We the members of the Hungarian nation' include Hungarians living abroad, even without an effective link to the State. At the same time, members of ethnic minorities living within the territory of the Hungarian state are not a constituent part of the Hungarian nation.[68]

[67] For constitutional transition in countries that are characterized by deep racial ethnic or religious animosities, see S. Issacharoff, 'Constitutionalizing Democracy in Fractured Societies', *Journal of International Affairs*, 58 (2004), 1, 73–93.

[68] See also Article XIV, granting non-Hungarian citizens asylum only if another country does not provide protection for them.

The constitutional expression regarding the 'nation torn apart in the storms of the last century' refers to the historical Hungary as believed to have existed in the Middle Ages, and certainly to those neighbouring territories where some two-and-a-half million Hungarians are still living today as a consequence of the post-world-war treaties of 1920 and 1947. The Fundamental Law therefore treats Hungarians living beyond the borders as members of a nation disunited by the international legal and political order. As a logical consequence, the legal provisions offer citizenship and even voting rights to them. These attributes make the Hungarian system similar to the Russian-type expansive nation-building policy. A constitution that identifies the nation as an 'intellectual and spiritual' constitutional community cannot be understood as a representative of integrative constitutions, but as a descendant of the Eastern European nationalist ideas and movements from the previous two centuries.[69]

Ex Post Facto *Law*

Comparative studies reveal that the preamble of a constitution is not only a solemn declaration, but may have normative strength.[70] The Hungarian example supports this finding. Article R of the Fundamental Law declares, 'The provisions of the Fundamental Law shall be interpreted in accordance with its objectives, the National Avowal contained therein and the achievements of our historical constitution.' Therefore, the basic principles, the institutional design, the relationship between state and churches, as well as fundamental rights, should be interpreted in accordance with the opening creed of the constitution. In addition, the Fundamental Law invalidates the first Hungarian written Constitution of 1949, which directly affects the validity of the 1989 Constitution. Importantly, the Fundamental Law was adopted according to formal procedural requirement set by the 1949 Constitution and it retains this two-thirds rule, contrary to what the preamble expresses. In this sense the Fundamental Law

[69] H. Lerner, *Making Constitutions in Deeply Divided Societies* (Cambridge University Press, 2011) p. 109. See also R. H. Pildes, 'Ethnic Identity and the Design of Democratic Institutions: A Dynamic Perspective' in S. Choudhry (ed.), *Constitutionalism in Divided Societies* (Oxford University Press, 2008).

[70] For a comparative study on normativity of preambles, see L. Orgad, 'The Preamble in Constitutional Interpretation', *International Journal of Constitutional Law*, 8(4) (2010), 714–38.

demonstrates legal discontinuity. What is more, the fourth amendment to the Fundamental Law explicitly repealed the decisions of the Constitutional Court taken prior to the entry into force of the Fundamental Law. As a consequence of the normative strength of the National Creed, the invalidation of the former Constitution and judicial precedents, the previously elaborated principles of the rule of law also ceased to exist. I offer three sets of examples of this.

As specified by Article 21, a new church listing system replaced the neutral registration by courts. According to the new rules, parliament is allowed to list the recognized churches and define the conditions for recognizing further churches. This provision expressly provides that a cardinal law on church status may require for recognition of churches a certain length of operations, membership, historical traditions and societal support. Based on this, parliament passed an Act listing 14 recognized churches, while the others – among them Christians, Muslims and Buddhists – would lose their church status. Their re-registration was a matter of agreement with the government. Finally, parliament recognized 32 churches, while around 90 per cent of the previously established churches lost their legal identities and entitlements to benefits for the purposes of faith-related activities.[71]

Article U offers a list of wrongdoings and crimes of the communist parties (the Hungarian Socialist Worker's Party and its legal predecessor) committed between 1945 and 1990. This legal text points out that the Hungarian Socialist Party (three-times winner of democratic elections after 1989, and currently a parliamentary opposition party) 'shares the responsibility of the state party – through the continuity in party leadership that bridged the old and the new party – as the legal successor to the Hungarian Socialist Worker's Party, as the inheritor of the illegally amassed wealth, and as the benefactor of the illegitimate advantages acquired during the transition.'[72] In line with the declarative list, this Article puts 'the society's sense of justice' above the rule of law. In this way, the Fundamental Law paves the way for reduction of

[71] From a comparative constitutional perspective, see R. Uitz, 'Freedom of Religion and Churches: Archaeology in a Constitution-making Assembly', Tóth (ed.), *Constitution*, pp. 197–235. The European Court of Human Rights declared that removing church status altogether constitutes a violation of freedoms of religion and assembly. *Magyar Keresztény Mennonita Egyház and Others v. Hungary*, Judgment of 8 April 2014.

[72] Elsewhere I argue that the Fundamental Law follows Carl Schmitt's idea on the distinction between friend and enemy. G. A. Tóth, 'Macht statt Recht: Deformation des Verfassungssystem in Ungarn', *Osteuropa*, 63(4) (2013), 23–6.

remuneration of, and retroactive criminal legislation against, communist party officials.[73]

The new constitutional regulation declares that the mandate of the President of the Supreme Court and of the President and members of the National Council of Justice shall terminate upon the entry into force of the Fundamental Law. In this way the chief justice, who was elected for six years in June 2009, was prematurely dismissed at the end of 2011.[74] Similarly, the Fundamental Law abolishes the institution of the Parliamentary Commissioner for Data Protection. As a substitute, it establishes an authority, which supervises the enforcement of the right to the protection of personal data and of the right to access data of public interest.[75] The Fundamental Law lowers the mandatory retirement age for judges from 70 to 62 years as of 1 January 2012. More than one hundred senior judges were thus forced to leave their offices. The Venice Commission estimates that nearly 10 per cent of Hungarian judges will retire in the near future, without a material justification. The Commission also criticizes the retroactive effect of the new regulation: 'A whole generation of judges, who were doing their jobs without obvious shortcomings and who were entitled – and expected – to continue to work as judges, have to retire.'[76]

Judicial Review

To reiterate, after the inaugural sitting of the newly elected 2010 parliament, the majority changed the regulation on the Constitutional Court. The Fundamental Law affirms those modifications. As regards Constitutional Justices' nomination process, the parliamentary majority is able to nominate candidates without working together with the

[73] For the prohibition of retroactive criminal jurisdiction with regard to crimes committed during the 1956 Hungarian Revolution, see *Korbely v. Hungary*, 19 September 2008.

[74] The European Court of Human Rights ruled in favour of the former President of the Supreme Court, declaring that the termination of his mandate before it had expired was a violation of his right of access to a court and freedom of speech. *Baka v. Hungary*, Judgment of 23 June 2016.

[75] The European Court of Justice ruled that the abrupt termination the Hungarian Data Protection Commissioner's term in office by the government constitutes an infringement of the independence of the Hungarian Data Protection Authority and is hence in breach of EU law. *European Commission v. Hungary*, C-288/12, Judgment of 8 April 2014.

[76] Venice Commission, Opinion No. 663/2012, para. 104–05. The European Court of Human Rights also concluded that dismissal of civil servants from public service without giving any reasons for that dismissal resulted is a violation of the right to fair trial. *K. M. C. v. Hungary*, Judgment of 10 July 2012.

opposition. The membership of the Court has been enlarged from 11 to 15, and the president of the Court will no longer be elected by his fellow justices but by parliament too. Due to this court-packing activity, up to now the parliamentary majority has elected 11 new justices. The two-thirds majority thus has absolute freedom to nominate and elect judges.

The Fundamental Law affects not only the independence but also the competences of the Constitutional Court. While it retains most of the competences of the Court, the changes are considerable. The new system consists of a French-type *a priori* constitutional control. The Government, the Speaker of the Parliament, and representatives submitting the Bill can initiate the preventive control of an act not yet signed by the Speaker. The parliamentary majority then decides whether it will ask the Court for an advisory opinion. In this way, the *a priori* control is in hands of the parliamentary majority, instead of being a protective tool for the minority. Moreover, the *ex post* review of the unconstitutionality of legislation is restricted: the Fundamental Law abolishes *actio popularis*. Only the Government, the Commissioner for Fundamental Rights, and one-quarter of the members of parliament can turn to the Constitutional Court, which means that according to the existing division of seats in parliament, all the opposition parties (from left to far right) would have to agree on a petition. As an improvement, the Fundamental Law introduces a German-type constitutional complaint (albeit with significant differences), making it possible to complain not only against a normative act but also against the violation of a fundamental right through a court decision without authorization of a normative act. The mechanism of individual complaint related to a concrete case includes the possibility to challenge the unconstitutional judicial application of a legal norm.[77]

Importantly, the regulation limits the Court's competences connected with financial matters. According to the new wording, 'as long as state debt exceeds half of the Gross Domestic Product', the Court may review

> [T]he Acts on the central budget, on the implementation of the budget, on central taxes, on duties and on contributions, on customs duties, and on the central conditions for local taxes as to their conformity with the Fundamental Law exclusively in connection with the rights to life and

[77] K. Kovács and G. A. Tóth, 'Aufstieg und Krise: Wirkung der deutschen Verfassungsgerichtbarkeit auf Ungarn' in M. Wrase und C. Boulanger (Hrsg.), *Die Politik des Verfassungsrechts* (Baden-Baden: Nomos, 2013), pp. 317–42.

> human dignity, to the protection of personal data, to freedom of thought, conscience and religion, or in connection with the rights related to Hungarian citizenship, and it may only annul these Acts for the violation of these rights.[78]

This means that the Constitutional Court may not assess these acts for example with regard to the principles of non-discrimination, rule of law, proportionality of burden-sharing, and the prevalence of the right to property. In order to understand the motivation behind the selection of rights, there is little point in searching for principled reasons. Hungarian case law reflects the reality that the Constitutional Court has annulled tax and other financial measures by referring to those rights and principles that are missing from the list. Property rights, principles of equal treatment, acquired rights and the so-called legitimate expectations in maintaining social benefits were the referenced values of the annulments.

Retrospectively, the Court issued a series of decisions which blocked the immediate implementation of 1995 cuts in the system of child support, sick pay, maternity leave, and other social programs by invalidating several parts of the Economic Stabilization Act, the government's IMF-required austerity program.[79] Since then the Court has reviewed several tax measures. It found, for instance, the arbitrarily issued property tax unconstitutional.[80] These cases were the symptoms of a theoretical democracy and separation-of-powers dilemma. If the Constitutional Court, without having political responsibility, frequently makes a policy choice better left to the governing majority, democratic decision-making is thwarted.[81] The government officials gave a definite answer to this problem when they made it clear that they saw no choice but to limit the power of the Constitutional Court. Otherwise the recent 'crisis taxes' imposed on banks, energy companies, foreign retail and telecommunication firms, and even confiscation of pension funds, social subsidies, and other individual interests might be deemed unconstitutional. Hungary faced a growing budget deficit and was on the verge of a severe economic crisis. To solve this, parliament chose to introduce the series of unconventional, 'windfall taxes' and budget policies instead of structural, social and economical reforms. The aims of modifications of the constitutional

[78] Article 37(4). [79] Judgments 43-45/1995 HCC. [80] Judgment 8/2010 HCC.

[81] Jeremy Waldron argues that allowing unelected judges to decide controversial political issues is contrary to the majoritarian democracy and denies the dignity of citizens. See J. Waldron, 'The Core of the Case against Judicial Review', *Yale Law Journal*, 115 (2006), 1346–60. See also a reply from Dworkin, in R. Dworkin, *Justice for Hedgehogs* (Cambridge, MA: The Belknap Press of Harvard University Press, 2011), pp. 483–5.

rules on taxation were to override settled constitutional case law and suspend a key veto player in the constitutional system.[82]

Conclusions

Constitutional transitions to and away from liberal democracy reveal different features of the rule of law. The rise of the Hungarian legal system based upon the 1989 Constitution and the emergence of a new regime founded by the 2011 Fundamental Law show important contrasts.

Procedurally, while the rival parties as partners in a joint political enterprise agreed upon the 1989 constitutional modifications, the adoption of the 2011 Fundamental Law lacked political consensus or compromise. As the phrase 'revolution under the rule of law' developed by the Constitutional Court indicates, the former transition was carried out on the basis of legality. Although the new constitutional system emerging after a so-called 'revolution in the polling-booth' echoes some formal rule-of-law requirements, it negates the validity of the previous constitutional system and retroactively interferes in legal relations.

Substantially, in 1989 the coordinated political procedure resulted in revolutionary outcomes embedded in the Constitution: democratic institutions and political pluralism replaced an authoritarian regime and the dominance of communist ideology. The judiciary, and most importantly the Constitutional Court, had a crucial say in implementing the rule-of-law requirements. The political system of the Fundamental Law, in contrast, represents a 'winner-takes-all' idea of democracy with a decisive omission, namely the *fairness* of elections does not matter.[83] In this sense, rule of law is a purely formalistic concept: roughly speaking, the parliamentary majority rules. As a consequence of this unrestrained rule by law, the constitution system replaces secular and pluralistic foundations with nationalist and certain religious ideologies, abolishes

[82] Venice Commission, Opinion No. 614/2011, para. 10.

[83] An ODIHR (Organization for Security and Cooperation in Europe's Office of Democratic Institutions and Human Rights) mission concluded that the 2014 parliamentary election was *not fair* and that the basic framework within which the election was run violated key OSCE guidelines. The governing party enjoyed an undue advantage because of partisan changes in election law, e.g., unequal suffrage, gerrymandering, restrictive campaign regulations, far-from-independent assessment of the election and biased media coverage that blurred the separation between political party and the State. *Hungary Parliamentary Elections 6 April 2014, OSCE/ODIHR Limited Election Observation Mission Final Report*, Warsaw, 11 July 2014.

institutional checks and balances, violates civil liberties, and discredits egalitarian principles.

The Lockean traditions of rule of law, which I portrayed as rule of law by a limited government, were influential during the development of the 1989 system. The Hobbesian conception, which I typified as rule of law by a sovereign government, proved in contrast to be arguably a powerful justificatory idea of the Fundamental Law. In my view, however, the new constitutional system does not follow a path from Hobbes to modern rule of law and limited parliamentarism, but rather leads to an authoritarian regime. The fallacious reference to the Hobbesian tradition seems a false justificatory idea for a legal system, which prefers not efficient but arbitrary central government to individual liberties.

In sum, this purely formalistic domain of law replaces the idea of 'rule of the people by the people for the people'. Under such circumstances, law as an unconstrained tool of a relative majority of the people serves aims that are not answerable to democratic and constitutional principles. As Thomas Paine warned us of the difference between constitutional and governmental issues, 'The Constitution of a Country is not the act of its Government, but of the People constituting a Government.'[84] In the world of the present, the lack of constitutional limits on a quasi-majoritarian government does not simply result in the emergence of an 'illiberal democracy'; in fact, it is not democratic at all.

[84] T. Paine, *Rights of Man* (New York: Dover Thrift Edition, 1999), p. 33.

PART III

Transnational Phenomena and International Developments

14

The EU and the Rule of Law – Naïveté or a Grand Design?

DIMITRY KOCHENOV*

Ideals and Realities of the Contemporary European Union

The European Union probably comes closest among a huge array of other legal-political systems to being a nearly ideal example of a cleavage between the ideals as proclaimed and the reality as practiced, and particularly so in the area of the rule of law – the key subject matter of this book. To start with, the EU is quite special in a number of crucial respects. This special character is in essence quite different from any particularities observed among states *sensu stricto.*[1] Indeed, it goes to the core of the EU's self-image and the account of it in the eyes of others. While the majority of law faculties in Europe teach EU law as constitutional law nowadays, the constitutional nature of the Union, although assumed,[2] is regularly questioned[3] – something one does not observe in the case of the majority of states. Moreover, the actual account of the nature of this contested constitution differs sharply from system to system, as every constitutional system of each of the member states will

* The author would like to thank all the colleagues who engaged with his thoughts, especially Professors Carlos Closa, Jan-Werner Müller, Gianluigi Palombella, Laurent Pech, Kim Lane Scheppele and the editors of this volume. A much shortened version of the argument presented in this chapter will appear as 'Self-Constitution through Unenforceable Promises' in Jiří Přibáň (ed.), *Self-Constitution of European Society* (Abingdon: Routledge, 2016).

1 This being said, it is not my intention here to advocate any *sui generis* nature of the Union, which has been persuasively disproved by Robert Schütze: R. Schütze, *From Dual to Cooperative Federalism* (Oxford University Press, 2009).

2 On the crucial importance of this presumption, see, J. H. H. Weiler and U. R. Haltern, 'The Autonomy of the Community Legal Order – Through the Looking Glass', *Harvard International Law Journal*, 37 (1996), 411, 422. Indeed, 'who cares what it "*really*" is' (at 422, emphasis added).

3 For the most compelling account, see, P. L. Lindseth, *Power and Legitimacy: Reconciling Europe and the Nation State* (Oxford University Press, 2010).

have its own explanation of the EU and the role it plays, not necessarily submitting to the narrative of constitutionalism as retold from Brussels and Luxembourg.[4] The differences of perspective in question are far from merely rhetorical, going to the essence of the crucial theoretical foundations instead. Reconciliatory strategies, even the most fashionable ones,[5] like all what was written on 'constitutional pluralism' in the EU in the recent years, are equally contested – often for very good reasons.[6] The same applies to the key particular elements of the law and principles of the EU. It is a democracy[7] – yet not quite, as the objectives of integration are pre-set and uncontestable,[8] turning it into a democracy of means, not the democracy of ends.[9] It offers citizenship,[10] but not quite: the majority of citizens' rights do not depend on this legal status, but rather on other considerations, particularly personal history of the bearer and her personal wealth or an ability to earn.[11] It has the aspiration for justice among its foundations[12] – yet it is not infrequently prone to generate injustice instead.[13] It is based on the rule of law,[14] yet crucial

4 G. Davies, 'Constitutional Disagreement in Europe and the Search for Legal Pluralism', *Eric Stein Paper* No. 1/2010 (Prague).

5 M. Avbelj and J. Komárek (eds.), *Constitutional Pluralism in the European Union and Beyond* (Oxford: Hart Publishing, 2013).

6 G. Letsas, 'Harmonic Law: The Case against Legal Pluralism' in J. Dickson and P. Eleftheriadis (eds.), *Philosophical Foundations of European Union Law* (Oxford University Press, 2013).

7 Democracy is one of the values on which the Union, together with its member states, is said to be built: Art. 2 TEU. See also A. von Bogdandy, 'The Prospect of a European Republic: What European Citizens are Voting On', *Common Market Law Review*, 42 (2005), 913.

8 G. Davies, 'Social Legitimacy and Purposive Power: The End, the Means and the Consent of the People' in D. Kochenov, G. de Búrca and A. Williams (eds.), *Europe's Justice Deficit?* (Oxford: Hart Publishing, 2015).

9 G. Peebles, '"A Very Eden of the Innate Rights of Man"? A Marxist Look at the European Union Treaties and Case Law', *Law and Social Inquiry*, 22 (1998), 581.

10 K. Lenaerts, '"*Civis europaeus sum*": From the Cross-Border Link to the Status of Citizen of the Union' in P. Cardonnel, A. Rosas and N. Wahl (eds.), *Constitutionalising the EU Judicial System: Essays in Honour of Pernilla Lindh* (Oxford: Hart Publishing, 2012).

11 D. Kochenov, 'Neo-Mediaeval Permutations of Personhood in the European Union' in L. Azoulai, S. Barbou des Places, E. Pataut (eds.), *Persons and Personhood in European Law* (Oxford: Hart Publishing, 2016).

12 D. Kochenov, 'The Ought of Justice' in Kochenov, de Búrca and Williams (eds.), *Europe's Justice Deficit?*

13 S. Douglas Schott, 'Justice, Injustice and the Rule of Law in the EU' in Kochenov, de Búrca and Williams (eds.), *Europe's Justice Deficit?*; D. Kukovec, 'Taking Change Seriously: The Rhetoric of Justice and the Reproduction of the Status Quo' in Kochenov, de Búrca and Williams (eds.), *Europe's Justice Deficit?*

14 Case 294/83 *Partie Ecologiste 'Les Verts'* v. *Parliament* [1986] ECR 1339, 23. See also Opinion 1/91 *EEA Agreement* [1991] ECR 6097.

elements of what the rule of law is essentially about are simply not part of the system.[15]

The enumeration of such disconnects can be continued *ad infinitum*. It is beyond any doubt that any legal-political system has an official façade and a day-to-day face. Yet, a growing amount of persuasive scholarly investigation[16] seems to demonstrate with an ever-crystallising clarity that the rift between law and reality in the EU – akin to Soviet constitutionalism, beautiful on paper, questionable at a closer scrutiny – is much broader than what we are used to assume. The critical work in assessing precisely how large this disconnect actually is, is very far from finished. The focus of this chapter in the scheme of things so grand would be disappointing to some, as the chapter only looks at one particular aspect of the rift, one corner of the EU rule of law story, thus supplying but a tiny brick to the edifice of approaching EU law critically.

The claim of the chapter is basic. The Union's vulnerability in the domain of values, including, but not confined to the rule of law,[17] which is more and more coming to light, is caused by a far-reaching systemic problem of the European Union's *design* and also by the modalities of its day-to-day *functioning*, both falling short of upholding the much-restated rule of law ideal for the Union. The two are intimately connected. Both are equally important. They have not been getting equal attention from the scholars and practitioners, however. While the literature has focused on restating EU's presumed rule of law nature,[18] the issue of the enforcement of EU rule of law and other values in the defiant member states, such as Hungary[19] or

15 G. Palombella, 'Beyond Legality – before Democracy: Rule of Law Caveats in a Two-Level System' in Closa and Kochenov (eds.), *Reinforcing Rule of Law*; D. Kochenov, 'EU Law without the Rule of Law. Is the Veneration of Autonomy Worth It?', *Yearbook of European Law*, 34 (2015).

16 Editorial, 'A Critical Turn in European Legal Studies', *Common Market Law Review*, 52 (2015).

17 For a most comprehensive treatment of EU Rule of Law, see, L. Pech, 'The Rule of Law as a Constitutional Principle of the European Union', *Jean Monnet Working Paper* No. 04/09 (NYU Law School, 2009). For a special 'Eastern-European' perspective, which is particularly important in the context of the on-going developments in the EU, see, J. Přibáň, 'From "Which Rule of Law?" to "The Rule of Which Law?": Post-Communist Experiences of European Legal Integration', *Hague Journal on the Rule of Law*, 1 (2009), 337.

18 M. L. Fernández Esteban, *The Rule of Law in the European Constitution* (The Hague: Kluwer Law International, 1999); L. Pech, 'The Rule of Law as a Constitutional Principle'; W. Schröder (ed.), *Strengthening the Rule of Law in Europe: From a Common Concept to Mechanisms of Implementation* (Oxford: Hart Publishing, 2016).

19 L. Sólyom, 'The Rise and Decline of Constitutional Culture in Hungary' in A. von Bogdandy and P. Sonnevend (eds.), *Constitutional Crisis in the European Constitutional Area: Theory, Law and Politics in Hungary and Romania* (Oxford: Hart Publishing, 2015);

Poland,[20] busy dismantling liberal democratic constitutionalism,[21] it is crucial to realise that Europe's structural constitutional vulnerability stretches far beyond enforcement issues *per se.*[22] Instead, it is rooted in the discrepancies between the EU's proclaimed constitutional structure as we find it in the Treaties and the reality marking the development of EU integration, as outlined above, allowing one to doubt whether the Union is actually abiding by the rule of law.[23] In the light of this structural deficiency, one can argue that the much-analysed systemic deficiency[24] in the area of values and, especially, the rule of law, was bound to emerge sooner or later, whether in Hungary, Poland or elsewhere, as the Union matured.[25] Dealing with it will necessarily require moving beyond preoccupation with enforcement which has engulfed all the recent literature on the subject and reforming the integration project at the core,[26] ensuring that democracy and the rule of law are endowed with a more important role to play in the context of the supranational law of the Union.

M. Bánkuti, G. Halmai and K. L. Scheppele, 'Hungary's Illiberal Turn: Disabling the Constitution', *Journal of Democracy*, 23 (2012), 138.

20 For an overview of destruction of independent constitutional judiciary in Poland, consult excellent syntheses of all the stages of the story by T. T. Koncewicz on the *Verfassungsblog*. See also The Venice Commission for Democracy through Law, Opinion on amendments to the Act of 25 June 2015 on the Constitutional Tribunal of Poland, CDL-AD(2016)001, Venice, 11 March 2016. Available at http://www.venice.coe.int/webforms/documents/?pdf=CDL-AD%282016%29001-e

21 On the types of constitutionalism, see V. Perju, 'Proportionality and Freedom – an Essay on Method in Constitutional Law', *Global Constitutionalism*, 1 (2012). For a broader analysis of the on-going processes, see, e. g., von Bogdandy and Sonnevend (eds.), *Constitutional Crisis.*

22 On the latter see, e.g. the contributions in C. Closa and D. Kochenov (eds.), *Reinforcing Rule of Law*; A. Jakab and D. Kochenov (eds.), *The Enforcement of EU Law and Values* (Oxford University Press, 2017 (forthcoming)); von Bogdandy and Sonnevend (eds.), *Constitutional Crisis*; J.-W. Müller, 'Safeguarding Democracy inside the EU: Brussels and the Future of Liberal Order', *Working Paper* No. 3 (Washington DC: Transatlantic Academy, 2013).

23 G. Palombella, 'The Rule of Law and its Core' in G. Palombella and N. Walker (eds.), *Relocating the Rule of Law* (Oxford: Hart Publishing, 2009); G. Palombella, 'Beyond Legality – before Democracy: Rule of Law Caveats in a Two-Level System' in Closa and Kochenov (eds.), *Reinforcing Rule of Law.*

24 A. von Bogdandy and M. Ioannidis, 'Systemic Deficiency in the Rule of Law: What It Is, What Has Been Done, What Can Be Done', *Common Market Law Review*, 51 (2014), 59.

25 See, for a broad discussion, Kochenov, de Búrca and Williams (eds.), *Europe's Justice Deficit?*

26 For a much more critical restatement of this particular argument, see D. Kochenov, 'EU Law without the Rule of Law. Is the Veneration of Autonomy Worth It?'; J. H. H. Weiler, 'Epilogue: Living in a Glass House: Europe, Democracy and the Rule of Law' in Closa and Kochenov (eds.), *Reinforcing Rule of Law.*

As the legal framework of EU law stands today, the rule of law, alongside democracy and human rights protection, is one of the values shared between the Union and the member states.[27] The provision aimed at ensuring that this indeed is the case is Article 7 TEU, which allows for the introduction of political sanctions against the member states that are suspected of breaching the values or that seem to be coming close to breaching the values.[28] This provision has been much criticised in the literature as not 'legal' enough and containing thresholds too high for the activation of political sanctions aimed at bringing deviant states into compliance.[29] This criticism, alongside the relatively problematic history of *ad hoc* sanctions against the member states perceived to be in breach,[30] prompted scholars and the institutions to come up with alternative routes for values enforcement. Especially, the stance of the Commission is interesting in this context: instead of deploying Article 7 TEU (as one of the possible initiators of the procedure contained therein), the institution opted for the introduction of a new, non-binding, 'pre-Article 7' procedure.[31] Replacing the solution of the outstanding problems with the introduction of new legal instruments did not work, however: instead of improving the

[27] Art. 2 TEU.

[28] For a detailed analysis of this provision, see C. Hillion, 'Overseeing the Rule of Law in the EU: Legal Mandate and Means' in C. Closa and D. Kochenov (eds.), *Reinforcing the Rule of Law*; L. F. M. Besselink, 'The Bite, the Bark and the Howl: Article 7 and the Rule of Law Initiatives' in Jakab and Kochenov (eds.), *The Enforcement of EU Law*.

[29] W. Sadurski, 'Adding Bite to a Bark: The Story of Article 7, EU Enlargement, and Jörg Haider', *Columbia Journal of European Law*, 16 (2010), 385; Besselink, 'The Bite, the Bark and the Howl'; B. Bugarič, 'Protecting Democracy inside the EU: On Article 7 TEU and the Hungarian Turn to Authoritarianism' in Closa and Kochenov (eds.), *Reinforcing the Rule of Law*.

[30] E.g., G. N. Toggenburg, 'La crisi austriaca: delicati equilibrismi sospesi tra molte dimensioni' (2001) Diritto pubblico comparato ed europeo, 735; Sadurski, 'Adding Bite to a Bark'; K. Lachmayer, 'Questioning the Basic Values – Hungary and Jörg Haider' in Jakab and Kochenov (eds.), *The Enforcement of EU Law*.

[31] European Commission, 'A New EU Framework to Strengthen the Rule of Law', Strasbourg, 11 March 2014, COM(2014) 158 final. The Legal Service of the Council was very critical of the proposal and concluded the following: '[T]he new EU framework for the Rule of Law as set out in the Commission's communication is not compatible with the principle of conferral which governs the competences of the institutions of the Union': Council of the European Union, Opinion of the Legal Service 10296/14, of 14 May 2014, para. 28. See D. Kochenov and L. Pech, 'Monitoring and Enforcement of the Rule of Law in the European Union: Rhetoric and Reality', *European Constitutional Law Review* (2015), for a detailed account why, legally speaking, the Council Legal Service's position on the Commission's pre-Article 7 is unsound. This issue will also be touched upon below.

climate of compliance, the new procedure in fact makes the use of Article 7 TEU impossible in the current circumstances. This means that the Commission's recent activation of the 'pre-Article 7' procedure against Poland is a low, rather than high point in the fight against backsliding on the rule of law among EU member states.[32]

Although numerous scholarly propositions have been made as to how to deal with the rule of law deficiencies in the EU to circumvent the perceived difficulties of Article 7 deployment (these are normally formulated in general terms, but, usually for good reasons, have specific member state(s) in mind),[33] the depth of the problem seems to be defying easy solutions,[34] implying the need to move *beyond* enforcement-dominated thinking in our analysis. Besides, solving the outstanding issues also implies pondering on which institution would be better placed to deal with the rule of law shortcomings. Only keeping our options open with regard to the possible actor to bring about change, as well as moving beyond enforcement as such, then constitutes the correct backdrop against which to assess the European Commission's pre-Article 7 procedure,[35] as well as numerous scholarly proposals and the Council's own rule of law dialogue:[36] all that is being done does not go deep enough at all, trying to solve only the enforcement problem, whereas the real issue spans as far as the very nature of the Union in Europe.

[32] D. Kochenov and L. Pech, 'Better Late than Never? On the Commission's Rule of Law Framework and Its First Activation', *Journal of Common Market Studies* 54(5) (2016), 1062.

[33] For a detailed analysis of all the key proposals on the table, P. Bárd, S. Carrera, E. Guild and D. Kochenov, 'An EU Mechanism on Democracy, the Rule of Law, and Fundamental Rights: Assessing the Need and Possibilities for the Establishment of an EU Scoreboard on Democracy, the Rule of Law and Fundamental Rights', European Parliament, Research Paper PE 579328 European Added Value Unit EPRS, April 2016; J.-W. Müller, 'The EU as a Militant Democracy, or: Are There Limits to Constitutional Mutations within the Member States', *Revista de Estudios Políticos*, 165 (2014). K. L. Scheppele, 'The Case for Systemic Infringement Actions' in Closa and Kochenov (eds.), *Reinforcing Rule of Law*. See also von Bogdandy and Sonnevend (eds.), *Constitutional Crisis*; D. Kochenov, 'On Policing Article 2 TEU Compliance – Reverse *Solange* and Systemic Infringements Analyzed', *Polish Yearbook of International Law*, XXXIII (2014), 145.

[34] Palombella, 'Beyond Legality – before Democracy'.

[35] For an analysis, see Kochenov and Pech, 'Monitoring and Enforcement'.

[36] Council of the EU, press release no. 16936/14, 3362nd Council meeting, General Affairs, Brussels, 16 December 2014, pp. 20–1. Cf. P. Oliver and J. Stefanelli, 'Strengthening the Rule of Law in the EU: The Council's Inaction', *Journal of Common Market Studies* 54(5) (2016), 1075.

The European Union is based on the principle of conferral,[37] i.e. the powers not transferred to the EU remain with the member states.[38] This is where first fundamental legal problems with the values of the Union arise: the values, the rule of law included, have never been delegated to the Union and thus fall outside of the material scope of Union law, called the '*acquis* of the Union' in legal eurospeak.[39] As a result, the legal position of values is not quite the same as 'ordinary' *acquis* of the European Union. This contribution states that the difference between the two – i.e. the values and the *acquis* ('the law') – is not confined to that of the scope of possible intervention on the part of the EU, but obviously covers the *substance* of the rules in question. The latter is infinitely clearer, once the letter and the spirit of the *acquis* is at stake as opposed to the 'values'. This holds true even for the pre-accession context, where the institutions, most notably the Commission, made an important and markedly unsuccessful attempt to bridge this divide.[40] There is a third difference between the two: values are infinitely more difficult to enforce (as well as to breach, one would presume) than the 'law': what is relatively easy and straightforward with the latter, is – still – an unchartered terrain with the former, which explains the excessive focus on the enforcement aspects of the practical operation of values in the literature today.

The starting point of this contribution is thus the triple difference between the law and values of European integration: legal scope, substance and enforceability. Looking at one of the three in separation from the other two will most likely be a meaningless exercise. To demonstrate how futile separate consideration of each of the three elements is most likely to be, the Commission's pre-Article 7 procedure deployed against Poland in January 2016, as well as, to a much lesser extent, the Council's rule of law dialogue is analysed. A much more fundamental problem plaguing the EU, whether we are to notice it or not, is the elephant in the room here: once the 'values' emerge as ephemeral – and thus inoperable, legally speaking at least, – at the three levels mentioned above, what is then the basis of the 'law'? This question, which is very far from being rhetorical, is worthy of a most

[37] Art. 5(1) TEU. [38] Art. 5(2) TEU.

[39] C. Delcourt, 'The *Acquis* Communautaire: Has the Concept Had Its Day?', *Common Market Law Review*, 38 (2001), 829.

[40] D. Kochenov, *EU Enlargement and the Failure of Conditionality: Pre-Accession Conditionality in the Field of Democracy and the Rule of Law* (The Hague: Kluwer Law International, 2008).

serious consideration, but will not make the centre of attention of this chapter.[41]

This contribution is dedicated, firstly, to the assessment of the systemic deficiencies which inform the rule of law problems on the EU's side, demonstrating that the problem we are facing actually lies, to a great degree (while not exclusively, of course), *outside* of Poland, Hungary or Romania,[42] i.e. in the realm of the European Union as such: the supranational *acquis*. I then approach the Commission's 'pre-Article 7' procedure critically, putting it in the context of the deficiencies, which the main bulk of this chapter outlines. To be clear: these are the EU-level, as opposed to the member-state-level deficiencies. The pre-Article 7 procedure is chosen since it provides a clear example of how the institutions can come up with answers that are most likely unworkable, simply by asking the wrong questions, questions that ignore an important part of the substance of the problem we are facing. The activation of the procedure thus only adds to the gravity of the problem instead of helping to find a solution. The conclusions drawn as a result of this brief investigation are worrisome: a much more serious reform of the Union seems to be required than the humble proposals which have been put forward so far.

EU Rule of Law: Design and Functioning at Different Levels

It is not for nothing that when one thinks about the EU, democracy or human rights protection would be the last thing to come to mind,[43] lagging as it is far behind bananas, sugar,[44] motorcycle trailers[45] or the prohibition to deport foreign prostitutes as long as they are not a burden on a social security system and contribute their hard work honestly to the host society.[46] This is because democracy and the rule of law are *not* EU's

[41] For more on this and related questions, see, A. Williams, *The Ethos of Europe: Values, Law and Justice in EU Law* (Cambridge, 2009); and Kochenov, de Búrca and Williams (eds.), *Europe's Justice Deficit?*

[42] For an excellent assessment of the situation in this country, see, V. Perju, 'The Romanian Double Executive and the 2012 Constitutional Crisis', *International Journal of Constitutional Law*, 13 (2015), 246.

[43] See further, A. Williams, *Human Rights: A Study in Irony* (Oxford University Press, 2004).

[44] E.g. A. Albi, 'From Banana Saga to a Sugar Saga and Beyond', *Common Market Law Review*, 47 (2010), 791.

[45] E.g., S. Enchelmaier, 'Moped Trailers, Michelson & Roos, Gysbrechts: The ECJ's Case Law on Goods Keeps on Moving', *Yearbook of European Law*, 29 (2010), 190.

[46] E.g. L. W. Gormley, 'Free Movement of Workers and Social Security: As the Waitress Said to the Bishop', *European Law Review*, 7 (1982), 399.

founding ideas, or, paraphrasing Joseph Weiler, not in the EU's 'DNA',[47] constant rhetorical adherence to both notwithstanding. In the context of the division of powers between the EU and the member states as interpreted at the moment, they are thus left seemingly entirely to the member states to care about.[48] The EU can thus do little when basic foundations of constitutionalism are disturbed in one or more member states. More problematically still, the Union's own adherence to the values it professes is not beyond doubt. This is a serious design flaw, which was probably difficult to anticipate from the very beginning: the issue only became problematic as a result of a certain path that the Union followed throughout its history: emerging as a dynamic federal constitutional system and digesting more and more competences. This meant that values turned from an image-related luxury item into an indispensable element of the legal-political climate in the EU.[49]

By and large the rearticulation of the Union from an ordinary treaty organisation into a constitutional system was not accompanied by a sufficient upgrade of the role played by the core values it is said to build upon. These do not inform the day-to-day functioning of EU law, either internally[50] or externally.[51] Let us not forget that the promotion of its values, including the rule of law, is an obligation lying on the Union in accordance with the Treaties.[52] Indeed, unless we take the Commission's

[47] J. H. H. Weiler, 'The Schuman Declaration as a Manifesto of Political Messianism' in J. Dickson and P. Eleftheriadis (eds.), *Philosophical Foundations of European Union Law* (Oxford University Press, 2012).

[48] The issue underlined by the Council Legal Service in its Opinion on the Commission's pre-Article 7 procedure.

[49] Schütze, *From Dual to Cooperative Federalism: The Changing Structure of European Law*. See also K. Lenaerts and K. Gutman, '"Federal Common Law" in the European Union: A Comparative Perspective from the United States', *American Journal of Comparative Law*, 54 (2006), 1; J-C. Piris, 'L'Union européenne: vers une nouvelle forme de fédéralisme?', *Revue trimestrielle de droit européenne*, 41 (2004), 23.

[50] J. H. H. Weiler, 'Europa: "Nous coalisons des Etats nous n'unissons pas des hommes"' in M. Cartabia and A. Simoncini (eds.), *La sostenibilità della democrazia nel XXI secolo* (Bologna: Il Mulino, 2009), p. 51; Williams, *The Ethos of Europe*.

[51] For critical engagements, see, M. Cremona, 'Values in EU Foreign Policy' in M. Evans and P. Koutrakos (eds.), *Beyond the Established Legal Orders: Policy Interconnections between the EU and the Rest of the World* (Oxford: Hart Publishing, 2011), p. 275; P. Leino and R. Petrov, 'Between "Common Values" and Competing Universals', *European Law Journal*, 15 (2009), 654.

[52] Art. 3(5) TEU. See, also, L. Pech, 'Promoting the Rule of Law Abroad: On the EU's Limited Contribution to the Shaping of an International Understanding of the Rule of Law' in D. Kochenov and F. Amtenbrink (eds.), *The European Union's Shaping of the International Legal Order* (Cambridge University Press, 2013), p. 108.

scribbles for granted, the EU's steering of countless issues directly related to the values at hand is more problematic than not. The EU is not about the values Article 2 TEU preaches, which any student of EU law and politics will readily confirm.[53] The EU's very self-definition is not about human rights, the rule of law or democracy.[54] EU law functions differently: there is a whole other set of principles which actually matter and are held dear: supremacy, direct effect and autonomy are the key trio coming to mind.[55] Operating together, they can set aside both national constitutional – and international human rights[56] and UN law constraints.[57] In the current crisis-rich environment,[58] the Union frequently stars as part of the problem, rather than part of the solution. The Union will need to change.

Such a change will, at least partially, mean a return to the promise of EU integration made in the days of the Union's inception.[59] A *fédération*

53 The crucial argument in this vein has been made, most powerfully, by Andrew Williams: A. Williams, 'Taking Values Seriously: Towards a Philosophy of EU Law', *Oxford Journal of Legal Studies*, 29 (2009), 549. See, also, J. H. H. Weiler's unpublished paper 'On the Distinction between Values and Virtues in the Process of European Integration'.

54 See, most recently, Opinion 2/13 (*ECHR Accession II*) [2014] ECLI:EU:C:2014:2454: para. 170, which states that the fundamental rights in the EU are 'interpret[ed] [. . .] within the framework of the structure and objectives of the EU'.

55 Procedural principles cannot possibly replace the lack of substantive attention to the core values encompassed by Art. 2 TEU, including the Rule of Law, threatening to cause justice deficit of the Union: D. Kochenov, G. de Búrca and A. Williams (eds.), *Europe's Justice Deficit?* Cf., D. Halberstam, '"It's the Autonomy, Stupid!" A Modest Defence of Opinion 2/13 on EU Accession to the ECHR, and the Way Forward' (2015) 16 *German Law Journal* 105; and P. Eeckhout, 'Opinion 2/13 on EU Accession to the ECHR and Judicial Dialogue – Autonomy or Autarky?', *Fordham International Law Journal*, 38 (2015), 955; D. Kochenov, 'Citizenship without Respect', *Jean Monnet Working Paper* (NYU Law School) No. 08/10, 2010.

56 Opinion 2/13 (*ECHR Accession II*) [2014] ECLI:EU:C:2014:2454; Kochenov, 'EU Law without the Rule of Law'.

57 On the *Kadi* saga, see, G. de Búrca, 'The European Court of Justice and the International Legal Order after *Kadi*', *Harvard International Law Journal*, 51 (2010), 1. See also, of course, C-584/10 *Kadi II* [2013] ECLI:EU:C:2013:518.

58 Three equally important facets of the current crisis can be outlined: values, justice, and economic and monetary. On the crisis of values, see e.g., Williams, 'Taking Values Seriously' and Weiler, 'On the Distinction'. On the crisis of justice: Kochenov, de Búrca and Williams (eds.), *Europe's Justice Deficit?* On the economic side of the crisis, see e.g., A. Menéndez, 'The Existential Crisis of the European Union', *German Law Journal*, 14 (2013), 453; M. Adams, F. Fabbrini and P. Larouche (eds.), *The Constitutionalisation of European Budgetary Constraints* (Oxford: Hart Publishing, 2014).

59 On the key aspects of dynamics of EU's legal history see, B. Davies and M. Rasmussen, 'Towards a New History of European Law', *Contemporary European History*, 21 (2012), 305.

européenne (the one mentioned in the Schuman Declaration) to be brought about via the creation of the internal market, stood for a line of developments significantly more far-reaching than the idea of economic integration as such. The former is value based – while the latter probably is not (at least not based on the values of Article 2), as Andrew Williams explained in his seminal work.[60]

Not the whole story was negative, though. Although the Union's ambition has gradually been scaled down to the market – call it a hijacking of the ends by the means[61] – *de facto* the Union started playing, mostly through negative integration, the role of the promoter of liberal and tolerant nationhood, as rightly characterised by Will Kymlicka – promoting a very clear idea of constitutionalism based on proportionality, tolerance and the taming of nationalism.[62] Besides, at the core of the Union there lay basic mutual respect among the member states: the Union would be impossible, should they obstruct the principle of mutual recognition.[63] This came down to frowning upon the ideology of 'thick' national identities, however glorified in some schoolbooks. The ultimate result is that the EU, subconsciously as it were, emerged as a promoter of *one* particular type of constitutionalism,[64] which is based on the rule of law understood through national democracy and the culture of justification implying human rights protection and strong judicial review. To be a member state of the EU in the context of these developments came to signify one thing – when approached from a systemic point of state-organisation at least: to stick to this particular type of constitutionalism, which is now reflected in Article 2 TEU and which also represents the most important condition to be fulfilled before joining the EU, as hinted at in Article 49 TEU.[65]

60 Williams, *The Ethos of Europe*.

61 D. Kochenov, 'The Citizenship Paradigm', *Cambridge Yearbook of European Legal Studies*, 15 (2013), 196.

62 W. Kymlicka, 'Liberal Nationalism and Cosmopolitan Justice' in S. Benhabib, *Another Cosmopolitanism* (Oxford University Press, 2006), p. 134. See also G. Davies, 'Humiliation of the State as a Constitutional Tactic' in F. Amtenbrink and P. van den Bergh (eds.), *The Constitutional Integrity of the European Union* (The Hague: T.M.C. Asser Press, 2010).

63 M. Poiares Maduro, 'So Close Yet So Far: The Paradoxes of Mutual Recognition', *Journal of European Public Policy*, 14 (2007); V. Mitsilegas, 'The Limits of Mutual Trust in Europe's Area of Freedom, Security and Justice: From automatic inter-State Cooperation to the Slow Emergence of the Individual', 31 (2012) *Yearbook of European Law*, 319.

64 Perju, 'Proportionality and Freedom – an Essay on Method in Constitutional Law', *Global Constitutionalism*, 334.

65 See e.g., D. Kochenov, *EU Enlargement and the Failure of Conditionality*, ch. 2.

The EU thus emerged as a vehicle of a negative market-based approach to the 'values' question, for which it is rightly criticised, e.g. by Alexander Somek and Andrew Williams, among numerous others.[66] Clearly, creating a market and questioning the state is not sufficient as a basis for a mature constitutional system, potentially creating a justice void at the supranational level[67] – and perpetuating the Union's inability to help the member states labouring hard to inflict a justice void on themselves, either through an outright embrace of Putin-style 'illiberal democracy', recently proclaimed as an ideal to strive for by the Hungarian Prime Minister Orbán,[68] an attack on the judiciary and the media, as in contemporary Poland,[69] or through failing to build a well-ordered and functioning modern state, as it the case in Greece[70] or Romania,[71] for instance. Outright defiance is thus not required to fall out of adherence to Article 2 TEU aspirations.

Moving beyond Article 7 TEU, which has been analysed in the literature in overwhelming detail (much of this analysis convincingly questioning the provision's effectiveness),[72] ordinary enforcement mechanisms designed to ensure that EU law works well in the member states – most notably, Articles 258, 259 and 260 TFEU – are always at our disposal. There is a very important problem here, however – it is too easy to expect of these provisions more than what they can deliver.

Even if it is presumed that violations of Article 2 TEU can be subject to the aforementioned procedures alongside with Article 7 TEU[73] – indeed, the very existence of Article 7 TEU clearly testifies to the intention of the drafters of the Treaty to ensure that Article 2 TEU is an enforceable legal provision, not merely a declaration – the fact that Article 2 law is somewhat different from the rest of the *acquis* is impossible to hide. The same

[66] E.g., A. Somek, 'The Preoccupation with Rights and the Embrace of Inclusion: A Critique' in Kochenov, de Búrca and Williams (eds.), *Europe's Justice Deficit?*

[67] S. Douglas-Scott, 'Justice, Injustice and the Rule of Law in the EU' in Kochenov, de Búrca and Williams (eds.), *Europe's Justice Deficit?*, p. 51.

[68] For the full text of the speech, see, *The Budapest Beacon*, 27 July 2014, available at: http://budapestbeacon.com/public-policy/full-text-of-viktor-orbans-speech-at-baile-tusnad-tusnadfurdo-of-26-july-2014/10592.

[69] Cf. Venice Commission, Report of 11 March 2016.

[70] M. Ioannidis, 'The Greek Case' in Jakab and Kochenov (eds.), *The Enforcement of EU Law.*

[71] Perju, 'The Romanian Double Executive', 246.

[72] E.g., B. Bugarič, 'Protecting Democracy inside the EU: on Article 7 TEU and the Hungarian Turn to Authoritarianism' in Closa and Kochenov (eds.), *Reinforcing the Rule of Law*; Besselink, 'The Bite, the Bark and the Howl'. See also, most importantly, Sadurski, 'Adding Bite to a Bark', 385.

[73] C. Hillion, 'Overseeing the Rule of Law in the EU: Legal Mandate and Means'.

applies to the violations: Article 2 TEU violations are not the same as ordinary *acquis* violations. Such differences are particularly acute in the in the context of one specific type of chronically non-compliant states, where, like in Hungary or Poland, non-compliance is *ideological* and cannot be explained with a reference to the lacking capacity, 'simple' corruption and outright sloppiness[74] – arguments one might deploy in the context of some South-East European countries, like Romania or Greece. Where chronic non-compliance is ideological, Article 260 TFEU becomes the *crux* of the whole story, as simple restatements of the breach under Article 258 TFEU (or Article 259 TFEU, for that matter)[75] will presumably not be enough.[76] The question of the effectiveness of fining against member states that have made an ideological choice favouring non-compliance is likely to remain open.

The fact thus seems to be that the EU not only suffers from inability to approach the values question, thus supplying a legitimate answer concerning what it stands for beyond the market – or a procedure to come up with such an answer by itself. It also lacks any ability to enforce the values as mentioned in Article 2 TEU in legal terms. The limitations of both Article 7 TEU and of the standard enforcement procedures in this context are quite straightforward, as the infringement procedures are profiled as confined to the scope of EU law *sensu stricto*, which makes it difficult to deploy them to protect the values viewed by many as outside of such scope,[77] while Article 7 TEU has simply never been applied, probably due to the high minimal thresholds to be reached for its activation.[78]

For many decades the Union has been consistently denying the very possibility that any Article 2 TEU problems could ever arise, presenting itself as solely working within the paradigm of the internal market, which

[74] R. Uitz, 'Can You Tell When an Illiberal Democracy Is in the Making? An Appeal to Comparative Constitutional Scholarship from Hungary', *I-CON*, 13 (2015), 279.

[75] See e.g., D. Kochenov, 'Biting Intergovernmentalism: The Case for the Reinvention of Article 259 TFEU to Make It a Viable Rule of Law Enforcement Tool', *The Hague Journal of the Rule of Law*, 7 (2015), 153.

[76] On the main deficiencies of the system, see, most importantly, B. Jack, 'Article 260(2) TFEU: An Effective Judicial Procedure for the Enforcement of Judgments?', *European Law Journal*, 19 (2013), 420; P. Wennerås, 'Sanctions against Member States under Article 260 TFEU: Alive, but not Kicking?', *Common Market Law Review*, 49 (2012), 145.

[77] But see, crucially, K. L. Scheppele, 'The Case for Systemic Infringement Actions' in Closa and Kochenov (eds.), *Reinforcing Rule of Law*; C. Hillion, 'Overseeing the Rule of Law in the EU'.

[78] Sadurski, 'Adding Bite to a Bark'.

denies serious treatment of the majority of the values and principles listed in Article 2 TEU. It is only in the context of the preparation of the Eastern enlargement that a fascinating situation arose, when the EU *de facto* ended up seemingly enforcing its foundational values through the pre-accession conditionality policy – to highly questionable results. The Failure of Conditionality in the fields of democracy and the rule of law, which I analysed elsewhere,[79] now stands overwhelmingly proven by, *inter alia*, the Hungarian developments.

The Union is thus generally powerless with regard to the *enforcement* of values and, more importantly, also their *content*. In fact, the very fact that we are now concerned with enforcing them seriously amounts to nothing else but conceding that the presumption that all the member states form a level playing field in terms of rule of law etc. – i.e. the fact that all of them actually adhere to the specific type of constitutionalism the EU set out to promote – does not always hold. This is something the European Court of Human Rights (ECt.HR) has already clearly hinted at in *M.S.S. v. Belgium and Greece*.[80] Acknowledging this alongside EU's obvious powerlessness as far as values are concerned is a potentially explosive combination in the Union built on member state equality and the principle of mutual recognition. In a situation where the core values are not respected by Hungary, for instance, we are not dealing with a member state revolting, for one reason or another, against a binding norm of European law. At the level of values, we are dealing with a *principally different member state*, with the Belarusianisation of the EU from the inside.[81]

Once the values of Article 2 EU are not observed, the essential presumptions behind the core of the Union no longer hold, which undermines the very essence of the integration exercise: mutual recognition becomes an untenable fiction, which the member states, nevertheless, are bound by EU law to adhere to: this is the core of what the autonomy of EU law stands for, as confirmed by the Court in the infamous Opinion 2/13.[82] Autonomy

[79] Kochenov, *EU Enlargement and the Failure of Conditionality*.

[80] *MSS v. Belgium and Greece* [2011] Application No. 30696/09. ECtHR reconfirmed its position in *Tarakhel v. Switzerland* [2014] Application No. 29217/12, dealing with the same issue and restating that the ECJ's 'systemic' standard articulated in *N.S. and others* (C-411/11 ECLI:EU:C:2011:865) and restated in *Abdullahi v. Bundesasylamt* (C-294/12 ECLI:EU:C:2013:813) is unacceptable under the ECHR.

[81] U. Belavusau, 'Case C-286/12 *Commission v. Hungary*', *Common Market Law Review*, 50 (2013), 1145.

[82] This point has been forcefully restated in the ECJ's Opinion 2/13 (*ECHR Accession II*) [2014] ECLI:EU:C:2014:2454. See, e.g., para. 192.

considerations in the context of EU law are usually prone to prevail over human rights and other values – including the rule of law – cherished in the national constitutional systems of the member states. Indeed, it would probably not be incorrect to argue that this would be the shortest possible summary of Opinion 2/13, which, in turn, summarised EU law as it stands. The consequences for the rule of law are drastic: all the principles invoked by the ECJ to justify giving EU law the upper hand in Opinion 2/13 are procedural, while the problems which the reliance on the ECHR is there to solve are substantive. Curing substantive deficiencies of the EU legal order with the remedies confined to autonomy and direct effect is a logical flaw plaguing the EU legal system, a condition that puzzles most renowned commentators.[83] One cannot quarrel about the roses when the forests are burning. To agree with Eleanor Sharpston and Daniel Sarmiento, 'in the balance between individual rights and primacy, the Court in Opinion 2/13 has fairly clearly sided with the latter. The losers under Opinion 2/13 are not the member states of the signatory States of the Council of Europe, but the individual citizens of the European Union'.[84] This is so, one must add, not only because of the potential reduction of the level of human rights protection. Rather, it is due to the fact that the EU, as Opinion 2/13 made clear, boasts an overwhelming potential to undermine the rule of law at the national level and this potential impact is not an empty threat.[85]

The question, then, is how to ensure that the EU's own vision of the rule of law – of which mutual trust without checking the substance of the Member States' adherence to values is an inherent part– does not undermine (or even destroy) adherence to the principle of the rule of law in the member states, which are, in fact, compliant with the values listed in Article 2 TEU.[86]

Clearly, horizontal *Solange* – i.e. allowing the member states to check each other's adherence to the values of Article 2 TEU and the *acquis* with the use of their own national system of courts and other institutions – if ever implemented, means nothing else but the end of all that we cherish in the Union, all its imperfections notwithstanding.[87] The legal fiction of

83 E.g., Eeckhout, 'Opinion 2/13'; Halberstam, 'It's the Autonomy, Stupid'.
84 E. Sharpston and D. Sarmiento, 'European Citizenship and Its New Union: Time to Move On?' in D. Kochenov (ed.), *EU Citizenship and Federalism: The Role of Rights* (Cambridge University Press, 2017 (forthcoming)).
85 See, further, Kochenov, 'EU Law without the Rule of Law?'.
86 For a detailed discussion of this dilemma, see, ibid.
87 But see, I. Canor, 'My Brother's Keeper? Horizontal *Solange*: "An Ever Close Distrust among the Peoples of Europe"', *Common Market Law Review*, 50 (2013).

'all the member states are good enough' is absolutely worth fighting for. But the only way to do it, it seems, consists in incorporating the values of Article 2 TEU in full into the realm of EU's *acquis*, thus rethinking our understanding of the scope of EU law and also approaching the difficult questions of the substance of values and of their effective enforcement.[88]

Attempts to Solve the Outstanding Problems: A Critique

The acute need to change the approach to values enforcement in the context where all the legal-political tools at hand are most likely unworkable drove the Commission, the guardian of the Treaties, to come up with the 'pre-Article 7' procedure.[89] In a nutshell, it comes down to outlining the steps that the Commission needs to take before it uses the right, which it enjoys under the Treaties, to activate Article 7 TEU. Before the Commission triggers the procedure it would thus engage in a productive dialogue with the member state suspected of falling short of complying with the rule of law requirements of Article 2 TEU. The design and the recent activation of the procedure against Poland has not contributed to solving the problems at hand.

Three crucial considerations inform the Commission's procedure. Firstly, it is equally applicable to all the member states without any discrimination, notwithstanding the fact that it is not based on any general monitoring across the board. Secondly, the proposal is *de facto* and also *de jure*, not decoupled from Article 7 TEU: it simply paves the way up to the Commission's use of its right, as set in the same provision, to trigger the procedure described therein. In other words, in a way it simply formalizes the preparatory steps that the Commission takes before Article 7 TEU is deployed. Thirdly, the proposed procedure is not to be deployed to the detriment of the standard, pre-existing enforcement procedures, which remain at the Commission's disposal.

What the Commission introduced is thus a minimal addition to the *acquis*. This saves the pre-Article 7 procedure from accusations that it is *ultra vires* in nature, as potentially defying the principle of conferral of Article 5(1) TEU – the point made by the Council Legal Service.[90] Although sensible at the first glance, the reference to conferral is probably less sound than what the legal service would like to claim, as the

[88] See, in the same vein, the contributions in von Bogdandy and Sonnevend, *Constitutional Crisis*.

[89] For a detailed analysis, see, Kochenov and Pech, 'Monitoring and Enforcement'.

[90] Opinion of the legal service of the Council.

procedure established by the Commission is, once again, but a part of what Article 7 TEU quite clearly implies, if not demands. The Commission can trigger the application of that provision and the pre-Article 7 procedure is simply an explanation of how the Commission plans to go about this. The consequences of this are clear: whatever the Commission might recommend or find is not binding on the member state, which is singled out as potentially non-compliant. The apparently soft nature is not the most fundamental flaw of the Commission's procedure, however. As demonstrated below, there are at least three crucial considerations which make the proposed procedure most likely useless in the medium- to long-term perspective. This being said, it would be difficult to deny that in the current legal-political climate in the EU it would be rather difficult to expect more of the Commission, so even a slightest move is a worthy addition to the existing palette of dysfunctional procedures at the Union's disposal.

While it is possible to criticise the Commission's proposal from the strictly legal point of view as the Council Legal Service has done, focusing, in particular, on the clarity (or the lack thereof) of the outline of the scope of EU law in the context of Article 2 TEU potential deployment, this contribution will adopt a different approach: effectiveness, also saying a couple of words about the sloppiness of the practical application of the new procedure in the context of the Commission's action against Poland. Indeed, how effective the proposed procedure is likely to be in solving the outstanding problems of the EU in the area of values enforcement is potentially as important as a legalistic dissection of it is.

Activation

What became abundantly clear following the new procedure's activation against Poland is that not only is it unhelpful, but it also undermines the deployment of Article 7 TEU proper.[91] The Commission made three strategic mistakes in dealing with Poland, which make Article 7 TEU much more difficult to use, thus undermining an already problematic instrument.

Firstly, activating the Pre-Article 7 Procedure implies that the Commission is not convinced that the situation is bad enough to warrant at least the shaming stage of Article 7, i.e. 7(1) TEU. From what we

[91] Kochenov and Pech, 'Better Late than Never?'

observe in Poland, this assessment of the Commission is most likely wrong.[92] So the activation of the mechanism only leads to the loss of time.

Secondly, activating the Pre-Article 7 Procedure instantaneously crippled Article 7, since now the 'pre-' step would rightly be regarded by any backsliding member state as necessary, making Article 7 TEU, which is complex enough to deploy already, even more difficult to use.

Lastly, activating the Pre-Article 7 Procedure in the current circumstances makes the deployment of the 'biting' part of Article 7, i.e. 7(3) TEU impossible. Since unanimity is required by 7(2) TEU, which is a necessary condition for moving on to the sanctioning part of 7(3) TEU, and given that Mr Orbán will make sure that there is no unanimity – a constellation which was all too easy to predict – starting the Pre-Article 7 Procedure against Poland alone without Hungary means that the Commission is *not* minded to actually use all the legal tools at its disposal. These mistakes allow questioning whether the Commission's PR move was actually meant to make a difference. The potential effectiveness of Article 7 TEU stands instantly undermined by the deployment of the procedure, which the Commission designed with an aim to help the activation of this article in the first place. The sloppiness of the first activation aside, it is worth looking at the legal nature and the potential effectiveness of the new procedure *sensu stricto*.

Criticism of the legal basis

Let us start with a word about the Council Legal Service's unhelpful reading of the limits to EU's powers. There can be no dispute that the values of Article 2 TEU do not make part of the traditional *acquis sensu stricto*, indeed, this is the key problem of the Union in the area of value enforcement, as has been argued also above – this, all the normative grounds for the Union intervention on behalf of the values notwithstanding.[93] To adopt an approach which is too inflexible in restating this, however, hardly helps anyone in an atmosphere where changing the Treaties to bring about a different legal reality is, no doubt, impossible: unanimity is of course required, and Hungary, Poland and other potentially problematic states cannot be expected, rationally speaking, to throw their weight behind a meaningful values-enforcement reform.

[92] See, Venice Commission, Report on Poland of 11 March 2016.

[93] C. Closa, 'Reinforcing the Rule of Law: Normative Arguments, Institutional Proposals and Procedural Limitations' in Closa and Kochenov (eds.), *Reinforcing Rule of Law*.

Having said this, numerous examples of sound logical constructions come to mind, which could clearly be deployed to back what the Commission introduced. The most important example from the history of EU law which could inform our thinking is the embrace of human rights by the supranational legal system in Europe. Something that has not been within the realm of EU law – remember *Stork*,[94] where the ECJ refused to take fundamental rights into consideration on the grounds that the EU does not have such competence – entered this realm and stayed.[95] It is easy to explain why: EU law would not be operational without human rights – and this is not simply to exaggerate the importance of *Solange* threats from the *Bundesverfassungsguericht* and *Corte Costituzionale*:[96] any *effet utile* hopes could be laid to rest without, just as the crucial transformation that turned the EU from an atypical international organization into a constitutional system.[97]

Approached in this sense, the rule of law (the member state level included) does not seem to be in any way different: can EU law exist without? As long as it cannot – and this answer cannot provoke much debate – the power to police the rule of law also in the member states is to be assumed – exactly what happened with the human rights story. Note that we are not speaking about inventing a wheel here, just about a repetition of a necessary step, well-tested in the past. The crucial difference consists in the fact that step no. 1 has been taken under pressure from the national courts, ready for *ideological* non-compliance for the reasons of respecting the law and the values of the legal systems they were entrusted to protect, which are now reflected in Article 2 TEU, while step no. 2 is to be taken under pressure from equally ideological non-compliance, but rooted, as opposed to the first step, in the failure to respect the law and values on which the Union and all its member states are built. The fact that one context of non-compliance was 'positive' while the second context is no doubt 'negative' cannot possibly change the nature of non-compliance with the values (and the law, for that matter), or diminish the EU's eagerness and desire to solve the outstanding problems, which emerge as a result.

[94] Case 1/58, *Stork v High Authority* [1959] ECR 17.

[95] For details, see, P. Alston (ed.), *EU Law and Human Rights* (Oxford University Press, 1999).

[96] See B. Davies, *Resisting the European Court of Justice* (Cambridge University Press, 2012).

[97] J. H. H. Weiler, 'The Transformation of Europe', *Yale Law Journal*, 100 (1991). See also his *The Constitution for Europe* (Cambridge University Press, 1998) and J. H. H. Weiler and G. de Búrca (eds.), *The Worlds of European Constitutionalism* (Cambridge University Press, 2011).

Plentiful sources of turning values into a somewhat more binding part of the law of the Union could be outlined. By claiming that the Commission does not have the competence to elaborate on how it plans to defend the rule of law in the EU by applying Article 7 TEU, the legal service of the Council is wrong in approaching the rule of law – which is the air any legal system breathes – as a luxury, which its *own law* seemingly prevents the EU from acquiring. Such an approach should be dismissed outright as lacking in coherence and potentially dangerous for both levels of law in the EU: the supranational and the national too, given the EU's essential conditioning – in all what it does – on entertaining and fostering the presumption that there is something akin to an equal level of compliance with the values all around the Union. In the atmosphere where *the presumption – not the compliance* – is policed with the use of EU law under the banner of EU rule of law, the Council Legal Service's position is irresponsible.

Turning to other analogies from which the EU can rightly draw inspiration in these difficult times, the pre-accession context is also to be named. The story of the pre-accession monitoring of democracy, the rule of law and other values is overwhelmingly telling. This is so not because of how dysfunctional the monitoring was. Indeed, it landed us with all the countries we now criticize as non-compliant with Article 2 TEU in the Union in the first place, while the Commission's regular reports were applauding compliance with what was then Article 6(1) TEU (as it then was) among all the new member-states-to-be, failing to ensure maturation of the institutions and lasting continuity of the change achieved. The Commission unquestionably enjoyed the competence to police Article 2 TEU matters, since Article 49 TEU then (and also now) requires to ensure that the new member states are fully compliant with the EU's values, not merely those elements thereof, which happen to fall within the scope of the *acquis*, since then – remember Weiler's DNA argument – we would not have *any* checks of compliance with democracy or the rule of law at all in the context of the pre-accession.

What is of crucial importance, such a competence was then enjoyed by the Union institutions for the first time in the EU's history. The use of the competence thus acquired led to a gradual forming a quasi-*acquis* on values, which can be vaguely distilled from the pre-accession monitoring documents.[98] While critics would no doubt point to the

[98] For an attempt, see e.g., D. Kochenov, 'Behind the Copenhagen Façade: The Meaning and Structure of the Copenhagen Political Criterion of Democracy and the Rule of Law', *European Integration online Papers*, 8(10) (2004).

important differences which exist between the 'internal' and the 'external' realms of the *acquis* in the competences field, what empowered the Commission to act in the realm of what is now Article 2 TEU, treating this provision as directly enforceable law, was a request from the European Council at Copenhagen in 1993 and the pre-accession reorientation of the Europe agreements,[99] i.e. a strong political decision and the rethinking of the law in force. No change of primary law was deemed to be required. Still now Article 49 TEU does not expressly mention either the principle of conditionality or the fact that the classical standard limitations of the scope of EU law do not apply to the pre-accession context, which this provision (very) vaguely regulates.

Both the example of the introduction of human rights protection into the edifice of EU law by the ECJ and the attempt to endow the values of what is now Article 2 TEU with substance by the Commission clearly testify to the plasticity of EU law, when the very *effet utile*, if not the survival of this legal system, is at stake. More examples could be given to support this point:[100] like the human brain, the EU legal system is flexible enough to ensure effective functioning against all odds. When push comes to shove and the legal system experiences a series of important shocks at its very base there is no room for excluding systemic legal arguments based on the considerations of the functionality of the law: the Commission definitely has all the competence in the world to run its pre-Article 7 procedure. In light of the above, the procedure is not only legal, but also possibly logical, once one moves beyond the activation problems. Yet, this picture is misleading.

[99] K. Inglis, 'The *Europe Agreements* Compared in the Light of Their Pre-Accession Reorientation', *Common Market Law Review*, 37 (2000), 1173.

[100] Especially the concept of the 'essence of rights' comes to mind, emerging from EU citizenship law and other fields: M. van den Brink, 'The Origins and the Potential Effects of the Substance of Rights Test' in Kochenov (ed.), *EU Citizenship and Federalism;* D. Kochenov, 'A Real European Citizenship; a New Jurisdiction Test; a Novel Chapter in the Development of the Union in Europe', *Columbia Journal of European Law*, 18 (2011), 56. For a clear proposal to apply this particular aspect of EU law's plasticity to the solution of Article 2 TEU enforcement problems, see, most importantly, A. von Bogdandy, C. Antpöller and M. Ioannidis, 'Enforcing European Values' in Jakab and Kochenov (eds.), *The Enforcement of EU Law*, as well as the earlier emanations of Professor von Bogdandy's proposal in the references. See also J. Croon-Gestefeld, 'Reverse Solange – Union Citizenship as a Detour on the Route to European Rights Protection against National Infringements' in Kochenov (ed.), *EU Citizenship.*

Effectiveness Considerations

The effectiveness of the procedure is fundamentally questionable. The change to be brought about as a result of the pre-Article 7 procedure's implementation will most likely be incapable of reverting the politics of consistent rule of law non-compliance in 'ideologically different' member states undergoing Belarusianisation. An emphasis on at least three aspects of the likely deficiency of pre-Article 7 can be made, in the light of the crucial deficiencies that the Union suffers from, as outlined above. As has been demonstrated, the EU does not actually have any *acquis* on values (outside of the pre-accession framework, which failed to produce sound results precisely in the values field); the EU does not have tools to formulate such *acquis*; the enforcement of values is lacking; the effectiveness of the current enforcement mechanisms – in particular the fines and lump-sums deployed against ideologically non-compliant member states – is inadequate in the values-enforcement field. Consequently, should the EU be serious about solving the outstanding issues with the operation of the rule of law, the key elements to consider should reach beyond mere enforcement to include the following aspects:

(a) the substance of values
(b) the procedure to alter the *acquis* on values and unquestionably extend the scope of EU law to cover the systemic departures from what Article 2 TEU presupposes
(c) elaboration of sound enforcement procedures in the sphere of Article 2 TEU *distinct* from what Articles 258 and 260 TFEU offer

Regrettably – but entirely not surprisingly – the pre-Article 7 procedure falls short of taking into account all the three elements outlined above, while also ignoring the context of simultaneous dealing with several problematic member states, rather than one, ruling out any effective deployment of Article 7 TEU, instead of helping its effectiveness. Moreover, beyond the point that the effectiveness of the mechanism can be questioned, it is quite arbitrary in terms of defining the values' substance, it does *not* extend the *acquis* to cover the values and it contains *no* enforcement procedures besides a threat to trigger Article 7 TEU, which, even if made credible, is now unfeasible in practice and is highly unlikely to be effective when applied to a principled illiberal government, non-compliant by virtue of consciously made ideological choices. It is not surprising, since it has at its foundation a picture of the EU which is already too optimistic to allow a clear outline of the outstanding problems. The main reason why the new procedure invoked against Poland, as well as the general scholarly trend of focusing uniquely on compliance, is too weak to be functional is, then, that it steers past all three indispensable issues to be tackled, should the enforcement of Article 2 TEU become a reality.

To Conclude

In light of the above, several observations are in order, once the work aiming at designing a new mechanism commences. EU values, as reflected in Article 2 TEU, objectively speaking, are not (and have never been) part of the *acquis*. This is precisely why the Copenhagen political criteria on democracy, the rule of law and human rights protection were formulated in the first place, roughly 20 years ago. The ECJ's attempts to deal *inter alia* with human rights and the rule of law as though these were part of the ordinary *acquis* are far from sufficient: the rule of law is turning into a purely procedural consideration of basic legality. In one example, paying compensation to the judges – what Orbán's government has done in Hungary following the Commission's win against the country in front of the ECJ – replaces the need to not destroy the independence of the courts.[101] Worse still, nods in the direction of the European Court of Human Rights, even in the most outrageous cases, are frequent and usually unhelpful, as the principles of the two legal systems often differ.[102] Take the case of *McCarthy* for instance, where the ECJ clarified that EU law could not help an EU citizen to prevent her husband, who was also the only bread-winner in a family in which one of the children was disabled and needed constant care, from being deported, because the mother was not working and was on social assistance, and thus unable to benefit from EU law, *de facto* punishing her for the disability of her child, that punishment taking the form of the destruction of her family.[103] As Gareth Davies has clearly demonstrated, the nods in the direction of the ECt.HR are futile and half-hearted.[104] The ECJ opens to question the very foundations of what

[101] K. L. Scheppele, 'Constitutional Coups and Judicial Review: How Transnational Institutions Can Strengthen Peak Courts at Times of Crisis (with Special Reference to Hungary)' *Transnational Law & Contemporary Problems*, 23 (2014), 51.

[102] G. Davies, 'A Right to Stay at Home: A Basis for Expanding European Family Rights' in D. Kochenov (ed.), *EU Citizenship and Federalism*.

[103] N. Nic Shuibhne, '(Some of) The Kids Are All Right: Comment on *McCarthy* and *Dereci*', *Common Market Law Review*, 49 (2012), 349.

[104] Davies, 'A Right to Stay at Home'.

EU law stands for. Where to find justice in the maze of a purely legalistic engagement with crucially important problems, usually reformulated as internal market governance issues, is thus a burning question.[105] In the context when the *acquis* is not about the values,[106] the EU at times emerges as a potent cause of injustice.[107]

In this general context, when the *acquis* and values are not synonymous, particularly the application of the Copenhagen criteria in the context of the recent enlargement rounds, there is a lesson of caution to be learned: the Commission has emerged as an institution which, when given all the responsibility for judging the preparedness of the new member states for accession, values compliance outside the scope of the *acquis* included, failed the exercise.[108] Here, to the void of substance also was added the lack of capability to generate such a substance, the lack of virtually any limitations emerging from the scope of the law – as discussed above – notwithstanding. Besides illustrating the EU's inbuilt limitations with regard to its ability to generate the substance of Article 2 TEU rules, the pre-accession context also sets off the alarm bell on in terms of institutional capacity: the Commission is probably not the best actor to entrust with the internal monitoring of member states' compliance with Article 2 TEU. It is highly unlikely that the

[105] For further analysis, see the contributions in Kochenov, de Búrca and Williams (eds.), *Europe's Justice Deficit?* Cf. D. Kochenov, 'On Tiles and Pillars: EU Citizenship as a Federal Denominator' in D. Kochenov (ed.), *EU Citizenship and Federalism: The Role of Rights*.

[106] Williams, *The Ethos of Europe*. For a general assessment of the *acquis* to uncover the ideology it reproduces and the biases in the knowledge it favours and blesses, see M. Bartl, 'Internal Market Rationality, Private Law and the Direction of the Union: Resuscitating the Market as the Object of the Political', *European Law Journal* (2015). See also, for a broader account, P. Agha, 'The Empire of Principle'.

[107] The Charter of Fundamental Rights emerges as a particularly cynical document in this regard: excluded from the scope of Article 2 TEU by virtue of the Charter's *ratione materiae* limitation clause in Article 51 CFR, it thus only applied to the *acquis sensu stricto*: part of the problem, rather than part of the solution. For a persuasive account of the Charter as a way to limit the reach of EU human rights obligations, see A. Knook, 'The Court, the Charter, and the Vertical Division of Powers in the European Union', *Common Market Law Review*, 42 (2005), 367; for a lament that the Charter is never used by the Commission in infringement actions, see A. Łazowski, 'Decoding a Legal Enigma: The Charter of Fundamental Rights of the European Union and Infringement Proceedings', *ERA Forum*, 14 (2013), 573. For a far-reaching proposal to revolutionize the current practice of the application of the Charter in the area of Article 2 TEU values through judicial activism, see A. Jakab, 'The EU Charter of Fundamental Rights as the Most Promising Way of Enforcing the Rule of Law against EU Member States' in Closa and Kochenov (eds.), *Reinforcing Rule of Law*.

[108] Kochenov, *EU Enlargement and the Failure of Conditionality*.

Commission's approach will radically change, raising a number of questions concerning who should be doing this job.

This is a fascinating question. The Copenhagen Commission proposed by Jan-Werner Müller, which is supposed to unite the wise men and women from a number of the member states commanding absolute respect and be endowed with some enforcement powers, as well as the potential to give binding advice to EU institutions, is definitely a workable idea[109] – even given the failure of the Copenhagen criteria, as enforced by the Commission, made obvious by the very fact that we are discussing Hungary, Poland and other states formerly fully subjected to the extensive pre-accession Copenhagen criteria-inspired scrutiny at this point. Acting on the assumption that the very ethos of the Copenhagen Commission would be radically different from that of the current Commission, Müller's proposal is worthy of most serious consideration. Of crucial importance here is the understanding that the formulation of the substance of values should not be outsourced, which would be the case if the Venice Commission, for instance,[110] were asked to do the job. The drawback of asking the Council of Europe to do something for the EU is obvious: it amounts to *outsourcing key constitutional issues*. This being said, it is also necessary to keep in mind that, given the overarching character of the values and principles established by Article 2 TEU, it is highly unlikely that the provision can be read as a sign of EU specificity, let alone uniqueness. The crucial symbolic value of being in charge of the proclaimed core of EU's constitutional system is worth the defying of outsourcing calls, however.

The solving of outstanding value problems should be done with care, gently. However imperfect, the EU is functioning well, boasting an obvious added value. Any new tools aimed at enforcement of Article 2 TEU compliance should thus unquestionably respect the key premise of European integration: EU federalism. Federalism's importance is twofold: it is a guarantee of preservation of diversity and a guarantee of preservation of liberty. Article 2 TEU should not be used as a pretext for a power-grab – even if this happens unintentionally. The risks are clear: the EU, with all its deficiencies, is not really very dangerous at the moment from the point of view of liberty and freedom (whatever the position one holds on Greek bailouts) only because it is constantly kept in

[109] J.-W. Müller, 'For a Copenhagen Commission: The Case Restated' in Closa and Kochenov (eds.), *Reinforcing Rule of Law*.

[110] K. Tuori, 'From Copenhagen to Venice' in Closa and Kochenov (eds.), *Reinforcing Rule of Law*.

check, whether we like it or not. In this context, putting an emphasis on the Charter of Fundamental Rights for instance, is highly problematic: general applicability of the Charter – something in favour of which Vice-President Reding (as she then was) used to argue – is likely to create more problems than it would solve: decentralized judicial review is not a panacea when the value core of the system is flimsy and often irrelevant at the moment when key decisions are taken.

Whichever mechanism is put in place to remedy the current problems, it is necessary to look at such mechanism's likelihood of effectiveness, keeping both the member states and EU citizens in mind. In this sense it is clear that copying the expulsion procedure of the Council of Europe (CoE) is not an option: rather than a way to improve the situation, it would amount to little besides making clear that the EU is powerless: by expelling a member state the EU would simply contribute to freezing a *status quo*, instead of taking responsibility to improve the situation on the ground. Moreover, expulsion of a member state would also ignore the interests of the EU citizens with regard to the nationality of the expelled state.[111] It is thus wonderful that Article 7 TEU is milder than its CoE Statute counterpart,[112] especially after the Commission undermined it through the activation of the pre-Article 7 procedure.[113] One should be equally realistic about the effectiveness of financial sanctions. Clearly, when nothing other than a regime change is required in order to comply, a member state will be happy to pay.[114] Moreover, shaming is not likely to work either. The amounts of fines are never unbearable (especially for a captured state). Besides, the 'ability to pay' is one of the criteria used by the ECJ in its case law on determining the amounts of fines and lump sums for the defiant member states to pay. The implications of this are far-reaching: it does not matter how the substance of Article 2 TEU values is established (by courts, the Commission, the Copenhagen Commission, the Venice Commission etc.) – enforcement is still a problem in the end if fines are not effective and kicking a member

[111] For more on this option, see B. Blagoyev, 'Expulsion of a Member State from the EU after Lisbon: Political Threat or a Legal Reality', *Tilburg Law Review*, 16 (2011), 191.

[112] Art. 8 of the Statute of the Council of Europe.

[113] Kochenov and Pech, 'Better Late than Never?'

[114] See, for the analysis of similar issues in the context of EU external relations law: N. Tocci, 'Can the EU Promote Democracy and Human Rights through the ENP? The Case for Refocusing on the Rule of Law' in M. Cremona and G. Meloni (eds.), 'The European Neighbourhood Policy: A Framework for Modernisation?', *EUI Working Paper* Law 2007/21, 23, at 29.

state out (thus seemingly eliminating the problem) is not an option. A better solution is needed.

The most mature answer to the outstanding problems should necessarily involve not only the reform of the enforcement mechanisms, but *the reform of the Union as such*, as the supranational law should be made more aware of the values it is obliged by the Treaties to respect and also, crucially, is obliged to aspire to protect at the national level and also at the supranational level. Instead of hiding behind the veil of procedural purity banners of autonomy, supremacy and the like, EU law should embrace the *rule of law* as an institutional ideal,[115] which implies, *inter alia*, eventual substantive limitations on the *acquis* of the Union, as well as taking Article 2 TEU values to heart in the context of the day-to-day functioning of the Union, elevating those values above the instrumentalism marking them today.

115 Cf., G. Palombella, *È possibile la legalità globale?* (Bologna: Il Mulino, 2012).

15

Constitutional Coups in EU Law

KIM LANE SCHEPPELE*

Introduction

Article 4 of the Treaty of the European Union (TEU) contains a microcosm of contradiction. It purports to announce the central principles of EU federalism by dividing jurisdiction between the EU and the Member States while still tying Member States to EU principles.

Article 4(3) TEU commits Member States to EU loyalty. As a matter of law, Member States are required to 'refrain from any measure which could jeopardise the attainment of the Union's objectives.'[1] The Union's objectives are very general and listed in Article 3 TEU. Among them are 'peace, its values and the well-being of its peoples.'[2]

The values referred to in Article 3 TEU point back to Article 2 TEU, where the commitments run broad and deep. The Union has pledged 'respect for human dignity, freedom, democracy, equality, the rule of law and respect for human rights, including the rights of persons belonging to minorities. These values are common to the Member States in a society in which pluralism, non discrimination, tolerance, justice, solidarity and equality between women and men prevail.'[3] The EU therefore is wedded to a particular vision of national constitutional order, one that contains classic liberal protections for citizens who retain rights of democratic self-determination in a nested polity bound by constraints of justice and solidarity.

But Article 4 also commits the EU to self-restraint in telling its Member States what specific sorts of constitutional orders they must

* Earlier versions of these ideas appeared in K. L. Scheppele, 'Constitutional Coups and Judicial Review: How Transnational Institutions Can Strengthen Peak Courts at Times of Crisis (with Special Reference to Hungary)', *Journal of Transnational Law & Contemporary Problems*, 23 (2014), 51 and K. L. Scheppele, 'Enforcing the Basic Principles of EU Law through Systemic Infringement Procedures' in C. Closa and D. Kochenov (eds.), *Reinforcing Rule of Law Oversight in the European Union* (Cambridge University Press, 2016).

[1] Art 4(3) TEU. [2] Art. 3(1) TEU. [3] Art. 2 TEU.

observe. Article 4(2) commits the Union to 'respect the equality of Member States before the Treaties as well as their national identities, inherent in their fundamental structures, political and constitutional.'[4] Article 4, then, anticipates pluralism in national constitutional commitments alongside loyalty to the values of the Union.

Article 4 therefore leaves open the question, 'How much leeway do EU Member States have in setting their own constitutional parameters?'

In this chapter, I will suggest that EU pluralism does not mean that 'anything goes'. What would the EU do with open dictatorship or a government that routinely violated the basic rights of its citizens? The EU has no mechanism for excluding such a state, but surely the EU could ostracize it under Article 7 TEU, which provides a mechanism for quarantining a state that violates values. But what should the EU do with Member State that attacks European values more subtly? What should the EU do with a Member State that has the form of a liberal, constitutional democracy without the content to go with it?

Such a constellation – democratic form without liberal constitutional content – is actually quite common these days in the world beyond the EU. Many questionably democratic-constitutionalist governments – think of Russia, Turkey or Ecuador – follow the forms of liberal constitutionalist democracy without commitment to liberal constitutional-democratic values. Such faux democracies hold elections even though they are not democratic in most other respects because it is nearly impossible to change the governing party or the leader. They may be practically (rather than morally) limited in how far they can engage in massive human rights violations, lest they run the risk of losing even their sham elections. But nonetheless they target particular opponents for second-class treatment, push out their dissidents and otherwise refuse to accept the principles of checked and limited government. When mass rights violations still occur in such states, they might take place at the hands of paramilitary groups while the official police simply disappear, making it hard to attribute the violations to the regime.[5] Even annexations of territory are legitimated after the fact with popular referenda to create the appearance of consent.[6] But the leaders of these faux democracies have no intention of ever leaving

[4] Art. 4(2) TEU.

[5] Human Rights Watch Report on Paramilitaries in Colombia (2011) though the peace agreement in process shows the current government's commitment to ending these practices; M. Peel, *A Swamp Full of Dollars: Pipelines and Paramilitaries at Nigeria's Oil Frontier* (London: IB Tauris, 2009).

[6] See, for example, Crimea. Or, as the Russian government would hasten to add, Kosovo.

power, so the system is rigged to keep elections from ever toppling them. Instead of a clean line between democracy and autocracy, then, we see a sliding scale of 'more or less' democracy, 'more or less' autocracy. These days, autocracy hides in the superficial forms of democratic states.

The political science literature is full of terms like 'managed democracy', 'competitive authoritarianism' and 'hybrid regimes' to describe various points on this scale as liberal democratic governments shade over into authoritarian regimes of varying degrees. The new quasi-authoritarians often operate in the name of no clear ideology, either being interested in power for power's sake or seeking to capture the state to divert public resources into private pockets. They seem less dangerous than twentieth-century authoritarians because they make no appeal to global hearts and minds. If we are all looking for another Hitler or a second Stalin in the twenty-first century, then, we probably will not find them. And of course, that's a very good thing. But it doesn't mean that serious threats to constitutional-democratic commitments are absent. Instead, today's autocrats are far more concerned with keeping up democratic appearances and denying that they violate rights.[7] They may even be scrupulous about the legality of everything they do. The threats to liberal, constitutional and democratic values are more insidious these days.

These concerns may seem quite far afield from the privileged space of the EU. The EU, of course, is supposed to be a club of *bona fide* democracies. All Member States were extensively checked at the door when they entered and were given a clean bill of constitutional-democratic health before they were admitted. Moreover, the EU is a trusting organization that must have believed that 'consolidated' democracies could never be tempted by backsliding.[8] Its treaties contain no procedure to throw out a Member State for violating the basic values of the Union. So what is the EU to do with a 'constitutional coup' in one of its Member States that turns one of its *bona fide* democracies into the sort of faux democracy that fails to live up to the values of Article 2?

The idea of a constitutional coup may seem a contradiction in terms, as it combines the positive ideal of a constitution with the unconstitutional reputation of a coup. The concept signals that constitutional coups have

[7] One of the best treatments of this phenomenon is W. J. Dobson, *The Dictator's Learning Curve: Inside the Global Battle for Democracy* (New York: Random House, 2012)

[8] In fact, the very definition of a consolidated democracy is that democracy has become 'the only game in town'. See J. Linz and A. Stephan, 'Toward Consolidated Democracies', *Journal of Democracy*, 7(2) (1996), 14.

elements of both. A *constitutional* coup is constitutional because there is no break in legality, never a moment when a government does something formally illegal to attain its desired goals. There is no violent seizure of power; no tanks are in the streets. (One can imagine that this, at least, would provoke an immediate EU reaction.) But a constitutional coup is nonetheless a *coup* because constitutional reform turns the prior liberal constitutional order on its head under circumstances of questionable legitimacy. Through a series of perfectly legal – if not always legitimate – moves, the leaders of a constitutional coup can fundamentally alter the key constitutional commitments of their state, including, in the extreme case, transforming a state in plain sight from a constitutional democracy to an quasi-authoritarian government and from a rights-respecting state to a state where its citizens have the full complement of rights only if they meet certain conditions – like supporting the governing party.

Can the EU intervene in such a case? On what basis, legally speaking? And with what tools?

This chapter examines these questions by focusing on a particular case of a constitutional coup in Europe – the post-2010 government of Viktor Orbán in Hungary. I will use this case to raise more fundamental questions about the ability of the EU to insist that its Member States honour the values of the Union in light of the potentially contradictory commands of Article 4 TEU.

The first section explains the basics of Hungary's constitutional coup. The second section describes how European institutions attempted to challenge the constitutional coup while it was in progress. In the final section, I will propose a new mechanism for dealing with constitutional coups within EU law.

Hungary's Constitutional Coup

The government of Prime Minister Viktor Orbán came to power in 2010 in a free and fair election in which the Fidesz (right) political party achieved a constitutional supermajority.[9] Under Hungary's disproportionate election law, 53 per cent of the party-list vote on election day was converted into slightly more than two-thirds of the seats in the parliament.[10] In a

[9] Technically, Fidesz won the election jointly with the Christian Democrats (KDNP) in a joint party list, but the Christian Democrats barely have a separate identity and have never deviated from the Fidesz party line on any issue, so from here on out I will refer to the government as the Fidesz government.

[10] For the election results, see http://electionresources.org/hu/assembly.php?election=2010.

constitutional system where constitutional amendments could be speedily accomplished with a one-time two-thirds vote in a unicameral parliament,[11] the government then proceeded in a perfectly legal and constitutional manner to turn the prior constitution on its head.[12] According to critics, the frenzy of legal change that Fidesz undertook in its first few years in office constituted an attempt to entrench one party in power for the foreseeable future.[13]

The Fidesz government inherited a constitution written in stages in 1989–1990. This post-communist constitution was created without any break in legality because all of the changes were accomplished by simply amending the 1949 constitution using that constitution's amendment rule.[14] Hungary pioneered the idea of the 'rule of law revolution'[15] because it accomplished a complete constitutional transformation by converting an anti-constitutional communist regime into a constitutional rule-of-law government without ever breaking the rule of law itself.[16] Because the

[11] The Constitution of the Republic of Hungary (1989–1990), Art. 24(3). For an English translation of the text, see www.constitution.org/cons/hungary.txt.

[12] M. Bánkuti, G. Halmai and K. L. Scheppele, 'From Separation of Powers to Government without Checks: Hungary's Old and New Constitutions' in G. Tóth, *Constitution for a Divided Nation: Hungary's Fundamental Law* (Budapest: Central European University Press, 2012).

[13] 'The Long March of Fidesz,' *The Economist*, January 7, 2012, available at: www.economist.com/node/21542422.

[14] Because the huge changes in 1989 were made by amendment rather than by writing a wholly new text, the constitution was still formally called 'Law XX of 1949, as amended', a title which disguised that the constitution had in fact been almost completely rewritten. Bánkuti, Halmai and Scheppele, 'Government without Checks'. In the present chapter, I will refer to the extensively amended Law XX of 1949 as the Hungarian Constitution 1989–90.

[15] The phrase was first used in the opinion by President László Sólyom in the Hungarian Constitutional Court's Retroactive Criminal Legislation Case, 11/1992 (III.5) AB hat., translated in L. Sólyom and G. Brunner (eds.), *Constitutional Judiciary in a New Democracy* (University of Michigan Press, 2000), p. 214. The phrase was repeated and explained in Sólyom. 'Introduction to the Decisions of the Constitutional Court of the Republic of Hungary', *Constitutional Judiciary*, p. 38.

[16] Formally, of course, this might also appear to be a constitutional coup because it accomplished a complete change of regime through constitutional means. As I stipulated in my definition of a constitutional coup above, however, a formally legal constitutional change that fundamentally alters the constitution needs an accompanying legitimating process to make it *not* a coup. I would argue that a series of ratification processes including elections, referenda and widespread acceptance of Constitutional Court decisions legitimated the 1989–90 constitutional coup. That said, a constitutional coup can theoretically work both ways – moving from a principled constitutional regime into an autocracy or the other way around. In this chapter, I am concentrating on the latter sorts of constitutional coups, where new leaders – often in the name of their democratic

1949 constitution could be amended by a single two-thirds vote of the parliament, the outgoing communist parliament could authorize a complete overhaul of the constitutional structure by amending huge swaths of the 1949 text with its two-thirds majority.[17] These changes were later confirmed by a series of popular referenda and elections. The new government constituted under this functionally new constitution learned to live under constitutional constraint even though the constitution remained lightly entrenched under the same amendment rule: a single two-thirds vote of the unicameral parliament was sufficient to change anything in the text.

When the first election law was written in 1990, the worry was that there would be too many small parties and that governments would therefore be unstable. So the 1990 election law, in effect through the 2010 election, was highly disproportionate and in fact made 'two-thirds governments' quite likely. Hungary's first post-communist two-thirds government served from 1994–1998 and consisted of a Socialist (MSzP) majority to which the liberal Free Democrats (SzDSz) added the heft to get to two-thirds. Showing substantial self-restraint by taking the authority to write a new constitution out of its hands alone, this government amended the constitution in 1995 to require a four-fifths vote to agree on a procedure under which any new constitution could be drafted.[18]

The supermajority Fidesz government elected in 2010 tipped its hand that it would launch a constitutional coup when it used its two-thirds majority to amend the constitution to remove the four-fifths rule.[19] This

mandates – attempt to subvert the constitutional-democratic governments they inherited in order to create a more autocratic system.

17 Bánkuti, Halmai and Scheppele, 'Government without Checks'.

18 The original amendment as it passed the parliament was Law XLIV of 1995 (MK 44/1995), creating Art. 24(5) of the Hungarian Constitution 1989–90.

19 There is a reasonable debate that could be had over whether the four-fifths rule was still legally valid at the time it was removed from the constitution. When the constitutional amendment creating Article 24(5) passed the parliament in 1995, the law containing the amendment said that the amendment would lapse in 1998, when the government of the day would have to stand for re-election again (Law XLIV/1995). The constitutional amendment, in other words, passed the parliament with a sunset clause. But when the constitutional text itself was modified by incorporating this amendment, there was no mention of a sunset, so the constitution in 2010 still formally contained that provision. Hungary, like most civil law constitutional systems, amends the constitution by incorporating the new provision in place of the old one rather than, as in the United States, simply tacking on the amendment to the end of the text, leaving the original formulation intact, but superseded elsewhere. The process of inserting the amendment into the existing constitution failed to include the sunset clause. As a result, some – and not just those in the governing party – believed that the 1995 constitutional amendment had indeed lapsed

was perfectly legal, as the four-fifths rule had not been entrenched any more deeply than the rest of the constitution. With that obstacle removed, the governing party could then start a new process to revise the constitution without needing the support of any opposition party.

Fidesz had not campaigned on a platform to rewrite the constitution, so it was not able to claim it had a popular mandate to do so, but the government set out to draft a new constitution anyway. The constitutional drafting process was itself controlled in all key aspects by the governing party. It lasted for about seven months, from October 2010 through April 2011, and it consisted of two disconnected stages: an inconsequential public stage and a consequential secret stage.

In stage one, which began in October 2010, a constitutional commission whose membership overlapped almost entirely with the membership of the Constitutional Committee of the Parliament was tasked with coming up with a list of principles that the new constitution should follow. In form, then, the Hungarian process followed the much-revered South African constitutional drafting procedure in which principles were defined in the first stage to guide drafting in the second stage.[20] This first-stage committee had open meetings, sought the opinions of civil society and eventually produced a list of principles. But the self-described 'democratic opposition' parties of the left walked out of this parliamentary committee when none of their proposals were accepted. The constitutional principles that resulted therefore reflected only those of the governing party and they were approved by resolution in the plenary session of the parliament by the Fidesz bloc on 7 March 2011.[21]

In stage two, that same resolution of 7 March 2011 gave MPs only *one week* to propose complete draft constitutions. But the resolution said that

because the original law limited its duration. Others thought that the four-fifths rule had become a permanent part of them constitution because it had stayed in the text for more than 15 years without objections from any political quarter. Regardless of one's position on the merits, however, the government after 2010 clearly wanted to remove any doubt about the validity of what it was about to do next by removing the four-fifths clause from the constitution, which it did in the law titled 'Constitutional Amendment of July 5th 2010' (with no formal law number in the parliament). The amendment was published in the official gazette, the Magyar Közlöny, at MK 113/2010 (5.VII).

20 Andrew Arato calls this sort of process 'post-sovereign' constitutional drafting because the responsibility for drafting is spread over several different 'sovereign' bodies and doesn't rest in a single constituent assembly. A. Arato, 'Redeeming the Still Redeemable: Post Sovereign Constitution Making,' *The International Journal of Politics, Culture, and Society*, 22 (2009), 427.

21 Parliamentary resolution 9/2011. (III. 9.) OGY was voted on March 7 but not published until two days later, which explains the citation. MK 9/2011 OGY, 24 MK 4717 (9.III).

a proposed constitution could be offered 'with or without' taking the draft principles into account. In other words, the first participatory stage of the constitutional drafting process in which public opinion, NGO views and opposition participation were solicited was entirely disconnected from the second, secret stage of the constitutional drafting process, in which draft proposals were prepared out of the public eye and did not have to take into account the results of the first stage of the process. In the end, no one ever publicly checked the final constitutional draft against the basic principles. The constitutional principles were never heard from again.

Stage two of the constitutional drafting process was entirely secret. There is no official record of just who was involved in the process, who was consulted, whose opinions were engaged, what alternatives were considered, or how the final draft was created. And there were certainly no public meetings, progress reports or even constitutional conceptions published in advance of the release of the proposed constitutional text. The whole process and all of its participants were secret.

The Fidesz constitution was unveiled as a full-blown, completed document on 14 March 2011 when it was introduced in the parliament as a private member's bill by two members of Fidesz bloc.[22] And while there were a few small changes added as the constitution hurtled to passage in just one month with the votes of only the Fidesz bloc, none of the amendments responded to opposition concerns.

The process through which the constitution was adopted was technically legal but fell far short of legitimate. Given that the opposition was ignored at every stage, the public had no meaningful input, and the constitution was drafted, debated and passed with the support of only the governing party, the constitution was a purely partisan document that did not even attempt to be inclusive.

But was the constitution otherwise compliant with European norms? Taking into account the new constitution,[23] the five substantial

[22] The private member's bill in the Hungarian Parliament is a parliamentary procedure that bypasses a variety of steps normally required of government bills. Before a government bill is introduced in the parliament, the bill requires both an impact assessment and consultation with the relevant agencies that would have to enforce the law as well as with the civil society groups that would be affected by the law. Because those stages are not required of a private member's bill, such a bill can navigate the parliament without its advocates having to confront any of the objections to the law that might come from opposition parties or from civil society groups.

[23] The government's translation of the Fundamental Law of Hungary can be found here: www.venice.coe.int/webforms/documents/?pdf=CDL-REF(2011)019-e.

constitutional amendments passed in the first three years of the new constitution, the cardinal laws[24] and the more than 800 new ordinary laws passed by the Fidesz government in its 2010–2014 term, I will describe the basic substantive features of the new system. I call this whole new legal structure the 'Fidesz constitution' even though not everything is in the single constitutional text or its amendments. Many elements of the system I describe are in 'cardinal' laws that require a two-thirds vote of the parliament and thus are almost as entrenched as the constitution itself. But the system functions as a whole, so should be assessed as such.

Gábor Tóth's chapter in this volume explains the system created after the 1989 'rule of law revolution' when the 1949 Stalinist constitution was substantially amended to produce a pluralistic, constitutional, democratic order that was established to respect the rule of law and protect human rights. The new constitution of 1989–90 maintained the unicameral parliamentary system that had been established in the communist era, but it created a Constitutional Court as the primary check on the fused legislative and executive power characteristic of parliamentary systems. Given its weighty responsibility in the 1989 constitutional design, the Constitutional Court was made highly accessible to the new democratic public in Hungary since anyone could challenge a law through abstract review before the Court (*actio popularis* jurisdiction). The Constitutional Court worked as a check because its institutional design made it very hard to capture. Before 2010, the procedure for electing judges to the Constitutional Court prevented the Court from being dominated by any one political fraction. Each judicial candidate to the Constitutional Court was first nominated by a majority of parliamentary parties before then being elected to the Court by a two-thirds vote of the parliament's members.[25] Because each judge or combination of judges appointed at any one time had to attract a wide array of support to get through this process, the Court always had a balance of different political views represented on the bench.[26]

[24] Cardinal laws are laws on especially important topics specified by the constitution that must be passed by a two-thirds vote of the parliament. A constitutional amendment requires an *absolute* two-thirds majority: two-thirds of all members of parliament. A cardinal law requires a *relative* two-thirds majority: two-thirds of a quorum of members of parliament. Cardinal laws are therefore easier, though *not much* easier, to pass than constitutional amendments, and much harder to pass than ordinary laws.

[25] Law XXXII/1989 on the Constitutional Court, Arts. 5–8, available in translation at www.refworld.org/docid/4c345b5b2.html.

[26] I can testify to this personally as I worked as a researcher at the Constitutional Court of Hungary from 1994–98.

The constitutional system created in 1989–90 provided many more checks on Hungary's unicameral parliamentary government.[27] There were so many different checks instituted after 1989 that the post-1989 constitutional system worked reliably to ensure that the operation of majoritarian political power didn't ride roughshod over minority rights, democratic guarantees and constitutional limitations. In short, after 1989, Hungary became a constitutional democracy that guaranteed the rule of law and protection of human rights. Hungary was admitted to the EU in 2004 on the basis of this constitutional system.[28]

By contrast with this robust system of complementary powers, the new 'Fidesz constitution' of 2011–12 removed virtually all of the checks that had been added after 1989. Each of the independent accountability offices was immediately restructured and restaffed, without permitting the incumbent officeholders to finish their terms. At the media council, election commission, ombudsmen's offices, state audit office, fiscal council and more, people who had been elected for their independent expertise by previous parliaments were removed before the end of their terms on the pretext of institutional reorganization, and their newly elected replacements have all been affiliated with the Fidesz governing party.[29] A sudden lowering of the judicial retirement age rid the bench of fully 10 per cent of the judges, including 20 per cent of the Supreme Court judges and many lower court presidents.[30] And a new system for appointing judges put the power to hire, fire, reassign, promote, demote and

27 A catalogue of these additional checks can be found in Bánkuti, Halmai and Scheppele, 'Government without Checks'. Gábor Tóth's chapter in this volume reviews many of the major ones.

28 In its final report on Hungary before Hungary was permitted to enter European Union, the European Commission noted: 'In its 1997 Opinion, the Commission concluded that Hungary fulfilled the political criteria. Since that time, the country has made considerable progress in further consolidating and deepening the stability of its institutions guaranteeing democracy, the rule of law, human rights and respect for the protection of minorities. This has been confirmed over the past year. Hungary continues to fulfil the Copenhagen political criteria.' *European Commission* (2003), Regular Report from the Commission on Hungary's Progress Towards Accession 33, available at: http://ec.europa.eu/enlargement/archives/pdf/key_documents/2003/cmr_hu_final_en.pdf.

29 For the details, see K. L. Scheppele, 'Hungary's Constitutional Revolution,' on *Paul Krugman, Conscience of a Liberal Blog*, 19 December 2011, available at: krugman.blogs.nytimes.com/2011/12/19/hungarys-constitutional-revolution/; Bánkuti, Halmai and Scheppele, 'Illiberal Turn' and Bánkuti, Halmai and Scheppele, 'Government without Checks'.

30 For more detail on this, see K. L. Scheppele, 'How to Evade the Constitution: The Constitutional Court's Decision on the Judicial Retirement Age,' *Verfassungsblog*, 9 August 2012, available at: www.verfassungsblog.de/evade-constitution-case-hungarian-constitutional-courts-decision-judicial-retirement-age/ and www.verfassungsblog.de/

discipline judges in the hands of an official close to the Fidesz party, who was herself elected to that job by a two-thirds vote of the Fidesz-dominated parliament.[31] Many of the powers of regional and local governments were moved to the national government as governance was radically centralized.

Because the Constitutional Court was the primary check on a government's power under the 1989 constitutional order, it came in for a particularly withering attack after 2010 when its power and independence were restricted in multiple ways. The system for electing constitutional judges was changed so that a single two-thirds vote of the parliament became sufficient to put a judge on the Court, abolishing the multiparty agreement that was once necessary for nomination.[32] The Fidesz constitution also expanded the number of judges from 11 to 15, which, taking advantage of normal rotation and retirements, allowed the Fidesz government to select without seeking either political consensus or balance 11 of the 15 judges on the Court in its first four years in office. The new constitutional judges have by and large behaved predictably; they have, with only a few exceptions, voted in lockstep for the Fidesz government position in each case that the Court has heard.

Nonetheless, the Constitutional Court continued to challenge the government as the constitutional coup progressed, at least until the time it was definitively packed. In case after case, the Court struck down various aspects of the government's revolution. The government's response was to pass an omnibus constitutional amendment in spring 2013 that ended the Court's attempts to challenge the government's constitutional coup. This Fourth Amendment to the 2011 constitution overturned practically all of the Constitutional Court's decisions that had ruled against the government by writing the impugned laws directly into

evade-constitution-case-hungarian-constitutional-courts-decision-judicial-retirement-age-part-ii/.

31 K. L. Scheppele, 'First, Let's Pick All the Judges,' on Paul Krugman, Conscience of a Liberal Blog, 12 March 2012, at: http://krugman.blogs.nytimes.com/2012/03/10/first-lets-pick-all-the-judges/ and J. Rozenberg, 'Meet Tünde Handó: In Hungary, One Woman Effectively Controls the Judiciary, and She Happens to be Married to the Author of its Constitution', *The Guardian*, 20 March 2012, available at: http://www.theguardian.com/law/2012/mar/20/tunde-hando-hungarian-judges.

32 Fundamental Law of Hungary, Art. 24(4), official translation available at: www.venice.coe.int/webforms/documents/?pdf=CDL-REF(2011)019-e. While the change was codified in the new constitution, it was initiated and took effect only one year after the Fidesz government came into power so that they could more quickly get their judges onto the bench. (Law LXII of 2011, published in the official gazette, the Magyar Közlöny, at MK 63/2011 (VI.14)).

the constitution itself. In addition, the Fourth Amendment barred the Constitutional Court from expanding review of constitutional questions beyond those it had been directly asked[33] and also explicitly prevented the Court from reviewing constitutional amendments for substantive conflicts with the constitution,[34] as the Court had threatened to do. Perhaps most tellingly, the Fourth Amendment nullified all of the decisions made by the Constitutional Court in its 22-year history before the new constitution took effect so that it could no longer use them as authority to challenge the government's revolutionary changes.[35] Through the Fourth Amendment, the Constitutional Court was made a prisoner of the Fidesz constitution, unable to assert its own sense of constitutional values against those of the government.

By the time of the election in 2014, no public institution in the country was in the hands of either the opposition or neutral experts. But the government's popularity had dropped as it consolidated power. From a high of 45 per cent approval at the time of the spring 2010 election when it won its two-thirds parliamentary majority, Fidesz' popularity sank to below 20 per cent as the constitutional changes were going into effect. The party's support then climbed to 35 per cent on the eve of the April 2014 election after the government forced through steep cuts in utility prices as a populist gesture. But under the election rules Fidesz inherited, a 35 per cent 'victory' would have cost the government its two-thirds supermajority and, with it, its ability to operate without constitutional constraint.

With this flagging support, the Fidesz government then rewrote the election law, as usual excluding the political opposition or the public from any participation in the project. The new constitution had cut the size of the parliament in half, so redistricting was necessary. And the new districts, with their borders written directly into a two-thirds law, were widely believed to be gerrymandered. Many other changes were made to the election law to ensure a Fidesz victory in the 2014 election. Fidesz was able to (just barely) regain its two-thirds majority, but this time with only 45 per cent of the vote (including a suspicious 95 per cent vote in favour of the governing party from Hungarians in the neighbouring states that put the government over the top to its constitutional majority).[36]

[33] Fourth Amendment, Art. 12(4). [34] Fourth Amendment, Art. 12(5).
[35] Fourth Amendment, Art. 19(2).
[36] The election law changes are detailed in my five-part series at the Krugman Blog, K. L. Scheppele, Hungary, an Election in Question, available at: http://krugman.blogs.nytimes.com/2014/02/28/hungary-an-election-in-question-part-1/?_r=0 with links there to subsequent posts.

In four years, the Fidesz government managed to create a system in which the law was no barrier to anything the government wanted to do and no other political party was able to challenge anything the government did. The government changed the law – and the constitution – at will whenever law got in the way. Most crucially, the new constitutional order entrenched a system of unchecked power. The Fidesz constitutional coup created a state outside the rule of law.

The European Response

It is often said that the European Commission is the guardian of the Treaties[37] and is therefore the main institution on the front lines of enforcement. The primary mechanism that the Commission has to enforce specific obligations under EU law is the infringement procedure, through which the Commission first files a reasoned complaint against a Member State alleging that the Member State has failed to comply with EU law. If the Member State fails to respond properly, the Commission may file an action against that Member State in the Court of Justice of the European Union (CJEU).[38] If the CJEU agrees that a Member State has violated EU law, the state will be ordered to comply and, if all else fails, serious monetary penalties may be levied against a Member State until it brings its laws and actions into line with EU law.[39]

The Commission has been quite active in criticizing Hungary quickly and strongly, but in the first five years of the Fidesz revolution, it brought only two infringement actions to the CJEU for elements of the constitutional coup. More infringement actions have been initiated for garden-variety violations of more specific violations of EU law, like late transposition of directives,[40] an affliction that affects virtually all Member States.

[37] In fact, the Commission says this about itself: 'As guardian of the Treaties, the Commission oversees the application of Union law under the control of the Court of Justice of the European Union.' From the Commission's website at http://europa.eu/legislation_summaries/glossary/european_commission_en.htm.

[38] The procedure is laid down in Art. 258 of the Treaty on the Functioning of the European Union (TFEU), available at: http://eur-lex.europa.eu/LexUriServ/LexUriServ.do?uri=OJ:C:2012:326:0047:0200:EN:PDF

[39] The levying of a financial penalty against a Member State for non-compliance requires a separate action at the CJEU, specified in Art. 260 TFEU.

[40] The 2013 report on infringement actions brought against specific Member States noted that the Commission brought 36 new infringement proceedings against Hungary in 2012, of which 26 were for late transposition of directives. Only four of these were eventually referred to the CJEU. Most of these actions had nothing to do with the constitutional coup. For example, while the constitutional coup was going on, the Commission lauded

The most dramatic infringement action related to Hungary's constitutional coup was the quick and creative action launched when the government suddenly lowered the judicial retirement age for ordinary judges, thereby removing from office the senior-most 10 per cent of the Hungarian judiciary. The main underlying issue was the threat to judicial independence posed by sudden changes in the legal qualifications to be a judge, but while commitment to the rule of law is a value protected under Article 2 TEU, the Commission decided to latch onto something more specific, and so it charged Hungary with age discrimination.[41] Recognizing that senior judges were being fired every day under the new law, the Commission asked the CJEU to expedite the case, and the Court did so, issuing a judgement on 2 November 2012.[42] The CJEU found Hungary in violation of the EU Directive establishing a general framework for equal treatment in employment and occupation. But, in the end, the Hungarian government did little to change its assault on the judiciary. While the government claims that it reinstated most of the judges, there are reasons to doubt that many of the judges returned.[43]

Hungary's speedy resolution of an outstanding action regarding the cages of laying hens and noted that Hungary had finally adjusted its national flood management rules. Report from the Commission, 30th Annual Report on Monitoring the Application of EU Law 30 (2012) [COM(2013) 726], available at: http://ec.europa.eu/eu_law/docs/docs_infringements/annual_report_30/sg_annual_r8eport_monitoring_eu_law_131023.pdf. Given all that was going on in Hungary in the first year of the new constitution, one might be forgiven for thinking that the European Commission had missed the most crucial problems.

41 Press Release, 'European Commission Launches Accelerated Infringement Proceedings against Hungary over the Independence of Its Central Bank and Data Protection Authorities as well as over Measures Affecting the Judiciary,' available at: http://europa.eu/rapid/press-release_IP-12-24_en.htm. Eventually, the Commission reached a settlement with Hungary on issues related to the Central Bank and proceeded only with the actions on the judicial retirement age and the firing of the data protection commissioner.

42 *European Commission v. Hungary*, C-286/12 [2012].

43 The Hungarian government claimed that nearly three-quarters of the judges returned to work. US Department of State, Bureau of Democracy, Human Rights and Labor, Country Reports on Human Rights Practices for 2014, Report on Hungary, at: www.state.gov/j/drl/rls/hrrpt/humanrightsreport/index.htm?year=2014&dlid=236532. But Gergely Mikó, president of Budapest's most important general jurisdiction court, said that 14 of the 70 judges on his court were forced by the change in the retirement age to retire but only one was reinstated. 'Efficiency of Criminal Procedures Increased, Metropolitan Court Leader Says', *MTI (Hungarian News Agency)*, 21 July 2013, at: www.politics.hu/20130721/efficiency-of-criminal-procedures-increased-metropolitan-court-leader-says/. So, on that particular key court the reinstatement rate was only 7 per cent instead of the 72 per cent the government claimed overall.

The other infringement action that touched on the constitutional coup dealt with the firing of the data protection commissioner. EU law requires each Member State to have an independent official who oversees compliance with data protection rules. And, as part of the reorganization of the ombudsman system in Hungary, the government had fired the incumbent data protection commissioner by closing his office and opening a newly named office that had a newly installed data protection officer.[44] The Commission brought an action against Hungary for infringing the data protection officer's independence, and the CJEU agreed that the prior officer's independence had been infringed with his firing.[45] But what could be the remedy? The Hungarian government argued that reinstating the prior data protection officer would mean firing the new one and repeating the infringement, so instead the Hungarian government gave the fired official €250,000 in compensation and everything went on as before.

In both cases, the Commission interpreted EU law narrowly and specifically in bringing infringement actions, so in the end it brought only those two actions that could be said to be about the core issues of the constitutional coup. Compliance that would roll back the Fidesz consolidation of power was achieved with neither action as the Commission asked for something that could not practically be done, which was reinstatement of fired officials long after their replacements had already been named. As the Fidesz government pointed out in its arguments before the CJEU, did the EU expect Fidesz to repeat the offense by firing those who had replaced the illegally fired officials?

That said, at the height of the constitutional coup in 2010–13, Commission President José Manuel Barroso and Commission Vice-President Viviane Reding were outspoken critics of the Hungarian government and repeatedly tried to talk PM Orbán into line with European norms. Barroso first warned the Hungarian government about its moves to seize control of the central bank.[46] This was quickly followed by a

[44] I have told the story, with documentation of the particulars, at K. L. Scheppele, 'Making Infringement Procedures More Effective: A Comment on Commission v. Hungary, Case C-288/12', *Eutopia*, 29 April 2014, available at: http://eutopialaw.com/2014/04/29/making-infringement-procedures-more-effective-a-comment-on-commission-v-hungary-case-c-28812-8-april-2014-grand-chamber/.

[45] *Commission v. Hungary*, C-288/12 [2014].

[46] The original letter, together with an account of the leaks, retributions and rumours surrounding the whole matter can be found at: 'Barroso's Letter to Viktor Orbán,' *Contrarian Hungarian Blog*, 21 December 2011, available at: http://thecontrarianhungarian.wordpress.com/2011/12/21/barrosos-letter-to-viktor-orban/.

public warning on the new constitution and its potential incompatibilities with European law.[47] After a number of criticisms of specific actions of the Hungarian government, Barroso openly transferred all interactions between the Commission and the Hungarian government to his office, a sign that a coordinated and serious response was needed.[48] At the time, Barroso was engaged in a heated correspondence with Orbán over whether the Fourth Amendment to the constitution which greatly reduced the independence and effectiveness of the Constitutional Court was compatible with European law.[49] Barroso then used his 2013 State of the Union speech to call for new Commission powers to be able to police democratic rights in the Member States.[50]

In the meantime, European Commission Vice-President Viviane Reding was engaged in her own efforts to develop tools to reinforce the rule of law across the EU. Reding launched a program to assess the independence and functioning of the courts in the Member States.[51] Her 'Justice Scoreboard' promised to evaluate the state of the rule of law and the independence of the judiciary across the EU. Originally developed in reaction to events in Hungary (also in Romania), the Scoreboard seemed to backfire when the first round of scoring put Hungary among the best countries in the EU for judicial performance.[52]

[47] MTI, 'Barroso: EC to Use All Powers to Ensure Hungary Complies with EU Principles', *Budapest Business Journal*, 12 January 2012, available at: www.bbj.hu/politics/barroso-ec-to-use-all-powers-to-ensure-hungary-complies-with-eu-principles_62299.

[48] MTI, 'Barroso to Personally Oversee Disputes over Controversial Hungarian Laws', *Politics.hu*, 22 March 2013, available at: www.politics.hu/20130322/barroso-to-personally-oversee-disputes-over-controversial-hungarian-legislation/.

[49] Statement from the President of the European Commission and the Secretary General of the Council of Europe on the vote by the Hungarian Parliament of the Fourth Amendment to the Hungarian Fundamental Law, 11 March 2013, available at: http://europa.eu/rapid/press-release_MEMO-13-201_en.htm; 'EU's Barroso Warns Hungary's Orban on Constitution', *Deutsche Welle*, 4 April 2013, available at: http://www.dw.de/eus-barroso-warns-hungarys-orban-on-constitution/a-16741178; European Commission, 'The European Commission Reiterates Its Serious Concerns over the Fourth Amendment to the Constitution of Hungary', 12 April 2013, available at: http://europa.eu/rapid/press-release_IP-13-327_en.htm.

[50] I. Traynor, 'European Commission Should Be Democracy Watchdog for EU, Chief Says', *Guardian*, 11 September 2013, available at: www.theguardian.com/world/2013/sep/11/eu-democratic-rights-european-commission. For the full speech, see http://europa.eu/rapid/press-release_SPEECH-13-684_en.htm.

[51] N. Vandystadt, 'Reding Aims to Place Justice in Member States under Surveillance,' *Europolitics*, 12 September 2012, available at: www.europolitics.info/reding-aims-to-place-justice-in-member-states-under-surveillance-art342885.html.

[52] European Commission, The EU Justice Scoreboard, available at: http://ec.europa.eu/justice/effective-justice/files/justice_scoreboard_communication_en.pdf.

On the one hand, this was not surprising in light of the fact that the data used for the 2013 scores came from 2010, before the Hungarian constitutional coup began. But the Justice Scoreboard used measures to assess the functioning of courts that would not likely reveal the extent of political control over the judiciary that the Orbán government was attempting.[53]

Throughout the Hungarian constitutional coup, EU officials were supremely self-conscious about being accused of using double standards and singling out particular countries for unfair treatment, so they attempted to develop general mechanisms that would clearly apply across the board. But as they did this, the government-friendly Hungarian media launched hate campaigns against EU officials, accusing them of singling Hungary out for special treatment because of political bias.[54] And Prime Minister Orbán himself joined the fray by accusing the EU of meddling in Hungarian affairs as the Soviet Union once did.[55] While the Commission often criticized Hungary, it did very little to follow up.

The European Parliament took a much tougher stance, despite having a working majority of conservative parties that might have been expected to be on the side of the conservative Hungarian government. After a series of resolutions in which the European Parliament warned that first the new media laws[56] and then the constitutional changes in Hungary[57] ran the risk of violating European norms, Hungary was referred for potentially breaching Article 2 TEU to the LIBE (Civil Liberties) Committee of the European Parliament on 12 February 2012, shortly after the new constitution came into effect.[58] The referring resolution

[53] I have been critical of checklist approaches to the rule of law in general. See K. L. Scheppele, 'The Rule of Law and the Frankenstate: Why Governance Checklists Do Not Work', *Governance*, 26(2013), 559.

[54] M. Torkos, 'Mrs Reding Will Not Resign – EU Justice Commissioner Is as Unfit for Her Job as László Kovács Was', *Magyar Nemzet*, 11 April 2013. Translated as 'Hungarian Paper Finds EU Commissioner "Unfit" to Oversee European Justice', *BBC Worldwide Monitoring*, 12 April 2013.

[55] K. Than, 'Hungary's Orban Accuses Europe of 'Soviet-style' Meddling', *Reuters*, 5 July 2013, available at: www.reuters.com/article/2013/07/05/us-hungary-eu-orban-idUSBRE9640BR20130705

[56] European Parliament Resolution of 10 March 2011 on Media Law in Hungary, available at: www.europarl.europa.eu/sides/getDoc.do?type=TA&reference=P7-TA-2011-0094&language=EN.

[57] European Parliament Resolution of 5 July 2011 on the Revised Hungarian Constitution, available at: www.europarl.europa.eu/sides/getDoc.do?pubRef=-//EP//NONSGML+TA+P7-TA-2011-0315+0+DOC+PDF+V0//EN.

[58] European Parliament Resolution of 16 February 2012 on the Recent Political Developments in Hungary (2012/2511(RSP)), available at: www.europarl.europa.eu/sides/getDoc.do?type=TA&reference=P7-TA-2012-0053&language=EN.

singled out a long list of particulars that caused concern, among them the independence of the judiciary, central bank and data protection authority; the freedom and pluralism of the media; the fairness of the new election law; the rights of political opposition; the restriction of freedom of religion through the required parliamentary registration of churches; and, of course, the restriction of the powers of the Constitutional Court.[59] The LIBE Committee was instructed to follow up to determine whether the recommendations of the European Commission, the Council of Europe and the Venice Commission had been adopted, and to present its conclusions in a report.

The 'Tavares Report', as it came to be called (after lead rapporteur and Portuguese Green MEP Rui Tavares) was approved by the parliament on 3 July 2013 with an overwhelming vote.[60] It became the strongest comprehensive statement yet about the Hungarian government's violation of European norms as well as the most ambitious program of action to counter Hungary's constitutional flight from Europe.[61]

The report began by noting that, while Member States of the EU have the competence to revise their constitutions under Article 4(2) TEU, those new constitutions must 'comply with commitments entered into by every Member State under the EU Accession Treaties, that is to say, the common values of the Union, the Charter and the ECHR.'[62] The report asserted that a new constitution should not set a lower bar of protection for fundamental rights than a previous constitution has established[63] and added that the core principles that national constitutions must protect include 'the common Union values of democracy and rule of law [that] require a strong system of representative democracy based on free elections and respecting the rights of the opposition.'[64]

Worries about the 'democratic system of checks and balances' led the report to criticize the way that the government had changed the Constitutional Court, adding new constitutional judgeships at just the moment when the new method for selecting these judges marginalized

[59] *Ibid.*, at point 4.

[60] The resolution passed with 370 in favour of the report, 248 against, with 82 abstentions, which signalled that there were many defections from alleged Fidesz allies in the European People's Party.

[61] European Parliament Resolution of 3 July 2013 on the Situation of Fundamental Rights: Standards and Practices in Hungary (Pursuant to the European Parliament Resolution of 16 February 2012) (2012/2130(INI)), available at: www.europarl.europa.eu/sides/getDoc.do?pubRef=-//EP//TEXT+TA+P7-TA-2013-0315+0+DOC+XML+V0//EN&language=EN.

[62] *Ibid.*, at para. 2. [63] *Ibid.*, at para. 6. [64] *Ibid.*, at para. 7.

any contribution of opposition parties.[65] Shifting power away from the Constitutional Court to the Hungarian Parliament worried the European Parliament, as did the repeal by the Fourth Amendment to the Fundamental Law of more than 20 years of constitutional jurisprudence.[66]

The report expressed alarm at the state of the ordinary judiciary, given that its independence was insufficiently safeguarded in the constitution. Inroads on the independence of the judiciary could be seen in the premature termination of the mandate of the president of the Supreme Court, the sudden lowering of the judicial retirement age, and the out-sized powers of the president of the National Judicial Office.[67]

Concerns about electoral reform, media pluralism and the failure of the Hungarian government to prevent active discrimination against Roma were highlighted in the report and the government was taken to task for failing to guarantee equal rights for lesbians and gays and for the homeless.[68] The new system for recognizing and registering churches was criticized for creating a situation incompatible with EU law.[69]

As the report's assessment section concluded, 'the systemic and general trend of repeatedly modifying the constitutional and legal frameworks in very short time frames, and the content of such modifications, are incompatible with the values referred to in Article 2 TEU' and the set of issues identified in the report, 'unless corrected in a timely and adequate manner . . . will result in a clear risk of serious breach of the values referred to in Article 2 TEU'.[70]

What, then, was to be done? Perhaps the most substantial recommendations in the report were addressed to the Commission, which was urged to act as the guardian of the Treaties and to take steps to enforce Article 2 as well as to ensure that the Commission understood the systemic nature of the risk and did not just produce an individualized list of separate complaints. The Commission was urged to adopt an 'Article 2 Alarm Agenda', which would require the Commission to monitor Hungary for compliance with Article 2 values. The Commission was urged not to conclude any ongoing negotiations Hungary until the country not only brought its legal system into compliance with Article 2 but also defused any risks of backsliding.[71] The Article 2 Alarm Agenda would therefore freeze ongoing negotiations across the board in Hungary in all areas of EU

[65] *Ibid.*, at para. 14. [66] *Ibid.*, at paras. 18–19. [67] *Ibid.*, at paras. 30–36.
[68] *Ibid.*, at paras. 44–55. [69] *Ibid.*, at para. 56. [70] *Ibid.*, at para. 58.
[71] *Ibid.*, at para. 70.

policy. While the Article 2 Alarm Agenda was proposed as a general remedy for a backsliding state, Hungary would be the first to go through the process.

In addition, the report recommended moving forward with the proposal for a Copenhagen Commission[72] to engage in continual review of Member States' compliance with the Copenhagen criteria. The report also encouraged the Commission to find ways to cut financial support for Member States that fail to honour EU values[73] and it encouraged beefing up the capacity of the Fundamental Rights Agency to address Member State compliance with Article 2.[74]

Crucially, the report provided a list of particular matters that the Hungarian government had to address in order to be in compliance with Article 2 TEU[75] and it proposed the creation of a 'trilogue' of Council, Commission and Parliament to ensure that the Hungarian government actually complied.[76] In the event that compliance was not forthcoming, the resolution suggested that Article 7 TEU procedure should be invoked.

Unfortunately, neither the European Commission nor the European Council responded to the Tavares Report and none of the proposals for monitoring or sanctioning were ever enacted. That said, the Commission, with its five-year term fast running out in 2014, started EU-wide discussions of mechanisms to ensure compliance with the rule of law in all Member States, without mentioning Hungary in particular.

In March 2014, the European Commission proposed a new 'rule-of-law mechanism' that provided a roadmap for gathering and assessing evidence that could lead to an Article 7 TEU procedure.[77] But the European Council's legal service almost immediately opined that this simple mechanism exceeded the powers of the Commission.[78] Nonetheless, the Commission seemed determined to go ahead.[79] In January 2016, the Commission

[72] *Ibid.*, at paras. 72 and 78. [73] *Ibid.*, at para. 74. [74] *Ibid.*, at para. 79.
[75] *Ibid.*, at para. 72. [76] *Ibid.*, at para. 86.
[77] Communication from the European Commission to the Council and the Parliament, a New EU Mechanism to Strengthen the Rule of Law, COM(2014) 158final/2, 19 March 2014.
[78] Opinion of the Council Legal Service, Commission's Communication on a New EU Mechanism to Strengthen the Rule of Law, at: http://data.consilium.europa.eu/doc/document/ST-10296-2014-INIT/en/pdf.
[79] Commission Statement: EU Framework for Democracy, Rule of Law and Fundamental Rights, Speech of First Vice-President Frans Timmermans to the European Parliament, Strasbourg, 12 February 2015, at: http://europa.eu/rapid/press-release_SPEECH-15-4402_en.htm. As I write (January 2016) the Commission has just decided to invoke the

actually invoked the rule-of-law mechanism to deal with the rapidly deteriorating situation in Poland. But it has not been used for Hungary.

In April 2014, the Fidesz government was returned to power in an election that the Office of Democratic Institutions and Human Rights (ODIHR) of the OSCE monitored. ODIHR, too, sounded the alarm on the constitutional coup. The election monitors found that in many different ways '[t]he main governing party enjoyed an undue advantage'. They reported numerous violations of international standards, including a failure to separate party and state, a biased media environment, a partisan Electoral Commission, lack of transparency in determining the electoral districts, and a generally un-level playing field.[80]

A 'free but unfair' election in the heart of the EU might have caused a major reaction, but the European elections followed in just one month, and for most of the rest of 2014, the European Commission was itself out of commission: nothing happened in Brussels because major European institutions were preparing for the election and then reorganizing themselves afterwards, and the actors who had been in the forefront of monitoring Hungary – Barroso and Reding at the Commission and Tavares in the Parliament – all left office. The new team, with First Vice President Frans Timmermans in charge of the 'rule-of-law' portfolio, criticized Hungary but did little to attempt to undo the already-consolidated constitutional coup.

From this review, one can see that European institutions were well aware of the seriousness of the constitutional changes in Hungary at the time they were happening. The Commission, Court of Justice and Parliament were on record as criticizing a one-sided constitution that didn't constrain the governing party. Each institution also concluded that Hungary was engaged in a serious violation of European values. None of these interventions or criticisms was effective at stopping the constitutional coup nor were any of the harsher sanctioning mechanisms that

rule of law procedure with regard to Poland, whose new far-right government has launched a constitutional coup of its own. Hungary, its constitutional coup consolidated, has still not triggered the rule-of-law mechanism.

80 ODIHR, Statement of Preliminary Findings and Conclusions, Hungary Parliamentary Election, 6 April 2014, available at: www.osce.org/odihr/elections/117205?download=true. For my analysis of the election, see K. L. Scheppele (with M. Bánkuti and Z. Réti), 'Legal But Not Fair,' *Paul Krugman, Conscience of a Liberal blog*, 13 April 2014, available at: krugman.blogs.nytimes.com/2014/04/13/legal-but-not-fair-hungary/ and K. L. Scheppele, 'Hungary and the End of Politics: How Victor Orbán Launched a Constitutional Coup and Created a One-Party State', *The Nation*, 6 May 2014, available at: www.thenation.com/article/hungary-and-end-politics/.

were available to European institutions used. With more bark than bite, European institutions made a racket but changed little on the ground. The Hungarian government finished its consolidation of power and then engineered its own re-election.

What Can Be Done?

The crisis of European values has caught European institutions by surprise, and they have been largely unprepared to act. Prospective Member States were required to run the gauntlet of the Copenhagen Criteria before being admitted to the EU, but the Treaties never adequately anticipated that commitments to the values in Article 2 of the Treaty of the European Union (TEU) might be substantially weakened after a Member State gained entry. As a result, the Treaties have no mechanism for throwing a state out if it persistently fails to respect the values of democracy, rule of law and human rights.[81] The 'nuclear option',[82] Article 7 TEU, permits the EU to remove a Member State's vote in the Council of the European Union.[83] But Article 7 TEU is more of a quarantine mechanism that would allow the healthy states to avoid being influenced by the pariah state than it is a mechanism for restoring Member State compliance with EU values.[84] Besides, Article 7 TEU has been widely thought to be unworkable as a practical sanction because supermajorities in the Council and Parliament are required for the success of this option, and party alignments at the EU level prevent the key parties from criticizing governments from allied states.[85] Even with the European Commission's new 'rule-of-law mechanism' that provides a roadmap for gathering and assessing evidence that could lead to an

[81] There is, of course, now a procedure for Member States to leave the EU of their own volition: Article 50 TEU. For an analysis: A. Łazowski, *Withdrawal from the European Union: A Legal Appraisal* (Elgar, 2015).

[82] Commission President José Manuel Barroso called Article 7 the 'nuclear option' in his State of the Union Speech in 2012 at http://europa.eu/rapid/press-release_SPEECH-12-596_en.htm.

[83] See C. Hillion, 'Overseeing the Rule of Law in the EU: Legal Mandate and Means' in Kochenov and Closa (eds.), *Reinforcing the Rule* (2016); W. Sadurski, 'Adding Bite to the Bark: The Story of EU Enlargement, Article 7 and Jörg Haider', *Columbia Journal of International Law*, 16 (2010), 385.

[84] I am indebted to Jan-Werner Müller for this idea.

[85] R. Daniel Keleman, 'Epp ♥ Orbán: Leading Figures in the European People's Party Are Sheltering The Orbán Regime in the Name of Partisan Politics', *Politico.EU*, 18 June 2015 at: www.politico.eu/article/epp-defends-hungary-orban-against-criticism/.

Article 7 TEU procedure,[86] nothing has followed yet in practice in the state farthest along in rewriting its constitutional order to create an illiberal state. Another proposal to create a 'Copenhagen Commission' to review Member States for their continued compliance with the Copenhagen Criteria[87] is widely assumed to require Treaty change.[88] Not only would Treaty change take a long time, but it requires unanimity. And any Member State that sees itself in the crosshairs of such a proposal has every incentive to veto the change.

What, then, can be done with the tools at hand to be more effective when states abandon European values? I propose rethinking the way that the Commission brings infringement procedures.[89] The Commission could signal systemic breach of fundamental Treaty obligations by a Member State by bundling a group of specific alleged violations together to argue before the Court of Justice that the infringement of EU law in a Member State is not minor or transient, but systemic and persistent and that it rises to the level of infringement of basic values of the Union. Unlike the usual infringement procedure in which narrowly focused elements of Member State action are singled out for attention one at a time,[90] a *systemic infringement procedure* would identify a pattern of state practice that, when the individual elements are added up, constitute an even more serious violation of a Member State's fundamental EU obligations than would the individual elements, taken separately. It is this pattern that would give rise to the finding of a systemic breach. By using the common infringement procedure in new ways, the Commission would be deploying a tried and true instrument but it would use this familiar method to achieve a more ambitious purpose.

[86] 'Communication from the European Commission to the Council and the Parliament: A New EU Mechanism to Strengthen the Rule of Law', COM(2014) 158final/2, 19 March 2014.

[87] The Copenhagen Commission was first proposed by my Princeton colleague Jan-Werner Müller, 'Should the EU Protect Democracy and the Rule of Law within Member States?', *European Law Journal*, 21 (2015), 141.

[88] Closa and Kochenov (eds.), *Reinforcing the Rule*, introduction.

[89] P. Craig and G. de Búrca, *EU Law: Texts, Cases Materials*, 6th edn (Oxford University press, 2015), pp. 431–53; S. Andersen, *The Enforcement of EU Law: The Role of the European Commission* (Oxford University Press, 2012).

[90] Wennerås has noted that the Commission seems to prefer bringing multiple separate actions of smaller bore rather than one larger action putting the pieces of a broader puzzle together. This piecemeal approach has made it more difficult for the Commission to win substantial remedies at the compliance and sanctioning stage. P. Wennerås, 'Making Effective Use of Article 260 TFEU' in Kochenov and Closa (eds.), *Reinforcing the Rule of Law*.

If a Member State is threatening the basic values of the Treaties or putting in doubt the legal guarantees presumed by EU law, it is probably violating more than one precise slice of EU law. Under present practice, the Commission picks its battles, so it currently fails to bring many actions that it might otherwise be justified in launching. As Wennerås notes, the Commission has a tendency to see problems as individual trees rather than as larger forests and to bring larger numbers of small cases rather than smaller numbers of large cases.[91] The CJEU has encouraged the Commission to consolidate actions to highlight more 'general and persistent' violations,[92] but the Commission uses this option infrequently.[93]

The sort of bundled action I propose is different from the uses we have seen thus far. Instead of simply documenting a pattern that shows EU law has been violated, the systemic infringement procedure would focus on claims that raise questions of a more fundamental sort, where the Member State's commitment to European values would be challenged through the way the action would be framed. The systemic infringement procedure would therefore be distinguished, by the seriousness and variety of the violations alleged in European constitutional terms, from the 'general and persistent' violation cases in which violation of a single source of EU law is proven by a pattern of separate instances.

Systemic infringement procedures before the Court could be structured doctrinally in one of several ways. First, and perhaps most ambitiously, they could directly allege that a pattern of Member State conduct violates one or more of the basic principles outlined in Article 2 TEU. This would have the disadvantage of being a novel form of legal action. A number of commentators believe that Article 2 TEU can only be enforced through Article 7 TEU, a distinctly political procedure.[94] But an increasing chorus of voices is starting to argue that CJEU enforcement of Article 2 TEU is thinkable. For example, former Commission Vice-President Reding suggested that the Commission might consider grounding an

[91] Wennerås, 'Making Effective Use'.

[92] See the discussion of this issue in Lenaerts et al., *EU Procedural Law* (Oxford University press, 2014), pp. 166–7 with many examples in the notes.

[93] Wennerås, 'Making Effective Use', at notes 51–60.

[94] M. Avbelj, 'The Inherent Limits of Law – the Case of Slovenia,' *Verfassungsblog*, 6 December 2013, at: www.verfassungsblog.de/en/the-inherent-limits-of-law-the-case-of-slovenia-2/ and P. Blokker, 'Systemic Infringement Action: An Effective Solution or Rather Part of the Problem?' *Verfassungsblog*, 5 December 2013, at: www.verfassungsblog.de/en/systemic-infringement-action-an-effective-solution-or-rather-part-of-the-problem-2/.

infringement action in Article 2 TEU.[95] Christophe Hillion makes the case more strongly, arguing that the Commission as guardian of the Treaties should be able to enforce Article 2 TEU to ward off more serious violations.[96] He envisions judicial enforcement of Article 2 as a precautionary measure seeking to dissuade offending Member States from engaging in conduct that might spur an Article 7 TEU procedure. Most recently, the 'Editorial Comments' in the Common Market Law Review noted that 'the Treaties neither restrain nor exclude the Court of Justice's jurisdiction in relation to Article 2 TEU. Had such limitation been wanted, the primary law-makers could have made it explicit.'[97]

To launch a novel action would take some serious work. In particular, many of the Article 2 values are stated very broadly, and critics say it would be difficult to create workable definitions of those general terms that would make Article 2 legally enforceable.[98] But one might start with the rule of law, which is not a mysterious concept to a judge. Surely, it includes the idea of judicial independence, and the CJEU already has a jurisprudence specifying what it means for other important EU institutions to be independent.[99] Using these standards, the CJEU could easily assess whether the independence of a Member State's judiciary had been compromised, something that would raise serious questions about the Member State's commitment to the rule of law as an Article 2 principle.

This sort of procedure would work to better capture the seriousness of what has happened in Hungary. The CJEU already found that the government of Hungary committed unlawful age discrimination when it suddenly lowered the judicial retirement age and fired the senior-most 10 per cent of its judiciary. But surely the problem was not *just* age discrimination. When criteria for holding office can be changed so that

[95] 'We could go further, by creating a new specific procedure to enforce the rule of law principle of Article 2 TEU against Member States by means of an infringement procedure brought by the Commission or another Member State before the Court of Justice.' Viviane Reding, Vice-President of the European Commission, 'The EU and the Rule of Law: What Next?' Speech given 4 September 2013, at http://europa.eu/rapid/press-release_SPEECH-13-677_en.htm.

[96] C. Hillion, 'Overseeing the Rule of Law in the EU: Legal Mandate and Means' in Kochenov and Closa (eds.), *Reinforcing the Rule.*

[97] Editorial Comments, 'Safeguarding EU Values in the Member States – Is Something Finally Happening?', *Common Market Law Review*, 52 (2015), 619, 622.

[98] *Ibid.*, at 625. But the author(s) then went on (at 626) to argue that the EU judiciary could also contribute to the clarification of Article 2 TEU.

[99] See, for example, the cases on the independence of data protection commissioners: Case C-288/12 *Commission v. Hungary* [2014] (GC); Case C-518/07 Commission v Germany [2010] (GC); Case C-614/10; Commission v Austria [2012] (GC).

current occupants of judgeships can be suddenly removed from office, this is also an infringement on the independence of the judiciary. In assessing what it means for an institution to be independent, the CJEU could take a page from its own jurisprudence on the independence of data protection officers in Member States. Hungary had just such a case before the Court when the office of data protection ombudsman was reorganized and the current occupant was fired before the end of his term. In that case, the CJEU said,

> 54. If it were permissible for every Member State to compel a supervisory authority to vacate office before serving its full term, in contravention of the rules and safeguards established in that regard by the legislation applicable, the threat of premature termination to which that authority would be exposed throughout its term of office could lead it to enter into a form of prior compliance with the political authority, which is incompatible with the requirement of independence.[100]

If one simply substitutes the word 'judge' for 'supervisory authority' in that paragraph, one would have a strong argument that the lowering of the judicial retirement age was not just age discrimination, but also a violation of judicial independence. The Court already has the tools, the standards and the existing jurisprudence to do this.

Finding that a country altered the job qualifications for sitting judges might be enough for a systemic infringement action, since it would mean establishing that it was not just one judge, but fully 10 per cent of the judiciary that had been fired in this way, showing a pattern of practice. But in the Hungarian case, there is much more, as we have seen. When the retirement age was lowered, the sitting president of the Supreme Court – too young to be affected by this change – was removed because the government changed the qualifications for his job and applied the changes immediately to him. Former Supreme Court President András Baka has since won a case at the European Court of Human Rights over his firing.[101] While the Hungarian government was ensuring a high level of turnover at the highest levels of the judiciary, it also radically overhauled the system of judicial appointments,[102] giving the power to appoint, promote, demote, reassign, discipline and remove judges to a single political official close to the government who, for two years, also

[100] Case C-288/12 *Commission v. Hungary* [2014].

[101] *Baka v. Hungary*, App. no. 20261/12 (ECtHR, 2012). The Hungarian government asked for reconsideration of the case, which is currently before a Grand Chamber of the Court. CITE THE GRAND JUDGMENT CASE.

[102] Scheppele, 'First, Let's Pick All the Judges'.

had the power to take cases from the courts to which they were assigned by law and move them to other courts around the country.[103] The Venice Commission[104] and the International Bar Association[105] found that these measures put the independence of the judiciary in danger.

A systemic infringement procedure could bring together this set of changes and allege that the independence of the judiciary has been infringed by each item separately, but even more comprehensively by the set together. The rule of law provision of Article 2 could provide a doctrinal anchor for this action. One doesn't have to have a precise definition that covers cases at the margins in order to identify a case that goes to the heart of a principle and one doesn't have to have a precise definition of every single value in Article 2 in order to be able to enforce the ones more amenable to adjudication.

But legal enforcement of the broad principles of Article 2 TEU is not the only theory under which a systemic infringement action could be framed. A systemic infringement procedure could argue, alternatively, that a systemic violation of the basic principles of EU law puts a Member State in violation of Article 4(3) TEU. This is familiar ground to the CJEU, which has already developed an extensive jurisprudence of 'sincere cooperation' or loyalty.[106] Using this rubric, the Commission would argue that the challenged laws and practices of the Member State systematically interfere with the operation of EU law in the Member State's jurisdiction and thus violate the Member State's loyalty obligations.

To see how this might work, consider reframing the proposed infringement procedure on the independence of the judiciary in Hungary as an

[103] Rozenberg, 'Meet Tünde Handó'.

[104] European Commission for Democracy through Law (Venice Commission), Opinion on Act CLXII of 2011 on the Legal Status and Remuneration of Judges and Act CLXI of 2011 on the Organisation and Administration of Courts of Hungary, adopted by the Venice Commission at its 90th Plenary Session (Venice, 16–17 March 2012), CDL-AD(2012)001-e, at: www.venice.coe.int/webforms/documents/?pdf=CDL-AD%282012%29001-e and Opinion on the Cardinal Acts on the Judiciary that were amended following the adoption of Opinion CDL-AD(2012)001 on Hungary, adopted by the Venice Commission at its 92nd Plenary Session (Venice, 12–13 October 2012), CDL-AD(2012)020-e, at: www.venice.coe.int/webforms/documents/?pdf=CDL-AD%282012%29020-e.

[105] International Bar Association's Human Rights Institute (IBAHRI), Courting Controversy: The Impact of the Recent Reforms on the Independence of the Judiciary and the Rule of Law in Hungary (September 2012), at: www.ibanet.org/Document/Default.aspx?DocumentUid=89D4991A-D61F-498A-BD21-0BAFFA6ABF17.

[106] For a comprehensive account of the loyalty principle in EU law, see M. Klamert, *The Principle of Loyalty in EU Law* (Oxford University Press, 2014).

Article 4(3) TEU action. National courts are, of course, also Union courts, since they are primary enforcers of EU law. If the national courts have been fundamentally reorganized in a Member State to be structurally dependent on political will, then the ability of the national courts to independently assess violations of EU law may be called into question. The laws themselves that tie judicial appointments to political influence could be given as evidence that the judiciary has ceased to be independent.

To make the case under Article 4(3) TEU, and to tie the matter more directly to the dangers of mistaken application of EU law, some concrete examples of political pressure being successfully applied to politically vulnerable judges would strengthen the case. Unfortunately, there are already such examples from Hungary, where political officials publicly attacked judicial decisions in cases involving EU law and judges afterwards changed their minds.[107] The strong attacks in the public press by governing party officials against particular judges and then the later compliance of other judges in the system with these partisan demands have given rise to the public view that the judiciary is now subject to political pressure.[108] A Member State in which judges publicly change their minds under political pressure cannot be said to have an independent judiciary. It becomes an EU law matter under Article 4(3) when national legal changes substantially infringe the independence of the judiciary and when the pressure extends to wrongly deciding cases in EU law.

[107] For example, in one case, a Slovakian driver who caused an accident that killed Hungarians appealed her criminal conviction and asked that her sentence be suspended while the appeal was pending. The initial judge granted her request for suspension but then the government attacked this judge for allowing her out of prison, arguing that the woman would flee back to Slovakia. That day, another judge reopened the case and sentenced the woman to jail time, despite the European Arrest Warrant that would have made the woman's extradition legally straightforward if she had in fact gone back to Slovakia. For one detailed account of the case, see E. Balogh, 'Political Interference with the Hungarian Judiciary', *Hungarian Spectrum*, 5 December 2013, available at: http://hungarianspectrum.org/2013/12/05/political-interference-with-the-hungarian-judiciary/. In another case, the Supreme Court reversed lower court judgments that had said that segregated Roma schools violated the Hungarian law that transposed the EU directive on equal treatment, after Fidesz officials criticized the lower courts and threatened to change the law. For more, see É. Balogh, 'The Hungarian Supreme Court Decided: Segregation Is Lawful in Parochial Schools', *Hungarian Spectrum blog*, 28 April 2015, available at: http://hungarianspectrum.org/2015/04/28/hungarian-supreme-court-decided-segregation-is-lawful-in-parochial-schools/.

[108] Both the Hungarian Association of Judges and the President of the Hungarian Supreme Court have issued warnings that incidents like this make it appear that judges are politically controlled; Balogh, 'Political Interference'.

In a third variant of the systemic infringement procedure, the Commission could allege that a Member State has engaged in a systemic violation of a particular substantive area of EU law through a pattern of conduct that adds up to more than the sum of the parts. As we have seen, the Commission has already done this with its 'general and persistent' jurisprudence. But a systemic infringement procedure could elevate the existing practice to permit it to reach cases that challenge EU values contained in Article 2 TEU, including the protection of human rights. Instead of using Article 2 TEU directly, the Commission could allege that a Member State's infringement of EU law rose to the level of violating individuals' rights under the Charter of Fundamental Rights.

Article 51 of the Charter limits the scope of the Charter to EU institutions and 'to the Member State only when they are implementing Union law.'[109] But if a Member State's systemic violation of EU law is sufficiently extreme, because the state misapplies EU law or fails to apply EU law, then the rights of EU citizens within that Member State may be endangered. Perhaps a critic might argue that the Charter should not apply where Member States misapply or do not apply EU law when they should. But that is a formalism bound to fail.[110]

If the Commission is the guardian of the Treaties – all Treaties, including the Charter – then it has an obligation to ensure that fundamental rights are protected when violated by Member State implementing EU law. Here, the Commission would not be bringing a case against a Member State that infringed a particular individual's right, but would instead bring an Article 258 TFEU action for situations in which the regular misapplication of EU law itself generated a pattern of rights violation.

Here, too, a Hungarian example might be helpful. The Commission might focus on Hungary's persistent violations of the Data Protection Directive.[111] Since it started in 2011 with a 'social consultation' on the new constitution, in which the government asked the public for its views but in a way that could not be taken into account in the drafting process because the questionnaire was sent out too late, the Hungarian

[109] Charter of Fundamental Rights, Article 51(1).

[110] See K. Lenaerts, 'Exploring the Limits of the EU Charter of Fundamental Rights', *European Constitutional Law Review*, 8 (2012), 375 (arguing that the Charter should apply to Member States' actions even when they have derogated from EU law). Surely, under this logic, Charter rights should apply to Member States misapplying EU law.

[111] Directive 95/46/EC of the European Parliament and of the Council of 24 October 1995 on the Protection of Individuals with Regard to the Processing of Personal Data and on the Free Movement of Such Data, OJ L 281.

government has repeatedly gathered the personally identifiable political opinions of individuals through these mass surveys without legal limitations on how the data may be used or how long it might be kept.[112] This is not just a violation of Article 8(1) of the Directive, which directly bans government collection of individually identifiable political opinion, but also a violation of Article 6(1) of the Directive that requires clear legal limits on the collection and use of personal data. Social consultations might also be a violation of Article 28(2) of the Directive, which requires the data protection officer to be involved in all personal data collection efforts, given that the data protection ombudsman had been fired when he brought a legal action against this data collection activity, claiming, among other things, that he had not been consulted before the questionnaires were went out. The Court has already established that the prior data protection ombudsman had been fired in violation of the Directive, which requires his complete independence.[113] It could examine the independence of the new data protection officer, who is currently housed in an agency nestled inside a government ministry, and who has not objected to the continued practice of social consultation. He dropped the case started by his predecessor challenging these data collection practices and did nothing to challenge repeated uses of social consultations, including one that was sent out in Spring 2015 on the migration crisis that directly implicates EU law.[114] A new European Parliament resolution against Hungary passed in June 2015 specifically criticized Hungary on the data protection issues, including the requirement that people provide personally identifiable information in response to questions about immigration.[115]

The collection of personally identifiable political opinions without legal limit is not just a violation of the Data Protection Directive, but

112 For the details, see K. L. Scheppele, 'Making Infringement Procedures More Effective: A Comment on Commission v. Hungary, Case C-288/12', *Eutopia*, 29 April 2014, available at: http://eutopialaw.com/2014/04/29/making-infringement-procedures-more-effective-a-comment-on-commission-v-hungary-case-c-28812-8-april-2014-grand-chamber/.

113 Case C-288/12 *Commission v. Hungary* [2014] (GC).

114 European Commission, 'Hungary: Government's National Consultation on Immigration and Terrorism Creates Widespread Debate,' European Website on Integration, at: https://ec.europa.eu/migrant-integration/news/hungary-governments-national-consultation-on-immigration-and-terrorism-creates-widespread-debate?pdf=1.

115 European Parliament Resolution of 10 June 2015 on the Situation in Hungary (2015/2700(RSP)) para 5, at: www.europarl.europa.eu/sides/getDoc.do?pubRef=-//EP//TEXT+TA+P8-TA-2015-0227+0+DOC+XML+V0//EN&language=EN.

also a violation of the individual right of data privacy protected by Article 8 of the Charter of Fundamental Rights.[116] If Hungary were to be found not just to have infringed EU law but also to have violated the fundamental rights of its citizens in doing so, then the shadow of Article 2 TEU would fall over the case because the basic values of the EU include the protection of fundamental rights. But, if the case were brought as a systemic violation of the Directive plus an allegation of the infringement of a particular right in the Charter, then the CJEU would not have to rule directly on Article 2. In fact, the same logic would apply to our earlier example of judicial independence, because the Commission could add to the bundled set of complaints mentioned there an allegation that these practices caused a violation of Article 47 of the Charter, the right to an effective remedy and a fair trial.[117]

Systemic infringement procedures identify the seriousness of violations committed by persistently challenging states by raising important EU principles in addition to more technical violations. They therefore also open up a different conversation about what compliance would mean. By grouping together a set of laws, decisions and practices to make a more general case, the Commission would be laying the ground for arguing that systemic violations of Member State obligations must be met with systemic compliance.

Regardless of the way in which it is ultimately grounded in EU law, a systemic infringement procedure would enable the Commission to signal to the Court of Justice a more general concern about deviation from core principles than would be allowed by a more narrowly tailored infringement action. It would also have the advantage of putting before the CJEU, all at one time, evidence of a *pattern* of violation so that the overall situation in a particular Member State would not be lost in a flurry of individual complaints, each of which might go to a different panel of judges at the Court. The CJEU could then either agree with the Commission that the set of allegations packaged together add up something more systemic in a way that violates basic EU values, or it could find that only some of the allegations within the set violate particular aspects of EU law. Just as with the 'general and persistent' cases, the CJEU would ultimately have to determine whether the larger pattern of infringement was demonstrated by the Commission.

If the CJEU agrees that a Member State's conduct rises to the level of a systemic violation, then compliance with the Court's judgement should

[116] Charter, Article 8. [117] Charter, Article 47.

also be systemic. In fact, that is actually the point of bringing a systemic infringement procedure in the first place. A Member State should not just be required to fix small technical violations in its implementation of EU law but should also be required to fix the systemic threat to EU values. Compliance should therefore be assessed differently than in a more highly tailored infringement action. A systemic infringement action should therefore open up a wider range of options for what would count as compliance, something to which the CJEU would contribute by finding a range of linked practices to be systemic violations of EU law.

If the Commission had brought the case about the change in the judicial retirement age as a values case violating the rule of law rather than an age discrimination case violating the rights of individuals, then compliance would have looked very different. If the CJEU had confirmed the systemic infringement, then the Hungarian government would have had to address more than the wishes of the specific judges affected by the one-off lowering of the retirement age. With a more systemic framing, compliance could instead have required measures to ensure that faith in the neutrality and objectivity of the judiciary was restored. This might include ensuring in law and practice that judges were secure in their positions and could not be arbitrarily dismissed, demoted or disciplined if they ruled against the government.

Some might object that the European Commission has no power to micromanage the detailed institutional arrangements of Member States, a very sensitive subject. As we have seen, the internal political structures of Member States are broadly protected by Article 4(2) TEU, which requires that the Union respect Member States' 'national identities, inherent in their fundamental structures, political and constitutional.' But surely the constitutional arrangements of Member States have to be broadly compliant with the values listed in Article 2 TEU and a Member State should not be allowed to hide behind an assertion of national identity to violate those basic values.

Conclusion

The European Union is experiencing a crisis of values, as some Member States are openly flouting the basic principles of EU law. Member States might claim that they are entitled to have any sort of constitutional system they want, citing Article 4(2) TEU for cover, but at some point, national pluralism hits the hard edge of common values. I have tried to explain in this chapter how a widespread agreement across European institutions should be enough to demonstrate when a Member State of the EU is no longer adhering to the European values that provide a limit to Member State pluralism.

Once Member States start deviating in crucial ways from the common values in Article 2 TEU, this threat might be addressed by EU political bodies invoking Article 7 TEU as a political mechanism. But even if a crisis of values represents a political problem, it is also at the same time a legal problem, as key provisions of EU law are being violated systematically without a meaningful attempt to address the violations. When violations are not neat and singular but plural and complex, the Commission needs to rise to the occasion and adapt the instruments at its disposal to meet the new challenges.

16

Peer Review in the Context of Constitutionalism and the Rule of Law

ANNE MEUWESE*

Introduction

> Neighbouring societies and governments may well be coping with similar problems and constraints, and may be finding ways to adapt rule of law, accountability, and transparency mechanisms to new and complex situations. In addition, few of the problems good governance is intended to attack are contained within national boundaries. Sharing ideas, experiences, and resources, coordinating rule-of-law functions on a regional basis, and peer review of governance procedures can all contribute to reforms appropriate to social realities, and can make better use of scarce resources.[1]

This quote has not been chosen for its authoritativeness but for how typical it is of how peer review is often presented in a context of rule of law promotion and constitutional reform: as instrumental to reform through mutual learning. As has been common wisdom in the private law realm for much longer, the development of public law, too, is the result of 'an irreversibly trans-jurisdictional search for adequate means to address common and border-crossing concerns'.[2] As a central ideal of contemporary public law, the rule of law then, at least in part, is 'a field of action and discourse that emerges through complex

* The author is grateful to The Netherlands Organization for Scientific Research for generously funding her research project 'You Need No Competence to Join In: Alternatives to Constitutional Law' with a Veni grant (451-11-032).

1 M. Johnston, 'Good Governance: Rule of Law, Transparency, and Accountability', working paper, 13.

2 G. P. Calliess and P. Zumbansen, *Rough Consensus and Running Code: A Theory of Transnational Private Law* (Oregon: Bloomsbury Publishing, 2010).

relationships among experts, national elites and global institutions'.[3] In this context we see the same 'rapprochement between institutional politics and social scientific analysis'[4] that has been observed in globalized networks more generally. The activities of interpretation of constitutional norms and rule of law standards and the formulation of constitutional desiderata become intertwined with the activities of learning about diverse national practices and translating this into useable knowledge.

This chapter aims to make a contribution to grasping how these evolutionary processes may be facilitated in more concrete terms to benefit not only learning with regard to constitutionalism and the rule of law but also the practice of challenging the conduct of public authorities. In order to do so we need to look beyond high-strung constitutional moments and include processes as mundane as to amount to a 'battle of advisors'.[5] To better comprehend the evolution of the fundamental ideals (and realities) that define states and national communities around the globe, it may well be worthwhile to include social norms in the picture and consider the impact of pressure.[6] This chapter offers some general reflections and a first inventory with regard to one specific mechanism occupying more and more ground in both practical proposals for furthering the rule of law and theoretical work on constitutionalism: peer review. In particular, this chapter explores the role that peer review as an instrument plays and could play in facilitating or steering constitutional development, in the context of rule of law promotion. This development occurs through two distinct behavioural mechanisms: challenging and learning. After a conceptual exploration, including an inventory of insights from research on peer review in different settings, we will look at some concrete instances of (budding) peer review processes with links to the rule of law in action and discourse.

[3] Y. Dezalay and B. Garth, *Lawyers and the Rule of Law in an Era of Globalization* (Routledge, 2011).

[4] A. Riles, *The Network Inside Out* (Ann Arbor, University of Michigan Press 2001), p. 174.

[5] M. Siems, *Comparative Law* (Cambridge University Press, 2014), p. 264. See also F. Schimmelfennig, 'A Comparison of the Rule of Law Promotion Policies of Major Western Powers' in M. Zürn, A. Nollkaemper and R. Peerenboom (eds.), *Rule of Law Dynamics: In an Era of International and Transnational Governance* (Cambridge University Press), pp. 111–32.

[6] Siems, *Comparative Law*, p. 237.

That the use of peer review in rule of law and constitutionalism settings is not as plainly upbeat as the quote at the beginning of this chapter suggests, has become clear in the wake of the European Commission's announcement that it plans to take on a role as a 'rule-of-law watchdog' by establishing a 'rule-of-law monitor'.[7] One of the controversial elements of this proposal is in fact the possible inclusion of a form of peer review.[8] The conclusion pinpoints the key challenges facing peer review in rule of law and constitutionalism settings and draws attention to a possible side effect of the application of peer review: increased transparency.

The Concept of Peer Review in the Context of Constitutionalism and the Rule of Law

The Notion of Review

For a concept used so much in daily and scholarly legal vocabulary, 'review' itself appears to be a poorly delineated concept. It is related to the 'checks' in 'checks and balances' and to 'control', but the latter is more general than 'review', which presupposes norms that set the standard for behaviour and an explicit appraisal in some form. The assumption is that one of the reasons we pass judgement on 'past performance' – behaviour or a course of action – is at least partly that we believe that this can have a positive impact on future performance. The central role of 'review' in public law is intimately linked to the silent acknowledgement that the inherently problematic ambition of this legal field, which could be summarized as 'getting government to comply with its own norms', requires constant iteration. 'Review' is about a judgement on a course of action, thus often focusing on the result ('in accordance with the law, yes or no?'). But it is also a process, with explicit and implicit norms, a methodology and a psychology. At the core of the notion of review is its 'challenge function'. Reviews focused

7 Remarks by President Barroso on the future of Justice and Home affairs and the Rule of Law initiative, 11 March 2014, available at http://europa.eu/rapid/press-release_SPEECH-14-204_en.htm.

8 For a defence of the inclusion of peer review, see E. M. H. Hirsch Ballin, 'Mutual Trust: The Virtue of Reciprocity Strengthening the Acceptance of the Rule of Law through Peer Review' in C. Closa and D. Kochenov (eds.), *Reinforcing the Rule of Law Oversight in the European Union* (Cambridge University Press, 2016).

on this 'are inherently regulatory in nature, so they can be unpleasant in practice', especially given that 'government agencies normally regulate others, they are themselves the regulated parties of a challenge function'.[9]

The concrete mechanisms perhaps most commonly associated with 'getting government to comply with its own norms' are parliamentary scrutiny and judicial review. These archetypical forms of 'review' potentially cover a wide range of public law norms.[10] In parliamentary systems scrutiny by parliament often hinges on the question regarding the aforementioned ministerial responsibility, but it can deal with almost any type of norm or standard given the open mandate of parliaments. Judicial review works with a set of principles and legal norms and often has standing rules for applicants as the main limitation. In this category, too, the review function is two-fold: a court telling a government agency that it cannot keep certain documents secret (challenging) also sends a signal that the agency in question might consider treating freedom of information requests differently in the future (learning). It appears though that in 'traditional' review settings, the challenging function, which ensures that public decisions do not go unchecked, remains key.

Beyond courts and judicial review, we can observe 'alternative' reviewers, who focus on behaviour and output of public authorities, stepping in.[11] Teubner in his recent book on Constitutional Fragments listed 'social-scientific and political performance reviews by authorities independent of the state – similar to audit courts – which render errors visible and avoidable' among 'the currently urgent constitutional self-limitations of the politics of the welfare

[9] R. B. Belzer, 'Principles for an Effective Regulatory Impact Analysis Challenge Function', *Horizons. Special Issue on Regulatory Strategy*, 10(3) (2009), 31–9, available at http://www.policyresearch.gc.ca/page.asp?pagenm=2009-0014_07.

[10] In some literature 'review' is equated with 'constitutional review' or 'the act of declaring a government action that violates some provisions of the constitution to be'. This is the case for instance in Tushnet's work, which actually explores the idea of 'review' beyond courts already but then limits it to achieving compliance with constitutional norms, which makes certainty regarding constitutional interpretation the main issue; M. Tushnet, *The New Constitutional Order* (Princeton University Press, 2003).

[11] C. Arndt, 'The Politics of Governance Ratings', *International Public Management Journal*, 11(3) (2008), 275–297; C. Arndt and C. Oman, 'Use and Abuses of Governance Indicators', *OECD Paris*, 2006.

state'.[12] Well-known is the range of specialized institutions such as courts of audit and ombuds institutions. Transgovernmental review by supranational or international actors, such as the OECD or the European Commission is a further category: international organizations that are increasingly active in assessing government actions, often based on performance measures that have been derived from a set of explicit or implicit public law norms. Then there is the possibility of self-review: many of the processes carried out inside governmental organizations, for instance in internal accountability offices, might be seen as 'review'. Finally, we see civil society groups like Statewatch or Transparency International acting as 'watchdogs' exposing rule-of-law wrongdoings.[13] Across all categories of 'alternative' review settings (see the table below), at least part of the debate concerns how governments should *learn* from the review results; it is not just the possibility of challenging that counts. The literature on policy learning hosts a vibrant debate regarding what role different instruments and architectures for comparative learning, such as benchmarking, peer review, checklists and facilitated coordination can play.[14]

Below, an overview of potential (alternative) forms of review which have the capacity to have an impact on the practice of constitutionalism and the rule of law is presented. They differ as to whether a formal competence is needed to bring about the review, what triggers the review, what limits their application, the issue of sanctioning and their potential for employing a 'peer-review modality'. What the types of review that are not 'judicial' or 'parliamentary' have in common is that the sanction for a negative outcome appears to centre around 'reputational damage'.

[12] G. Teubner, *Constitutional Fragments: Societal Constitutionalism and Globalization* (Oxford University Press, 2012), p. 87.

[13] R. B. Chavez, 'The Rule of Law and Courts in Democratizing Regimes', in K. E. Whittington, R. D. Keleman and G. A. Caldeira (eds.), *The Oxford Handbook of Law and Politics* (Oxford Handbook Online, 2008), pp. 63–80, p. 72.

[14] C. A. Dunlop and C. M. Radaelli, 'Systematizing Policy Learning: Vrom Monolith to Dimensions', *Political Studies*, 31(3) (2013), 599–619. See also S. Borrás and C. M. Radaelli, 'The Politics of Governance Architectures: Creation, Change and Effects of the EU Lisbon Strategy', *Journal of European Public Policy*, 18(4) (2011), 463–84.

	Based on formal competences	What triggers review?	What limits review?	Sanction	Peer review potential?	Primarily learning or challenging?
Judicial review	Yes	Case	Standing Judiciability Case-based	Invalidation decision	Very informally	Challenging
Parliamentary review	Yes	Formal report Incident	Time Political dynamics	Removal Change in policy	Very informally	Challenging
Specialized public review Audit, ombuds, commissions	Yes (but stretched)	Complaint Routine	Mandate	Reputation damage	Limited	Learning
Transgovernmental review OECD, European Commission	Yes (but stretched)	Own agenda	Mandate Information	Reputation damage Threat of sanction (fine, expulsion)	Yes	Challenging and learning
Self-review Internal accountability offices	No	Routine Incident	Lack of incentives/ sanctions	Prevention of external sanctions	Yes	Learning
Specialized private review NGOs	No	Routine Agenda	Information	Reputation damage	Facilitating at most	Challenging and learning

The Notion of 'Peer'

As the accompanying table already suggests, a great difficulty with the concept of peer review in a public law context – and a crucial difference with scientific peer review – is the proper identification of 'peers'. The idea that peers, as 'equals' or 'colleagues', are best placed to pass judgement on one's actions and outputs appears to fit a scientific context better than a political or constitutional one. Government actors tend to derive their mandate from a basis in national public law and this may be expected to strongly shape their identity.

Although the Magna Carta already mentioned the term ('lawful judgement of his peers'),[15] what we understand by the word 'peer' is intrinsically subjective. It is difficult to force a 'peer' on someone. In the judicial world the acceptance of foreign judges as fellow professionals[16] appears to be on the rise and is conceptually relatively clear, but this is not necessarily the case for, say, environmental inspectors or even government ministers. Colleagues from another country who at first glance might be 'peers' may be dealing with a completely different mandate or politico-administrative environment. What is the responsibility of a minister in one country may be up to an agency director in another.

'Peers' could emerge at four different analytical levels of actorship, often used in diffusion studies:

1. the individual level (colleagues appraising each other; difficult to track down and less likely to have a measurable impact in a rule-of-law context)
2. the agency level (agencies or other public bodies with a specialized task engaging one another in dialogue about their procedures and performance)
3. the state level (countries reviewing countries – often with involvement of international organizations as facilitators)
4. the global level (dialogues between inter-, supra- or transnational bodies with involvement of transnational epistemic communities)

For the purpose of exploring the potential of peer review to strengthen the rule of law and constitutionalism, the third level is the most relevant,

[15] 'No freeman is to be taken or imprisoned or disseised of his free tenement or of his liberties or free customs, or outlawed or exiled or in any way ruined, nor will we go against such a man or send against him save by lawful judgement of his peers or by the law of the land. To no-one will we sell or deny or delay right or justice.'

[16] Siems, *Comparative Law*, p. 148; A.-M. Slaughter, 'A Global Community of Courts', *Harvard International Law Journal*, 44 (2003), 191–219, at 193.

given that, as a matter of public law,[17] the nation state is still the primary setting in which the rule of law materializes. However, since the role of cross-border dialogues among regulatory officials has been the subject of more research, we will also engage with the second level in this chapter in order to collect some insights into the way peer review works.[18]

The Notion of 'Peer Review'

'Peer review' as discussed in this paper is distinct from 'scientific peer review', the process 'in which independent scientists comment on the technical underpinnings of proposed regulations',[19] but also from 'regulatory peer review',[20] which is related to the evidential underpinning of concrete regulations. The latter form of peer review has been qualified as 'a recently pursued form of political control of the bureaucracy'.[21] However, 'review' as a public law mechanism, even in the most traditional sense of 'judicial review', does not exist purely for the sake of keeping tabs on governmental power, but also for the sake of governmental learning. Peer review as it is beginning to occur in a rule of law context[22] is a:

> [M]ethod by which countries can assess the quality and effectiveness of their policies, legislation, policy environments and key institutions [providing] a forum where policies can be explained and discussed, where information can be sought and concerns expressed, on a non-confrontational and non-adversarial basis. The feedback provides the reviewee with a yardstick for measuring its system against those of other peers while also informing the reviewing countries.[23]

Roughly, there are two distinct approaches to peer review as employed in an international or transnational context. One is focused on compliance

[17] The concept of 'rule of law', of course, can and should be extended to other fields, such as company law, as well. See the contribution by Krygier in this volume.

[18] A.-M. Slaughter, 'Agencies on the Loose? Holding Government Networks Accountable' in G. A. Bermann, M. Herdegen and P. Lindseth (eds.), *Transatlantic Regulatory Cooperation* (Oxford University Press, 2000), pp. 521–46.

[19] S. Shapiro and D. Guston, 'Procedural Control of the Bureaucracy, Peer Review, and Epistemic Drift', *Journal of Public Administration Research and Theory*, 17(4) (2007), 535–51.

[20] C. F. Sabel and J. Zeitlin 'Learning from Difference: The New Architecture of Experimentalist Governance in the EU', *European Law Journal*, 14(3) (2008), 271–327.

[21] Shapiro and Guston, 'Procedural Control of the Bureaucracy'.

[22] E. M. H. Hirsch Ballin, 'Mutual Trust: The Virtue of Reciprocity Strengthening the Acceptance of the Rule of Law through Peer Review' in Closa and Kochenov (eds.), *Reinforcing the Rule of Law*.

[23] OECD, *Peer Review: Merits and Approaches in a Trade and Competition Context*, 2002.

with existing standards. The other emphasizes the potential for 'policy or institutional learning', also regarding the appropriate rule-of-law standards.[24] The distinct functions of 'challenging' and 'learning' can both be applicable within the former approach. A peer review mechanism directed at achieving greater compliance with the norms already agreed upon within the community at hand may try to achieve this by calling out review subjects for specific violations (challenging) or by aiming at more systemic feedback directed at reform (learning).

Peer reviews are often undertaken in the framework of an international organization. For instance, the Directorate-General Enlargement of the European Commission coordinates the Technical Assistance and Information Exchange instrument (TAIEX) which aims at increasing understanding of EU legislation in 'partner administrations' and may include 'monitoring and analysis of progress through Peer Reviews or Assessment Missions'. To give another example, sometimes the development of 'rule of law' peer review takes place in the private sphere: the ACE Practitioners' Network (part of the ACE Electoral Knowledge Network) assembles 'election professionals' and next to the dissemination of best practices also facilitates peer review in the field of elections.[25]

Beyond the rule of law context, Braithwaite and Drahos suggest that regulatory dialogues are a key way in which government officials deal with the uncertainties of the world.[26] Through such dialogues, officials discover the state of their relations with their counterparts in other jurisdictions as well as information about regulatory cooperation among officials in other jurisdictions. Moreover, these authors contend, 'webs of dialogue', compared to more coercive mechanisms, are relatively good at delivering effective forms of global regulation because they (1) define issues, (2) enhance the contracting environment so that complex interdependency and issue linkage can motivate agreement and compliance, (3) constitute normative commitments, (4) institutionalize habits of compliance and (5) institutionalize informal praise and shame for defection from the regime. That national government or agency officials will or would identify with foreign counterparts is not obvious. But once it occurs, the psychology behind transnational peer review for agency employees is clear: feeling part of an international effort working

[24] R. Bossong, 'Peer Reviews in the Fight against Terrorism: A Hidden Dimension of European Security Governance,' *Cooperation and Conflict*, 47(4) (2012), 519–38.

[25] www.aceproject.org/.

[26] J. Braithwaite and P. Drahos, *Global Business Regulation* (Cambridge University Press, 2000).

towards the same policy goals appeals more than being part of a vast government bureaucracy with countless objectives.[27]

These dialogues, or 'transnational networks' of agencies, sometimes come to involve an explicit form of peer review.[28] These are likely to review for performance norms and procedural or 'input-oriented' norms, such as transparency requirements (see next section). As Majone points out, there is a clear link between the formal and social existence of a 'duty to give reasons' and opportunities for peer review.[29] That said, transgovernmental networks typically do not adopt binding rules or agreements, but are far more likely to formulate model codes or compilations of 'best practices'. So, '[a]t least in theory the risk exists that the participating agencies commit themselves more to the internationally defined aims than the aims as laid down in their by-laws, when they feel more accountable to "peer" agencies.'[30] This puts the spotlight on the normative frameworks used in peer reviews, especially when their nets are cast more widely as is likely the case for rule-of-law peer reviews (see next section).

A different way to reflect on the emergence of 'peer review' in a context of constitutionalism and the rule of law is to analyse to what extent transnational dialogues as loose phenomena start incorporating peer review mechanisms. Alexander Somek has written that 'peer review' as a notion 'most adequately captures [the] spirit' of the European Convention on Human Rights.[31] He links the emergence of peer review – in both formal and informal capacities – to what he views as the 'third stage' in the development of constitutionalism. Peer review provides an opportunity for authority to be earned 'on the basis of explaining one's own practice with an eye to what and how the peer group is doing'. Authority, then, is no longer earned through practical reason ('constitutionalism 2.0') but through 'mutual engagement'[32] ('constitutionalism

[27] B. de Jonge, 'Legal Approaches of Purposes: The Case of Independent Agencies', *OECD* (2007); Expert Meeting OECD, 'Designing Independent and Accountable Regulatory Authorities for High Quality Regulation' (London, 2005), 143.

[28] M. Everson, G. Majone, L. Metcalfe and G. Schout, 'The Role of Specialised Agencies in Decentralising EU Governance' (2001), 59 and 213. Available at: http://ec.europa.eu/governance/governance_eu/decentral_en.htm.

[29] G. Majone, 'The Regulatory State and Its Legitimacy Problems', *West European Politics*, 22 (1999), 1–24, 14.

[30] B. de Jonge, 'Legal Approaches'.

[31] A. Somek, *The Cosmopolitan Constitution* (Oxford University Press, 2014), p. 18.

[32] Somek cites Kumm for this term: M. Kumm, 'The Cosmopolitan Turn in Constitutionalism: on the Relationship between Constitutionalism in and beyond the State' in J. L. Dunoff and J. P. Trachtman (eds.), *Ruling the World? Constitutionalism,*

3.0').[33] The universalization of public reason is a precondition for this transformation to happen.[34] Yet, this is exactly where the tension resides. Is there a risk in states awarding 'peers' a certain degree of authority over their domestic processes? Participants in peer reviews, mainly government officials, enter into relatively open dialogue with their foreign counterparts and learn about approaches to governance problems that differ from their own system's solutions. This may motivate them to contribute to 'change' that states and/or citizens may not have otherwise chosen to adopt. Depending on who is steering the normative agenda behind the peer review and what this normative agenda is, there may in fact be an accountability problem.

Collected Insights on Peer Review in Different Settings

Now that informal or formal systems of peer review are coming to be seen as crucial features of contemporary constitutionalism,[35] the question arises, to what extent can we, and do we wish to, take on-board insights from the context of sector-specific peer reviews and agency-level peer reviews. As peer review in the rule of law context is an emerging instrument, there are no empirical insights available as to how, exactly, it operates. Peer review (outside a research context) has been dealt with in the literature, but usually not from a perspective of furthering compliance with general public law norms and promoting the rule of law. For instance, the OECD peer reviews have been addressed in the literature on policy convergence, which often sees the realization of convergence as the ultimate measure of success. Learning in a rule of law context may not be about convergence so much. Much of the international relations literature which has described the role of the World Bank and the Organisation for Economic Co-operation and Development (OECD) in designing and legitimizing best practices has focused on the respective influence of these organizations[36] and/or on methodological aspects of the review process. When looking at their effects on the constitutional environment, however, this is less clear-cut. The fact that the peer reviews tend to rely an odd mix between 'universally excepted public law achievements', such as the rule of law as an 'idea' or the principle of due process,

International Law, and Global Governance (Cambridge University Press, 2009), pp. 258–324, p. 309.

[33] Somek, *The Cosmopolitan Constitution*, p. 178. [34] *Ibid.*, p. 176. [35] *Ibid.*, p. 18.

[36] The Peer Review Observatory Maastricht.

and very technical norms included in indicators does not make this assessment any easier.

Some research has been done as well into the social mechanisms underlying country-level peer review. The importance of knowledge-triggered routines, aided by socialization processes, which can unconsciously shape collectively desired behaviour by member states is being emphasized.[37] For instance, in the field of European Security Governance, 'the varied interaction patterns of national professionals and EU officials during these peer reviews'[38] are seen as a matter of socialization.[39] Basic ingredients of country peer reviews in the OECD context have been found to include value sharing among participants, 'mutual trust regarding the dissemination of accurate data, confirmation of a standard level of commitment from the member states and credibility of the OECD.'[40] The importance of mutual trust appears to be both the reason why some commentators argue in favour of including a strong and regular form of peer review in the Rule-of-Law monitor and the reason why many do not see it as a realistic option.

Another insight from research on agency-level peer review to take seriously is that this type of review tends to suffer from the habit of using it to ratify rather than improve behaviour and performance.[41] From the specific context of regulatory peer review we know that it can lead to great investment in research on the part of nongovernmental participants but also to a politicization of the whole process.[42] In a policy-specific context, peer review has been shown to have 'contributed not so much to "emulation", "harmonization" or "penetration" of policies, but more to the strengthening of élite networks and policy communities'.[43] One would expect 'persuasion' to be the dominant behavioural mechanism in peer review, but it may in fact be 'congratulation' that is the

[37] OECD 2004: 4, Porter and Webb 2007: 4–5. [38] Bossong, 'Peer Reviews in the Fight'.

[39] B. Bernstein, 'A Sociolinguistic Approach to Socialization' in R. Boudon and M. Cherkaoui (eds.), *Central Currents in Social Theory: Contemporary Sociological Theory* (London: Sage, 2000), pp. 319–58; J. Lempp and J. Altenschmidt, 'Supranationalization through Socialization in the Council of the European Union' (Portsmouth, UACES conference, 2007); M. Weber, 'Bureaucracy and Education' in R. Boudon and M. Cherkaoui (eds.), *Central Currents in Social Theory: The Roots of Sociological Theory, 1700–1920*, vol. 1 (London, Sage, 2000), pp. 300–3.

[40] Rendak, 'Monitoring and Surveillance', p. 228.

[41] Belzer, 'Principles for an Effective Regulatory Impact Analysis'.

[42] Shapiro and Guston, 'Procedural Control of the Bureaucracy'.

[43] B. Casey and M. Gold, 'Peer Review of Labour Market Programmes in the European Union: What Can Countries Really Learn from One Another?', *Journal of European Public Policy*, 12(1) (2005), 23–43.

driving force. Peer review as a proper vehicle of *change* therefore seems a slow track, in the light of findings such as this: '[e]ven peer reviews that are conducted under the voluntary initiative of national actors who wanted to show the working of their own particular solution, rather than a valuable exercise in mutual knowledge and understanding, are often described as ways of achieving a consensus among member states. Everyone wants to be nice to each other, and everyone is recognized as having done something good'.[44] Information and experience sharing, technical assistance and capacity building then appear to be the main functions of this type of alternative review.

The solution for 'foreignness' offered by Braithwaite and Drahos, namely 'that accountable government does not seek to constrain the sources of knowledge brought to bear on a particular governance problem, but rather the ways in which that knowledge is acted on',[45] points to a possible Achilles' heel of rule-of-law peer review. In the 'constitutionalism 3.0 model', the communal source of knowledge is directly linked to authority. The question of the domestic implications of a peer review process resulting in a demand for change is the ultimate litmus test for the new-found source of authority. As the early experiences with invoking the new 'pre-Article 7' procedure by the European Commission against Poland show, if the 'peer-ness' of the reviewers is not without dispute, peer review may result in a defensive attitude and further entrenchment on the part of the domestic actors.[46] Within the paradigm of peer review, if communality and learning are crucial features, is there still room for sanctions if a state under scrutiny fails to act on critical feedback? And if there are no sanctions, in order to optimally facilitate learning, can peer review ever be effective?

The Normative Framework of 'Rule of Law' Peer Reviews

Rule of law promotion is a field in which constitutional norms are actively socially conceived of and perhaps even constituted; where attempts are made to turn the 'constitutional ideal' into the 'constitutional real' by encouraging 'behavioural regularities which actors observe in order to show that they are desirable partners of cooperative endeavours'.[47] This ties in with a regulatory perspective on law which emphasizes the objective

[44] N. Stame, 'The European Project', 132.
[45] Braithwaite and Drahos, *Global Business Regulation*, pp. 532–3.
[46] See the contributions by Kochenov and Scheppele in this volume.
[47] E. Posner, *Law and Social Norms* (Cambridge, MA: Harvard University Press, 2009).

of shaping socially valued behaviour through standard setting and monitoring.[48] Translated to constitutionalism, this perspective points to a central behavioural issue: getting public actors to comply with rule of law norms – and with their spirit rather than just their letter. On this specific point the mutual engagement that peer review is capable of bringing may play a catalysing role. Also, norm formation and practical compliance may turn out to be linked in an iterative process.

In peer-review processes, both formal constitutional and administrative law rules and rules drafted by non-state organizations irrespective of national borders (e.g. NGOs or groups of academics) may play a role.[49] Private reviewers or even their public counterparts with a relatively fluid mandate, such as ombudsmen, can latch onto the appetite for learning (see the table). Since certain peer reviews are mechanisms for which formal legal competences are not prerequisite we may need to deal with myriad norms that can appear on their radar. Even a more formal and official type of peer review carries an enormous potential for norm innovation. However, this is where peer reviews at the agency level may well differ from peer reviews at the state level. If we see peer review as instrumental in earning authority in the eyes of fellow nation states, a certain level of consensus regarding norms and standards and their appropriate application appears inevitable. It may be the case, though, that consensus occurs on a fairly abstract level (e.g. the importance of judicial independence) and norm innovation on the more concrete level with which peer reviews inevitably need to engage (e.g. which side jobs are considered acceptable for members of the judiciary).

While appealing to 'universally acknowledged' achievements in public law, such as the rule of law, or fundamental rights protection standards, peers can take the space to put forward concrete norm innovations. Because peer review usually does not lead to any binding sanction in the sense of a decision being rendered void, there is less pressure on the quality or even the legitimacy of the review process. At the same time, because alternative reviewers lack the evident legitimacy of parliaments or courts, they need to demonstrate that they can achieve effects on the ground and will therefore have an incentive to experiment. A normative agenda can thus be furthered by initiating a review system. The archetypical case of this is the category of transgovernmental reviewers such as

[48] M. Bronwen and K. Yeung, *An Introduction to Law and Regulation: Text and Materials* (Cambridge University Press, 2007); C. Parker et al., *Regulating Law* (Oxford University Press, 2004).

[49] Siems, *Comparative Law*, p. 249.

the OECD, the World Bank and the European Commission (see the table).

A first category of norms at the basis of peer reviews could be the prominent public law norms linked to more visible aspects of the rule of law: fundamental rights, prohibitions against criminal offences, fraud and corruption. A further category consists of performance norms: governments are expected to have their finances in order, to care about traffic safety and to prevent disasters. A third category is more procedural or 'input-oriented' and concerns transparency norms, participation standards and the duty to give reasons. Finally there is a category which hovers at the margins of constitutionalism and rule of law norms and consists of values such as goodness, integrity and responsiveness.

An important aspect of the normative frameworks of 'rule of law' peer reviews deals not with the norms applied as such, but with the way in which they are turned into a methodological element of peer reviews. One method employed, for instance, in the OMC context is benchmarking. With this method the biggest problem is the 'multi-formity of values, in particular the contextual differences between countries and the institutional and organizational differences'.[50] Another is the identification of best practices. The way in which they are sometimes used has been criticized in the literature,[51] and the concept itself has been the object of intense debate:[52] '[a]part from the question of who is legitimated to say that something is the best, practices can be 'best' in one context but not in another, and in any case even their imitation requires a lot of adaptation. The Danish system of industrial relations, now very fashionable in Brussels, cannot be imposed on everybody'.[53] Obviously, the same goes for best practices in the area of the rule of law. Still the back-and-forth between norm innovation and norm consensus goes to the heart of how

[50] J. Hakvoort and H. Klaassen, 'International Benchmarking of Public Organizations: A Critical Approach' in *New Public Management in Europe*, pp. 107–34, p. 133.

[51] A. Garapon, 'A New Approach for Promoting Judicial Integrity' in R. Peerenboom (ed.), *Judicial Independence in China* (Cambridge University Press, 2010), pp. 37–51; K. Hendley, 'The Rule of Law and Economic Development in a Global Era' in A. Sarat (ed.), *The Blackwell Companion to Law and Society* (Malden MA: Blackwell, 2004), pp. 605–23.

[52] M. Q. Patton, 'Evaluation, Knowledge Management, Best Practices, and High Quality Lessons Learned', *American Journal of Evaluation*, 22(3) (2001), 329–36; B. Perrin, 'How Evaluation Can Help Make Knowledge Management Real' in R. Rist and N. Stame (eds.), *From Studies to Streams: Managing Evaluative Systems* (New Brunswick, NJ: Transaction Publishers 2006), pp. 23–45.

[53] N. Stame, 'The European Project, Federalism and Evaluation', *Evaluation*, 14 (2008), 117–40, 132.

peer review can contribute to the simultaneous development of the ideal and the practice of the rule of law and constitutionalism. If we look at ideals as designs of the real in the future, which still demand realization and specification, they embody the projection of a state of affairs that has yet to come and can be strived for. This projection occurs quite literally in the normative framework of peer review settings and other alternative review mechanisms, in which the benchmark reveals the 'realistic ideal'.

A further and well-documented technique applied in alternative review settings and with the potential to be used in peer reviews relies on the use of indicators,[54] which has been connected to the rise of a 'hypermodernist conception of government'.[55] The 'first generation' of good governance indices is mostly focused on substance, aiming to rank countries according to their output regarding such norms as political rights and freedom of information. The indicators of the 'second generation' are of a more procedural nature, providing comparative information on policy processes. Here too, the link with formal public law norms often remains unarticulated. For instance, the World Bank Good Governance Indicators are loaded with assumptions regarding how a government should be organized and should treat its citizens, but these cannot be traced back to any theory of governance.[56] This of course does not mean that the effects on the development of public law are not there. As Nelken puts it, '[w]hat is at issue here however, is the way using indicators for governance transform 'facts' (data) into norms and 'standards' – as well as *vice-versa*'.[57] If legal scholarship engages with indexes, rankings and indicators, it is often in a critical manner and inspired by normative concerns. For instance, Scheppele dismisses the use of rule-of-law 'checklists' because she finds that they have no way of taking into account any combined detrimental impact of two 'positive' rule-of-law features.[58] The example she gives is the situation in Hungary,

[54] K. E. Davis, B. Kingsbury and S. E. Merry 'Indicators as a Technology of Global Governance', *Law and Society Review*, 46(1) (2012), 71–104, at 73–4. See also Ginsburg and Versteeg in this volume.

[55] C. Pollitt, '"Moderation in All Things": International Comparison of Governance Quality', *Financial Accountability & Management*, 27(4) (2011), 437–57.

[56] Arndt and Oman, 'Use and Abuses'.

[57] D. Nelken, 'Contesting Global Indicators' in S. E. Merry, K. Davis and B. Kingsbury (eds.), *The Quiet Power of Indicators: Measuring Governance, Corruption, and Rule of Law* (Cambridge University Press, 2014).

[58] K. Lane Scheppele, 'The Rule of Law and the Frankenstate: Why Governance Checklists Do Not Work', *Governance: An International Journal of Policy, Administration, and Institutions*, 26(4) (2013), 559–62.

where the simultaneous occurrence of two constitutional changes, namely constitutional amendment by a single two-thirds vote and a move away from a multiple party system, each of which individually would have passed the checklist, but which together produced a reckless constitutional amendment. However, review mechanisms such as the World Justice Project (WJP) Rule of Law index purposefully defy the notion that the rule of law cannot be defined or measured.[59] In fact, by measuring it, the index simultaneously defines the rule of law through its methodological choices. The 'factors', each with subfactors, are limited government powers, absence of corruption, order and security, fundamental rights, open government, regulatory enforcement, civil justice and criminal justice. A weak point in its claim to show compliance with rule-of-law norms is the methodology, which relies exclusively on interviews with lawyers and polling of the general public. A strong point appears to be its capacity to create a communicative practice around the rule of law. For instance, the inclusion of the effectiveness of the right to water prompts water experts to talk to lawyers. Of course questions remain regarding the access of certain underprivileged groups to the indicators. As Nelken points out, 'those ... who are more positive about the indicators they describe, see it as one of their key virtues that they expose the issues they deal with to debate'.[60] So if the combination with peer review would somehow leave indicators tried, tested and adapted they could contribute to a shared understanding of what encouraging the rule of law as a globalized ideal actually means in practice.

Instances of 'Rule of Law' Peer Reviews

In this section three distinct settings in which dedicated rule of law peer reviews are emerging will be discussed: the OECD peer reviews, African Peer Review Mechanism and the EU Rule of Law monitor.

OECD Peer Reviews

The Organisation for Economic Co-operation and Development (OECD), which has on occasion called itself 'the house of best practice',[61] probably

[59] See the contribution by Ginsburg and Versteeg in this volume.
[60] Nelken, 'Contesting Global Indicators'.
[61] This phrase is attributed to Angel Gurria, Secretary General of the OECD, for instance in a letter addressed to him, sent by ECA Watch on 18 November 2008, http://www.eca-watch.org/problems/fora/oecd/ECA_Watch_letter_to_OECD_Gurria_18nov08.pdf.

has the widest experience with peer review outside the context of science and regulation in a narrow sense. Peer review has even been an important catalyst for the organizational evolution of the OECD since its inception in 1961.[62] This was possible because of the OECD's limited and largely homogenous membership.[63] For lack of the ability to employ hierarchy, 'review' (of regulatory regimes, economic trends, and policy performance) combined with the use of peer pressure is a well-known OECD strategy. In conformity with its mandate as an international organization, none of the OECD peer reviews deal with rule of law issues exclusively or explicitly, but many touch upon institutional and constitutional issues. The spillover to the rule of law context becomes clear, for instance, from the 2012 Recommendation of the Council on Regulatory Policy and Governance which stipulates that an effective regulatory policy includes 'a consistent policy covering the role of functions of regulatory agencies in order to provide greater confidence that regulatory decisions are made on an objective, impartial and consistent basis, without conflict of interest, bias or improper influence.' Another example of an assessment of institutional values in OECD context is when a 'peer review' of DG Competition led to the conclusion that its multiple roles raised concerns regarding the absence of checks and balances.[64]

Apart from the OECD's numerous 'surveys' and performance reviews (e.g. Environmental Performance Reviews), which are not *peer* reviews, the OECD facilitates a number of formal 'peer review' processes. Within the OECD, peer review is carried out in several policy areas and, across those areas, does not follow a standardized pattern, although all contain a basis for proceeding, an agreed set of principles, standards and criteria against which the country performance is to be reviewed, designated actors to carry out the peer review and a set of procedures leading to the final result of the peer review.[65] This makes for very process-oriented peer reviews. Also, whether the focus is on 'compliance with existing standards' or on 'policy or institutional learning' does not immediately become clear.

62 N. Rendak, 'Monitoring and Surveillance of the International Monetary System: What Can Be Learnt from the Trade Field?' in T. Cottier, R. M. Lastra, C. Tietje and L. Satragno (eds.), *The Rule of Law in Monetary Affairs* (Cambridge University Press, 2014), p. 227.

63 *Ibid.*

64 P. Marsden, 'European Competition Law and the Rule of Law' in R. McCorquodale (ed.), *The Rule of Law in International and Comparative Context* (British Institute of International and Comparative Law, 2010), p. 111.

65 F. Pagani, 'Feature Peer Review as a Tool for Co-Operation and Change: An Analysis of an OECD Working Method', 17.

The peer reviews within the Development Assistance Committee (DAC) Members' Development Co-Operation programmes establish the effectiveness of development strategies and structures with the aim of increasing the effectiveness of member countries' investment. Each DAC member country is peer reviewed roughly every four years by 'examiners' from two DAC member states. These reviews usually do not look at 'rule-of-law performance' by the country under review but at most at the manner in which the countries 'help partner countries establish the rule of law, particularly as it applies to contract and property rights, an effectively functioning labour market and a state that guarantees physical safety'.[66] However, sometimes there is a direct spillover to normative judgements regarding 'rule of law' behaviour:

> Spain's understanding of governance is citizen-centric, comprehensive and political. Realisation of citizens' human rights, their equal access to opportunities, resources and services and their effective participation in decision-making guide Spain's work in core governance areas such as promotion of democracy, rule of law and public administration reform. Spain's engagement in the political realm conveys a strong commitment to political pluralism as well as to dialogue and political consensus-building. Activities include, for instance, the strengthening of political parties and trade unions, strengthening of parliaments and legislative processes as well as electoral processes and bodies, support to civil society and enhancing processes for its empowerment.[67]

Without drawing any conclusions regarding the evidence-base or impact of such statements the phenomenon that dialogues regarding what good governance and the rule of law mean in ideal and real terms can also take place in peer reviews with a fairly unrelated purpose, is worth pointing out.

Another kind of OECD peer reviews includes those that are part of the OECD's work on 'regulatory policy'.[68] From the outset the organization's take on 'regulatory quality' has been a mix of 'efficient markets' and 'effective governance'.[69] To help achieve these goals the OECD

[66] DAC peer review of The Netherlands 2011, 46, available at http://www.oecd.org/dac/peer-reviews/49011988.pdf

[67] OECD, DAC Peer Review Spain, 62.

[68] T. Jakobi, 'Regulating Regulation? The Regulatory Policy of the OECD', working paper 2 June 2012.

[69] 1997 OECD Report to Ministers on Regulatory Reform, which contained the OECD's first integrated policy framework for regulatory reform.

undertakes detailed country reviews, based on both self-assessment and peer review. The normative framework of these reviews, the outcome of which takes the form of a final report, is based on the OECD's regulatory reform programme. In 1999, Japan became the first country to be 'peer reviewed' and Kazakhstan was among the most recent, in the spring of 2014.[70] These peer reviews touch upon 'rule of law concerns' more directly, certainly as governance has become the focus more and more in recent years.

For the sake of comparability and cost reduction, each report has the same structure: four thematic chapters covering economy-wide policy and institutional issues, two sectoral chapters, and a concluding chapter that presents approximately 70 to 80 concrete policy recommendations for each country. Although particular countries are appointed to review one another, usually with two countries each appointing one expert to a review team (e.g. Denmark and the Czech Republic recently reviewed Kazakhstan), the OECD is more than a mere 'facilitator'. Apart from the fact that there are also two OECD experts on each team, data collection is based on written responses to detailed OECD questionnaires from the reviewed government, followed by 'on-site' missions to the country, where the team meets with Government officials, trade unions, business, academia and public interest groups. Each chapter of the draft country review is peer reviewed by the relevant specialized committee (e.g. the Public Management Committee). The final complete report is then peer reviewed by an 'Ad hoc Multidisciplinary Group of Experts', which means that the reports reflect the input and views of all OECD member governments and the European Commission. The final report is 'independent in that it is published under the responsibility of the OECD Secretary General, and the reviewed country is not asked to agree with its contents.'[71]

The OECD peer reviews appear to have the following four functions:

1. Policy dialogue: 'during the peer review process, countries systematically exchange information, attitudes and views on policy decisions and their application. This dialogue can be the basis for further co-operation, through, for example, the adoption of new policy guidelines, recommendations or even the negotiation of legal undertakings.'[72]

[70] www.oecd-ilibrary.org/governance/oecd-reviews-of-regulatory-reform_19900481.
[71] *Ibid.* [72] Pagani, 'Feature Peer Review', p. 11.

2. Transparency: 'the reviewed country has the chance, in the course of a peer review, to present and clarify national rules, practices and procedures and explain their rationale'.[73]
3. Capacity building: 'peer review is a mutual learning process in which best practices are exchanged. The process can therefore serve as an important capacity building instrument – not only for the country under review, but also for countries participating in the process as examiners, or simply as members of the responsible collective body.'[74]
4. Compliance: '[a]n important function of peer review is to monitor and enhance compliance by countries with internationally agreed policies, standards, and principles.'[75]

One example of how peer reviews can be a useful check on self-assessment involves the quality of the law-making process in The Netherlands. In the 2010 OECD peer review report it was concluded that consultation is a weak point in the Dutch system. In contrast to this conclusion, the OECD indicators report 2009, which is based on self-assessment through a questionnaire, states for The Netherlands that formal processes for consultation 'always' exist for both new primary laws and new subordinate regulations.[76]

In the OECD context it has been proposed that the effectiveness of peer review depends on the presence of the following cumulative factors:

(a) value sharing and convergence among participating countries on the criteria for evaluating performance
(b) commitment of the participating countries in terms of human and financial resources, and full engagement in the process
(c) mutual trust, since the peer review process is a cooperative and non-adversarial process (it is also recognized that the peer review process can, itself, contribute to this confidence building.)
(d) credibility, which is linked with the objectivity, transparency and the quality of the work (as Pagani points out, 'the main threat to the credibility of the process is the possibility of attempts by the reviewed State to unduly influence the final outcome.')[77]

[73] *Ibid.* [74] *Ibid.*, p. 12. [75] *Ibid.*, p. 12.
[76] OECD Regulatory Policy Committee, Indicators of Regulatory Management Systems 2009, p. 102.
[77] Pagani concludes, *ibid.*, pp. 12–13.

African Peer Review Mechanism

The main example of 'peer review in a Rule-of-Law context' outside the Western world is the African Peer Review Mechanism (APRM).[78] This mechanism is very wide in scope, but promotion of constitutional democracy, political competition and the rule of law is part of it.[79] The indicators used here are in the institutional sphere (e.g. 'Establishment of Office of the Registrar of Political Parties' or the adoption of a media act). As happens within the OECD, self-assessment is combined with peer review, but within the APRM the latter follows the former and has a more direct relationship with it. On the basis of a Country Self-Assessment Report (CSAR) and the National Plan of Action (NPoA) produced by participating countries themselves, the documentary basis for the peer review, called the Country Review Report (CRR), is facilitated by a central secretariat. The report is mainly document-based and focuses on three main questions: how accurately does the CSAR identify the main problems faced by the country, to what extent does the NPoA address these issues, and what is the nature of civil society participation in the production of the CSAR and the NPoA? The interactive part of the peer review then takes place among heads of state and government of participating countries – the APRM Forum – during summits of the African Union. An evaluation of the APRM has found that this high-level forum has actually made it difficult for the reviews to receive proper attention.[80] Also, the way this particular peer review process is organized means the country's self-assessment report and NPoA 'are given maximum prominence, thereby relegating implementation of the NPoA to a subordinate position'.[81] A further important finding is that whereas the Country Review Reports, the basis for the peer review (although it is unclear to what extent these are actually written by the secretariat rather than by the 'peer') are made public but the Country Self-Assessment Reports are not. Finally it is important to note that, according to Bing-Pappoe the APRM has been 'sold' as 'African in origin and strategic purpose'[82] but that the

[78] Memorandum of Understanding on the African Peer Review Mechanism: the MOU, NEPAD, 2003. http://sites.dbsa.org/aprm/index3.php; Adotey Bing-Pappoe, 'Reviewing Africa's Peer Review Mechanism. A Seven Country Survey', 2010, http://www.pacweb.org/Documents/APRM/APRM_Seven_countries_March2010-E.pdf.

[79] Progress Reports from Ghana and Kenya on Democracy and Political Governance.

[80] A. Bing-Pappoe, 'Reviewing Africa's Peer Review Mechanism. A Seven Country Survey', p. 9.

[81] *Ibid.*, pp. 19–20. [82] *Ibid.*, p. 22.

financing of the NPoA increasingly takes place through 'normal development' channels, threatening 'African ownership of the APRM'.

EU Rule of Law Monitor

In the EU 'peer review' has appeared as part of the 'Open Method of Coordination'[83] and other specific areas,[84] but more recently and more explicitly in a 'Rule-of-Law' context also in the debate on the establishment of a 'Rule of Law' monitoring framework (hereafter referred to as the 'Monitor').[85] Heavily promoted by The Netherlands from the start,[86] and in possible competition with the EU Justice Scoreboard,[87] the initiative for such a Monitor was put forward without a Treaty change. A legal argument can be made that the need to have sufficient instruments to guarantee the proper functioning of the rule of law in the member states follows from the acceptance that rule-of-law values forms the constitutional basis for European integration (Art. 2 TEU).[88]

The main debate at the moment is divided between preferences for an 'ad hoc mechanism' as proposed by the Commission and pleas for a procedure

[83] W. Kerber and M. Eckardt, 'Policy Learning in Europe: The Open Method of Co-Ordination and Laboratory Federalism Policy Learning in Europe: The Open Method of Co-Ordination and Laboratory Federalism,' *Journal of European Public Policy*, 14(2) (2007), 37–41; A. Schäfer, 'A New Form of Governance? Comparing the Open Method of Co-Ordination to Multilateral Surveillance by the IMF and the OECD,' *Journal of European Public Policy*, 13(1) (2006), 37–41.

[84] Bossong, 'Peer Reviews in the Fight'.

[85] On 11 March, a year after a joint letter from The Netherlands, Germany, Denmark and Finland calling for the development of a new mechanism to protect the Union's fundamental values, the European Commission ('the Commission') published its Communication 'A new EU Framework to Strengthen the Rule of Law'. COM (2014), 158.

[86] Advisory Council on International Affairs (AIV), advisory report: 'The Rule of Law: Safeguard for European Citizens and Foundation of European Cooperation', No. 87, January 2014, available in English at http://www.aiv-advies.nl/ContentSuite/upload/aiv/doc/webversie_AIV87_ENG_2(1).pdf; This AIV advisory report was submitted to the House of Representatives on 30 January 2014, see annex to Parliamentary Paper 33750-V no. 61. See also the Letter of 28 April 2014 from the Minister of Foreign Affairs enclosing the government's combined response to this report; English summary available at http://www.aiv-advies.nl/ContentSuite/template/aiv/adv/collection_single.asp?id=1942&adv_id=3398&page=regeringsreacties&language=UK&print=1; See also, Dutch House of Representatives, motions introduced by MPs Henk Jan Ormel and Klaas Dijkhoff in 2012 and Mark Verheijen in 2013.

[87] COM (2014) 155.

[88] See Kochenov and Scheppele in this volume. See also C. Closa, D. Kochenov, and J. H. H. Weiler, 'Reinforcing Rule of Law Oversight in the European Union,' *EUI Working Papers, RSCAS 2014/25*, 2014 for an extensive discussion of the normative and legal basis.

revolving around regular peer review as recommended by the Dutch Advisory Council on International Affairs (AIV).[89] Back in 2009 the Stockholm programme, which was put forward by the Justice and Home Affairs Council under the Swedish presidency and adopted by the European Council, also included the possibility of, where appropriate, using 'an evaluation mechanism based on the well-established system of peer-evaluation'.[90] Of course combining the *ad hoc* and regular mechanisms – as the Dutch government favours – is possible too: a mechanism which enables the European Union (through the Commission?) to respond on an *ad hoc* basis to acute threats to the rule of law on top of regular monitoring of all member states. Whether proper 'peer review' is the best format for such monitoring is a further question of course. The AIV does propose this, but without a very strong peer element, in the sense that the review teams appear to consist of a large number of experts who are not necessarily there because of their nationality:

1. A committee of experts draws up a report on the basis of consultations with relevant organisations, covering a number of cross-sectoral issues (a restricted number to keep the peer reviews manageable in scope), and a number of focal points for specific countries. The European Commission should provide the secretariat for the committee of experts.
2. The report is discussed by representatives of the member states at an official level (the actual peer review), leading to draft operational conclusions/recommendations.
3. These draft conclusions/recommendations are adopted by the Council. The results of the reviews should also be submitted to the Justice and Home Affairs Council, which will supervise the follow-up. The EP should be informed of both the recommendations and the follow-up.[91]

The not-so-strongly national 'peer element' may be an advantage: EU law has already attempted to make use of 'peer mechanisms' in, for instance, the infringement procedure, in which member states have the right to take one another to court, but they rarely do. Participants in a roundtable in Florence deemed the effect of 'peer pressure' in case of a breach of rule-

[89] Advisory Council, 'The Rule of Law: Safeguard for European Citizens and Foundation for European Cooperation' (No. 87, January 2014), available at http://aiv-advies.nl/download/57da03fa-3410-4aba-af05-663cb780df72.pdf. (AIV advisory report), 36–7.

[90] Hirsch Ballin, 'Mutual Trust: the Virtue of Reciprocity' in Closa and Kochenov (eds.), *Reinforcing the Rule of Law*.

[91] AIV advisory report.

of-law values among member states 'limited', although this assessment was not necessarily made in a peer *review* context.[92]

A big institutional risk of this new instrument would be that legal mechanisms in a Council of Europe context would be undermined because actors prefer this new political mechanism. Of course competition between the two types of mechanism could be minimized or used to good end by incorporating the Venice criteria, informally already in use by EU Institutions, into the future Monitor.[93] Another way of making the Monitor less political in nature is by attaching sanctions. A further risk in that case is undermining the acceptance of the Monitor itself through sanctions that are perceived as too harsh and taking the instrument away from its core of 'constructive dialogue on the basis of objective information'. Financial sanctions in particular may make member states reconsider the wisdom of the Monitor. This is though, where *peer* review has an edge: 'all countries will be evaluated, and all will be evaluators too with the opportunities to share their ideas and expertise.'[94] Hirsch Ballin has pointed to an advantage of a fundamental nature: since the rule of law depends on reciprocal respect and mutual trust, the best way of promoting it may be to enshrine these values in the *way* in which we do this.[95]

Further issues are the exact role of the European Commission (in coordinating reviews but also as a possible object of review itself) and the involvement of civil society groups as possible experts in peer reviews. A final important element of any official use of peer review in the EU context is the normative framework. As indicated above, it is probably in the interest of the Monitor not to become overly politicized. Therefore, the temptation to work with indicators may be great. Yet, the experiences with the use of 'Rule-of-Law indicators' by the European Union, in the context of the Cooperation and Verification Mechanism for instance, are very mixed.[96] One of the things to take on board as peer review is being

92 Closa, Kochenov and Weiler, 'Reinforcing Rule of Law', p. 19.

93 See in the context in particular the Report of the Venice Commission of 4 April 2011 Study No. 512/2009 (CDL-AD(2011)003rev), which lists criteria for the Rule of Law that are cited by the European Commission in its Communication 'A New EU Framework to Strengthen the Rule of Law'. COM (2014) 158.

94 Johnston, 'Good governance', 22.

95 E. M. H. Hirsch Ballin, 'Mutual Trust: The Virtue of Reciprocity Strengthening the Acceptance of the Rule of Law through Peer Review' in Closa and Kochenov (eds.), *Reinforcing the Rule of Law*.

96 M. A. Vachudova and A. Spendzharova, *The EU's Cooperation and Verification Mechanism: Fighting Corruption in Bulgaria and Romania after EU Accession* (Swedish Institute for European Policy Studies, 2012); Nelken 'Contesting Global Indicators'.

considered for inclusion in a European Union Rule-of-Law monitor, is that peer reviews are relatively open processes, but also susceptible to normative commitments that are never made explicit and that can introduce biases that may go unnoticed. This brings us back to a point made in the previous section: methodology is of crucial importance in any peer review process because detailed methodological choices, such as the way various indicators are formulated, are what connect the normative commitments (stated or unstated) to the outcomes.

Concluding Remarks

As the analysis above has shown, in the context of constitutionalism and the rule of law, we find both mechanisms explicitly designed as peer reviews and a broader tendency to mimic the phenomenon within existing supra-national regimes. In Somek's 'constitutionalism 3.0' model, the price states have to pay for a continued claim to authority – of a new, community-based kind – is to subject themselves to a communal review process that may include an evolution of the normative framework over time. The emergence of informal and formal peer reviews is the 'practical implication of the simultaneous retention and abdication of sovereign authority in the field of human rights'.[97] Peer review as it is envisaged by 'constitutionalists 3.0' would have difficulty identifying the political principals required for a control function. The community of states willing to engage in dialogue is the new-found source of authority. Whereas in more specific peer reviews between regulatory agencies the 'foreign' source of knowledge is often considered problematic, this very source appears key in rule of law peer reviews. Here the difference between 'control' and a 'challenge function' seems important. As the popularity of alternative reviewers reveals, even if 'control' is not an option for lack of political leverage, and even if it is not always effective, the claim to a legitimate 'challenge function' can be earned, but possibly through a long-term investment in a 'learning function'.

There may be a side effect to the use of peer review that is interesting in the context of rule-of-law promotion. We have to face the risk that peer review makes participants too complacent to have proper challenging or learning functions, but we can also embrace the hope that it may lead to some self-restraint among actors through the effects that it has on

[97] Somek, *The Cosmopolitan Constitution*, p. 17.

transparency.[98] In the context of global dialogues among regulators or judges or legislators it has already been put forward that if this dialogue 'changes minds and practices in unexpected ways, the best solution does seem to be transparency, in the form of full disclosure of sources'.[99] In general, transparency is expected to lead to better decision-making because it becomes less attractive for governmental actors to prioritize vested interests. Peer reviews certainly do not equal transparency. But in the process, a lot of information has to be dug up, shared and translated, thus possibly helping to instil an institutional habit of openness in the reviewed actor. Also, although not all reports may be made public, it gets noticed when that does not happen. The role of peer review in constitutional development may be hard to pin down, but it appears it could play a role in shaping the expectations of the actors involved regarding at least some process-oriented norms, and therefore at least regarding the rule of law in a thin sense.

[98] OECD, *Peer Review: Merits and Approaches in a Trade and Competition Context*.
[99] Braithwaite and Drahos, *Global Business Regulation*, p. 535.

17

Constitutional Correlates of the Rule of Law

TOM GINSBURG AND MILA VERSTEEG*

Introduction

The rule of law (RoL) is the central political ideal of our time, a lynchpin of democracy, justice and development. So broad is the consensus that the RoL is important that even countries that do not fully implement it still pay lip service to its value. Yet, despite the normative consensus, we still do not have a clear understanding of where respect for the RoL comes from and how it is sustained. For billions of people, the RoL remains an aspiration only; understanding how the RoL is realized has the potential to improve lives in a concrete way on a vast scale.

Constitutions are a central institution for any understanding of the RoL.[1] As the highest law of the state, constitutions contain the laws that must prevail if the RoL is to be achieved. Constitutions help ensure that those in power work for the public rather than for private gain; they define the rules for making rules of law and help to ensure the enforcement of those rules. Moreover, constitutions define the limits on sovereign power and can serve as focal point for coordinating enforcement when rulers transgress the stated limits on their powers.[2]

In many countries, however, constitutions fail to live up to their potential.[3] In some countries, constitutions remain a dead letter and thus do little to advance the RoL.[4] In other countries, constitutions

* The writers would like to thank Anne Meuwese for helpful comments and suggestions.

1 D. B. Rodriguez, M. D. McCubbins, and B. R. Weingast, 'Rule of Law Unplugged', *Emory Law Journal*, 59(6) (2010), 1455–94, at 1476.

2 B. R. Weingast, 'Political Foundations of Democracy and the Rule of Law', *American Political Science Review*, 91(2) (1997), 245–63; J. Carey, 'Parchment, Equilibria, and Institutions', *Comparative Political Studies*, 33 (2000), 735–61.

3 Rodriguez, 'Rule of Law Unplugged', 1476.

4 G. Sartori, 'Constitutionalism: A Preliminary Discussion', *American Political Science Review*, 56(4) (1962), 853–64; D. S. Law and M. Versteeg, 'Sham Constitutions', *California Law Review*, 101(4) (2013), 863–952.

include many aspirations that are difficult to fulfil and can clash with each other. Other constitutions are highly unstable: in any given year, some five to ten countries draft new constitutions.[5] Thus, for a variety of reasons, including political instability and poor drafting, constitutions can fail to promote, and perhaps even undermine, the RoL.

Understanding how constitutions can build respect for the RoL is a crucially important question. Yet, remarkably little is known about the empirical relationship between constitutions and the RoL. In this chapter, we offer a first but preliminary empirical exploration of their relationship. We focus on three constitutional features: (i) the direct protection of the RoL in the constitution, (ii) the inclusion of rights and (iii) the establishment of judicial review, that is, a mandate for a Supreme Court or Constitutional Court to invalidate legislation that contradicts the constitution. While each of these has been offered as recipe for building the RoL, we find that none of them is associated with respect for the RoL in practice. First, we find that countries that explicitly protect the RoL in their constitutions have lower RoL scores than those that do not include such protections. Second, we find a negative relationship between the number of constitutional rights and RoL scores. The more rights a constitution enshrines, the worse its RoL performance. This holds true when considering both the full catalogue of rights (including socio-economic rights, minority rights, environmental rights, and group rights) and civil and political rights alone. Indeed, of the 100+ constitutional rights we consider, only two are positively and statistically significantly associated with the RoL (the right to a timely trial and the freedom to choose one's education). We suggest that the protection of numerous constitutional rights can contradict some of the core requirements of the RoL, such as the possibility of compliance, consistency, and congruence. Third, we find that constitutions that explicitly establish judicial review have lower RoL scores than those that do not. While none of our findings suggest that these constitutional features undermine respect for the RoL, they indicate that constitutional texts alone do little to improve the RoL.

It is important to note the limitations of our analysis. First, we do not make any causal claims, as the relationship between constitutions and the RoL is complex and multi-directional. Specifically, constitutions can create the RoL, but respect for the RoL can also affect constitutions. Where respect for the RoL prevails, stable constitutions might emerge

[5] Z. Elkins, T. Ginsburg, and J. Melton, *The Endurance of National Constitutions* (New York: Cambridge University Press, 2009), at pp. 122–46.

and rulers might accept genuine constraints on their power, turning constitutions into something more than mere parchment barriers (to use James Madison's famous phrase).[6] Conversely, where respect for the RoL is absent, constitutions might fail to be implemented. What is more, in the absence of respect for the RoL, constitution-makers might be more likely to proclaim its importance and adopt more rights and judicial review as aspirations for a better future. The result is that in countries where there is little respect for the RoL, constitutions might be more aspirational in nature. Because the effects are so difficult to disentangle, this chapter merely shows correlations and raises questions for future research. A second possible limitation of this chapter is that it assumes that the RoL can be measured. In reality, the measurement of the RoL is complex and subject to numerous critiques.[7] We do not resolve any of these critiques and recognize that our assumption that the RoL can be measured is controversial. A final limitation of our inquiry is its scope: we consider a small set of constitutional features and focus on constitutional texts, not actual practices. This chapter, thus, is merely a first step in what is ultimately an entire research agenda.

The remainder of this chapter unfolds as follows. We will start with some conceptual clarifications and will then theorize how the RoL, constitutions and constitutionalism relate to each other. After this, the question whether certain substantive constitutional features are associated with higher RoL scores will be explored. We end with a conclusion.

Rule of Law, Constitutions and Constitutionalism

We start with some definitions. Specifically, we distinguish RoL from constitutions and constitutionalism.[8]

The Rule of Law

While the concept of the RoL is surrounded by substantial theoretical confusion,[9] Lon Fuller's definition remains canonical and serves as the

[6] Federalist 48, in *The Federalist Papers* 79, C. Rossiter (ed.) (New York: Signet Classics, 2003).

[7] S. Merry, *The Seductions of Quantification: Global Governance, Human Rights, and the Rise of Indicator Culture* (University of Chicago Press, 2016).

[8] This section partly draws on M. Versteeg and T. Ginsburg, 'Measuring the Rule of Law: A Comparison of Indicators', *Law and Social Inquiry* (2016).

[9] Rodriguez, 'Rule of Law Unplugged', 1455–94.

starting point for many RoL theories. According to Fuller,[10] there are eight procedural requirements for the RoL:

1. **Generality**, meaning that required conduct is stated in general rules that are broadly applicable
2. **Publicity**, meaning that rules are publicly announced
3. **Prospectivity**, meaning that rules will not be changed retroactively
4. **Clarity**, meaning that rules are understandable for all
5. **Consistency**, meaning that rules are not inconsistent or contradictory
6. **Possibility of compliance**, meaning that rules do not demand conduct that is impossible to conform to
7. **Stability**, meaning that rules are stable and not subject to frequent change
8. **Congruence** between the rules as announced and their actual administration

Fuller's version is 'thin' because it makes no demand that laws be 'good' in any substantive sense. A thin version of the RoL can also be achieved without the presence of democracy or human rights, for example. Numerous legal theorists have since built on this definition, adding further procedural and functional elements to Fuller's list. For instance, scholars have singled out judicial independence and judicial review as further functional components of the RoL. Joseph Raz, for example, notes that

> [s]ince just about any matter arising under any law can be subject to a conclusive court judgment, it is obvious that it is futile to guide one's action on the basis of the law if when the matter comes to adjudication the courts will not apply the law and will act for some other reasons.[11]

Other theorists have added more substantive values. These theorists argue that Fuller's definition merely requires rule *by* law and does not demand that the law be normatively reasonable or just. They contend instead that the RoL requires some thicker content. Friedrich Hayek, for example, suggests that the RoL includes 'the recognition of the inalienable right of the individual, inviolable rights of man.'[12] Ronald Dworkin argues that the RoL is not merely a rulebook, but that the concept is

[10] L. L. Fuller, *The Morality of Law* (New Haven: Yale University Press, 1969), pp. 33–39.

[11] J. Raz, 'The Rule of Law and Its Virtue' in J. Raz (ed.), *The Authority of Law: Essays on Law and Morality* (New York: Oxford University Press, 1979), p. 227.

[12] F. Hayek, *The Road to Serfdom* (Chicago: University of Chicago Press, 1944), p. 88, cited in Rodriguez, 'Rule of Law Unplugged', 1455–94 at 1469–74.

necessarily substantive and includes equality and rights.[13] Many other theorists include various additional substantive values in their definitions of the RoL.

Once substantive values are incorporated into the definition of the RoL, the concept becomes harder to separate from neighbouring concepts. Joseph Raz argues that once the RoL means the 'rule of good law, then to explain its nature is to propound a complete social philosophy' with the result that 'the term lacks any useful function.'[14] In other words, when substantive values are incorporated into the RoL, the concept becomes synonymous with those values and might lose analytical value on its own.

Despite such theoretical disagreements over the RoL, different organizations that measure and quantify the RoL tend to reach very similar conclusions about which countries respect the RoL and which countries do not.[15] In our previous research, we compared and contrasted different well-known and widely used RoL indexes and found that three of these indexes were nearly identical to each other (with their pairwise correlations all exceeding 0.95). These are the indexes by the World Governance Indicator project of the World Bank (WGI), the Heritage Foundation, and the World Justice Project (WJP). We argued that this finding is striking because these indicators all build very different substantive values into their definitions of the RoL. Specifically, the WGI's index is heavily focused on law and order; the Heritage Foundation's index incorporates private property, the absence of corruption, and the free market; and the WJP's index includes human rights along with a range of other values. The stark convergence between these indexes, we concluded, likely results from some underlying latent variable, such as a general demand for government impartiality.[16]

In this chapter, we abstract from the nuances of measuring and defining the RoL and primarily rely on the RoL as measured by the WGI. This indicator purports to capture 'perceptions of the extent to which agents have confidence in and abide by the rules of society, and in particular the quality of contract enforcement, property rights, the police, and the

[13] Rodriguez, 'Rule of Law Unplugged', 1470.
[14] Raz, 'The Rule of Law and Its Virtue', p. 211.
[15] Versteeg and Ginsburg, 'Measuring the Rule of Law', at 9.
[16] In addition, we noted that the fact that all these measures rely on expert judgements also contributes to their convergence.

courts, as well as the likelihood of crime and violence.'[17] While frequently criticized,[18] this index has the widest country coverage and is thus most useful for our present purpose of examining correlations. Since the values on this index are closely correlated with those of the WJP and the Heritage Foundation, we believe there is little at stake in our choice to use this measure. Thus, in the remainder of this chapter, we primarily rely on the WGI's RoL index and specifically its values for the year 2011.

Constitutions

A constitution is a written document that usually sets out the basic structure of government and limits on government power. As with the RoL, there are different ways to define a constitution. Some definitions are functional: a legal document is a constitution when it performs certain functions, such as setting up a government, dividing powers, and defining substantive limits on these powers in the form of rights. Other definitions are essentialist in nature: a document is constitutional when it is entrenched or includes certain higher values. Yet other definitions are nominal: a document is a constitution when a nation calls it a constitution or regards it as such.[19]

Regardless of the definition, written constitutions can induce respect for the RoL, for several reasons. First, constitutions almost by definition must provide for a process for making binding law, advancing Fuller's requirement of generality of rules. Second, constitutions typically require that laws be publicly debated and promulgated, advancing the requirement of publicity. Third, many constitutions explicitly prohibit the retroactive application of legislation, requiring that laws be prospective. To illustrate, the US Constitution stipulates that '[n]o Bill of Attainder or

[17] D. Kaufmann, A. Kraay, and M. Mastruzzi, 'The Worldwide Governance Indicators: Methodology and Analytical Issues', World Bank Policy Research Working Paper No. 5430 (2010). For a more in-depth discussion, see Versteeg and Ginsburg, 'Measuring the Rule of Law', at 15.

[18] M. J. Kurtz and A. Schrank, 'Growth and Governance: Models, Measures, and Mechanisms', *Journal of Politics*, 69(2) (2007), 538–54; T. Ginsburg, 'Pitfalls of Measuring the Rule of Law', *Hague Journal on the Rule of Law*, 2(3) (2011), 269–80 at 271; M. A. Thomas, 'What Do the Worldwide Governance Indicators Measure?' *European Journal of Development Research*, 22 (2010), 1–54 at 18.

[19] M. Versteeg and E. Zackin, 'American Constitutional Exceptionalism Revisited', *University of Chicago Law Review*, 81 (2014), 1641–1707; K. L. Cope and M. Versteeg, 'Constitutions' in J. D. Wright (ed.), *International Encyclopedia of the Social and Behavioural Sciences*, 2nd edn (Oxford: Elsevier, 2015), pp. 710–15.

ex post facto Law shall be passed.'[20] Today, 82 per cent of all constitutions prohibit retroactive law.[21] Fourth, constitutions tend to limit the ability of government to change the rules by providing entrenched amendment procedures. These provisions allow constitutions to enhance their own stability and the stability of the legal system as a whole.

Constitutions can also provide clarity. If the nation's founding document is written clearly, it can provide basic rules that are understandable to all. A clear document should also be consistent and exclude contradictory rules. However, not all constitutions accomplish the goals of clarity and consistency and, in some cases, these goals might not even be desirable. Cass Sunstein argues that constitutions are best thought of as 'incompletely theorized agreements' that rely on ambiguity in the face of deep moral disagreement and partisan division.[22] By keeping the purposes and underlying theory of constitutional rules vague, constitutions may allow people with deeply conflicting motives to live together.[23] This suggests that ambiguity may advance the conditions of agreement on a text, which may in turn undermine clarity and/or consistency and thus the RoL.

Finally, constitutions typically define rights for citizens and, as such, stipulate substantive limits on government power. While Fuller does not explicitly include a constrained government as a criterion for the RoL, the insight that power needs constraints is key in many accounts on the foundations of the RoL. Barry Weingast, for example, suggests that by defining transgressions of sovereign power, written texts can serve as focal points to coordinate enforcement action, which is foundational for the RoL.[24]

Importantly, however, the inclusion of rights can also be in tension with the RoL. Specifically, when constitutions include a large number of rights, they can become aspirational in nature. Aspirational constitutions require

[20] U.S. Constitution, Article 1, Section 9.

[21] Data from the Comparative Constitutions Project as of 2014.

[22] C. R. Sunstein, 'Incompletely Theorized Agreements', *Harvard Law Review*, 108 (1995), 1733–72.

[23] H. Lerner, *Making Constitutions in Deeply Divided Societies* (Cambridge University Press, 2011); A. Bali and H. Lerner, 'Religion in Constitution-Writing: A Theoretical Framework', unpublished draft, on file with authors (2014); C. B. Lombardi, 'The Constitution as an Agreement to Agree: The Social and Political Foundations (and Effects) of the 1971 Egyptian Constitution' in D. J. Galligan and Mila Versteeg (eds.), *The Social and Political Foundations of Constitutions* (Cambridge University Press, 2013), pp. 398–425; G. L. Negretto, *Making Constitutions: Presidents, Parties, and Institutional Choice in Latin America* (New York: Cambridge University Press, 2013), pp. 43–69.

[24] Carey, 'Parchment, Equilibria and Institutions', 735–61; Weingast, 'Political Foundations', 245–63.

the government to work towards goals that are only achievable in the distant future. These might include universal rights to minimum standards of living or health care if adopted in impoverished countries. Consider the 2008 Constitution of Ecuador: in addition to a standard catalogue of civil liberties, it guarantees the right to culturally appropriate food, breastfeeding facilities, and free psychological care for persons with disabilities, among others. The document also grants rights directly to *Pacha Mama* (Mother Earth). When numerous goals are declared to be constitutional rights, it becomes nearly impossible for governments to fully comply with them. Many of these rights can only be realized through sustained policy efforts and institutional transformation. Moreover, such aspirational rights may clash with each other, undermining Fuller's demand of consistency. To illustrate, it is not clear how a government can reconcile the requirements of secure property rights with a right to an adequate standard of living. Aspirational constitutions also fall short on Fuller's requirement of congruence. When constitutions are aspirational, they are not congruent with their actual implementation. It is unclear, therefore, how constitutional rights relate to the RoL.

Constitutionalism

A constitution is not the same as constitutionalism. Constitutionalism, perhaps as complicated a concept as the RoL, is described as 'evocative and persuasive in its connotations yet cloudy in its analytic and descriptive content.'[25] For most theorists, constitutionalism denotes limited government and constraints on government power. Andras Sajó, for instance, notes that 'a constitution impregnated with the ideas of constitutionalism is about limited power.'[26] Likewise, Friedrich Hayek observes that constitutionalism means that 'all power rests on the understanding that it will be exercised according to commonly accepted principles.'[27] Under such a definition, constitutions that merely enable, but do not constrain, governments fall short of constitutionalism. For example, communist constitutions, which provided no constraints on government but instead described

[25] T. C. Grey, 'Constitutionalism: An Analytic Framework' in J. W. Chapman and J. R. Pennock (eds.), *Constitutionalism* (New York: New York University Press, 1979), pp. 189–209 at p. 189.

[26] A. Sajó, *Limiting Government: An Introduction to Constitutionalism* (New York: Central European University Press, 1999), p. 2.

[27] F. A. Hayek, *The Constitution of Liberty* (Chicago: University of Chicago Press, 1960), p. 181.

a 'vision ... in attractive but abstract terms of what "future" society will become', did not provide constitutionalism.[28] African and Arab countries are also commonly characterized as possessing constitutions without constitutionalism.[29]

Another way to define constitutionalism is as a constitution that is congruent with its actual administration. Hardin, for example, suggests that constitutionalism means that a constitution can actually 'maintain social order' and 'resolve prisoner's dilemma and other interactions, including other coordination problems.'[30] Hardin urges that 'good' constitutions do not exist and that constitutionalism is about the document's consequences (whether it manages to coordinate) rather than whether it comports with higher values, including limited government.[31] For Hardin, then, dead letter constitutions do not provide constitutionalism, yet undesirable documents that successfully set conventions and solve coordination problems do provide constitutionalism. Even an authoritarian constitution that does not constrain government power can serve as a coordination device.[32]

For our purposes, we do not need to settle on a definition of constitutionalism. Instead, it is sufficient to note that having a constitution is not the same as having constitutionalism and that, in many parts of the world, there are 'constitutions without constitutionalism.'[33] In the remainder of this chapter, we focus solely on constitutional texts.

The Constitutional Content of RoL-Respecting Countries

Written constitutions can be crucial in underpinning the RoL, yet they can also fall short of some of the most basic requirements for the RoL, for example when they lack clarity or generality. In this section, we offer a

28 Sajó, *Limiting Government*, p. 1.

29 H. W. O. Okoth-Ogendo, 'Constitutions without Constitutionalism: Reflections on an African Political Paradox' in D. Greenberg, St. N. Katz, M. B. Oliviero, and S. C. Wheatley (eds.), *Constitutionalism and Democracy: Transitions in the Contemporary World* (New York: Oxford University Press, 1993), pp. 65–82; N. J. Brown, *Constitutions in a Non-Constitutional World: Arab Basic Laws and the Prospects for Accountable Government* (Albany: State University of New York Press, 2001), pp. 6–7.

30 R. Hardin, 'Why a Constitution?' in M. Versteeg and D. Galligan (eds.), *The Social and Political*, pp. 51–72 at 63.

31 *Ibid.*, p. 52.

32 T. Ginsburg and A. Simpser (eds.), *Constitutions in Authoritarian Regimes* (Cambridge University Press, 2013), pp. 1–24.

33 Okoth-Ogendo, 'Constitutions without Constitutionalism', pp. 65–82; Brown, *Constitutions in a Non-Constitutional World*, p. 10.

preliminary exploration of which constitutional features appear to be conducive to the RoL in practice. Specifically, we explore the empirical connection between the RoL and rights, judicial review, and explicit constitutional references to the RoL. We focus on these features because they are connected to the RoL on theoretical grounds.

We have to begin with an important caveat: in exploring the association between constitutional features and respect for the RoL, we merely show correlations. We deliberately refrain from more sophisticated statistical analyses for two reasons. First, constitutions are not only a crucial condition for the RoL, but the RoL is likely also an important predictor of constitutions and constitutionalism, which makes it difficult to make causal claims. Second, some of the constitutional features whose connection to the RoL we explore here might be built into RoL indexes.[34] As mentioned previously, our goal for this chapter is to provide an initial exploration of the plausibility of certain hypotheses and to raise questions for future research.

Mentioning the RoL

Many constitutions today pay lip service to the RoL. They commonly declare the RoL to be one of the nation's founding principles, or articulate it as a guideline for government action. To illustrate, the 2004 Constitution of Afghanistan declares its intention to '[f]orm a civil society void of oppression, atrocity, discrimination as well as violence, based on rule of law, social justice, protecting integrity and human rights, and attaining peoples' freedoms and fundamental rights.'[35] Likewise, the post-apartheid constitution of South Africa declared that it is 'a sovereign, democratic state founded on the following values ... [s]upremacy of the constitution and the rule of law.'[36] China's 1982 Constitution states that '[t]he People's Republic of China exercises power in accordance with the law and establishes a socialist country under the rule of law.'[37] The 2013 Constitution of Zimbabwe mentions the RoL no fewer than seven times.[38]

[34] Versteeg and Ginsburg, 'Measuring the Rule of Law', at 15–22.

[35] Constitution of Afghanistan 2014, Preamble.

[36] Constitution of South Africa 1996, Article 1.

[37] Constitution of China, 1982, Revised 2005, Article 5.

[38] See Constitution of Zimbabwe (2013), Preamble ('Recognising the need to entrench democracy, good, transparent and accountable governance and the rule of law[.]'); Id., art. 3.1 ('Zimbabwe is founded on respect for the following values and principles[...]the

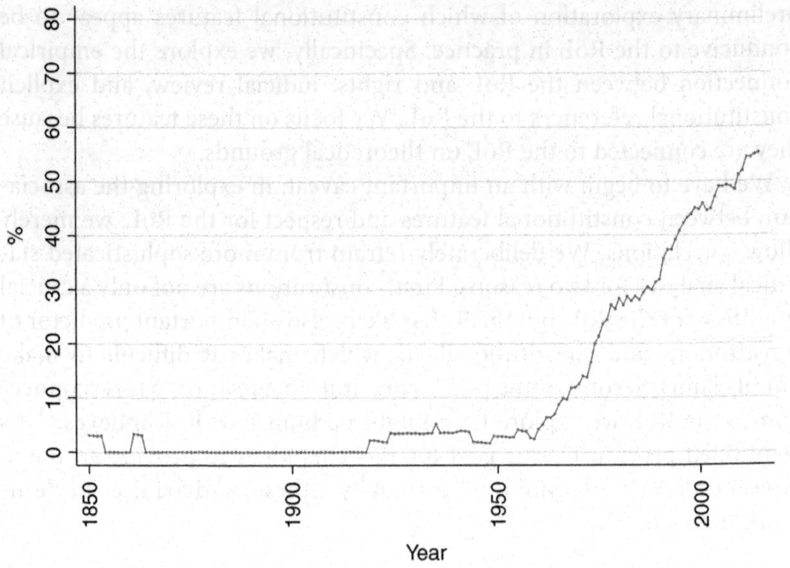

Figure 17.1 Percentage of Constitutions that Make Explicit Reference to the Rule of Law.

Indeed, there is a strong trend among constitution-makers towards explicitly protecting the RoL. Figure 17.1 depicts the percentage of written constitutions that reference the RoL in some form over time. The data plotted in this figure is based on coding that has been conducted by the Comparative Constitutions Project.[39] Figure 17.1 reveals that as of 1950, fewer than 3 per cent of all constitutions referenced the RoL, while today more than half (55 per cent) of all constitutions do. Indeed, the growing constitutional references to the RoL fairly closely track the 'Rule-of-Law Revival' (to use Carothers' term)[40] in the academic literature and

rule of law[.]'); Id., art. 90.2 ('The President must . . . ensure protection of the fundamental human rights and freedoms and the rule of law'); Id., art 114.4 ('The functions of the Attorney-General are . . . to promote, protect and uphold the rule of law and to defend the public interest'); Id, art 164 ('The independence, impartiality and effectiveness of the courts are central to the rule of law and democratic governance'); Id., art. 165.1 ('In exercising judicial authority, members of the judiciary must be guided by the following principles . . . c. the role of the courts is paramount in safeguarding human rights and freedoms and the rule of law'); Id., art. 206.3 ('In particular, the protection of national security must be pursued with the utmost respect for . . . the rule of law').

39 See www.comparativeconstitutionsproject.org (last accessed November 29, 2015).

40 T. Carothers, 'The Rule of Law Revival', *Foreign Affairs*, 77(2) (1998), 95–106.

policy circles, as the graph shows a particularly steep increase in the 1990s.

The constitutional protection of the RoL does not guarantee respect for the RoL in practice. References to the RoL are not usually justiciable and might be primarily aspirational. If such references are primarily aspirational, the somewhat paradoxical result might be that countries in which the RoL remains unrealized are more likely to pay lip service to its importance in their founding documents.

Our data suggests that the relationship between mentioning the RoL and respecting it in practice is indeed negative. To measure actual respect for the RoL, we use the WGI's RoL Index. This indicator ranges from −2.67 to 2, whereby higher scores denote more respect for the RoL. We find that the average RoL score for countries that mention the RoL in their constitution is −0.266, while the average RoL score for those that do not mention the RoL is 0.077. A t-test shows that the difference in these means is statistically significant at the 5 per cent level. When calculating a correlation coefficient between mentioning the RoL in the constitution and actual respect for the RoL, we find that it is negative (the correlation coefficient is −0.1738) and statistically significant at the 5 per cent level (p-value 0.0189). This negative correlation suggests that the relationship is, at best, aspirational: countries that have little respect for the RoL are most likely to declare its importance in their founding documents.

Constitutional Rights

Rights are not part of Fuller's classical definition of the RoL. A thin version of the RoL need not involve protection of particular human rights.[41] Many theorists, however, do consider respect for basic rights crucial to the RoL. As touched upon before, according to Ronald Dworkin the RoL is not merely a rulebook, but also includes respect for rights. He further explains that the RoL 'assumes that citizens have moral rights and duties with respect to one another, and political rights against the state as a whole. It insists that these moral and political rights be recognized in positive law, so that they may be enforced upon the demand of the individual citizen through courts or other judicial institutions of the familiar type, so far as this is practicable.'[42]

[41] R. Peerenboom, 'Human Rights and Rule of Law: What's the Relationship?', *Georgetown Journal of International Law*, 36(1) (2005), 815–945.

[42] R. M. Dworkin, *Political Judges and the Rule of Law* (London: The British Academy, 1980), pp. 11–12.

Constitutions are crucial in defining rights. The constitution declares certain rights to be higher values, which cannot be overturned by subsequent legislation or regulation. Indeed, constitutions in a growing number of countries protect an ever-expanding number of rights.[43] One conjecture, therefore, is that where constitutions protect more rights, the country will also do better in respecting the RoL.

Yet rights can also undermine respect for the RoL. While thick conceptions of the RoL include rights, the protection of constitutional rights can sometimes clash with thin conceptions of the RoL. Specifically, once a large number of rights are protected by the constitution, it might fall short of Fuller's requirement of the possibility of compliance. Some rights, such as the right to free healthcare or education, might take time to implement and cannot be complied with immediately. Moreover, once many values are declared to be rights, they might be in competition with each other, undermining Fuller's requirement of consistency. Eric Posner argues, in the context of international human rights law, that the coexistence of many competing rights claims effectively free governments from real constraints.[44] Posner contends that by committing to a 'huge number of vague rights that encompass nearly all human activity,' states are basically free to pick and choose the rights that they want to focus on, because it is impossible to protect all these rights, often with competing values, equally.[45] In sum, when constitutions protect many rights, they might lose congruence with their administration and thus undermine the RoL.

Our data provides some support for this thesis. Specifically, when we correlate a measure that captures the total number of rights that a country enshrines in its constitution with the WGI's RoL index, the correlation coefficient is negative (–0.267) and statistically significant at the 1 per cent level (p-value is 0.0003). Our measure of the total number of rights is based on the coding of 108 possible rights, including civil and political rights, socio-economic rights, third-generation rights, and other more esoteric rights.[46] Figure 17.2 plots countries' RoL scores against the number of rights in their constitutions, along with a regression line. It

43 D. S. Law and M. Versteeg, 'The Evolution and Ideology of Global Constitutionalism', *California Law Review*, 99 (2011), at 123.

44 E. Posner, *The Twilight of Human Rights* (New York: Oxford University Press, 2014).

45 *Ibid.*

46 These are the same rights used by B. Goderis and M. Versteeg in 'The Diffusion of Constitutional Rights', *International Review of Law and Economics*, 39(1) (2014), 18–19. Appendix 17.1 provides the full list of rights.

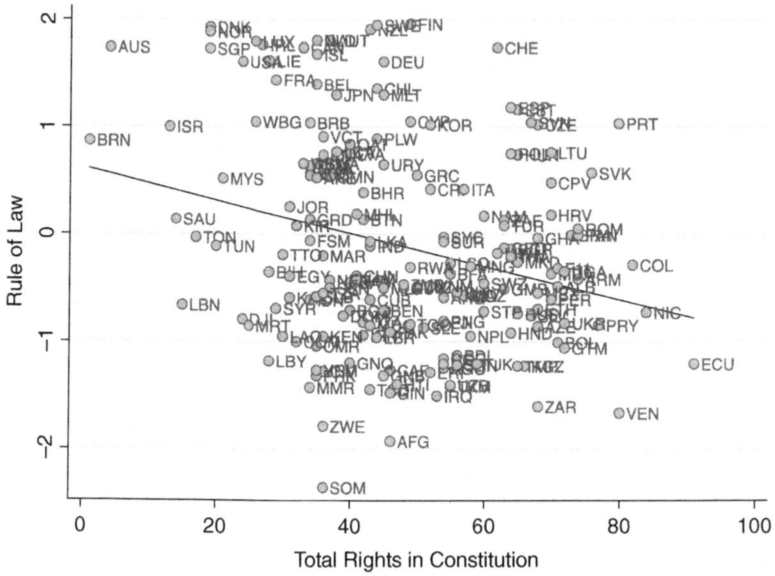

Figure 17.2 Total Number of Rights in Constitutions versus *De Facto* Rule of Law Scores.

shows that some of the countries with the highest RoL records (e.g. Australia, Brunei, or Israel) enshrine few rights in their constitution, while countries with the largest number of rights in their constitution (e.g. Ecuador, Venezuela) have notoriously weak RoL records. While it is important to emphasize that this does not represent a causal relationship, it suggests that the relationship between constitutional rights and the RoL might be negative. Perhaps this is because in weak-RoL environments, citizens demand more rights in the hope of improving performance over time, but it is not clear if this strategy is effective.

The reader might object that this picture would be different if we were to limit our analysis to civil and political rights. Commentators often suggest that civil and political rights are easier to implement than social and economic rights, since the former mainly require the government to refrain from action (e.g. not to torture any of its citizens), while the latter require government action.[47] We therefore repeated the same empirical exercise for a set of 31 civil and political rights. This exercise revealed no

[47] At the same time, the strict distinction between positive and negative rights is problematic on theoretical grounds. See e.g. S. Holmes and C. R. Sunstein, *Why Liberty Depends on Taxes* (New York: W.W. Norton & Company, 1999), pp. 3–5.

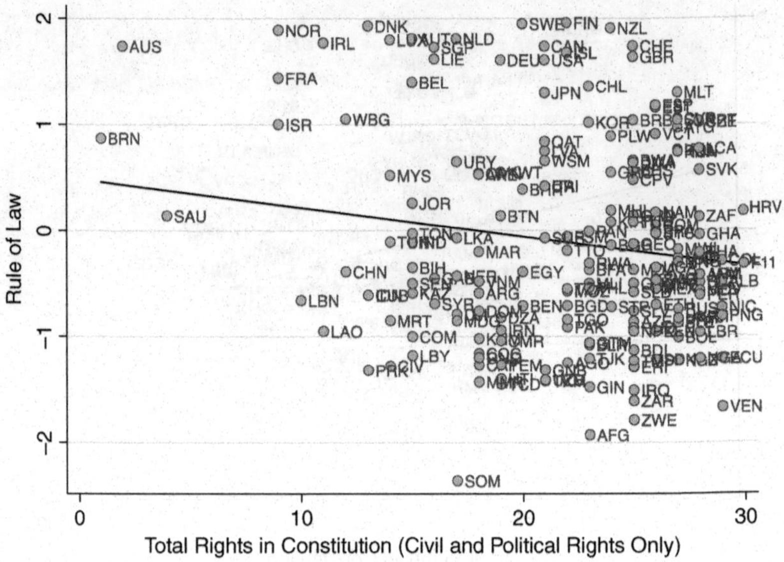

Figure 17.3 Total Number of Civil and Political Rights versus De Facto Rule of Law Scores.

evidence that civil and political constitutional rights are associated with better RoL scores. Indeed, the correlation between civil and political rights and actual RoL scores is again negative (−0.156) and statistically significant at the 5 per cent level. This indicates that constitutional rights protections do little to improve respect for the RoL.

Another possible objection to this analysis is that the WGI's RoL measure captures a thin version of the RoL, which does not include rights. As stated above, the WGI's index emphasizes property rights, contract enforcement and security. To explore whether this affects our results, we repeated the same exercise using an RoL measure from the World Justice Project (WJP) that includes respect for rights as one of its components.[48] This alternative measure yields results that are essentially the same: the correlation between the WJP's RoL measure and the full

48 The World Justice Project (2014) defines the RoL as follows: 'The government and its officials and agents as well as individuals and private entities are accountable under the law. The laws are clear, publicized, stable, and just; are applied evenly; and protect fundamental rights, including the security of persons and property. The process by which the laws are enacted, administered, and enforced is accessible, fair, and efficient. Justice is delivered timely by competent, ethical, and independent representatives and neutrals who are of sufficient number, have adequate resources, and reflect the makeup of

rights index is −0.34 and statistically significant at the 1 per cent level, while its correlation with the civil and political rights index is −0.28 and statistically significant at the 1 per cent level. This suggests that our choice of RoL index does not drive our finding on the relationship between constitutional rights and the RoL.

While an increased number of constitutional rights does not appear to be associated with improved RoL, it remains possible that certain rights are by themselves conducive to the RoL. One candidate is the prohibition of *ex post facto* laws, which is meant to directly safeguard Fuller's requirement of prospectivity. As mentioned above some 82 per cent of all written constitutions contained such a prohibition, but the correlation between this right and the RoL is negative, albeit not statistically significant (correlation coefficient −0.091, p-value 0.22). Indeed, of the 108 rights that featured in our initial analysis, only two are positive and statistically significant at the 5 per cent level: the requirement of a timely trial and the freedom to choose one's education.[49] The overwhelming majority of rights (84 of 108) are negatively correlated with the RoL. While this exercise is based on correlations only, it suggests that enshrining constitutional rights in the constitution by itself does little to improve the RoL around the world. We recognize that this finding is somewhat troubling, especially since many RoL practitioners and theorists have emphasized the importance of constitutional rights in building the RoL. Future research is needed to further explore this relationship.

Judicial Review

Judicial review is not part of Fuller's definition of the RoL. Yet constitutional theorists, especially in the United States, often consider it to be critical for the RoL. Justice Marshall's famous opinion in *Marbury v. Madison* suggests that the RoL requires courts to exercise judicial review. According to Marshall, the US government was meant to be 'a government of laws, and not of men', and that it 'will certainly cease to deserve this high appellation if the laws furnish no remedy for the violation of a vested legal right.'[50] More broadly, a neutral third party is seen as

the communities they serve.' *World Justice Project*. Who We Are http://worldjusticeproject.org/who-we-are (accessed November 2014).

49 When evaluating statistical significance at the 10 per cent level, equality regardless of ancestry and the prohibition of the death penalty are also positively and statistically significantly associated with the RoL.

50 *Marbury v. Madison*, 5 U.S. (1 Cranch) 137, 163 (1803).

essential to ensuring that laws are adjudicated consistently with procedural requirements.[51] Under this logic, realization of the RoL requires the establishment of judicial review.

Judicial review is often provided for in the constitution's text. In previous research, we have shown that no fewer than 83 per cent of all constitutions today establish judicial review.[52] Yet countries that constitutionally establish judicial review do not have higher RoL scores. Instead, the correlation is negative (–0.1934) and statistically significant at the 1 per cent level (p-value 0.0085). The average RoL score of countries that do not establish judicial review in their constitutions is 0.341, while the average score of those that do is –0.194. A t-test shows that this difference in means is statistically significant at the 1 per cent level.

However, the constitutional text might not provide an accurate reflection of whether judicial review is actually exercised. In the United States, the Supreme Court decided it could review the constitutionality of laws despite the arguable silence of the constitution on judicial review.[53] Conversely, judicial review might be provided for in the constitution, but not exercised in practice. These kinds of discrepancies suggest that we should be cautious to suggest that judicial review and the RoL are unrelated, as our measure is based on the constitutional text alone. What is more, since our analysis is based only on correlations, it does not rule out the possibility that judicial review *does* improve respect for the RoL. It could be that countries with well-established traditions of the RoL do not feel a need to adopt judicial review, but that judicial review makes a difference in countries without such traditions. Our findings suggest, however, that a mere declaration that courts possess the power of judicial review is likely insufficient to improve respect for the RoL.

Conclusion

In this brief contribution, we have explored the relationship between written constitutions and the RoL. We found that a number of

[51] Rodriguez, 'Rule of Law Unplugged', 1476; Raz, 'The Rule of Law and Its Virtue', p. 216.

[52] T. Ginsburg and M. Versteeg, 'Why Do Countries Adopt Constitutional Review?', *Journal of Law, Economics and Organization*, 30(3) (2014), 587–622.

[53] Likewise, in Israel, the Supreme Court decided it had the power of judicial review even though the Israeli Basic Laws did not grant this power. See C.A. 6821/93, *United Mizrahi Bank Ltd. v. Migdal Cooperative Village*, 49 (4) P.D. 221.

constitutional features that are commonly associated with the RoL do not appear to be associated with respect for the RoL in practice. Specifically, constitutional rights and judicial review do not appear to translate into improved RoL scores. Also, mentioning the RoL in the text of the constitution has no such effect. While further research is required, these findings suggest that a constitution's text alone does not build respect for the RoL. While it is possible that written constitutions are necessary, our analysis suggests that by themselves they are not sufficient.

Our analysis probably raises more questions than it answers. First, we have not sought to establish any causal relationship, as doing so is notoriously complex with observational data. The correlates of the RoL that we presented suggest that some relationships do exist, but future research is needed to establish this. Second, even if constitutional features such as rights and judicial review do not affect the RoL by themselves, they could still be important when they are combined with other features. For example, it is possible that rights and judicial review only matter when there is an independent judiciary. Alternatively, it is possible that rights and judicial review matter only in democracies.[54]

Perhaps most importantly, it is possible and indeed likely that constitutional features are conducive to the RoL only when they are actually effective in practice. Thus, it might be that constitutional practices, not written constitutional texts, produce the RoL. This brings to the fore the longstanding question of how constitutions actually become effective in practice.[55] We do not purport to have an answer to this question. But it deserves mentioning that respect for the RoL is a likely part of any explanation for why constitutions matter: constitutions that are adopted in the face of a strong RoL tradition are more likely to be effective. One possibility, therefore, is that respect for the RoL is a precondition for an effective constitution. Our contribution provides little insight into these rather difficult questions. But it does reinforce the idea that simply writing new constitutions with attractive features, by itself, is insufficient to create respect for the rule of law.

[54] B. A. Simmons, *Mobilizing for Human Rights: International Law in Domestic Politics* (New York, Cambridge University Press, 2009), pp. 135–42.

[55] See e.g. A. Chilton and M. Versteeg, 'Do Constitutional Rights Make a Difference', *American Journal of Political Science*, 60(3) (2016).

Appendix 17.1 *108 Constitutional rights*

I. Political, democratic and accountability rights	
Right to freedom of religion	Right to a remedy
Freedom of expression	Right to petition
Right to assembly	Right to information about government
Right to association	Right to compensation
Right to vote	Right to resist
Freedom of press	Right to amparo
Freedom to form political parties	
II. Life, liberty, physical integrity and privacy	
Prohibition of arbitrary arrest and detention	Right to establish private schools
Right to privacy of the home	Freedom of education
Right to privacy of communication	Right to privacy of family life
Freedom of movement	Right to protection of one's reputation
Prohibition of torture	Prohibition of death penalty
Right to life	Right to privacy of personal data
Right not to be expelled	Free development of personality
Prohibition of slavery	Rights for unborn children
Right to personal privacy	Right to bear arms
Artistic freedom	
III. Fair trial	
Right of access to court	Right to remain silent
Prohibition of *ex post facto* laws	Right to a timely trial
Presumption of innocence	Right to an interpreter
Right to defence	Right to fair trial
Right to counsel	Right to appeal
Right to public trial	Rights for prisoners
Prohibition of double jeopardy	Right to due process
IV. Equality rights	
General equality clause	Equality regardless of nationality
Gender equality	Equality regardless of place of origin
Racial equality	Equality regardless of disability
Religious equality	Age equality
Equality regardless of belief/ philosophy	Equality regardless of education
Equality regardless of political opinion	Equality regardless of tribe

Appendix 17.1 (*cont.*)

Equality regardless of social status	Equality regardless of ancestry
Linguistic equality	Equality regardless of caste
Economic equality	Equality regardless of sexual orientation
Ethnic equality	Equality regardless of HIV/aids
V. Socio-economic rights	
Right to property	Right to work for the government
Right to education	Right to favourable working conditions
Right to work	Intellectual property
Right to form trade unions	Right to sport
Right to health	Right to strike
Right to social security	Right to adequate standard of living
Freedom of enterprise	Prohibition of child labour
Right to rest	Prohibition of confiscation
Right to minimum wage	Right to food
Right to housing	Right to water
VI. Women, children and family	
Right to establish a family	Rights for elderly people
Rights for children	Protection of women
Special protection of mothers	Gender equality in labour
Right to get married	Right to maternity leave
Equality of husband and wife	
VII. Third-generation rights	
Right to a healthy environment	Schooling right for minorities
Right to culture	Rights for consumers
Protection of minority language	Right for minorities to use indigenous lands
Right to preserve customs	Rights for victims of crimes
Right to asylum	Representation right for minorities
Special protection of minorities	Autonomy for minorities
Rights for handicapped people	

INDEX

Lightning Source UK Ltd.
Milton Keynes UK
UKOW06n0650270817
308031UK00013B/217/P

9 781107 151857